The New Chicago

The New Chicago

A Social and Cultural Analysis

EDITED BY

*John P. Koval, Larry Bennett,
Michael I. J. Bennett, Fassil Demissie,
Roberta Garner, and Kiljoong Kim*

TEMPLE UNIVERSITY PRESS
Philadelphia

Temple University Press
1601 North Broad Street
Philadelphia PA 19122
www.temple.edu/tempress

♾ The paper used in this publication meets the requirements of the American National
Standard for Information Sciences—Permanence of Paper for Printed Library Materials,
ANSI Z39.48-1992

Library of Congress Cataloging-in-Publication Data

The new Chicago : a social and cultural analysis / edited by John P. Koval . . . [et al.].
    p.   cm.
    Includes bibliographical references and index.
    ISBN 1-59213-087-9 (cloth : alk. paper) — ISBN 1-59213-088-7 (pbk. : alk. paper)
    1. Chicago (Ill.)—Social conditions.   2. City planning—Illinois—Chicago.
  3. Immigrants—Illinois—Chicago.   I. Koval, John P. (John Patrick), 1935– .

HN80.C5N49 2006
307.1′4160977311—dc22

                              2005056850

2   4   6   8   9   7   5   3   1

Contents

Preface   ix

PART I.   INTRODUCTION

1   An Overview and Point of View   3
John P. Koval

PART II.   CONVERGING FORCES

2   Globalization and the Remaking of Chicago   19
Fassil Demissie

3   Economic Restructuring: Chicago's Precarious Balance   32
David Moberg

4   Chicago's New Politics of Growth   44
Larry Bennett

5   The Physical Transformation of Metropolitan Chicago   56

    Chicago's Central Area   56
    Charles S. Suchar

    The Emergent Suburban Landscape   77
    Kenneth Fidel

6   Race Relations Chicago Style: Past, Present, and Future   82
Michael I. J. Bennett and Richard T. Schaefer

PART III.   THE IMMIGRANT PRESENCE

7   Chicago: The Immigrant Capital of the Heartland   97
John P. Koval and Kenneth Fidel

 8   Latinos of the New Chicago   105
     Rob Paral

 9   New Chicago Polonia: Urban and Suburban   115
     Mary Patrice Erdmans

10   Asian Indians in Chicago   128
     Padma Rangaswamy

11   Re-Visioning Filipino American Communities: Evolving Identities,
     Issues, and Organizations   141
     Yvonne M. Lau

12   The Korean Presence in Chicago   154
     Kiljoong Kim

13   Chicago's Chinese Americans: From Chinatown and Beyond   168
     Yvonne M. Lau

14   Immigrants from the Arab World   182
     Louise Cainkar

15   Immigrants at Work   197
     John P. Koval

PART IV.   CONTESTED REINVENTION AND CIVIC AGENCY:
           TEN CASE STUDIES

16   The Rebirth of Bronzeville: Contested Space and Contrasting Visions   213
     Michael I. J. Bennett

17   Devon Avenue: A World Market   221
     Padma Rangaswamy

18   The Affordable Housing Crisis in the Chicago Region   231
     Aurie A. Pinneck and Howard Stanback

19   Back to Its Roots: The Industrial Areas Foundation and United Power for
     Action and Justice   239
     David Moberg

20   Chicago School Reform: Advancing the Global City Agenda   248
     Pauline Lipman

21   Police and the Globalizing City: Innovation and Contested Reinvention 259
     David Plebanski and Roberta Garner

22   Transforming Public Housing   269
     Larry Bennett

23   Regionalism in a Historically Divided Metropolis   277
     Larry Bennett

24   Coalition Politics at America's Premier Transportation Hub   286
     Joseph Schwieterman

25   Urban Beautification: The Construction of a New Identity in Chicago   295
     Costas Spirou

PART V.   CONCLUSION

26   Learning from Chicago   305
     Roberta Garner

     References   319

     About the Contributors   341

     Index   343

Maps follow page 212

Preface

THIS BOOK is unusual on several counts. Its most persistent and unnerving characteristic was expressed by our university's Academic Vice-President when the book editors met with him to ask for extraordinary support to bring the project to life. "It's too ambitious" was the frank appraisal of our historian-trained administrator. Our college Dean concurred, but in the wake of our presentations to each, they gave us their full and unwavering support for the duration of the project.

Another unusual characteristic of this book is the reality of six editors—a bit odd for sure because it is difficult to get more than two academics to agree on anything. The book began with three like-minded editors—John Koval, Michael Bennett, and Fassil Demissie—who had begun by planning a very different book, a book examining the impact of immigrants and immigration on contemporary Chicago. As we discussed our project, it expanded to a much larger and more exciting intellectual challenge: the analysis of social, political, demographic, economic, and cultural change in the Chicago region. Deciding to forge ahead with this larger agenda, we looked for colleagues to expand the team.

The first colleague we approached to join us in this conceptualizing and writing venture, Roberta Garner, passionately rejected the offer—because she was reluctant to reexperience the frustrations of working with other authors, coordinating schedules, and enforcing deadlines. Intellectual arm wrestling finally won out, and three became four. Larry Bennett actually offered to join us and convinced us that we

needed him more than we knew (he was right), and four became five. Lastly, we each recognized that our project called for a social scientist conversant in the use and management of census data and other large data sets. Five, then, became six with the recruitment of Kiljoong Kim.

Planning the book became a six-person year-long colloquium on urban analysis and change. After that year we knew what kind of a book we wanted to produce, what its content and chapter subjects should be, and how it should flow. We also thought we knew most of the people we wanted to produce it with, so the next challenge was to bring them on board.

Moving ahead proved sensitive on two counts. First, many of us—speaking both of editors and contributors—were strangers to each other, and not one of us knew everyone else both personally and intellectually. So first we had to prove to our potential team that our project could be realized and that it would be worth the risk of time and effort. Second, with twenty contributors we faced the danger of generating nearly that many distinct book agendas with little to unify them except a single book jacket and a common title.

We brought all the potential contributors together for two workshops. The first day-long workshop had two goals: (1) to introduce ourselves to our prospective co-authors and to each other, as well as (2) to introduce them to our project, the parameters of a common theme, and a common set of what we had now identified as "converging forces." We agreed beforehand that if, after our presentation at this workshop, anyone felt they could not write within the parameters of our common theme and its "converging forces," they would simply be dis-invited.

This first workshop roundly confirmed an early caveat expressed by one of the editors: "Working with a group of academics is as difficult as herding a bunch of cats." The first couple of hours were not pleasant. The group was testy, contentious, argumentative, challenging, and, not surprisingly, proposed writing several books other than the one we had in mind. However, as the day-long discussion played out, we realized that a consensus was being reached and that no one would drop out or be dis-invited.

Six months later, when we convened our second workshop, we knew each other, had worked one-on-one with each other, discussed all contributing author chapter outlines or rough drafts, and given our contributors feedback, editorial comments, and recommendations. We now all felt very comfortable with each other. The workshop focused almost entirely on integrating and cross-referencing ideas and themes, smoothing out the bumps in the road rather than mapping a new one. The last year of creating the book has been one of intense work. We experienced one especially rocky episode when nearly everyone's first chapter drafts ran way too long (editors' fault), and page lengths had to be markedly reduced. Lots of frustration, some anger, but no anarchy. Thank the gods for six editors.

Writing and editing a book is, inevitably, a humbling experience. For no matter how much ego and self-confidence may be possessed by authors, somewhere in the process the need to admit that "this book wouldn't have been possible without…" becomes overridingly clear. In our case that realization hit early. When the book was still only a glimmer and a hope, Richard Meister, our Vice-President of Academic Affairs, and Michael Mezey, the Dean of DePaul's Liberal Arts college—following their initial (but not to be repeated) "too ambitious" shots across our bow—provided us with positive and unstinting support. This is not a pro forma "thank you," but a deeply felt one. We were also lucky enough to find research assistance among a crowd of enthusiastic, generous, and talented M.A. and B.A. students who did much of the traditionally thankless, unglamorous backstage work. So another heartfelt and warm thank you to: Erin Curtin, Nandhini Gulasingam, Leo Hernandez, Rasa Karbauskaite, Mike Lorr, Ryan Orr, Jennifer Richardson, Tait Runnfeldt-Medina, Krysten Ryba, Elizabeth Valvo, Kathy Von Ohlen, Bijan Warner, and Mark Wodziak.

Lastly our thanks go to the editorial staff of Temple University Press. To our first editor Peter Wissoker for "liking big books," and to our current editor, Alex Holzman, for stepping in and letting us know that he was fully supportive of our project. To our production coordinator, Joanne Bowser, and copy editor, Joann Woy, for doing what they do best—taking and polishing our prose and, at times, our ideas—and to each and every one of the above, as well as our chapter authors, for contributing to an ambitious book from which we can all derive a sense of well-earned achievement.

The New Chicago

PART I

Introduction

John P. Koval

1   An Overview and Point of View

IT WAS FIRST said back in the 1880s: "Chicago is the most American of cities and to know America, you must understand Chicago"[1] (Miller 1997, 17; d'Eramo 2002, 8). The claim holds up to this day for two complementary reasons—one mythic and one real. Mythically, the Midwest is America's "heartland"—the region that speaks to the imagined core of our national identity: what the country stands for and how it wishes to be defined. Chicago is our heartland's capital. The city's unique status might also be attributable to a fundamental reality. The birth of Chicago and the birth of industrial America were contemporaneous. By the 1920s, Chicago had emerged as the poster-city of America's industrial power when the nation itself came to be recognized as the world's industrial giant. To this day, it still has the largest industrial labor force of any American city.

Chicago is also the urban reality that affirms America's conceit that "We are a country of immigrants." It is our only major city that had, from its beginning, an immigrant core contained within an immigrant skin. Our major eastern cities have distinctive Yankee foundations that became wrapped in immigrant skins later in their histories. Similarly, America's western cities were peopled, in the first instance, by migrants—mostly migrants from the Midwest. Only recently have they experienced substantial immigration from outside the continent.

The origins of the United States' self-image, dating from the colonial period and the first decades of the new republic, are grounded in the East—Boston, New York, Philadelphia—cities that once were predominantly white, Anglo-Saxon, and Protestant. Chicago has never been that. No one would accuse Chicago—the city of the "dese," "dose," and "da" people—of being a WASP city. It has no colonial past: only an immigrant and industrial history and a postindustrial present. It unambiguously represents what this country became by the late nineteenth century and illustrates our first major economic transformation from a predominantly rural agricultural country to a predominantly urban industrial country. This transformation began shortly before the Civil War. It continued over the next one hundred years, into the decade of the 1970s, when the second transformation began. This transformed postindustrial Chicago, the immigrant capital of the Midwest Chicago, the Chicago with the most manufacturing jobs in the country *and* the most high-tech jobs in the country (Markusen et al. 2001), is "the New Chicago" of this book.

This book has several purposes. First, to affirm that the social, cultural, economic, and political change that is taking place nationally and internationally is as momentous as the Industrial Revolution in terms of its transformative power. Second, to embed in this case study of Chicago a conception of global change that highlights the components and dynamics of a postindustrial society and world distinct from that of the Industrial Revolution. Third, to identify a select number of converging forces that have produced a new Chicago and to describe and illustrate their consequences and interplay in that urban setting. Fourth, to show that the consequences and interplay of the converging forces exemplified in Chicago are reflected in other urban areas in this country, as well as urban centers in other developed countries.

WHY "THE NEW CHICAGO?"

The title of this book makes a bold statement. Why *The New Chicago*, rather than *The Renewed Chicago* or *The Evolved Chicago* or *The Postmodern Chicago*? Because the change is so radical that the concept "new" gives us the right kind of intellectual jolt needed to begin the process of making meaning and enhancing the understanding of this truly significant process. If we do have a "new" Chicago, then what makes it new? Answer: its people; its basic economy; its political character; its physical landscape; its local, regional, and national influence; and its role in a global world—economically, politically, socially, culturally.

The old Chicago followed a trajectory initiated by a series of events beginning around the Civil War—perhaps the Great Fire of 1871 is an apt starting point. This trajectory was fairly well defined by the mid 1920s and, as indicated earlier, continued through the early 1970s, with elaborations but no fundamental alterations. Then, a new series of events changed the trajectory and started in motion a network of factors that make it abundantly clear that, by the year 2000, a new Chicago arose, not simply a renewed Chicago. The bending of the old trajectory and the shaping of the new was, in retrospect, most sharply delineated during the two decades of 1970s and 1980s.

Forces for Change

The Industrial Revolution of the 19th century was only one of a number of forces that led to the evolution of modern society (Watson 1980, 8). The Reformation, the Enlightenment, and the French Revolution, along with the Industrial Revolution, were a set of converging forces that moved Western society into the Industrial Age and beyond.

Back in another time, when radio was king, each incredible feat of the Lone Ranger and Tonto ended with an anonymous voice asking, "Who was that masked man?" In the aftermath of any dramatic event, we too search for meaning and perspective. Historians typically date the origin of the Industrial Revolution in England to about 1750. Yet, as best we know, it wasn't until 1848 that John Stuart Mill coined the term "Industrial Revolution," and it was not until 1884—nearly 150 years later—that Arnold Toynbee added perspective to this era in his "Lectures on the Industrial Revolution in England" (OED Online, 2000). It took time, in other words, for participants to grasp the revolutionary nature of their age. The same may well be said of our time.

The New Economy

The ongoing economic transformation of the present is revolutionary in two significant ways: (1) a knowledge-based, computer-driven information technology and service sector is rapidly emerging as the economy's most dominant force, and (2) a bifurcated labor force, metaphorically dubbed "the hourglass economy," is emerging as a result. Two additional changes of no small consequence flow from this dual economic transformation: (3) mobility stagnates and placement in the economic hierarchy increasingly becomes linked to the acquisition of educational credentials and (4) location in the upper or lower segment of the hourglass economy is intimately related to race and ethnicity.

The hallmark of the Industrial Revolution was the replacement of agricultural production by industrial production as the dominant economic activity. The hallmark of our present revolution is the replacement of industrialization with computer-driven information and service technology as the dominant economic activity.

With the arrival of industrialization, this country did not become postagricultural, just as with the arrival of a high-technology service and information economy it did not become postindustrial. In both instances, "hyper-agricultural" and "hyper-industrial" are more fitting descriptors of the change in the sense that, first, machine technology penetrated agriculture and, now, computer-based technology is penetrating into agriculture, industry, and other sectors, especially the information and knowledge management arenas. Agriculture quickly adopted the new forms of mechanization and techniques of the Industrial Age and later the new technology of the Computer Age. The result? In place of the once "revolutionary" horse-drawn McCormick reaper, we now have 500-horsepower, diesel-engine, self-steering, quadruple dual-wheeled tractors, with seven on-board microprocessors (to monitor soil moisture, yield levels, etc.), with a satellite-linked geo-positioning system to map and locate soil conditions. This computer-controlled machine enables one farmer to till as many as 3,500 acres—when 100 years ago one farmer would max out at 50 acres; a 70-fold increase in manpower productivity. Coupling this technology with the technology of bio-agriculture, farmers in the Midwest now look to top off their corn yield at 200 bushels per acre when, a short 40 years ago, 100 bushels per acre was reason for smug satisfaction. Little wonder that 1.6 percent of our labor force produces (actually overproduces) all the foodstuffs required for a nation with 295 million stomachs (U.S. Department of Labor 2002). The Industrial Age didn't cause us to "de-agriculturalize"; rather, we hyper-agriculturalized.

Contemporary industry is following suit. The infusion of mechanization and computer-based technology into the production process has resulted in markedly increased productivity using significantly less manpower. The height of our manpower commitment to manufacturing occurred during the early 1940s, with 32% of the labor force employed in manufacturing. In 2000, that proportion was just below 13%, and it is expected to drop to 9.2% by 2012 (Berman 2004, 77). Still, thanks to hyper-productivity in 2000, that 13% produced more than eleven times what the 32% produced in 1940 (Forbes 2004, 3)—and we're only getting better. For example, manufacturing productivity increased 4.0% between 1995 and 2000 and 4.8% between 2000 and 2003 (Forbes 2004, 3). Unfortunately, productivity growth means that companies can produce more goods without adding more workers; in fact, these data show that the manufacturing sector of our economy now produces eleven times more goods using 65% fewer workers than it did 65 years ago.

In Chicago's case, this transformation began in the early 1970s. In the early and mid 1950s, there were three times as many manufacturing jobs as service jobs in the Chicago metropolitan areas. By 2001, nearly two-and-a-half times as many service jobs existed as compared to manufacturing jobs. This economic transformation is still in process and is projected to reverse the service-to-manufacturing jobs ratios of the 1950s.

As wrenching as the transformation from a manufacturing economy to a service- and information-based economy may be—in terms of occupational obsolescence, re-training, learning new occupational and economic systems, and the like—it might well be tolerable if the middle-class lifestyle of the majority could be maintained. This does not appear to be the case. Wage gaps and increasing inequality in the economy have been an item of public discussion and media focus for some time now. The economic hourglass of the new economy greatly exacerbates that trend. Although, as Milkman and Dwyer have said "... the fact that the newly generated jobs ... are so sharply polarized is an alarming portent of the likely shape of the future employment structure" (Milkman and Dwyer 2002, 12), one unfortunate characteristic of our society is that impending crises, regardless of the level of surety, rarely gain public action until they are upon us.

To ratchet up the situation even further, race and ethnicity must be placed in the picture. Given the history of race in America and the size and distinctive educational and skill mismatch of the majority of Latino immigrants to this country, the following Department of Labor prediction is particularly relevant:

> The hourglass economy will continue to be fed and shaped: the fastest and largest occupational growth is predicted to occur among professional and related occupations, and ... occupations requiring a postsecondary vocational award or an academic degree, which account for 29 percent of all jobs in 2000, will account for 42 percent of total job growth from 2000 to 2010. (Hecker 2001, 57)

The sharp economic polarization that occurs because of the tight link between educational credentials and advanced skills with better paying occupations bodes a near caste-like system as a by-product of the American version of the new economy.

CHICAGO AS CASE STUDY

Chicago is the most studied American city— thanks to the birth of American sociology at the University of Chicago and the Chicago School's employment of the city as its research laboratory. Generations of social scientists and urbanologists cut their intellectual teeth on *The City*, Concentric Zone Theory, *The Gang, The Delinquent Boy, The Jack Roller, The Professional Thief, The Hobo, The Unadjusted Girl, The Marginal Man, Black Metropolis,* and the classic *The Polish Peasant in Europe and America*— all products of the University of Chicago, researched in Chicago, but intended to be "particularly representative cases" generalizable beyond Chicago. Usage of the generalizing article "The," rather than the particularizing article "A" in the studies cited above is mute but clear evidence of their intentional commitment to this principle.

Chicago was the unquestioned paradigmatic city for the social sciences since the Chicago School was established in the 1920s until it was partially displaced by the political economy approach in the 1970s (Savage and Ward 1993, 7–33). More recently, urban researchers elsewhere claim that the Chicago School model simply doesn't apply to "their" city, and proponents of "an emergent postmodern urbanism" (Dear 2000, 99) are identifying new models. According to Beauregard (2003), claims are now staked out by the Los Angeles School (Dear 2000; Soja 1989), and paradigmatic Miami (Nijman 2000), Boston (Erlich and Dreier 1999), and Las Vegas (Gottdeiner, Collins, and Dickens 1999).

The inter-city competition for paradigmatic status has been sharply criticized for having "slipped into an academic boosterism at odds with a critical theoretical enterprise" (Beauregard 2003, 183)—an *enterprise* being, presumably, the development of urban theory untainted by the suspicion of mixing scholarship with partisan rhetoric. But the core of the issue can't be brushed aside or dismissed simply because of boosterism and exaggerated claims.

The fundamental reality is that the Chicago School's paradigm was dominant precisely because most urban analysts saw a goodness of fit between it and other extant and emerging urban-industrial cities. This is simply no longer the case. A consensus presently exists among urban theorists that the old paradigm doesn't fit the urban realities of our time. The search for a new model is clearly underway, and it is highly unlikely that a "winner" will be crowned on the basis of who amasses the most superlatives. Also, it may well be the case that a "one-size-fits-all" paradigm may not emerge. The emergence of several pretenders to the crown is, on balance, a good omen, however. The task at hand calls for isolating the essential attributes of a changed contemporary urban society; the more concepts that vie for the title "essential" in a contested terrain, the greater the likelihood that viable postmodern urban paradigms will emerge.

Case studies have at least two purposes: One, to present a detailed description and analysis of a single case that, when combined with and compared to other similar case studies, can contribute to theory as one element in a comparative analysis. And two, to serve as a primary source, a paradigm, for understanding a phenomenon by being "a particular (case) that in its very particularity reveals the generality that otherwise could not be defined" (Arendt 1982, 77). Put another way, a paradigmatic case study is "the place where it all comes together " (Soja 1989, 221). In this latter instance, the case study is the basis for that theorizing that produces the paradigm since, in Robert Beauregard's terms, "... the point of paradigmatic theorizing is to isolate the essential attributes of the case so that it can subsume other cases" (Beauregard 2003, 190).

This study asserts Chicago's representativeness as the most "typical" of American cities. Once this case is made, the analysis of Chicago's transformation takes on greater meaning: the expectation that such an analysis will provide insight into the essential ingredients of understanding transformations in other U.S. cities and, perhaps, other cities in the advanced-capitalist world. Our study, then, is inductive, and we are developing theory about urban change and globalization based on a case study of the City of Chicago. And, to close the circle, we are asserting that, in spite of and because of incredible change, Chicago is still the paradigmatic city for urban studies.

A POINT OF VIEW: CONVERGING FORCES

Daniel Burnham, the architect of a new Chicago after the Great Fire of 1871, was in the right place at the right time with the right vision. His credo, "Make no little plans, they have no magic to stir men's blood," rallied citizens and power brokers to create the phoenix that is present-day Chicago. His credo was also a challenge and a point of view. The plan of this book is not little; not for the sake of stirring men's blood, but because the scope and character of the subject matter requires it. And, rather than magic, we have employed a multifaceted conceptual lens to create a vision of a changing Chicago in a changing world.

The major organizing concept of this book is that five converging forces have significantly transformed and continue to transform the city of Chicago and its metropolitan region. Understanding these forces give us a perspective on the experience of residents and move us toward a clearer understanding of the present and its effect on the future. What follows is an introduction to these converging forces, some evidence to support our contention that a new Chicago has emerged and, last, a discussion of how an analysis of Chicago's transformation can contribute to an understanding of our postmodern world.

Globalization

Globalization, like pornography, is hard to define. Unlike pornography, however, it can be hard to recognize even when seen. "The international movement of capital, goods, and people" is a conventional but unidimensional definition of globalization. Perhaps more consequential for rank-and-file urban residents are the local effects produced by broad-scale transformations of the economy and the increased geographic mobility of populations, ideas, and technology.

Moreover, when an urban region has attained the scale of Chicago's metropolitan area, the local effects of globalization may very well be reconfigured as new elements give shape to emerging social and economic networks at the global scale.

At the same time, Chicago's governmental, business, and civic leadership is anxious to advance the city's claim to global or "world-class" status. Although self-promotion is nothing new to a metropolis whose most durable monicker—The Windy City—is not a meteorological reference, current efforts to promote Chicago as a center for the arts, culture, entertainment, business services, and tourism represent a sharp break from older identities such as "Hog Butcher to the World." In fact, until the most recent decade, an unmistakable air of civic desperation was revealed by such efforts as the unsuccessful campaign, in the mid 1980s, to mount a Chicago World's Fair in 1992. However, during the 1990s, Chicago's successful hosting of internationally heralded events, including the World Cup soccer championship (preliminary round, 1994) and the Democratic Party National Convention (1996), began to rejuvenate the city's national and international reputation. In addition, a massive program of public-works investment, combined with a private residential real estate boom since the mid1990s has substantially re-glamorized Chicago's downtown core and surrounding environs. Given these recent trends, many Chicagoans seem to think once more of their metropolis as a prosperous and dynamic urban center. As we explore the remaining converging forces, this theme of Chicago's renewed economic dynamism—and its perception as a global "player"—threads its way through many of the specific discussions.

Economic Restructuring

Industrial America's economy boomed during the 1950s and 1960s, and all boats were being lifted by a tide of mobility that was systemic, or structural, at base:

Most employed men experienced significant economic mobility during the postwar years, but this mobility was mostly structural, brought about by the transformation of the occupational system itself, rather than through individual advancement within a fixed occupational wage hierarchy. . . . A man got on the escalator simply by taking and holding a job, and then simply watched his income rise steadily as the nation's entire occupational wage structure shifted upward. (Massey and Hirst 1998, 56)

As it turns out, the 1950s and 1960s were the last hurrah for America's industrial hegemony. The United States was evolving a postindustrial, high-technology, knowledge-based service economy, and the transition would be stressful and telling.

The 1970s and 1980s were not kind to much of Chicago's labor force. It is now reasonably clear that, during those two decades, the winds of change were beginning to blow, bringing in a new economic era. First came deindustrialization in the Rust Belt cities of the Midwest. The human cost was high. Chicago lost 32% of all manufacturing jobs between 1969 and 1983—dropping from a high of nearly one million to less than 600,000 (See Chapters 2 and 3). The decimation of Chicago's broad-shouldered, blue-collar labor force was beginning. Then, on its heels, came a restructuring of the business sector that was similarly devastating for white-collar workers. Massey and Hirst put it simply: "The period 1969–1989 brought a stagnation of structural mobility . . . and a growing polarization of the occupational wage structure" (Massey and Hirst 1998, 56). The net result was a series of proactive and reactive efforts by many players with differing interests, differing definitions of the situation, and differing goals. Government at all levels, major and minor businesses and industries, labor unions, investment bankers, and venture capitalists all weighed in. Analysts cleaned up that very messy process by using the simple label of "economic restructuring."

Over the last three decades, the economic restructuring of Chicago has included several components. Three merit special attention: the transformation of metropolitan Chicago's industrial base, the transformation of metropolitan Chicago's labor force, and the geographic restructuring of industry and labor.

Economic Transformations: Industry, Labor, Geography. The major blow to Chicago's traditional economy was a one-two punch delivered during the 1970s and 1980s. First came the rise of service jobs and the service economy; second, a near-simultaneous decline in manufacturing jobs and the manufacturing economy. During the mid 1950s, manufacturing jobs in Chicago outnumbered service jobs by a 3.2-to-1 ratio. In 2001, service jobs outnumbered manufacturing jobs by a 2.2-to-1 ratio, with 1982 being the crossover year for the numeric dominance of service economy jobs (Bureau of Labor Statistics 2001).

The stress of economic restructuring and the rise of globalization caused management to rethink how to optimize labor utilization and restructure the existing labor force. Such thinking took two forms. One form was the acceleration of a long-term trend: Enterprises became more capital intensive and less labor intensive, replacing workers with technology. (The phrase "capital-intensive industries," like "job furloughs," is a spin-doctor expression that masks some hard realities for workers. One East Chicago steel mill reduced its labor force by eighteen thousand jobs—one-fifth of its peak labor force—and still produced four times the amount of steel in 1998 as in 1985, thanks to an infusion of high technology via capital investments. The slashing of the labor force was, perhaps, not too little, but most certainly too late. That same steel mill filed for Chapter 11 of the Federal Bankruptcy Code in December of 2000—an oft-repeated event in the industrial Midwest.)

A second type of labor force restructuring aimed at the greater optimization of labor through a radically new creation: the contingent labor force. This innovation reduces the labor force to a few "core" jobs and, as need dictates, brings in a "just-in-time" contingent labor force from the periphery. The work force mobilized by temporary help agencies doubled in size between 1982 and 1989 and doubled again between 1989 and 1997 (Gonas 1998; Mishel, Bernstein, and Schmitt 1999). One temp agency executive refers to his and other agencies as the ATM's of the job market (Castro 1997, 44). In Illinois, a state whose statistics are dominated by Chicago, at the peak of the economic cycle in 1998, as many as one-half of all vacancies in manufacturing were filled by temporary workers. Temp agencies and the contingent labor forces they supply exist at both ends of the occupational spectrum—the trained and skilled as well as unskilled employees. Mitchell Fromstein, former president of Manpower Inc., recently proclaimed that the United States is going from just-in-time manufacturing to just-in-time employment (Peck and Theodore 2001, 476).

As business and industry in Chicago was being transformed, so too was its geography. The death of some industries and the massive decline of others, not only left sectoral holes in Chicago's economy but also physical holes, such as the 100+ still-vacant acres in Chicago's South Side left by the demise of Wisconsin Steel. Similar holes in the economic and physical landscape exist as a result of the exporting of some businesses and industries "offshore" to other countries.

This geographic restructuring also is seen in the movement of existing businesses and industries to Chicago's six collar counties, especially Cook and DuPage, accompanied by the rise of new business and industry in those and other collar counties. Since 1960, the physical location of major portions of the Chicago Metropolitan Area's economy has tilted significantly toward suburbia. Chicago experienced a greater than 50% decline in the number of manufacturing establishments within the city limits between 1960 and 2001, while, in contrast, the collar counties roughly doubled their numbers over that same period.

The geographic restructuring of the economy also produced a geographic restructuring of the labor force; as business and industry moved to suburbia, so too did their labor forces. Nearly 80% of metropolitan Chicago's labor force lived in the city in 1955; less than a third did so by 2000. During this 45-year span, the geography of where workers work versus where they live has undergone a near 100% change; in 1955, the Chicago-to–collar country worker residence ratio was approximately an 80–20 split, with the city of Chicago being the residential heavyweight. By 2000, the ratios had reversed; the collar counties now dominate in a (roughly) 70–30 split, highlighting yet another indicator of a sub-

stantial but gradual geographic change occurring over the decades and adding up to a radical reversal of situations when we compare 1955 to 2002.

The Shape of the Present. Two additional important factors, race and ethnicity and *industrial* and *occupational* niches are not so obviously linked to economic restructuring. Economic restructuring, combined with immigration and superimposed over existing racial and ethnic occupational conditions, includes the phenomenon of racially and ethnically linked *industrial* and *occupational niches*. In this case, a niche refers to an industry or occupation with disproportionately high numbers of one racial or ethnic group—to the extent that the occupation of that industry becomes "theirs." Construction workers in Chicago know full well that, for example, "drywall work is Mexican work." In the dry cleaning industry, approximately two-thirds of Chicago's over 3,000 establishments are owned by Koreans (Holli 1995, 491), and "somewhere between 84% and 86%" of all Dunkin' Donut franchises in the metropolitan area are owned by Indians or Pakistanis (Dunkin' Donuts 1998). These illustrations are the tip of a substantial iceberg and reflect the racial and ethnic dimension of economic and labor force restructuring.

As in any transition, a passing of the old occurs and the emergence of the new. Yet, the old does not fall off the flat edge of the Earth, but typically coexists along with the new, sometimes for long periods. A case can be made that Chicago has two different yet coexisting economies. One is a shrinking but still very much alive industrial-based economy characterized by good pay and a large white- and blue-collar middle class. It is typified by union jobs in manufacturing and construction and a substantial number of government jobs. The other economy consists of service and IT occupations with a two-tiered system of inequality. The upper segment is characterized by high skill and pay, job security, and high prestige. The lower tier offers low pay and little job security, and it consists of low-skill and low-prestige occupations. The metaphor is an hourglass; the economic differences are profound.

Political Managerialism and Chicago's New Politics of Growth

Politics and Chicago are synonymous. In particular, mayoral politics has been integral in forging Chicago's national and, in many cases, international reputation. Although city politics over the past four decades represents a major converging force in shaping the new Chicago, the allocation of resources and power by three specific mayors reflects their different responses to social, economic, and political changes in the city: Mayors Richard J. Daley, Harold Washington, and Richard M. Daley. Each has played a significant role in forming Chicago's external image and internal workings. Each has responded differently to the shifting racial and ethnic mosaic that comprises the city. Building on the momentum created by the civil rights movement of the 1960s, black, Latino, and liberal white leaders constructed a political coalition that rocked the heretofore unbeatable Chicago Democratic Machine of Richard J. Daley and led to its first major defeats during the early 1970s.

It took a while to get there. Blacks, Latinos, and liberal, progressive whites coalesced in the mid to late 1960s around anti-Machine strategies, flexed their collective muscle and, in 1972, ousted Mayor Richard J. Daley and his delegation from the floor of the National Democratic Convention meeting in Chicago. The growing disaffection of black leaders and voters over what they perceived as inadequate returns for their long-term investments in and loyalty to the city's regular Democratic organization led to defections from the organization by prominent black politicians and sequential waves of voter revolts. By 1983, the stage was set for the election of Harold Washington as Chicago's first African American mayor. The Daley machine survived but never completely recovered from this defeat. City and county jobs, street-cleaning schedules, and garbage pick-up priorities required re-negotiation with new power brokers from the city's black and Latino wards. Meanwhile, the expansion of the Chicago region diluted the city's legislative influence in the Illinois state capital of Springfield and forced Chicago Democrats to move more cautiously when seeking to bring state resources to bear on the city's multiple problems.

Although his late father's Democratic machine was in shreds by the time Richard M. Daley ascended to the mayoralty, in many respects Chicago's second Mayor Daley has grasped power in the city just as effectively as did his father. In the city's most recent mayoral election, in February of 2003, Richard M. Daley carried 79% of the votes cast and won majorities in each of the city's 50 wards. Although a few of the mayor's allies in the Chicago City Council faced ward-level challenges in the 2003 election, just as from 1999 to 2003, the current city council counts no more than three to four consistent mayoral critics among its 50 members (Washburn 2003, 4). Beyond mayor–council relations, Richard M. Daley has built a powerful base of support, drawn both from the elite circles of the city's business and civic leadership and from the city's older working-class, newer Latino, and growing professional populations. As mayor, Daley has promoted significant overhauls of Chicago's public schools, the much-criticized Chicago Housing Authority, and even the police department. In part, the political strength of Richard M. Daley must be attributed to his recasting of the image of Chicago city governance, downplaying its traditions of party influence and patronage, and emphasizing popular new approaches to government derived from the world of corporate management. Furthermore, the current Mayor Daley's success is a function of the city's evident success during the 1990s, a decade during which substantial portions of the central city experienced new infusions of commercial and residential investment, the first decade since the World War II era in which the decennial U.S. census registered an overall population gain for the city.

The Transformation of Space

Space and the transformation of space is a major component of the cultural canvas we all experience. We celebrate the birth of places with cornerstones, provide temporary immortality with historical landmarks, and mourn their passing with monuments. When we speak of "going home," we mean not only returning to people but also returning to place and space. Space is also one of the great interpersonal and cross-cultural identifiers. After asking a stranger, "What do you do?" we then typically ask, "Where are you from?" When we change space, we change ourselves. We use space to reinforce our sense of self as well as to shape it. Our structure and use of space is a public statement of who we are, who we want to be, and how we want others to define us. Public space, the physical urban environment we call Chicago, also collectively announces who we are and what we declare ourselves to be. This space too serves to shape our individual self-concept as well as our collective one.

The new Chicago has a new face. Over the course of the last two decades, the city and its metropolitan area has undergone a radical kind of spatial, structural, and aesthetic cosmetic surgery. Chicago's new face is the result of a team of practitioners at work: city, state, and local government; planners and architects; business and industry; large and small-scale developers; communities; interest groups; and individual property owners—to name but a few.

The City. Recently, a reporter for the *Chicago Tribune* was assailed by many Chicago-lovers for writing a story asserting the city no longer had an identity (*Chicago Tribune* 24 January 2003). Yet, the reporter was merely reporting a true but less than obvious reality. Some changes creep up on us relatively unnoticed until one day, we suddenly notice that the workplaces of the service and high-tech industry do not spout smoke and grit nor do their employees drive pickup trucks, carry lunch pails, wear steel-toed work boots, or stop off for a beer and chaser on the way home from work before trudging off to their 16" summer softball game. Yes, Chicago has fewer local taverns and more wine bars and fitness centers. Yes, Chicago has fewer broad shoulders and more firm pecs. The steel mills are mostly gone, and manufacturing continues to decline. White ethnic immigrants of the past have mostly assimilated, whereas more recent immigrants provide testimony to the reality of ethnic succession. So, indeed, the old Chicago image doesn't really fit any more.

The city's physical transformation has pretty much gone hand in hand with its economic transformation. And, because we cannot create more space, the city has engaged in the process of subtraction before addition. Much, but not all, of that subtraction serves two elements of the city's new economy: tourism, a booming and multilayered new multimillion dollar industry, which is new in the sense that it has only recently been institutionalized as an industry; and the knowledge-based, service and high-tech world of business and commerce. The stockyards are long gone. High-rise public housing, a mistake in the first place, is soon to be history. West Madison, once the main street of Chicago's Skid Row, has been transformed into a "nice" mixed-use commercial street, as has Maxwell Street, Chicago's down-home version of London's Portobello Road. An impoverished black neighborhood on Chicago's near West Side was demolished to provide a home for the Chicago Bulls and creeping gentrification. The site of one of Chicago's two large, urban, commercial food markets—South Water Street, once the distribution center for many of Chicago's wholesale fruit and vegetable vendors—is currently being incorporated into the University of Illinois at Chicago (UIC) campus. The other, the Randolph Street Market—the distribution center for meat, poultry, and fish purveyors—is slowly but surely evolving into an area of urban lofts and chic restaurants. Some areas, such as the 100+ acres left by long-dead Wisconsin Steel on Chicago's far South Side, are still vacant pits waiting to be redefined and transformed.

The addition side of this equation is truly impressive. Chicago probably has not seen such rapid and comprehensive change since the Great Fire. And, as in the community response after the Fire, participation in this change process is extensive. It's as if some unspoken common accord has been reached and, simultaneously, a cascade of government, civic, business, and citizen projects have rippled throughout the city and much of the metropolitan area. Wholesale projects of renewal, expansion, conversion, and replacement can be seen almost everywhere. Class and race have not been neutralized, however; after all, this is still Chicago, the place where clout was perfected, so not all interests are served equally.

The spatial transformation is also a racial and class transformation. For decades, urbanologists warned of the likelihood, if not the certainty, that America's inner cities would soon become minority ghettos surrounded by a suburban belt of middle- and upper-middle-class whites—another failed prophesy, as it turns out. For, in the face of continued racial and minority spatial segregation, Chicago is undergoing large-scale gentrification (both black and white), utilizing a new version of urban renewal, that has gone from trend to movement to near mania. And, in the process, gentrification has become a dirty word for many. Since "location, location, location"—in this case closeness to work, restaurants, the lakefront, and entertainment—is the dominant value, neighborhoods close to the Loop are experiencing the greatest transformation.

A new, relatively large, and unheralded army of well-trained, well-educated, and well-paid professionals and administrators—the labor pool of an economically restructuring city—now calls the city home. Attracted to the lifestyle, amenities, and convenience of the city, they have become a relentless force for change. In some instances, they enjoy one-stop living in newly developed and developing high-rise communities—the city's answer to suburbia's gated communities. In other instances, entire neighborhoods are being transformed. For a generation, Lincoln Park and Hyde Park stood out as beachheads of up-scale urbanity on the north and south side of the Loop, and they did not appear likely to be joined by similar additional bastions. It wasn't until the early 1990s, with the rise of the new economy, that Lincoln Park and Hyde Park changed from isolated urban anomalies to new urban models. Soon, neighborhoods like Wicker Park, Bucktown, the Near West Side, and Dearborn Park emerged as new zones of urban gentrification. Some were formed largely through the rehab of existing housing stock, others by tear-downs and new construction.

The initial transformation took place in north and near north communities, in which the working class was simply driven out by force—the force of the checkbook. The checkbook has become a weapon of mass destruction in working-class and poor neighborhoods. It has produced a tide of rising property costs,

followed by a tide of rising property taxes, followed by a tide of departing working-class and poor residents. That tide soon spread westward and then southward and, most surprising of all to urbanologists, to that innermost part of the inner city, the Loop. Aside from experiencing the physical transformation brought about by government, business, and commercial interests, the Loop and environs, for the first time in Chicago's history, is becoming a major residential area. Here, high-rise villages and communities—interspersed with warehouse conversions—are literally popping up like so many mushrooms on a summer morning. The net result is the rise of a new residential city.

The Metropolitan Area. Although we continue to use a "city–suburb" vocabulary in speaking about major metropolitan areas and their environs, the reality is that most major cities in the country, Chicago included, are surrounded by a number of edge and satellite cities with vigorous, growing, and broad-scope economies. With few exceptions, these cities are increasingly areas of job growth and are the major cause for the "reverse commuting" of City of Chicago dwellers, who clog the expressways in the morning and evenings in their to-and-fro work-to-home exodus.

The intense suburbanization of America's cities during the 1950s and 1960s initially produced bedroom communities in which workers slept in their suburban homes and commuted to the city for work. Services and retail sales businesses soon followed these households to the suburbs and, by the 1970s and 1980s, so too did major businesses and industry. Currently, more people, more jobs, more businesses, and more industry exist in Chicago's six collar counties than do in Chicago itself. This is a relatively new and radical change that has morphed bedroom communities into edge cities like Rosemont, Oakbrook, Hinsdale, and Schaumburg as well as satellite cities like Aurora, Naperville, Waukegan, and Elgin—replete with high-rise corporate campuses, vast industrial parks, and major hotel chains spiking a prairie skyline that sprouted nothing higher than corn stalks a few short years ago.

Race, Ethnicity, and Immigration

The Chicago story has long been a story of migration and immigration. It once was the immigrant capital of the American heartland, and it currently ranks among the top five immigrant cities in America. A hundred and fifty years ago, during the 1850s and 1860s, about half of Chicago's population was foreign-born. Over the decades, that proportion declined, until it reached its low of 11.1% foreign-born in 1970. Since then, this figure has risen steadily and, by 2000, the proportion of foreign-born Chicagoans stood at 21.7% (INS, 1972–2000). On-going research suggests that this proportion may now be closer to 25% (WSJ.com. 2003).

Post World War II Chicago has seen two major demographic shifts. One, a white urban outflow—the movement of large numbers of the white community to the suburbs—and the other, the change of a white majority–black minority, two-race city into a geographically segregated multiracial, multiethnic city. The white urban decline began during the 1950s and accelerated over the next two decades. The 1980s and 1990s saw a slowing of the white exodus and, by 2000, stabilization. In turn, the white population in suburbia maintained a constant growth rate from the 1980s to 2000 and will probably do so into the foreseeable future.

The history of race relations in Chicago has always been less than admirable, and while statistically contemporary Chicago can be described as a multiracial, multiethnic city, in reality that less-than-admirable past is still with us. Demographic change over the past 20 years has resulted in a city with nearly equal proportions of whites and African Americans and, by 2004, a near similar proportion of Hispanics. The statistics are deceptive, however, in that significant racial and ethnic segregation still exists throughout the city. It is difficult to miss the irony in that, recently, analysts have downgraded Chicago from being *the* most racially segregated city in the country to simply *one of* the most racially segregated cities in the country. As the racial-ethnic residential map in Chapter 8 amply demonstrates, Chicago's south- and west-side neighborhoods are black, its south-central and west-central neighborhoods are Hispanic, its north and northwest neighborhoods are white, and small clusters of Asian and immigrant Eastern European neighborhoods dot near-South and near-North neighborhoods.

In the early days, new arrivals to Chicago from eastern and southern Europe were complemented by the migration from south to north of black Americans who sought new economic and social freedoms within their own country. Current patterns of newly arriving residents to Chicago are a cultural and ethnic kaleidoscope drawn from all continents. The five most numerous immigrant groups are illustrative of this wide range of national origins: Mexican, Polish, Indian, Filipino, and Korean.

While Chicago remains among the nation's most racially segregated cites, jazz and blues music attracts multiethnic groups to clubs in predominately white North Side neighborhoods. Ethnic areas, such as the Mexican communities of Pilsen and Little Village, and Chinatown and the South Asian-dominated portions of Devon Avenue, attract restaurant patrons from throughout the city, even as many immigrant families migrate outward and add to the ethnic and cultural mix of Chicago's collar counties. In addition, diverse groups of new and old residents intersect in the classroom, workplace, and commercial and recreational venues in a constant, if mostly informal, exchange of world cultures that in many ways reflects the immigration data. Observing residential interactions in the city is like viewing the shifting colors and patterns of the aggregated particles of a kaleidoscope.

CONTESTED REINVENTON

We call the convergence of these five forces—globalization, economic restructuring, political managerialism, transformation of space, and race, ethnicity, and immigration—a process of "contested reinvention." Contested reinvention speaks to the various visions, advocates, and modes of urban transformation that have played out in Chicago over the past two generations. With respect to vision, the new Chicago has been variously conceived as a postindustrial corporate center (by two generations of civic boosters, as well as by a series of city planning documents), as a racially inclusive city holding onto a substantial share of its mid twentieth century industrial base (notably by economic development officials in the Harold Washington administration), as an amenity-rich playground for the contemporary upper-middle class (the current Daley mayoral administration), and as an efficiently organized, environmentally sustainable economic region (by the authors of 1998's *Chicago Metropolis 2020* plan). And as a cluster of more or less progressive neighborhoods by various grassroots organizations.

As for advocacy, Chicago's older polarization of voices—Democratic Party insiders versus anti-Machine advocates and central city versus suburban leaders—has given way to a complicated mix of governmental reformers and traditionalists (read patronage- and contract-hungry political insiders). Others with development interests, whom John Logan and Harvey Molotch (1987) have called "place entrepreneurs," as well as metropolitan-oriented business and civic leaders, neighborhood activists, and new constituency (recent immigrant populations, gays and lesbians) advocates are also players. This partial cataloging of local voices is not meant to suggest that contemporary Chicago has become, if you will, a war of all against all, but it does speak to the complexity of interests seeking to shape key features of the emergent metropolitan community.

The modes by which this transformation will occur vary from the explicitly defined visions of a new Chicago revealed by various city planning documents to the especially grand *Chicago Metropolis 2020* plan. In the chapters that follow, however, we also discuss the less self-conscious transformations of neighborhood space produced by new patterns of immigrant settlement, or by the emergence of commercial enclaves such as the gay-oriented "Boys Town" in the Lake View neighborhood and the gallery-and-entertainment districts of River North and Wicker Park. Of course, such neighborhood transformations often produce conflict between working-class outgoers and prosperous incomers, and even between the first-wave of student–artist gentrifiers and subsequent loft and condominium purchasers. But, contested reinvention also speaks to the *parallel* changes reflected by

gentrification in some sections of the city, new immigrant settlement in both central city and suburban communities, and the efforts of some suburban towns to create new, downtown-like commercial cores. In short, we can assert that a new Chicago is emerging. Because of the multiple dreams at work across this metropolis, the multiple dreamers, and the unpredictability of many of their interactions, we also recognize that our central aim of defining the predominant directions of change will probably elude our powers of prognostication.

Thus, with this introductory chapter— *Part I* of *The New Chicago*—we have explained the scale and purpose of our enterprise and, as well, we have outlined our primary lines of analysis. In *Part II* of the book, we disaggregate the five converging forces and deal in detail with each in separate chapters. Because we believe the five converging forces are *essential* for understanding how a new Chicago emerged, it becomes especially important to elaborate on the role of each in that process. We see these forces in part as structural pilings that serve as a foundation for a new Chicago and in part as interrelated strands of a strong spider-like web in which no movement or activity takes place in one strand without affecting all the others.

Part III has several chapters dedicated to past and present ethnic and racial groups. Because people energize and bring alive the four other converging forces, and because immigration is dramatically altering the human composition and culture of Chicago, extensive description and analysis is contained here. For, as complex as other converging forces are, the human forces are even more complex and produce distinctive and ever-changing dynamics. Black and white relations, while still evolving and never static, have a long and exceptionally uneven history in Chicago, and we will analyze the emerging patterns of the "postmodern" construction of race and race relations. Immigration over the past quarter-century has added new cultures, races, and religions to Chicago's social mix that further alter the politics, economy, geography, and culture of metropolitan Chicago. Not only are there new players, but players who—by their very presence—change the nature of existing, older social dynamics and add a new and even more complex set of dynamics of their own. While large numbers are no guarantee of social, political, or economic influence, we have limited our analysis of Chicago immigrants to those seven groups that constitute approximately 60% of all legal immigrants to Chicago since 1972: immigrants from Mexico, Poland, India, the Philippines, Korean, China, and the Middle East.

Part IV consists of a series of case studies on selected topics and issues. A metropolitan area like Chicago is a vast and multilayered network of actors, organizations, institutions, geographies, and interest groups, daunting in its complexity. In turn, people, organizations, and government in Chicago are responding to the converging forces and also trying to give shape to the new Chicago in an intentional fashion. The vignettes in this section were chosen: (1) to simplify this complexity by examining in detail a selective series of issues, or cases, of recent or current vintage that, collectively, have contributed to making Chicago what it is today and (2) to illustrate some of the main lines of active reshaping pursued by various groups in the region. The case studies are intended to illustrate the effect of converging forces on social and political institutions and organizations, as well reveal the role of people, interest groups, organizations, and governments in the framing, processing, and outcomes of these forces.

Part V, the final section of the book, does two things. First, it reintroduces the overall point of view of the book—the converging forces—and the case studies and merges them into an integrated description of a new Chicago in a global world. Second, it takes these "lessons from the Chicago experience" and moves beyond them to identify principles and processes found in the Chicago story that might apply to other urban areas in this country and to other regions of our postindustrial world. It ends with a glimpse of different cultures waiting to be born.

NOTE

Acknowledgments. My thanks to Larry Bennett for being a thoughtful and helpful critic as well as enriching this chapter by writing the two sections: "Political Managerialism" and "Contested Reinvention."

1. James Bryce, the British Ambassador to the United States, appears to have been the first person to make this claim (in 1888). Since that time, several other observers and scholars made near-identical statements about Chicago, the latest being Mayor Richard M. Daley, hardly a nonpartisan urban analyst.

PART II

Converging Forces

2 Globalization and the Remaking of Chicago

THIS CHAPTER EXPLORES the fundamental transformation that has taken place in contemporary Chicago in relation to both the globalization process and associated rise of neo-liberal approaches to public policy. In the first portion of this chapter, I present a general framework for interpreting globalization. Here, globalization is presented as one aspect of a new accumulation regime in which global cities play a pivotal role in the circulation of capital, commodities, images, and people. I emphasize the centrality of global cities as strategic sites in the functional repositioning of cities within nation states and across the globe. Against this background, I review one aspect of the globalization process, namely the deindustrialization of Chicago's economy, which has led to a significant loss of manufacturing employment while concentrating attendant social costs on the city's working poor and racial minority populations. The last section considers the specific transformation of Chicago's central business district (CBD) for corporate services, retail activity, tourism, culture, and upscale residential development. This transformation, which has been spearheaded by Chicago's corporate elites and municipal leadership, expresses the broader neo-liberal agenda to transform parts of the city made obsolete by mid to late twentieth century deindustrialization. The chapter concludes with an assessment of the social implications of the type of downtown redevelopment that has occurred in Chicago since the 1980s.

REVISITING THE CONTESTED MEANING OF GLOBALIZATION

Many scholars have examined the contours and depth of the globalization process and its effect on cities and regions across the world. They have analyzed the degree to which globalization has set in motion processes such as deindustrialization, defined as the shift to service-based economies and the introduction of new, advanced information technologies; the privatization of public services; and the growth of low-wage and casual employment, unemployment, urban poverty, and racial and social polarization. At the same time, the traditional role and function of particular cities has been redefined as these cities emerge as strategic sites for new types of capital, commodity, and information accumulation and circulation, thereby contributing to the emergence of a redefined hierarchy of cities (Friedmann 1986; Sassen 1991, 1994). On the political front, these economic and social transformations have typically been accompanied by a neo-liberal urban agenda to revitalize inner cities through restructuring the institutions of local government to support sustained and intensified urban redevelopment (Brenner and Theodore 2002). The neo-liberal urban agenda is spearheaded by local corporate elites and allied municipal leaders intent on responding to the dictates of globalization (as it is conventionally understood) and typically in consonance with redefined national urban policies (Sites 2003).

David Harvey (1989a) argues that globalization is a manifestation of the worldwide condensation of space and time, in which space grows smaller and time more instantaneous. He calls this process "time-space compression," in which the speeding up of economic and social processes has experientially shrunk the globe, so that distance and time no longer appear to be major constraints on the organization of human activity (Inda and Rosaldo 2002, 6). For Harvey, the process of time-space compression (and hence of globalization) is neither incremental nor continuous. Rather, it occurs in discrete phases consisting of short, concentrated bursts inherent in the capitalist economic system and manifesting itself in periodic crises of overaccumulation (Inda and Rosaldo 2002, 6). Anthony Giddens, on the other hand, considers globalization to involve a profound reorganization of time and space in social and cultural life; his work emphasizes the stretching of social life across time and space. Giddens (1990, 14) captures this process with his notion of "time-space distanciation," referring to the "condition under which time and space are organized as to connect presence and absence."

For both Harvey and Giddens, globalization involves a fundamental transformation of social and cultural life, which in turn produces new kinds of cities and a globe-spanning urban system. David Held and his co-authors (1999, 2) suggest that cities are strategic nodes for the "widening, deepening and speeding up of world-wide interconnectedness in all aspects of social life." Because cities provide the dense technological infrastructure and expertise that enables transnational corporations to coordinate and control worldwide economic activity, they have emerged as the primary site for incoming and outgoing of foreign investment, labor, transport, and communications, processes that compress and unify the dense, networked infrastructure of the globalized world.

As local urban, regional, and national economies merge into a single networked global system, so the argument goes, they form a new urban hierarchy, with the positions of particular cities dependent on their ability to attract and facilitate global flows of capital, labor,

commodities, cultures, images, and information. At the top are the command and control centers of the world economy—by virtually universal assent, New York, London, and Tokyo—that are closely linked to a second tier of cities including Amsterdam, Chicago, Frankfurt, Los Angeles, and Paris (Sassen 1991; Abu-Lughod 1999). As urban theorist John Friedmann (1986, 318) has argued, the "form and extent of a city's integration into the world economy and the functions assigned to the city in the new spatial division of labor will be decisive in determining any structural changes occurring within it."

Yet, skeptics have pointed out striking differences among global cities in terms of economic base, spatial organization, and social structure. Global cities sharing the same command-center functions—and therefore presumably aligned in terms of world historical experience—do not mirror one another in all the ways predicted by the world-city hypothesis. For example, Tokyo and New York are both global cities, but Tokyo has not experienced anything like the severe manufacturing decline or racial and spatial dislocation experienced by New York, much less Chicago. New York is located at the eastern end of an industrial belt stretching from the U.S. East Coast to the upper Midwest and, like Chicago, New York has experienced massive deindustrialization and rising racial and social inequality (Hill and Kim 2000). But New York does not have the deeply entrenched, hyper-segregated residential structure that sociologists Douglas Massey and Nancy Denton (1993) have identified as a defining feature of postindustrial Chicago. Commenting on race and geography in these two cities (as well as Los Angeles), Janet Abu-Lughod (2000, 12) has noted that, "neither New York nor Los Angeles has the same degree of cleavage as Chicago between the central city and its politically powerful 'white' collar counties. And it is this cleavage, which was the result of racism, that stands in the way of a solution." Indeed, it is Abu-Lughod's view that the crucial factors of race, residential hyper-segregation, and concentrated poverty are major stumbling blocks as Chicago strives to solidify its status as a global city.

GLOBALIZATION AND URBAN RESTRUCTURING

One major development of the post-World War II period was the increasing dominance of transnational corporations, particularly those based in the United States, Europe, and Japan, to invest in overseas production and manufacturing operations. In the late 1950s to early 1960s, 20 percent of U.S. machinery plants, 25 percent of all new chemical plants, and 30 percent of all new transportation equipment was located abroad. By the 1970s, almost 70 percent of U.S. imports were transactions between domestic and transnational subsidiaries, and 40 percent of all world trade was "intra-firm" (Knox 1997, 19).

The growth of transnational economic activity was accelerated by the deregulation of financial and currency markets as well as new technological developments in transport and communication. These new technologies gave transnational companies the flexibility to exploit differential labor costs between countries. The corporate implementation of globalization strategies clearly opened new possibilities for reducing labor costs, generating what has been called the new international division of labor.

The performance of cities and regions is increasingly affected by forces external to their specific geographical context. Contemporary urban restructuring is characterized by:

- Increasing internationalization of metropolitan regions in terms of both capital and labor (Soja 1991), producing the formation of the "world city" (Castells 1993) or the "global city" (Sassen 1991)
- Changing power relations between the public and private sector, which, on the local and regional level of government, is manifest by the deregulation of planning controls and the reworking of other governmental regulations in favor of entrepreneurialism (Harvey 1989b) and the attraction of foreign investments
- Industrial restructuring and consequent shifts in production patterns and labor structures, characterized by deindustrialization (in many areas of North America and Western Europe) and by the growth of command and control functions in the central areas of a few global cities (Sassen 1991)
- Increasing social and economic polarization, symbolized by the emergence of the "dual city" (Mollenkopf and Castells 1991), which is marked by a simultaneous concentration of an executive-professional-managerial technocracy and an urban underclass (Soja 1991)
- Emergence of postmodern urban landscapes (Zukin 1992), characterized by new modes of urban culture and consumption, physically marked by an aesthetic form of postmodern urban architecture directed at "the selling of place" (Harvey 1993)

Obviously, the foregoing trends—particularly that of cities becoming greater or lesser conduits for the characteristic transactions linking global economic players and the redefinition of local urban geography, institutional composition, and social structure—play out in different ways in different metropolitan regions. Chicago is one city whose continued economic might is unquestionable, but whose particular role or positioning within the emergent network of global cities is less certain. Moreover, local elite anxiety over the city's future has been a subtext for much of its planning and redevelopment activity as far back as the 1950s.

JUST HOW GLOBAL IS CHICAGO?

A generation ago, planning scholar Robert Cohen (1981) constructed a "multinational index" for American cities, to situate them within the emergent international urban hierarchy. Cohen's index compared the percentage of a city's *Fortune* 500 firms to total foreign sales. For example, in the New York Standard Metropolitan Statistical Area (SMSA), *Fortune* 500 firms accounted for 40.5 percent of all foreign sales and 30.3 percent of total sales. Dividing the first percentage by the second, Cohen derived a multinational index of 1.43. Cohen further proposed that, when most of the corporations domiciled in a city had extensive international operations, the city's score on the multinational index would be 1.0 or higher; as such, the city was ranked as an "international city."

Those metropolitan areas with some firms having international subsidiaries, scoring between 0.7 and 0.9, Cohen characterized as "national cities." Chicago, as scored by Cohen, was a "national" rather than an "international city." By analyzing the percentage of total deposits represented by foreign deposits among for the nation's top 300 banks, Cohen (1981) also constructed a "multinational banking index." Using this mode of classification, several "international" corporate centers dropped to a "national" or "regional" status, whereas Chicago moved up the ranking to "international" center.

A more recently published "roster of world cities" (Beaverstock et al. 1999) was constructed by assessing the presence of advanced producer services, namely accountancy, advertising, banking, and law. A grouping of "alpha" world cities was headed by London, New York, and Paris, with Chicago, Frankfurt, Hong Kong, Los Angeles, Milan, and Singapore also earning this status. A second tier of "beta" world cities included Madrid, Mexico City, San Francisco, Sao Paulo, and Sydney. Saskia Sassen's (1994) assessment of global cities focuses on postindustrial production for producers, financial services, and global financial markets, yielding a smaller top tier consisting of London, New York, and Tokyo. Sociologist Janet Abu-Lughod's (1999; 2000) recently produced historical assessment of urban development in Chicago, Los Angeles, and New York characterizes each as a global city, though with widely varying trajectories of development and local socioeconomic landscapes.

If global cities are defined in terms of locally headquartered *Fortune* 500 corporations, Chicago ranks only fourth among U.S. cities (behind New York, Houston, and Atlanta). On the other hand, Abu-Lughod (1999, 411) has noted that the value of transactions through the Chicago Mercantile Exchange far exceeds those of New York or any other global financial center. Until just the last several years, Chicago also dominated the global market in futures and options trading, in 1991 having issued 60 percent of all such contracts (Sassen 1994, 91). Clearly, scholars differ among themselves when it comes to defining a global city. Just as evidently, the acceleration of economic processes associated with the contemporary world economy means that

the fortunes of particular cities can shift dramatically, sometimes within a matter of years. In Chicago's case, its current global significance is not based on the same economic formula—national geographic and railroad centrality, long production–line assembly processes, and a domination of a variety of heavy equipment and consumer products markets—that brought it to prominence a century ago. On the one hand, forces associated with globalization have buffeted Chicago's older industrial economy; on the other hand, local business, governmental, and civic elites have attempted to define a new role for their city within a rapidly changing global economic context.

GLOBALIZATION AND CHICAGO: A GALE OF CREATIVE DESTRUCTION

During his 1989 mayoral campaign, Richard M. Daley told an audience, "The city is changing. You're not going to see factories back . . . I think you have to look at the financial markets—banking, service industry, the development of O'Hare Field, tourism, trade. This is going to be an international city" (Phillips-Fein 1998, 28). While the Mayor was echoing the popular understanding of globalization, it is important to specify the particular factors that have altered Chicago's economy in recent decades.

Over the past 30 years, a steady erosion has occurred of the American Midwest's industrial base. Thousands of the region's once bustling factories, warehouses, and steel plants, formerly the backbone of America's industrial might, have permanently shut down or relocated to the South, West, or overseas. A complex set of factors, including capital flight, global competition, automation, and production decentralization, has resulted in major setbacks for local urban economies in the region (Bluestone and Harrison 1982; Sugrue 1996). By 1973 and the first Middle East oil crisis, the ongoing decline of the Midwest industrial belt was unmistakable. Coincidentally, the nation witnessed the emergence of "Sunbelt" industries (microelectronics, medical instruments, bio-engineering, etc.), spawned in part by post-World War II defense spending, in regions that had previously lagged economically (Markusen, Hall, and Glasmeier 1986).

No region was hit as hard by this restructuring process as the Midwest. Richard Hill and Cynthia Negrey (1987) examined the Midwest manufacturing employment decline for the period from 1979 to 1985, and they concluded that the Midwest suffered especially from the national decline in the "metal-bending" industries. Furthermore, while the rest of the nation compensated for employment loss in these declining industries through growth in other economic sectors, the Midwest did not. A few years later, Ann Markusen and Virginia Carlson (1989) reported that the region lost nearly one million industrial jobs between 1977 and 1986, further noting that differentials in employment rates between the region and the nation were primarily the result of sectoral shifts in the national economy away from the traditional manufacturing enterprises and toward military defense, finance, and business services. The trends observed in the Midwest region did not by-pass Chicago. Indeed, the genesis of Chicago's deindustrialization can be located in the early post–World War II era.

Like other Midwestern cities, the economy of Chicago underwent significant changes between the late 1960s and the mid 1990s, changes that were intensified by the globalization process. In the initial stage of the deindustrialization process, manufacturing relocation to suburban areas was a key marker. In Chicago, the citywide distribution of manufacturing employment, during the period from 1958 to 1972, actually grew from 329,000 to 389,000. However, from 1972 to 2000, manufacturing employment plunged by nearly 267,000 jobs (Dept. of City Planning 1958; U.S. Department of Labor 2002).

THE EFFECT ON CHICAGO COMMUNITIES

The restructuring of manufacturing and the suburbanization of jobs have had a profound impact on the geography of local employment, producing devastating effects in the city Chicago and its neighborhoods. From the stockyards to the far South Side, economic restructuring, deindustrialization, and the shifting geography of employment have especially undermined working-class African American and Latino neighborhoods. These neighborhoods have been further marginalized by punitive public policies regarding housing, education, and transportation, which have deepened and concentrated poverty.

The sectoral and geographic restructuring of the Chicago economy hit African American communities hardest. In 1950, fully one-third of all black workers in Chicago were employed in manufacturing (Wacquant 1989). One major consequence of the geographic shift of employment has been to fracture the employment networks of many inner-city residents, who find themselves trapped in low-income, poorly serviced neighborhoods that are at a considerable distance from suburban centers of employment growth (Theodore 1998). These circumstances have "hurt most of those seeking their first jobs—young adults, particularly those who are black and facing greatly magnified competition by the rapid black concentration of this age segment in the central cities" (Lichter 1988, 789). In interviews that the University of Chicago's Urban Poverty Project conducted with employers, "it was found that many directors of personnel express considerable reticence at the prospect of hiring young black males and openly acknowledge that they, or their colleagues, do not consider them fit for employment because of insufficient work ethic, education or proper work experience" (Wacquant 1989, 512). With few opportunities to capitalize on work experience and skills, many inner-city working-class residents, particularly African Americans and Hispanics, have endured long spells of unemployment, typically turning to poorly paying service-sector and dead-end jobs (Wilson 1996).

The economically viable neighborhoods of what, during the pre-World War II era, was known as the "Black Metropolis" and, in particular, the dense network of social ties giving people a sense of place, have been obliterated as deindustrialization has torn at the social fabric of community. As with other ghettos around the country, whose predominant institutions have become liquor stores and storefront churches, the physical face of African American neighborhoods on Chicago's South and West Sides, far more than statistics, offers graphic demonstration of the ultimate effects of the passage of Chicago's older, industrially centered economy.

NEW ECONOMIC ACTIVITIES

Even as manufacturing jobs have moved out of central cities to suburbs, the Sunbelt, and beyond, new economic activities have begun to cluster in the nation's major cities. Although scores of transnational companies have long been located in major cities and engaged in international trade, a report released by the U.S. Department of Commerce (2001), reveals that, by 1995, in 253 selected U.S. Metropolitan Statistical Areas, export earnings totaled more than $467 billion, an increase of nearly 13 percent over the previous year. For example, in 1995, Los Angeles County gained 93,000 jobs, and surrounding areas gained another 50,000 jobs through growth in business services, tourism, entertainment, and wholesaling, all in part attributable to international trade. Since 1990, one estimate places the growth in Los Angeles area jobs caused by global trade at 300,000 (Kotkin 1996). Janet Abu-Lughod (1995, 182–3) notes: "... it is clear that even if we may have some reservations about American urbanized regions [being] truly of world significance, foreign investors do not share our doubts. They single out New York, New Jersey, Illinois, and California as the preferred outlets for their investment."

Foreign direct investment and international trade plays an important role in urban development by stimulating the economic growth and capital inflows that generate tax revenues, as well as increases in regional and personal income. At the same time, these processes also create the institutional and technical infrastructure that can yield sustained export and import business. Those cities that have a robust economic activity related to foreign-directed investment (FDI) and international trade can accelerate their growth because exports generate significant employment and increase productivity. In Illinois, FDI plays a significant role in economic

vitality, making the state the number one destination of foreign investment in the Midwest. Currently, 5,800 foreign firms employ approximately 350,000 Illinois residents.

Since the early 1990s, the value of exports from the Chicago Metropolitan region has steadily increased. Between 1993 and 1999, the value of exports to North American Free Trade Agreement (NAFTA) countries as well as to the rest of the world has increased, with subsequent implications for employment and local economic development. The bulk of exports from the Chicago Metropolitan Statistical Area are to NAFTA countries (Canada and Mexico), Japan, and the rest of Asia and Europe and stood at well over $21 billion in 1999. Chicago was in sixth place behind San Jose/Bellevue/Everett, San Jose, Detroit, New York, and Los Angeles among metropolitan regions with the fastest growing export sales between 1993 and 1999 (cited in Madigan 2004, 57)

Commentators on the emergence of global cities, notably Saskia Sassen (1996, 1991, 1988), emphasize the economic dynamism of those core urban areas that feature a dense mix of commercial and governmental institutions combined with business-service enterprises, such as law, accounting, and communications. In these geographic spaces, highly trained labor forces engage in transactions requiring specialized skills, typically conducted via face-to-face meetings. Nevertheless, a contradictory spatial trend is embodied by the locational choices of many high-technology firms—whose operations often are not subject to "anchoring" geographic imperatives—in favor of "edge city" or even altogether nonurban sites (Garreau 1991). Prominent American edge cities include "the Route 128 area outside Boston, the Schaumburg area outside Chicago, the Perimeter Center of north Atlanta's Beltway, Irvine outside Los Angeles, and King of Prussia outside Philadelphia. These edge cities ... now have substantial office space, large retail complexes, corporate headquarters, and clean production facilities, as well as residential and recreational areas that are eagerly sought after by globally oriented firms" (Rondinelli et al. 1998, 82).

As a consequence—and apart from local specifics such as the bottom-line performance

TABLE 2.1. Downtown Chicago: Percentage Change in Employment by Major Sectors

Year	Manufacturing[1]		Nonmanufacturing[2]	
	Loop	Outer Ring	Loop	Outer Ring
1965	5.3	33.3	94.7	66.7
1970	6.6	31.4	93.4	68.6
1975	5.5	26.3	94.5	73.7
1979*	5.3	23.2	94.7	76.8
1984*	3.8	22.1	96.2	77.9
1990	4.8	13.1	95.0	86.7
1995	4.4	10.2	95.5	89.7
2000	3.4	7.3	96.2	92.3

[1] Manufacturing includes durable and nondurable goods.
[2] Nonmanufacturing includes construction, transportation, communication, utilities, wholesale trade, retail trade, finance, insurance, real estate, services, and miscellaneous.
* Data for 1980 and 1985 are not available.
Sources: Illinois Department of Employment Security historical data "Where Workers Work," 1957–1984 and 1988–2000, and UI (Unemployment Insurance Act) covered in the city of Chicago by Geographic District, 1957–1984.

of the firms headquartered in a particular city— major cities of the early to mid twentieth-century industrial era have no guarantee of evolving into postindustrial service centers of equal prominence. Table 2.1 offers some evidence of how the economy of central Chicago has changed over the last two generations, with the city's central business district divided between the traditional Loop and the "Outer Ring" (business areas adjoining the Loop on the north, west, and south). Historically, employment figures have revealed a striking division of labor between the Loop and adjoining areas, with the Loop's employment dominated by retailing, finance, and business management. And, in fact, the Loop's longstanding employment profile has persisted even into the present. But, until well after World War II, Outer Ring areas continued to sustain a substantial number of light manufacturing enterprises (Rast 1999). As Table 2.1 reveals, as late as 1970, nearly one-third of the workers in the Outer Ring were employed in manufacturing. However, two generations of industrial decline in the Outer Ring has reduced its manufacturing workforce to less than one-tenth. Since the 1980s, the Outer Ring has been

transformed by commercial and residential gentrification, with abandoned factories and warehouses converted to residential lofts and condominiums, and the newly developed residential complexes often linked by suburban-style shopping corridors.

THE NEO-LIBERAL AGENDA AND DOWNTOWN DEVELOPMENT

During the late 1960s and early 1970s, neo-liberal ideology emerged as a strategic response to the fiscal crisis engulfing American cities and metropolitan regions. Drawing on intellectual roots traceable to the early post-World War II writings of Friedrich Hayek and Milton Friedman—and galvanized by crucial events such as the New York City fiscal collapse of the mid 1970s—neo-liberal doctrines were "deployed to justify, among other projects, the deregulation of the state control over major industries, assaults on organized labor, the reduction of corporate taxes, the shrinking or privatization of public services, the dismantling of welfare programs, the enhancement of international capital mobility, the intensification of interlocality competition, and the criminalization of the poor" (Brenner and Theodore 2002).

Neo-liberal ideology has been incorporated into the urban policy agenda of local governments to rejuvenate urban redevelopment through deregulation, privatization, and increased fiscal austerity. In particular, a variety of urban policies to stem the devaluation of older fixed capital in the downtown through place-marketing, local tax abatements, urban development corporations, public–private partnerships, new strategies of social and spatial control, property redevelopment schemes, and other institutional modifications have been put on the agenda of many city governments. These urban policy strategies were designed to refashion urban space as an arena both for market-oriented economic growth and for elite consumption practices.

Larry Bennett (1999, 7–8) discusses three conditions contributing to the emergence of new modes of urban development. First, the demise of federally sponsored urban renewal programs meant that "cities had to identity and perfect their own methods of stimulating private investment." Second, municipal leaders found new methods for attracting private investment, luring tourists, and reviving declining neighborhoods. And third, a variety of small-scale, scattered entrepreneurial redevelopment initiatives that seemed to produce positive local effects began to be imitated across the United States.

The extent of devaluation and the spatial restructuring of the existing physical capital during the late 1960s and 1970s varied from city to city; in many American cities, the process reached the stage of wholesale inner-city abandonment. In Chicago, the process began in the years immediately following World War II, when the city's economy began to decline and the central business district (CBD) suffered from falling property values and declining retail sales, even as manufacturing jobs were steadily being lost to the suburbs (Berry et al. 1976; McDonald 1984). As Bennett (1989, 161) has observed, "the post-World War II economic evolution of Chicago, as well as the city government's response to population loss and the decline of older industries, parallel the experience of other U.S. cities."

THE CIVIC VISION

By the mid 1950s, consensus was growing among Chicago's business elite that, if the city was to retain its historic role as a major economic hub for the region and beyond, the economic decline engulfing the CBD had to reversed. The first major consensus on the future of Chicago's downtown was articulated in the "Development Plan for the Central Area of Chicago," which was issued in 1958 by the Department of City Planning. To improve access to the Loop for the workforce and shoppers, the plan proposed a network of expressways between the central city and outlying suburbs, with designated parking facilities on the periphery of the Loop. In addition, the plan anticipated substantial residential development in the areas immediately north and south of the Loop. Although a number of the plan's elements were not realized, the 1958 Development Plan clearly, defined the initial thrust of

Loop revitalization, particularly the creation of the Civic Center/Daley Plaza, the development of a University of Illinois campus on the Near West Side, and the designation of the North Side Sandburg Village urban renewal district. These projects were a major boost to local revitalization efforts, following nearly a quarter-century during which no significant new construction had been undertaken in the Loop.

As such, central-city revitalization, spearheaded by city's leading corporations and municipal officials, went beyond the CBD and aimed, in quite fundamental ways, to redesign the city's future. The entire period of Richard J. Daley's 21-year mayoralty, from 1955 to 1976, was marked by overlapping developments in which the mayor, municipal planning and redevelopment agencies, and the city's business leadership undertook efforts to transform the city (Bennett 1989). In the initial phase, large-scale redevelopment focused on infrastructural investment as a crucial element for the circulation of capital and labor, particularly through the expansion of the city's transport system. This program was supported by state, federal, and private expenditures. In addition, private–public partnership projects undertook targeted neighborhood residential developments and the construction of headquarters for national retail and global companies such as Sears and Standard Oil, shopping and tourist facilities such as the Water Tower on the Near North Side, as well as numerous other office buildings. The local coalition assembled for this task had the shape of a fairly characteristic, growth-oriented "urban regime"—a City Hall and business elite collaboration with the aim of jump-starting a new vision of urban centrality—as described by political scientist Clarence Stone (1989). Indeed, these shared visions and the institutions designed to transform the city had far-reaching effects beyond the CBD and constituted major initiatives to transform not only Chicago but also the region as a whole.

The general transformation of Chicago from a largely manufacturing base to an office-dominated financial and service economy was directly manifest in the physical transformation of the Loop. Prior to the early 1970s, the Loop and adjoining areas to the north, west, and south entered a period of stagnation marked by falling property values, declining retail sales, job losses, and depopulation. As many of the manufacturing plants closed or relocated out of the Outer Ring, the economic vitality of these districts was significantly eroded. The reorientation of the Loop—and indeed the physical expansion of the Loop—toward services and the intensification of residential development, have been the main objectives of the city's leading corporate leaders, who have been instrumental in supporting various downtown redevelopment plans for the Loop.

During the Richard J. Daley era, the Chicago Central Area Committee (CCAC) was probably the most important local business organization supporting downtown redevelopment. In cooperation with the city government, the CCAC released a controversial document known as "Chicago 21: A Plan for Central Area Communities" in 1973. In a much more explicit way than the 1958 Development Plan, "Chicago 21" advocated the physical expansion of downtown business, leisure, and cultural institutions into the working-class residential and light-manufacturing districts on the Loop's northern, western, and southern margins:

> Two functional assumptions of the proposed Plan are that the Chicago Central Business District should continue as the dominant focus of commerce and culture for the entire Metropolitan Area and that the Central Communities should serve as the transportation hub, the seat of government, office and business center, cultural and entertainment center and central market place. . . . Residence, work, recreation, goods and services should be brought closer together. Significant areas of vacant land can be developed under new concepts of city living.

From "Chicago 21" and its sponsors emerged the Dearborn Park residential development, a middle- to upper-income "new town in town," situated directly south of the Loop. With the city government providing infrastructure improvements, Dearborn Park has been variously interpreted as a much-needed boost in the drive to reintroduce high-income residents to Chicago's near-downtown areas and as a physical barrier between the central business district and the low-income communities of the Near South Side (Emmons 1977; Suttles 1990; Wille 1997; Rast 1999).

A decade following the release of "Chicago 21," an updated Central Area Plan was released, the broad aims of which were perfectly consistent with its predecessor documents of 1958 and 1973 (Squires et. al. 1987). However, with the election of Harold Washington as Chicago mayor in 1983, the city government's 30-year commitment to unbridled downtown transformation was—for the time being—put on hold. However, during the ensuing years, a large part of the vision articulated in particular by "Chicago 21" has become a reality under the stewardship of Mayor Richard M. Daley. The strategy of reversing the economic decline and transforming and expanding the Loop through the support of high-density office development and retailing as well as the reintroduction of a substantial downtown residential population, have been top priorities of the current city administration. A distinctive feature of the second Mayor Daley's strategy of downtown transformation and global city repositioning (as discussed at length by Costas Spirou in Chapter 25) has been the municipal government's sophisticated deployment of resources in support of cultural enhancement and physical beautification, primarily in and around the Loop. Yet, coincidentally, the "other side of the municipal policy coin" has been the aggressive scaling down and transformation of public housing, especially those Chicago Housing Authority developments in the vicinity of the city's physically expanded, multifunctional downtown district (see Chapter 22).

REDESIGNING CENTRAL CHICAGO AS A GLOBAL WORK AND LEISURE ZONE

The social, spatial, and governmental restructuring of downtown Chicago, in part defined through local decision-making processes, also bears the mark of broader phenomena shaping cities and regions across the globe. The specificity of redevelopment activities across this nation has been crystallized through the implementation of a particular array of neo-liberal policy responses to urban economic decline. The remaking of industrial Chicago as a business-services center, linked to associated "leisure" functions including convention and trade show hosting as well as more conventional tourism, and finally as a center for the arts and upscale retailing, represents the defining economic trajectory of the new Chicago. As manufacturing and industrial activities give way to service activities, Chicago has refashioned its downtown space to cater to professionals, tourists, conventioneers, and other visitors (Judd and Fainstein 1999).

Following two decades of what sociologist Richard Child Hill (1986, 102–09) once termed the "corporate-center" strategy of urban redevelopment in Chicago—in effect, the single-minded focus on retaining corporate headquarters—a more broadly based business, residential, and leisure facilities strategy of redevelopment began to emerge in the 1980s. One indicator of this trend can be seen in the pattern of investment evident in the period from 1979 to 1984. According to a study conducted by Mary Ludgin and Louis Masotti (1985), Chicago was experiencing an unprecedented building boom in office, rental and condominium, hotel, retail/recreation, and educational facility development within this half-decade. In the course of just six years, Ludgin and Masotti noted that 167 projects involving new and upgraded office space, residential units, retail spaces, and hotel rooms were completed, and close to $4.5 billion was invested. A further $2.2 billion was invested during 1985–86 in 148 new, adaptive reuse, or renovation projects in the expanding downtown area that Ludgin and Masotti dubbed the "Super Loop" (demarcated by North and Cermak Avenues to the north and south, Racine Avenue at the western boundary, and the lakefront to the east). In this two-year period, the intensity of investment in the Loop exceeded even the previous six years (Ludgin and Masotti 1986).

Much of the investment in the adaptive reuse and rehabilitation of existing buildings was facilitated by the federal Economic Recovery Act of 1981 (specifically, the tax code incentives for building rehab, which were subsequently rescinded), providing generous tax credits for construction costs incurred in the rehabilitation of many older buildings: 25 percent for buildings on the National Register of Historic Places, 20 percent for nonlandmark buildings over 30 years old. In addition, the coincidental amending of the Chicago Building Code in 1981 simplified the processes of upgrading and/or converting existing buildings. The evident result of these federal and local measures was a substantial increase in local reuse and rehabilitation projects. Moreover, the upsurge in rehabilitation was associated with an upsurge in smaller-scale development projects. For example, the 68 new construction projects completed during 1979–84 cost $2.77 billion, while the 99 completed rehabilitations cost only $565.8 million. It is clear that rehabilitations—with their relatively small costs, federal tax subsidy, and often accelerated construction timetables—became very attractive to local developers and contributed substantially to the investment boom in near-Loop sections of Chicago's central area.

Central area investment during the 1980s, while still concentrated in the Loop, also flowed into adjoining areas to the north, west, and south, significantly improving the climate for the further infusion of capital and intensification of office, retail, hotel, and residential development. Of the investments made in Chicago's central area neighborhoods, the Loop absorbed 40 percent. However, the Streeterville/North Michigan Avenue area just to the north and east of the Loop received nearly $2 billion in investment. Much of this was devoted to commercial expansion by retailers such as Neiman Marcus, Bloomingdale's, and Saks Fifth Avenue, but major projects also included facilities for Northwestern and Loyola Universities, the completion of the NBC Tower, a major hotel project, and the renovation of the North Pier entertainment complex. These retail and institutional developments also increased demand for adjoining condominium and apartment developments (Ludgin 1989, 14). Similar trends were evident in the West Loop/River West, East Loop, River North, South Loop, and Near South Sides. Within Ludgin and Masotti's Super Loop, only in the Near West Side—at that time still viewed as a risky area and the location of several Chicago Housing Authority developments—did new investment seem to lag. But since the early to mid

1990s, even the Near West Side has begun to receive a tremendous volume of commercial and residential investment.

During the 1950s and 1960s, Chicago's strategy of central area revitalization had been anchored primarily in supporting office, headquarters, and institutional development, with specific enclaves also set aside for high-rise residential projects. These efforts produced a physical makeover of the Loop but did little to hold the headquarters of firms intent on relocation or which had been absorbed through corporate takeovers. Residentially, among the city's central neighborhoods, only the near North Side managed to retain a significant population of much-desired professionals, office workers, and other prosperous urbanites. However, by the 1980s, the varieties of commercial investment in the Loop and adjoining areas, as well as the mix of residential construction and rehabilitation were, in fact, remaking the face of central Chicago. Commenting at the end of the 1980s, Alicia Mazur, who later headed the city's department of planning, noted that "Downtown Chicago was prosperous in the 1980s as it had ever been before" (Mazur 1991, 1). Much of the investment in central Chicago came from abroad. Although figures are not available for the preceding years, institutional real estate transactions increased dramatically in the late 1980s, before peaking at $4.5 billion in 1989. Japanese transnational capital investment was involved in about half of the roughly $11 billion in investments made between 1986 and 1990 in central Chicago (Mazur 1991, 18).

LOCAL GLOBALIZATION FROM THE TOP DOWN AND THE BOTTOM UP

In this chapter, I have traced a complicated playing out of forces that includes large-scale economic transformations that have changed the relationships among cities globally and restructured the local economies of many cities—Chicago included; neo-liberal policy trends that have shaped characteristic policy initiatives in American cities; and the evolution of a sequence of not altogether coherent redevelopment "visions" for Chicago. For example, during the

1950s and for a decade and more beyond, globalizing pressures were not much on the minds of civic leaders and municipal officials leading the local redevelopment campaign. Instead, their main concerns were buttressing the Loop as a new-style business center and bringing the affluent middle class back to the city. Downtown and near-downtown investment trends during the 1980s—to some degree a response to publicly initiated redevelopment efforts, in some measure a consequence of broader economic forces—began to dramatically reshape the physical face of central Chicago. Only during the 1990s, and to a considerable extent because of the initiatives of Mayor Richard M. Daley, has a redevelopment vision squarely defining Chicago as a global city emerged. In concluding this chapter, I will discuss two issues that have appeared in conjunction with the articulation and implementation of this vision: (1) the socially uneven effects of the current wave of central-area gentrification, and (2) the parallel processes globalizing Chicago in ways more or less unanticipated by the city's municipal and civic leadership.

As Chicago's central area has become an increasingly attractive place in which to live as well as work, it has begun to attract large numbers of middle-class professionals, corporate managers, and other office workers with significant disposable income. Collectively, they have begun to influence the use of space in downtown and beyond through their desires and lifestyles. The conversion of work spaces into expensive condos, the building of new office spaces for major corporations, and the establishment of upscale restaurants, boutiques, bars, and night clubs have dramatically altered Chicago's downtown cityscape (see Chapter 5). Sociologist Sharon Zukin (1998) has identified downtown-living professionals and office workers as a consumption group whose preferences increasingly determine the entertainment and amenity offerings of postindustrial downtowns.

Yet, directly linked to these shifts in space, amenities, and residency are more complicated matters of uneven social effect and benefit. For example, one of the major consequences of stepped-up office, retail, and residential development in central Chicago has been, in effect, the "pricing out" of less competitive residential uses such as single-room occupancy hotels (SROs). As SROs close or withdraw from near-downtown locations, their residents must either fend for themselves in a local housing market experiencing substantial inflationary pressure or accept housing in neighborhoods that are not necessarily of their choosing or convenient from the standpoint of their limited financial means. Downtown redevelopment has had an explicitly racial dimension as well. As one developer suggested when commercial and residential conversions within the Loop began to pick up speed, "I'll tell you what's wrong with the Loop. It's people's conception of it. And the conception they have about it is one word: Black, B-L-A-C-K. Black" (quoted in Rast 1999, 31). Clearly, the first stage of the remaking of central Chicago turned, in part, on the dispersal of undesirable minority groups and working-class families, whose physical presence could threaten newcomers and whose spending habits would not fuel much in the way of new, upscale commercial activity.

The successful "creation" of space or the re-designing of existing places for consumption is itself part of a wider reassessment of the desirability of urban living, a reassessment that has proceeded in all advanced industrial nations (Bagguley, Mark-Lawson, and Shapiro 1990; Smith 1988). From the 1930s on, cities within advanced industrial countries became increasingly suburbanized, particularly in the United States, whose federal government heavily subsidized suburban residential development. But, beginning in the 1970s, the post-World War II outward flow of the middle class ebbed as a portion of the more affluent population rediscovered, and ultimately gentrified, large sections of the inner city—a "process of middle class replacing the working class; increasing property values; alternation in the built environment and the emergence of a new urban style of life" (Savage and Warde 1993, 80).

The reshaping of central Chicago, of course, is not simply directed at enhancing amenities for local workers and residents. Among the contemporary economic functions of Chicago, and key to the city's self-conception as a global city, is its prominence as a host of conventions and trade shows and as a tourist destination. Municipally supported efforts to boost tourism in Chicago have involved: (1) the displacement of older economic functions, principally manufacturing, providing material and symbolic spaces available for adaptive recycling; (2) the commodification of culture, to be consumed in designated entertainment venues; (3) the beautification of central Chicago and adjoining neighborhoods for middle-class households; (4) place-marketing for local, regional, and international consumers; (5) the revaluation of central Chicago as a space of leisure, entertainment, culture, and education; and (6) the investment in hotels and convention facilities (Lloyd 2002, 518). The net result of these strategies has been (at least until the post-September 11, 2001) a substantially increased flow of tourists and conventioneers to the city. For example, in 1998, 4,530,000 overnight visits to the city occurred by persons attending organizational meetings of one type or another. Chicago and Cook County also ranked first among convention sites in the United States (Clark et al. 2002). As a major convention center, Chicago continues to lead the nation and world in square feet of convention space, and suburban Rosemont ranks 10th in the country, providing additional convention space for the metropolitan region. Political scientists Dennis Judd and Dick Simpson estimate that $8 billion of convention- and tourist-generated spending annually flowed into Chicago's economy in the years preceding 2001. In addition, tourism and convention business boosted several of the municipal government's revenue streams, notably sales tax revenue, which jumped from $54 million in 1989, the year of Richard M. Daley's election as mayor, to $145 million in 1999 (Judd and Simpson 2003, 1058).

Yet, as several of this volume's subsequent chapters detail, the top-down "repositioning" of Chicago as a global city has been paralleled by bottom-up processes involving renewed immigration to the city—principally by Mexicans, but also including substantial numbers of other groups from Central America, the Caribbean, Asia, and Middle East—as well as the formation of ethnic-inflected business districts, such as the Mexican-American dominated 26th Street corridor on the city's Southwest Side and the Devon Avenue "world market" on the far North Side (see Chapter 17). New cultural organizations and nationality-inscribed festivals continue to be a hallmark of Chicago's civic identity, with the city government frequently offering resources to support these initiatives. Coincidentally, new efforts to reinterpret the city's longstanding heritage of racial and ethnic pluralism have sometimes proceeded with highly contested aims and associated means. In Chapter 16, Michael Bennett discusses the redevelopment of Bronzeville, the heart of Chicago's early to mid twentieth-century racial ghetto, a neighborhood improvement campaign directly intended to build heritage tourism, but one that has been beset by criticism of its seeming means to that end: "black gentrification" and removal of the neighborhood's low-income, public-housing population. In short, although Chicago is globalizing in ways apprehended and, to the extent possible, guided by its civic, business, and governmental elites, even as these guided changes occur, global immigration and new community formation by immigrants are recasting the city's outlying neighborhoods and broader cultural identity in ways that are only partially captured by the elite discourses and practices intended to recast the "City of Broad Shoulders" as "global Chicago."

NOTE

Acknowledgments. I would like to thank Sandra Jackson and Larry Bennett, who read various drafts of the paper and provided critical comments and suggestions.

David Moberg

3   Economic Restructuring: Chicago's Precarious Balance

AFTER SPURRING CITIES across the country into a bidding war for its favors, Boeing Corporation announced, in March 2001, that it was moving its corporate headquarters from its long-time Seattle home to downtown Chicago. Although $56 million in public subsidies brought only 450 jobs, Chicago political and business leaders celebrated the capture of the nation's leading exporter and iconic global corporation as proof of the city's intrinsic attractions as a world corporate center (McCourt, Leroy, and Mattera 2003; Reed 2003).

On the other hand, relatively little fanfare erupted when Brach's Confections Inc. announced two months earlier its plans to shut down the world's largest candy manufacturing plant at the end of 2003. It was easy to see the loss of roughly 1,000 jobs on Chicago's still-poor West Side as an episode in the oft-told "Rust Belt" story of a fading industrial past giving way to a postindustrial service and knowledge economy. The company's transfer of production to Mexico followed more than half a million other manufacturing jobs that, over the decades since World War II, had largely moved out of the central city to the suburbs, to the South, and to foreign countries (Ginsburg, Jin, and McCann 1994).

But what looks like a paradigmatic tale of the emergence of a new Chicago economy is not so clear and simple. After all, both Boeing and Brach's are manufacturing companies. Globally, manufacturing obviously has not died. Neither has it all migrated. At the time Brach's was closing, metropolitan Chicago had the largest number of manufacturing jobs of any U.S. metropolis. Despite other shutdowns, Chicago was still the candy capital of the country, and even without its once-famous stockyards, it was by far the national leader in food processing.

Brach's was a local icon, cited by *Industry Week* (Verespej 1999) as one example of why Chicago was the premier location for manufacturing in the United States. But, starting in 1986, Brach's was subjected to a wave of corporate buyouts and spin-offs that imposed shifting and disastrous marketing strategies. Despite many years of both pressure and assistance (including $10 million from the city), community groups and the workers' union could not persuade the changing cast of owners and managers that they could succeed by improving technology and training workers rather than pursuing cheaper workers (and sugar) across the border (Ginsburg, Jin, and McCann 1994; Langley 2003).

Attracting Boeing was a public relations coup, but it also raised troubling questions. If the subsidy wasn't critical, as a key Boeing executive said, what did the outsized enticement say about Chicago's confidence in its own merits? Might the $56 million have been better spent on improving schools, fixing infrastructure, training workers, or enriching cultural life? Ultimately, Boeing generated far fewer ancillary economic benefits than projected in the rosy, never-released analysis justifying the public subsidies. Another Chicago corporate giant, Arthur Andersen, had prepared the analysis not long before that one-time symbol of Chicago's strength in business services folded in the aftermath of the Enron debacle (McCourt, Leroy, and Mattera 2003; Reed 2003).

The city's roster of corporate headquarters remained mixed, despite optimistic projections that Boeing heralded the beginning of a new era. Starting in 1998, Chicago had lost a string of headquarters, such as Amoco, Ameritech, and Inland Steel, mostly to corporate takeovers.[1] In January 2004, J. P. Morgan Chase & Co. bought Bank One, depriving Chicago of the headquarters for its largest bank. Also, corporate headquarters were nearly as likely to be in the suburbs as in the central city (*Chicago Tribune* 18 May 2003); *Economic Focus* 2002).

Nevertheless, both suburbs and city could take comfort in the dramatic growth of business services, such as architecture, personnel, and consulting firms, which provided specialized assistance to the corporate managers of far-flung empires.[2] In one of the nation's fastest-growing employment sectors, with moderately above-average salaries, metropolitan Chicago was either first or second nationally in the number of business service workers, depending on who's counting (World Business Chicago or the Harvard Cluster Mapping Project), and many of those jobs were in the city.

Also, despite its lingering Rust-Belt image, metropolitan Chicago had the largest concentration of high-tech workers of any urban region in the country (and tied with Washington, D.C. for the greatest number of information technology jobs). The city ranked considerably lower in the proportion of all workers in high-tech and in the ratio of high-tech manufacturing to services (whereas cities like San Jose and Seattle ranked at the top), and it lagged on measures of innovation and rate of growth (Markusen et al. 2001). But Chicago's history as an electronics and telecommunications center left a legacy of companies, research institutions, and skilled workers that could be a foundation for growth.

The wired world, analysts like Saskia Sassen have argued, does not eliminate the need for personal contacts among the decision-makers, professional advisors, and technical elite of the business world. Consequently, certain key cities—especially in their traditional cores—were likely to be centers of corporate control for the global economy (Sassen 1991). Yet, just as cities like Chicago were gearing up to compete for global-city status, growing indications

hinted that many highly skilled, business professional jobs—computer programmers, software engineers, architects, securities analysts, and others—could be outsourced to India, China, and other lower-wage locations, as were the manufacturing jobs before them (Engardio, Bernstein, and Kripalani 2003).

CHICAGO: REGIONAL CAPITAL WITH A GLOBAL REACH

So what, if anything, do Boeing and Brach's reveal about the new Chicago economy? First, Chicago is increasingly globalized, shaped for both good and ill by the force of global markets in goods, services, capital, and labor and by the strategies of global corporations. Workers at factories like Brach's got the short end. Many new business professionals are winners—at least for the moment. However, ultimately, globalization and related factors, such as a declining union movement, contributed to growing economic inequality and insecurity.

Chicago will have to adapt to the constraints and opportunities posed by globalization, but it is not a "global city" that can be reasonably confident of a controlling position like that enjoyed by New York, London, and Tokyo. Despite the growing presence of foreign multinationals, significant trade, and a renewed and varied influx of immigrants, metropolitan Chicago remained, in the early twenty-first century, a strong regional capital with a global reach. Its best opportunity to extend its global importance may depend as much on the health of the wider Great Lakes region as on the steps both the city and metropolitan Chicago take locally to shape their economic future.

It is not simply greater global interconnectedness that is shaping Chicago and other cities or that defines most contemporary conceptions of a "global city" (Sassen 1991). Rather, contemporary globalization embodies a distinctive set of rules for an economic game that are heavily influenced by global corporations. With different rules, such as stronger worker rights around the world, an end to U.S. farm subsidies, the cancellation of most less-developed country debt, or a "Tobin tax"[3] on currency and financial transactions, Chicago would still be a globalized city, but one with different opportunities.

More broadly, the Boeing and Brach's cases both underscore how market relationships have intensified and penetrated more deeply into social and economic life, a political and economic process driven partly by globalization. For example, deregulated financial markets spurred the market in corporate control, which subjects to the solvent of financial calculations ties that might have bound parts of corporations together or business facilities to a particular location. Cheap transportation and communications provide technical means for a geographic dispersal of factories and offices, but a distinct business strategy, often shaped by short-term profit horizons, is the driving force behind the often frenzied relocation of operations. Just as Brach's can be easily detached from Chicago, other corporate centers of control, like Boeing's head office, increasingly separate themselves from the gritty reality of the enterprises they manage and the cities or nations where they have headquarters. While the corporate centers retain control over dispersed and contingent empires (Harrison 1994), managers devote much effort to managing risk—such as through the Chicago futures markets—and, above all, to shifting risk to employees, contractors, governments, and the general public.

There are implications for cities like Chicago in these intensified trends. One economic rationale for cities is that they provide agglomeration advantages, such as large labor pools, nearby suppliers, easy transportation, ready customers, and a climate of both cooperation and competition that generates useful information. A variety of networks of businesses develop, including both industrial districts made up of small firms, such as the old printers' row or garment districts in Chicago's Loop outskirts, and those networks formed around a government institution or a dominant corporation, the most common pattern in Chicago as it industrialized. These relationships often made businesses more efficient, but in the process they created a kind of "stickiness," or reason to stay in place (Markusen 1996). Even ownership made a difference. A privately held business run by owners who live in the same area, or a worker-owned business, is

likely to be less mobile than publicly held multinationals, which were disproportionately quick to relocate out of both the city and the country (Squires et al. 1987).

In the newly globalized world of intensified market relations, capital becomes ever more "slippery" (Markusen 1996). The capitalist ideal of liquidity is exemplified in the global financial markets, but both people and places can suffer from an excess liquidity of investment and employment. Stickiness can yield economic benefits, for example, through stimulating businesses to increase productivity by building on human skills, cooperative community relationships, or technical innovation to cut costs rather than fleeing to lower-wage locations.

COHESION AND CONTRADICTIONS IN THE CITY'S DEVELOPMENT

Advantages of a specific physical location have often been the starting point for sticky urban agglomeration. Historically, Chicago grew as the junction between the Great Lakes and the Mississippi River system, then between eastern and western rail networks and, most recently, as a national airline hub. Although highway traffic after World War II contributed to sprawl and business migration from the central city, the metropolis remained a hub for truck traffic, and it remains the third largest intermodal container port in the world, after Hong Kong and Singapore.

At first primarily a city of wholesale trade, Chicago secured its prominence in competition with other cities, historian William Cronon wrote, by greater control of capital from far-flung creditors that financed its growth as a manufacturing center, especially after 1860 (Cronon 1991, 11, 305). Chicago became an instrument for imperial dreams of imposing the market on nature, and the idea of the city and the businesses that grew there were intertwined, most intimately in a development like Pullman.

It was nevertheless a cohesion filled with contradictions, as the Pullman strike, the Haymarket incident, the great railroad strike of 1877, and other industrial conflicts made clear. The "white city" of the Columbian Exposition symbolized the unity of purpose Chicago's elite felt at the end of the nineteenth century, but that vision attempted to conceal the conflicts within the city under the exposition's gleaming white plaster (Trachtenberg 1982). Clashes occurred between the visions of entrepreneurs like Gustavus Swift and Cyrus McCormick and those of socialist, anarchist, trade union, and other working class leaders, like Eugene Debs. By the late nineteenth century, prominent reformers from the city's elite and middle class (including Jane Addams) wanted to reduce raw class conflict and improve the lives of workers in order to make the city flourish, thus laying the groundwork for modern liberalism (Schneirov 1998). Although employers resisted mightily, Chicago's union movement triumphed in organizing steel, meatpacking, electrical machinery, farm equipment, and other major industries, raising the living standards of workers dramatically and stabilizing both workers' lives and local community economies (Cohen 1990). In addition, there were urban visionaries like Daniel Burnham, whose turn-of-the-century advice to "make no little plans" still reverberates in a metropolis that, a century later, often has a hard time making even little plans.

From the late nineteenth century onwards, Chicago was a diverse center for manufacturing, transportation, and trade, growing out of its role as metropolis of the Great West. Increasingly, the city itself also generated new enterprises to serve its needs, from modern department stores to the first skyscrapers. Its central industries, like the slaughterhouses, the steel mills, and the grain elevators, not only created huge workplaces but also generated a wide range of smaller, related businesses that supplied or used the products of those core industries. Chicago's central position in the rail networks made it a logical place for the Pullman company to build train cars or for General Motors to manufacture locomotives, but it also nurtured the rise of mass merchandisers, like Sears and Montgomery Ward.

Chicago was a hotbed of technological innovation even beyond its role in developing the Great West. Although manufacturing dominated, the city was also a center for finance, business services, medicine, and education. Most thriving Midwestern industrial cities depended more heavily on one or a few related industries, such as autos, steel, or machine tools, but by the late nineteenth century, Chicago could claim unusual economic diversity. That diversity was remarkably well knitted together because the economic linkages among businesses made working in Chicago efficient.

After the interruption of earlier progress by the Depression, many Chicago companies flourished through contracts generated by the needs of World War II, from Motorola's communications technology to the South Side steel mills. However, increased military spending immediately after the war stimulated a shift of industry to the Sunbelt and fostered new industries, such as air transport and semiconductors, in which Chicago played a relatively minor role (Markusen 1991).

In the era after World War II, prosperity returned, but two contradictions reshaped the metropolitan region. First, the expanding population of African Americans was largely excluded from the core economy. As a result of this discrimination and inequality, much of the urban social tension shifted from the condition of workers and their relations with employers to the relationships between blacks and whites.

Second, Chicago began losing manufacturing jobs to the expanding suburbs, where land was cheaper and more readily available for new or expanding businesses. Population rapidly grew in the suburbs as the central city stagnated, then shrank, before modestly rebounding in the 1990s for the first time in four decades.

Rapid suburbanization, including the shift of much manufacturing to outlying areas at an even faster rate than the population shift, shaped both the political and economic development of Chicago (Chicago Case Study Working Group 2001). The expanding metropolis was not incorporated into one governmental unit. Rather, it evolved as an overlapping maze of 1,300 units of local government (Johnson 2001, 57). This created new, perverse private and public incentives and new contradictions in economic development that shaped—and ultimately hurt—the metropolitan area.

Politics often shapes economic development, just as the economy in turn influences politics. Certainly, federal policies drove suburbanization (Dreier, Mollenkopf, and Swanstrom 2001), and state politics stymied the natural expansion of Chicago's geographic growth. But local political responses to these changes also had an effect. Mayor Richard J. Daley built an "urban growth coalition" that focused on downtown real estate development and new property-tax revenue more than on manufacturing (Rast 1999). But when manufacturing collapsed, many analysts either saw it as inevitable or blamed taxes, regulations, and high workers' wages. Often, the blame rested more on bloated management, lack of innovation, underinvestment, or short-term strategic focus, as well as flawed government policies on research, trade, education, and public investment.

FROM MANUFACTURING TO BUSINESS SERVICES

From the early 1980s, Chicago and the Midwest reeled from recession and economic turbulence on many fronts. Manufacturing even began to slip in the suburbs. Services, especially business services, dominated the entire metropolitan economy, and the suburbs had the lion's share of all employment, even if the central city remained the prime location for many good jobs.

In 1970, slightly more than half of the roughly three million jobs in the metropolitan area were in Chicago. By 2000, jobs in the central city had declined by 12.2 percent to 1.2 million, but employment in the rest of the metropolitan area increased by 80 percent, to a total of 3.9 million jobs. While metropolitan Chicago led the nation in the absolute number of new jobs during the 1990s and ranked second among the five biggest metropolitan areas in the rate of job growth, its annual growth rate of 1.3 percent was below the national average of 1.8 percent (Mayor's Council of Technology Advisors n.d.; World Business Chicago n.d. [2003]).

In 1970, the unemployment rate of Chicago proper was below the national average but, by 1980, it was slightly above average, then double the national average in both 1990 and 2000. By contrast, the unemployment rate for the suburbs remained generally below the national average over the three decades (SOCDS). With the collapse of the 1990s financial bubble, the tech sector crisis and, most particularly, a renewed

structural decline in manufacturing, in 2002, metropolitan Chicago was leading the nation in absolute numbers of jobs lost (Gardner et al. 2002, 9; Taylor 2003). The great success of the late 1990s was at least stalled.

Manufacturing employment in the central city began declining in the 1950s, then dropped catastrophically, although employment increased in the rest of the metropolitan area. Except for some limited cyclical recovery, manufacturing employment in Chicago plummeted again during the 1980s (by 32 percent) and, for the first time, declined in the suburbs as well (SOCDS). Then, despite the boom of the 1990s, manufacturing continued its sharp drop in the city (by 24 percent), while remaining nearly stable in the suburbs. Big losers in the city included primary metal and fabricated metal products, electronic and electrical equipment, apparel, printing and publishing, instruments, and chemicals, all under significant global pressures, except for printing. Manufacturing was still more important in Chicago than in most other big urban areas, but smoky mills, clanging presses, and fast assembly—or disassembly—lines no longer defined the regional economy as much as it had in the past.[4]

Survivors of the 1980s debacle often reorganized their operations, invested in new technology, shifted products, trained or empowered workers, or cooperated among themselves to boost productivity while maintaining production. Yet, in many cases, survival came at a financial cost even for workers who remained employed. Between 1979 and 2000, real manufacturing wages fell 17 percent in Illinois, compared to 10 percent nationally (Gardner et al. 2002).

Yet most manufacturing jobs still pay relatively well compared to the service sector, are more likely to be unionized, yield more rapid productivity growth, and generate more secondary jobs. The remaining manufacturing jobs typically require increasing levels of education and skill, and metropolitan Chicago manufacturing faces a serious problem in finding and training enough skilled workers (Banks, Hellwig and MacLaren 2000; Chicago Federation of Labor and Center for Labor and Community Research 2001).

Despite the recession of the early 1990s and a "jobless recovery," some favorable turns occurred in Chicago's economic activity. First, a slight reversal occurred in the four-decade history of population loss in Chicago proper, in large part as a result of increased immigration and higher immigrant birth rates. Second, strong gains were made in employment for the metropolitan region, especially from specialized services to large multinational corporations (SOCDS).

Business services were important for both the number and quality of jobs (compared with much of the service sector) and for the export income they generated. Several subcategories were disproportionately located in the Chicago area, effectively providing metropolitan Chicago export employment for more than 100,000 workers in fields such as public relations, accounting, personnel supply, and advertising, according to World Business Chicago. Although skills and salaries varied greatly, business service jobs typically paid well above average for the region.[5]

CHALLENGES TO CHICAGO'S FUTURE AS A "GLOBAL CITY"

Saskia Sassen, the influential urban sociologist, argues that global cities have a new role as producers of services, such as the work of lawyers and financial specialists, for the demanding task of managing global corporate empires. These services thrive on face-to-face interaction among business and professional people in city centers, which is more effective than communication at a distance by telephone or the Internet (Sassen 1991).

At first blush, this certainly seems to be happening in Chicago, with its expansion of business services, construction of new Loop office buildings, recycling of older office buildings into downtown condominiums, and the creation of new and more affluent residential neighborhoods near the Loop.

By most accounts, Chicago clearly ranks among the second tier of global cities, in the company of cities such as Hong Kong and Frankfurt. Some economic strategists envision a "global Chicago," with a central city featuring more of both multinational corporate headquarters and related financial, professional, and service firms. But even the relatively flush decade of the 1990s contained some worrisome signals.

First, while Chicago pursues corporate headquarters and their elite business service partners for the city center, corporate headquarters have been shifting to suburbs and "edge cities." Consequently, Sassen argues that " 'the center' now has many centers, as the business activities associated with downtown spread into the suburbs" (Sassen 2004). But if "instant cyber-touch" permits this redefinition of the center for corporate headquarters, businesses serving global corporations may also not be a reliable engine for central city employment growth.

Second, a detailed analysis of Chicago's economy during the 1990s raises questions about the quality and quantity of future growth. For example, personnel supply services constitute by far the largest business service category and the category with the largest increase during the 1990s. But this industry includes not only executive recruiters and global giants, such as Manpower, but also proliferating day-labor agencies, like Laborama or Ready Men, which are concentrated in Latino neighborhoods. While about a fifth of temporary workers are professionals, most temp jobs are low-wage, degraded versions of former full-time office and laborer jobs (Peck and Theodore 2001).

Some higher-end corporate service jobs, such as engineering and architectural services, research and testing services, and advertising, grew slowly or even declined during the 1990s. A dramatic decline even occurred in sectors that serve global corporations, such as legal services (down by 25 percent, for a loss of more than 8,000 jobs) and depository institutions (a 17 percent loss, typically in banks). However, employment doubled at nondepository financial institutions, which include currency exchanges and payday loan offices—unlikely servants to global business.

During the 1990s, security and commodity brokers increased by nearly half, a byproduct of the stock bubble, but the subsequent bust almost certainly reduced those numbers, at least temporarily. Job prospects are at risk as the city's futures, options, and stock exchanges face both rising global competition and a shift from the open outcry system—and its face-to-face interactions—to electronic trading. Overall, employment in the broad category of finance, insurance, and real estate, as a share of total employment, declined after the stock bust—at a rate slightly faster than the national average—in both the city and the metropolitan area (SOCDS; Economic Report of the President 2004).

Third, corporations will likely subcontract more managerial activities, thus generating demand for public relations, data management, and other business services. But, as economist David Gordon argued, for decades, corporations in the United States have had a much higher ratio of managerial to nonmanagerial workers and greater workplace conflict than that of competitors from countries like Germany, Japan, and Sweden (Gordon 1996). Those more cooperative economies performed better in terms of investment, productivity growth, inflation, and unemployment. If U.S. corporations maintain high managerial burdens, then workers are more likely to lose jobs or income in a competitive global economy. But if corporations turn more cooperative and efficient, then the need may be reduced for some business services on which Chicago depends.

Fourth, many of the jobs that strategists hope will grow rapidly in the new global Chicago are now being performed at a fraction of the cost by well-educated workers in India, China, Russia, and other newly industrializing or transition countries. Management consultants—a business service growth industry in Chicago—now tell businesses that they must relocate both blue- and white-collar work to China and elsewhere if they want to succeed (Engardio, Bernstein, and Kripilani 2003; Goodman 2003; Roberts and Luce 2003; Uchitelle 2003).

CHALLENGES TO THE "HIGH ROAD" ADAPTATION TO GLOBALIZATION

The new challenge of globalization strikes at the heart of even the more progressive strategies of adaptation to global competitive pressures and capital mobility, such as educating workers to perform higher-skilled, better-paying jobs even as lower-wage workers in developing countries do tasks like sewing clothes or assembling automobiles. But millions of educated workers in both the rich and poor countries are moving up the same skill ladder, applying downward income pressure even on those jobs that may remain in the United States.

Inspired by the success of Silicon Valley, Chicago strategists have also longingly looked for salvation from manufacturing losses through the development of high-tech industries, such as biotechnology, business software, nanotechnology, or advanced manufacturing and materials. But metropolitan Chicago's large supply of science and technology workers is distributed throughout a wide range of both "new" industries, from pharmaceutical companies (such as Abbott Laboratories and Baxter Pharmaceuticals) to electronics firms (such as Motorola or Tellabs), and "old" industries, from steel mills to machine tool and fastener makers. Indeed, Chicago ranks quite low in high-tech specialization (Markusen 2001) and just below the national average in the number of patents per employee (Porter n.d.).

Metropolitan Chicago has also not been especially hospitable to new technology businesses. Very little venture capital is available. The region's universities and research centers have, until recently, done little to link research to local business development (Johnson 2001). Also, the required critical mass of workers has rarely existed in any particular emerging high-tech industry to create an environment of intellectual exchange, cooperation, public institutional support, and competition that can stimulate the growth of new companies in a geographic region. The symbol of the region's high-tech slip-ups is Marc Andreessen, who developed the computer code for an Internet browser as a student at the University of Illinois but had to go to California to find venture capital to launch his business, Netscape. Also, the local giant, Motorola, has faltered, losing an early lead in the cell phone business. In 2003, it closed its five-year-old, $100 million factory in the collar-county town of Harvard, where 5,000 workers once were making and distributing cell phones. Now that building may become an indoor water park, an unwelcome symbol for the region's high-tech hopes (Tita 2003a, b).

Many urban economic development analysts argue that innovation is nurtured by the clustering of businesses in a particular industry, whether around a dominant firm or as a district of small businesses. Chicago has a large number of highly concentrated clusters of related businesses, making goods for trade rather than for local consumption, in which the metropolitan area's share of national employment is greater than its share of the national work force. But Chicago is not known for one or two hallmark industries, such as computers and aerospace in Seattle, finance in New York, or entertainment in Los Angeles or Las Vegas. Local leaders are proud that Chicago is, according to one study, the most diverse urban economy in the nation. While diversity helped Chicago rebound from the 1980s manufacturing collapse, it is no guarantor of future success. The varied cities following Chicago in the diversity ranking are questionable models: Little Rock, Baltimore, Salt Lake City, and Buffalo (Moody's Investors Service 2003).

Indeed, in most of Chicago's strongest industrial clusters, the metropolitan area was losing share throughout the 1990s, not an indication of growing strength. According to the Cluster Mapping Project of Harvard University's Institute for Strategy and Competitiveness (Porter n.d.), Chicago gained national share among its most concentrated clusters only in the processed food industry and the education and knowledge cluster. Chicago remained the leading metropolitan area for employment in metal manufacturing, food, plastics, communications equipment, production technology, lighting and electrical equipment, heavy machinery, and medical devices. It also had a very high relative concentration in other clusters: transportation and logistics (second among all metropolitan areas), publishing and printing (second), distribution services (third), chemical products (second), business services (second), and financial services (third). Yet, at the same time, it was losing national share in all those clusters, suggesting that they were not serving as the needed seedbeds of innovation and superior economic growth.

The focus on diversity leaves unanswered a big question: What will be the engines of both job and income growth for the Chicago region? The strongest sectors have been lagging behind national averages in employment growth. Many of the biggest corporate pillars—United Airlines, McDonald's, Allstate, Sears, Motorola, and even the new star, Boeing—are experiencing hard times for varied reasons. Outside takeovers continue to undermine the city's position as a corporate decision center. Chicago's big-business exhibition and convention business faces Sunbelt competition (Orlando and Las Vegas), economic doldrums, and post-9/11 travel jitters. Even a rapidly growing local film industry has been undercut by the industry's shift to foreign locales: Toronto often serves as the backdrop for television shows or movies supposedly set in Chicago, according to a *New York Times* report (Bernstein 2003).

At the start of the new century, neither high-tech nor financial industries are poised to be the new drivers of a growing economy. Despite efforts to retain manufacturing and upgrade workforce skills and technology, manufacturing is unlikely to yield job growth. Business services, perhaps even education, have promise but also vulnerabilities. In all those sectors, a base exists that could be developed, but it seems likely that, in 2020, Chicago's leaders will still be touting diversity rather than a new job-generating champion.

INEQUALITY: THE ECONOMIC AND SOCIAL THREAT

The economic challenge for the city is not simply to create jobs, but to generate adequate income from good jobs. In the competition to attract businesses, pressure always exists to sell a city as offering cheap labor, but the prospect of earning low incomes does not attract talented people. If workers earn more, they can invest in their homes, buy goods and services for local consumption, and strengthen their communities, making the city even more attractive. An economically thriving population can afford to pay for the schools and infrastructure that make the city more livable and businesses more productive. But raising average incomes is not enough. The metropolitan area will be more likely to thrive if there is greater economic equality among individuals and among communities. Urban regions with higher economic inequality typically grow more slowly, hurting both central-city and suburban residents (Dreier, Mollenkopf, and Swanstrom 2001; Moberg 1995).

Inequality has grown both among different geographical communities within the metropolitan region and among households. From 1989 to 1999, an increase occurred in the percentage of families in the metropolitan area in the lowest quintile of national income and in the highest quintile, but a decrease occurred in the broad middle-income quintiles (SOCDS). By 2000, household income was more unequal in metropolitan Chicago than in the nation as a whole. Among the central cities of the 40 largest metropolitan areas, the city of Chicago ranked fifteenth in income inequality in 1999 (Rodgers and Lazere 2004).

But metropolitan Chicago scored even worse in the contrast between poverty levels in the city and its suburbs. With its central-city poverty rate 3.5 times the poverty rate in the suburbs, metropolitan Chicago was the eighth most unequal urban region in terms of poverty level (Rodgers and Lazere 2004). The suburbs are richer than the city largely because many suburbanites work at well-paid jobs in the city, even though suburban corporate headquarters also increasingly provide high-paid jobs (Dreier, Mollenkopf, and Swanstrom 2001). Suburban workers prosper disproportionately from the higher wages in the city, but they pay local taxes to support communities that escape much of the costs of social inequality.

Sassen argues that increasing inequality is "built into the new growth sectors" of global cities (Sassen 2004). That is partly because of the intrinsic effects of competition in the global labor market, but it also reflects the lack of unionization in many growth sectors. Although Chicago has long been a union stronghold, unions represented only 19 percent of metropolitan area workers in 2002, more than the 13 percent nationally, but a decline from the 22 percent of workers in unions during the mid 1980s. Yet, unions representing janitors and hotel workers have recently won significant

gains for these workers, suggesting that current levels of inequality are not intrinsic to the new economy.

Just as inequality exists among workers and families, the disparities among geographic communities, including individual suburbs and city neighborhoods, are deepened by the exodus of manufacturing from the central city and by suburban sprawl. Because of persistent discrimination and the historically high degree of racial segregation in Chicago, the mismatch between the skills of black inner-city residents and service and manufacturing jobs in the suburbs is particularly severe (Wilson 1987). Sprawl also has created huge public and private external costs—such as traffic congestion and environmental destruction—and shifted public spending away from modernizing inner suburb and city infrastructure. On balance, the social costs of sprawl have roughly equaled the private benefits. Sprawl thus transfers income from low- and middle-income workers to upper-income business owners, especially if one takes into account the state's highly regressive taxes (Persky and Wiewel 2000; Chicago Case Study Working Group 2001; Gardner et al. 2002). Suburban growth thus made it harder, even if the good will existed, to reduce racially based economic inequalities and to resolve the racial contradiction in post-war Chicago urban development.

Although businesses that sell goods and services outside the region typically have a disproportionate effect on the region by stimulating the growth of related jobs, roughly two-thirds of all jobs provide goods and services for local consumption (Porter n.d.). These local businesses, from grocery and hardware stores to restaurants and theaters, affect both the economic vitality and livability of the diverse microeconomies within the broader urban region, from depressed and depopulated communities like Lawndale on the city's West Side to wealthy Kenilworth in the north suburbs.

Although the influx of new immigrants to Chicago has strengthened many neighborhood economies, the central city overall is undersupplied with retail stores. Many businesses fled—just as banks deprived the same neighborhoods of credit—because they did not want to serve black neighborhoods. By the late 1990s, the federal government estimated that Chicago had a "retail gap" of $9.9 billion, second only to New York. But, because land is scarce and the suburban "big box" store has emerged as the retail model, initiatives by retailers to replicate their suburban-style stores often conflict with the need to preserve manufacturing jobs. After concluding that the city gained more economically from manufacturing than from retail or residential development, Mayor Harold Washington protected several key manufacturing districts from real estate speculation (Clavel and Wiewel 1991). Also, anti-union discount retailers, such as Wal-Mart, put downward pressure on wages and benefits and are likely to lead to a net loss of jobs (Mehta, Baiman, and Persky 2004). In 2004, community and labor critics of Wal-Mart proposed that future "big box" retailers meet certain minimum standards on wages, hiring, and other policies.

CREATING AN ECONOMICALLY COHERENT REGION

Beyond such problems as the mismatch between job location and willing workers or the inequities of tax revenue among different jurisdictions, this dispersal of jobs through a large number of competing municipalities unravels the metropolitan area's economic coherence. As major firms or factories moved out, small businesses whose fates had once been linked to them failed, followed, or adapted to a more national market. A few local businesses still benefit from their proximity to one of the remaining giants, and some local suppliers to big corporations such as McDonald's have expanded their national or global operations (Gupta 2004). Ford is also creating a new supplier park close to its South-Side assembly plant.

Businesses now rely on ties within the Midwest or Great Lakes region much in the way that they once looked to links within the city or metropolitan region. During the 1990s, the average firm in the Chicago region relied much more on external customers and suppliers than in previous decades. But, despite the growing importance of international trade, especially with Canada and Mexico, Illinois companies' trade with other states is roughly four to five times larger than trade with other countries (Hewings n.d.).

Chicago could thus gain greatly from a strategy to develop the region: strengthening the manufacturing base, providing business services, and developing new high-tech firms that complement the region's needs. This refocusing of the region's economic ambitions does imply two strategic changes.

First, the political will would be necessary for the entire region to stop its low-road strategy of attempting to compete in the world—and often among the states and cities of the region—by offering cheap labor, lower taxes, and direct public subsidies. Instead, a commitment to a high-road regional strategy is necessary, one that emphasizes research, education, skilled workers, high wages, innovation, and productivity (Swinney 1998). Trying to pursue both is impossible. The low road continually undermines the potential for the high road.

For the region to be more economically integrated, it needs a dramatic increase in infrastructure spending designed to increase regional efficiency, such as upgrading existing streets, expanding public transportation, and making Chicago the hub of a high-speed rail network. Despite substantial infrastructure investment in Chicago during the 1990s, key areas were neglected (such as upgrading the city's intermodal freight capacity), and public investment was often misguided (especially tax increment financing for Loop businesses) (*PRAGmatics* 2002).

Before Chicago can hope to implement a vision of an integrated Midwestern region, it must first confront the political and economic conflicts within the metropolis itself. Part of the business elite, as well as many neighborhood groups and labor unions, now recognize the need for a regional approach that includes control of sprawl, balanced growth, improved energy and transportation efficiency, a strengthened manufacturing sector, and enhanced education and training.

Ultimately, regionalism will only work effectively if strategies are also implemented to share tax revenues throughout the region, starting with state efforts to equalize funding for public schools, but including more regional tax sharing as well. Growing disparity among local governments' capacity to raise revenues feeds on itself in a spiral of growing inequality. From 1980 to 1993, 26 suburbs (mainly black and poor to start with) lost tax base by as much as 36 percent, but the tax base increased by more than 48 percent in 77 suburbs (mainly white and affluent) (Chicago Case Study Working Group 2001).

Regionalism—whether it spans metropolitan Chicago or the Midwest—will be most successful if leaders can unite a divided metropolis around a vision of self-consciously creating good jobs and communities for all, rather than relying on the trickle-down effects from an increasingly unequal region. Chicago was initially "the city of the [nineteenth] century" (Miller 1997) partly because it embodied a vision of both the city and its industries opening up the Great West. It was riven with class conflict, but it had a vitality that was captured in the classic odes to Chicago by Carl Sandburg, who was a keen socialist critic of the city. Chicago in this era was rough-edged, but it was also coherent.

THE FUTURE OF CHICAGO IN A GLOBAL ECONOMY

In the decades after World War II, Chicago lost much of that vitality, as people and jobs, especially in manufacturing industries, moved to suburbs not integrated within one metropolitan area, and as racial discrimination divided the central city and fed the suburban exodus. As businesses moved out or simply folded, the metropolitan region became less politically and economically coherent as well. Inequalities grew, among individuals and communities, and these inequalities undercut the economy of the entire region.

The form that globalization took exacerbated the tensions within the urban region, putting severe pressure on traded-goods manufacturers, but opening new opportunities for corporations to move production to meet short-term performance goals. Globalization reinforced the trend toward the dominance of financial interests and the transformation of corporate power into remote strategic centers distanced from routines of production, whether of candies or airplanes, and from the communities in which they operated.

These tendencies towards a less coherent and less egalitarian metropolis deepened even during the 1990s, but after a horrendous previous decade of manufacturing job losses and economic hardship, there was a tenuous recovery of both economic and population growth. Surviving manufacturers had reorganized and reinvested to survive, new business service firms were expanding in the central city, and a renaissance occurred around the Loop and even in some outlying neighborhoods. New efforts were made to exploit Chicago's historic advantages and economic legacy, to enrich the amenities of community and cultural life, and to give new focus to the neglected needs of deprived communities and of the region.

A growing awareness has arisen of Chicago's economic role in the wider world. With the forces of globalization nibbling away at highly skilled white-collar jobs, as well as both skilled and unskilled blue-collar jobs, it is becoming difficult to make increasingly slippery jobs stick in the city or metropolitan area. Local government can foster supportive cultures among businesses in common industries and professions, guarantee adequate infrastructure, and improve education and both basic and advanced job skills, but it needs more progressively generated revenue from regional, state, and federal governments. Local government can also encourage management cooperation with workers and an organized voice for workers themselves, but Chicago's economy could benefit as well from closer cooperation with universities and research centers and from a greater variety of investment and credit, including both more venture capital and more neighborhood capital (such as lending by community-oriented development banks).

If Chicago is to become a global city, it is likely to do so by first becoming an integrated metropolis that serves as the capital of a more integrated Midwestern region. Globalization is full of contradictions for Chicago, destroying and creating opportunities, generating inequalities, and encouraging a less parochial outlook while ungluing local ties that bind. Chicago's hold on the business service firms that cater to the needs of global corporations, as well as the headquarters of many of those corporations, will depend on the health of the Midwest region and the quality of life in the metropolitan area. In the end, local government can have little effect, even with its most generous subsidies and tax breaks, on the shifting winds of globalization and markets for corporate control. It may achieve most by focusing on the skills of its citizens and the quality of life in the region (Markusen 1996).

Far from being a Rust Belt relic, high-tech incubator, or global city, the new Chicago economy is precariously balanced, retaining a diminished but transformed legacy of industrial greatness and expanding its potential as a center of high-skilled services. Chicago is the globally important capital of a region larger than nearly all other national economies, yet it lacks metropolitan political and economic coherence. It also lacks the commitment to renewal that would create a more integrated, egalitarian region. Those shortcomings are as much a threat to the region's economic future as are the shifting winds of national politics or economic globalization.

NOTES

1. Looking only at the biggest companies, Chicago's share of corporate headquarters dropped by 40 percent over two decades. But, by other measures, the metropolitan region was second to New York and growing (counting corporations with 2,500 or more employees) or in fourth place and declining (counting corporations with more than 500 employees) (Klier and Testa 2001; Strahler 2003).

2. An increase of 42.7 percent occurred in professional and business services employment (NAICS code 54) in metropolitan Chicago from 1990 to 2000, according to U.S. Census Bureau figures compiled by Glen D. Marker, Director of Research, World Business Chicago.

3. Named after economist James Tobin, who first proposed it, a very small tax on international financial transactions could dampen speculation and some of its destabilizing effects (ul Haq, Kaul, and Grunberg 1996).

4. Although 14.1 percent of the national workforce was employed in manufacturing in 2000, 16.5 percent of metropolitan Chicago (and 14.2 percent of the city) worked in manufacturing. That represented a dramatic drop from about 32 percent in both the city and suburbs in 1970 (SOCDS).

5. The average business service wage in Chicago in 2001 was $61,173, compared to the $52,235 regional average for traded industries (goods and services sold outside the metropolitan region), according to Harvard Business School Professor Michael Porter's Institute for Strategy and Competitiveness Cluster Mapping Project (http://data.isc.hbs.edu).

Larry Bennett

4   Chicago's New Politics of Growth

APART FROM MICHAEL JORDAN and Al Capone, Chicago's most prominent citizen has been Richard J. Daley, mayor from the spring of 1955 until his death in late 1976. Many Chicagoans suppose that Daley invented the Democratic Party machine that monopolized local political power during the middle decades of the twentieth century, although more accurately, Daley should be viewed as the innovative legatee of his precursors, Anton Cermak and Ed Kelly. What even close observers of Chicago politics sometimes fail to recognize is that there were two Richard J. Daley machines, the first a reasonably harmonious racial–ethnic choir that accompanied Daley's first two terms, the second an internally contentious organization exercising imperfect control over a racially polarized, economically wasting city. This second machine emerged during the last ten years of Daley's mayoralty.

The evolution of the first Daley machine into the second resulted from a powerful social movement, the civil rights crusade in Chicago, coupled with Richard J. Daley's reaction to his only serious challenge for reelection, in 1963. Chicago-based civil rights campaigning began in 1960, with an initial focus on the city's segregated public schools (Anderson and Pickering 1987; Ralph 1993). By undermining the party loyalty of a core Daley constituency—African Americans of the older South Side "Black Belt" and the more recently settled "plantation wards" of the West Side—civil rights activism disrupted the leadership cadres and patterns of political privilege that had bound black voters to the Democratic Party. In the spring 1963 mayoral

race, Daley's Republican challenger was a former Democrat, Benjamin Adamowski, who—in addition to attacking Daley's expansionist fiscal record—explicitly appealed to "white ethnic" voters by claiming that Daley was overly beholden to African Americans and, as a consequence, was betraying decades of faithful voting by the city's European-descended residents. Although in percentage terms, Daley handily defeated Adamowski by carrying 55 percent of the vote, historian Roger Biles (1995, 80) estimates that "Adamowski actually won 51 percent of the ballots cast by white voters, receiving solid support from his fellow Polish Americans and also faring especially well in wards adjacent to the expanding Black Belt." Biles (1995, 83) further comments: "Thereafter, in his actions as well as his rhetoric, the mayor began playing to his white constituency in response to a series of highly charged racial controversies. His decision to redirect the machine's support from the increasingly black river wards to the peripheral bungalow belt set the stage for the turbulent times to follow."

As historian Paul Kleppner (1985) and political scientist William Grimshaw (1992) have documented, Richard J. Daley's latter years coincided with a substantial erosion of the Democratic Party's hold on the Chicago electorate. Daley continued to pummel his Republican opponents, winning each of his last three general elections with over 70 percent of the vote, but turn-out declined with each successive campaign. By the time Daley defeated John Hoellen in 1975, his winning total exceeded Benjamin Adamowski's losing tally in 1963 by a mere 2,000 votes. Clearly cognizant of Daley's growing intransigence in the face of their insistent civil rights claims, African Americans accounted for much of the fall-off in his electoral support. Grimshaw (1992, 140) observes that Daley "left his successors to cope with a black electorate that had been severely suppressed and denied representation and which was therefore ripe for revolt."

The first Daley machine had sought to incorporate African American political ambitions within the encompassing logic of ethnic politics, presuming that black political leaders would strive for the types of rewards—the opportunity to seek prominent public office, control of patronage jobs, and privileged access to city services—that had long defined the aspirations of the city's immigrant and ethnic politicians. However, as the 1950s gave way to the 1960s, Daley's increasing tendency to directly intervene in African American ward-level politics deviated sharply from the ethnic pattern, in which local cadres earned organizational rewards by virtue of local electioneering success. Daley personally installed ward-level African American leaders and did not especially concern himself with whether they could sustain efficient party operations. From Daley's perspective, more critical than either campaigning or management skills was his delegate ward bosses' disinclination to advocate civil rights–inspired governmental initiatives or to seek more expansive shares of the machine's traditional fund of resources, either of which might fray the pattern of racial, ethnic, and geographic alliances that bound together the Democratic Party ward organizations (Grimshaw 1992, 91–114).

From the standpoint of African Americans, the transition from the first to second Daley machine was marked by what Grimshaw characterizes as a growing "productivity-rewards contradiction." As early as the mid-1950s, African Americans had become a principal supplier of the Democratic Party's citywide electoral majorities, but in terms of access to important public offices, patronage, and basic services, the city's black elite and rank and file alike did not receive their "fair shares." In the second Daley machine, white ethnic Chicago's privileged access to office-holding, entry-level public employment, and decent-quality neighborhood services represented the mayor's main claim to loyalty on the city's white far South, Southwest, and Northwest Sides (Edsall 1989).

Despite the overarching significance of race as a defining political cleavage in mid-century Chicago, the differences between the first and second Daley machines transcended matters strictly related to race and ethnic succession within the Democratic Party. During the 1950s and early 1960s, Richard J. Daley governed a prospering city whose municipal government possessed fiscal resources sufficient to earn it the reputation as "the city that works." Federal government funds were also brought to bear on massive public works initiatives, such as the development of the city's expressway network, the expansion of its rail transit system, and the construction of more than 20,000 units of public housing. During Daley's last decade as mayor, fiscal crises struck the city's public school and transit systems, and the decay of public infrastructure was visible across Chicago (Biles 1995, 209–20; Fuchs 1992, 120–24; Orlebeke 1983). Coincidentally, the city's population began to slope downward even as its suburbs boomed. In 1974, Daley managed to bail out the Chicago Transit Authority by prompting the state legislature to create a six-county Regional Transit Authority (RTA), whose board composition and financial structure were highly advantageous to the city of Chicago. However, when membership on the RTA board was reworked a few years after the mayor's death, the Chicago "delegation" was reduced to a minority (Fuchs 1992, 199). Although the elderly Richard J. Daley still commanded influence in Springfield, Illinois' state capital, the growing imperative to seek state and suburban governmental cooperation would require subsequent mayors to maneuver in a political environment much less subject to domination by the fifth floor of Chicago's City Hall.

THE HAROLD WASHINGTON INTERREGNUM

Richard J. Daley's immediate successors as mayor were Michael Bilandic and Jane Byrne. Bilandic had served as alderman from Daley's home 11th ward and was initially selected as interim mayor by the city council, which preferred a new man without discernible ambition or charisma. In a remarkable Democratic Party primary election, in February 1979, Bilandic was upset by a disaffected former Daley protégé, Jane Byrne. Swept to victory with solid support from Chicago's African American wards, Byrne will be long remembered as riding to victory on the winds of one of the city's most horrendous snow storms, a blizzard that paralyzed Bilandic's municipal administration. Following an easy general-election victory, Byrne presided over four years of politics as turbulent as the winter storms of 1979. Largely beyond Mayor Byrne's control was the city's continuing economic slide. Well within her power—and evidently the intent of several of her controversial administrative appointments—was to stoke the city's long-smoldering black–white political tensions and thereby reduce the likelihood of a challenge from the late mayor's son, Richard M. Daley (Grimshaw 1992, 159–61). However, in a mayoral election season just as surprising as 1979, 1983 brought an insurgent African American, Harold Washington, to Chicago's mayoralty. Unlike the Bilandic-Byrne period, Washington's four and one-half years in office brought much innovation to city government, setting in motion policy trends that carried through to Richard M. Daley's administration in the 1990s.

Harold Washington was swept into City Hall by three movements, the most powerful being the last massing of the civil rights insurgency that had originated in the 1960s. Among Washington's key campaign organizers was Al Raby, whose Coordinating Council of Community Organizations had brought Martin Luther King, Jr. to Chicago in 1965. In the final months of Jane Byrne's mayoralty, African American dissatisfaction had produced a Jesse Jackson-led boycott of the City-sponsored ChicagoFest summer entertainment events. In mid-1982, a coalition of grassroots groups sponsored a voter registration drive that increased the eligible black electorate by 125,000 and which, in turn, drew Congressman Washington into the Democratic mayoral primary (Gills 1991; Kleppner 1985, 144–51).

By far the largest number of Harold Washington's votes in the 1983 primary and general

elections were cast by African Americans. However, from an organizational standpoint, and in terms of the crucial 10 to 15 percent of the white vote carried by Washington, two other forces made important contributions to Washington's victory (*Chicago Politics 1990* 1990, 42–45). Washington benefited from the vigorous support of dozens of grassroots organizations either advocating better city government services or directly working in community development. Such groups had begun to proliferate during the 1960s, but had been viewed quite unsympathetically by mayors Daley, Bilandic, and Byrne (Ferman 1996, 66–75). As the Washington campaign began to craft its message in 1983, grassroots activists contributed a neighborhood development component to the platform, while across the city neighborhood organizations supported the ongoing voter registration effort. Washington—a one-time Young Democrat and Daley organization–sponsored state legislator—had broken ranks with the regular Democratic Party during the mid-1970s. His campaign appeal was explicitly anti-machine and, as such, also won support among white, "independent" Democratic voters in wards such as the South Side 5th and North Side 43rd and 44th wards, strongholds of what were known at the time as Lakefront Liberal voters (*Chicago Politics 1990* 1990, 42).

In some respects, the Washington mayoralty can be compared to the experience of first-time black mayors such as Richard Hatcher in Gary, Indiana, Maynard Jackson in Atlanta, or Wilson Goode in Philadelphia (Keiser 1997). Like Hatcher, Jackson, and Goode, Washington triumphed in a racially polarized election and, once in office, found himself in charge of a city government subject to substantial fiscal constraints. As a result, among the more visible programmatic emphases of the Washington administration was the introduction of affirmative action targets for municipal hiring and contracting. Such initiatives, as political scientist Peter Eisinger (1984, 250) has noted, represent an "effort by black mayors to use their control of city hall to enhance income making opportunities for their black constituents." Unlike seeking to restructure the fundamentals of municipal policy or jump-start the local economy, these moves are within the decision-making reach of those chief executives leading cash-strapped municipalities. Harold Washington also agreed to a settlement of the longstanding Shakman litigation (a lawsuit dating from the early 1970s, in which the plaintiff had successfully argued that patronage practices in Chicago local government employment violated provisions of the U.S. Constitution's First and Fourteenth amendments) and, in so doing, pledging that the city government would no longer use political criteria in screening applicants for rank-and-file municipal employment (Biles 1995, 188; Grimshaw 1992, 188). Although settling the Shakman case did not directly benefit African American constituents, the broader meaning of this commitment was unmistakable: No longer would city government positions represent the financial safety net supporting individuals—mainly drawn from Chicago's European-descended ethnic groups—whose core mission was working the city's 3,000 election precincts.

Yet, apart from his commitment to achieving "racial fairness," Harold Washington—unlike Hatcher, Jackson, or Goode—pursued a more daring policy program reflecting the "urban populist" thinking advanced by various American and British activists during the 1980s (Gyford 1985; Swanstrom 1988). For example, economic development officials in the Washington administration implemented a variety of projects aimed at stemming the city's loss of manufacturers and well-paying industrial jobs. Some of these ventures, such as the series of "sectoral committees" aimed at determining which elements of Chicago's industrial base remained on sound footing, probably accomplished little of a substantive nature. In contrast, several elements of the neighborhood development agenda forged during the Washington years—targeted industrial development initiatives, such as planned manufacturing districts and model industrial corridors, as well as the commitment to high levels of neighborhood infrastructure investment—have continued to be significant policy commitments (Giloth 1996; Rast 1999).

Clearly, the defining feature of the Washington mayoralty was the much publicized "council wars" that divided the mayor and Chicago City Council from 1983 until the municipal special election of 1986 (Grimshaw 1992, 182–86; Rivlin 1992). Shortly after Washington's election, Democratic machine–affiliated aldermen Edward Vrdolyak and Edward Burke organized a 29-member majority bloc in the council committed to opposing and, if possible, discrediting Washington initiatives. The Vrdolyak–Burke "29" held up various Washington proposals, but probably more important, produced an ongoing atmosphere of uncertainty regarding Chicago governance. In turn, the perceived shakiness of Harold Washington's hold on city government—a topic given much coverage by local news media—had a tangible effect on Washington-administration policy making. For example, the Washington administration's decision to cooperate with the owners of the Chicago White Sox in the construction of a new Comiskey Park—which required the demolition of several blocks of a stable African American neighborhood—was largely because of Harold Washington's unwillingness to be proclaimed the "mayor who lost the Sox" (Spirou and Bennett 2003, 59–82). Some prospective elements of the Washington program, such as comprehensive reform of the Chicago Public Schools and the Chicago Housing Authority, barely made it onto the radar screen of an otherwise embattled administration.

By 1986, special election results in several West Side wards gave Harold Washington a 25-25 split in the 50-member city council, and the mayor's "deciding vote" in the case of ties meant that Washington could finally overcome the Vrdolyak–Burke bloc. Yet, in the 1987 mayoral race, Washington once more encountered serious challenges in the primary and general elections, winning each contest with approximately 54 percent of the vote. Although Harold Washington for the first time seemed to be the unchallenged leader of city government, his hold on the city's electorate remained tenuous. The Washington era came to an abrupt end on November 25, 1987, when the mayor suffered a fatal heart attack. In the next week, Chicago's city council performed an eerie reenactment of the last days of 1976, once again selecting an unheralded back bencher, 20th ward alderman Eugene Sawyer, to serve as interim mayor (Rivlin 1992, 403–20).

Until unseated by Richard M. Daley in 1989, Eugene Sawyer presided over a city government still subject to powerful, racially inflected cross-pressures. On one side, African American "loyalists" to Harold Washington sought to engineer the unseating of Sawyer, even as "realists" supporting the council-designated mayor worked to cement black control of City Hall. Among the largely white bloc of city council members loyal to the memory of Richard J. Daley—as well as among Democratic Party activists outside the city council—there was intense maneuvering to determine who would challenge Sawyer in the special mayoral election of 1989 (Grimshaw 1992, 197–206).

Ultimately, Cook County State's Attorney Richard M. Daley emerged as the front-runner among old-style Democrats, and the political ineptitude of both Sawyer and his chief African American antagonist, Alderman Tim Evans, produced the break-up of the Washington coalitions of 1983 and 1987. Neither Sawyer nor Evans seemed to recognize the realities of Chicago's electoral demography during the mid-1980s. African Americans and whites were nearly matched numerically, which meant that neither group could overwhelm the other electorally so long as each mustered comparable levels of voter turnout. As a result, coalition building was necessary, as indeed, had been demonstrated by Harold Washington. This logic never penetrated the Sawyer and Evans camps, which lost relatively high-turnout contests with Richard M. Daley in the 1989 primary and general elections, respectively. By 1989, Richard M. Daley had succeeded Washington as the political leader most attuned to Chicago's evenly balanced electoral forces. Daley not only won back white independents but linked his nearly universal appeal among "white ethnic" voters to strong support among Latino voters (*Chicago Politics 1990* 1990, 46–47).

CHICAGO'S SECOND MAYOR DALEY

Cook County State's Attorney Richard M. Daley's second effort to win the Chicago mayoralty, in 1989, was widely anticipated. In the years following his defeat in the Democratic primary of 1983, Daley had avoided the racial sparring between Democratic Party loyalists and Harold Washington's supporters. Daley also managed the state's attorney office in an evidently competent and clearly uncontroversial manner. Consequently, given the widespread public disapproval both of Mayor Eugene Sawyer's performance and of the factional African American feuding over whether or not Sawyer was Harold Washington's true and worthy heir, Daley was, for many Chicagoans, a welcome entrant to the mayoral contest in 1989. At that time, however, few could have ascribed anything like a coherent program to Daley. During his campaign, he had advanced a carefully elusive agenda, often focusing, as in the following statement, on his determination to move the city past the divisive 1980s:

> We wanted to win, but more than that, we wanted to win in a way that would make us proud and set a positive tone for the city. The late Mayor Washington opened city government to many citizens who felt excluded and ignored. As long as I'm mayor, those doors will remain open to all our citizens (Dold and Hardy 1989).

Having served as mayor for a decade and a half, Richard M. Daley's program can now be specified in some detail. But before addressing Daley's performance, two contextual factors—which are extremely important in defining the parameters of Daley's vision as mayor—ought to be noted. In the first instance, Daley's record can be usefully viewed from the broader perspective of national trends in the fortunes of central cities, urban policy, and the practice of his fellow big-city mayors. Richard M Daley's mayoralty has coincided with an era that, according to Peter Eisinger (1998, 319) "has placed a premium on local public management skills and discouraged grand visions of social and racial reform." Although Eisinger derives his analysis from the connection between federal policy "devolution" and new patterns of mayoral politics, which give primacy to managerial acumen over visionary political leadership, another crucial shaper of the urban political landscape of the 1990s was the national economic boom. Even as Richard M. Daley—like Edward Rendell of Philadelphia, Richard Riordan of Los Angeles, and John Norquist of

Milwaukee—presented himself as a responsible public manager, he committed his city government to a program of civic beautification and public works that would have been unthinkable in the fiscally pinched 1970s. As such, Daley has, in the minds of many Chicagoans, delivered a much more livable city, even as he has adopted a political pose that tends to deflect partisan attack. Characteristically, when opponents of the current Mayor Daley criticize his record, he responds by proclaiming himself a steward of the public weal, not a political man.

Then there is the matter of Richard J. and Richard M. Daley, which sometimes is reduced to the assertion that the contemporary mayor of Chicago is but an updated version of his father. From a characterological standpoint, there is much that links the two. Richard J. Daley was a notorious mangler of the English language, and his son, likewise, is uneasy in the company of reporters or when called to speak spontaneously. For both mayors Daley, their evident affection for the city of Chicago has been an ambiguous virtue: on the one hand prodding them to envision grand physical projects, on the other hand leading them to construe criticism of the city—or worse, of their administrations—in a highly personal manner. But apart from the clear intertwining of their personalities, the programmatic orientation of Richard M. Daley can be clearly distinguished from his father's. For example, the current Mayor Daley has advanced an image of Chicago as a global center for corporate management and services, "new economy" entrepreneurship, and the arts much more vigorously than had his father, who for all his efforts devoted to rebuilding downtown Chicago, retained the view that his was essentially a blue-collar city (Rakove 1975, 43–89). Furthermore, the current mayor's support of "green" initiatives, such as dedicated bicycle lanes on city streets and rooftop gardens on downtown buildings, or even more dramatically, his overtures to the city's gay and lesbian organizations, are decided departures from his father's milieu of ethnic-inflected ward organizations and his overriding concern with the delivery of basic city services.

Clearly, the centerpiece of Richard M. Daley's mayoralty has been the promotion of Chicago as a cosmopolitan city whose global importance is manifest equally by its economic and cultural spheres. Chicago's rise to prominence as an industrial center in the nineteenth century derived from the city's geographic centrality and pivotal position within the North American railway network. Richard M. Daley has aggressively sought to sustain an updated version of Chicago's historic "centrality," notably by expanding the downtown McCormick Place convention complex and O'Hare Airport on the city's northwestern edge (see Chapter 24).

Although corporate relocations have only a modest direct effect on large cities' economic fortunes, their symbolic resonance is substantial. The Daley administration has not hesitated to influence corporate locational choices. In this regard, the Daley administration's signal triumph was the relocation of the Boeing Corporation's headquarters from Seattle to Chicago in 2001, a corporate decision that was seeded by a $60 million City of Chicago–State of Illinois incentive package (Washburn and Ciokajlo 2001).

Apart from investing in such direct and indirect economic development initiatives, a second crucial element of the Daley administration's global city initiative has been the physical upgrading of the Loop and its adjoining neighborhoods, a series of initiatives that has also yielded a substantial increase in the residential population of the city's near-downtown neighborhoods (see Chapters 5 and 25). As downtown Chicago's parks, streets, and plazas have been beautified, a remarkable transformation of near-downtown land uses has proceeded apace. The distribution of central-area land uses in industrial-era Chicago, as so richly documented by the early Chicago School urban sociologists, featured a relatively concentrated commercial core (which, when enclosed by elevated transit lines became known as the Loop), hemmed in on its north, west, and south sides by an expansive industrial–transportation belt (Park, Burgess, and McKenzie 1925). By the 1970s, the decline of railroad traffic and the withdrawal of manufacturers from this horseshoe-shaped area had produced a highly visible emblem of Chicago's decline as an industrial center. Then, although very gradually at first, galleries and restaurants began to reoccupy sections of this near-downtown industrial wasteland, whose north side section was redubbed River North by the early 1980s. Since the mid-1990s, a boom in residential conversion and new construction has brought thousands of new households into the neighborhoods adjoining the Loop. In part, the Daley administration's role in facilitating the residential transformation of near-Loop areas has been a matter of its downtown-directed public works and civic beautification program. More subtly, the Daley administration has used fiscal incentives, notably tax increment financing (TIF) to support private investment in these areas, and has "streamlined" planning approval processes to speed the planning and construction of new residential projects (Neighborhood Capital Budget Group 2002; Washburn 1998b).

Nor do business supports and the encouragement of near-Loop residential development exhaust the menu of Daley administration initiatives aimed at promoting Chicago as a global city. In a variety of ways, the city's current administration has also used fiscal resources and public works investments to trumpet Chicago's artistic import and cultural diversity. Within blocks of City Hall, a "theatre district" has emerged, in part induced by the Daley's administration's fiscal support for the renovations of the Oriental and Palace Theatres (Sharoff 1999). Across Chicago, public works expenditures have been used to "thematize" neighborhood commercial areas, such as the mid-South Side Bronzeville area, "Greektown" on the Near West Side, and the north Halsted Street commercial area between Belmont Avenue and Addison Street. The latter project—involving sidewalk widening and the installation of ornamental planters and multi-colored curb-side pylons—generated heated debate between supporters of the beautification scheme and opponents, many of whom objected to its implicit ghettoization of the North Side's gay population (Banchero 1997).

In addition to the myriad techniques by which the Richard M. Daley administration has pursued its global-city agenda, the second major focus of the current Mayor Daley's program is management reform. Mayor Daley's most ambitious managerial and public policy initiatives have involved the ongoing restructuring of the Chicago Public Schools and the Chicago Housing Authority, which are discussed in detail in Chapters 20 and 22. In Chapter 21, David Plebanski and Roberta Garner survey Chicago's approach to community policing, another of Mayor Daley's central managerial initiatives. In some respects, Richard M. Daley's passion for more up-to-date and tightly structured public management can be directly linked to his global-city program. For example, the mixed-income redevelopment of public housing sites and the establishment of new magnet high schools further the mayor's aim of boosting the population of affluent central-area dwellers. Like his father, the current Mayor Daley links "good politics" to "good government," although in the younger Mayor Daley's case, the claim of managerial competence clearly takes precedence. Having noted this contrast between Chicago's two Mayor Daleys, it also clear that, in one crucial respect, their managerial inclinations are quite comparable. Each of these three Richard M. Daley managerial initiatives has been criticized for imposing reform in a "top-down" fashion that is unresponsive to grassroots or broader public sentiment.

The third leg of Mayor Daley's program might be termed "elite inclusion," to distinguish it from the more free-wheeling grassroots inclusion of the Washington years. In dealing with various public policy problems—factory shutdowns, the debate over whether to impose a "linkage fee" on new downtown development, the continuing poor performance of local schools—Harold Washington appointed commissions or convened city-wide "summits" to discuss policy innovation (Bennett 1987). More generally, community organizations supplied many of the appointees to Washington's administration. Combined with his explicit appeals for support from Latino and "independent" white voters, this relatively open decision-making style was intended to draw new blood into the city's policy-making circles and distinguish Washington's openness from the top-down approach of "Boss Daley."

Richard M. Daley relies on a small circle of advisors to guide decision making, but he has forged public alliances with prominent minority political figures. In the early 1990s, Daley won the support of one of Washington's most vocal city council allies, Luis Gutierrez, who subsequently captured a U.S. congressional seat. An even more steadfast ally of Daley has been John Stroger, the first African American to be elected president of the Cook County Board of Commissioners. Richard M. Daley has also supported the initiatives of gay and lesbian advocacy groups, and his top administration includes many female appointees. Although personal access to the mayor is quite limited, and new city policy only emerges from his handful of trusted aides, Richard M. Daley's leadership is cemented by the nearly universal endorsement of the city's business, civic, and political leadership.

CHICAGO POLITICS, RICHARD M. DALEY-STYLE

The means selected by a chief executive to identify crucial public policy matters, to analyze these issues and produce plans for action, and to implement action straddle the boundary between policy and politics. For Harold Washington, the "opening up" of decision making in Chicago was both a reflection of the movement-style campaign (itself rooted in Civil Rights-era rhetoric and tactics) that swept him into office and a substantive commitment to rebuilding the long-neglected neighborhoods of rank-and-file Chicagoans. Richard M. Daley's practice of elite inclusion signals his recognition that racial, ethnic, and lifestyle diversity is a hallmark of the new Chicago. At that same time, Mayor Daley and his coterie of advisors are careful political entrepreneurs, attuned to the still-vigorous culture of Democratic Party politics in Chicago and masterful deployers of political resources. In the early 1990s, William Grimshaw described Richard M. Daley as a practitioner of "machine politics, reform style." A decade later, a useful reworking of Grimshaw's characterization might be "crony managerialism." In any event, the current Mayor Daley has synthesized a potent amalgam of old- and new-style Chicago politicking and, in so doing, achieved a tight grip on city government (Simpson 2001, 247–94).

Unlike his father, who on his dying day retained the position of 11th ward Democratic Party committeeman, Richard M. Daley does not hold a formal political party position. Moreover, the City of Chicago's acceptance of the Shakman settlement in the early 1980s substantially reduced the number of "patronage" jobs in municipal government. Nevertheless, in the 20 years since the resolution of the Shakman suits, the Republican Party has not made a comeback in Chicago politics. Indeed, Richard M. Daley controls the affairs of Chicago like no mayor since his father, although the current Mayor Daley's domination of civic affairs turns on a set of local power relations that is much more fluid than those characterizing the 1950s or early 1960s. Across the city of Chicago, the once-monolithic phalanx of Democratic Party ward organizations, today, looks more like a patchwork quilt. On the city's Northwest Side, 33rd ward alderman and Democratic Party committeeman Richard Mell commands a local organization that looks, in many respects, like a mid-twentieth century operation (Fremon 1988, 218–23; Reardon 1996). Mell's organization includes a small army of patronage-supported campaign workers and has the capacity to contact every local household. Mell indeed possesses sufficient campaigning resources to extend his influence into adjoining wards and state legislative districts, thereby placing allies in important elective offices. Illinois' current governor, Rod Blagojevich (as well as being Richard Mell's son-in-law), is a product of the Mell organization, having previously served as a Northwest Side state legislator and U.S. congressman before winning the 2002 gubernatorial race. Richard Mell, for his part, does not challenge Mayor Daley in city council. At the same time, Mayor Daley's support of the Blagojevich gubernatorial candidacy no doubt derived from something critical the prospective governor could offer Mayor Daley: steadfast support for continued expansion of O'Hare Airport (Ford 2002).

The ranks of Chicago's Democratic Party leadership include a few other major players on the scale of Richard Mell, such as 14th ward alderman Edward Burke and state House of Representatives leader Michael Madigan, both ward committeemen directing efficient local campaigning operations. Yet in several of the north lakefront wards, as well as much of African American Chicago, Democratic Party ward organizations possess neither the activist base nor rank-and-file loyalty that typified ward organizations in the early Richard J. Daley era. In many respects, this state of affairs suits the interest of Richard M. Daley perfectly well. The mayor's name recognition gives him a tremendous advantage over any prospective challenger and, as the city's record-setting campaign fundraiser, Mayor Daley can mount citywide, media-oriented campaigns of the sort never imagined by his father (Gierzynski, Kleppner, and Lewis 1996). Moreover, the relative weakness of many of the city's Democratic Party ward organizations increases the mayor's leverage with city council members, whose reputations often rise and fall depending on the mayor's delivering adequate public services or otherwise sponsoring or withholding projects desired by their constituents.

In recent years, the most telling development in local electoral politicking has been the emergence of the Hispanic Democratic Organization (HDO), which is headed by Victor Reyes, a former aide to Richard M. Daley. Functionally speaking, HDO is a mobile political unit with the capacity to flood campaign workers into electoral districts with substantial Latino populations. Since its formation in the early 1990s, the HDO has invariably worked on behalf of candidates supported by Mayor Daley. The *Chicago Tribune* has reported that the HDO can mobilize more than 1,000 campaign workers, with half of the group's members holding city government jobs, usually in agencies hiring large numbers of manual workers. However, the HDO has not earned the universal admiration of Democratic Party activists, as indicated by one ward-based politician's comment to *Tribune* reporters: "A lot of organizations feel they're being cannibalized . . . It's a faster track to promotions" (Cohen, Mota, and Martin 2002). In effect, sustaining the HDO's activist ranks siphons off political resources that might otherwise flow into ward organizations. Nevertheless, Mayor Daley's electoral success initially derived in part from his ability to win Latino votes, and as the Latino electorate in Chicago increases Daley will very likely continue to ally himself with the HDO.

Richard M. Daley's political base of support also includes a network of lobbyists, former office-holders, and businessmen whose careers have linked political and business entrepreneurship. This group's defining skill, the capacity to offer various forms of political assistance to the mayor—tactical advice, access to campaign contributors, support from one or another civic organization—while also managing to win preferential municipal policy decisions, has caused local journalists to coin a new term: "pinstripe patronage." In some instances, such as the Chicago Transit Authority's 1999 sale of a valuable parcel of land in the upscale Lincoln Park neighborhood to a real estate team including acquaintances of the mayor, the linkage between government decision makers and business "insiders" was probably nothing more than the mayor's ubiquitous networking at elite social and civic gatherings (Mendell and Washburn 1999). In other cases, politically canny business firms have used inside knowledge of municipal purchasing practices to win contracts, or have actually engaged in financial manipulation to enlist official support for their contract bids. For example, in 1998 11th ward alderman Patrick Huels—the mayor's city council floor leader—resigned from the council when journalists revealed that he had received a personal loan of $1.25 million from a businessman who had won $65 million in city contracts (Washburn and Martin 1997). In early 2001, three prominent associates of Mayor Daley, Jeremiah Joyce, a long-time political advisor, Oscar D'Angelo, a West Side real estate investor with Democratic Party connections running back to the Richard J. Daley era, and Victor Reyes (of the HDO) were revealed to have earned substantial fees advising private concessionaires at O'Hare Airport (Cohen and Martin 2001). In addition to perpetuating the widely held assumption that "clout" remains a force in City Hall decision making, the frequency of these revelations has also undercut Mayor Daley's claim that his advocacy of service privatization is rooted in its promise to improve governmental performance.

It is also possible that the accumulation of insider scandals could produce a serious erosion of Mayor Daley's public support. Throughout 2004 and 2005, Chicago news media reported on a sequence of scandals involving politically rigged city contracting and favoritism in City hiring (Spielman 2004b; Washburn and Cohen 2005). By the spring and summer of 2005, waves of dismissals and federal indictments had swept through the leadership ranks of the City's departments of Streets and Sanitation, Transportation, and Water Management, as well as a unit working directly for Mayor Daley, the Office of Intergovernmental Affairs (Washburn and Mihalopoulos 2005; Mihalopoulos and O'Connor 2005). For the first time since the early 1990s, political commentators began to discuss an upcoming mayoral election (in early 2007) as if a serious contest might be in the offing. It is also presumed that Democratic Congressman Jesse Jackson, Jr., if he chooses to challenge Mayor Daley in the 2007 election, could be a formidable candidate. Nevertheless, even in the wake of Richard M. Daley's most difficult two years since becoming mayor, any challenger in the next mayoral election will encounter a number of substantial obstacles: the incumbent's multimillion dollar campaign war chest, the absence of organized political opposition (certainly not the Republican Party, nor for that matter the mobilized grassroots organization network so instrumental to Harold Washington's victory in 1983), and a numerically reduced, Daley-tilting voting population.

Beyond Chicago's city limits, Mayor Daley's record has verged on the schizophrenic. Since the mid 1990s, he has been a regular participant at meetings of the Metropolitan Mayors Caucus, an organization convening the chief elected officials from municipalities across the metropolitan region (Hamilton 2002). And, on occasion, the City of Chicago has worked closely with suburban officials, for example, by joining in the drafting of a model municipal ordinance restricting firearms sales and ownership (Washburn 2002). In other instances, such as the O'Hare Airport–Third Airport debate, the City of Chicago's stance has been willfully at odds with the wishes of many suburban municipalities. Quite remarkably, even though Mayor Daley and former Illinois Governor George Ryan reached a settlement in 2001 that authorized an expansion of O'Hare coupled with further planning of the south-suburban air

terminus, the mayor then proceeded as if he had made no commitment of support for the new airport (Washburn and Hilkevitch 2001; Hilkevitch and Washburn 2001). Otherwise, Mayor Daley and Governor Ryan often worked closely on initiatives sought by the City, notably the very quick state approval of the redevelopment of lakefront Soldier Field. Conversely, Daley had regularly warred with Ryan's predecessor, Jim Edgar, over a variety of projects: the governor's proposal to add a sports arena to the McCormick Place complex, a previous plan—supported by Mayor Daley—to renovate Soldier Field, and the mayor's proposal to convert a small airport near downtown Chicago, Meigs Field, to a lakeside park (Kass and Pearson 1996; Baade and Sanderson 1997). While Mayor Daley appears to recognize the inescapable reality that the city of Chicago's fortunes are very much joined to the fortunes of its metropolitan region, and moreover, that its fiscal fortunes very much depend on the good will of the governor and state legislature, he has yet to consistently pursue a politics of regional and intergovernmental collaboration.

CHICAGO AND THE TWENTY-FIRST CENTURY

Among commentators on American cities in the twentieth century, the great intellectual bookends are Jane Jacobs and Lewis Mumford. Jacobs, especially through her book *The Death and Life of Great American Cities* (1961), has probably been the most powerful intellectual force shaping how late twentieth century city planners and local activists interpret neighborhood-level processes. Jacobs' great insight was to propose that the unplanned, collective behavior of city residents exercises a determinative influence on how well buildings, streets, and public places work to support human activities. This view of cities has produced contemporary city planning initiatives that emphasize mixed-use development, "redensification" of central cities, and around-the-clock patterns of activity. Mumford (1986), Jacobs' occasional antagonist, has only recently received a revival of attention by advocates of "new regionalist" solutions to urban problems. In contrast to Jacobs' miniaturist analysis of urban street life and the routines of neighborhood interaction, Mumford was a large-scale thinker, who, in his major work, *The City in History* (1961), framed his examination of cities within the long arc of human history. For Mumford, cities could not be understood without exploring their role in such fundamental human enterprises as economic accumulation and war making. Ultimately, Mumford did not share Jacobs' enthusiasm for "great cities." Rather, his utopian sensibility proposed that a more environmentally sustainable, regional form of urbanization was the appropriate corrective to twentieth century mega-cities.

If, indeed, the company of planners, politicians, and activists can be divided between the Jacobsites and the Mumfordites, Richard M. Daley is clearly one of the former. The quality-of-life improvements that Daley has brought to Chicago have tended to be outgrowths of the mayor's attention to the city's physical details. Chicago, in the 1970s, looked and acted the part of a declining Rust Belt city. Parks, neighborhood play-lots, and public buildings had fallen into physical decay. Surrounding the city's still-impressive downtown core was a band of emptying-out industrial districts straddled by run-down working-class residential areas. And even during the mayoralty of Harold Washington, the city's political arena seemed to be defined by an inexorable dispute between mobilized racial factions, each determined to claim a disproportionate share of what seemed to be an ever-shrinking pool of public resources.

Richard M. Daley's Chicago is a much more physically impressive and collectively optimistic city. Schools have been renovated, and neighborhood play-lots across the city have been fitted out with new swings, monkey bars, and sandboxes. Much of the residential development that has occurred north, west, and south of the Loop has adopted the "New Urbanist" preference for low-rise, rowhouse-style site planning. Contemporary Chicago architects and developers trip over themselves to assert that their developments will restore links in the city's "traditional street system" that were obliterated by Corbusian mega-projects built in the 1950s and 1960s.

Richard M. Daley's commitment to reviving Chicago as a city of traditional-looking neighborhood architecture, "themed" residential areas, and spruced-up public spaces has set the tone for the rush of near-downtown development during the 1990s.

Daley's Jacobsite physical design predilections, of course, cannot directly account for the suppressing of race- and ethnicity-inflected political conflict, but his careful management of racial politics via elite inclusion would probably not be possible in the absence of the city's rejuvenated economy and sense of optimism, both of which have been given substantial fuel by the residential rebuilding of central Chicago. Moreover, the opportunities for politically connected African Americans and Latinos to participate in residential development consortiums, or to bid on city contracts for various public works improvements, are legion. In short, for the first time since the mid-1960s, Chicago appears to be a thriving city offering economic opportunities to all.

It is from the Mumfordite vantage point that Richard M. Daley's performance is less impressive. Chicago's relatively modest increase in residents during the 1990s boosted the city's population back toward the three million mark but, even so, the central city's portion of the metropolitan figure is less than half. Richard M. Daley, at best, has been an ambivalent supporter of measures to bring coherence and cooperation to Chicago metropolitan affairs. When it has served his political purposes, the mayor has been willing to work with suburban officials on specific matters of mutual concern. Nevertheless, the City of Chicago's endorsement of regional policy initiatives has been quite circumscribed. The most obvious failure to "think regionally" is represented by the longstanding debates over whether O'Hare Airport can continue to expand, and relatedly, whether a new south-suburban airport should be constructed. But Chicago and its neighboring jurisdictions fail to cooperate on a variety of other significant matters. For example, in spite of many pleas to integrate their urban and commuter lines, the Chicago Transit Authority and the Regional Transit Authority have made very little progress in providing inter-system transfer points or an integrated passenger fare system. Similarly, one of the hallmarks of the Daley program in the 1990s, the demolition of high-rise public housing developments, has failed to anticipate a crucial human effect. As the number of public housing units within the city of Chicago is reduced, former Chicago Housing Authority (CHA) residents—armed with housing vouchers—have begun to fan out across Chicago and several of its adjoining suburbs. Several years into its Plan for Transformation, the CHA has demonstrated no inclination to work with outlying municipalities (or, for that matter, with community organizations in Chicago neighborhoods) to ensure that public housing relocatees find decent housing, accessible social services, and reasonably welcoming new communities.

In the first years of the new millennium, Chicago officials and their suburban counterparts can appropriately view the future with a degree of optimism. The 1990s were a good decade for city and region. The city of Chicago's status as a dynamic economic center, richly endowed with major cultural institutions and an energetic creative community, worked to the benefit of residents throughout the region. Moreover, unlike several coastal metropolises, the late 1990s collapse of the high-tech economy did not strike Chicago with overwhelming force. However, the Chicago region's sense of collective destiny was not greatly advanced during this decade. Many suburbanites continue to view Chicago as a corrupt central city dominated by machine politicians. For their part, the city's political leaders have only begun to consider whether the fortunes of Chicago might not be greatly enhanced through a more concerted engagement with metropolitan solutions to approaching public policy dilemmas in the areas of affordable housing, transportation, and the environment.

5 The Physical Transformation of Metropolitan Chicago

Chicago's Central Area

Charles S. Suchar

She outgrows her prophecies faster than she can make them. She is always a novelty; for she is never the Chicago you saw when you passed through the last time.

—Mark Twain, *Life on the Mississippi*

MARK TWAIN'S observations of Chicago, made more than a century ago, could not be more appropriate today. Although the last quarter of the twentieth century was witness to a most impressive array of changes and transformations that characterized many urban centers in the United States, this was especially the case in Chicago. These changes were responses to and the consequences of historical, social, economic, cultural, and political forces that, taken together, have helped to reinvigorate city life, change the physical and material character of the central city, and point the direction of the city's future form—its urban morphology. Chicago, said by Nelson Algren to be "on the make" has, in a way, been on the "remake," transformed through a complex set of characteristics that have impacted its people, especially its physical topography and landscape, the built environment in which community is experienced.

A major reversal of urban development has taken place within the city of Chicago. At one time, Chicago had a central area where the middle and upper social classes were dominant—a pattern common to other major world cities. With the development of industry and the city's impressive growth through immigration and migration, Chicago's central area became increasingly an area for the working class and those at the bottom of the social stratification system. Suburbanization and public policy in the years preceding and following World War II provided added ingredients to transform an industrially based economy and social order. Neighborhoods and populations tied to that economy and social order changed when industrial production began to leave the city. These neighborhoods went into decline, experiencing a devaluation or "devalorization" of real estate and property (Smith 1986).

In addition to these economic changes in the city and its neighborhoods, poorly planned national and local solutions to the housing needs of residents and the physical deterioration of certain neighborhoods gave rise to additional social problems that began to affect these communities as well. As we approached the last decades of the twentieth century, much of these economic and physical changes began to occur in earnest. However, the changes leading to a "revalorization" and redevelopment of the central city have had to compete with conditions that have remained very much within the central city. The tension between the Chicago that was and the Chicago that is emerging leads to the city's central area becoming a "contested area," a region of competing social lifestyles, social class interests, race relations, and a physical environment that reflects these social characteristics.

VISIONS OF CENTRAL CHICAGO'S FUTURE

The Chicago Central Area Plan

In July 2002, the City of Chicago's Departments of Planning and Development and

Transportation released a draft of their *Chicago Central Area Plan* (City of Chicago 2002). The plan was prepared for the Mayor's Central Area Plan Steering Committee and took its place as the latest in a series of historically significant urban planning documents dating back to *The Plan of Chicago* (1909) by Daniel Burnham and Edward Bennett, which established the very identifiable face of much of central Chicago. Intervening central area plans in 1958, 1973, and 1983 had contributed important ideas for the revamping of Chicago's physical infrastructure and cityscape: the Daley Civic Center, McCormick Place, redevelopment of Navy Pier, extension of public transportation lines to the airports, the building of new expressways, and the expansion of green space and parks, to name just a few of the significant changes to Chicago's more famous features. The 2002 central area plan provided a conception of Chicago's central area that was radically different from that of previous plans. It reflected the significant social, economic, and cultural changes since the last (1983) plan, and it dramatically foretold of a very different central city area envisioned by its planners, civic and business leaders, and politicians.

The 2002 central area plan, projecting forward to the year 2020, emphasized an expanded West Loop office area that would anchor the economic revitalization of the city. It included the development of what it termed "mixed-use," high-density urban corridors in the West Loop that combined new high-rise office buildings, hotels, and commercial structures and a new transportation system of busways and integrated public transport. The latter would link the new, expanded downtown with other parts of the central area and beyond. It envisioned an integration of central city residential neighborhoods already in development, with new, central area neighborhoods yet to be developed. In many ways, this latter projection and the already-present residential developments upon which it was based, are among the most significant and extensive central city physical transformations to be found or planned for in Chicago.

The 2002 plan also envisioned a central city area of revitalized green spaces, open-spaces, neighborhood parks, and waterfronts, especially along the north and south branches of the Chicago River. It included plans for specific district transformations in the Near North Side, but particularly for areas adjacent to the already developing South Loop and the changing Near South Side. These included an extension of the Michigan Avenue and Wabash and State Streets residential corridors in the South Loop, as well as a revitalized "Motor Row" (a former automobile sales district, long stagnant and decaying); a Cermak Road mixed-use corridor of hotels and housing that would link McCormick Place with Chinatown, Motor Row, and the developing Near South Side; and an additional south by southwest Loop Corridor along Roosevelt Road, linking these developments to a revitalized Near West Side and areas around the University of Illinois at Chicago campus such as the new University Village. The newly projected South River neighborhoods that extend between the South Loop and Chinatown and through to north Bridgeport (Chinatown South) would border a revitalized Chicago River and "promenade" that the planners viewed as anchoring the revitalization of a decaying former railroad and largely derelict Rust Belt region.

The combined effect of these changes to the central Chicago area, as projected by the 2002 city planning document, is truly striking when taken as a whole. The near $30 billion price tag that would pay for the planned changes is equally impressive. The plan projects this development over an approximately 18-year period, to the year 2020, although a number of the physical manifestations of these central-area plans are already visibly evident, as photography and systematic observation will attest.

The Metropolis 2020 Plan

Another vision of the future Chicago (Chicago Metropolis 2020 2003; see also Johnson 1998, 2001), one based on a broader metropolitan view of Chicago's six-county region, is contained in a document released by the Chicago Metropolis 2020 organization—a nonprofit civic group created by The Commercial Club of Chicago in 1999. Because the Chicago Metropolis 2020 organization and its ongoing planning efforts are examined in detail elsewhere in this volume, only the basic outline of its 2003 "Choices for the Chicago Region" report is noted here. That the target date for this plan is the same as the City's Central Area Plan is no accident, since the latter was written in full recognition of the basic framework of the initial Chicago Metropolis 2020 plan, which was released several years prior to the City's plan.

"Choices for the Chicago Region" shares several characteristics with the Central Area plan and its vision. At the core of the metropolitan regional plan is an emphasis on efficient and effective public transportation links between suburbs and city, residence, work, and recreation, and an improved regional environment with sustainable growth and protected open spaces. The difference between this broader, metropolitan plan and that of the Central Area plan is that "Choices for the Chicago Region" includes a much more decentralized view of development needs, favoring regional, multiple-nuclei development, while at the same time seeking efficiencies and functional integration of resources, services, and amenities.

The plan calls for a regional effort to distribute affordable housing and assure equitable educational opportunities. It calls for an investment in and development of strong regional cities that would work in partnership with the city of Chicago. To accomplish these goals on a regional scale, the plan calls for, among other things, coordinated transportation and land-use planning and, most significantly, a revenue and tax-sharing system that is based on a broader geographical base than individual communities presently have. As might be expected, in a period of a declining national economy and significant state and local government budgetary shortfalls, the revenue and funding recommendations, especially in the 2002–03 reports, seem very optimistic—if not slightly more pipe-dream than practical solution. The revenue-sharing scheme also includes politically sensitive issues that would have been difficult to surmount even under good economic conditions.

The implications of "Choices for the Chicago Region" for the physical transformation of the metropolitan area would principally rest with the goals of linking public transportation (and land-use policy) to walkable distances between residential, work, and shopping and recreational facilities and those services that would ease traffic congestion in a growing metropolitan population. In addition to the preservation of open space and the encouragement of redevelopment to make best use of the available resources in the built environment, the plan also promotes affordable, mixed-income residential development near job centers, schools, services, and public transit centers that would create metropolitan development nodes and concentrations, thus eliminating the need to travel great distances, especially by automobile (see Chapter 23, for a more comprehensive exposition of Chicago Metropolis 2020's vision).

THE VISION IN LIGHT OF OTHER CHANGES IN CHICAGO'S NEIGHBORHOODS

What do these visions of Chicago and its metropolitan region reveal? These views of the future Chicago see a city vastly different from the industrial city that emerged in the last quarter of the nineteenth century and as it existed during the first three-quarters of the twentieth century. Chicago, hog-butcher to the world, the manufacturing center for clothing, steel, and food-products, with a city center devoted to retailing and trade, had become, especially in the last quarter of the twentieth century, a postindustrial city. As such, its physical presence reflected a fair amount of fatigue, decay, and obsolescence in the former industrial central-city hub, built environment, and physical infrastructure.

But, while this devolution was taking place in its industrial identity and function, Chicago was also experiencing a significant social and cultural revitalization of its central city neighborhoods—a postindustrial, social, economic, and cultural transformation of significant proportions. "Central city" and certainly "inner city" had begun to mean different things by the late 1970s and early 1980s in Chicago, particularly on the city's Near North Side. By the 1990s, the revalorization or revaluing of the central city area was clear: It had become a very attractive area for increasingly well–educated, younger, and upwardly mobile urban professionals. Lincoln Park, the Near North Side, Wicker Park, Bucktown, and other gentrifying neighborhoods just to the north of the central-city area, had already been in significant stages of development. Downtown and the Loop had been replaced by residential place-names—South Loop, Printer's Row, Dearborn Park, Near West Side, River North, River West, Museum Park, Streeterville, East Loop—that had been rarely used before in popular discourse on the city's neighborhoods. These designations were unrecognized as neighborhoods, and their emerging use is testimony to the effect of the realtor's inventive, creative, and powerful labeling ability.

On the basis of this neighborhood transformation (very little of it the direct consequence of either of the earlier central area plans of 1973 and 1983), the 2002 plan projected its vision of the future of central Chicago. In fact, it might be argued that much of the 2002 *Central Area Plan*, and also components of "Choices for the Chicago Region," would not have been possible without these earlier neighborhood transformations.

While names and plans for new communities were being touted for the central city, places like Cabrini-Green, Taylor Homes, ABLA Homes, Stateway Gardens, Henry Horner Homes— some of Chicago's decaying and infamous public housing projects—were also undergoing long-needed transformations. Although peculiarly absent in the planning documents of the city and elsewhere, these plans would also potentially impact and transform the urban landscape of the central city. The *Central Area Plan* contains few references to the issues of resident displacement, housing replacement, social class and racial tensions, and the city's plans for responding to these problems. In fact, much of the *Central Area Plan* and various Chicago Metropolis 2020 documents, while mentioning the need for "affordable housing" and noting the massive decline in rental units during the decade of the 1990s (e.g., Chicago Metropolis 2020 2001, 28–32), makes surprisingly little mention of many of these serious problems affecting the residents of these communities.

CHICAGO TAKING SHAPE BEFORE OUR EYES

Beginning in the spring and summer of 2002 and extending to the summer of 2003, the series of photographs in this chapter highlights the physical transformations that were most reflective of the new central area cityscape. This photodocumentary project follows upon an extensive visual documentation of the gentrifying communities in both Chicago and in Europe (Suchar 1992, 1994, 1997, 2004a, 2004b).

The most recent photographic documentation of Chicago's central area revealed a landscape in significant stages of redevelopment. The most noticeable and extensive changes have taken place within an area of longstanding interest to urban sociologists.

More than 80 years ago, the pioneering work of Robert E. Park, Ernest W. Burgess, and Roderick D. McKenzie in the landmark book *The City* (1925), and in subsequent studies by disciples at the University of Chicago (known as the "Chicago School" within the discipline of sociology), drew particular attention to the pattern of urban development and urban growth taking place within the city of Chicago and postulated a "concentric zone theory."

Of particular interest to sociologists for several generations were the zones in the center of the city, most especially the area labeled the "Zone in Transition"—an area almost exactly co-extensive with the "Central Area" of Chicago discussed in the previous section. This area became the object of the present visual documentation for the very reason that it reflected the greatest amount of contiguous physical transformation taking place within the city over the past 10 to 15 years and that it resonated with and reflected this longstanding, even traditional perspective within urban studies. Map 5.1 (see color insert) details the specific sites and locations for the photographs included in this chapter.

Park, Burgess and McKenzie labeled the "zone in transition" as such because it reflected dominant traits of instability and change, due to two leading factors: the invasion of industry—the influx and growth of an industrial base just outside the Loop or central business district—and the subsequent population succession, especially due to the effect of immigration, the movement of large groupings of people in and out of the densely populated area. This movement was based in large part on the relative weight of the affordability of the port-of-entry residence and proximity to work versus the more negative attributes of this zone, its "moral region," and the resultant normative and behavioral environment. Although the central area of Chicago had made enormous changes over the three quarters of century since the original Chicago School formulation, it still was a zone in transition, in some measure precisely because of qualities related to its (former) industrial character and the population succession or changes that have more recently taken place within the area. The present photographic effort entailed documenting these changes and characteristics, in part to assess the current state of the area's transitional character against this longer historical process of transformation.

Finally, another interesting and re-emerging physical reality important in Chicago's earliest growth, which appears to be equally significant in its present and future postindustrial development, is the influence of the Chicago River. The River, as well as the more immediately prominent lakefront to the east, structurally helps to establish those geographic conditions that produce significant social, cultural, ecological, and urban morphological consequences. Most recently, the Chicago River has reemerged as a geographic centerpiece in the redevelopment of many neighborhoods in the central area. The current photographic project attempted to document the transformation of the River's function as a physical anchorage for this development. It is difficult to avoid noticing how this feature of Chicago's geography has been a constant in central area revalorization.

THE SOUTH LOOP

The photography of central area city neighborhoods reveals a significant amount of new construction, building renovation and refitting, and a massive amount of functional transformation of formerly commercial and industrial property.

The most notable physical changes are extensions of central city residential developments, such as the expansion of the South Loop along the State–Wabash–Michigan Avenue corridor. These developments are linked by connections to the southwest Loop and Near West Side developments.

A series of photographs document several different and important characteristics of this development process. For example, with the Prudential Building and buildings on north Michigan Avenue in the background, Photos 5.1 and 5.2 show quite different examples of the upscale townhouses of Museum Park, newly constructed in 2001–02, in an entirely new neighborhood, over former railway land.

The quality of the construction and the location signal a major change in the central city and South Loop urban form and in the function of the built environment. Chicago's elite social classes during the nineteenth century once built their magnificent urban mansions just a few blocks farther south of this area on Prairie Avenue, and the vestiges of this area have helped form a nucleus for current development.

The presence of a Chicago public school within the South Loop neighborhood of Dearborn Park (Photo 5.3) and a collection of children playing in its playground, demonstrate the demographic changes to the area, particularly the influx of middle class families.

A formerly problematic area beset by deteriorating and vacant warehouses, commercial and manufacturing properties, and the remnants of a more tawdry entertainment district, the South Loop area has been redeveloped into a large-sized, upper-middle and upper class residential district with a growing number of service establishments on the major north–south streets of Wabash and Michigan Avenue (such as a large Jewel Food store, which opened in 2002). These new structures are a clear example of neighborhood gentrification and may be only the leading edge of further changes to come.

The architecture of this new Chicago neighborhood looks surprisingly similar to that found in other gentrified communities on the Near North Side of the city, such as Lincoln Park. The houses along State Street just south of Roosevelt Road are modern-day replicas of

PHOTO 5.1. Row houses in the Museum Park neighborhood. Note the Prudential Building in the background and buildings along Michigan Avenue. The location of single-family residencies in proximity to the south Loop harkens back to a century ago, when Prairie Avenue was home to Chicago's commercial elite. This upscale neighborhood is one of the most recent additions to the south Loop development that includes the adjacent Dearborn Park area immediately to the west.
Source. All photos by author.

Chicago balloon-frame houses. The townhouses of Museum Park share a close resemblance to the row houses to be found in sister gentrified communities surrounding the central city area as well. The developers of these housing complexes have copied architectural styles that have proven themselves in the marketplace as desirable for a clientele able to afford the half-million dollar minimum starting sale prices.

In the summer of 2003, the *Chicago Tribune* (Corfman 2003b) reported development plans for a new neighborhood immediately to the west of Dearborn Park, and referred to it as "Riverside Park" to be built over a former railroad yard and include 5,000 new residences, a very large home-furnishings store, and total

of "600,000 square feet of retail space including restaurants and cabarets as well as stores . . . ," all bordering the south branch of the Chicago River (Photo 5.4). The planned development will occupy more than 10.2 million square feet of space.

THE NEAR SOUTHWEST SIDE

Immediately to the west of the Riverside Park development, along the "Roosevelt Corridor," rests one of the more controversial residential projects to be created in Chicago in recent years—the $700 million University Village (Handley 2002a): the new 68 acre residential community replacing the famed Maxwell Street

PHOTO 5.2. Townhouses in the Museum Park neighborhood. These particular three- and four-storey homes in the foreground of the photograph are at the high end of the market in this area. Visible in the background and looming over these single-family residencies is a building that was undergoing conversion to a condominium complex.

PHOTO 5.3. South Loop Public School—a Chicago public school in the south Loop neighborhood of Dearborn Park. For observers of central-city development, the presence of a public school in proximity to the south downtown area marks a particularly salient departure from the area's former physical and social character. The building of the institutional infrastructure of a neighborhood commences at a slow but seemingly deliberate pace.

PHOTO 5.4. The South Branch of the Chicago River and the signs of development along its shores. The new neighborhood of Riverside Park is planned for the area to the south of this site, on the opposite side of Roosevelt Road.

Market area near the University of Illinois at Chicago (Photos 5.5 and 5.6). The photographs show this area, made famous by both its Jewish and Chicago Blues heritage, as the last remaining buildings were about to be torn down to make way for this massive mixed-use development. Where once stood rows of clothing stores, street vendors selling just about anything and everything with the refrain "you've gotta have this," and hot dog stands selling the famous "Maxwell Market Polish Sausage and Fries," now stand row upon row of condominiums and townhouses, mid-rise apartment buildings, and the dormitories making up University Village.

The southern end of this half-mile-long development abuts the northeastern corner of the old Water Market (the fruit, vegetable, and meat market of the city's Near Southwest Side) and the northern edge of the Pilsen neighborhood. This historically significant area appeared on old Hull House-produced maps that documented the many different ethnic groups—Eastern European Jews, Italians, Greeks, Polish,

Bohemians—that settled when it was a multilingual, multi-ethnic "port of entry" from the turn of the last century into the 1930s. It now joins the expanding swath of urban redevelopment taking shape on the Near South Side and Southwest sides of Chicago's central city area.

For many years, one small public park—Arrigo Park—epitomized the sharp boundary that some neighborhoods manifest between poverty and middle class affluence. This thin dividing line of social class and race can be seen between one of the most deteriorated public housing projects in Chicago—the Chicago Housing Authority (CHA)'s ABLA project on the south end of the park, built between 1935 and 1965—and a middle-and upper-middle class area on the north end of the park, the Little Italy community, a mix of the longstanding Italian population and a significant number of gentrifying residents. Much of ABLA has been demolished by the CHA or has been scheduled for demolition. Although rehabilitation has

PHOTO 5.5. One of the remaining commercial structures on Maxwell Street just before the wrecking ball eliminated the last vestiges of the old market area to clear the way for the building of University Village.

yet to commence, the CHA envisions a mixed-income development that will include approximately one-third each of new public housing units, affordable housing units, and market-rate units. This mixed-income development, totaling nearly 2,500 units and now called the Roosevelt Square project, would transform the 100 acres of neglected housing and bring some hoped-for relief to the physical blight that ABLA has long represented. The real issue is the closing of approximately 3,600 units of public housing and the displacement of their residents, for whom CHA will need to find alternative accommodations. (Chapter 22 contains a discussion of public housing in Chicago and ABLA's history of planned development.) This dilemma confronts other central Chicago areas struggling with the aftermath of failed 1950s and 1960s urban solutions affecting the poor (and African Americans specifically) in the "inner city."

THE NEAR SOUTH SIDE

The southward expansion of development projecting from the South Loop along the State Street corridor and extending, sporadically, as far south as 54th Street encompasses one of the most extensive concentrations of public housing and poverty in the country. Hilliard Homes, Harold Ickes Homes, Dearborn Homes, Stateway Gardens, and Robert Taylor Homes, are in various stages of transformation. Only Harold Ickes and Dearborn Homes are possible

PHOTO 5.6. The building of University Village drew significant protest from groups that held to the belief that the Maxwell Street area might still be saved from the wrecker's ball. Needless to say, their efforts were largely futile, and the project proceeded as planned.

exceptions to the trajectory of change. Of the group, Robert Taylor has seen the most significant demolition of its buildings. In August 2003, plans were announced for a 2,400 unit mixed-income neighborhood for the Taylor site (along with coordinated off-site development) with significant retail space included (Almada 2003). Stateway Gardens was largely demolished by the end of 2003, and the Ida B. Wells public housing project to the east of it, the oldest in Chicago, is also scheduled for demolition and redevelopment as a mixed-income community. Finally, the Hilliard Homes are undergoing rehabilitation and are awaiting a mixed-income development that will add two new towers to the complex and offer a significant link to the "Cermak Corridor" plan for McCormick Place-to-Chinatown redevelopment.

The CHA, in receivership in the early to mid-1990s, has made significant strides in finding new methods of financing the rehabilitation and redevelopment of public housing (see Chapter 22). Most recently, the CHA is turning increasingly to the private sector for joint-development projects and hence the market or public partnerships that envision mixed-income communities at Hilliard, Stateway Gardens, and many other CHA sites.

Made possible by the U.S. Office of Housing and Urban Development (HUD)'s 1992 HOPE VI program, the effort initially affected the Cabrini-Green Housing Project on the Near North Side, in 1998–99. The transformation of public housing has been long-overdue but still beset by many problems, not the least of which is finding strategies for adequately placing thousands of displaced families who will not qualify for or choose to live in these redeveloped projects. The physical improvements to the neighborhoods in which these new and planned for projects are located are already quite visible, marking a considerable departure from the desperate conditions in which Chicago's poorest residents have lived for decades.

SOUTHWEST SIDE CORRIDOR

To the west of this South Side corridor of development along State Street, paralleling the Dan Ryan Expressway and continuing the transformation of south central Chicago, the changes to Chinatown and Bridgeport reflect complex economic, social, and cultural realities that interweave with the larger macro-transformations. A severe housing shortage produced by an expanding population, overcrowding, and confining physical, social, cultural, and economic barriers had, through the 1970s and 1980s, placed significant limits on the Chinatown community. Westward, physical expansion was limited by the Chicago River, the railroad lines, the interstate highway system, and an adjoining industrial corridor.

In the meantime, an expansion of the Chinese community occurred to the south into the northern portion of the Bridgeport neighborhood. Bridgeport itself was undergoing a population swing, with increasing numbers of Latinos joining Chinese in a southward movement into what was formerly a predominantly white, working-class community. The Chinese community had a particular need for family-accommodating middle-class housing, senior citizen housing, and economic development away from the Chinatown commercial core along Wentworth and Cermak Road. This need was alleviated by several important development projects on Archer Avenue and Cermak, a senior citizen facility, row upon row of new townhouses, and Ping Tom Park along the railway property of the Burlington-Northern and Santa Fe (Photo 5.7).

THE NEAR WEST SIDE

The neighborhood west of the Kennedy Expressway and north of the Eisenhower Expressway, immediately to the west of downtown and including Greek Town is an area of the city that slowly began to change in character starting in the late 1970s. This mixed area of manufacturing, warehouses, a variety of other small business establishments, nonprofit organizations,

educational institutions, public housing, and even television studios, was among the earliest to make a significant transformation to residential housing, and it did so with a vengeance. The area might be dubbed the loft apartment capital of central Chicago. The sheer concentration of renovated buildings that began to convert to condominiums and "loft-style" apartments is staggering. A recent *Chicago Tribune* article (Handley 2002b) quoted Eric Sedler, at that time president of the West Loop Gate community organization, as indicating that 2,000 residential units were then under construction in the West Loop, a segment of the near West Side close to the Kennedy Expressway and Halsted Street.

A close inspection of Photos 5.8 and 5.9, taken in this area, shows both renovations and new construction with advertisements indicating "luxury lofts," "loft-style condos," and the Europeanized "lofthaus," revealing a number of important characteristics common to residential development in this area.

The "loft-style" and associated character of this new residential community clearly can be seen in the advertisements that sell this particular urban lifestyle, which values proximity to downtown, open living quarters, and a postindustrial aesthetic. This aesthetic uses exposed brick, pipes, utility fixtures, floor-to-ceiling windows, and luxury appointments such as industrial-grade kitchen appliances, granite countertops, and elaborate electronic systems for security, communication, and entertainment. Although some buildings, such as the 950 Monroe Building (Photo 5.8) contain "luxury lofts," others also have "set-aside" affordable housing units selling at an approximately 20 to 25 percent reduction from market rate prices. (Because of a city zoning incentive program encouraging such projects, the Chicago Plan for Affordable Neighborhoods, approximately 10 percent of units are designated as "set-asides.") The vast majority of these new loft apartments and condominiums have, however, a high-end market value and are aimed particularly at a clientele of affluent urban professionals. Singles, couples without school-aged children, "empty-nesters" wanting an unusual apartment location, and real estate speculators have made

PHOTO 5.7. Ping Tom Park, designed by Ernest Wong, along the South Branch of the Chicago River in the expanded Chinatown community. The Park is sited along the river and the railway line of the Burlington-Northern and Santa Fe Railroad. Visible in the photograph are remnants of the industrial heritage of this section of the neighborhood (including a converted warehouse that belonged to Carson Pirie Scott and Co. and a near century-old railroad bridge still in service). Adjacent to the park is a major townhouse development that has extended the residential capacity of this community long in need of additional housing.

this fledgling residential area a "hot" location with significant sites pre-sold at a rate of nearly 25 percent before completion.

The West Loop neighborhood extends northwards across Fulton Street, Grand Avenue, and the Chicago and Northwestern Railroad tracks—a community referred to as River West by some. The neighborhood now encompasses an unusual area of formerly deserted lots, expressway overpasses, and old railway lines.

THE NEAR NORTHWEST
SIDE—RIVER NORTH

In 2002–03, standing at the corner of Halsted Street and Chicago Avenue, looking north, east, and south, the casual observer could see the backside of Chicago's famed skyline taking on a different appearance. Against the skyscrapers, one would have seen tall cranes dotting the near horizon and the steel beam outline of nearly a dozen new structures emerging along the north branch of the Chicago River. Photographs taken in 2002 and 2003 reflect the nature of this physical transformation, the density of construction and rehabilitation, and the upscale, exclusive nature of the new residential developments on both sides of the north branch of the river. Three photographs illustrate salient characteristics of the community taking shape in this area of central Chicago.

A pivotal development in the North River area is the renovation of the former Montgomery Ward Catalogue complex off Chicago Avenue (Photo 5.10). It stands at the northern

PHOTO 5.8. The marketing of new "luxury loft" condominiums and apartments particularly aims at the lifestyle interests and demographic profiles of young urban professionals. The economic and social infrastructure of a neighborhood, with convenience groceries, cleaning shops, hair salons, and a multitude of additional services, is fast developing in the area.

PHOTO 5.9. A sign announcing the building of a Europeanized version of a new loft building in this near West Side neighborhood.

PHOTO 5.10. The Montgomery Ward building development project along the North Branch of the Chicago River (visible in the extreme left-hand side of the photograph) is one of the anchors of the "River North" redevelopment. Also visible are several of the many high-density apartment and condominium construction projects that were visible in the summer of 2002.

end of this development area, between the upscale development to the south and the southern portion of the Cabrini-Green public housing project to its immediate north and east. Recent interventions by the city, which include a $32 million tax increment financing (TIF) subsidy, have provided public incentives to the approximately $250 million project (Corfman 2003a). The latter subsidy is largely in exchange for a substantial number of units in the development property north of Chicago Avenue being reserved for affordable housing (30 percent), half of those for former CHA residents. The financing for this project points to the complexity of such large development ventures in the central area: a Chicago-based development company, Centrum Properties; a New York financier, Angelo Gordon and Co.; an Atlanta-based real

estate lender, Column Financial Inc.; the City of Chicago; and The Chicago Housing Authority are the principal participants.

The ongoing redevelopment of the Montgomery Ward area is a spur to new development to the south, but much of the latter is decidedly different in several ways. Gated communities were rare in the city of Chicago until quite recently. As Photo 5.11 attests, this is no longer the case.

On the west bank of the Chicago River off Erie Street (and within sight of the Montgomery Ward complex), just opposite the East Bank Club, stands a quite exclusive and gated townhouse development (Photos 5.11 and 5.12).

With current market prices in the million dollar range, these luxury units along the Chicago River are harbingers of what might be

PHOTO 5.11. A gated luxury residential development on the North Branch of the Chicago River opposite the East Bank Club ("Kinzie Park"), off Kinzie Street. Such gated communities were rare in Chicago until quite recently. Both banks of the river in this section of the near North Side have seen significant development during the past few years.

considered Chicago's new "Gold Coast," reflecting the changes in desirability, value, function, and look of Chicago River-side real estate.

The valuable stretch of the North Branch of the River from Wolf Point to the Montgomery Ward riverside development (and ultimately North to Goose Island) is gradually taking shape, with a premium being placed on high-density, upscale, market-rate housing with robust in-fill development. The attractiveness of the River North area as a "lifestyle" community is quite apparent. The neighborhood's proximity to downtown, the established restaurant and entertainment center of River North along Wells Street from Chicago Avenue to the river, and the art gallery district enclave to south of Chicago Avenue make for a real estate de-

veloper's dream set of ingredients to spark the interest of well-heeled consumers. Money, real estate, culture, cuisine, and proximity to centralized power mark what urban sociologist Sharon Zukin refers to as "landscapes of power." The shared social consumption characteristics and proclivities of the new urban elite who inhabit these new central city urban zones are quite a change from those who inhabited the zone in transition identified by the earliest sociologists commenting on Chicago's central area (Zukin 1991, 179–215).

Despite the robustness of development along the River North community, all is not tranquil. Photo 5.12, depicting the gated community of townhouses off Erie Street, also shows a 37-story tower at Lake and Canal Streets. This is The

PHOTO 5.12. Luxury townhouses along the North Branch of the Chicago River and several luxury high-rise condominium developments in the background. A slow economy and worrisome vacancy rates in some of the high-density developments during 2001–03 have caused some concern among financial investors and developers.

Residencies at River Bend, a new luxury condominium development. In August 2003, it was announced that the developer of this project, B.J. Spathies, was unable to pay off loans totaling $44.5 million, because of a 32 percent vacancy rate, and that a foreclosure auction of the development entity that owns the unsold units was imminent (Corfman 2003c). The decline in demand for such housing is attributable to the sagging economy in 2001–03, the increase in condominium prices, and overbuilding. This decline has concerned developers and particularly the lending companies who finance these projects. As in the case of other projects, the River Bend condominium is financed by a number of lending banks from as far away as New York (Lehman Brothers Holdings, Inc.) and

California (Construction Lending Corporation of America). Although Chicago enjoys a reputation as a good city for new housing investment by such firms, the current slowness of the luxury housing market may affect such development. The office vacancy rate in the River North area has also increased in the past several years, from a rate of 9.24 percent in 1999 to 25.3 percent in 2002 (Black's Guide 2002–03). This rate is highest in the central area, with the exception of the south Loop, where the 2002–03 vacancy rate was at 31.67 percent (Black's Guide 2002–03).

With the demise of Cabrini-Green public housing, the trajectory of Near North Side development is quite clear. A helicopter passenger flying over the northern portions of central

Chicago would discern a nearly continuous region of redevelopment, tear-downs, new housing starts, high-density high-rise, low-density single-family structures, and the ubiquitous market-rate townhouse development stretching from the Loop, up along the North Branch of the Chicago River. This development stretches past the former Cabrini-Green public housing project or, as parts of the area are now called, "the North Town Village" and "Orchard Street" developments, into gentrified Lincoln Park, Wicker Park, and Bucktown, and continuing through other North Side neighborhoods undergoing transformation (Photo 5.13). The region surrounding Cabrini-Green, however, has most recently become a focal point for some innovative planning and attendant controversy that reflect tensions over land-use and conflicting resident interests.

In January 2004, plans were announced (by developers, the CHA, and political supporters) for a two-phase SRO and mixed-income housing development, featuring the design of famed architect Helmut Jahn, to be located at Division Street and Clybourn Avenue. The plan's announcement immediately revealed a considerable amount of disagreement among various parties as to its viability, with former CHA residents and adjacent property owners' associations casting doubtful interpretations (with different concerns) on the project's eventual success (Deering 2004). The contest over land use in this area of the central city, particularly in former industrial and public land, reveals the potential for more significant and wider community divisions as many different interests clash over the use and control of this rapidly changing cityscape and real estate.

PHOTO 5.13. "North Park Village" under construction in 2002. This mixed-income development on the western edge of the Cabrini-Green Public Housing (one of the CHA high-rises is visible in the background) is among the first developments made possible by HUD's HOPE VI program.

PHOTO 5.14. A shopping mall on the 2000 North block of Clybourn Avenue. This entire stretch of Clybourn, extending south to North Avenue and paralleling the North Branch of the Chicago River contains block after block of strip malls similar to this one. These shopping malls serve numerous functions, benefiting both residents, the remaining industrial entities in the PMD between them and the river, and their constituent commercial enterprises.

Developers and other commercial interests in this portion of the central city have found a most effective means of linking parcels of market-rate development: the street-paralleling commercial strip mall. Borrowing the concept from the suburbs, strip malls line streets such Clybourn and Elston Avenues, but serve a complex set of functions (Suchar 2004a, 2004b). First, they serve as an interstitial zone, commercial bridges uniting communities separated for many years by natural, physical, and social barriers: Near North, Wicker Park, and Bucktown from Lincoln Park, for example. These ubiquitous strip-malls (Photo 5.14) offer the advantages of automobile-accessible parking for shoppers in a parking-deficient central city.

Finally, the strip malls are important buffers between the new residential areas and the remaining pockets of industry along the Chicago River. As such, they serve the needs of residents, industrialists, community and neighborhood organizations, and the politicians wishing to maintain a peaceful coexistence as central area development pushes forward.

Lincoln Park, historically the leading edge of community revitalization and transformation in central area Chicago, deserves special mention as an example of the extensiveness of gentrification and the manner in which it has served as an impetus for physical change in contiguous areas of the central city. With a population of approximately 68,000 residents in 2003, Lincoln Park ranked first among all Chicago neighborhoods in median housing prices. From its eastern lakefront boundary to its western river edge, and from North Avenue to Diversey Parkway, the neighborhood is perhaps the most gentrified community within the city and is often used as the benchmark for comparisons with other developing neighborhoods.

The "Clybourn Corridor," a three-quarter-mile area of strip shopping centers bordering a city-designated Planned Manufacturing District (PMD) represents a particular form of revalorization—the revaluing of formerly devalued or devalorized industrial, commercial, and residential real estate on the postindustrial western edge of the neighborhood along the Chicago River (Smith 1986; Suchar 2004a, 2004b). The area in question represents some unusually sharp contrasts in the physical look and quality of the built environment. These

PHOTO 5.15. The 2000 block of Magnolia St. (Magnolia and Clybourn Streets). The siting of new construction so close to the industrial area's collection of former factories and warehouses produces some startling visual contrasts. Houses approaching the million dollar value front on industrial lots, buildings, and commercial developments.

contrasts between new residential and older industrial properties are illustrated in Photo 5.15. A home, more commonly seen in suburbia rather than in central Chicago, stands near a former warehouse and factory.

Equally startling at times are the results of other "tear-downs" (houses completely removed and usually replaced by much larger and more expensive structures) when seen in juxtaposition to older housing, a topic of significant controversy in the community. As shown in Photo 5.16, the scale of the new brick and cinder block housing differs dramatically from that of the old working class wooden structures on the 900 W. block of Concord Place.

The cycle of housing transformation in such gentrified communities often moves through three phases. Initially, older houses are gutted and the rehab work (mostly internal) entails putting in new plumbing, electrical wiring, new walls, support structures, flooring, and furnaces and heating and cooling systems, as well as eliminating pests such as termites and rodents. The second phase of rehabilitation includes "building-out and up," where additional rooms and space are added to the existing structure, often building back to the alley limits of the property line. Most recently, the phenomenon of

"tear-downs," the complete replacement of the building, by-passing rehabilitation, is becoming more common. When the cost of retrofitting the property and full rehabilitation competes with the cost of new construction, the urban romanticism of earlier pioneers gives way to the luxury townhouse or urban mansion, and new "old" construction. That the going market price-tag on such properties is at least twice to three times that of rehabbed units is added incentive to builders and developers. In this way, scattered sections of Lincoln Park have become bastions of the urban rich, with property values no longer quoted in the hundred thousands of "K's" but in the number of "Mils." This third phase of housing transformation in such neighborhoods demarcates a new form of revalorization that distinguishes the gradients of upper-middle class and upper class housing and class status.

A power struggle may be taking shape for control of a newly contested area within the city, caused by the revalorization of the central area. The opposing forces of the market place and public sector needs and the clash of lifestyles and social class differences—the consequences of Chicago's decades-old segregated racial heritage—may provide fuel to the contest unless political, social, and cultural solutions

PHOTO 5.16. The 900 block of Concord Place. A typical collection of older cottages and the new construction residential units that have replaced the torn-down structures.

are aggressively pursued early enough to forestall negative outcomes. The hope of many of Chicago's less affluent and often marginalized residents is that the central city may still become a more inclusive area, meeting the needs and aspirations of a diverse community. This is not however, the current trajectory of development and change.

DISINVESTMENT TO REINVESTMENT: THE CONSEQUENCES OF URBAN REVALORIZATION

Segments of Chicago that, early in the city's formation, were critical to the development of industry and manufacturing and that offered adjacent space for modest working class homes and community life, fell into decline, in a classic, postindustrial pattern of devalorization. That process of decline included the departure of the manufacturing sectors of Chicago's economy from the central city. As a result of this disinvestment, other social forces affected the character of Chicago's central area neighborhoods: suburbanization; commercial decline; physical deterioration of housing and community infrastructure; population succession, in the form of

the in- and out-migration of waves of temporary residents; and the establishment of longer-lasting enclaves of new residents, due to public policy decisions such as the building of concentrated public housing for the poor. In turn, some neighborhoods experienced attendant changes in various institutional investments and resources as well—in schools, religious institutions, hospitals, and community organizations.

Many social and cultural forces then contributed to a process of revalorization in Chicago's central area. The reinvestment in central city living by urban pioneers and gentrifiers has been explained by many scholars (Hannigan 1995, Smith 1996). The social class shifts and attendant cultural and lifestyle changes have infused central area neighborhoods with younger, more educated, less family-oriented, upwardly mobile professionals who have come to almost stereotypically characterize the central area. The vast amount of physical neighborhood improvement associated with the arrival of these new residents has come with some significant costs, most especially the displacement of remaining segments of the neighborhood's earlier working class and less advantaged residents. It is, however, the pace and extensiveness of this more current development that is most surprising.

Sharon Zukin's conception of "inner city" and "landscape of power" (one might add "zone in transition"), provides contrasting characterizations of the central area that signify a historical trajectory of change that is probably less uniform and homogenous than is commonly thought. Pockets of social class, lifestyle, ethnic, and racial variation reflect a more complex, cosmopolitan configuration to the demographic composition of the central area's population. The actual or planned built environments that provide shelter, space for commercial development, and the infrastructure of services to sustain such urban transformation are highly dependent on market forces (e.g., financial lending and investment practices, developer entrepreneurship) and political and governmental regulation and decision-making (e.g., zoning regulation, ward politics, tax-incentives, municipal services, transportation policy, and government subsidies).

At present, the forces that control this transformation are greatly influenced by and responsive to the needs, interests, and spending capital—the "power of consumption"—of people who have come to inhabit this "landscape of power." In Chicago, this new urban elite has already affected what Zukin calls the "critical infrastructure"

> ...through which cultural values are appreciated. They conduct walking tours through seedy neighborhoods, pointing out art and history amid decline. They visit restaurants writing up reactions to dishes... By these activities, the critical infrastructure establish and unify a new perspective for viewing and consuming the values of place—but by so doing they also establish their market values.
>
> From this point of view, gentrification—like cuisine—is transformed from a place-defining into a *market-defining* process.... For developers, centrality is a geographical space; for gentrifiers it is a built environment. But for the population that is socially or economically displaced from older cities, centrality is a struggle between

their own segmented vernacular and a coherent landscape of power." (Zukin 1991, 215)

In Chicago, this segment of the population already has established the prism through which culture, lifestyle, and issues of "community development" are viewed. Through neighborhood organizations, block clubs, political engagement and influence, and the control and influence over consumer-driven recreational and commercial development, this new urban elite has come to dominate the attention and "place and market defining" characteristics of this urban landscape.

Chicago's pattern of physical development reflects a cityscape and landscape of power that, while striving for coherence, lacks the overall communal integration that would auger well for its future. Different racial, ethnic, cultural, and social class constituencies are wary of private and public intentions for the "new Chicago." These groups have too many unanswered questions about their future stake and role in and benefits from the many changes that have taken place in the city. The building of an integrated, coherent central area, utilizing coordinated planning and problem solving and benefiting the widest possible number of residents in its many different sectors, is a most formidable task. City government, the private business sector, community organizations and institutions, and citizen and resident groups must find the will and means by which to achieve a common ground for dialogue and understanding. These constituencies need to establish a vision and agenda for community planning that recognizes the interests, rights, hopes, and aspirations of all Chicagoans, regardless of background and status. If centrality brings with it power, that power, for the common good, needs to be carefully allocated and shared. The future and strength of Chicago, like all great cities, lies in its heterogeneity and diversity and in the common-ground of aspirations achieved and hopes realized.

The Emergent Suburban Landscape

Kenneth Fidel

CHICAGO'S SUBURBAN region is comprised of multiple independent political entities, with different and often conflicting agendas and degrees of control over the physical environment and different potential urban fortunes (Logan and Molotch 1987). Each of the more than 280 communities in the six-county region has its own land use zoning ordinances and regulations, with little coordination between surrounding communities or region-wide uniformity. Towns are subject to different social concerns, available resources, and susceptibility to the demands of economic and social interests. Like Chicago, suburban towns are affected by globalization, immigration, and economic restructuring—converging forces that are largely beyond local control.

CREATING THE EDGELESS CITY

Approximately two-thirds of the Chicago region's population lives in the suburbs, and their proportion of the regional population will increase in coming decades. The Northeastern Illinois Planning Commission projects total population growth from 2000 to 2030 for the area's two most populous counties, Cook and DuPage, at 10 percent and 11 percent, respectively. Projections for Lake, Kane, McHenry, and Will counties are 31 percent, 71 percent, 73 percent, and 121 percent, respectively (Northeastern Illinois Planning Commission 2003). Others predict that, 30 years from now, some fringe towns will have populations exceeding 125,000, replicating the experience of suburbs like Naperville

over the past 30 years and Mokena and New Lenox over the past 15 years. As a consequence of suburban expansion, both the Census Bureau and the Northeastern Illinois Planning Commission have enlarged their definitions of the Metropolitan Region and, tellingly, so too has the real estate industry.

Suburban population growth is driven by natural increase and immigration to the metropolitan area, social factors such as the desire for improved housing and a better quality of life, and economic factors such as the movement of jobs to the suburbs and the lower cost of housing at the urban fringe. One outcome of current patterns of suburban population growth is the dispersal of households over a large area, with low population densities and dispersed commercial and industrial sites. This settlement pattern is termed "the edgeless city," and it more closely resembles the Los Angeles model of suburban sprawl than the older urban model of suburbs surrounding a dominant central city (Lang and Talbott 2003).

In the past, expansion of the built area beyond the city limits was closely tied to access to public transportation. Today, the most important determinant of expansion at the periphery is access to the highway system created by the Illinois Tollway Authority, the Illinois Department of Transportation, and the interstate system (Boarnet and Haughwout 2000). The current wisdom is that the suburban region is expanding outward at a rate of approximately 5 miles per decade. Around the peripheral arc of towns surrounding Chicago, small farming communities such as Manteno, Morris, Plano, Oswego, Genoa,

Huntley, Belvedere, and Harvard are experiencing the early stages of transformation to bedroom communities characterized by new, large-scale, single-family housing developments.

For developers, the urban–rural boundary provides relatively low-cost land that, in combination with economies of scale, makes tract housing more readily affordable for working and middle class households. National builders, until recently not a significant presence in the Chicago region, are purchasing large farm properties on which they are building thousands of new homes and transforming existent communities. For example, in Manhattan, a town in Will County, one developer is building 3,600 new homes, and the population is expected to triple over the next few years (Munson 2004).

Housing prices are an important factor in the appeal of communities at the suburban fringe. In distant communities such as Oswego, new home prices are currently a bit more than $130 per square foot, approximately one-half the cost of a similar home in a less distant, more established suburb such as Naperville. In McHenry County, average home prices are currently 25 percent cheaper than for comparable houses in adjacent Lake County (Handley 2004).

RACIAL INTEGRATION

Although whites make up the greatest portion of suburban population increase, some suburban racial integration has occurred (Kahn 2001). During the 1990s, Chicago's suburban African American population increased by 153,670 persons, and the Latino population increased by 367,000 persons (Singer et al. 2003). In 1980, African Americans constituted at least 5 percent of the population of 17 suburban communities; a decade later that number had increased to 28 communities; and by 2000, to 64 communities. For the most part, however, African American suburbanization entails movement to communities that already have a significant African American presence. As the movement of jobs to the outer edges of the region continues, the mismatch between African American settlement patterns and available jobs is exacerbated (Stoll

2005). The Latino population, on the other hand, is widely dispersed across the suburban region, with a number of areas of concentration, such as the towns of Cicero and West Chicago.

THE SECTORAL DIVISION

The expansion of the suburban region has not substantially changed the larger pattern of community social status across the region. Chicago's suburban region can be visualized as an arc around the city, divided into five wedge-shaped segments. The northern sector is best characterized in terms of wealthy and upper-middle class communities and relatively little poverty, except in a few towns such as North Chicago, Waukegan, and Highwood. Other than North Chicago, there are no industrial towns. Middle class suburbs and light industry characterize the northwestern sector. O'Hare Airport is a major economic engine for this part of the metropolitan region, and the Woodfield-Hoffman Estates area contains concentrations of white-collar jobs. The central sector is characterized by a wide array of communities, including working class towns such as Cicero and centers of wealth such as Oakbrook Terrace, Hinsdale, and Burr Ridge. The I-88 high-tech corridor, with its offices, light industry, and shopping, runs the length of the central sector. Middle and working class communities and both light and heavy industry characterize the southwest sector. Much of the recent growth in regional population is occurring at the fringes of this sector. The southern sector contains working class and poor communities as well as considerable heavy industry. The transformation of the region from an industrial center to a post-industrial, service-oriented economy has greatly affected many of the southern and southwestern sector communities by way of reduced property tax revenues and increased unemployment. Many of the towns in the southern sector are the physical extension of Chicago's south side African American community, and deindustrialization has maintained if not exacerbated poverty levels.

THE MIGRATION OF JOBS

The same incentives that encourage new housing construction at the periphery of the region also drive the outward expansion of office, warehouse, industrial, and transportation facilities beyond the existent built environment. Important benefits include more rapid movement of goods and people, lower land values, lower property taxes, and more receptive and pliable local governments. Like new housing developments, stand-alone commercial, transportation, and industrial facilities on non-contiguous sites now define the urban–rural boundary and act as magnets for yet other projects of all types (Fox 2004).

As measures of sprawl, approximately 67 percent of jobs are located in the area between 10 and 35 miles from the central business district (CBD) (Kahn 2001), and 46 percent of the area's office space is located in the suburbs, reflecting the shift in the locus of commerce from the city to the suburbs (Lang and LeFurgy 2003). Suburban office concentrations are found in secondary downtowns located in older regional centers such as Evanston, which house all the facilities and services of a CBD, and in edge cities such as the Oakbrook complex and the contiguous "high-tech corridor" extending westward along I-88. Lang and LeFurgy (2003) estimate that nearly 20 percent of the region's office space is now located in edge cities. These concentrations form social and cultural nuclei that increasingly compete with the Loop and Michigan Avenue as commercial, cultural, and entertainment centers. They differ from the CBD in the availability of parking and in the absence of traditional institutions such as museums.

Elsewhere, large office complexes have been developed along the region's interstate highways. A number of large firms have moved their headquarters from the CBD to suburban sites, including Sears and SBC in the Hoffman Estates area and the Brunswick Corporation in the Deefield–Lake Forest area. Many other companies are now located along the high-tech corridor adjacent to I-88, close to Hinsdale, Burr Ridge, and farther west Naperville and Saint Charles, and to the south in Orland Park, with

its access to I-294 and I-80. Along major area roads, such as River Road near O'Hare Airport and Illinois Route 21 between Glenview and Libertyville, new office and hotel complexes form commercial strips, similar to but not nearly as densely sited as the concentrations of businesses in the Loop or along Michigan Avenue. These sites offer a number of advantages, including the ability to create a tailored physical environment characterized by both internal and external spaciousness, enhanced security, parking, and technologically advanced utilities. Joel Garreau (1991) suggests that, among other reasons for relocating offices to the suburbs, corporate executives may value proximity to the communities in which they live.

Industrial and warehousing facilities began moving from the city to the suburbs more than 100 years ago, as exemplified by the construction of Pullman (in the 1880s) beyond what was then the city limits. South and southwest of the city, numerous older industrial sites exist, many predating World War II and, in some instances, now abandoned (Campaign for Sensible Growth 2003). Increasingly, companies and government agencies view the older commercial, industrial, and transportation facilities in Chicago as obsolete and dysfunctional, and see the construction of new facilities beyond the current urbanized region as an important, if not necessary, measure for maintaining the economic viability of the metropolitan region. The opportunity to construct modern, more functional facilities with greater ease of access makes movement to outlying communities a rational course. An early indicator of a trend that continues to this day was the construction of the Chrysler plant at Belvedere, built more than 30 years ago. A more recent example is the relocation of rail facilities to Joliet and Rochelle, approximately 30 and 80 miles respectively from downtown Chicago. However, the enormous and now closed Motorola plant at Harvard, built some 12 years ago, exemplifies the ephemeral nature of land and facility usage in a global era.

Although construction of a Peotone airport, some 35 miles south of downtown Chicago, is presently on hold, efforts to gain approval for the project continue and appear to be gaining momentum. Construction of a new airport would have dramatic and wide-ranging effects on the far south and southwestern sectors of the region, including infrastructure expansion, new jobs, new housing, and population increase, thus expanding the size of the region and further exacerbating sprawl-related problems.

DOWNTOWN REVITALIZATION

Since the end of World War II, many suburbs have lost their local shopping and small businesses, in large measure because of their inability to compete with malls, big-box stores, and new office complexes. Some suburbs have successfully redeveloped their downtown areas, attracting new business and new housing. The city of Oak Park, immediately west of Chicago, may well be the earliest local case of suburban downtown renewal. Oak Park has three advantages: rapid transportation connecting the town to both the Loop and the western suburbs, policies encouraging population diversity, and a well-maintained housing stock, including a significant architectural legacy. The two most notable current examples of downtown revitalization are Evanston, immediately adjacent to Chicago along the north shore of Lake Michigan, whose advantages also include rapid transportation to the CBD and the presence of Northwestern University, and Naperville, immediately adjacent to the I-88 corridor, where the downtown has been transformed into a lively shopping and entertainment venue. Naperville's success at revitalizing its downtown contributed significantly to *Money* magazine (Schurenberg 2005) selecting it as the Midwest's best town to live in with a population over 100,000.

Other towns, such as Highland Park, Des Plaines, and Arlington Heights have also attempted significant downtown revitalization with varying degrees of success. Not all attempts at downtown revitalization are on a grand scale, multifaceted, or necessarily successful; nor do all plans come to fruition or have their projections met. In some communities, such as north suburban Buffalo Grove, downtown redevelopment is characterized by the market-driven construction of large condominium complexes. In far

southern Park Forest, a community built shortly after World War II and made famous by William Whyte's book *The Organization Man,* the effort to revalorize the downtown consists of the construction of new stores and apartment houses. In southwest Oak Lawn, the cornerstone of revitalization efforts is the construction of a new commuter rail station, and in Roselle, downtown redevelopment consists of a handful of new shops.

THE FUTURE

Suburban sprawl characterized by spacious homes, large lots, and low population density is essentially irrational in an age when average household size is decreasing and the costs of infrastructure development, utilities, and transportation are increasing. Yet, as jobs move away from the center of Chicago, living on the region's periphery becomes a more acceptable and, in some respects, more rational choice for many households than it had been in the past. Data from the 2000 census indicate that "more than one-third of metro area residents work more than 10 miles from the city center, and almost half of all commutes take place between a suburban home and a suburban job" (Lang and Talbott 2003). In 2000, over 800,000 persons were working in a county other than their county of residence (U.S. Census Bureau 2003b).

The housing built today will be sold and resold over the coming decades. The dispersed pattern of low-density settlement and workplace sites make traditional forms of mass transit uneconomical. Yet, in the final analysis, the viability of living in outlying communities depends on access to highways and relatively low-cost gasoline. Although some higher-density residential developments are being built, they represent only a small portion of the region's increasing housing stock. In the suburban portion of the six-county area, between January 2000 and April 2004, 135,515 residential unit permits were issued, of which only 22,140 (16.3 percent) were for units in multi-unit buildings (Northeastern Illinois Planning Commission 2000–2004).

Given current patterns of suburban development, we can expect the continued outward migration of jobs and people to result in a fragmented, multinucleated suburban region that closely resembles the Los Angeles model. This is likely to have a number of significant effects on the nature and characteristics of the metropolitan region, including population loss in Chicago and many inner-ring suburbs, a shift in regional political power to the suburbs, further deterioration of the public transportation network, and declining support for important regional cultural and educational institutions located in the central city. At the level of individual behavior and psychology, we are likely to see a population that is locally oriented, perhaps more urban but less urbane. An obvious need exists for effective regional planning and the establishment of a development boundary. We need to encourage higher-density population settlement and a more effective public transportation system that is better able to move people between their suburban homes, their jobs, and their shopping places.

Michael I. J. Bennett and Richard T. Schaefer

---

6   Race Relations Chicago Style: Past, Present, and Future

THE INTRODUCTORY chapter in this volume quotes Miller and d'Eramo's description of Chicago as the "most American of cities," believing, "to know America, you must understand Chicago" (Miller 1997, 17; d'Eramo 2002). This chapter details the past, present, and projected future components of conflict, contest, and collaboration among the racial groups that make up Chicago and its metropolitan region, with an emphasis on black, white, and Latino relationships.

DEFINING WHITENESS

Race has little to do with biology. Even the latest research from the Human Genome Project documents the difficulty of labeling as "race" clusters of characteristics as distinctive to any human grouping. Race is a social construct that allows the dominant group, the oppressor, to identify who is privileged and who is not. As definitions of race crystallized, this defining and redefining of people in Chicago reflected American society as a whole.

Michael Omi and Howard Winant (1994) coined the term "racial formation" to connote the socio-historical process by which racial categories are created, inhibited, transformed, and destroyed. Those in power depend on racist structure to define groups. The Native American people who had settled along the shore of Lake Michigan quickly became seen as "outsiders" in their own land, and were subjected to federal policy and military campaigns that largely disregarded tribal differences and treated indigenous people collectively as hostile (Winant 2003).

Racial formation in Chicago manifested itself among people who, by today's standards, would be considered white. German, Polish, Irish, and Italian immigrants and their children were regarded as unworthy of the privileges extended to the descendants of settlers of English extraction. The different immigrant groups did not move into Chicago's social environment randomly, and acceptance was not automatic.

For example, Irish immigrants arrived to find anti-Roman Catholic prejudice running at a feverish pitch. The nineteenth-century stereotyping of the Irish was accepted as fact: Irish Catholics were the "most depraved, debased, worthless, and irredeemable drunkards," proclaimed the *Chicago Tribune* (Cohen and Taylor 2000, 19). Prominent national figures, such as the inventor and painter Samuel F. B. Morse, fanned local anti-Irish fervor, warning that the Pope planned to move the Vatican to the Mississippi Valley (Duff 1971, 34).

William Julius Wilson (1978, 2–3) describes three stages of "black-white contact" in America—"pre-industrial, industrial, and modern industrial"—each shaped by a combination of the economic and political arrangements reigning at the time. In his terms, the pre-industrial, slavery period was characterized by "plantation economy and racial-caste oppression"; the industrial period, running from the end of the nineteenth century through the 1940s, featured "industrial expansion, class conflict, and racial oppression"; and the modern industrial period, roughly the 1950s through the

1970s, was a time of "progressive transition from racial inequalities to class inequalities." The latter two stages characterize the Chicago experience, however, with one significant alteration to Wilson's third stage: Although evidence indicated growing class inequities, race remained a prominent stumbling block to black social, economic, and political progress.

The situation in Chicago illustrates Derrick Bell's description of the dynamics surrounding blacks in America as "faces at the bottom of the well." As long as other groups—whites, in particular—can look down the long dark shaft of America's social and economic well and see faces looking up—black faces, in particular—they will always share a comforting feeling of hegemony (Bell 1992).

THE BEGINNINGS OF THE BLACK METROPOLIS (1900–1950s)

The presence of African Americans in Chicago increased sharply after World War I, when the black population leaped from 44,000 in 1910 to 277,000 in 1940. The growth was almost entirely from the northern migration of blacks fleeing the Jim Crow culture of the former slave-holding states. Although northern industrial cities like Chicago offered more opportunities to newcomers, many migrants encountered less acceptance than they had anticipated in the housing and labor markets.

During the first half of the twentieth century, overt segregation was one of the starkest realities to confront African Americans new to Chicago. Unlike Irish, Polish, Jewish, or Italian immigrants from Europe, who may have sought out enclaves of their fellow countrymen for linguistic and cultural reasons, blacks found themselves confined through systematic, long-term discrimination to a densely packed section on Chicago's South Side. The population of this "Black Belt," stretching from 26th to 47th Streets between the Rock Island railroad tracks on the west and Cottage Grove Avenue on the east, was more than four times as dense as the rest of the city.

White resistance to black mobility, characterized by fire-bombings and rock-throwing incidents to limit blacks' residential choices, grew so violent in Chicago that it became national news. Author Dempsey Travis (1981, 20) noted that "the expansion of the 'Black Belt' in Chicago could be measured by the bombings: between July 1, 1917, and March 1, 1921, bombings occurred on an average of once every twenty days." White-initiated rioting in the summer of 1919 broke out when a young black swimmer drifted into the traditionally white beach area of Lake Michigan. The violence that followed left the boy and 36 other people dead, and brought out the State Militia to restore order (Chicago Commission of Race Relations 1922; Spear 1967).

Bombings were the penalty levied on black families who slipped through the restrictive covenant barriers erected to deter them from buying homes in white areas. By 1930, 75 percent of Chicago's residential property was in areas of restrictive covenants where white owners agreed not to sell or rent to blacks. A pivotal court case opposing these covenants, *Lee v. Hansberry*, was the basis of the celebrated play and movie, *A Raisin in the Sun*, written by the plaintiff's daughter, Lorraine Hansberry. In 1938, her real estate developer father tried to purchase a house for his black relatives in the last island of white residents living in Washington Park, just south of the Black Belt. The Illinois State Supreme Court ruled against Hansberry in the ensuing court case. However, the case set the stage for an eventual victory when, in 1948, the U.S. Supreme Court refused to honor the covenants in the case of *Shelley v. Kramer* involving a legal team from the NAACP (Plotkin 1999; Drake and Cayton 1993, 184).

SPATIAL BATTLES: CONFRONTING RESISTANCE

To Dr. Martin Luther King, Jr., Chicago was the poster city for Northern racism and the most ghettoized city in America. He made residential segregation the target of his northern campaign. Launching his "End the Slums" campaign in 1966, King looked at Chicago's vibrant central business district, the Loop, just a few miles east of the impoverished West Side neighborhood where he was living, and remarked, "This is truly an island of poverty amidst an ocean of plenty" (Oates 1982, 379).

That summer, King marshaled a coalition of civic, religious, and community-based organizations to march into Marquette Park and Gage Park, two white neighborhoods notorious for resisting black integration. Again, Chicago made national headlines, as mobs of whites were caught on camera hurling bricks, bottles, and debris at King and his multiracial followers. They marched to demand a city-wide debate to open up housing opportunities for black Chicagoans.

Some working-class black families, aided by unscrupulous white "panic peddlers," successfully crossed the divide to purchase homes in traditionally white neighborhoods only to encounter more sophisticated forms of housing discrimination. In the early 1970s, a group of Jesuit seminarians led by a West Side parish priest and later legend, Father Jack Egan, organized the Contract Buyers League (CBL), a civil rights effort unique to Chicago, to confront the racist real estate sales practice of contract sales.

Contract buying rose out of a trio of deep-seated motives. Black working-class residents dreaming of home ownership and looking for an escape from the resource-deprived ghetto became the dubious beneficiaries of whites vested in maintaining a geographic distance (and discrete borders) away from blacks. Their primary incentive was to sell their homes to blacks so that they could move further away from blacks. White realtors sniffing a quick profit used scare tactics to stimulate panic selling. Scooping up houses from whites at bargain prices, they resold them to blacks at inflated prices. The exploitation was compounded when white-run financial institutions refused conventional mortgage financing to blacks, thus enabling realtors to sell "on contract," without a mortgage. The structure of the contracts prevented buyers from realizing any equity in their property until the house was paid in full. Missing even one monthly payment put contract buyers at risk of repossession of their homes and the loss of everything they owned (Frisbie 2002; Travis 1981).

THE EMERGENCE OF THE BLACK MIDDLE CLASS AND THE PERSISTENCE OF RACISM

In the next section, we trace how Wilson's third phase, that of the "declining significance of race" was truncated in Chicago, so that the significance of race did not decline as rapidly or completely as expected in the Civil Rights era. This truncated trajectory is evident in four areas: housing and residential patterns, occupations and the economy; education; and politics.

Housing

The effect of white flight on inner-city America was apparent by the late 1960s, when major cities exploded in a rash of violence caused by racial tensions. This violence culminated in a series of riots across the country following the assassination of Dr. King. Whites who fled the inner-city in record numbers to settle in the suburbs were soon followed by white-owned businesses and financial institutions. Those financial institutions that remained accelerated their practice of "redlining," drawing a red line around those areas undergoing racial change—initially from white to black, and later from white to Latino. Within these redlined areas, conventional mortgages were refused to new arrivals and, in the case of insurance companies, new home owners were charged premiums two to three times higher than those paid by previous owners. Financial institutions defended the practice as a way to shield their depositors from losses inherent in lending in "high-risk" areas.

Whatever the explanation, redlining is institutional racism. Studies by the Woodstock Institute, a Chicago-based financial industry watchdog, found that areas were redlined even before incoming residents' financial capabilities were systematically assessed. The only assessment done was of the newcomers' skin color and the socioeconomic characteristics ascribed to that assessment (Woodstock Institute 2002a, 2002b). Redlining exacerbated the physical deterioration of neighborhoods and contributed to the self-fulfilling prophecy of urban decline. It made certain that communities excluded from the traditional sources of credit and capital that enable people to buy and maintain homes, rehabilitate and maintain large apartment buildings, purchase inventory or expand businesses would experience the downward spiral of deterioration, deferred maintenance, vacancy, abandonment, and demolition. In most communities, the result was the displacement of poor, mostly black residents from low-rent housing that was later demolished.

At the opposite end of the redlining and disinvestment spiral stood investors eager to profit from the low purchase prices. These buyers used their investments to convert rental units into condominiums and to renovate larger single-family homes, thus sending property values and tax bills upward and beyond the reach of low- and fixed-income residents. Displacement by gentrification was the result.

From the late 1960s through the mid 1980s, community-based organizations, some enlightened financial institutions, and the federal and city government joined to craft collective strategies to address neighborhood decline. Shorebank Corporation, the nation's first community development bank holding company, attempted to create one prominent model to develop communities while limiting gentrification. Organized in 1971, the Illinois Neighborhood Development Corporation (now known as Shorebank) offered the most comprehensive approach to reversing the gentrification trend through a concentrated effort to "greenline" communities (Bennett 1980). Formed by an interracial group of Chicago bankers, civil rights activists, business people, and representatives of local and national foundations and religious organizations, Shorebank's goal was to establish a sustainable source of capital and credit, rooted in a local neighborhood, that could become an engine for social and economic development. Revitalization without displacement was the primary aim, utilizing programs that addressed those employment, housing, and education issues rooted in institutionalized racism.

In 1973, the corporation purchased a local community financial institution, South Shore Bank, in Chicago's South Shore neighborhood. Five years later, the holding company capitalized two nonbank development subsidiaries and attracted philanthropic support to create a nonprofit affiliate (Taub 1994; Osborne 1988). Shorebank Corporation pioneered locally focused Community Development Finance Institutions (CDFIs) as a conglomerate of development tools. During the 1990s, the Shorebank model inspired new legislation that broadened the scope of federal support for CDFIs.

Shorebank and other revitalization agents walked a development tightrope, delicately balanced between the displacement brought on by disinvestment and the displacement caused by reinvestment or gentrification.

The early portraits of gentrifying neighborhoods featured upwardly mobile, often young, white professionals. Reversing the white flight phenomenon, these "urban pioneers" risked their savings to reinvest in houses and apartment buildings in deteriorating neighborhoods where property values had plummeted. On Chicago's North Side, investments by them and real estate speculators led to a development boom that priced working class whites and Latinos out of the now-prestigious Lincoln Park neighborhood. On the South Side, young African American professionals acquired once subdivided apartment buildings and large single-family homes and rehabilitated them into stunning graystones and upscale rental units, also beyond the reach of the working class. Gentrification has become an issue primarily of class, not race, prompting one to ask if race in the new Chicago is less significant than class and wealth in terms of quality of life for racial and ethnic minorities (Map 6.1, color insert).

JOBS AND ECONOMIC RESTRUCTURING

Fifteen years after the Great Migration[1] and midway between the two World Wars, the Great Depression began. More than a decade of urbanization during a period of industrial expansion had not brought blacks the skilled-labor, clerical, professional, and business jobs and occupations proportionate to their numbers. Blacks clung precariously to the margins of the economy. As former sharecroppers and underpaid, Southern-city workers, they had "bettered their conditions," but had not equaled the rapid progress that white European immigrants had made in the 15 years between 1895 and 1910 (the high mark of European immigration into the city). Unlike their white counterparts, blacks had been barred from competing freely, *as individuals*, for whatever job they aspired to or were qualified for. The result of these limitations was the crystallization of a *job ceiling* (Drake and Cayton 1993, 223).

In the segmented labor force, "Negro jobs" and "white men's jobs" existed. Negro jobs consisted of servant, service, semi-skilled, and un-skilled occupations. During the 1940s, for example, 94 percent of the nation's train-car porters were black, and four out of 10 of them lived in Chicago (Drake and Cayton 1993, 235). Starting with Roosevelt's New Deal programs of the mid 1930s, government funding became available for job creation in black communities and the employment of black professionals. "Blacks were employed for the first time as statisticians, lawyers, engineers, architects, economists, office managers, case aides, librarians, and interviewers. Lower-level white-collar positions for secretaries, clerks, and stenographers also became available. Despite the fact that many of these jobs involved the administration of governmental programs, for blacks they represented the first real breakthrough in a racially segregated labor market" (Wilson 1978, 126). Wilson pointed out that "one of the most significant contributions to black occupational differentiation during and following the New Deal era was the improved relationship between black workers and labor unions" (Wilson 1978, 126). As a result, although black unemployment was disproportionately high by 1940, those blacks who were working saw their share of semiskilled and skilled jobs increase from 17.2 percent in 1940 to 29.1 percent in 1950. This represented upward mobility into the middle-class during the decade of the 1940s.

In Chicago, this also marked the beginning of a bifurcated social and economic stratification within black society. With the loosening of residential restrictions, middle-class and upper-working-class residents exited the Black Metropolis for neighborhoods to the south and west, leaving behind those with the fewest resources and the most circumscribed residential choices. In contrast to Wilson, Douglas Massey and some other researchers refuse to fully attribute the deterioration of black communities to the outward migration of blacks of means. In an interview with Chicago writer Studs Terkel (Terkel 1992, 92), Massey said, "I don't think black neighborhoods deteriorated because of the departure of middle-class blacks. . . . It happened because stable working-class blacks became poor blacks over the past fifteen years. They moved down the income hierarchy from working class—or lower middle class—to poverty status."

According to Massey, the restructured economy that eliminated higher paying blue-collar jobs in the "steel mills, auto industry, and other factories" sent blacks with limited education into a downward economic spiral that affected the next generations of their families and their neighborhoods.

Employment and income data indicate that, for black Americans, not all boats rise with the tide. When the American economy experiences periods of boom, blacks are in a perpetual state of depression (Jargowsky 1997; Wilson 1987).

Black Transformation and Stagnation. The economic transformation brought on a massive decline in manufacturing jobs and had a devastating effect on many sectors of the city's population. Hardest hit were minority residents who had limited education and few marketable skills. In Chapter 3, David Moberg describes how economic restructuring and deindustrialization have ushered in low-wage service jobs to replace the higher-wage manufacturing jobs that had once enabled workers with limited education to support their families adequately.

During a period from the late 1960s through the 1970s, blacks hurried up the socioeconomic ladder into the middle class (Herring 1997). But, by the end of the next decade, the bubble had burst. The confluence of racially discriminatory residential patterns and deindustrialization affected both the social and economic life chances of blacks in Chicago. "A history of discrimination and oppression created a huge black underclass, and the technological and economic revolutions have combined to ensure it a permanent status," observed Wilson (Wilson 1978, 22).

TABLE 6.1. African American Top Occupations: 1980, 1990, 2000

Year	Male	n	Female	n
1980	Janitors and cleaners	21,535	Nursing aides, orderlies, and attendants	17,373
	Laborers, except construction	11,988	Secretaries	16,571
	Machine operators, not specified	10,666	General office clerks	14,288
	Truck drivers	8,422	Cashiers	14,187
	Managers and administrators	8,285	Teachers, elementary school	13,371
	Assemblers	7,929	Assemblers	10,103
	Guards and police, except public service	7,144	Typists	10,087
	Supervisors, production occupations	6,824	Machine operators, not specified	7,422
	Cooks	5,945	Maids and housemen	7,183
	Construction laborers	5,747	Child care workers	6,933
1990	Janitors and cleaners	19,806	Cashiers	24,153
	Truck drivers	15,306	Nursing aides, orderlies, and attendants	21,441
	Cooks	11,640	Secretaries	19,278
	Guards and police, except public service	9,552	Teachers, elementary school	15,216
	Laborers, except construction	8,739	General office clerks	11,211
	Stock handlers and baggers	8,361	Typists	8,352
	Managers and administrators, n.e.c.	7,386	Registered nurses	8,151
	Assemblers	6,351	Postal clerks, except mail carriers	8,013
	Freight, stock, and material handlers	6,315	Data-entry keyers	7,269
	Postal clerks, except mail carriers	6,045	Cooks	6,756
2000	Driver/sales workers and truck drivers	19,060	Cashiers	24,030
	Janitors and building cleaners	17,568	Nursing, psychiatric, and home health aides	23,744
	Laborers and freight, stock, and material movers	16,997	Secretaries and administrative assistants	20,951
	Security guards and gaming surveillance officers	10,639	Customer service representatives	16,409
			Elementary and middle school teachers	12,923
	Stock clerks and order fillers	9,988	Retail salespersons	12,195
	Retail salespersons	8,593	Child care workers	11,558
	Cooks	8,282	Office clerks, general	10,814
	Industrial truck and tractor operators	6,204	Registered nurses	10,596
	Cashiers	6,052	First-line supervisors/managers of office	8,973
	Bus drivers	5,696		

Source. Reproduced from U.S. Census 2000, 1 percent Public Use Microdata Samples (PUMS).

Notwithstanding surface appearances of a transformed economy, a review of the occupational concentrations of African Americans illustrates how little has changed in Chicago during the last 20 years. As shown in Table 6.1, African Americans, especially males, remain concentrated in jobs requiring little formal education beyond high school and that offer little promise of significant upward social mobility. African American women fare somewhat better, with a greater concentration in the teaching profession, as elementary school teachers. Both genders are grossly underrepresented in occupations that might be associated with the new economy, such as information systems, finance, and health management. Two generations later, the pattern of a segmented labor force noted earlier in the 1940s persists.

In his portrayal of an "hourglass economy," John Koval further demonstrates the disproportionate effects blacks and Latinos suffer as a result of these transitions. In his depiction, whites and some East Asians occupy the upper chamber of the hourglass, blacks and Latinos occupy the lower chambers, and the middle chamber continues to shrink (see Chapter 15).

Although every group realized advancements during the 1990s, when poverty and unemployment among all racial and ethnic groups fell in the city and the region as a whole, the income gap persisted. In 1999, nearly 30 percent of Chicago's blacks, 20 percent of Latinos, and nearly 18 percent of Asians lived in poverty. By comparison, just 8.2 percent of the city's whites reported incomes below the poverty line.

Dramatic confirmation of white privilege came from a study published by sociologist Devah Pager in 2003. Pager sent four men out as trained testers to look for entry-level jobs requiring no experience or special training. Devah chose Milwaukee, Wisconsin, a city with a black historic experience arguably similar to Chicago's. All four men were 23-year-old college students, who presented themselves as high school graduates with similar job histories.

Their reception in the job market, from 350 potential employers, was vastly different. The reason? Two of the testers were black and two were white. One tester in each pair also indicated on his job application that he had served 18 months in jail for a felony conviction (for possession of cocaine with intent to distribute). Not surprisingly, applicants with a prison record received significantly fewer call-backs. Yet, as significant a difference as a criminal record made, even more important was race. Thirty-four percent of the white male job applicants with no jail record received call-backs compared with 17 percent of white applicants with a jail record. For the black testers, only 14 percent of the applications containing no history of incarceration and 5 percent with a record were called back. A white job applicant with a jail record received 3 percent more call-backs than a black applicant with no criminal record. Whiteness has a privilege even when it comes to jail time (Pager 2003).

Wilson (1996) reflects on the data from a survey of Chicago-area employers and concludes that "African Americans, more than any other major racial or ethnic group, face negative employer perceptions about their qualifications and their work ethic" and, as a result, have more difficulty in being hired (p. 111). In essence, racial discrimination may be declining, but it remains a persistent element in social and economic dynamics.

Education: The Social and Economic Escalator

Much of the gains into the middle class that blacks experienced during the 1950s and 1960s can be attributed to expanded opportunities in the labor market, ushered in by improved labor union relations, new clerical- and professional-level employment created by governments, and government-enforced antidiscrimination policies. However, the true escalator to the upper reaches of society was (and is) college degrees, and access to quality education was still unavailable to the majority of blacks, who came from resource-barren ghetto schools. In Chicago, where schools were never segregated by law or seldom even by overt exclusionary practices, residential segregation ensured that they were segregated by race.

Although segregated schools may be more the result of patterns of residential discrimination than overtly racist school policies, the two elements in combination have had a devastating effect on educational equity. Minority students find themselves in those schools with the most meager educational resources and the shabbiest facilities.

Dr. King came to Chicago in 1965 at the invitation of Al Raby, the convener of the Coordinating Council of Chicago Community Organizations (CCCO). Raby had assembled the organization three years earlier from a coalition of 34 civic, church-based, and civil rights groups to fight the de facto school segregation Travis wrote about. More specifically, the struggle began as a campaign to oust the current Chicago Public Schools Superintendent Benjamin Willis (Oates 1982). Raby and CCCO reasoned that King's intervention would raise their campaign for educational equity to the national stage.

Willis' response to overcrowding in black neighborhood schools had been to install trailers, dubbed "Willis wagons," on school playgrounds and to institute a double-shift school day of four hours each "instead of integrating the adjacent and usually half-empty white school" (Lemann 1991, 91). Although the movement did not net all the gains its organizers sought, the massive demonstrations Raby's CCCO staged contributed to Willis's resignation in 1965.

Chicago political figures, business and civic leaders, residents, and community-based organizations have participated in a rash of measures to address the persistent failings of the city's public schools. In 1988, the Illinois State Legislature passed a measure essentially placing the major governance authority of the schools in the hands of parents and community representatives, through local school councils. This school reform effort to channel participation from the bottom-up met resistance from educational professionals at the school sites and within the hierarchy of the board of education. In the end, meaningful attempts at resident and parent control were stifled.

Current statistics indicate that this situation is exacerbated by the high drop-out rate (or what some observers call the "push-out" rate) among young black males, the group now furthest from the labor force. In 2001–02, the drop-out rate among black male high school students in Chicago was reported at 25.8 percent, compared to 15.6 percent for white students and 15.3 percent for Latinos (Olszewski 2003).

Race and Politics

In early 1966, CCCO joined with Dr. King's Southern Christian Leadership Conference (SCLC) to form the Chicago Freedom Movement. Instead of following Raby's lead and focusing on schools, the reconstituted campaign made the elimination of slums and slum housing its first priority. Offended by the implication that something was wrong with "his city," Chicago's legendary Mayor Richard J. Daley confronted King's attack by labeling him "an outsider" and unleashing a battery of social service and housing inspection programs funded by the new federal Office of Economic Opportunity and Model Cities programs. Chicago proved an insurmountable obstacle to King's nonviolent mass demonstrations against poverty and inequality for reasons that King's aides had predicted. Daley organized his Machine-controlled "Negro aldermen" to oppose King's efforts in their South and West Side wards (Oates 1982, 395). Daley bought them by giving them influence over land-use decisions and a select number of municipal jobs in their wards (Dawson 1994; Lemann 1991; Greenstone and Peterson 1973).

Blacks had not always been allied with Chicago's Democratic Machine. During the Depression years of the 1930s, employment and housing interests pushed economically vulnerable blacks to shift their traditional allegiance from the Republican "Party of Lincoln" to the party of the "New Deal" Democrats. In the 1932 presidential election, less than 25 percent of black Chicagoans voted for Roosevelt. But in the mayoral election three years later, 80 percent of the black vote went to the Democrats. By the next presidential election, 50 percent of the black vote went to the Democratic candidate. In 1934, this shift spelled the defeat of Oscar DePriest, a Republican and the first black congressman elected from the North following the Civil War; he was beaten by black Democrat Arthur Mitchell (Frazier 1957).

From the broad view, it took nearly 50 years for black Chicagoans to demonstrate their independence from a blind allegiance to the Regular Democratic Organization. A contributing factor was the death of Mayor Daley in 1976, which split the seemingly impregnable Machine into pieces. Two subsequent mayors were unable to reassemble the parts. Black political action reached its apex in Chicago in 1983, with the election of Harold Washington, the city's first black mayor. Many veterans of the Chicago Freedom Movement that King and Raby had led emerged to lead that political victory; Raby himself was Washington's campaign manager.

For that election, "the city's black community, often divided by political bickering, came together with an unprecedented degree of political unity," Dawson pointed out (1994, 3–4). It took a coalition of blacks, progressive or reform-minded whites, and a significant portion of Latino voters to win that victory. Race, ethnicity, and broader civic interests combined to produce a political response greater than any of its elements alone. Washington's election lit hopes for an ongoing coalition that would use the resources and power of city government for balanced growth. Hopes were high for a dual-focus administration committed to upgrading neighborhoods while investing in the central business district, affordable housing for low-to moderate-income residents, and the replacement of special-interest job creation by truly rational planning (Giloth 1991, 2002; Clavel and Wiewel 1991).

The seeds were planted, but hopes all but died along with Washington in 1987. Chapter 4 in this volume paints a vivid picture of the disarray and power-grabbing that followed the mayor's death. When the dust settled, the political force of what had appeared to be a unified black community was muffled by factional strife from within that community.

Two images of black political strength present themselves. One portrays prominent black politicians such as State Senate President Emil Jones and John Stroger, president of the Cook County Board and 8th Ward committeeman, who, respectively, wield influence over the state and county political apparatus. The other image shows a black electorate that is divided over issues such as the dismantling of public housing and the migration of displaced residents into neighboring black middle-class areas; the placement of new low-income housing developments; and, most recently, the revamping of the city's public schools (Patillo-McCoy 1999). This divisiveness reflects Wilson's notion that class trumps race.

The expanded scope of black political interests also can be seen in examples such as Congressman Jesse Jackson, Jr.'s 2nd Congressional District in the South suburbs of Chicago, two-thirds of which is composed of middle-class African Americans. These black voters have distanced themselves from city issues and are much more conservative than their central-city counterparts.

And there is Barack Obama, born in Hawaii, to a black father from Kenya and a white mother from Kansas. He built his public career as a community organizer in Chicago, focusing on low-income neighborhoods, and then as a state senator from the integrated, liberal city neighborhood of Hyde Park, dominated by the University of Chicago (where he is a member of the law school faculty). In 2004, Illinois voters sent him to Washington as the state's first African American male senator (in 1992, Illinois elected Carol Moseley Braun as the first African American female senator to the U.S. Senate). On the road to his historic victory in 2004, Obama beat six Democratic candidates in the primary—four whites, one Latino, and one African American—by a margin of 53 percent. His face-off against a youthful, white Republican millionaire in the general election was cut short when a scandal forced his opponent out

of the race. His opponent was subsequently replaced by a conservative black Republican imported from Maryland. That race, between a liberal mixed-race candidate and a black conservative who focused on anti-gay, right-wing rhetoric, was not lost on political pundits, locally and nationally (Fornek 2004, Chase and Mendell 2004).

While Obama's victory buoyed blacks in Chicago and throughout the state, his election was more one of symbolic significance than evidence of an invigorated black political strategy. Obama's obligation to represent state-wide interests will leave him hard pressed to contribute to a black political agenda, except where it coincides with class-based issues such as jobs, health care, and education. Even these issues illustrate the fragmented class interests threatening the formation of a unified, black political agenda. Another significant threat to such consolidation of power is the changing demographics of Chicago's electorate. Although blacks are proportionately overrepresented among registered voters (they make up 37 percent of the population and 39 percent of registered voters), Chicago's older population is disproportionately white. Although they may make up only 32 percent of the population, the white population in Chicago constitutes 45 percent of registered voters (Johnson 2002).

Added to this mix is an influx of Mexican American residents, emboldened since the demise of the Washington coalition to establish their own political base. The fall 2004 legislative term included 13 Latino state legislators, the most ever. Where previously most of the Latino legislators (who come largely from Chicago) participated with the Black Caucus, their growing numbers and statewide representation since then have given them incentive to form their own Latino caucus. Eight Latino aldermen now serve on Chicago's City Council, and a movement is afoot to add two more predominantly Latino wards. The major impediment facing this emerging political voice is that the Latino populations younger demographics and lower rates of citizenship translate to an under-representation at the polls. Latinos total 26 percent of Chicago's population, but only 13 percent of registered voters (Johnson 2002).

Although vestiges of Washington-era collaborations remain among blacks, Latinos, and progressive whites, these coalitions most often center on jobs, education, and affordable housing rather than political matters (Herring, Bennett, and Gills 2000). Limited discussions between blacks and Latinos are underway at the city and state levels to identify a common political agenda. Now that Chicago's combined population of blacks (36.7 percent) and Mexicans (18 percent) is greater than 54 percent, several neighborhood leaders are trying to leverage coalition work on community development into a revitalized "black and brown political coalition" (Betancur and Gills 2000, 23).

However, the relationship between blacks and Latinos city-wide has a long way to go before political collaborations are likely to bear fruit. Data from a recent survey in Berwyn and Cicero, two communities west of Chicago, indicated perceived tensions between the two groups. Table 6.2 tallies responses to the question, "How much tension would you say there is between Latinos and African Americans in the Chicago area?"

Literary discourse delineates modern and postmodern turns in the emerging reactions to racial contest and conflict. The modern politics of change were articulated in grand notions of liberation struggles for universal rights and freedoms for all, with Marxism often presented as a primary example. The postmodern politics of change focuses more on identity politics, described by Best and Kellner (2004, 1) as "a politics in which individuals construct their cultural and political identities through engaging struggles or associations that advance the interests of the groups with which they identify."

Race relations in the new Chicago reflect what Best and Kellner call a "reconstructive postmodernism that combines modern and post modern politics" (p. 3). This is analogous to the framework used in this book to analyze the forces converging to shape a new Chicago—contested reinvention. Wilson, in his analysis of interactions between blacks and whites, and the consequences of deepening class distinctions on black-on-black relationships, moves his discussion toward a largely socioeconomic conceptualization of a "declining significance of race" and elevated influence of class. It is becoming more apparent that myriad factors will contribute to the diminishing political strength of African Americans in this city.

RACE, ETHNICITY, AND THE FUTURE OF THE NEW CHICAGO: METROPOLITAN VIEW

Subsequent chapters in this volume will detail the different residential patterns of new ethnic arrivals to the Chicago metropolitan area, including substantial numbers of Spanish-speaking Mexicans and Central Americans, and Arabic-speaking Middle Easterners of Muslim backgrounds. For example, in Chapter 8, Rob Paral documents that 49.7 percent of all Mexican immigrants in 2000 settled in the suburbs. And, much like the formation of distinct ethnic enclaves in the city during the first half of the twentieth century, the refractions found in immigration data and residential interactions in the suburbs—even more than the city itself—is like viewing the shifting colors and patterns in the aggregated particles of a kaleidoscope.

An analysis of residential patterns in the 2000 Census shows little national change, despite growing racial and ethnic diversity in the nation. The Chicago metropolitan area is no exception (Hancock and Kim 2003; Lewis Mumford Center 2002). Racial segregation is empirically calculated using a segregation index or index of dissimilarity. The index ranges from 0 to 100, indicating what percentage of a group would have to move to achieve even residential patterns. For example, Chicago's index of 80.9 for black-white segregation means that about 81 percent of either blacks or whites would have to move to

TABLE 6.2. Berwyn-Cicero Latino Survey: Perceived Tension between Latino and African Americans

A great deal	14.1 percent
Some	38.3 percent
Very little	22.9 percent
Don't know	20.6 percent

create census tracts with the same balance as the metropolitan area as a whole.

In the twenty-first century, the white residents of metropolitan Chicago still exist in what Feagin and O'Brien (2003) term a "white bubble" of racially segregated communities of schools, places of worship, and even workplaces. Whites may encounter African Americans, but mostly in role-defined situations, such as clerk and security officer, not as neighbor or good friend. This segregated existence in metropolitan Chicago precludes any prolonged, significant equal-status contact across the color line. Even when prolonged white–black interaction occurs, such as among co-workers, it rarely extends beyond limited work-defined social roles or to family–family interaction.

Chicago's first black suburban populations emerged in inner-ring towns and villages just south of the city. This first wave of black suburban settlers did not find the plush commercial and residential resources of the whites who preceded them in their moves west and north of the city. The small south-suburban industrial towns of Robbins, Harvey, Ford Heights, Phoenix, and Dixmoor, with their predominantly black populations, are the five poorest suburbs in metropolitan Chicago. They exemplify the downward spiral brought on by massive job loss from economic restructuring.

Economic factors exacerbate the spatial separation among racial groups (see Map 6.2, color insert). Concentrations of poverty have been in decline nationwide and in metropolitan Chicago. During the 1990s, the population in those 15 areas having the highest poverty levels, generally African American, declined 43 percent in population (Jargowsky 2003), whereas the segregation index remained relatively unchanged. Blacks may be moving out of poverty areas, but not necessarily because of upward social mobility. It is more likely that they are relocating to another predominantly black enclave, far away from the "white bubble." An analysis of 2000 Census data reveals that the city's black middle class is much more likely than whites to live near poverty areas—in Chicago, 78 percent of the black middle class resided a half-mile within a high poverty area, compared with 24 percent of the white middle class (Mendell and

Little 2003). Map 6.2 illustrates the highly concentrated residential pattern in Chicago based on the 2000 Census.

Affordability is the primary housing issue for the new Chicago. Echoing Bell's notion, race will always be a prominent factor in determining most social and economic arrangements in America. Center stage in the new Chicago, however, is Wilson's emphasis on the role of class, as seen from an economic standpoint.

In January 2004, the Affordable Housing Planning and Appeal Act took effect (Toomey 2004, 10). This new state law mandates that each town in Illinois have at least 10 percent of housing stock in the affordable range or forward a plan by April 2004 indicating how it will achieve that goal by 2009. Affordability for the seven counties surrounding Chicago is pegged at "$125,000 for sale units and $775 for rentals" (Toomey 2004, 10). The agency monitoring this law is the Illinois Housing Development Authority, which is headed by an African American who indicated that a primary goal of this policy is "to promote social diversity." The policy's focus on economic criteria diminishes racial diversity as an apparent objective. But, through this policy, the intricate connection between economics and race could effectively extend housing choices for lower-income African Americans and Latinos into previously unaffordable suburbs.

A study commissioned in 2001 by the Leadership Council for Metropolitan Open Communities, an organization dating back to 1966 and Dr. King's Chicago campaign against residential racial discrimination, declares: "Whites and people of color are not only moving in different geographical directions, they are experiencing different levels of access to and benefits from important opportunities such as public education, employment, and wealth accumulation" (Powell 2001, 1).

All evidence points to continuing unequal access to quality education, particularly for blacks and Latinos, because of the persistence of segregated schools. In 2004, a study released by Harvard Professor Gary Orfield indicates that progress toward desegregation peaked in the 1980s. According to Orfield (2004), black and Latino families moving to the suburbs has created hundreds of new segregated and unequal schools, which seems to frustrate middle-class minority families' dreams of access to better schools. The report predicted that the suburbs soon could be threatened with the same problems of ghettoization that affects big urban areas. Orfield (2004) warned that such a development "would bring the nation closer to the 'nightmare' of 'two school systems' and 'two housing markets.'"

Evidence suggests that blacks have not escaped the binds of racial stigmatization by migrating to the suburbs. A study conducted by the Legal Assistance Foundation of Metropolitan Chicago and the Chicago Urban League used matched-pair testing to gauge the extent to which race affected the employment opportunities of black residents in the Chicago suburbs. The study, *Racial Preference and Suburban Employment Opportunities*, found that, in the case of equally matched white and black job seekers with appropriate qualifications and experience for the position advertised by area retailers, the white job applicants were twice as likely to be called back as the blacks. In its analysis of the data, the Chicago Urban League concluded that the study actually understated the extent to which "deeply entrenched racism still blocks equal opportunity for blacks in the labor market" (Legal Assistance Foundation of Metropolitan Chicago and Chicago Urban League 2003, 3).

More than a century has passed since blacks began arriving in Chicago. In the early decades, black life went largely unnoticed and was free of interracial friction. Until the 1970s, blacks were confined to a specific geographic area through written covenants among white land owners. When African Americans ventured outside their prescribed occupations or neighborhoods, they met with resistance, even violence. Today, blacks are still confined, albeit to a broader geographic area that extends to portions of the suburbs. This confinement is largely the consequence of meager economic resources. Future and existing employment opportunities, and the means to enhance their economic resources, continue to elude a major portion of the black population of metropolitan Chicago. Constraints in residential choice continue to negatively affect blacks' access to the quality of education demanded for jobs requiring increasingly higher levels of knowledge and skill.

Although periodically blacks have exercised muscle through pressure groups, voting, or token administrative positions, their effect on lasting change to their social and economic status has been minimal. Today's chief unknowns center on the effect of metropolitan dispersion, slow as it is, and factional political competition from the expanding Latino population. If a comparison of past to current trends is predictive of the future, blacks in the new Chicago will be struggling with many of the same housing, employment, and education issues they faced in the old Chicago.

NOTE

1. The Great Migration is identified as that period when African Americans migrated from the rural South in two distinct waves—first from 1840 to 1900, then between 1910 and 1920—to find work and economic liberation in the North.

PART III

The Immigrant Presence

John P. Koval and Kenneth Fidel

7   Chicago: The Immigrant Capital of the Heartland

WHEN OSCAR HANDLIN (1951) wrote, "Once I thought to write a history of the immigrants in America. Then I discovered that the immigrants were American history," he could just as easily have been talking about Chicago then as now. One hundred and fifty years ago, approximately half of Chicago's population was foreign-born. Then, the Alien Immigration Acts of the 1920s, the Great Depression, and two world wars dramatically reduced the flow, and the proportion of the city's foreign-born population declined to a low of 11 percent by the 1970s.

Nearly 40 years have passed since the Kennedy-inspired Immigration Reform Act of 1965 changed the rules for legal immigration to this country, effectively doing away with the restrictive national quotas established during the 1920s. Since then, an unprecedented number of immigrants have come to the United States. During the 1990s alone, the known immigrant in-flow to the United States averaged nearly 978,000 per year, with little evidence of abatement (U.S. Department of Homeland Security 2003, 11). Most recent immigrants have settled in a relatively few large urban centers, one of which is Chicago. This new "Great Migration" differs from previous in-migrations in that the migrants are now predominantly from Latin American and Asia, and they are more diverse in terms of their race, ethnicity, religion, and human capital than were previous waves of immigrants. As a result, the Chicago of today has a global population that matches its global economy.

Today, the city and region are also greatly different from what they had been 100 years ago. Third-wave immigrants arriving in Chicago between 1880 and 1914 (Martin and Midgley 2003, 13) came primarily from central, eastern, and southern Europe. The largest group, numbering approximately 800,000 persons, came from Poland, with smaller but significant numbers from countries such as Italy, Russia, the Ukraine, Greece, Slovakia, Hungary, Bohemia, Serbia, Croatia, Romania, and the Ottoman Empire. At the time, those regions of Europe and the Middle East were considered backward parts of the world, and indeed, these immigrants were primarily of rural and small town origins, and most had little or no education and few skills. For the most part, these immigrants were Christians, with the greatest number Roman Catholic and the remaining belonging to various Orthodox denominations. A large number of Jews also added to the mix of immigrants.

CONTEMPORARY IMMIGRATION: 1950–2000

Post World War II immigration has had two phases. Soon after the war immigrants and refugees from Western Europe and parts of Eastern Europe, taking advantage of a two-year window for immigration allowed under the Displaced Persons Act of 1948, were the New Americans. This was a relatively short and geographically focused immigration burst that sharply declined with the rebuilding of Western Europe and the re-establishment of its economy. The next period of large-scale immigration began in 1965 and continues to the present. Asian

TABLE 7.1. Distribution of the Foreign-Born Population and Citizenship Status by County

County	Foreign Born	Entered 1990–2000	Naturalized Citizens	Not Citizens
Cook	1,064,703	473,265	420,739	643,964
DuPage	138,656	62,177	61,601	77,055
Kane	63,516	32,408	18,252	45,264
Lake	95,536	45,092	35,300	60,236
McHenry	18,764	8,614	7,253	11,511
Will	35,715	14,192	15,449	20,266
Total	1,416,890	635,748	558,594	858,296
Chicago	628,903	291,785	223,984	404,919

Source: U.S. Census Bureau, Census 2000 Summary File 1 (SF 3).

and Latino immigrants dominate this migration and for the most part do not replicate the social or cultural characteristics of either earlier immigrants or the native born population. On the one hand, current immigrants are asked to adapt to new economic, religious, civic, social, and cultural environments, while on the other hand, they are also causal agents, inducing economic, religious, civic, social, and cultural change.

Over the past 30 years, Chicago has become home to over 1.4 million immigrants from over 200 locales and speaking nearly as many different languages (Table 7.1). Approximately two-thirds of the foreign-born population resides in the six counties of the Chicago metropolitan area and came to this country after 1979; 44 percent came here during the decade of the 1990s. By 2000, 21.7 percent of city residents and 17.5 percent of metropolitan Chicago residents were foreign-born. These proportions are expected to increase over time. In 2001, for example, 233,690 people moved into the Chicago metropolitan area, approximately 640 persons per day, with nearly two-in-five coming from abroad. Of 152 large metropolitan areas in the country, this in-migration was second in number only to that of Los Angeles (Brooking Institution Center 2000).

Of the nearly 1.5 million foreign-born persons living in the six-county Chicago metropolitan area in 2000, nearly 61 percent were not citizens. Immigrants living in the city of Chicago were only slightly more likely than suburban residents to have come to this country during the 1990s and slightly less likely to be citizens (64.4 percent).

The current immigrant population in the Chicago metropolitan area is distinctive on

several counts and differs from previous immigrants in a number of important ways. First, contemporary immigrants differ from previous immigrants in terms of the global geography they represent. The majority come from three regions: 47.9 percent come from Latin America, with Mexicans accounting for 85 percent of all Latino immigrants; 26.4 percent come from Europe, with Poles and Russians accounting for 50.4 percent of all European immigrants; 20.6 percent come from Asia, with Indians and Filipinos constituting 43.4 percent of all Asian immigrants; 2.4 percent come from the Middle East; and 1.3 percent come from Sub-Saharan Africa. The remaining 1.4 percent come from other regions of the world. A closer look finds persons from all the Balkan nations as well as from the Baltic countries and Ireland. In addition, small numbers of immigrants came also from western and central Asia, including Iran, Turkey, and the Arab countries. Asian immigrants have also arrived from countries such as China, Pakistan, Vietnam, Laos, and Cambodia. Immigration from Africa is much lower, with the largest numbers coming from north and west Africa, Nigeria in particular. Although Mexicans are by far the largest group of Latino immigrants coming to the region, in recent years, the number of people coming from Central and South America has increased.

Second, immigrants come with very different human capital. In the past, immigrants were largely rural and poorly educated. Today's immigrants include significant numbers of persons of urban origins, and many are highly educated, holding bachelor's degrees and higher. Indian and Filipino immigrants, for example, are likely to be English-speaking and college educated. Poles, on the other hand, include a high proportion of skilled blue-collar and construction workers, many of whom do not speak English when they arrive. Mexicans more typically come from agricultural backgrounds (Papademetriou 2004, 51), speak little or no English on arrival, and many lack the skills most valued in our postindustrial economy.

Third, immigrants come from different cultural backgrounds in regard to family structure, religion, and child-rearing practices. Although the great majority of European and Latin American immigrants are at least nominally Christian and predominantly Roman Catholic, immigrants from other parts of the world contribute to a more heterogeneous religious community. Increasing numbers of Hindus, Sikhs, Sunni and Shia Muslims, Buddhists, and Confucians are present. Yet other cultural differences are related to immigrants' many different regional, language, and social-class backgrounds.

No agreed upon technique exists for measuring complex racial and ethnic diversity. But if Chicago is a major immigrant capital, it is also a highly diverse community. For example:

- Chicago has the second largest African American community in the United States.
- Chicago has the second largest Mexican community in the United States.
- Chicago has the third largest Latino community in the United States.
- Chicago has the fourth largest Asian community in the United States.
- Chicago has the third largest Arab community in the United States.
- In the decade from 1990 to 2000, Chicago's Mexican population percentage growth and absolute number growth was the largest of any major city in the nation.
- Chicago was the third largest receiver-city of legal immigrants to the United States in 2002. (U.S. Bureau of the Census, 2000)

Still, numbers alone do not communicate the human dimension of current immigration or help understand the quality of life in ethnic villages like Pilsen and Little Village for Mexicans, Korea Town, the Indian Market Place of Devon

Avenue. Nor do numbers fully encompass the ethnicizing of occupations such as nursing by Filipinos, dry cleaning establishments by Koreans, and dry-wall installation by Mexicans, or the challenge and complexity of teaching in a high school where as many as 30 different languages might be spoken. "Demographic shift" is a rather banal label to attach to the sizeable quantitative and qualitative human and institutional transitions that are now such a dynamic part of Chicago's present and future. The chapters that follow are intended to enrich this introductory overview and bring out more fully the depth, character, and quality of the immigrant presence in Chicago.

WHY IS CHICAGO AN IMMIGRANT CAPITAL?

Certainly, the anticipation of experiencing Chicago's raw and bitter winters or its hot and humid summers is not a draw for immigrants. Among many pull factors, one stands out: *economic opportunity*. The U.S. economy provides immigrants from less-developed countries the opportunity to earn five to ten times more for their labor than would be possible in their country of origin. In the words of one immigrant, "All you have to do is work and money pours from the spigot." For example, business was so good at a poultry packing plant in Chicago's Randolph Street Market that, when the supervisor announced that a swing shift was going to be added, the nearly all-Mexican immigrant day crew protested. They wanted to work both shifts.

Yet, the opportunity structure of the region is undergoing change. The global labor market is a two-lane international highway that both workers and jobs travel. Enormous wage differences exist for the same work in different global locales and, not surprisingly, this makes a difference in the location of jobs and industries. Chicago's Motorola Corporation, for example, has plants throughout the world. Its "fully loaded" cost— employee pay, benefits, taxes, and the like— for a Mexican national working in its cellular telephone plant in Nogales, Mexico, is approximately $8,000 a year. The "fully loaded" cost to

Motorola for an assembler in its Schaumburg, Illinois plant is $50,000 a year—a 6.25-to-1 cost ratio. Even more dramatically, a cell-phone assembler for Motorola in China costs Motorola a grand total of $3,500 annually—a >14-to-1 ratio (Motorola 2003).

For many workers, merely stepping across the Rio Grande or investing in a red-eye flight from Hong Kong can increase earnings by 625 to 1,400 percent. Wage differences are, at one and the same time, both a pull factor for immigrants and an inducement for employers to relocate their plants to another country. To a great extent, because of the latter, the Chicago metropolitan region is experiencing both unprecedented immigration and deindustrialization and transformation to a postindustrial economy.

ECONOMIC DIVERSITY

Carl Sandburg's 1916 characterization of Chicago as "hog butcher for the world," although not entirely hyperbole, obscured a more complex reality about the Chicago of that time.[1] At the same time that Sandburg wrote his poem, Aaron Montgomery Ward and Richard Warren Sears were inventing a new form of commerce called the mail order catalog; Cyrus McCormick's factory (later to become the International Harvester Company) was supplying agricultural plows and harvesters to the world; Marshall Field was defining and refining the meaning of department store; the Chicago Board of Trade and the Chicago Mercantile Exchange were being birthed; and, 25 miles down the road, in northern Indiana, the new U.S. Steel Corporation was founded by Judge Elbert H. Gary and J. P. Morgan. Hog butcher? That and much more.

The Chicago of the past was the archetypal industrial city, in which large numbers of jobs were available in the primary and secondary sectors of the economy. Thousands of workers with few skills found employment in a variety of industries producing steel, farm equipment, railroad engines and rolling stock, wire, and telephone equipment. Other jobs were available in the food industry, in the stockyards, and in cereal production, as well as in the clothing and shoe indus-

tries. Then, as now, singly and collectively, immigrants had a kind of economic compass that pointed them to destinations like Chicago and other industrial capitals. (Chapters 8 through 15 deal more extensively with Chicago's complex economic mosaic and the role immigrants play in enriching its character.)

Economic diversity was an early characteristic of Chicago that attracted workers from many different countries. This has not changed. Current immigrants enter an economic environment even more diverse than that of the past. The manufacturing sector, although declining, is still the largest in the country. Chicago's Information Age high-tech labor force is also the largest in the nation. As the region's health care Mecca, Chicago's professional and technical medical community, fueled in part by immigrants, is exceptionally large and growing, as is its hospitality and leisure industry and a host of related service occupations. Chicago's changing economy also reflects its growing economic diversity. And, in part because of its immigrant population, it remains a national and international magnet for professionals, managers, entrepreneurs, and workers across a wide economic spectrum. A recent study identified Chicago as the most economically diverse city in the United States (Markusen et al. 2001), and the Census Bureau has identified Chicago as one of the few central cities that continues to attract large numbers of recent college graduates. So, Chicago continues to be the immigrant capital of the Midwest.

IMMIGRANT RESIDENTIAL PATTERNS

Previous immigrants to the United States mainly came from agrarian backgrounds. On arrival in this country, they settled in central cities, not because of the lure of city lights, but because that was where the jobs were. The rapid suburbanization of America's population during the 1950s and 1960s initially produced bedroom communities from which workers commuted to jobs in the city. In the mid 1950s, regardless of where individuals lived in the metropolitan area, they were likely to work in the city of Chicago. Over time, shopping, services, industry, and offices followed the suburbanites so that, by 1980, a majority of both the region's population and jobs were located in the suburbs. Today, more people and more jobs reside in suburban Cook and the collar counties than in Chicago. The changed balance of people and jobs between the city and its suburbs is in part a function of the city losing jobs both to the suburbs and other places. However, it is also a function of the creation of new jobs in the suburbs, especially in Cook and DuPage counties, and of new immigrants moving directly to suburban communities. So, for example, the correlation between DuPage County being home to the largest number of area Mexican immigrants outside of Cook County is likely a reflection of the fact that it also houses the largest number of jobs in the region outside of Cook County.

That is not to say that older, inner-city immigrant communities are passing out of existence. Within the city, a few examples of stable or expanding ethnic neighborhoods include:

- The Polish neighborhoods along the corridors created by Archer Avenue on the Southwest Side and the neighborhood along the Milwaukee Avenue—"Polish Broadway"—corridor on the Northwest Side
- The Mexican neighborhoods of Pilsen and Little Village, extending west from Chicago's Near South Side
- The Chinatown neighborhood on the Near South Side
- The traditional and expanded port-of-entry mini-U.N. neighborhoods of Albany Park, Rogers Park, Edgewater, and Lincoln Square on the North Side

In at least three cases, population growth, fueled largely by current immigration, coupled with income growth among community residents has resulted in the expansion of ethnic enclaves into immediately contiguous areas. Examples of this phenomenon include the expansion of the Chinese settlement into the Bridgeport neighborhood and former South Loop railroad properties, the extension of the Mexican community across the city boundary into suburban Cicero and Berwyn, and the movement of Poles to suburban Niles, Park Ridge, Elmwood Park, and Bridgeview.

As Map 7.1 (see color insert) shows, different patterns of immigrant residential expansion occur beyond the city limits. Immigrants Poles have generally extended the boundaries of existing in-city communities into adjacent southwest and northwest inner-ring suburbs. By contrast, the pattern of immigrant Mexican settlement is more widely dispersed across the six-county region, creating a number of concentrations, particularly in larger suburban communities such as Elgin, Aurora, Carpentersville, and Waukegan.

Filipino immigrants are also widely dispersed, mostly in western and northwestern communities—primarily in DuPage, northern Will County, and northern Lake County. Indian immigrants are most highly concentrated in the western suburbs of DuPage County, and clusters of other Asian immigrants reside in the western, northwestern, and northern suburbs of Cook, DuPage, and Lake Counties. To date, very little immigrant settlement has occurred in the more distant Will, Kane, and McHenry counties.

Two other settlement patterns deserve notice. First, Chicago's North Shore remains mostly a high-income white preserve. In 2000, with the exception of Evanston (65 percent white), 95 percent of residents of all other North Shore communities were white. Second, Chicago's South and West Side African American communities are isolated from all immigrant populations—with the exception of immigrant businesses located in or adjacent to black neighborhoods and portions of Latino communities, such as Little Village (Brooking Institution 2003, 22). For all practical purposes, the discriminatory tradition of ethnic groups distancing themselves from African Americans both socially and physically continues today, as seen in the settlement patterns of current immigrants (Massey and Denton 1993).

TRANSNATIONALISM

Historically, immigration meant breaking ties with family, friends, and institutions in one's place of origin (Martin and Widgren 2002, 4). This is no longer characteristic of immigration, and an increasing number of immigrants are now able to maintain a transnational lifestyle and identity (Levitt 2001). Maintaining ties to relatives and friends in the place of origin has been enabled by dramatic reductions in the cost of telephoning other countries (now little more than the cost of a local phone call) and the Internet. Cable and satellite television, videos, and other news and entertainment media also allow immigrants to stay abreast of events, politics, and culture in their homelands. One hundred years ago, the trip from Europe to the United States was long and arduous for those with enough economic resources to afford it and practically impossible for those less well off. Most immigrants either never returned to visit their homelands or, if they did, it was only once in a lifetime. Today, it is not unusual for immigrants to make multiple trips back to their place of origin and, in some instances, to routinely spend a part of the year there, in essence living a transnational life. Air travel has dramatically shortened the time it takes to travel between the United States and various immigrant homelands, thus making the cost of the trip affordable in terms of time and money. For example, the trip from Turkey to Chicago is 11 hours nonstop; from India to Chicago, the trip is 18 hours long nonstop. Among Mexican immigrants, it is common to return to Mexico for vacations or during holidays. At Christmas time, the southern border crossings are crowded, as long lines of cars, vans, and pick-up trucks, full loaded with gifts, make their way from the United States to Mexico.

The ability to move back and forth between Chicago and a place of origin, to maintain regular contact with friends and relatives, to access home-based television and other mass media and, for many, living in an immigrant enclave makes a transnational identity viable and even normal. This form of partial assimilation is supported by various public policies and other features of contemporary American society, including the willingness of the federal government to recognize dual nationality, economic and political interests that profit from immigrants maintaining a sense of foreign national identity, and an often publicly expressed ideology that the United States is a pluralistic society in which dual cultural identities and the preservation of ethnic traditions and language are not problematic.

IMMIGRANTS AS AGENTS OF CHANGE

That "people make the city" is simple in conception and exceptionally relevant in the Chicago of 2004. The large number of post-1965 immigrants, and now their children and grandchildren, are subject to the structural and social changes that affect everyone in the region, and are themselves important contributors to determining the social and economic fate of the region, both today and in the foreseeable future. Sheer numbers make immigrants important actors in the life and fate of Chicago and its region. The 1.4 million immigrants who have come to the region during the past 40 years are prime movers in remaking and reshaping the city—socially, culturally, physically, politically and, perhaps, spiritually.

The majority of arriving immigrants come here as young adults, and their presence is visible in virtually every public place in the city and the suburbs. A metropolitan shopper, participating in the global economy at suburban Ikea's all-everything store, would have to be exceptionally insensitive not to recognize the veritable United Nations–type character of the store's clientele. Indeed, although admittedly Ikea shoppers do not constitute a random sample of Chicago's population, on any given day an observer would be hard pressed to describe the race and ethnicity of the shoppers in simple terms other than their extensive heterogeneity.

Even Chicago's traditional geography is being reshaped. Not only has Pilsen's Slavic community been transformed into a Latino community, but so too have its physical symbols. Mexican religious and cultural wall murals abound on the sides of public buildings, and the traditional church statuary reflecting the Eastern European presence now shares space with the Latino statuary, tapestries of Our Lady of Guadeloupe, and a mixture of pre-Columbian and Spanish-Catholic cultural and religious symbolism. Churches that once were the cultural expression of solemn Eastern European "Catholicity" now celebrate the Mass and other religious rituals to the accompaniment of Spanish guitars and unabashedly public displays of religious devotion. This type of cultural transformation can be multiplied several times over. Mosques in the basements of coffee shops and cafes near the cab barns of Pakistani and Middle-Eastern taxi drivers can also now be found in neighborhoods where mainstream Protestants claim they feel like foreigners in their own country and, in many cases, disliking it. Recently, in one suburban community, a Moslem group purchased a vacant building with the intention of turning it into a mosque and local residents protested, demanding that the village government prevent this incursion.

The phenomenon of ethnic succession is perhaps no more evident than in Chicago's changing physical landscape. Racial and cultural change at the street and neighborhood level is visible in the signage, colors, banners, and architecture that announce an immigrant group's presence and ability to control the local environment. This change is evident not only in the proliferation of ethnic restaurants in all parts of the city and suburbs, but in the groups of people, young and old, who gather on stoops and in the chatter of shoppers in local grocery stores.

One cannot ride the subway train without encountering people from different countries and hearing foreign languages spoken by adults going to or from work or by students who speak English at school but their parents' native tongue at home and among friends. It is not unusual to see whole families of recent immigrants posing in front of some well-known landmark, scenic vista, or building for a photo to be sent back home to family and friends who have not yet arrived. Likewise, one cannot enter a major department store, either downtown or at a suburban shopping mall, without noticing the presence of immigrants either as customers or as employees.

THE IMMIGRANT EFFECT

The coming chapters of *The New Chicago* profile seven significant immigrant groupings: Poles, Latinos, Asian Indians, Filipinos, Koreans, Chinese, and Middle Easterners (including Arabs and Assyrians). In most instances, immigration to Chicago from other countries began long before the 1960s. In the case of the Poles, immigration from their home country was a significant source of Chicago's population explosion during the two decades preceding World War I. Thus, these profiles of contemporary immigrants span many decades, from one population flow that began to affect Chicago's cultural and neighborhood mosaic nearly a century ago to the newest arriving ethic groups. The patterns of residential settlement, absorption within the local economy, formation of Chicago-based cultural institutions, and maintenance of ties with home regions vary substantially. Of the six "new immigrant" groupings we examine, Latinos—whose local population is numerically dominated by individuals of Mexican origin and descent—have residentially settled and otherwise assumed a role within Chicago's economy and cultural life that is most reminiscent of the "old immigrant" populations of the late nineteenth and early twentieth centuries. To note but a pair of examples, two distinctive Mexican-American neighborhoods—Pilsen and Little Village—have emerged on the city's Southwest Side, and Chicago's City Council currently includes several Mexican-American aldermen who represent wards in this section of the city.

It is important to bear in mind that the effect of Chicago's current wave of immigration resonates across a local cultural, neighborhood, and political landscape that has long reflected the presence of "new arrivals." Contemporary Chicago never experienced the type of culture shock that coursed through Los Angeles after the 1960s, as that city's transplanted "Midwestern ethos" was reinterpreted by growing African American, Latino, and Asian populations (Fogelson 1993, 186–228; Sonenshein 1993, 26). Indeed, the cultural ferment one observes in contemporary Chicago neighborhoods such as West Ridge (through which Devon Avenue runs, see Chapter 17 in this volume) or Logan Square (in which gentrification, Latino population expansion, and extant Polish neighborhoods converge) is strikingly similar to the complex processes of neighborhood change in central and western Queens, New York, as documented by anthropologist Roger Sanjek in *The Future of Us All* (1998).

As a consequence, one of the most evident effects of the resurgence of immigration to the Chicago region has been the adaptation to new groups and conditions by older, immigrant-oriented institutions. Probably the most notable instance of this phenomenon has been the "ethnic succession" of many Roman Catholic parishes across the city, as older European-descended congregants have departed to be replaced by incoming and characteristically Catholic Latinos. Apart from Chicago's large Roman Catholic archdiocese, various neighborhood-level social-service agencies—including several settlement houses founded during the early 1900s—have recast their missions and redefined their service populations during the last two decades.

However, the formation of inner-city ethnic enclaves—clearly the most visible effect of late nineteenth- and early twentieth-century immigration on Chicago's cityscape—has not been nearly so characteristic of the current wave of immigration. In some cases, social class, education, and occupational variations within a particular immigrant grouping has produced a more dispersed pattern of settlement, as is quite evident among the Chicago region's Asian Indians. And, although a number of ethnic occupational-entrepreneurial "niches" have been carved out by new immigrant populations—Polish construction workers, Mexican landscapers, Filipino hospital attendants, and so on—the formation of dense networks of ethnic- or immigrant-specific businesses within extensive residential areas dominated by these same population groups is not typical of contemporary Chicago.

More generally, as Chicago's economy has moved from its extensive base in an array of manufacturing sectors toward a more diversified economy that includes significant business-service functions and growing entertainment, leisure, and tourist-oriented sectors, immigrants have taken their places throughout the emerging occupational hierarchy produced by the new Chicago economy. In so doing, they have produced a local cosmopolitanism that is distinctive over the long arc of Chicago's development. Whereas the Chicago of 1904 was far more a city of immigrants than is the Chicago of 2004, that older Chicago was also beset by intercommunal tensions and a considerable degree of politically inspired ethnic exclusion. Ethnicity was a ready tool for politicians aiming to build loyal constituencies and, in the early days, some portion of in-group loyalty was built on out-group antipathy. Interracial relations, as well as some specific interimmigrant relationships, in contemporary Chicago have not achieved perfect harmony, but in a metropolitan region that is increasingly conscious of global economic and cultural linkages—and among whose immigrant populations a considerable degree of transoceanic commuting is now commonplace—immigrants and the cultural and economic vitality they bring with them are a prominent and generally appreciated feature of the new Chicago.

NOTE

1. Curiously, this is the only phrase from Sandburg's long and elaborate description of the Chicago of his time that has stuck in the public's mind.

Rob Paral

8 Latinos of the New Chicago

FEW GROUPS embody the new Chicago as well as Latinos.[1] The Latino population has many of the characteristics associated with a dynamic and rapidly evolving modern city. These include a strong immigrant presence, a heritage distinct from Anglo traditions, bilingualism, heavy participation in new labor force sectors such as service jobs, and ongoing, rapid dispersion across many city neighborhoods and suburbs.

Although the Latino population has been present since the early years of the twentieth century, its numbers have become substantial only in the last few decades. The 329,000 "Spanish-speaking" persons tallied by the 1970 census more than quadrupled to 1.4 million persons by 2000. The Latino population has burgeoned mainly because of federal immigration admissions policies that were liberalized in 1965; the arrival of Puerto Ricans, many of whom departed their island homeland for economic reasons similar to those facing other Latino immigrants; and a relatively high birthrate among Latina women in the United States.

Latinos share a heritage of Spanish language use, roots in Latin America, and often, other traditions, such as Catholicism. However, the community consists of numerous national-origin groups, each having its own cultural preferences, histories, and affiliations. In the six-county Chicago area, the largest group by far consists of the 1,072,747 persons of Mexican origin, followed by 149,517 of Puerto Rican origin. Other large groups include 19,943 Guatemalans, 17,018 Cubans, and 12,467 Ecuadorians.

Notwithstanding the diversity among Latinos, the population overall has undergone a return to its roots: the Mexican-origin population, which appeared in the area during the early decades of the twentieth century and well ahead of the Puerto Ricans who arrived after World War II, has been increasing its share of the overall Latino population. Persons of Mexican origin made up 72.9 percent of the Latino population in 1990, but 75.7 percent in 2000. This has occurred because some groups, such as Cubans and Puerto Ricans, have been growing at very low rates and newer arrivals from Central and South America are still low in number. Thus, the Latino population of metropolitan Chicago has become arguably less "Latino" and increasingly more "Mexican."

Latinos are more likely than most groups to live in the city of Chicago. Some 53.6 percent of metro-area Latinos live in Chicago, compared with 32.0 percent of non-Latinos. In Chicago, several identifiable Latino areas include a contiguous set of community areas comprising the Lower West Side, South Lawndale and—below the south branch of the Chicago River and the Stevenson expressway—Bridgeport, McKinley Park, Brighton Park, New City, and Gage Park. Another principal area of Latino residence is the set of Near Northwest Side community areas including West Town, Humboldt Park, Logan Square, Hermosa, and Belmont Cragin. These two main areas, one on the North Side and the other on the South Side, are merely two of the larger concentrations of Latino population. During the 1980s, it was possible to describe most Latinos as living in these major centers, but today Latinos in Chicago are actually found in many neighborhoods, including Uptown and

Edgewater along the lake on the far North Side, and in South Chicago, the site of some of the earliest Latino residents: Mexican immigrants who came to work in the steel mills in the early 1900s.

Suburbanization is an increasing trend among Latinos. The community is dispersed across many suburbs, but key areas of residence may be identified. These include the Cicero-Berwyn area, which is contiguous with the large Latino community on Chicago's West Side. Also within the inner ring of Cook County suburbs are Melrose Park, Franklin Park, and Stone Park. Substantial populations of Latinos are found close to or within the satellite cities that ring the periphery of the metro area: Waukegan, Elgin, Aurora, and Joliet.

Latinos are highly visible in city neighborhoods and suburban areas, in part because of high levels of business ownership. In Chicago-area commercial strips, such as 26th Street, 18th Street, Milwaukee Avenue and many others, Spanish-language advertising is prevalent and, in some areas, is the dominant language of signs and billboards. The same is true of Cermak Road in Cicero and, in many suburban shopping strips, it is common to find Latino-owned businesses. In many areas, the numerous small Latino businesses—selling produce, music, food, and other items—create the sense of liveliness, entrepreneurship, and economic development that one associates with healthy neighborhoods.

As Latinos are relative newcomers to metro Chicago, a pertinent question is: How have Latinos been received by the society? Certainly, their experience is unlike the resistance—too often organized and violent—visited upon the African American community. No parallels exist in Chicago Latino history to the deadly 1919 race riots of Chicago or the anti-black hate groups that existed in Cicero and the Chicago neighborhood of Marquette Park during the 1970s. Indeed, according to the index of dissimilarity for Chicago, which measures the percent of persons who must move for a group to achieve a random geographic distribution with whites, Latinos have a score of 63.5, compared to a score of 88.3 for blacks (Institute for Metropolitan Affairs and Office for Social Policy Research

2002).[2] Thus, Latinos are significantly less segregated than blacks in the city of Chicago.

The Latino experience in integration, however, has not been smooth. During the 1990s, as Latinos (primarily Mexicans) moved into Cicero in large numbers, their reception was marked by oppressive governmental efforts to control their inflow and behavior. For example, the town tried to limit the number of persons who could live in a housing unit (a policy rescinded after intervention by the U.S. Justice Department), children were prevented by ordinance from playing basketball in alleyways or on sidewalks, and public schools demanded five forms of identification from students attempting to enroll (Institute for Latino Studies 2002). Elgin has been charged by the U.S. Department of Housing and Urban Development with discriminatory enforcement of housing codes against Latinos, and courtroom testimony charged Mt. Prospect with unfair targeting of Latino motorists (almost half of Mt. Prospect arrests during the late 1990s were of Latinos, who made up only 6 percent of total residents) (Paral 2000).

Although the area's Latino population is diverse in terms of the national origins of its members and the large numbers of both U.S.-born and foreign-born Latinos, Mexican immigrants in particular are a key component of the population. The remainder of this article discusses the effect of Mexican immigrants on the growth and characteristics of Latinos overall and on the larger society of metro Chicago.

Few groups have such a dramatic demographic effect on metropolitan Chicago as Mexican immigrants. The number of foreign-born persons from Mexico grew by 115 percent during the 1990s alone, reaching 582,000, or 7 percent, of the entire regional population. In particular economic sectors and geographic areas, the growth of Mexican immigrants is felt even more keenly. The metro Chicago workforce grew by a net of 269,000 workers during the 1990s, and 49 percent of this growth is attributable solely to Mexican immigration. Mexican immigrants comprise one of ten residents in the city of Chicago and are either a majority or a significant portion of the population in numerous suburbs, including inner-ring Cook County communities such as

Cicero, Stone Park, and Franklin Park, and also outer-ring communities such as Waukegan, Carpentersville, Elgin, West Chicago, and Aurora.

Evidence is contradictory on the rate at which Mexicans are moving, succeeding economically, and experiencing social and political integration. On one hand, a traveler through the metropolitan region can see many signs of certain economic vitality within the Mexican foreign-born population. Wherever Mexican immigrants reside, local commercial districts seem healthy and thriving. The presence of Mexican workers in many service-sector jobs, such as in restaurants and hotels, give the correct impression of a community with a high rate of labor-force participation.

Other indicators of the progress of Mexican immigrants are not so encouraging. Census data reveal that Mexican immigrants have among the lowest level of education among all immigrant groups, and their schooling is well below that of native-born groups such as whites and African Americans. Only 3 percent of Mexican immigrants have a college degree, and only 34 percent have a high school diploma. Although rates of employment are high among Mexican immigrants, they are largely employed in service and low-wage manufacturing-sector jobs that offer few opportunities for significant wage increases or benefits. Many Mexican immigrants have undocumented immigration status, which severely limits their employment outlook and exposes them to exploitation.

DEMOGRAPHIC HISTORY AND SETTLEMENT PATTERNS OF MEXICAN IMMIGRANTS

The growth of the Mexican population has proceeded more or less steadily during the twentieth century (Figure 8.1). The arrival of Mexican immigrants to metropolitan Chicago may be dated to the World War I era. By 1920, the census reported 1,755 Mexican foreign-born persons in the area. Twenty years later, the number of Mexican immigrants had grown to 8,525; by 1950, the population reached 10,785, accompanied, of course by growing numbers of Mexicans born in the United States. During the past thirty

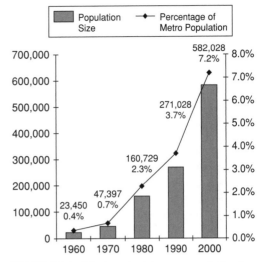

FIGURE 8.1. Mexican immigrant population in metro Chicago.
Source: U.S. Census: 1960–2000

years, Mexican immigration to metropolitan Chicago has accelerated at a rapid rate. The Mexican foreign-born population in metropolitan Chicago stood at 47,397 in 1970, 160,729 in 1980, and 271,028 in 1990. The community's size surpassed .5 million during the 1990s, reaching 582,028 by 2000. The actual number of Mexican immigrants in all these periods is doubtlessly higher, given undercounting by the decennial census.

Early Mexican immigrants arrived in the Chicago area to work in steel mills, packing houses, and rail yards (Año Nuevo Kerr 1975). Some workers were recruited as strike-breakers, whereas others were attracted to urban jobs that paid better than beet-harvesting and other agricultural work in the Midwest. The stock market crash and Great Depression discouraged Mexican immigration, but not enough to reverse the trajectory of growth. Subsequent labor demands created new job openings in Chicago for migrants.

Although Chicago's predominance as a center of meat packing, rail traffic, and steel manufacture waned during the last decades of the twentieth century, the region spawned new jobs in manufacturing and services that have maintained Chicago as one of the leading centers of economic activity in the United States. As a result, the area continues to be a magnet for Mexican immigration, in 1999 ranking second among U.S. metropolitan areas (after the Los Angeles area) in the number of new legal immigrants arriving from Mexico (U.S. Immigration and Naturalization Service 2002).

The 2000 census reported that the largest Chicago community areas having a Mexican population were South Lawndale (42,422 Mexican foreign-born) and the lower West Side (20,529); the third largest community area was Brighton Park (17,609). This latter area is contiguous with and directly south of South Lawndale, thus representing a further amassing of Mexican foreign-born population on the West and Near Southwest Sides of the city. Some of the major institutions created by and for the Mexican community are found on the Near Southwest Side communities. These include the Mexican Fine Arts Museum at 19th and Ashland, which is the largest Mexican art museum in the United States; the Alivio Medical Facilities at 21st and Morgan and at 24th and Western; and community service organizations such as Instituto del Progreso Latino at 27th and Blue Island.

Although some of the larger and more established Mexican organizations are concentrated on the South Side, the Mexican immigrant community has nevertheless become more dispersed in Chicago. Some 15,321 Mexican immigrants lived in Logan Square on the city's North Side in 2000, 11,122 lived in West Town, and 10,820 lived in Albany Park. At the same time, the Mexican immigrant population has been expanding in the suburbs at a faster rate than in the city of Chicago. By 2000, the suburban Mexican population of 289,463 persons had become nearly as large as its Chicago counterpart (292,565 persons).

Suburban centers of Mexican immigration include Elgin, Aurora, Waukegan, Joliet, Carpentersville, West Chicago, Cicero, and Franklin Park. The settlement patterns of the suburban Mexican immigrants contrast with those of Asian and Europeans. Asian immigration centers are in north and northwest Cook County suburbs and in DuPage County, whereas European immigrants in the suburbs are concentrated in northern Cook County suburbs. With some exceptions, principally in northwest Cook County, the settlement patterns of Mexicans generally do not overlap those of Asians or Europeans.

ROLE OF MEXICAN IMMIGRATION IN REGIONAL POPULATION CHANGE

The number of Mexican immigrants is increasing rapidly, and the growth of this population is fueling larger demographic shifts in metropolitan Chicago. The large numbers of Mexican immigrants arriving in recent years is seen in the fact that fully 28.1 percent of Mexican immigrants in metro Chicago reported to the 2000 census that they arrived within the last five years. In fact, the 1990s increase in Mexican foreign-born population accounts for more than a third—37.4 percent—of the net regional growth over the decade (Table 8.1).

In turn, the high numbers of newly arriving Mexican immigrants are responsible for the majority of growth in the larger Mexican American population (consisting of both native- and foreign-born persons). Although 47.1 percent of the Mexican-origin population was foreign born in 1990, by 2000 some 55.3 percent of the population was comprised of immigrants. In other words, the Mexican-origin population became more, not less foreign-born during the 1990s. This fact is more striking in light of the high birth rate of Mexican-origin women who live in the United States and give birth to native-born babies. The birth rate of Mexican-origin women—3.1 births per woman in 1990—is high compared to other groups (2.1 for white non-Latinas, 2.4 for African Americans),[3] yet this high birthrate is nevertheless outpaced by immigration as a contributing factor to Mexican American population growth.

TABLE 8.1. Portion of Metro Chicago Population Change Caused by Latino Groups

	Net change, 1990–2000	% of Net population change
Total	830,544	
Mexican foreign-born	311,000	37.4
Mexican American	478,031	57.6
Latino	568,211	68.4

Increases in the Mexican American population—due largely to immigration—are responsible in turn for the majority of growth in the larger Latino population. During the 1970–2000 period, for example, the Mexican American (native- and foreign-born persons of Mexican origin) portion of the Latino population has surpassed the growth of other Latinos overall. Mexican Americans comprised 32.6 percent of Latinos in 1970, but made up 63.6 percent in 1980, 70.5 percent in 1990, and 74.9 percent in 2000. Mexican American growth accounts for well over half—57.6 percent—of net regional growth in the 1990s.

Finally, with Mexican immigration at its core, the Latino population has been growing impressively in recent decades, increasing by 75.8 percent during the 1970s, by 40.6 percent during the 1980s, and by 67.9 percent during the 1990s. Growth of the Latino population during the 1990s, in fact, is responsible for the great majority—68.4 percent—of the overall population change in the region. One could argue that our regional population growth is built on Mexican immigration.

SOCIOECONOMIC STATUS AND PROGRESS OVER TIME

Social and economic data from the U.S. Census Bureau show that Mexican immigrants have the lowest socioeconomic status among major immigrant groups in the metropolitan Chicago area. As seen in Table 8.2, Mexican immigrants have lower education levels than either other large foreign-born populations or the native-born white population.[4] For example, 33.5 percent of Mexican immigrants have a high school degree compared to 69.3 percent of Polish immigrants and 90.9 percent of native-born whites. At \$42,000, the median household income of Mexican immigrants is below that of all other groups. Mexican immigrant income is fully \$19,000 lower than that of the typical white household.

With regard to poverty levels, Mexican immigrants have a double-digit rate of 16.1 percent, while each of the other groups has a poverty level below 10 percent. The low levels of education among Mexican immigrants doubtlessly help to explain their disadvantaged position in the regional labor market. Two-thirds of Mexican immigrant workers, 66.6 percent, are employed in service and laborer jobs, whereas the other major immigrant groups and native-born whites have less than half of their employed population working in service and labor occupations.[5]

As noted in Table 8.2, the household incomes of Mexican immigrants fall well below that of native-born whites and other large immigrant groups, with Mexican immigrant households having income equivalent to \$0.69 for each dollar of income in a white household. As seen in Table 8.3, this income gap has worsened over time. During the 1980–2000 period, Mexican household incomes (adjusted for inflation) grew by 16.1 percent, lower than the growth in each of the other major immigrant groups (except that of Poles) and well below the 23.5 percent growth in median household income among native-born whites.

The income gap has grown even more sharply between native-born whites and recent Mexican immigrants, that is, those who have been in the country for less than 10 years. Although these recent immigrants had household incomes that amounted to 64.6 percent of the income of

TABLE 8.2. Comparative Socioeconomic Status of Mexican Immigrants

	% with high school degree	% with B.A. degree	HH income	% Poverty rate	% in service and laborer occupations
FB Mexico	33.5	3.4	\$42,000	16.1	66.6
FB Poland	69.3	16.0	44,000	6.5	48.6
FB India	87.5	65.8	65,000	5.0	19.1
FB Philippines	94.8	64.9	73,300	2.2	24.4
FB China	77.4	52.5	58,500	9.0	28.3
Native-born white	90.9	37.4	61,000	3.9	18.3

Note: FB = foreign-born.

TABLE 8.3. Percent Growth in Median Household Income, 1979–1999 (Inflation Adjusted)

FB Mexico	16.1
FB Mexico arrived <10 years	10.0
FB Poland	14.9
FB India	17.2
FB Philippines	18.8
FB China/Hong Kong/Taiwan	25.0
Native-born white	23.5

Note: FB = foreign-born.

whites in 1979, by 1999, their incomes equaled only 57.6 percent of white income. The growing income differentials suggest that Mexican immigrants, especially new arrivals, are increasingly isolated, at least economically, from the majority white population in metropolitan Chicago.

Household incomes among Mexican immigrants are the product of complex factors including education, language ability, and access to social networks. One important factor is that Mexican immigrant incomes in metropolitan Chicago have been tied to the fate of the manufacturing industry, which has historically paid relatively high wages to unskilled workers and which has been in decline, with the metro Chicago economy losing more than 254,000 manufacturing jobs in the last two decades.

In 1980, a clear majority (57.5 percent) of Mexican immigrants in metro Chicago worked in manufacturing. By 2000, however, less than half (42.7 percent) of these immigrants were in manufacturing. The serious effect of this shift on Mexican immigrant income is seen in the significantly inferior earnings of Mexican workers in nonmanufacturing jobs. In 1999, Mexican immigrant manufacturing workers had median household incomes of $48,900, nearly $9,000 more per year than all other Mexican households, which had median incomes of $40,000.

GENERATIONAL PROGRESS OF MEXICAN IMMIGRANTS

A key question for immigrant-receiving societies like metropolitan Chicago is the socioeconomic legacy of immigration, that is, the social and economic status of the children of the immigrants. At issue is whether the U.S.-born children of low-income Mexican immigrants having relatively little formal education, high poverty rates, and low household incomes, will be able to progress beyond the achievements of their parents.

Having been born in this country, the children of Mexican immigrants presumably will not have significant language and acculturation barriers, and they will have had access to a higher level of public education than their parents. However, some indications suggest that, at least in some regions, native-born Mexican Americans have been experiencing poor economic performance. Ortiz, for example, in a study of Mexicans in the Los Angeles region, followed the progress of a cohort of whites, U.S.-born Mexicans, and African Americans over the course of two decades. He found that U.S.-born Mexicans have been falling behind whites and African Americans in terms of their earnings (Ortiz 1996).

Native-born Mexican Americans in the Chicago area show signs of slow progress similar to those identified by Ortiz in Los Angeles. Although the native-born Mexican Americans have substantially exceeded the educational levels of their parents (having, for example a high school completion rate of 72.5 percent, compared with 33.9 percent for immigrants), their educational levels in terms of high school and college completion are nevertheless slightly below those of African Americans. Whites, meanwhile, have a high school completion rate of 90.9 percent, well in excess of the native-born Mexican rate. Whites are also more than twice as likely to have a college degree as native-born Mexicans.

The achievement of exceeding their parents' educational levels has unfortunately led to little economic payoff for the children of Mexican immigrants. The $42,020 median household income of the native-born Mexicans *is virtually the same as that of the Mexican immigrant households.* A similar story is seen in poverty levels of the U.S.-born Mexicans: Some 15.9 percent are living in poverty, nearly the same percentage as their parents (15.8 percent).[6]

A thorough examination of the factors hindering native-born Mexican American advancement is beyond the scope of this article, but

TABLE 8.4. Education, Income, and Poverty of Mexican Origin and Race Groups in Metro Chicago, 2000

	% with high school diploma	% with B.A.	Median HH income	% Poverty rate	% in service and laborer jobs
FB Mexico	33.9	3.4	$42,000	15.8	66.6
NB Mexican origin	72.5	15.0	42,020	15.9	31.5
NB African American	73.6	16.1	34,000	24.8	34.0
NB Asian	95.0	58.1	55,000	4.6	16.7
NB Non-Latino white	90.9	37.4	61,000	3.9	18.3

Note: Income and poverty data are reported for 1999. FB = foreign-born; NB = native-born.

overall educational levels among the population are doubtlessly lowered by the well-documented high dropout rate of Latino high school students. Household income, in turn, is clearly hindered by the relatively high percentage of native-born Mexicans in service and laborer jobs (31.5 percent).

A striking set of circumstances exist with regard to the status of both foreign- and native-born Mexicans compared to that of blacks (Table 8.4). Both foreign- and native-born Mexicans have lower educational levels than blacks, yet their household incomes exceed those of blacks by about $8,000. A picture emerges of an aggregate Mexican economic experience that, among the first-generation of immigrants, already is superior to that of blacks, a status that is maintained by the descendants of those immigrants. Further investigation is called for into the factors permitting Mexican-origin persons to exceed the aggregate economic position of blacks. These factors are likely to include a more frequent presence of two or more wage earners among Mexican households than among blacks, and discrimination in education, the workplace, and other areas.

Notwithstanding the income levels showing U.S.-born Mexicans to have an aggregate economic situation higher than that of blacks, my analysis of changes in income levels during the 1990s shows a trend of low growth for the U.S.-born Mexicans and a widening gap between them and all other major racial groups. It also shows that native-born Mexicans saw their status weaken in comparison to Mexican immigrants.

As seen in Table 8.5, the median incomes of native-born Mexican households increased by 7.7 percent during the twenty-year period

from 1979 to 1999. This rate of growth was far behind that of native-born whites (who experienced a 23.5 percent increase in income), blacks (28.4 percent increase), and even foreign-born Mexicans (16.1 percent increase). (African Americans outpaced all groups in household income growth, an increase tempered somewhat by the fact that this group began with a low base of $26,489 in 1979.)

The disparate rates of income growth between native-born Mexican Americans and native-born whites have led to an increasing gap in prosperity between these groups. As seen in Figure 8.2, although native-born Mexican American incomes amounted to 79.0 percent of native-born whites in 1979, by 1999 this amount had fallen to 68.9 percent. Amazingly, over the period 1979–1999, native-born Mexican Americans in metro Chicago saw their incomes fall to a level nearly equal to that of Mexican immigrants, who actually maintained their income vis-à-vis that of whites during the 1990s.

EFFECT OF IMMIGRATION POLICY

National immigration policy, and particularly its implications for undocumented immigrants,

TABLE 8.5. Percent Growth in Median Household Income, 1979–1999 (Inflation Adjusted), in Metro Chicago

FB Mexico	16.1
NB Mexican origin	7.7
NB African American	28.4
NB Asian	23.5
BB Non-Latino white	23.5

Note: FB = foreign-born; NB = native-born.

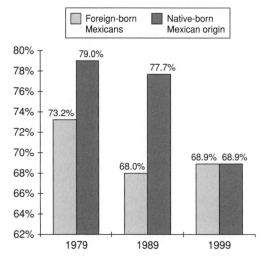

FIGURE 8.2. Houshold income as percentage of white income.
Source: U.S. Census: 1980, 1990, 2000.

has significant meaning for Mexican immigrants. Many Mexicans have an illegal status, and policies related to illegal immigration have been tightened in recent years.

Up to now, this chapter has not distinguished among the different immigrant status categories that apply to Mexican immigrants. Most Mexican immigrants to the United States fall into three categories. *Legal immigrants* (and those who subsequently naturalize) are those Mexican nationals who have been awarded lawful permanent residence status. *Undocumented immigrants* are those residing in violation of federal immigration law. A third category consists of *temporary workers* admitted primarily to fill labor shortages. Most Mexican immigrants with temporary employment visas work in agriculture, and relatively few of these reside in Illinois.

For the Mexican population of metropolitan Chicago, undocumented immigration status constrains an individual's ability to socially and economically integrate into this society. The lack of legal status for a young person often means that formal education terminates at high school, because undocumented immigrants enrolling in state universities are assessed the high tuition rates applicable to foreign students. Working-age undocumented immigrants may become stuck in a job because it is necessary to secure and present false documents to change employment. Adult undocumented immigrants are unable to vote or serve on juries, and persons of all ages may simply be reluctant to interact with government officials, such as police officers. Given these serious consequences of undocumented status, it is important to assess the overall extent of illegal immigration among the Mexican immigrant community.

Size and Scope of Undocumented Mexican Immigrant Population

Substantial numbers of Mexican immigrants in the metro Chicago area have an undocumented immigration status. One indication of the size and scope of the undocumented Mexican population is the discrepancy between data from the U.S. Immigration and Naturalization Service on legal entries and data collected by the 2000 census on foreign-born Mexicans.

According to the INS, approximately 79,000 legal Mexican immigrants entered the United States during the 1990s with the intention of residing in Illinois. In contrast, the 2000 Census found about 305,000 foreign-born Mexicans in the state who reported coming here during the 1990s. These data represent a ratio of about three undocumented arrivals for each legal arrival during the 1990s. In other words, the majority—about three-quarters—of recent Mexican immigrants may be undocumented. (I stress "recent" 1990s arrivals, as opposed to all Mexican immigrants.)

The high percentage of recent Mexican immigrants who are undocumented should cause policy makers and advocates to rethink the status of Mexican immigrants. By virtue of their lack of legal permanent residence, the majority of incoming Mexican immigrants find most social safety net programs to be irrelevant, because access to programs like food stamps or regular Medicaid requires a green card. Some of the basic programs funded by philanthropic and government agencies to serve immigrants, such as naturalization, are also unhelpful to this population. When dealing with undocumented immigrants, the question is how to provide assistance to needy persons when they are ineligible for existing programs. Undocumented immigrants also have needs that do not confront legal immigrants, such as how to interact with local government representatives (including police departments) in ways that do not place them in jeopardy of deportation.

It may be assumed that large numbers of undocumented Mexican immigrants are likely to reside permanently in the United States. For many of these individuals, it would make sense to legalize their status, given that legal immigrants are more likely to achieve stable economic status (and pay taxes) and to participate civically (by voting, serving on juries, and the like). In recent years, however, the barriers to legal status for undocumented Mexican immigrants have become more, not less, formidable.

Barriers to Legal Immigration Status

The concept of family reunification has been the cornerstone of U.S. immigration policy since 1965, when Congress mostly eliminated national-origin quotas and developed an immigration system in which most arrivals must be sponsored by a close relative. In the last few decades, however, the development and expansion of other legal immigrant categories (including refugees, immigrants admitted to fill labor shortages, and others) have lowered the percentage of legal arrivals who have been sponsored by family.

Yet family reunification, which represents a declining portion of overall immigrant admission decisions, is much more important to Mexican immigrants than to most other groups. For example, nationally, in 1998, 68.5 percent of legal Mexican immigrants entered the country under the provisions of family reunification (Paral 2002).[7] For non-Mexicans, only 41.2 percent of legal arrivals entered under family reunification. During the same period, 45.3 percent of non-Mexican legal arrivals to the United States were granted permanent or temporary residence on the basis of their filling a labor need. Only 29.3 percent of Mexicans were admitted on this basis.

The preponderance of family-based entry for legal Mexican arrivals is largely because of the requirements that most employment-based legal arrivals have relatively high occupational skills. Given their socioeconomic status, Mexican entries are too often unable to avail themselves of visas and work permits based on labor market needs. At the same time, and unfortunately for the Mexican-origin population, lengthy backlogs and waiting periods apply for persons applying for U.S. residence through family reunification.

While the family-based system of legal immigration—so important to Mexicans—is backlogged, U.S. employers have nevertheless demonstrated a growing reliance on Mexican immigrant labor. Nationally, between 1990 and 2000, the percent of all U.S. workers who were born in Mexico doubled, from 2.0 to 4.0 percent (Paral 2002). In metropolitan Chicago, 48.7 percent of the net growth of the labor force is attributable to Mexican immigration (Norkewicz and Paral 2003). Clearly, a "disconnect" exists between U.S. needs for Mexican workers and the legal systems in place to facilitate the migration of those workers. This disconnectedness promotes undocumented immigration.

A new barrier to legal Mexican immigration was installed in 1996 as part of the welfare reform act of that year, when Congress raised the income requirements of persons seeking to sponsor an immigrant. As of that year, immigrant sponsors must have incomes of at least 125 percent of the federal poverty level. According to 1990 census data, some 22.6 percent of Mexican American householders in Illinois would not meet this income standard. For low-income Mexican American households, family reunification too often comes through undocumented immigration.

Another hurdle to legal status involves those undocumented Mexicans in the United States who have applied for a legal immigrant visa and been notified that they have been awarded such a visa. During the 1990s, a catch-22–like situation developed that often prevented them from adjusting their status. Current immigration law mandates that undocumented immigrants residing in the United States must have applied for legal status by April 2001, if they wish to adjust their status while remaining in the United States. Immigrants who have not applied by that date would have to return to Mexico to receive an immigrant visa. However, in 1996, Congress instituted severe penalties on immigrants who attempt to enter the United States after having previously resided here in an undocumented status. Any person who had more than 12 months of illegal residence here would be barred from entering for 10 years. The effect of these policies is that undocumented Mexican immigrants who become otherwise eligible for an immigrant visa may decide not to return to Mexico to accept that visa, given that they would be barred for 10 years from returning to the United States. Thus, the undocumented immigrant may decide to remain in undocumented status here in the United States.

As undocumented Mexican workers and their families enter metro Chicago, many of them eventually qualify for legal immigration status. Roughly 90,000 Illinois Mexican immigrants acquired legal status through the legalization programs enacted by IRCA in 1986. A more common and ongoing way to legalize involves the eventual acquisition of legal permanent resident status—such as through marriage—*after* a period of illegal residence. The cumulative effect of IRCA legalizations and other means through which the undocumented regularize their status mean that a substantial portion of currently legal Mexican immigrants have at one point been undocumented. It is easy to see why immigration policy has such a severe effect on the Mexican-origin population in the Chicago area.

CONCLUSION

This chapter draws a portrait of Latino and Mexican immigrant communities that are burgeoning in size and extending their residential patterns across the metropolitan area. Indeed, Latino population growth, with Mexican immigration at its core, is a key factor in the overall population growth of the region. Mexican immigrants, however, have socioeconomic levels well below those of other immigrant groups. Of particular concern, the children and grandchildren of the immigrants—U.S.-born persons of Mexican ancestry—are experiencing very low levels of income growth and are actually falling behind other groups over time. At the beginning of this chapter, I described Latinos as a group that embodies the new Chicago in terms of their rapid growth, geographic dispersion, cultural roots apart from Anglo traditions, and other characteristics. The decline in Mexican immigrant and Mexican American household income against that of whites suggests that Latinos embody the new Chicago in still another way: as a group on the disadvantaged side of a widening economic gap within the region.

NOTES

1. Persons of Latino origin may be of any race. Latino is an ethnicity that generally refers to persons who trace their ancestry to Spanish-speaking portions of Latin America and to Spain.

2. The Dissimilarity Index runs from 0 (for complete integration) to 100 (for complete segregation).

3. Birthrate data are for ever-married women.

4. Immigrants from Poland, India, the Philippines, and China are natural comparison groups for an analysis of Mexican immigrants. These groups are, respectively, the second through fifth largest immigrant groups in the Chicago area and, together with Mexicans, they comprise nearly two-thirds (or 64.3 percent) of the entire foreign-born population.

5. "Service and laborer" jobs in this report include workers who are employed in service occupations and in production, transportation, and material-moving occupations. These occupations represent the lowest-paid jobs in the region.

6. A comparison of foreign-born and native-born Mexican-origin persons might suffer from the inclusion of native-born children of Mexican immigrants: The current economic situation of these children is that of their immigrant parents. To examine the effect of factoring out native-born children of immigrant parents, Current Population Survey data for 1998–2001 was used to compare second-generation and foreign-born Mexican householders. The analysis revealed comparable trends in education, i.e., native-born Mexicans having education levels above their parents but lower than African Americans. Household incomes of second-generation Mexicans, however, were $40,000, only about $4,000 higher than foreign-born Mexican households, which average $35,602.

7. The population in this analysis consisted of persons awarded permanent legal status and persons given permission to work temporarily.

Mary Patrice Erdmans

9   New Chicago Polonia: Urban and Suburban

POLES HAVE BEEN immigrating to Chicago for over a century. Immigrant numbers peaked in the first decade of the twentieth century and by the time national quotas were introduced during the 1920s, almost half a million Poles and their children were living in Chicago. During the middle of the twentieth century, Polish migration was limited to mostly postwar refugees, but in the last decades, a new surge of immigrants arrived. These contemporary immigrants are similar to the earlier arrivals in that most of them are coming in search of jobs and a better life, many of them work as skilled laborers or in service positions, and a significant number do not initially intend to stay permanently. This recent migrant wave differs, however, in that today immigrants are more educated, they are more likely to have had managerial and professional occupations in Poland and, because of the changes in immigration policy, the newcomers are not classified only as "immigrants" but also as political refugees and undocumented workers. Another difference is that, while the majority of immigrants continue to live in the city in the old Polish neighborhoods, an increasing number of new arrivals are resettling in nonethnic suburban communities. Today, over a million Poles and their descendents live in the larger Chicago metropolitan region and, although the newcomers make up only a small percent of the total population, they have a noticeable presence in the city and the suburbs.

THE NEW IMMIGRANTS: EDUCATED AND UNDOCUMENTED TRANSNATIONAL WORKERS

In 2000, 133,797 foreign-born Poles were living in metropolitan Chicago (along with nearly 900,000 Americans of Polish heritage). The presence of new Polish immigrants in Chicago is a consequence of larger global patterns, which include cold war conflicts and the dismantling of the Soviet Union, as well as neoliberal U.S. immigration policies that support capital's need for low-wage labor. During the first half of the 1960s, roughly 7,000 Poles were admitted into the United States annually; the 1965 policy revisions cut this rate in half for the next 20 years. Despite this rate reduction, the migration cohort grew steadily throughout the 1970s and 1980s with the arrival of political refugees and temporary visitors. The 1968 upheaval in Poland produced the first wave of refugees, but the largest numbers came after the national strikes in Poland in 1976 and the formation of the trade union *Niezalezny Samorzadny Zwiazek Zawodowy* (Independent Self-Governing Trades Union), popularly known as *Solidarnosc* (Solidarity) in 1980. In December 1981, the Polish state declared martial law, disbanded Solidarity, and jailed opposition activists. The United States, always receptive to political exiles from communist countries, admitted more than 40,000 Polish refugees during the 1980s.

In addition, over the last 30 years, an increasing number of temporary nonimmigrants arrived, particularly "visitors for pleasure," known within the community as *wakacjusze* (vacationers) or *turysci* (tourists). Many of these vacationers overstayed their visas for significant periods (in some cases, for decades) and worked without authorization. Their numbers rose from an average of 24,000 admitted annually during the 1970s, to 36,000 during the 1980s, to almost 52,000 annually during the 1990s.[1] Although the majority of *wakacjusze* intended to return to Poland, estimates made during the mid 1980s indicated that roughly a third had overextended their visas, and that 95,000 Poles were living (and working) illegally in the United States. Efforts to reduce this population through the 1986 Immigration Reform and Control Act (IRCA) gave amnesty to more than 16,000 Poles and another 2,000 of their dependents. A decade later, estimates of the illegal Polish population dropped to 70,000.

The number of permanent immigrants also has grown steadily. Just over 42,000 Polish immigrants arrived during the 1970s; this doubled to almost 82,000 during the 1980s. During the 1990s, more than 180,000 Poles were admitted into the United States.

Metropolitan Chicago attracted the largest share of the new immigrants. One-third of all Polish immigrants in the United States live in Illinois (mostly in the Chicago metropolitan region). Between 1972 and 2000, roughly 100,000 Poles immigrated to the Chicago metropolitan region, and two-thirds of them came during the last decade of the century (Figure 9.1). During the early 1990s, an average of 11,000 new Polish immigrants resettled annually in Chicago.

The increase in immigration during the 1990s is explained by a variety of factors. First, not all new admissions were new arrivals. The recipients of the 1986 IRCA program arrived during the 1970s and 1980s, but they were not officially admitted until after they received amnesty. As a result, most of them were entered on the books during the early 1990s.

More significantly, the increase in Polish immigration during the 1990s is explained by the instability of the economic system in Poland, the established nature of the migration flow itself,

and changes in U.S. immigration policy. Prior to 1989, Poles often said they chose to emigrate because of the political oppression and economic limitations of the communist system in Poland (Erdmans 1998). But the communist system imploded in 1989. Almost immediately after Poles voted the communists out of office, the new leaders began to dismantle the centralized command economy and establish the institutional structures for a free-market system. For some groups, the collapse of the communist state increased their opportunities in Poland and thereby discouraged emigration (Kolarska-Bobinska 1993,108; Lipinski-Wnuk 1993; Czapinski 1995). The young, educated, urban population was best positioned to take advantage of new business initiatives; jobs in new technology markets (e.g., computers and telecommunications); economic and development aid provided by the United States, Sweden, and Germany; and managerial, skilled, and unskilled positions in Western companies like Pepsico and Bell Telephone. More vulnerable groups, however, fared better under the socialist system, including retirees and those with less education. Moreover, without state subsidies, several large industries collapsed—mining in Lower Silesia, textiles in Lodz, and shipbuilding along the Baltic coast. In these regions, the transition to capitalism led to the displacement of workers. In addition, farmers lost state subsidies, and the younger generation left the farms to look for work in cities at home and abroad. Finally, under communism, artists, writers, sculptors, and actors were state workers supported by stipends. Today, they depend on a still-developing market.

With unemployment rates as high as 12 to 15 percent during the 1990s (and as high as 25 percent for 15- to 24-year-olds), the "liberalization" of Poland and the move toward a more capitalist economy has left many Poles still looking for work and wages *za granice* (abroad). The introduction of capitalist markets created unequal rates of development as well as high rates of inflation. The privatization of Poland has outpaced the democratization of Poland, and growing poverty, unemployment, underemployment, and social inequality sustain the large pool of potential emigrants lined up

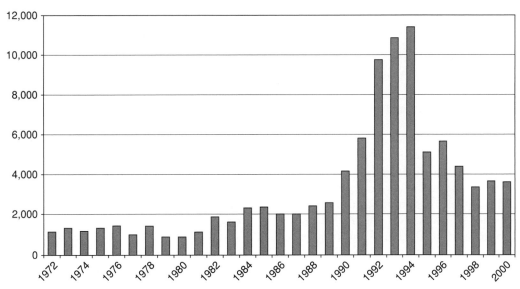

FIGURE 9.1. Polish immigrants to Illinois, 1972–2000.
Source: U.S. Immigration and Naturalization Service.

outside the American embassies in Warsaw and Krakow, waiting for a chance to come to Chicago to earn the "green."

Poland is still in transition, and this unsettled state encourages emigration even among the more educated. Even people in a relatively good position in Poland to take advantage of the new market, given the opportunity to come to the United States, often take the Green Card Gamble.[2] Although some actively pursue this route, others more or less fall into the opportunity. One woman explained her situation this way:

My godmother she sent the application for green card for everyone in her family, I'm her godchild, and for my family. And I was studying Polish philology, and I was on the fourth year of my university, I was thinking about staying at the university. I wanted to go to Jagiellonian to the class of the creative writing. I never thought to emigrate. And then I won. Nobody else but I. And then it was at the beginning of the 1993, I was at the beginning of my fourth year in the university. And then I said, 'I won't go.' And they said, my family, 'You should try. People are paying $10,000 to have a green card. You have to try. It's a chance that you've got.' I have to try.

Ask why she emigrated, another woman, who had been a dentist in Poland, explained:

I hope I don't mess up your research because I didn't come here because I wanted to. I came here only because my husband's biggest dream was to live in the United States. And he had an uncle who was working in Germany [and] after World War II, he decided he didn't want to go back to Poland, so he decided to emigrate to the United States in 1953. Since then, until my husband came to the United States in 1991, he visited maybe three times. But they exchanged letters, and my husband was in love with the United States. And he wanted to come. He came, and he won the lottery. We were not married at the time. But we had been dating six years. 'Why don't you come, and you can be a legal immigrant?' I said, I'm not going to come, I just come for honeymoon, and my honeymoon has lasted nine years.

Even when it is possible to live a satisfying and fulfilling life in Poland, Poles continue to go abroad because migration to the United States (and Germany and Canada) is part of a national habit for Poles. As Douglas Massey (1987) has shown in association with the migration of Mexicans to the United States, although economic factors stimulate the onset of emigration, cultural and social factors better explain the continuation of migration. In the example above, the cultural habits are evident in her husband's "dream" to come to the United States, and his uncle who was living in Chicago represents the social factors.

Given the cultural and social factors that sustain old migrant flows, even when economic conditions improve, we can expect emigration to continue from Poland. Peter Stalker argues in *Workers Without Frontiers* that emigration rates often drop when the wage ratio between sending and receiving countries equalizes, which is expected to occur with free-market practices and globalization. He found, however, that emigration often increases initially after the introduction of free-trade practices because markets are unstable during the transition stage (2000, 57). And the more rapid the changes, the more disruptive they are. In Poland's case, the "shock therapy" introduced to jumpstart the economy destabilized certain labor markets. Development itself may encourage emigration by "shaking people loose from their communities, raising new possibilities, and providing them with the funds to travel" (103). Stalker's model factors in the complex of mechanisms that influence the migrant flow, including established networks that minimize the costs of migration, the affordability of travel, the openness of borders and receptivity of policies for professionals, the Internet as an information node, and the presence of family (and a community) in the receiving country. In sum, although wage ratios are important, other factors come into play, especially in old migration flows.

In addition to the economic instability in Poland and the maturity of the migrant wave, immigration increased during the 1990s because of more open U.S. immigration policy. The Immigration Act of 1990 created more permanent visas and temporary work visas. First, it raised the ceiling for all immigrants from 270,000 annually to a level of 700,000 for 1992–1994, and then to 675,000 beginning in 1995. Included under the numerical cap were slots for "diversity immigrants," defined as aliens from countries adversely affected by the 1965 Immigration

Act. This included Poles and, between 1992 and 1996, more than 50,000 Poles were admitted under this program. Second, this act expanded categories and ceilings for nonimmigrants arriving for cultural exchange, business, employment, and tourism. The United States needs workers in certain industries, and Poles often work in two of these—construction and domestic services. Neoliberal practices, designed to deregulate the economy and allow both labor and capital to move more freely, translate into the high immigration ceilings in advanced economies that allow for the inflow of low-wage labor.

These policy changes brought a larger number of migrants to the United States, willing to work longer hours, for less pay, and with fewer benefits than their native-born counterparts. In the case of Polish migrants, many of these workers employed in changing bedpans, roofing buildings, and working in maintenance are well educated, and they arrive with skilled technical and professional training (Erdmans 1996). For immigrants arriving in Chicago during the 1980s, 76 percent had at least a high school and 18 percent had at least a bachelor's degree; for those arriving during the 1990s, 64 percent had at least a high school degree, and 12 percent had at least a bachelor's degree. This drop in educational level reflects, I would argue, the absence of political refugees during the 1990s and the increase in temporary migrants (including undocumented workers).

During the last 25 years, an increase has occurred in the percent of Polish immigrants who had professional and managerial occupations as well as technical, sales, and administrative positions in Poland; at the same time, the percent of operators, fabricators, and laborers has decreased (Figure 9.2). For men, the percent of skilled workers doubled from 21 percent in 1972 to 46 percent in 2000. For women, those who had held professional and managerial positions in Poland almost doubled during that same period. In 2000, just over a quarter of female immigrants had professional and managerial positions in Poland, and another 43 percent were in technical, sales, and administrative support occupations. In addition, roughly one-fifth of the

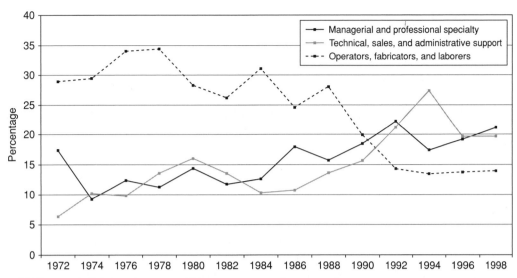

FIGURE 9.2. Polish immigrants to Chicago metro area by occupation.

women were in service positions, and this has remained steady over the past quarter of a century.

Although their education and skills help them to secure jobs, many immigrants pay a steep price for their newness, expressed in the Polish phrase *emigracja to deklasacja* ("emigration leads to downward class mobility," whereby class is assessed as much by status indicators as by economic indicators).

Compared to the native-born Polish American population (which has rates similar to the general white population), Polish immigrants are more likely to work in semi- and low-skilled positions (almost twice as likely if they are new arrivals) and in the service sector (again almost twice as likely if they are new arrivals). Over time, the foreign-born population begins to resemble their native-born counterparts, but they still remain slightly overrepresented in service and manual labor occupations (U.S. Census of the Population 1993a, 365–66). Several factors influence this decline in occupational status, including lack of a green card, family obligations that require newcomers to find work immediately instead of first learning English and recertifying their degrees, and the perception that further education in the United States will not always pay off monetarily.

COMMUNITY BUILDING IN CHICAGO POLONIA

Polonia refers to a community of Poles living abroad and their descendants. Chicago Polonia has been and continues to be one of the largest, most vibrant Polonias in the world. In this new century, it has more than 100 Polish organizations, three prominent Polish-language radio stations with 217 different programs, four television stations, three daily newspapers, and more than two dozen magazines, both weeklies and monthlies. There are fifteen Polish bookstores, and city-wide events include the May 3rd Constitution Day parade, the Polish Film Festival, Taste of Polonia Festival, and the Festival Polonaise.

At the beginning of the last century, the heart of the Polish community was *Trojska Polska* (the Polish Triangle) at the intersection of Milwaukee, Division, and Ashland Avenues. Along with this North Side neighborhood, a large community of Polish immigrants who emigrated mostly from the mountain region of southeastern Poland settled on the Southwest Side of Chicago during the late 1800s, near the meatpacking industries (known as the Back of the Yards community). Today, new Polish immigrants settle along the tracks laid down by their predecessors—along Milwaukee and Archer Avenues, at the southwest and northwest edges of the city, and in the suburbs (see Map 9.1, color insert).

Anchored by the spires of the first Polish churches in Chicago, St. Stanislaus Kotska (1867) and Holy Trinity (1872), *Trojska Polska,* also known as the Polish Downtown, was home to the large ethnic insurance fraternal organizations (e.g., the Polish National Alliance and the Polish Roman Catholic Union), the Polish Museum of America, and the Chopin Theatre, as well as to numerous Polish restaurants, stores, and professionals providing services to the Polish community. At the beginning of the twentieth century, St. Stanislaus Kotska was one of the largest parishes in the United States, with 8,000 families registered (40,000 parishioners), almost all Polish. By mid-century, the neighborhood started to decline as the processes of suburbanization, urban renewal, and racial integration pushed and pulled the second and third generations north up Milwaukee and eventually into the suburbs. During the 1950s, the newly constructed Kennedy Expressway dissected the community and contributed to the tailspin as residents moved out, businesses closed, property values plummeted, buildings were boarded up, and low-income and transient populations moved into the area, a majority of whom were racial minorities.

In West Town (made up of the Wicker Park and Bucktown neighborhoods), where the Polish Triangle is located, the white population dropped from 98 percent to 55 percent between 1960 and 1980. By 1981, St. Stanislaus Kotska had only 850 families registered; today, this parish serves an aging Polish community and a growing Latino community, mostly Mexican. On Sunday, two Masses are celebrated in English, one in Polish, and three in Spanish. By 2000, 40 percent of the population in the tract where St. Stanislaus is situated was Latino (80 percent of them were Mexican), and only 9.5 percent (N = 8,326) of the total West Town population was Polish (a third of them were foreign-born).

Despite this decline in the Polish population, the Polish Triangle has witnessed a renaissance of Polish culture with the Kennar Art Gallery, home of Polish sculptor Jerzy Kennar, who immigrated to America in 1978, and the 1112 Gallery whose curator, Christopher Kamyszew, also organizes Polish Film Festivals in Chicago (as well as New York and Los Angeles). In addition, the Polish Museum and Library have been refurbished, and the Chopin Theatre reopened. The few Polish immigrants moving into the area are often well-educated professionals who work in the city.

Two blocks up the street from St. Stanislaus, in the vicinity of Holy Trinity Church, a new Polish intellectual community is taking hold. Originally a diocesan parish, today Holy Trinity is a mission church designated to serve the Polish immigrant community. All its priests are foreign-born Poles, and its Masses are all celebrated in Polish. More than 600 children are enrolled in its Polish Saturday classes, and the four Sunday Masses attract hundreds of worshipers, with standing room only on the holidays. Polish consulate members attend Holy Trinity, as well as many well-educated newcomers, some of them driving in from their suburban homes. The parish is unique in that it serves the larger metropolitan immigrant community and not the local neighborhood. As is evident, very few Poles live in this neighborhood; most of them have moved north.

CONSUMER-SERVICE IMMIGRANT COMMUNITIES: *JACKOWO* AND BELMONT-CENTRAL

Three-quarters of all new arrivals resettle in the city, mostly on the Northwest Side. When the Poles began moving out of the Polish Triangle at mid-century, they moved North up Milwaukee Avenue. By the time the newest wave of immigrants began arriving in the 1970s, a new Polonian center was already established near St. Hyacinth's parish. Known as *Jackowo,* this Polonian neighborhood also shares its borders with Mexican neighborhoods.

In 1990, the highest concentration of Polish immigrants was near St. Hyacinth Church, in an area known as Jackowo (see Map 9.1). In tract 2105, where St. Hyacinth is located, 65 percent of the population was Polish and 81 percent of the Poles were immigrants (N = 3,880). By 2000, however, this tract was 65 percent Latino (N = 5,341) and only 30 percent Polish (but 86 percent of the Poles were immigrants). In this community, the Poles were concentrated in the areas surrounding Milwaukee Avenue and St. Hyacinth parish (on the block where the church is located, only 28 percent of the population was Latino).

Today, Jackowo hangs on as the heart of Chicago's Polonia, primarily because of St. Hyacinth parish and the retail and professional services in the area. Founded in 1894, St. Hyacinth had almost 4,000 registered families in 1990 (40 percent of whom were new immigrants) and again as many nonregistered Polish families who attend Mass (the majority are new immigrants). For the past 15 years, as many as 10,000 Poles attend weekly one of the sixteen Polish-language Masses (four on Sundays and two each weekday), more than 4,000 Easter baskets are Blessed on Holy Saturday, and at least 2,000 people participate in the Feast of the Corpus Christi in June. The neighborhood surrounding St. Hyacinth is composed of single-family dwellings, two-flats, and small apartment buildings. The newest immigrants rent apartments, rooms, and sometimes only a 10-by-20-foot space cordoned off by a sheet in a basement. Renters are often undocumented workers not intending to stay permanently in the United States, or they are the newest arrivals, who quickly move into other (better) neighborhoods once they are oriented.

Jackowo's Polish concourse on Milwaukee Avenue has shortened over the last 20 years. During the late 1980s, the block between Central Park and Diversey was a trilingual community, home to a Polish bookstore, several Polish restaurants, and numerous store signs advertising "Mowimy po Polsku" and "Hablamos Espanol." Today, the Polish bookstore, restaurants, and "Mowimy po Polsku" placards are gone from this block, and Spanish has become the *lingua franca*.

One block north, however, it is still indisputably Polish urban space. In the summer of 2002, more than 90 percent of the stores had Polish-language signs and/or names, and only five had any Spanish-language signs (and this included the laundromat, where the sign asking customers to please mind their children was written in Spanish but not in English or Polish). More than half (56 percent) of the 85 stores on the block have the same name and sell the same goods or provide the same services as they did in 1989. One of the new businesses, however, is a Mexican restaurant sandwiched between the Polish florist and a Polish department store.

Although Jackowo businesses provide goods and services in Polish, Jackowo does not resemble a traditional ethnic neighborhood. No ethnic organizations are present in the community, the Polish Welfare Office is not located there, nor are the fraternal, political, cultural, or intellectual organizations. The Poles attending the Masses and shopping in the stores come from the entire Chicago metropolitan region, and the transient shoppers do not contribute to building a community, although they do stabilize the area as a market region. Mostly this is an immigrant consumer-service community of retail shops and professional offices that includes Polish-speaking doctors, dentists, lawyers, and accountants as well as meat markets and delicatessens, liquor stores, bakeries, florists, travel agencies, and the central shipping company, Polamer. The businesses that have expanded over the last fifteen years are those providing immigrants services (travel agencies, passport and visa services, translators, and shipping companies) as well as the deli-liquor stores. On this strip, only three restaurants and three bars are present (there are more herbalists than bars), and few public places are available for gathering or community-building—no theaters, concert halls, auditoriums, libraries, or even parks. It is not a companionate neighborhood, but an urban strip where Poles buy goods and receive services.

Jackowo is well known in Poland, and new arrivals quickly find their way to the community. It is a central place to shop, and it even has tourist appeal—visitors from Poland come to see St. Hyacinth the same way they go to visit the Sears Tower. Despite these attractions, however, it does not have a good reputation. New immigrants refer to the area as a place "with a lot of primitivism and simplicity" that "looks sloppy" and has a lot of "people who drink and swear." One Pole said, "I only go there to see the dentist. I was down there last week at ten in the morning and people were drunk already." Another said that, in Jackowo, there are "mostly more poor people, recent immigrants, those who came just shortly and this is more like a ghetto."

Farther west, on Belmont Avenue, is a newer Polonian community considerably more attractive to immigrants than Jackowo. Today, the Central and Belmont intersection is known as "the center of Polonia." According to the 1990 census, in the tracts adjacent to this intersection, a third to a half of the population was Polish, and half of the Polish population was foreign-born. Throughout the 1990s, this section continued to attract new Polish immigrants so that, by 2000, half of the population was Polish and over three-quarters of them were immigrants. Just south of Belmont, the Polish population decreases, and the Latino population increases. In tract 1511, bordering on Belmont, half the population is Polish and 20 percent is Latino; one tract south, the Polish population drops to 34 percent, and the Latino population rises to 41 percent. One farther tract south, 68 percent of the population is Latino and only 20 percent is Polish.

The Belmont-Central community looks like a traditional Polish neighborhood, with more owner-occupied homes, long-term renters, and more public ethnic space in bookstores, cafes, and the library. In addition, numerous professional, retail, and immigrant-service businesses are present, as well as restaurants, nightclubs, the headquarters for a Polish-language newspaper (*Kurier*), and a Polish medical clinic. Of interest, however, is the recent marketing strategy of using "European" rather than "Polish" for businesses: European Foot and Ankle; European Optical; Continental Café; European Kwiaty (*kwiaty* is flowers in Polish); European Quality Tuck-pointing; European Motors; and European Music. Despite the pan-ethnic symbols, the area is predominantly Polish.

The local neighborhood library, Portage-Cragin, houses the second largest Polish-language collection in the Chicago Public Library system (the first is housed in the Harold Washington central library). Helen Ziolkowska,

an immigrant who arrived in 1974 with a degree in Polish philology from Jagiellonian University and started working at the branch in 1984, was instrumental in amassing the 7,000-volume collection that includes fiction, reference books, and nonfiction work on Poland. After 1989, a proliferation of English-language books was translated into Polish, and today, Danielle Steele and Edith Wharton are found on the shelves next to Henryk Sienkiewicz and other classic Polish writers. Ziolkowska is representative of the large number of educated immigrants from Poland, and her professional life is dedicated to meeting the needs of and expanding the spaces for educated immigrants. She started a Polish-language book club at the branch in 2002 (two others are at branches in Northwest neighborhoods and a fourth is on the South Side), and she is also the founder and editor of *Glos Nauczyciela,* a quarterly journal for Polish educators, established in 1985. New immigrants created a demand for bilingual services in city offices, schools, and institutions, and they also supply the teachers, librarians, and professional bilingual personnel to meet these needs. Polish bilingual programs, started in 1978, enrolled more than 300 students city wide by 1990, and this number jumped to 4,300 students by 1998 (Coleman 2004).

The city also expanded its collection of Polish-language materials in the library system. The Slavic Librarian of the Literature and Language Division at the Harold Washington Library, Maria Zakrzewska, an immigrant with a master's degree in philology from Poland, began working at the Chicago Public Library (CPL) in 1993. In 1995, she applied for and received a grant for $21,000 to build the Polish-language collection, which dates back to 1883. Currently, the library has approximately 15,000 Polish-language volumes in its collection as well as five daily newspapers from Poland and twelve magazines. Eleven branches of the Chicago Public Library have Polish collections along with five suburban public libraries (the Skokie Public library houses the largest collection, containing 630 Polish-language books). This growth in Polish collections at suburban libraries parallels the growth of suburban Polish residents.

SUBURBAN POLES: EDUCATED PROFESSIONALS AND SKILLED LABORERS

Although temporary immigrants and recent arrivals often resettle in traditional Polish quarters in the city, an increasing number of immigrants are moving to suburban communities. Between 1983 and 1998, the number of new arrivals listing a suburban zip code as their intended residence more than doubled from 16 to 36 percent (U.S. Immigration and Naturalization Service 1983–1998). In addition, within five to ten years after arrival, many immigrants buy homes in the suburbs. This represents a marked difference from earlier immigrants, many of whom lived and died in the urban neighborhoods and whose descendants had assimilated culturally and structurally before moving into the suburbs. The suburbs on the northwest and southwest borders of the city (those adjacent to the Polish communities in the city) experienced the largest influx of new immigrants (Map 9.2, color insert).

Immigrants' move to the suburbs reflects a general population trend. From 1960 to 1990, the overall city population declined, especially the white population, whereas the population outside the city increased, in Cook and the collar counties. According to the 2000 census, 60 percent of all people reporting some Polish ancestry in Cook County lived outside of the city. Most Polish immigrants and Polish Americans are moving for the same reasons as the general white population—better public schools, more affordable housing, and increased quality of life (e.g., larger yards, better air quality, lower crime rates). Suburban life also represents social mobility—as immigrants become established and more secure in their occupations, they want to "move up," and moving up often involves moving out of the city. One immigrant said: "In the Polish mentality, for young immigrants this is a step up: You made it in America, you move to the suburbs." Asked why he moved to the suburbs instead of buying a house in the Belmont-Central neighborhood where his medical practice is located, one doctor said, "My status is such that I can afford something nicer, bigger, more independent. You want something bigger, some comfort, to live in the house with no neighbors below or above. Status. Comfort. So people are moving, when they are somewhat richer, they are moving outside."

Moving out of the urban community also means moving away from encroaching minority communities. Poles in America quickly develop stereotypes that indict blacks and Latinos as undesirable neighbors. One Polish priest stated that Polish immigrants were moving out of the city "because blacks, Asians, and Spanish-speaking people [were] moving more into the city. The black community is coming, more and more, along the CTA, you know." Several Polish realtors and priests made similar comments:

- "[They are] moving away from Mexicans. . . [They] move to escape the Mexicans."
- "Clients prefer all-white neighborhoods. This constitutes a better neighborhood for them."
- "A better neighborhood has better schools and is usually white. Polish immigrants want a white neighborhood."
- "Churches are being overrun by Hispanics. They don't want to live by blacks or Hispanics."
- "How about Asians? They prefer to live by whites than Asians."
- "[They] don't want to live near people of color. They are worried property values will go down. . . . They have a really bad attitude toward living near people of color. I shouldn't even be telling you this."
- "They want to live in a good neighborhood. And a good neighborhood is usually white, but they will never escape the Mexicans. There are so many of them. They are everywhere."

Where Poles live also suggests they prefer white neighborhoods. According to an article in the *Chicago Sun-Times* (June 7, 1992), Polish Americans tend to move to suburban towns that have more Germans, Italians, and Irish than racial minorities. In 1990, in city tracts with the highest concentration of Poles, there were no African Americans; by 2000, less than 3 percent of the *Jackowo* community was African American.

Polish immigrants who move to the suburbs tend to be homeowners rather than renters, permanent immigrants rather than working vacationers, and better-educated professionals and skilled laborers rather than low-skilled workers (Grammich 1992). Although knowledge of English is not a necessity, it is easier to make the move if they are not dependent on a Polish-language community. One realtor explained: "Polish immigrants coming to the United States are better educated, and the city is not as attractive to them." While English-proficient immigrants are more likely to "go suburban," speaking English is less necessary if they move to more Polish-populated suburbs such as Harwood Heights, Niles, Norridge, Des Plaines, and Park Ridge, where they can rent Polish videos, visit Polish dentists, and find bilingual cashiers at chain stores. Shoppers can buy the *Dziennik Zwiazkowy* in their local Osco or Jewel, and residents can socialize with compatriots at Polish sports clubs and social groups organized in places like Des Plaines and Park Ridge.

The immigrants buying homes in the suburbs usually have been in the United States five to ten years. They have moderate incomes and buy houses in the range of $120,000 to $300,000. Their move often corresponds with their children's educational needs (e.g., moving to the suburbs when the child is entering high school). Leona Stagg, a former Chicago English-as-second-language (ESL) instructor stated: "These immigrant parents will secure two or three jobs, save their money, then move to the suburbs, where they feel the best possible education is available to their children.... They most likely will not need a Polish bilingual program at their new suburban school" (Coleman 2004, 35).

Although the bilingual programs are located in the city schools, in the suburbs, Polish children are more likely to attend Polish Saturday Schools that teach Polish language, history, geography, literature, and culture three hours a week (usually on Saturday mornings). Parents pay tuition for the schools (the classes are often held in the classrooms of parochial schools), which covers the nominal costs of the teachers ($10 per hour in 2002), most of whom are immigrants themselves with master's degrees from Polish universities. The materials for the elementary and high school courses are developed, compiled, and distributed by the Polish Teachers Association in America, which is located in Chicago. In 1983, there were 18 Polish Saturday Schools, with 130 teachers and 3,000 students; by 2002, there were 27 schools with 647 teachers and 13,425 students. Before 1974, only one of the schools was located in the suburbs; today, over half of them are.

In the suburbs, Polish immigrants are more visible than later-generation Polish Americans, who often marry outside the ethnic group, no longer speak Polish, and are more evenly dispersed throughout the suburbs. The new Polish immigrants are not assimilated Americans. In the suburbs, the Polish presence is visible, but it is tucked between the national chains. For example, in a strip mall at the corner of Lawrence and Harlem, across from the Old Warsaw Restaurant, Rich's Food and Liquors advertises in Polish and hires only Polish immigrants, many of whom do not speak English well. Next to the liquor store is a Polish calling card–phone store, a Polamer (shipping company), and an Avis Car Rental, Office Max, Copy Max, and an Italian restaurant. Polish business owners share space with other ethnic retail shops. Nearby, on Lawrence, another strip mall holds the Aztec Mexican Restaurant, Sobieski's Deli, a Filipino restaurant, and a Polish video store. In Niles, Harwood Heights, and Des Plaines, a variety of professional shingles with Polish last names (e.g., doctors, dentists, accountants, lawyers, travel agents) are visible, as is an occasional Polish deli, and signs for Polish realtors and construction companies abound, but no "Mowimy po Polsku" signs are visible in the windows (yet). Although the Polish presence in the suburbs is noticeable, unlike in *Jackowo* and Belmont Central, it does not define the community.

With the delis, video stores, and professional services, many immigrant needs are met in the suburbs, but not all of them. Krystina Flaherty, a Polish immigrant and Director of the European American Ministry for the Archdiocese of Chicago said:

> Everything moved out there. They don't want to come to the city [because] all the Polish stores, moved there—Polamer, Koligowski Sausage and, when you have that, people say, well why not churches? They used to go [into the city]

shopping for the Polish food, stop for the Mass, and then go home. Now they don't need to do that because they have all these things available where they are. So they think, people are very comfortable with their nice homes and shopping malls, so what's missing? The missing part would be a Mass. The problem is, from the church point of view, that there are not too many services offered for ethnicity in general in the suburbs. Suburbs are perceived as very American.

Even when immigrants are comfortable speaking English to buy toothpaste, they prefer to pray in Polish. As Flaherty said: "I know many people who are living in the suburbs, driving a Volvo; they have a huge villa and speak perfect English and still prefer to go to a Polish Mass." The archdiocese is slowly responding to meet this preference.

PARISH LIFE IN THE SUBURBS: INTEGRATING POLISHNESS TO MAINTAIN CATHOLICISM

The presence of immigrants in the suburbs has led to an increased number of Roman Catholic churches offering Masses and other services in Polish. Unlike their urban counterparts, however, immigrants today are not building "Polish" churches but instead are integrating themselves into Roman Catholic parishes with the help of Polish-speaking priests. The function of the Polish-speaking priest is not to retain Polishness, but to maintain Catholicism. Prayer and spiritual attachments are deep, emotional, and more easily accessible through one's native language. One immigrant said, "Praying in Polish has a special feeling. It helps to connect me." To maintain her Catholicism, she attends a Saturday Polish Mass for herself and a Sunday English Mass with her children.

In the Chicago metropolitan region, 54 churches offer Polish masses, and one-third of these are located in suburban parishes. The traditional "Polish" churches in the cities are larger, often celebrate several Masses in Polish, and they have Polish-speaking priests in residence. In comparison, suburban churches are more likely to offer only one Mass in Polish, often celebrated by a visiting priest. These suburban churches are not defined as "Polish parishes" but, instead, as parishes with a Polish Mass. Even a parish such as St. John Brebeuf in Des Plaines, where Polish immigrants make up 40 percent of its members, the resident Polish priest stated, "This is not a Polish parish." Whereas in the past, urban ethnic churches attracted a particular group to the exclusion of others, today Polish- or Spanish-speaking priests serve the purpose of opening the door wider, not creating a wall. One Polish suburban priest stated: "We believe Jesus is the same in your language, in my language. Jesus connects us. When we have to express our emotion in English, in Polish, in Spanish, it is okay, you can. But we in the Catholic Church have one very good point to connect all the nations.... Jesus will never divide, Jesus always connects.... It is a Catholic church, not Polish."

The initiative for Polish-speaking Masses comes from the parishioners, not the archdioceses, and more requests for Polish Masses are made than can be satisfied because of a shortage of Polish-speaking priests. The diocese keeps adding more Polish-language Masses "but there is never enough," said Flaherty. "And that creates the problem, because there are no resources available." In 2002, the archdiocese had 30 priests from Poland and a few more arrive each summer. The recruitment of Polish priests is aided by changes in immigration policy through the Immigration Act of 1990, which added a new category for workers in religious occupations (R1 visas). According to the *Statistical Yearbook of Immigration and Naturalization*, between 1993 and 1997, the United States admitted 60 to 65 Polish priests annually; in 1998, this number increased to 144, and to 177 the following year.

The Polish-language Masses in suburban parishes often attract immigrants from beyond the parish boundary and, at times, even from surrounding archdioceses (e.g., Joliet). On some Sundays or special holidays, 1,000 or more worshippers may overwhelm a church, creating parking problems and safety issues. The community within which the church is located can resent the intrusion of these "outsiders" who are not always respectful. One priest said: "They park everywhere: on sidewalks, people's lawns.

Nobody cleans up. Nobody takes care of it. That's why there is a conflict. It used to be, 'I'm from *Jackowo*, I'm from *Brunowo*.' That's their neighborhood. Now they're coming from Naperville. What do they care?"

In these cases, the Polish-language Mass does not necessarily build a geographic community, but instead serves a clientele's language needs. St. Zachary Catholic Church, in Des Plaines, a parish of roughly 2,400 families, has mostly white parishioners (Irish, Italian, Polish) with a growing Latino population. Although only 10 percent of the parishioners are Polish immigrants, the Polish-language Mass on Saturday attracts 600 to 700 devotees from neighboring suburbs, including Arlington Heights, Park Ridge, and Mount Prospect. The visiting priest who says the mass travels from Indiana.

St. John Brebeuf, in Niles, a northwest suburb located along Milwaukee Avenue, is one of the few suburban churches that has a Polish-speaking priest in residence. The parish is comprised of roughly 3,000 families; 40 percent are Polish immigrants, many of whom joined the parish in the last 10 years. Twenty years ago, Mass was celebrated in Polish by a visiting Jesuit priest, but in 2002, Father Galek, a Polish immigrant priest, joined the parish. Today, the visiting Jesuit priest celebrates the Saturday Mass (400 people attend on average). The resident Polish priest celebrates the Sunday noon Mass in Polish (for roughly 1,000 people), as well as the English-language Masses for the other parishioners. Half of those who attend the Polish-language Masses are parishioners, and the rest come from surrounding suburbs. In addition to the two Polish Masses, a Wednesday evening Marion worship group is offered for Polish-speaking parishioners, along with a Bible study group and a first-Friday devotion. The parish also features a Polish Saturday school. The Poles have changed the parish in other ways, including an increased number of processions during the holidays (e.g., Lent and Corpus Christi) that include more Polish banners. Father Galek maintains, however, that Poles have not changed the church in any significant ways, that the immigrants strengthen the church by bringing in new members, and that the church serves Catholics, not Poles. He states that, for new immigrants, the "experience of the Mass in the Polish language is better for them. . . . We care that the Polish community becomes good Catholic Americans."

Krystina Flaherty often hears Americans criticize the Polish-language Mass as potentially fragmenting the church and taking away from the parish "because they don't bond if they go to a Polish parish. My answer to them is, if there is no Polish [Mass] they won't go at all, so instead of losing people, it's at least better that they hang on." She said the suburban priests resent the ethnic-language Masses more than urban priests, who are used to the multiethnic community and "don't make a big deal out of it. If we were to open up more Masses in Polish in the inner city, we would not have half of the problems that we have in the suburbs." Regarding resistance to Polish-language Masses in the suburbs, Flaherty said, "I think the bottom line is that the suburbs don't want to be called ethnic. They all want to be Americanized. The churches in the city were built by the immigrants, so they become the 'Polish' church. But in the suburbs, there is an American church."

Polish-language Masses recapitulate the larger pattern of Polish immigration in the suburbs in that immigrants are not creating Polish neighborhoods, nor are they residing in the suburbs as assimilated, nonethnic Americans. Instead, they are being incorporated into nonethnic suburbs as Polish immigrants.

CONCLUSION

Emigration from Poland has existed for over a century, and it will continue for as long as the United States keeps open its borders, because cultural and social factors keep the sending and receiving country linked. In some regions of Poland, emigration has become embedded in the collective memory of the villages: It is written into songs, it finds its face on gravestones, and it is expressed in the material growth of the village (Erdmans 1999). For these villages, Chicago is an intimate component of their economy and culture. For example, almost every one of the 300 residents in Dlugopole in the province of Nowy Sacz has a close relative living in Chicago. The wealth of the villages of Nowy Sacz is reflected in the large two- and three-story "Chicago houses" so named because of their source of capital, not their architectural style (Hundley 1998). Marriages, births, and deaths that happen in Chicago are recorded in the parish books in Poland. And most important, the money continues to flow from the labor of immigrants to their families in Poland. Between 1994 and 1999, Polish workers' remittances to Poland from the United States totaled $4.4 billion.

During the 1990s, two of every five Polish newcomers to the United States settled in the Chicago metropolitan region, as did almost half the Polish refugees of the 1980s. They settled here because of habit, because they knew people here, and because the established ethnic and immigrant community made it easier to locate jobs and housing, secure bank loans, and find a doctor, priest, or herbalist who spoke Polish. Social networks attract new immigrants because they are conduits for information, reduce the risk of working illegally, and counter the threat of loneliness with restaurants, nightclubs, churches, theaters, sports clubs, and media. Polish-language newspapers and employment agencies help new immigrants find jobs and facilitate their incorporation into American society. And finally, because of the way our immigration laws are designed, family networks bring in new immigrants. Neoliberal migration policies, global inequality, national habits, thick social networks, and ethnic institutional completeness ensure the continuation of Polish immigration to Chicago.

When they arrive, the new immigrants settle both within and beside the old established Polonian neighborhoods. The two types of neighborhoods discussed in this article represent old and new forms of integration. The immigrants in the *Jackowo* and Belmont–Central areas are living in ethnic Polish communities, working, praying, socializing, and shopping with other immigrants. They reproduce old patterns of resettlement and represent new Polonia in old neighborhoods. Polish immigrants finding homes in the suburbs represent new patterns of integration. Unlike their Polish Americans counterparts who assimilated before suburbanizing, the new immigrants are in the process of culturally assimilating even as they are more rapidly structurally assimilating into labor markets and educational institutions. They move into the suburbs as immigrants, not homogenized ethnic whites and, as such, they bring some cultural variation (though not racial variation) into "white-bread" suburbia.

NOTES

1. *Annual Report of the Immigration and Naturalization Service*, 1960–76; *Statistical Yearbook of the Immigration and Naturalization Service*, 1977–99. Tables: immigrants admitted by selected class of admission and region and selected country of birth; nonimmigrants admitted by class of admission and region and selected country of birth.

2. This is the name of a television series in Poland produced and directed by Slawomir Grunberg.

Padma Rangaswamy

10   Asian Indians in Chicago

ONE OF THE earliest immigrants of Indian origin to have made his home in Chicago is Chandra Lachman Singh, whose adventurous life remains a little-known immigrant saga. He came to New York from Grenada in 1911. He traveled to Chicago, where he worked in a restaurant on Wabash Avenue before being inducted into the army in 1918. He served in World War I, became a naturalized citizen, and purchased and managed residential properties in Lincoln Park and Hyde Park. Between 1929 and 1932, he and his wife went to India, where they worked with Mahatma Gandhi and the Indian National Congress for the Indian independence movement. He lost all his Chicago properties during the Depression and experimented with homesteading in Brazil before he returned to Chicago and lived out the remainder of his life in Hyde Park; he died in 1989.[1] His first days in Chicago predated the arrival of substantial numbers of Indians to this city by more than 50 years yet, his adventurism, entrepreneurship, resilience, love for the homeland and the adopted country, and globalism—all reflected in his checkered career—he foreshadowed a future and presaged the experiences of thousands of Indians who would pour into Chicago after 1965 and form a thriving community here by 2000.

The rapid growth of the Asian Indian population in Chicago has to be understood not merely as a one-way stream of migration from India to America, but, as in the case of Chandra Lachman Singh, in a global context, as a constantly evolving migratory network or *oikumene* (Rangaswamy 2000, 15–40). This network is the result of an interplay of various global phenomena—started by legislative and economic forces that opened the gates to immigration, fuelled by social and cultural factors that encouraged family reunification and chain migration, and finally consolidated by communications and technological advancements that revolutionized the very notion of immigration and created a new breed of "Global Indian."

HISTORICAL OVERVIEW AND THE CHICAGO CONTEXT

Asian Indians recorded the highest growth rate among all Asian groups in the 2000 census, making up 16.4 percent of the Asian American population and 0.6 percent of the general U.S. population. Although their immigration history in the United States goes back to the first decade of the nineteenth century (when about 7,000 Sikhs migrated from the Punjab to California), they have long been denied free entry and citizenship rights under racist immigration laws. After World War II, India was allotted a quota of 100 immigrants; not until 1965, with the Civil Rights movement in full swing, did Congress change the immigration laws to drop racial quotas and allow Asians to migrate in large numbers under a preferential quota system that gave high priority to skilled professionals. Meanwhile, a new generation of Indians, born after India gained independence from the British in 1947, but still deeply influenced by the colonial legacy, was looking abroad for economic opportunities. India itself was caught in the quagmire of a socialist economy and could not provide employment for all its engineers, doctors, and scientists, trained in its own Western-style institutions. Emigration from India to the United Kingdom was attractive during the 1950s, but less desirable in the 1960s because of increased racial conflicts and tighter immigration laws. America became the favored alternative. Travel in search of new adventure was not seen as a one-way street, but as an opportunity to explore new vistas. So, thousands of middle-class, well-educated urbanites from India boarded jet planes for New York, convinced they would return home some day. More than 30 years later, they were still coming, to both the Atlantic and Pacific coasts, and fanning out to all the major metropolitan cities of the United States, including Chicago. They raised families, sponsored relatives, diversified their population, and built strong, vibrant communities. They did go back home, but only for visits. Home was now America. In the years since they first came, they were joined by Indians from other parts of the world. Chicago's Indians include those who fled political persecution in Fiji, escaped Idi Amin's terror in Uganda, sought better economic opportunities than Canada offered, or left behind racial conflict in Trinidad. The "Chicago Indian" is the local Indian of Hyde Park or Devon Avenue or even Oakbrook or Skokie, but he or she is also unmistakably the Global Indian who maintains contact with India or the country of origin through a worldwide network sustained by family ties, trade relations, and religious, political, economic, and cultural connections.

The evolution of these new Indians, who are at once rooted in the neighborhood and globally wired, can be traced back to the 1940s, when Indian students and academics began arriving in small numbers at the University of Chicago and the Illinois Institute of Technology. Most came on Indian government scholarships and were required to return home on completion of their studies. Many chose to stay on, and these became the pioneers of a new immigrant population. Short-term visitors to Chicago during the early 1960s included about 45 engineers who trained in heavy industrial engineering at U.S. Steel and Inland Steel (Indo-American Center 2003). Among the early arrivals was Subrahmanyam Chandrasekhar (1910–95) who

accepted a faculty position at the University of Chicago in 1937, and went on to win the Nobel Prize for physics in 1983. (Another notable Indian who made his mark early in Chicago was Swami Vivekananda, who attended the first World's Parliament of Religions in 1893. He visited the Midwest frequently thereafter, leading to the establishment of the Vedanta Society of Chicago in Hyde Park in 1930.) During the 1960s, it is estimated that 350 or so Indians lived in the Chicago area.

GROWTH AND DIVERSIFICATION

The first substantial wave of immigrants to settle in Chicago after the 1965 immigration-reform law consisted almost entirely of doctors, scientists, engineers, academics, and other professionals. They came with their immediate families and, because of their high skill levels, fluency with the English language (a result of the British colonial heritage), and familiarity with Western ways, they advanced rapidly in their careers and settled in affluent suburban neighborhoods. Soon they sent for their relatives, mainly siblings and parents, under the family reunification clause of the same 1965 act. By 1980, when Indians were counted as a separate category for the first time in the U.S. census, they numbered 31,858 in the six-country Chicago metropolitan area. With each subsequent decade, their numbers have almost doubled, keeping pace with the growth of the national Asian Indian population. By the year 2000, Asian Indians became the largest group (nearly 30 percent) of Asian Americans in Illinois (Table 10.1).

The settlement patterns of Indians in Chicago have been influenced by their employment opportunities, which have shifted increasingly from the city to the suburbs since the 1950s. When Indians first came, plenty of jobs for engineers and scientists still existed in the manufacturing industries, but in subsequent decades these jobs declined in Chicago, although they continued to grow in the collar counties. More and more Indians settled directly in the suburbs, where they had access to existing support systems and new job opportunities. Still, the city population of Asian Indians also grew

TABLE 10.1. Asian Indian Population in the United States and Illinois Counties, 1980–2000

	1980	1990	2000	Growth rate 1990-2000 (%)	Asian population 2000	Asian Indians as % Asian population 2000
U.S. POPULATION	226,545,805	248,709,873	281,421,906	13		
ASIAN (U.S.)	3,466,874	6,908,638	10,242,998	48		
ASIAN INDIAN (U.S.)	387,223	815,447	1,678,765	106		16
ASIAN INDIAN (Illinois)	35,749	64,200	124,723	94	423,603	7
By county						
Cook	23,062	39,225	71,194	82	260,170	27
DuPage	6,381	14,172	30,730	117	71,252	43
Kane	510	754	1,615	114	7,296	22
Lake	1,012	2,257	5,476	143	25,105	22
McHenry	130	305	1,136	272	3,782	30
Will	763	1,279	3,549	177	11,125	32
Total six county metropolitan areas	31,858	57,992	113,700	96		
Chicago*	11,209	16,386	25,004	53	125,974	20
Suburbs	20,649	41,606	88,696	113	252,756	35

* In Cook county.

Source: U.S. Census 1980, 1990, 2000.

Note: The Asian (U.S.) category includes Bangladeshi, Burmese, Cambodians, Hmong, Indonesian, Laotian, Pakistani, Sri Lankan, and Thai.

steadily, from to 11,209 in 1980 to 16,386 in 1990 to 25,004 in 2000 (see Table 10.1). Statistically, in 1980, for every Indian living in the city, nearly two (1.8) lived in the suburbs; by 2000, that number had increased to more than three (3.5). Both Cook and DuPage counties, which recorded the highest job-growth rates, especially along the west and northwest research corridors, also saw the most substantial increases in the Indian population.

In DuPage County, Asian Indians are most concentrated in the western suburbs of Naperville and Glendale Heights. In Cook County, the highest concentrations live in the north and northwest suburbs of Schaumburg, Skokie, Hoffman Estates, and Mount Prospect Table 10.2.

Other Cook County suburbs with large concentrations of foreign born Asian Indians are Niles, Des Plaines, Bartlett, Palatine, Wheeling, Franklin Park, Schiller Park, and Elk Grove Village According to the 2000 census, the number of foreign-born Indians in the six-county metro area stands at 83,173, and Chicago continues to be a beacon for new immigrants from India.

The spread of Indians to the suburbs was accompanied by their strengthening presence in the city, especially in northern neighborhoods such as West Ridge, North Park, and Albany Park. (For a more detailed look at the growth of the retail business community on Devon Avenue in West Ridge, see Chapter 17, "Devon Avenue: A World Market.") Smaller concentrations of Asian Indians in the city are to be found in the university and medical communities in Hyde Park and the Near West Side. Both the suburban spread and city concentration are associated with changes in the socioeconomic character of the Indian community, from an elite group of professionals during the 1970s to a broader workforce that included shopkeepers, factory workers, and retail clerks during the 1980s. Those family members who followed the early Indian immigrants often lacked professional skills. They set up shops and small businesses along Devon Avenue to provide ethnic services and goods for a growing immigrant population. Whereas the 1970s immigrants were employed by manufacturing firms such as Harza Engineering and Sargent and Lundy, and by universities and research institutions such as Fermilab, Argonne, Bell Labs, and Amoco, the relatives whom they sponsored during the 1980s later joined the sales force of insurance

TABLE 10.2. Asian Indian Population in Selected Illinois Suburbs, 1980–2000

Suburb	1980	1990	2000	Growth rate % 1990 to 2000	Asian	% Asian
Naperville	327	1,468	5,126	249	12,380	41
Schaumburg	541	1,218	4,864	299	10,697	45
Skokie	880	2,292	3,944	72	13,483	29
Hoffman Estates	497	1,347	3,233	140	7,461	43
Mount Prospect	458	1,291	3,166	145	6,292	50
Glendale Heights	593	1,177	2,728	132	6,345	43
Des Plaines	482	1,051	2,216	111	4,492	49
Hanover Park	453	964	2,193	127	4,574	48
Palatine	149	240	2,132	788	4,953	43
Carol Stream	243	646	1,995	209	4,531	44
Woodridge	290	637	1,705	168	3,485	49
Addison	445	1,087	1,645	51	2,850	58
Morton Grove	223	622	1,497	141	4,980	30
Lombard	317	642	1,471	129	2,982	49
Wheeling	150	545	1,428	162	3,193	45
Niles	266	557	1,322	137	3,812	35
Westmont	299	570	1,274	124	2,935	43
Downers Grove	448	698	1,211	73	2,782	44
Evanston	314	632	1,149	82	4,524	25
Bolingbrook	406	566	1,146	102	3,591	32
Elk Grove Village	508	637	1,135	78	3,051	37
Oakbrook	151	736	918	25	1,750	52
Wheaton	261	531	786	48	2,687	29
Elmhurst	277	504	772	53	1,568	49
Bensenville	212	619	757	22	1,318	57
Forest Park	443	540	402	−26	1,071	38
Chicago	11,209	16,386	25,004	53	423,603	6

Source: U.S. Censuses, 1980, 1990, and 2000.

companies such as MetLife, New York Life, and Prudential.

The percentage of Indian immigrants admitted to the Chicago Metropolitan area under the Managerial and Professional Specialty declined from a high of 92 percent in 1972 to 52 percent in 1998, although it remained higher than for any other immigrant group from 1977 to 1996. The figures for Technical, Sales, and Administrative support rose from a low of 4 percent in 1972 to 15 percent in 1998. The Operators, Fabricators, and Laborers category for Indians has remained the lowest of all immigrant groups. Those who spoke little English joined the blue-collar workforce as taxi drivers, shop assistants, and assembly-line workers. The more enterprising among them became franchisees, and soon the city and suburbs were dotted with Indian-owned and operated Dunkin' Donuts, Subways, Pak-Mails, and gas stations.[2]

Sometimes, even the professionally trained preferred to go into business for themselves, disillusioned by discrimination in the corporate workplace or unable to find suitable employment in the recessionary environment of the 1980s. Second-generation professional Indians responded to the revitalization of the Chicago downtown business district and the resultant gentrification by moving into high-rise apartments in the Loop and Near North neighborhoods, such as Lincoln Park and Wicker Park.

IMPLICATIONS OF A GLOBAL SERVICE ECONOMY

While Chicago was shifting from a manufacturing to an information-based economy, the Indian economy was undergoing some dramatic changes that affected immigration to the United

States in complex ways. Since independence, India had followed a socialist economic policy designed to address the desperate poverty of its masses. A series of five-year plans set industrialization goals to be attained by a state-controlled industrial sector but, far from alleviating India's poverty, the policy stifled initiative or bogged it down in red tape, resulting in what was called the "Hindu rate of growth." Beginning in the 1990s, the Congress government instituted a series of changes that slashed tariffs, invited external competition, and made the rupee convertible on world money markets. Changes in the world economy were not lost on Indians planning to immigrate to America. Word of the decline of the manufacturing sector in the United States spread in India, where more and more immigrant applicants were preparing themselves for life in America by obtaining skills in the service sector, as computer programmers, management consultants, or physical therapists.Educational levels among Asian Indians are the highest in the six-county metropolitan area. Nearly two-thirds (64.8 percent) of Asian Indians have a bachelor's degree; 31.5 percent have a master's, professional, or doctorate degree A boom in software development occurred in India, which soon became the world's largest supplier of programmers. The computer industry spawned rapid and remarkable wealth in the Indian immigrant community, more so in California than in Illinois, where the economy is more diversified. But, highly qualified Indians also complained of being exploited and having to work much harder than their white counterparts for less pay.

Other fields in which new employment opportunities opened up for Indians in Chicago included special services, such as priests in the Indian religious institutions that sprang up across the Chicago region, or chefs in the expanding Indian restaurant industry. By 2003, many teachers trained in India were migrating to fill vacancies in Chicago-area schools after being interviewed via the Internet (*Indian Reporter* 4 April 2003). In an opposite trend, many U.S.-born Indian professionals returned to India to live the good life in their homeland, while would-be immigrants were discouraged from making the move because of a thriving economy and improved job prospects at home.

The liberalization of the Indian economy resulted in increased business interaction between Chicago's Indians and their homeland. Not only did they invest their dollars in emerging markets in India to provide badly needed infrastructure and technical expertise, they also helped U.S.-based companies such as AT&T, Lucent, GE, Motorola, and Hewitt Associates with their Indian operations by moving back to India to provide managerial and technical support. In another globalizing trend, American companies looked to India to set up their backroom offices for remote outsourcing, in which customer-service calls placed from the United Service about computer problems, credit card bills, and Internet accounts were answered by call centers in New Delhi, Mumbai, or Bangalore by specially trained "American-speaking" college graduates. Major companies with call centers in India include GE, American Express, Citibank, and British Airways. So, although advanced satellite communications technology enables Indian Americans and American companies to span the globe and conduct transnational business, it also reduces immigration by making it more attractive for Indians to stay in their homeland.

SOCIOECONOMIC DIVIDE

A detailed look at different sets of income figures for Asian Indians in Illinois and a comparison with other groups shows that, behind the image of a prosperous community, disturbing signs of inequalities emerge. Income distribution patterns among Asian Indian households in Illinois show that, although a fairly healthy proportion (40 percent) occupy the $50,000 to $100,000 income bracket, a significant section (nearly 15 percent) also occupies the under-$25,000 category (Table 10.3).

As with other immigrant groups, those who live in Cook County have the lowest income (Table 10.4), but the income disparities between Cook and other counties is not as wide for Asian Indians as it is for other groups.

We need to look beyond county figures for the real economic divide in the community, which exists between Asian Indians living in

TABLE 10.3. Income Distribution for Asian Indian Households in Illinois, 2000

Income	Households	%
Less than $10,000	2,169	6
$10,000 to $14,999	977	3
$15,000 to $19,999	1,027	3
$20,000 to $24,999	1,383	4
$25,000 to $29,999	1,370	4
$30,000 to $34,999	1,688	4
$35,000 to $39,999	1,543	4
$40,000 to $44,999	1,626	4
$45,000 to $49,999	1,560	4
$50,000 to $59,999	3,649	10
$60,000 to $74,999	6,056	16
$75,000 to $99,999	5,734	15
$100,000 to $124,999	3,521	9
$125,000 to $149,999	2,110	6
$150,000 to $199,999	1,982	5
$200,000 or more	1,964	5
Total	38,359	

Source: U.S. Census, 2000.

the city and the suburbs. For example, the median household income for Asian Indians in Chicago is only $42,979, compared with $72,073 in Schaumburg and $72,875 in Des Plaines, all of which are within Cook County (Table 10.5).

But not all suburbs have affluent Indians, either. In DuPage County, for example, Naperville's Asian Indians enjoy a median family income of $96,926, compared with Glendale Heights Asian Indians, whose family income averages $57,019.

Yet another indication of income disparities is seen in the high poverty levels of Asian Indians in Chicago compared with those in Illinois and the United States as a whole (Table 10.6).

In Chicago, the numbers of Asian Indians living in poverty in different categories (such as female heads of households and children under 18) is much greater than among Asian Indians elsewhere. This issue is demanding increasing attention, as seen in the growing number of Asian Indian social service agencies in Chicago. It shatters the model-minority myth and shows that the Asian Indian community is beset by the same problems that afflict other immigrant groups in the city.

BUILDING A COHERENT COMMUNITY

Even as Asian Indians have developed class disparities, evolving from an elite vanguard group to a socioeconomically diversified lot, they have organized themselves along national, religious, linguistic, professional, gender, and even age-related issues, marshaling their resources and technical expertise to build a variety of institutions that are at once local and global in nature.

Among the earliest of the pan-Indian immigrant organizations in Chicago were the India League of America (1972), renamed the ILA Foundation, and the Federation of India Associations, which organizes Indian Independence Day celebrations on Devon Avenue. Other organizations, such as the National Federation of Indian American Associations and the Association of Indians in America (which helped obtain a separate U.S. census category and minority status for Asian Indians), are headquartered in New York and have chapters in Chicago.[3] Over the years, the increased immigration of diverse groups from all parts of India (India has 30 states and 18 official languages) has enabled Indians to organize along narrower lines as Gujaratis, Punjabis, Tamils, Malayalees, Bengalis, and the

TABLE 10.4. Median Household Income for Asians in the Six-County Area

	Cook County	DuPage County	Kane County	Lake County	McHenry County	Will County	Chicago PMSA*
Philippines	$63,925	$77,082	$75,707	$77,418	$85,355	$72,614	$68,273
India	$60,428	$76,555	$70,104	$81,090	$76,783	$81,721	$65,509
Korea	$40,955	$61,522	$68,750	$77,190	–	$81,131	$45,334
China/Taiwan	$44,040	$91,393	$87,208	$94,506	$58,000	$84,500	$52,465
Total	$45,922	$67,887	$59,351	$66,973	$64,826	$62,238	$51,680

Source: U.S. Census, 2000.
Note: PMSA = Primary Metropolitan Statistical Area.

TABLE 10.5. Income Levels for Asian Indians, 2000 (in Illinois counties and select Chicago suburbs with Asian Indian populations over 1,000)

Geography	Total Asian Indian population	Median household income in 1999 ($)	Median family income in 1999 ($)	Per capita income in 1999($)	Male median earnings in 1999($)	Female median earnings in 1999($)
Illinois	123,275	64,969	70,331	26,094	51,101	31,928
BY COUNTY						
Cook	71,194	60,428	64,955	24,114	45,432	30,864
DuPage	30,730	76,555	78,970	28,240	59,252	34,688
Kane	1,615	70,104	70,560	22,647	50,962	29,609
Lake	5,476	81,090	90,580	32,105	60,827	40,638
McHenry	1,136	76,783	78,239	33,904	42,419	28,250
Will	3,549	81,721	88,718	27,942	65,313	31,042
BY PLACE						
Chicago City	24,208	42,979	49,500	21,262	36,860	32,470
Naperville city	4,674	92,686	96,926	31,557	78,092	52,829
Schaumburg village	4,529	72,073	75,739	33,111	60,858	31,182
Skokie village	3,845	66,071	66,173	20,697	36,738	28,320
Mount Prospect village	3,155	57,955	59,176	19,337	44,135	21,563
Glendale Heights village	2,780	57,063	57,019	14,857	35,216	22,184
Hoffman Estates village	2,740	66,250	66,892	20,262	45,125	27,670
Palatine village	2,210	66,818	68,750	25,663	56,419	36,146
Des Plaines city	1,953	72,875	72,875	19,098	40,362	30,000
Hanover Park village	1,895	60,625	61,250	17,340	35,845	23,382
Carol Stream village	1,823	62,885	63,510	21,193	41,554	30,871
Addison village	1,652	61,304	61,685	21,910	43,456	24,417
Woodridge village	1,644	60,817	59,833	27,879	52,857	28,359
Morton Grove	1,532	72,171	72,171	18,983	48,309	35,326
Aurora city	1,495	73,929	80,024	27,540	67,188	35,650
Wheeling village	1,398	68,514	68,784	24,691	46,635	30,852
Niles village	1,366	68,646	63,295	17,120	32,054	31,458
Westmont village	1,352	66,875	75,696	23,883	55,179	41,615
Downers Grove village	1,341	82,809	87,992	27,728	62,396	33,393
Lombard village	1,304	65,353	65,929	24,596	61,402	29,861
Streamwood village	1,236	72,292	72,500	25,977	51,364	34,773
Evanston city	1,204	71,667	84,023	28,157	68,500	37,656
Bolingbrook village	1,091	83,264	92,144	25,388	60,865	27,336
Elk Grove Village village	1,068	83,376	84,438	33,183	55,714	25,521

Source: U.S. Census, 2000 (SF4).

like. Scores of regional cultural organizations exist within the Chicago area, with membership ranging from less than a hundred families to thousands. Each of these groups celebrates the regional cuisine, music and dance, arts and crafts, and special festivals particular to their own region in India. This trend must be seen in light of the changes India itself was undergoing during the 1980s and 1990s—the assertion of regionalism, the devolution of power from the center to greater autonomy for the states, and the shift from central, one-party Congress rule to rule by a coalition of regional parties. Diver-

sification may go hand-in-hand with stability in India, and there is no reason to believe it could not be the same for a pluralistic Indian immigrant population in Chicago.

Organizing along these lines has helped Chicagoans extend the idea of community well beyond geographical boundaries to include India and the rest of the world. Scattered as they are in the Chicago metropolitan area, individuals can come together physically as Indians for major association events, while also connecting in less tangible ways via the Internet to promote common causes. Every one of these associations

TABLE 10.6. Poverty Levels for Asian Indians, 2000

Poverty status in 1999 (below poverty level)	U.S.	Illinois	Chicago
Families	27,947	1,526	667
Percent below poverty level	7	5	13
Families w female householder, no husband present	4,410	246	97
Percent below poverty level	22	18	24
Individuals	157,516	9,167	4,334
Percent below poverty level	10	8	19
Elderly (65 years & over)	5,542	152	31
Percent below poverty level	9	4	5
Related children under 18 yrs.	37,547	2,289	1,146
Percent below poverty level	9	8	25

Source: U.S. Census 2000: Profile of Selected Economic Characteristics. Summary File #4.

has a well-constructed website kept up-to-date by a tech-savvy immigrant population.

Although no official count exists of the religious affiliation of immigrant groups in the U.S. census, it is estimated that 80 percent of Chicago's Indians are Hindu, reflecting roughly the same proportion as in the homeland. Muslims in India comprise less than 15 percent of the total population, but it is difficult to estimate the proportion of Chicago's Indian Muslims because they form a religious cohort with Muslims from other South Asian countries, such as Pakistan and Bangladesh. Indeed, South Asian Muslims tend to worship with Muslims of other nationalities, including Muslims from Central Asia and the Middle East as well as African Americans. According to the Islamic Circle of North America, forty-four mosques exist in metropolitan Chicago (See Chapter 14). Other significant religious groups include Christians (both Catholic and Protestant), Zoroastrians, Jains, and Sikhs. Each of these religious groups has flourished in Chicago, its members transplanting many of their religious practices from the homeland, but also transforming them in unique ways to suit their new environment.

The politicization of Hindu religious groups in India with the growth of the Bharatiya Janata Party (BJP) has been tied to the growth of similar movements in Chicago's Indian immigrant community, especially among the Hindu Swayamsevak Sangh, which is said to have about fifty active members in the greater Chicago area and is part of the Rashtriya Swayamsevak Sangh, a Hindu nationalist grassroots organization in India. The Hindu Students' Councils are very active on U.S. university campuses, and the Vishwa Hindu Parishad, a religious body closely tied to India's ruling Bharatiya Janata Party, has an active chapter in Chicago. Hindus and Muslims voice their concerns over religious extremism in India and display their solidarity conspicuously in parades and symbolic marches through neighborhoods where Hindus and Muslims live and work together, as on Devon Avenue. However, they tend to lead distinctly separate social lives because their social and cultural activities are very often faith based.

No matter what their religion, Chicago's Indians use their involvement with religious groups not only to practice their faith, but also for social, cultural, charitable, and political purposes. The different religious structures are not just intriguing additions to Chicago's architectural landscape, they provide immigrants with an oasis or safe haven where they can be themselves, as though they were back in the homeland. Indians also give back to their homeland through these institutions, by making charitable donations to specific causes and by promoting the spread of their religious heritage here in America.

Religion is the means by which Indians gather on a worldwide scale at global conventions, so that they can connect with Hindus, Muslims, Christians, and other beliefs from other parts of the world. For many immigrants, religious activity is much more intense here than it was in the homeland, where they were likely to take it for granted. Particularly after the terrorist attacks of September 11, 2001, Indians have become aware of a new vulnerability and the need to educate their fellow Americans about their religion. Global terrorism has necessitated a new kind of activism among Indian immigrants. Not only Muslims and Sikhs, who are immediately targeted because of their names or their appearance, but all South Asians have become aware that they are likely to be mistakenly targeted for their ethnicity.

Chicago has an astonishing variety of home-grown institutions that cater to the cultural needs of the Indian community and spread its influence among the broader population. Parents who desired to impart Indian culture to their children through artistic traditions spurred a demand for dance and music schools, and soon a variety of them sprang up, each one devoted to a different classical or folk tradition. A new genre of fusion is emerging as dancers trained in the Indian classical tradition blend with Western dance practitioners, and the strains of sitar music harmonize with Afro-Latin reggae rhythms in innovative bands. *Mehndi* (henna tattoo) salons have opened up throughout the Chicago area, staffed by South Asians, but catering to a much wider population. Other examples are of Bollywood[4] movies playing in major multiplex movie theaters in the suburbs of Warrenville and Barrington on the same day they are released in India. Indians are also spreading the popularity of the one game they are passionate about—cricket. Little known in the United States but widely played in England's former colonies (including Pakistan, Bangladesh, Sri Lanka, and countries of Africa and the Caribbean), the game is propagated in Chicago by immigrants from all these colonies. Several leagues play competitive cricket in tournaments throughout the Chicago area.

CREATING A POLITICAL AGENDA

A vital step toward being involved in American politics is acquiring citizenship, and Indians have been doing that in steadily increasing numbers, mainly to take advantage of laws that enable citizens to sponsor new family members for immigration and to qualify for Social Security and welfare benefits. About 41 percent of Asian Indians in Illinois are naturalized citizens (Table 10.7).

The earliest immigrants are most likely to be naturalized. Eighty-five percent of those who entered before 1980 are naturalized, as are 61 percent of those who came between 1980 and 1989.

TABLE 10.7. Nativity, Citizenship Status, and Year of Entry for Asian Indians in Illinois, 2000

Nativity & year of entry	Asian Indian	%
Native	32,476	26.3
Foreign born	90,799	73.7
Naturalized citizen	36,868	40.6
Not a citizen	53,931	59.4
Entered 1990 to March 2000	48,577	53.5
Naturalized citizen	6,577	13.5
Not a citizen	42,000	86.5
Entered 1980 to 1989	23,153	25.5
Naturalized citizen	14,025	60.6
Not a citizen	9,128	39.4
Entered before 1980	19,069	21.0
Naturalized citizen	16,266	85.3
Not a citizen	2,803	14.7
Total Population	123,275	

Source: U.S. Census 2000: Nativity, Citizenship, Year of Entry, and Region of Birth, (Summary File #4).

Among those who arrived between 1990 and March 2000, only 14 percent are naturalized. This is understandable, because many of them may not even qualify for citizenship. The number of registered voters, however, is still far below citizenship levels; thus, the Indo-American Democratic Organization (IADO) organizes periodic voter registration drives to encourage Indians to become more politically involved. IADO was founded in Chicago in 1980, and it lobbies on behalf of the Indian American community on issues such as immigration, affirmative action, education, social security, health care reform, and hate crimes. It works with local politicians sympathetic to Indian American issues and promotes India's interests with Washington lawmakers through the India Caucus. (The Congressional Caucus on India was formed in 1994, with a view to educating members of Congress on issues relating to India and enabling them to influence policy in India's favor.)

However, IADO's attempts to get Indians elected to political office have not borne fruit. This is partly because Indians are widely scattered in the suburbs and don't have the geographical concentration conducive to forming effective voting blocks, as the Latinos and African Americans in Chicago have been able to achieve. After the 2000 census figures were released, IADO did try to address redistricting issues in the north and northwest, where Indians have some sort of concentration, but this effort did not meet with much success. In 2003, only two Indians occupied elected office in the Chicago area: Niles Township Collector Pramod Shah and Skokie trustee Usha Kamaria. Rena Van Tine, associate judge in Cook County, is the first Indian American judge in the United States. Others who are recognized and rewarded for their fund-raising efforts and interest in politics include Niranjan Shah, appointed Trustee of the University of Illinois, and Iftekar Shareef, appointed Trustee of Northeastern Illinois University in 2003. Many members of Chicago's Indian American community were part of President Clinton's entourage when he visited India in March 2000. Politicians running for office seek IADO's official endorsement, but also woo prominent donors who hold the purse strings.[5] IADO officers lament that many wealthy Indians prefer to act in their individual capacity, by donating to the campaign funds of front-runners such as Hillary Clinton for New York senator and Rod Blagojevich for Illinois governor. Although this gains high visibility for the individual donors and helps them curry favor with the elected politicians, it does little for the community as a whole.

Grassroots community activists tend to be more coalition-oriented, and rely on partnerships under the Asian American umbrella or with other minority groups on issues of common concern. For example, members of the Indian American community are appointed to the Governor's Advisory Council on Asian American Affairs and are part of the Asian American Coalition of Chicago, Asian Health Coalition of Illinois, and the Asian American Coalition Committee at the University of Illinois. A number of Indian American organizations co-sponsored a bill with other groups representing Asian American populations to introduce the study of Asian American history into the Illinois school curriculum. They also fought, albeit unsuccessfully, to be included in the city's "set-aside" program, which benefited other minority communities seen to be less advantaged than Asian Americans. When it comes to immigration issues, civil rights, or voter registration drives, Indian Americans may work with Latino and African American groups in the city for greater effect. Indian American politics in Illinois are still at a nascent stage, but the ability of Indian Americans to get elected in other parts of the country has been a source of inspiration.[6]

Homeland politics continues to generate excitement in the community for several reasons. Ties to India remain strong because three-quarters (75.4 percent) of Asian Indians are foreign-born and nearly half (49.6 percent) are relatively young, between the ages of 20 and 44 (U.S. Census 2000). The continuous flow of new immigrants from India keeps connections to the homeland alive, and the Indian government has recently taken concrete steps (such as approving dual citizenship and hosting conventions that draw nonresident Indians from all over the world) to cultivate new connections with Indian Americans. Different political parties in India maintain ties with Indians in Chicago through organizations such as Overseas Friends of the BJP and Overseas Friends of Congress. The involvement of expatriates in homeland politics is always controversial and particularly so in the Indian community, where the specter of religious fundamentalism looms large. Although religious conflict in India spurs some of Chicago's Asian Indians to politico-religious activism, domestic and global politics on the post 9/11 war on terror has left Asian Indians scared and confused. On the one hand, they want to build solidarity with their fellow Indians who are Muslims and Sikhs and particularly vulnerable; on the other hand, to avoid trouble, the tendency exists to distance themselves from Pakistanis and Muslims from other countries black-listed by Homeland Security. The more they are exhorted to shed the baggage of homeland politics, the more it seems to dog them in an increasingly shrinking globalized world.

GENDER AND INTERGENERATIONAL ISSUES

Indian women have migrated to the Chicago area in as large numbers as Indian men, and have even exceeded their numbers in some years when they came to join their husbands (according to data from the U.S. Immigration and Naturalization Service 1972–98). A majority of these women are educated professionals—according to the 2000 census, the percentage of females in the managerial and professional category in Illinois is 51.4 percent. Although census figures tell a story of prosperity and high achievement among professional women, the parallel growth of an undocumented and unprotected labor sector also exists, where females work under difficult conditions at poorly paid jobs. A significant percentage (12.5 percent for Asian Indian women in Illinois compared with the state-wide figure of 8.3 percent for Illinois women) work in production jobs. Many women work in family-owned establishments, such as in the back rooms of restaurants on Devon Avenue, or in the unorganized sector as baby-sitters, domestics, or self-employed providers of goods and services to the Indian community.

No matter what the socioeconomic level of Indian women, they are vulnerable to the same gender-related exploitation as other American women. *Apna Ghar,* a Chicago shelter geared to the needs of South Asian women, has served over 3,800 domestic-violence clients since its inception in 1990. Apna Ghar is part of a network of such organizations that have sprung up throughout the United States and Canada. The women who seek help range from wealthy suburbanites and professionals to illiterate women who were brought as immigrant wives from villages in India and abandoned by their husbands. Another special-interest gender-related support group in the community is *Khuli Zaban* for South Asian gays and lesbians in Chicago.

An interesting aspect of these service organizations is their ability to draw upon national and international resources. Social activists and artists operate as if national borders did not exist, moving between Chicago and Delhi or Mumbai with remarkable speed and ease of travel. As for those who need these social services, at least here in the Midwest, a dearth of studies exist on the lower-income population and minority issues. Gender and labor activism are subjects much better documented among the Asian Indian communities of the East and West Coasts.

For the second generation, the main issues revolve around gender, sexuality, and career choices. Many Indian youth have followed the path set down by their parents and have pursued high-paying professions in engineering, medicine, and law. However, rebellion also arises in the ranks, and more and more young Indians are choosing their own paths and opting for lower-paying or riskier professions including show business, primary education, and social service. Young women complain that their parents subject them to stricter standards regarding dating and sexual behavior than they do men, while both men and women feel the pressure to adhere to Indian customs and resist Americanization. Suicide among Indian youth who feel these pressures is a cause for concern, but the community is not yet willing to acknowledge or discuss these matters openly.

The growth of the youth population has been accompanied by a rapid increase in the number of aging Indians. Of the four leading contemporary immigrant groups to the Chicago metro area, Indians have the highest average age. This higher average is partly caused by an increasing number of elderly and retired parents who immigrate to join their adult children. (India has no state-sponsored social security system, and the elderly are usually provided for by the family. All Indians, regardless of religion, feel morally bound to support their elderly parents.) But adjusting to life in America is particularly difficult for the elderly. Research on Indian American elders in Chicago, done by the Indo-American Center located in the heart of Chicago's South Asian business district, has shown that they experience loneliness, economic and social vulnerability, and are disadvantaged by the lack of linguistically appropriate health care and social services, subsidized housing, and accessible transportation.

NOT WHITE OR BLACK BUT BROWN

Indians in Chicago have enjoyed vigorous growth as a community for nearly 40 years, thanks in part to demographic diversity in terms of age, class, occupation, gender, and settlement patterns. Another key factor may have been the ambiguity in the minds of other Chicagoans regarding the racial identity of Indians. How else to account for the fact that, in a city notorious for violent racial conflict and structurally racist practices such as redlining, Indians have emerged relatively unscathed? The early immigrants were not at all sure of this outcome. During the 1970s, fierce controversy raged in the community as to which racial category Indians should identify themselves. Some community members advocated a low profile and recommended trying to merge into the white population by categorizing themselves as "Other" in the census, whereas others lobbied vigorously to be classified as a "minority" group because they felt they were discriminated against and disadvantaged just as much as blacks (Elkhanialy and Nicholas 1976). Indians were counted as a separate category under the Asian American umbrella for the very first time in the 1980 census and, since then, it has been possible to track the growth and make-up of the community in quantitative terms. This classification may have long-term implications for the Indian community. Given their generally high professional and economic status, and the fact that they are not seen as "black," are they likely to get more and more absorbed into the mainstream? Or, will their cultural distinctiveness, their tendency to intermarry within their own ethnic group, and their desire to maintain strong links to the homeland keep them perpetually apart, rendering them more vulnerable to discrimination as has happened in other countries where Indians have a longer history as an immigrant population? Will this lead to an increasing proportion of lower-income Indians in the population?

Chicago's Asian Indians share many of the same concerns faced by other Chicagoans—economic and social threats to the community stemming from socioeconomic inequalities and the sharing of political power and limited resources with other immigrants while also making significant cultural contributions to life of the city. Other important issues are civil rights—especially after 9/11, a tightening of immigration laws, and stringent visa restrictions. Asian Indians also worry about lack of education and

employment opportunities, and the dearth of health and human services as the number of underinsured and unskilled increase in their midst. They know they have a long way to go in terms of fair political representation, and they are concerned about a growing class divide between the haves and have-nots in their own community. These issues affect even those who don't think of themselves as immigrants. But, beyond these concerns shared with other Chicagoans, Asian Indians have an identity that is truly global in nature. As prolific users of the Internet and members of international organizations, through their frequency of international travel, and connectivity via the telecommuncations network, their direct access to products and services throughout the world, and their strong links to the homeland, they have shown that immigration is no longer a simple matter of relocating from one part of the world to another. It is, instead, a matter of being an integral part of a dense web of international relationships that affects every aspect of their lives. On one hand, its homogenizing effects are seen in the way Indians are becoming Chicagoans and integrating into American society. On the other hand, it has helped Chicago's Indians keep their individual culture alive and spread it far beyond their original homeland.

NOTES

1. Interview conducted by the author and Lakshmi Menon with Singh's daughter and son-in-law Shiela and Aspy Tantra, at their home in Hyde Park on January 15, 2003. Singh's grandparents migrated from Patna in eastern India to Grenada as indentured labor under the British, who shipped millions of Indians to the Caribbean and other colonies to replace slave labor in the plantations during the mid nineteenth century. Singh's wife Nerissa, also of Indian origin from Grenada, became the first woman to earn a medical degree from the Chicago Medical School, in 1959.

2. Indians built their niches in the workforce, as did other immigrant groups, because of many different factors. Whereas the success of the vanguard group is attributed to their educational and professional skills, the success of later arrivals in the franchising industry is attributed to their thrifty ways, ability to bring in large amounts of capital, and willingness to put in

long hours working with family members, all qualities needed to turn around failing businesses. Immigration laws that allowed Asian Indians to bring in workers as family members rather than through labor certification laws also helped them consolidate their businesses.

3. For details on these and other religious, cultural, and social organizations in the Chicago area, see *Namaste America.*

4. Similar to Hollywood, the U.S. film capital, Bollywood is named after Bombay, India. and represents the largest film industry and has the widest audience within and outside of India.

5. IADO Political Action Committee Report is filed with the Illinois State Board of Elections and advertised in Chicago's Asian Indian media. *Indian Reporter,* March 15, 2002.

6. Kumar Barve was elected to the Maryland legislature in 1991 and elevated to House Majority Leader in 2003; Satveer Chaudhury rose from the Minnesota House (1996) to the Senate (2000) and to Majority Whip (2002). Republican Bobby Jindal's run for governor of Louisiana in 2003, and his surprisingly strong showing in the preliminary rounds, opened the eyes of other Indian Americans to possibilities beyond the Democratic Party.

Yvonne M. Lau

11   Re-Visioning Filipino American Communities: Evolving Identities, Issues, and Organizations

CHICAGO AS A MECCA FOR
YESTERDAY'S PENSIONADOS AND
TODAY'S FILIPINAS

The first recorded group of Filipinos arrived in Illinois 100 years ago. In 1906, shortly after America's victory in the Spanish American War, 178 Filipino college students were sponsored by the government to study in the United States. Nearly a quarter (24 percent) of the "pensionados" entered schools in Illinois, including the University of Chicago and the University of Illinois. This early migration of educated Filipinos to the Chicago region, spurred by the colonialist relationship between the United States and the Philippines, would set the context for future Filipino occupational groups. Despite changing patterns in occupational preferences and in the gendered migration of labor, the flow of transnational workers continues today as, especially, Filipinas (women born in the Philippines) are recruited to Chicago to fulfill the fluctuating needs of the American labor market.

Unlike the larger Filipino concentrations of agricultural and migrant workers in Hawaii and the West Coast during the late nineteenth and early twentieth centuries, Chicago's *Pinoy* (referring to male Filipinos who entered the United States prior to World War II) community was highly educated. Although part-time or former students who stayed in Chicago were mostly limited to service or low-level white-collar jobs because of discriminatory labor practices, Chicago retained its reputation as an educational mecca. This image was fueled by success stories told by the first wave of elite pensionados who returned

to the Philippines, Chicago degrees in-hand, ready to help lead in the administration of the Islands (Posadas and Guyotte 1990).

Today, Filipino Americans in Chicago, with the highest median household income of any immigrant group, are generally regarded as upwardly mobile, affluent professionals who have easily "assimilated" into Chicago and suburban neighborhoods. Although specific demographic trends will be discussed later, the overall images and socioeconomic indicators associated with Filipino Americans are overwhelmingly positive, to the degree that Filipino American leaders complain about their invisibility. Yet, despite individual or family success stories, the current status and future health of the larger Filipino American community is perceived to be problematic. Although it is challenging to attain consensus from Chicago's diverse Filipino American communities, given the divisions of class, occupation, region, generation, and the like, recent interviews with a cross-section of key community leaders and observers indicate that community factionalism dominates discussions on the current state of the Filipino American community.

The Persistent Gaze on Unity

Appointed and elected leaders affiliated with nonprofit agencies and community-based organizations express concern that the Filipino American community has become dysfunctional and ineffective in addressing community problems and needs. Although the first (pre–World War II) and second (1945–64) waves of

Filipino migration created a more concentrated and homogeneous community residing within Chicago, the third wave of post-1965 immigrants has generated numerous subgroups with competing interests and needs. Given that the continuing influx of immigrants and demand for overseas Filipino workers widens the diversity of the overall population, community residents and organizational representatives are aware of the growing divide between early Filipinos, Filipino Americans, and recent immigrants. Expressing a wide range of opinions on how the Filipino American community reached this level of fragmentation, interviewees are anxious about a range of issues, especially affecting family and community welfare.

The persistent preoccupation or debate about "unity" among Filipinos is not a recent phenomenon. It spans a hundred years, especially among Filipinos living abroad and here in the Midwest. The early pensionados recognized the importance of group unity when working with members of some indigenous tribes at the 1904 St. Louis World's Fair's Philippine Reservation exhibit; after this popular exhibit, Filipinos became stereotyped as wild, tribal savages. These earliest Filipino students felt under attack, and were compelled to create a united front, presenting their homeland as a model case for independence. Controversy over how their homeland should be depicted at the Chicago World's Fair in 1933 again provoked a call for unity and temporarily united the Chicago-based Filipino community (Posadas and Guyotte 1990). The overall importance of moving American popular opinion toward embracing the image of a civilized nation, deserving of independence, provided a common agenda for the different Filipino immigrant and student communities.

Today, while conflicts involving community events like the Rizal Day commemorations have diminished—focusing instead on the annual Philippine Independence Week—leadership wars are common. Honoring Dr. Jose Rizal, who became the Philippines' national hero by his publicizing of Spanish misrule and subsequent execution, Rizal Days were started by the pensionados. In the early 1930s, three competing Rizal celebrations involving a

banquet, dance, and queen contest occurred on the same evenings. A split in the original Filipino Association of Chicago erupted over disagreements about the length of the speaker's table. The community complained about repercussions from this "lack of unity" because it fueled the stereotypical public perceptions of Filipinos as "inferior—and incapable of governing themselves as a nation" (Posadas and Guyotte 1990). In recent years, vying for leadership for June's Philippine Independence Week celebrations presents continuing challenges to the public mandate for unity in the face of community factionalism.

Transnational Ties and Community Linkages

Today, despite overcoming overt racism and achieving some measures of success, rising individual or group mobility has not necessarily led toward full assimilation or a stronger Filipino American community. Participation in Filipino activities, including ethnic-based organizations and community life, is still meaningful for the upwardly mobile. Attaining high socioeconomic status does not negate interest in homeland politics and community affairs, however. As discussed in later sections, the spiraling growth of Filipino American organizations—250 organizations are registered at the Chicago office of the Philippine Consulate—and community-based institutions should not indicate a waning interest in Filipino American affairs. To the contrary, the quest for community recognition has created an organizational and community culture in which the pressures abound to be viewed as a leader and be recognized as a winner. According to some community observers, volunteerism or participation in a majority of Filipino-based organizations is only coveted when one can be elected as an officer of the group, not serve as a mere member.

Consequently, this chapter investigates both quantitative and qualitative indicators of well-being for the Filipino American community in metropolitan Chicago. Using Census 2000 data, quantitative indicators will highlight the aggregate socioeconomic status of Filipino American residents in Chicago and the metropolitan, six-county area. Contributing to the literature on ethnicity and identity, this chapter also integrates ethnographic research to uncover the process of forming ethnic and national identities. The degree to which "Filipinoness" or "Filipino Americanness" may reflect transnational and constructed identities serves as another focus.

Of all the immigrant groups coming to New Chicago, Filipino Americans may enjoy the distinction of representing the group with the longest record of transnational ties between the homeland and Chicago. With the first group of 42 pensionados admitted to Chicago schools in 1906, successive waves of Filipino immigrants, and a second group of nurses recruited to work at Cook County Hospital during the 1930s, linkages were established that would foster ongoing economic, social, and political exchanges. Investigating the past and current experiences of Filipino Americans in Chicago offers rich data to understand the factors shaping multifaceted and transnational identities.

Research on Filipino immigrants in the United States, including those in Chicago, must be contextualized within the history of United States–Philippines relations, which has been marked by colonialism and occupation. Filipino migration to Chicago—one of our major immigrant cities—cannot be viewed as merely a linear process of arrival, adjustment, and assimilation to the host society. For Filipino immigrants, acculturation to U.S. society and capitalism started not at the juncture of immigration, but in the homeland, where U.S. institutions and mores had already influenced their lives and opportunity structures. Compared to other Asian immigrant groups, Filipinos alone carry the unique burden of emigrating from a former U.S. colony, thus leading to their formation both as a racialized minority in the United States and as transnational migrants shaped by colonialism and capital investments in the Philippines (Lowe 1996, 8).

Expanding the concept of racial formation, Filipino American racial formation partially stems from economic, social, and political interaction between the United States and the Philippines; from U.S. (neo)colonialism in the Philippines; and from the position of the homeland within the global racial order (Espiritu 1995, 26).

Consequently, any study of Filipino Americans must consider their dual histories of being a racialized minority in the United States and as colonized nationals while in their homeland. Investigating the lives and experiences of Filipino Americans in Chicago requires that we consider their convergent status as colonized nationals, transnational immigrants, and a racialized minority. Such a study must also address how the experiences of colonialism and migration affect and change Filipino Americans, and how they decide to shape and reformulate their social worlds and communities in the United States.

EARLY HISTORY: THE SEEDS OF A FILIPINO AMERICAN COMMUNITY

Most of the pensionados of the early 1900s intended to secure their higher education and return to the Philippines to help build and modernize their homeland. World wars and changing immigration policies deterred some from returning and stranded others as permanent exiles.

By 1920, 154 Filipinos were counted in Chicago by the U.S. Census. Twenty years later, the population had risen to 1,740. Unofficial estimates placed about 5,000 Filipinos as living in Chicago prior to World War II (Posadas and Guyotte 1998, 139). Typically, during this period, most of the Filipino settlers in the Chicago area were males with some college experience who had to work to support their education. Available jobs were confined to the service industry as menial laborers, for example, busboys, waiters, and bellhops. Several hundred found jobs with the Pullman Company, as attendants and porters. The U.S. Post Office was viewed as a better employer, because it provided security and relative affluence. More than 200 Filipino Americans were employed as clerks and laborers, leading to the formation of the Filipino Postal Club. The latter contributed to the invisible history of early Asian American activism, when it successfully resisted attempts by the American

Legion to have Filipinos dismissed from the federal civil service (Posadas and Guyotte 1990). As one post-World War II Filipina interviewee describes: "Al, my husband, came to Chicago in 1924, having worked on the pineapple plantations in Hawaii. The best job he could get was at the main post office, downtown on Canal. After he worked his way through Northwestern, getting his engineering degree in 1931, he couldn't get a job as an engineer... there were many highly educated at the P.O."

From 1898 until 1934, Filipinos were classified as U.S. nationals and provided unrestricted entry to the United States as replacement labor (as opposed to earlier legal exclusion of Chinese and other Asian groups), yet they were not eligible for citizenship. Fueled by the intensifying anti-Asian movement on the Pacific Coast from the 1920s through the 1930s, public sentiment against Filipinos grew, erupting into riots and massacres. In California, legislative testimony reflected negative stereotypes, characterizing Filipinos as economic threats and social menaces. Anti-miscegenation laws were expanded to include Filipinos. By 1934, the Tydings-McDuffy Act was passed to grant the Philippines independence in ten years (which was delayed until 1946 by World War II), thereby reclassifying Filipinos from U.S. nationals to aliens; their immigration was limited to 50 per year (Dela Cruz and Agbayani-Siewert 2003, 47).

In recognition of contributions in U.S. military service during World War II, the Filipino annual quota was raised to 100 in 1946. More significantly, those Filipinos already in the United States became eligible for naturalized citizenship. Until 1965, this paved the way for the majority of Filipinos who entered the United States to be admitted as nonquota immigrants, following the family reunification goals of the McCarran-Walter Act of 1952 (Posadas 1999, 31). Also, under the War Brides Act of 1945, Filipino American families finally appeared in the United States. Filipina wives, children, and fiancées of U.S. servicemen were allowed entry into the United States as nonquota immigrants (Acierto 1994, 70). By 1960, 2,725 Filipinos were counted in the Chicago area, reflecting the small numbers of early *manongs*, elderly men who arrived before the 1930s (Posadas 1999, 164).

POST-1965 IMMIGRATION: CHANGING DEMOGRAPHICS

With the passage of the 1965 Immigration Act, Filipino immigration surged, as many entered the United States through the occupational and family preferences priority of the Act. Although initially new Filipino American immigrants entered through the professional preference of HI-B visas, especially as physicians and nurses, family links also accounted for a significant number of new arrivals. Nationally, between 1966 and 1991, larger percentages of Filipinos entered through exempt and preference-driven family reunification. Those who entered under occupational preferences accounted for merely 10 percent of the annual total of immigrants from the Philippines to the United States between 1977 and 1991 (Posadas 1999, 36).

For the Chicago region, data follow some of the national patterns reflecting the dominance of immigrants entering through family preferences. Available admissions data starting from 1972 indicate that 77 percent of Filipinos entered as "new arrivals," with the majority through family preferences, whereas 23 percent secured an "adjusted" status with a majority of those categorized as "professionals/highly skilled immigrants, spouse and children." Through two decades, the dominance of new arrivals over adjusted-status immigrants has continued. In 1998, 78 percent of Filipinos entered as new arrivals, and 22 percent received their adjusted permanent residency status.

In Illinois, Filipino Americans represent the second largest Asian population after Asian Indians, numbering 100,338 residents. By state, Illinois ranks as the third largest concentration of Filipino Americans, surpassed by top-ranked California, home to 46 percent of Filipino Americans (N = 1,098,321) and second-ranked Hawaii (Dela Cruz and Agbayani-Siewert 2003, 46).

Chicago Hospitals Beckon: We Want You!

Filipino immigration to Illinois has remained fairly constant during the past three decades. A peak of 4,608 immigrants was recorded in 1976 (Figure 11.1), with a significant decline into the early 1980s. This earlier period of family-driven immigration is also marked by the peak influx of immigrant children (Chapter 12, Table 12.1). Through the mid 1970s, after a massive call for foreign health care professionals to fill the labor shortages in American hospitals was answered, immigration again declined. U.S. medical associations lobbied for restrictions, particularly against foreign medical graduates (FMGs). The Eilberg Act and the Health Professions Educational Assistant Act of 1976 drastically curtailed the entry of Filipino physicians. Immigrants entering through occupational preferences were required to have a firm job offer from an U.S. employer. FMGs were also required to pass either the National Board of Medical Examiners' or the Visa Qualifying Exams to demonstrate competency before qualifying for admission (Ong and Liu 1994, 60). Because of these increasing constraints, Filipino FMGs admitted to the United States were disproportionately hired by inner-city hospitals granted waivers to hire FMGs.

The higher numbers of Filipina women entering Illinois over Filipino men can be explained by the persistent shortages of nurses in the United States and the steady recruitment of Filipina nurses by Chicago-based hospitals and agencies. A recent study by the National Institutes of Health (NIH) reveals that 50,000 nurses

have left the Philippines in the last three years. Although the Philippines Overseas Employment administration reported that only 715 nurses had left for the United States between 2000 and 2002, it is speculated that U.S. hospitals were directly recruiting the health workers as immigrants (Rivera 2004, 7). One Filipino American nurse interviewee confirms this trend, saying "at University of Chicago hospitals, we have a special recruiter that goes to the Philippines. This goes in cycles, but after some labor problems this year, and a threat of a strike, they intensified their efforts to get more Filipino nurses."

For example, registered nurses constitute the largest occupational group (N = 7,292) of Filipina immigrants (see Appendix Table 15.8 in Chapter 15). In addition, Filipina immigrants consistently outnumbered their male counterparts from 1972 through 2000 (see Figure 11.1). Their representation as nursing and health care aides, and as physicians and surgeons, has also contributed to their roles as first arrivals, paving the way for later waves of immediate and extended family members.

Historically, it is important to note that, while the Immigration Act of 1965 reflected and fueled demand for foreign health professionals, the migration of Filipina nurses to Chicago started decades earlier. A group of Filipina

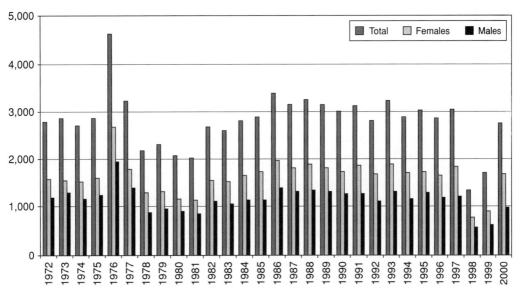

FIGURE 11.1. Filipino immigration to Illinois, 1972–2000.
Source: U.S. Immigration and Naturalization Service Data, 1972–2000.

nurses started working at Cook County Hospital during the 1930s, and others arrived before1965 under exchange programs. Such programs were very popular during the 1950s and 1960s, when American hospitals sought relief from the postwar nursing shortage by recruiting Filipinos for several years; sometimes, these nurses would stay in the United States permanently (Osterman 2004).

The continuing exodus of Filipina nurses from the Philippines dates back to early twentieth-century colonial rule, when an Americanized hospital training system was developed in the Philippines. Beyond the dominant immigrant narrative of being pulled to developed countries like the United States for individual economic pursuits, Filipina nurses become part of the gendered, transnational migrant work force. The imperialist legacy of racialized social hierarchies continues today, influencing the reception and integration of Filipino nurses in the United States.

The development and export of a Filipino nursing labor force results from collaborative transnational processes and the interdependence between American and Philippine nurses, government officials, professional nursing organizations, and hospital administrators (Choy 2003, 6).

In nursing today, Filipinos represent 43 percent (38,000) of the 4 percent of foreign-trained nurses employed in the United States nationwide (Zarembo 2004). The overarching representation of Filipinos in the overall health care, social service, and education industries should also be noted. The gendered domination of Filipinas in these industries can also be seen, with 54 percent of women and 23 percent of men working in these three sectors in the Chicago metro area (Table 15.6 in Chapter 15). Finally, the over-representation of both foreign-born Filipino men and women as registered nurses, physicians and surgeons, nursing and health aides, home care aides, lab technicians, and medical assistants points to the historical and continuing demand for foreign health care professionals in the American labor market that led to revisions in immigration laws and preferences.

Recent aggressive recruitment by different segments of the U.S. health care industry has led to a new hybrid transnational worker, the "RN-MDs" or nurses (male or female) who were formerly physicians in the Philippines (Zarembo 2004). It has been noted that "a nursing degree has long been the fastest way out of the Philippines" (Zarembo 2004). Despite the downward mobility of physicians being retrained as nurses (59 percent said it was "degrading"), 75 percent of those surveyed said that money drove their decision, spurred by the hopes of immediately earning in the United States four times a physician's salary in the Philippines, with salaries in the United States starting at $50,000 and above (Zarembo 2004).

An aging U.S. population and continued nursing-school closings have intensified the demand for qualified nurses. Some hospitals offer recruiters as much as $18,000 for each foreign nurse contracted (Osterman 2004, 2:2). Responding to America's pleas for nurses, about 2,000 to 4,000 physicians are currently in nursing schools in the Philippines (Zarembo 2004).

Throughout the past decade, the increasing percentages of Filipino immigrants entering through family preferences as service workers suggest lower levels of human capital brought over in the persons of relatives of third-wave professionals. With increasing numbers of new immigrants at-risk, their needs will be one of the priority areas for emerging advocacy and community groups. Facing greater immigration barriers and occupational restrictions in transferring their human capital, higher proportions of recent Filipino immigrants experience limited mobility. Along with the rising numbers of undocumented workers, the escalating ratios of these low-skilled, less-advantaged groups serve to challenge the dominant narrative of Filipino immigrant success and model assimilation.

RESIDENTIAL CONCENTRATIONS: CHICAGOANS AND SUBURBANITES

In 1970, the Filipino American population in Chicago totaled 9,497. Twenty years later, Chicago's Filipino population had risen to 29,309, metropolitan Chicago having a Filipino population of 63,182. Filipino Americans in the

Chicago metropolitan area now number 95, 928, a 52 percent increase since 1990. The vast majority of Filipino Americans reside in the six-county Chicago metropolitan area (Map 11.1, color insert). In the city-based Chicago Filipino American community, the numbers declined slightly to 28,423, a 3 percent decrease, thus showing a residential preference for suburban communities.

The following suburbs, in descending order, show the highest concentration of Filipino Americans: Skokie, Glendale Heights, Waukegan, Morton Grove, Bolingbrook, Hanover Park, Bartlett, Schaumburg, Carol Stream, and Des Plaines. With the opening of suburban developments to increasing numbers of minorities during the 1970s, upwardly mobile Filipino Americans joined other non-white and immigrant groups in seeking neighborhoods with good schools, co-ethnic networks and services, and overall, a better quality of life.

Looking at the table of median household income in the six-county area for the largest Asian immigrant groups (Chapter 12, Table 12.2), in Cook and McHenry Counties, Filipino Americans have the highest household income, $63,925 and $85,355, respectively. Within the Chicago Primary Metropolitan Statistical Area (PMSA) and the City of Chicago, Filipino Americans represent the highest median household income, $68,273 and $55,164, respectively. Conversely, they have the lowest poverty rates among the major immigrant groups.

For Filipino Americans in Chicago, 7 percent of the population lives below poverty level; in the suburbs, this number falls to less than 2 percent. They also represent the lowest percentages of linguistically isolated Asian immigrants at 11 percent (to a high of 49 percent for Vietnamese), according to the Asian American Institute. Among the largest immigrant groups in Chicago, at 80 percent, Filipino Americans have the second highest English-proficient population, just below the rate for Polish immigrants. This is despite their having the highest proportion of foreign-born (61 percent) compared with all other major immigrant groups. Consequently, their higher human capital and legacy of colonial Americanization provides greater access to suburban living and mainstream neighbor-hoods. Of the foreign-born population in the six-county area, 20,755 Filipino Americans live in Chicago and 37,924 live in the suburbs.

Filipino Americans as Exemplary Model Minorities?

Despite the popular perceptions of higher socio-economic status, access to suburban lifestyles, and overall upward mobility associated with Filipino Americans, greater scrutiny leads to mixed indicators. Given the dominance and continuing influx of the foreign-born population both into the City of Chicago and the metropolitan area, the most widely used indicator of success—median household income—remains problematic. Both Filipino immigrant and Filipino American families tend to live in extended family and multigenerational households (Mendoza 2003, 23). Throughout my research, many Filipinos emphasized how close family networks of obligations necessitate such common multihousehold arrangements, with new arrivals staying with relatives for extended periods. Another contributing factor to larger household size may be the delayed independence of working young adults, especially Filipinas, who tend to live with their families until marriage.

Demographers in Asian American studies have critiqued the reliance of median household income in depicting Asian Americans as model minorities, preferring per capita income as a more reliable measure, because of the higher ratio of workers in Asian Pacific American (APA) households (Shinagawa 1996, 76). In the 1990 Census data, almost 20 percent of APA households had three or more workers, compared with the general U.S. population, in which 13 percent of households have three or more workers. Among the largest Asian Pacific American groups, Filipino Americans had the highest percentage of households with three or more workers, at 30 percent. The second highest group was Vietnamese Americans, at 21 percent (Shinagawa 1996, 110).

Nationwide, Asian Americans are likely to come from larger families and grow up in two-parent households. The average household size for Asian Pacific American families is higher than for all U.S. families. In 2000, the average household size was 3.61 for Asian Pacific American families, but 3.14 for all U.S. families (Nishioka 2003, 30). Among Filipino Americans in the Chicago metropolitan area, the largest households are found in the outlying counties (Lake = 3.57), with smaller numbers in Chicago (2.83).

Consequently, when median household income is used to cast Filipino Americans as the most successfully assimilated immigrant and Asian American group, greater use of disaggregated, individual-based data should be considered. As many sociologists have observed, the disproportionate reliance on education by Asian Americans as the sole mobility path has resulted in lower individual incomes across occupations, suggesting some level of underemployment or discrimination of Asian Americans. Using the equity model, Kim concludes that, for Asian Americans, the investment for attaining socioeconomic status is higher than for whites (Kim 1995, 93). Both Asian immigrant and native-born Chinese, Japanese, and Filipino males earn less than white males under equivalent conditions of investment (Kim, Hurh, and Fernandez 1989).

The model-minority stereotype linked to Asian Americans in general dominates public discourse and overshadows the widening bimodality of many Asian American groups. Filipino Americans in the Chicago metropolitan area may be found in both low- and high-income niches. Dominated by an expanding pool of foreign-born workers, the Filipino American occupational profile shows signs of this growing polarity. In 2000, among foreign-born Filipino American women (Chapter 15, Appendix Table 8), Filipina registered nurses are the largest group (7,292). Other dominant occupational groups include health technicians, nursing and health aides (1,422), and hospital-affiliated Filipina physicians and surgeons (1,004). Home care aides (726) and licensed practical and vocational nurses (526) are likely to be found in nursing and private homes.

Among foreign-born Filipino men (Chapter 15, Table 15.7), large numbers also cluster in the health care industry, with the top group being physicians and surgeons (956). Other large clusters include registered nurses (756), laborers (618), cooks (572), electricians, machinists, janitors, and parking lot attendants.

Filipino higher educational attainment, both as Chicago and suburban residents, also leads to a pattern of higher human capital: 49 percent of Filipino Americans in Chicago and 53 percent of Filipino Americans in the suburbs have college degrees, and another 11 percent of both city and suburban residents hold master's, professional, or advanced degrees. This equal representation of highly educated Filipino American professionals residing in the city and suburbs contrasts with other recent Asian immigrant groups; among Chinese American professionals, 21 percent of similarly degreed professionals reside in Chicago, compared with 43 percent of suburban residents. The greater representation of linguistically independent Filipino Americans working in civil service, government, and managerial occupations located in the central core of Chicago may require and facilitate city residence. (The City of Chicago maintains a city-residence requirement for most of its employees throughout its agencies, including the Chicago Public Schools.)

Among Filipino Americans in the suburbs, 85 percent are English-proficient, compared with 72 percent of Filipino Americans in Chicago. Their greater human capital and U.S. colonial legacy have also facilitated their transition into becoming U.S. citizens; 61 percent of Filipino Americans in both Chicago and the suburbs are naturalized citizens.

Filipino Americans in Chicago are typically found in neighborhoods that cluster on the North Side of the city (Map 11.2, color insert). The ten top community areas for Filipino Americans include Albany Park, Irving Park, West Ridge, Lincoln Square, Edgewater, Portage Park, Belmont Cragin, Lake View, Uptown, and North Park. This residential and business pattern of concentration toward the north part of the city mirrors most of the other Asian immigrant communities and the historical neighborhood preferences of Filipino Americans.

When the first Filipino American Community Center was established by the Filipino American Council of Chicago (FACC), first on the North Side along Webster Avenue during the

1960s and then on Irving Park as the Rizal Center in 1974, this reflected the higher numbers of Filipino Americans and their more visible presence in the North Side neighborhoods.

Racial barriers in Chicago also limited home ownership and dispersal of Filipino Americans to changing neighborhoods undergoing ethnic and racial succession. As recently as 1970, only 15 percent of Filipino Americans in Chicago were homeowners—despite higher education and income—compared with 56 percent in San Diego and 49 percent in Seattle (Posadas and Guyotte 1998, 148). For Filipino Americans in Chicago, race mattered more than ethnicity or class.

Early Filipino Americans may have relied on residential dispersion as a protective strategy to minimize the effects of racism and discrimination, explaining why Filipino Americans in Chicago never developed an ethnic enclave, for residents or businesses. Entering as colonized nationals and bringing over higher levels of human capital including English proficiency skills, later waves of Filipino immigrants were similarly not dependent on a traditional ethnic enclave. Although they gravitated toward residential neighborhoods where they knew people or were convenient to jobs and schools, they were not searching to locate within a Filipino business or residential cluster.

The early dominance of professionals and skilled workers, globally recruited into awaiting positions, also did not allow the formation of a critical mass of entrepreneurs needed to build a commercial or business enclave. This third wave of immigrants, entering the United States after 1965, generally held college or professional degrees or came as former civil servants. Post-independence, civil service was held in high regard and viewed as a secure occupation. Such salaried civil servants however, arrived with less capital and were less likely to start a business. In 1990, only about 3 percent of Filipino Americans were self-employed, making them fifth among all Asian American groups in entrepreneurship (Posadas 1999, 79).

With less need for a business enclave, Mr. Alex Cirera, a community leader and newspaper publisher comments: "Filipinos quickly integrated into mainstream society. Speaking English wasn't a problem.... We've been occupied for so long.... Western culture is mixed with us ... we have education and can assimilate into the city or suburbs."

CONSTRUCTING AND MAINTAINING IDENTITIES: A CONTINUUM OF CHOICES

How do we conceptualize the dimensions of "Filipino Americanness" or degrees of "Filipinoness" in the United States? Carrying the legacy of a Spanish and American colonial past in which regional and hometown allegiances prevailed, do the majority of immigrant Filipino Americans even identify as Filipino Americans? Or do they retain their provincial ties as Illokanos or Visayans, as did the first waves of Filipino immigrants? The transformation from Philippine hometown native to Filipino American starts as the native crosses the U.S. border. Yet the "process of negotiating not only Filipinoness but, even more, Filipino Americanness," continues in the new settlement, particularly in certain sites (Bonus, 171).

Yen Le Espiritu's work on identity-formation among Filipino Americans distinguishes between how immigrant Filipinos and second-generation Filipino Americans offer new constructions of Filipinoness and Americanness. Espiritu suggests that for upwardly mobile immigrants, "symbolic ethnicity" may be all that remains. Second-generation immigrants may only seek occasional opportunities to express their ethnic identity, not wanting to be too involved in their ethnic culture or participate in ethnic organizations (Espiritu 2002, 24). In delineating differences between first- and second-generation perspectives, she describes that, for immigrant Filipinos, "ethnicity is deeply subjective, concrete, and cultural ... [while] for the second generation, it is largely cognitive, intermittent, and political, forged out of their confrontation with and struggle against dominant culture" (Espiritu 1994, 17).

Consequently, studying intergenerational differences enhances an understanding of the continuum of differences between each generation's connection and engagement in that culture. Recent immigrants may share a Filipino ethnic identity that is constantly refueled by daily practices including using native dialects, observing rituals identified with Filipino Catholicism, shopping in Filipino markets, and socializing with co-ethnics. Second-generation Filipino Americans may engage in ethnic behavior that is "largely symbolic, characterized by a nostalgic but unacquainted allegiance to an imagined past" (Espiritu 1994, 5).

Filipino Americans have access to multiple identities, and they negotiate using one for some settings and another for other situations. Self-identifying as Filipino American might be necessary to be considered for the Filipino American Youth Leaders Fellowship Program—an immersion trip to the Philippines sponsored by Chevron Texaco—but checking the Asian Pacific American box may be pragmatic for minority scholarships. Given changes in national and global politics, including race-based and immigration policies, strategies for self-identification along a racial–ethnic continuum may vary over time. More recent changes in the Philippines policy of allowing Filipinos to retain dual citizenship facilitate the retention of transnational identities.

Second-generation Filipino Americans are particularly susceptible to hearing the dialogue of racial domination in the United States. Unlike their parents or 1.5-generation (immigrant children who arrive in the United States before their adolescent years with bi-lingual proficiency) members who are familiar with another life and social ties "back home," second-generation members have been raised without the specific roles that fuel ethnicity. Moreover, as minorities, they have to simultaneously navigate racist acts that remind them that they will always be excluded and overcome pressures for assimilation. In describing second-generation Filipino Americans, "the majority do not live in an ethnic neighborhood, attend school with other Filipino children, or belong to Filipino organizations" (Espiritu 2002, 24). In contrast, although contemporary Filipino American residents in the Chicago metro area reveal strong patterns of participation in Filipino organizations, for most second-generation Filipino

Americans, their ethnic activities are more symbolic.

Espiritu argues that, because Filipino Americans are actively engaged in resisting racism, racial categorization, and American nativism, Filipino immigrants intensely retain their connections to the Philippines (Espiritu 1995, 27). Although Filipino Americans may not contextualize their ties to the homeland to "resisting racism" but to deep-seated familial obligations, they are proud that they have succeeded enough in America to help their relatives back home. Whether through sending regular remittances, *balikbayan* (large "homecoming" boxes full of gifts sent back to relatives) containers, or engaging in volunteer projects to benefit the homeland, Filipino Americans have taken the role of transnationals; they actively maintain relationships between the United States and the Philippines. As Filipino Americans balance their transnational with their racialized identities imposed by U.S. culture and confront pressures to assimilate or acculturate, they construct a new hybrid culture. Using their lived experiences to develop this continuum of degrees of acting Filipino American in the Chicago metropolitan area, I will draw from Espiritu's contention that this distinct hybrid culture is not "simply an extension of the 'original' or of the mainstream 'American' culture" (Espiritu 2002, 24).

Constructing a Continuum: Growing Up Filipino in Chicago—What's Important to Me?

This section attempts to construct a "degree of ethnicity continuum," recognizing that ethnicity is socially constructed through people's social interactions with others. Decisions on whether to label oneself Filipino, American, or Filipino American raise questions on what it means to be Filipino, how that identity influences choices, and how one learns to be Filipino. The majority of 1.5- and second-generation Filipino Americans live in two worlds. Growing up in white-dominated neighborhoods or towns, these Filipino Americans typically spent weekdays with non-Filipinos and weekends dominated by activities with extended families and co-ethnics. With parents who mainly work in white-dominated institutions and having non-Filipino friends from school or the neighborhood, second-generation Filipino Americans recall weekends full of gatherings, pot-luck dinners, parties, church activities, or community events (including Filipino groups based on hometown, provincial, professional, religious, cultural, social, civic, or alumni organizations). Although depending on the degree of participation of their parents in ethnic-based organizations or their networks of relatives and fictive or "adopted" kin, young Filipino Americans' experiences vary from being family- or community-dominated, but always involving other Filipinos.

Level One—Involved with Family or Extended Kin

At the minimum, Filipino Americans socialize with extended or adopted family members on most weekends. For those who live in white-dominated communities or outlying suburbs, the weekends are periods during which their families can relax and be comfortable with other co-ethnics. Although some Filipino Americans have clustered in Chicago's North Side neighborhoods, they seldom see co-ethnics on a daily social basis. The weekends then, contrast with weekdays, during which time Filipino Americans are racially isolated. Socializing with co-ethnics on weekends allows them to release their tensions from dealing with difficult work conditions. They rely on their co-ethnics as a support system, one that provides strong family networks. The development of strong fictive kinship networks are fueled by one of the most pressing issues facing Filipino Americans in Chicago and nationally: immigration and family reunification issues. The long separation of Filipino Americans from immediate family members encourages the integration and "adoption" of close friends or distant relatives as family.

Level Two—Participating in Family, Extended Kin, and Church Functions

Because most Filipino Americans are Catholic, many family events reflect religious devotion and festivities. As one second-generation Filipino American describes it: "Filipino Americans have a strong relationship with God. We long for traditional Filipino church rituals." Given the numbers of Filipino Americans in the Chicago metropolitan area and their high visibility in certain residential areas, Philippine-based religious customs are widely practiced. For many Filipino American families, attending or being involved with church functions usually means celebrating with co-ethnics. Consequently, locating Filipino Americans on this second level of the continuum describes Filipino Americans who most likely attend services in a parish with some presence of Filipino Americans and who may participate in organizing activities for Filipino Americans in the parish.

Level Three—All of the Above Plus "Community" Organizations

Of all the Asian American communities in Chicago, Filipino Americans stand out in their formation and participation in a wide range of community organizations. Although some might regard Filipino Americans as having assimilated easily and having little use for ethnic organizations, the large number of Filipino-based organizations, estimated at 250 to 400, indicates otherwise. Across varying degrees of commitment or activism, Filipino Americans express their longing to be involved with an organization that promotes Filipino American culture and heritage.

Posadas discusses the reputation of Filipino Americans as organizers and joiners. She describes how Filipino Americans "define and re-define attachments outside of their family networks . . . Being born and growing up in a Philippine town, province, or region establishes a central basis for organization-building among Filipinos in the U.S." (Posadas 1999, 61). On meeting new co-ethnics, Filipino Americans will ask "Where did you come from?" to establish the person's dialect and region in the homeland (Munoz 2002, 53). This connection is the basis for many Filipino American organizations in urban areas, and it provides new immigrants particularly with an antidote against individual prejudice and U.S. nativism.

Previous studies focus on how Filipino Americans manage to reconcile thwarted mobility with desires for recognition and visibility. I am also motivated to discover where Filipino Americans have found "refuge in places where they can be among and enjoy the company of people who are like them and therefore are likely to treat them in more positive ways" (Bonus, 54).

Similar to the regional research biases prevalent in Asian American Studies, which has focused more attention on Asian American communities in California and Hawaii, research on contemporary Filipino American community life seldom includes Chicago. Despite the pioneering work of historian Barbara Posadas on pre-1965 Filipino Americans, attention on Filipino Americans in Chicago and Midwestern communities has been minimal. Yet where else should a study of Filipino American community organizations begin if not in Chicago, where pensionados formed organizations shortly after their arrival in 1906 (Posadas and Guyotte 1990, 3)?

Efforts to build the first Filipino American community center in the United States, the Dr. Jose Rizal Memorial Center, started in Chicago with the incorporation of the National Filipino American Council in 1953. In 1966, the first Filipino Community Center Building was purchased for the community at 1113 Webster Ave (Acierto 1999, 39). Soon outgrowing the space, fundraising efforts started for the current Dr. Jose Rizal Memorial Center at 1332 West Irving Park, leading to its purchase in 1974 (Acierto 1999, 40).

Filipino American community organizations in Chicago have a long history, some having been started by first- and second-wave Filipinos. Although many new organizations have formed through the interests and efforts of third-wave immigrants, the rich legacy of Filipino and Filipino American organizational networks reflects the continuing needs and demands of Filipino Americans to claim spaces to communicate with co-ethnics about daily experiences and shared issues. Joining Filipino-related organizations provides Filipino Americans with opportunities to maintain their transnational identities and cultivate new interests in Filipino American community affairs.

FINAL HOPES: RE-VISIONING COMMUNITY

As the community matures and leadership shifts to more second-generation Filipino Americans, perhaps this drive for success and assimilation will provoke a critical mass of leaders to reorient their thinking on community issues. Interviewees mention the need for Filipino Americans to improve on a sense of identity and develop representative organizations that are community-focused instead of individual-focused. Consensus concurs that Filipino Americans should work to establish cooperation, improve living conditions, and offer assistance to other Filipino Americans, especially new arrivals. A newly-formed task force, Operation Mango, has investigated the social and psychological needs of the immigrant community. It found, for example, that many need help related to immigration—particularly legal assistance and related immigration services.

Given the immense resources and human capital available to Filipino Americans in Chicago, once a stronger sense of unity prevails, Filipino Americans could become more visible and be recognized as a viable and integral part of the whole community. Such a unified presence would enable the Filipino American community to become politically empowered within the larger society and contribute to community success and community-building.

In upcoming elections, four Filipino Americans are running for elected office in various suburban races. Filipino Americans are quickly becoming the most visible and active Asian American community in electoral politics. As one candidate conveys, "I want to make a difference for our Filipino American and local community . . . I want to be viewed as a player!"

Building community for Filipino Americans goes beyond relying on one model of community empowerment. Some may choose

to invest and expend their financial and social capital only on homeland-based or Filipino American-based projects; others on pan-
Asian American ventures; still others may focus
on mainstream organizations. Whatever vehicles or agendas are chosen, both Filipino immigrants and Filipino Americans retain their myriad facets of identity and cultural roots. Across
varying levels of Filipinoness and Filipino Americanness, Chicago's Filipino Americans are embracing their cultural and ethnic identities, some
more visibly than others. Whether they choose
to join affinity organizations or affirm their cultural and ethnic ties among family and friends,
Filipino Americans are engaged in building
community and constructing their own sense
of ethnicity.

NOTE

Acknowledgments. Special acknowledgments and
dedication in memory of my father, McKee Lau, who
was in the Foreign Service in the Philippines before
immigrating to the United States, and for my mother,
Grace Lau, who has shared so many stories about living
in the Philippines.

Research for this chapter would not have been possible without the support and commitment of more than
50 Filipino Americans—Chicago community leaders,
residents, and students who graciously agreed to be
interviewed from 2003–4. Although I cannot identify
all participants, I thank the following visionary individuals for sharing their personal stories and inspiring
me to develop this chapter: Dr. Maria Acierto, Sylvia
Acierto, Alex Cirera, Casey Chinsio, Jerry Clarito, Naisy
Dolar, Carmen Estacio, Ben Lumicao, Alana Mariano,
Alpha Nicolasin, and Rey Villar Jr.

Kiljoong Kim

12 The Korean Presence in Chicago

A BRIEF history of Koreans in the United States covers just over 100 years. In Chicago, the initial composition of the Korean community was certainly unique, and its history has had a large effect decades later. Issues universal to all immigrants also apply to Koreans, such as changing expectations of gender roles and a growing generation gap. However, issues that not all immigrants directly faced, such as the Korean community's intimate and sometimes violent relationship with the African American community, also form part of this history. Above all, Koreans have always prided themselves on resilience and perseverance, and their small but stable community in Chicago certainly reflects those characteristics.

KOREAN IMMIGRANT HISTORY

Although Korean immigrants made their way to the United States as early as 1903, the early part of Korean immigrant history is for the most part confined to Hawaii and the West Coast. The combination of two factors motivated Koreans to consider leaving the homeland and seek opportunities elsewhere: unstable political and economic conditions in Korea and a high demand for agricultural labor in Hawaii. Despite the Naturalization Law of 1790 that reserved the rights to U.S. citizenship only to whites, circumstances in the homeland caused Koreans to seek other places to live. Japan's declaration of Korea as a "protectorate" in 1905, which began 40 years of colonization, led many to flee as political refugees. Poverty in Korea during the early

1900s also contributed to the increased interest in Hawaii and other places where famine and drought were not everlasting concerns.

Economic opportunity, specifically a demand for physical labor in the agricultural sector, might have brought Koreans into the United States, but a lack of institutional support prohibited them from numerical growth and from forming collective political strength. Also, although most Koreans of the early days migrated for opportunities in agricultural labor, only one-seventh of them had been farmers in Korea; the remainder came from metropolitan areas (Lee 1989). Sugar plantations in Hawaii attracted 7,200 Korean laborers to Hawaii between 1903 and 1905 (Min 1998). By 1920, a total of about 8,000 were believed to have made it to the United States (Takaki 1989). Most settled in northern California, although some ventured inland as far as Chicago, seeking business opportunities that were labor intensive and had minimal capital investment. However, the National Origins Act of 1924 barred the entry of women from Asian countries such as Korea, thus preventing population growth in a group in which males already constituted 75 percent of immigrants in 1920 (Takaki 1989).

In contrast to the first wave of Korean immigrants, who were predominantly men, the next opportunity for Koreans to enter the country occurred partly through the War Brides Act of 1946, which allowed the entry of Asian women who married U.S. soldiers overseas. This particular group increased as the United States became heavily involved in the Korean War, in 1950, as did the number of orphans adopted by American citizens. As a result, about 15,000 Koreans moved to the United States between 1950 and 1964 (Min 1998).

The long-term effect of the War Brides Act lingered well into the 1950s and 1960s, as the uneven gender distribution shifted and Korean women became greatly over-represented. For example, in 1958, the first year that Immigration and Naturalization Service (INS) officially distinguished Koreans from Chinese and Japanese, 425 Korean males were counted and 765 females. When broken down by age, the population consisted of 46 Koreans males between the ages of 20 and 23 and 322 Korean females in the same age group. This gap persisted through 1977, with 12,116 male and 18,801 female Koreans living in the United States. Those between the ages of 20 and 23 had the largest gender gap: 2,373 males and 6,335 females. As seen in Figure 12.1, this trend continues today, and female Korean immigrants have outnumbered their counterparts for every year since 1972.

A sizable number of Korean students also were present in universities across the country. Although they neither arrived with permanent resident status nor had the intention to stay after their education, they nevertheless started to make their group identity known in Korean communities. Massive number of graduates from American institutions also affected the homeland, as a number of alumni associations for American universities started forming in Korea, mostly for those who had received advanced degrees in the United States and then returned to South Korea. In a culture in which school ties are an integral part of the networking processes in professional settings, such formations have a significant influence in social interactions.

After the Immigration and Naturalization Act of 1965, economic opportunity and political freedom continued to be the primary reasons for Korean immigration to United States, and the number of immigrants dramatically increased in 1970s. More than 30,000 Koreans immigrated to the United States annually between 1976 and 1990, constituting the third largest immigrant group during that period, behind Mexicans and Filipinos. Consequently, the estimated number of Koreans grew rapidly: from 79,598 in 1970 to 354,529 in 1980, 797,304 in 1990, and 1,076,872 in 2000, according to the U.S. Census. Considering that 82 percent of Koreans were foreign born in 1980 and 80.2 percent (864,125 out of 1,076,872) in 2000, it is evident that they are in a relatively early phase of immigrant history.

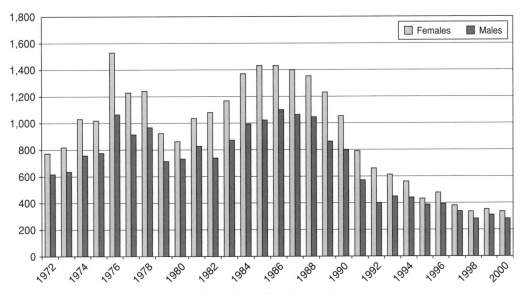

FIGURE 12.1. Korean immigrants to Illinois by gender, 1972–2000.
Source: Immigration and Naturalization Service, 1972–2000.

Although selective migration brought students and laborers to the United States during the early part of Korean immigrant history, their demographic characteristics during the 1970s and 1980s can be summarized as a professional, business-oriented group with strong educational background (Portes and Rumbaut 1990). This trend continued into the 1990s, although the overall number of immigrants decreased as the standard of living and the economy of the homeland improved dramatically and the political environment stabilized.

The perceptions of Korean immigrants, however, appear to be different from what the data suggest. Many Korean Americans believe that, as the number of immigrants arriving on the invitation from Koreans with U.S. citizenship increased, the overall educational level of Korean immigrants began to decline. They also believe that it has led to an increase in the proportion of immigrants who have difficulties adapting and assimilating to the new culture.

These shifts in the composition of immigrants have an important long-term implication. Whereas earlier immigrants left Korea either to escape adverse circumstances (with the intent to return upon accumulation of individual wealth or democratization of the homeland) or to seek economic opportunities in the United States, the later wave of immigrants were mostly families seeking better lives for their children and having the intention of settling in the United States to achieve that goal. Because of the extremely competitive college entrance procedure in South Korea, many choose to migrate for better educational opportunities, despite having to give up their social and socioeconomic status in the homeland, preferring to face instead the hardships of the immigrant lifestyle. As indicated in Table 12.1, the influx of Korean immigrants to Illinois since 1972 contains a higher proportion of children than other large immigrant groups. This cohort eventually created a pool of first-generation immigrants that defied the stereotype of a group with a high language barrier and lack of cultural understanding. Rather, it resulted in significant foreign-born population having a U.S. education and bilingual ability. This group of immigrants often strives to distinguish itself from the older first generation by labeling themselves as the 1.5 generation. In fact, this group tends to politically align itself more closely with second-generation Korean Americans within the community, having less focus on the issues of the homeland and being more concentrated on local issues.

For Korean immigrants, two significant changes occurred during the past 30 years. First, these "new immigrants"—historian Yoon-Jin Kim's reference to immigrants who came after 1965—are quite different from earlier Korean immigrants in that "they are generally well-educated urban middle-class immigrants from a rapidly changing industrial, capitalist, and modernizing country" (Kim 1991, 76). Second, even though Los Angeles was initially the overwhelming favorite destination for Koreans, an increasing number of immigrants slowly expanded into other metropolitan areas, including Chicago. Although they may not have been entirely familiar with American lifestyles, the urbanization and Westernization of South Korea

TABLE 12.1. Percentage of Immigrant Children Under 16 to Illinois

Year	Koreans	Indians	Filipinos	Mexicans	Polish
1975	36.1%	18.8%	23.3%	37.6%	23.2%
1980	28.2%	23.8%	12.3%	23.8%	19.9%
1985	35.7%	18.2%	19.0%	15.3%	18.3%
1990	29.1%	18.9%	21.7%	19.8%	23.1%
1995	38.1%	21.7%	19.9%	34.8%	24.9%
2000	34.0%	14.2%	12.2%	25.5%	28.6%
Annual Average (1972–2000)	31.7%	18.8%	20.3%	27.0%	22.1%

Sources: Immigration and Naturalization Service, 1972–2000.

since 1960s encouraged Korean immigrants to seek out major metropolitan areas in the United States.

The economic success of South Korea during the past 25 years has had an effect on emigrants to the United States. Unlike emigrants during the earlier part of the century, who fled economic and political hardships in the homeland without starting capital, many of today's emigrants have different backgrounds and initial capital. The South Korean government policy on these emigrants over time also reflects the nation's economic advancement. Until 1981, no emigrant was allowed to relocate outside the country taking with them their cash or assets. The transition from a developing country to an industrialized country made these limitations on asset transfer necessary. This restriction naturally skewed the emigrant population to those who were simply seeking opportunities to work overseas and willing to start their lives without any initial capital. The South Korean government increased the amount of allowance for emigrants from $200,000 per household in 1988 to $200,000 per head of household plus $100,000 for each family member in 1995. Those emigrating for the purpose of investing were allowed to take up to $500,000 out of the country. As of January 1, 2001, all limitations were lifted under the condition that verification of sources with the Korean Internal Revenue Service is required in case of $100,000 or over. This change is likely to have a greater impact on the composition of Korean emigrants in the near future, particularly as it coincides with the growth of the Korean economy and the increasing participation of South Korea in the global economy.

Although the Census Bureau estimates that approximately 1 million Koreans and 1.2 million persons with any racial–ethnic combination that includes Korean live in the United States, those in the Korean community believe they are grossly undercounted. Although it is unlikely that the number approaches 6 million (*100 Year History of Korean Immigration to America: Story of Korean Diaspora 1903–2003*, 2002), as argued by some, undocumented immigrants and those who failed to be counted during Census 2000 because of linguistic barriers might have contributed to some undercount.

SETTLEMENT AND NECESSITY OF ASSIMILATION

Historically, many immigrant groups congregated in densely populated residential areas, mostly in inner-city areas, to create environments in which those with similar cultural backgrounds can form an affordable community filled with social and religious institutions, shops, and restaurants. In this way, it is possible for some groups and individuals to survive without ever assimilating to the mainstream culture.

In today's context of Korean immigration, another option to assimilation or isolation is present within the Korean American community. Just as Korean immigrants and students returned to Korea upon its independence in 1945, many Koreans who came to the United States in recent years choose to go back after a short period of the immigrant experience. A number of factors are attributed to such a phenomenon: First, the rapid economic growth in South Korea has resulted in a higher standard of living, more business opportunities, and political stabilization. Second, an inability to assimilate to the American lifestyle, and a subsequent inability to tap into its economic and employment opportunities, may also play a part. As indicated by Figure 12.2, the number of Korean immigrants to the United States who returned to South Korea peaked during early 1990s. In 1992, in addition to riots in number of metropolitan areas (including Los Angeles and Chicago) that affected Korean immigrants, a civilian presidential administration was elected in South Korea for the first time in decades. Although the number of Koreans who returned to South Korea was on the rise before this, over a third of the 71,968 immigrants (37.4 percent) who returned between 1980 and 2001 had done so in the years following those two events.

KOREANS IN CHICAGO

During the earlier part of the twentieth century, the presence of Koreans in Chicago was largely unknown. A total of 27 Koreans in 1920 and 64 in 1930 were believed to have resided in Chicago,

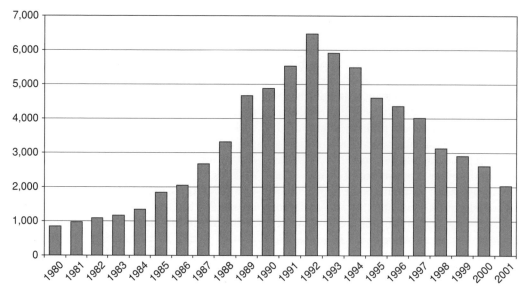

FIGURE 12.2. Korean immigrants to U.S. that returned to Korea, 1980–2001.
Source: South Korean Ministry of Foreign Affairs and Trade.

after moving from Hawaii to seek nonplantation work (U.S. Census; *70 Years' History* 1995).

Despite such small numbers, Chicago's first Korean Student Association was formed in 1918, and the first Korean church was established in 1923. The role of students became increasingly significant during the 1930s, when Korean students regularly gathered at the University of Chicago's International House to discuss the movement underway in Korea to seek independence from Japanese occupation.

The beginning of World War II and a subsequent labor shortage provided economic opportunities for Koreans in Chicago, and those who were able to accumulate enough capital opened restaurants and grocery stores. Despite such opportunities, the number of Koreans in Chicago remained consistent. By the end of the war, many chose to return to Korea, as the defeat of Japan finally ended colonization.

By and large, the students returned to Korea whereas most other immigrants stayed. Almost no incoming students arrived between 1945 and 1950 but, after 1960, when Koreans in the Chicago area began to increase, most newcomers were students. By 1962, the Korean American Association was formed by students in the area. Many of these students eventually became immigrants holding white-collar profes-

sions. Unlike the organization formed in 1918, which focused on the issues of the homeland and its independence from Japanese occupation, the focus in the 1960s was primarily on the issues affecting those who intended to settle in Chicago.

Thousands of Koreans had migrated to the United States by the 1970s, and commercial areas that consisted mostly of restaurants and grocery stores for Koreans began to form in the Lincoln Park and Lakeview neighborhoods along Clark Street in Chicago. The first Korean restaurant, *Sammee*, opened at 3370 North Clark Street in 1969, and it stayed at the same location until the 1990s, when gentrification forced it to close. Because many Japanese were already settled in the area, it was easier for Koreans to establish in that area than to compete with white ethnic groups or blacks.

Although many came from Korea with a college education and professional experience, most had difficulty landing comparable positions in the mainstream economic structure of the United States. Many medical doctors, for example, spent years after migration seeking full accreditation, and many never managed to qualify. Even after attaining professional validity, many Korean professionals, including medical doctors, established private practices in Korean business areas. These commercial formations, however, developed very slowly and were small in proportion to the population they served.

Aside from students, a large proportion of Korean nurses and coal miners (who had initially migrated to West Germany) and agricultural workers (who had previously migrated to South Africa) settled in Chicago, as well as professionals such as doctors and martial arts instructors. It is speculated that job opportunities in Chicago's industrial sector attracted those Koreans from other countries.

Having lived the immigrant experience once before, those from West Germany adjusted more easily to the new culture, compared with those who came directly from Korea. The Fellow Workers' Club, established in 1973, by this subgroup is still in existence today. Their prominence within the Korean community grew to the point at which socialization patterns divided the Korean community between former students and those who had come from Germany, with both groups competing for the community's leadership positions. While most students eventually became professionals and somewhat assimilated by establishing in suburban areas, those from West Germany explored small-business options.

Koreans who continued their occupations in the health care profession settled in Lincoln Park and Lakeview, near their hospitals and near Korean commercial areas on Clark Street, whereas others expanded further north along Lake Michigan to Uptown, Edgewater, and Rogers Park. Because of such vastly different backgrounds, Korean communities in Chicago had residential patterns more scattered than the typical pockets formed by European immigrants of previous years.

Koreans in Chicago during these early years defied the explanations given for the development of ethnic groups by such scholars as Louis Wirth, who saw the city as being comprised of a number of various ethnic groups, dwelling in clustered areas that formed "ghetto-like" slums for cultural and economic reasons. Although a concentration of businesses geared toward Koreans in the aforementioned Clark Street area in Lakeview did exist, other institutions had established themselves in a number of different areas of the city. In fact, this pattern still persists

today; while commercial concentration follows residential trends, no ethnic enclaves form where commercial areas co-exist with a dense residential population of a same group.

According to an estimate from the Census Bureau, 7,313 Koreans lived in the Chicago metropolitan area in 1970. Not surprisingly, considering the effects of the War Brides Act, 60 percent of them were females. By 1980, the estimate for the same area increased to 21,484, with a narrowed gender gap (53 percent females). Considering the massive migration from Korea during this decade—the number of Koreans in the nation almost quadrupled in 10 years—the Korean population did not necessarily grow at the same rate in the Chicago area. Around this time, the main Korean commercial area migrated from Clark Street to Lawrence Avenue, further north and west. Consequently, a small concentration of Korean residents moved from the Lincoln Park and Lakeview areas to Lawrence Avenue and the surrounding neighborhoods, such as Edgewater, Albany Park, Lincoln Square, Uptown, West Ridge, Rogers Park, and Irving Park. Again, the pattern shows a scattering around the north side of the city, rather than a large pocket. The relatively affordable rents and proximity to Lawrence Avenue made the areas quite popular for many years. Lawrence Avenue, which was once referred to as "a second Clark Street" by Korean immigrants, became the main Korean commercial strip for the next two decades, and it took over the role as the symbolic center for the Korean community in Chicago.

By 1990, 35,328 Koreans were estimated to be living in the area. Once again, although the national number of Koreans more than doubled through massive migration, in the Chicago area, the population only grew by 64 percent from 1980. The estimate from Census 2000 shows the Korean population experienced moderate growth during the 1990s, both nationwide and locally, at 35 percent and 28 percent respectively. (Incidentally, the local population of 45,515 is slightly less than the cumulative number of Korean immigrants in Illinois between 1972 and 2000, which may indicate that Chicago is a transitory location for a sizable number of Korean immigrants.)

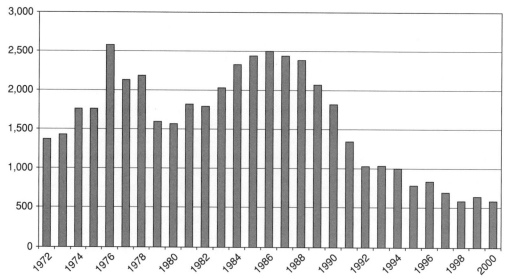

FIGURE 12.3. Korean immigrants to Illinois, 1972–2000.
Source: Immigration and Naturalization Service, 1972–2000.

During the 1990s, the Korean community thrived in Chicago: Lawrence Avenue was densely populated with Korean restaurants, grocery stores, churches, pharmacies, book stores, herbal stores, and even comic book stores. In 1993, Lawrence Avenue was officially named "Seoul Drive" between Kedzie Avenue and Pulaski Avenue. It was an acknowledgment of Koreans' influence in Chicago, but many Korean Americans also felt that such recognition came a little late, seeing that residential suburbanization already started taking some of the commercial Korean businesses out of the area.

As indicated in Figure 12.3, the number of Korean immigrants moving to Illinois has declined dramatically in recent years. Over 80 percent of the 47,200 Koreans who came during this period arrived prior to 1990. This trend reflects the national trend during the same period, although the proportion of Korean immigrants coming to Illinois never exceeded 8 percent of the total number of Koreans immigrating to the United States. Considering that only 12.3 percent of all Korean Americans live in the Midwest region (Census 2000), such a low proportion of arrival is to be expected.

As was the case with the national estimates, Koreans in Chicago also believed they have been undercounted by the Census Bureau in 2000. Again, although the number may not have been 150,000, as suggested by some, the actual figure is likely to be somewhere between the Census estimate and 150,000.

As far as residential patterns are concerned, most Koreans firmly believe in the American dream through suburbanization and buy a house in the suburbs as soon as they can afford it. The Korean cultural emphasis on education and upward mobility through education is also reflected in their migration pattern. Although Koreans in the Chicago area are believed to be quite dispersed, they often congregate to areas with reputable public school systems. Initially, many first-ring north and northwestern suburbs with reputable school systems such as Skokie, Lincolnwood, Niles, Glenview, Morton Grove, and Schaumburg attracted many Koreans because of their proximity to the city (Map 12.1, color insert). By the early 2000s, so many Koreans had left Chicago that the Korean commercial areas along Lawrence Avenue started to shrink in size. Suburban expansion has reached Lake County, an affluent county north of Chicago, where Koreans are the only Asian ethnic group with a sizable presence. The Census 2000 (SF4) identified more than twice as many Korean immigrants in the six-county suburban areas (24,321) as in the city (10,011).

Such a desire for spatial upward mobility is facilitated by a high number of financial institutions, including mortgage companies, banks, and real estate agencies that are either owned by Koreans or have services tailored to the Korean population. The Korean Business Directory of 2002–03 lists 60 mortgage corporations and lending companies, 93 banks, and 172 real estate agents and agencies. Of these listings, 122 were listed in the 847 area code (north and northwestern suburbs), whereas only 53 were listed in 312 and 773 area codes in the city.

As many upwardly mobile Korean immigrants moved to the suburbs, they became scattered around the region, no longer supporting a central commercial area like old Clark Street or Lawrence Avenue. Instead, these businesses began to occupy bits and pieces of strip malls in various locations of commercial venue. Although clusters of these Korean shops exist around the north and northwestern suburbs, a symbolic central location no longer exists to identify Koreans. Those who have observed the Korean community in Chicago for a long time are concerned about the loss of cohesiveness resulting from this lack of physical concentration.

As widely dispersed residential patterns started to spread in the suburban area, the income disparity by geography among Korean Americans in Chicago has become fairly severe (Table 12.2). Those in the suburban areas earn far more than those in the city, and this inequality is quite dramatic compared with other predominant ethnic immigrants.

THE CONFLICT BETWEEN ECONOMIC ACHIEVEMENTS AND SOCIAL ISSUES

Political Participation and Interests

As the Korean community grew, its leaders encouraged immigrants to become U.S. citizens to increase participation in the political process. In addition to the language barrier, there also existed a general lack of understanding of the mainstream culture and the political system, which resulted in a lack of political participation. However, it would be a mistake to conclude that this translates to a lack of interest in the political process.

Mainstream observers have constantly labeled most Asian ethnic groups, including Koreans, as being apolitical, passive groups with a low level of participation and interests. But immigrants typically have different means of socialization that drive their political interests. Therefore, a traditional model for political participation does not always apply. According to the traditional model, those who are older, with higher incomes and educational levels, are more likely to be involved in the political process. If such a model were to be applied to immigrants, a higher level of participation would be expected among Asian Americans. In contrast, the patterns in which immigrants socialize depend on their foreign-born status and English proficiency (Cho 1999); thus, the likelihood of their voting does not necessarily increase with income. Similarly, first-generation immigrants educated in Korea do not necessarily have a better understanding of the American political system, just as higher education in other

TABLE 12.2. Median Household Income in Six-County Area for Asian Ethnic Groups

	Cook County	DuPage County	Kane County	Lake County	McHenry County	Will County	Chicago PMSA	City of Chicago
Philippines	$63,925	$77,082	$75,707	$77,418	$85,355	$72,614	$68,273	$55,164
India	$60,428	$76,555	$70,104	$81,090	$76,783	$81,721	$65,509	$42,979
Korea	$40,955	$61,522	$68,750	$77,190	—	$81,131	$45,334	$20,401
China/Taiwan	$44,040	$91,393	$87,208	$94,506	$58,000	$84,500	$52,465	$36,853
Total Population	$45,922	$67,887	$59,351	$66,973	$64,826	$62,238	$51,680	$38,625

Sources: U.S. Census Bureau, 2000, SF4.

countries does not contribute greatly to the knowledge of political systems outside the home country.

In fact, in the case of Korean immigrants, as the more affluent and better-educated came to the United States, political interests for Korean Americans heightened, but focused primarily on homeland politics rather than on local or national interests in America. Korean American newspapers played a crucial role in the 1983 military coup d'état in South Korea. Although all sources of media within Korea were banned from reporting the event, Korean American newspapers were one of the few sources available to spread the news. During the 1980s' military dictatorship in South Korea, a political struggle divided the Korean community in Chicago between those who were anti-government and those who supported the government. By late 1980s, as South Korea became democratic, this division dissolved.

Because of the shrinking Korean population in the city and its scattered residential patterns, traditional support for local elective positions, such as mayors and aldermen, is not likely to be formed. If the Korean American population in the area were to stabilize at its current size, the number may not be large enough to draw interest from regional politicians. Nevertheless, interest in politics, especially in local politics, is slowly rising among 1.5- and second-generation Korean Americans. Organizations are forming, primarily fostered by professionals in the legal and medical fields, to increase ethnic influence in the area. It remains to be seen if such interests will coalesce within the group or will grow into a coalition with other ethnic groups.

GENDER ROLES

The role of Korean women in formal economic structures had already started changing in the early part of the last century, and their increased participation and cultural tolerance in the labor force has challenged traditional women's roles in general. But, to this day, a common understanding of a woman's professional career path is based on the deep-seated Confucian philosophy that such a career would cease to exist

upon marriage, and the perception is that most women prefer to be full-time homemakers.

In the immigrant community, however, women are expected to contribute as much as men in the labor force, especially in the context of an entrepreneurship based on family members as laborers. As is the case in many patriarchal societies, conflicts arise when external economic factors force the role of women to change while domestic roles remain the same. Typically, this means that, in addition to working an equal amount of hours outside the home, women are still expected to fulfill the domestic duties of cooking, raising children, and other household chores. As a result, an increasing number of immigrant women challenge the traditional authority of their husbands.

As indicated in Figure 12.4, the proportion of immigrants holding managerial and professional specialty occupations prior to their arrival is similar among females and males. Although this pattern may not be generalized in South Korean society, it suggests a pattern of selective migration, in which, particularly for females, those who have had white-collar occupations are more likely to leave their country and migrate.

The higher proportions of professional and managerial occupations for women, however, are not necessarily transferable when they migrate. Just as similarly high proportions of labor-force participation for professional and managerial workers have occurred between males and females, as shown in Table 12.3, similar proportions of them redistributed and diversified themselves into different sectors, starting with manufacturing in 1980s and later into retail-oriented, entrepreneurial sectors. Although professional and managerial occupations did not dissipate completely, the trend suggests a decline in occupational status for Korean-immigrant men and women. These transitions are not likely to be willful but rather a consequence of lacking the linguistic skills and cultural understanding necessary for success in a new country.

The even distribution of the labor force has an important implication for Korean immigrants in Chicago area. Despite a historically disproportionate dominance in sheer numbers of females over males, much of the focus given to Korean entrepreneurship includes mostly male

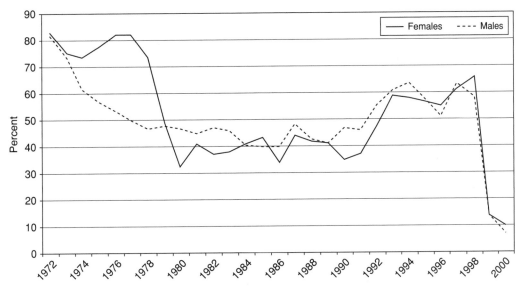

FIGURE 12.4. Occupation of Korean immigrants by gender, managerial, and professional specialty, 1972–2000.
Source: Immigration and Naturalization Service, 1972–2000.

ownership. Because women's roles still contain domestic responsibilities, a similar distribution of occupation did not translate into a similar level of income.

THE ROLE OF MEDIA AND SOCIAL–RELIGIOUS INSTITUTIONS

One of the first forms of Korean media in Chicago was an hour-long Saturday evening AM radio program started in 1970, by the Korean American Association. Today, despite the lack of residential concentration amongst Koreans in Chicago area, other means of communication and community bind the groups together. Three major newspapers are printed in Korean, and two radio and two television stations offer a variety of entertainment and news programs. With satellite technology, newspapers are able to print on the same day locally as in Korea, and the 9 o'clock evening news and latest Korean soap operas can be viewed virtually instantaneously here.

In addition to providing entertainment and news from the homeland, the Korean media increasingly plays an important role in connecting what could otherwise be a community highly

TABLE 12.3. Major Industries for Korean Immigrants by Gender (in Percent) 1980–2000

	1980		1990		2000	
	Males	Females	Males	Females	Males	Females
Manufacturing	14.8	9.1	13.8	16.3	36.4	35.2
Retail Trade	15.0	17.4	17.8	16.7	11.6	11.6
Professional and Related Services	12.1	9.6	4.6	4.2	4.7	1.1
Arts, Entertainment, Recreation, and Food Services	5.3	12.2	5.6	7.8	5.1	5.6
Business, Repair, and Other Services	12.1	15.1	22.1	19.5	8.0	6.4
Educational, Health, and Social Services	5.0	19.7	11.1	15.3	15.3	30.7
Total (N)	5,501	5,341	9,447	9,327	11,838	12,070

Sources: PUMS, 1980–2000.

isolated by the language barrier that exists between it and the mainstream culture. Local sections in the newspapers and local television news report events not only in the Korean community in Chicago but also for the area in general, so that even those who do not comprehend English can catch up on general issues. Such means of mass communication play a vital role during elections or census taking. The significance of these media outlets is increasing beyond the Chicago metropolitan area and throughout the Midwest region, where the Korean population is steadily rising.

Religious institutions are another important form of community for Koreans in Chicago. During the earlier days of Korean immigrant history in Chicago, churches, in addition to being places of worship, were the only formal setting offered for socialization. Although a virtually even distribution exists between Buddhists and Christians in South Korea, an overwhelming number of Christian churches are present in Chicago, whereas Buddhist temples are far less represented. The Korean Business Directory of 2002–03 lists 263 Christian churches in the six-county area, whereas only six Buddhist temples are listed. Of 263 churches, 173 were located in the 847 area code (north and northwestern suburbs) and 58 were located in the city. Interestingly, five of six Buddhist temples are located on the North Side. Many scholars, including historian Youn-Jin Kim, do not necessarily believe that more Christians migrate but rather, many become Christians after immigration, sometimes for practical purposes (Kim 1991, 279). Those who convert believe the American lifestyle is mostly based on Christian beliefs, and they believe conversion will enhance their (or more importantly, their children's) chance of assimilation.

INTERACTIONS AND CONFLICT WITH AFRICAN AMERICANS

During the 1980s Koreans started to collaborate with African Americans for civil rights. This effort was hardly publicized, and focus was given instead to those Korean entrepreneurs who had became successful in black Chicagoan neighborhoods and caused resentment among the black residents.

Many Korean immigrants perceived blacks as inferior and were suspicious of them, although many Korean businesses' primary clientele was African American. When the riots occurred in Los Angeles in 1992, the effect was felt in Chicago, as tension grew between Koreans and African Americans. When the Chicago Bulls basketball team won the National Basketball Association Championship, a riot similar to that which occurred in Los Angeles damaged a number of South Side businesses, quite a few owned by Koreans.

Understanding this clash requires a comprehension of two distinct cultures competing for limited space and resources. Although such competition between ethnic groups has occurred previously among many different minority groups in many different cities, the story behind these two groups tells a tale slightly different from the traditional interethnic competition of the early twentieth century.

Chicago's history of racial segregation is well documented, especially when it comes to African Americans, who have been confined to the South and West Sides of the city for decades. Large parts of these areas have remained impoverished because of institutional racism and political ignorance. Korean immigrants found modest economic success with their small shops in those areas. Being abandoned by the mainstream economy meant a lack of access to retailers by the residents of the area and, for Korean entrepreneurs, that translated to a captured clientele for merchandise ranging from everyday household items to apparel and wigs.

It is important to note, however, that Koreans had no interest in establishing roots in these traditionally African American neighborhoods. Rather, their goal was generating revenue and accumulating capital. Many commuted well over an hour from their North Side or northern suburb homes to stores along Roosevelt Avenue or even further south to 83rd Street. Furthermore, initially, most of these entrepreneurs had no interest in establishing relationships with their clients and customers: They were often suspicious of blacks, based on stereotypes. Combined with a lack of cultural understanding from both parties, conflict was inevitable.

Koreans criticized blacks for being crime-prone and not trustworthy, and hired guards for their stores specifically to look for shoplifters. Blacks criticized Koreans for being greedy, arrogant, and rude. Koreans resented violence and boycotts directed toward their stores and blacks resented the stores for refusing to hire black employees from the community. Not many Koreans were aware of the historical context responsible for creating such impoverished areas for blacks. And the African American community did not understand Korean immigrant culture, which had an essentially different way of interacting and had the added difficulty of learning a new language.

Korean entrepreneurs were determined to maximize profit by minimizing cost. This meant working longer hours and bringing in family members or relatives to work, rather than hiring strangers. This phenomenon is not unusual among many immigrant cultures, where family goals often dominate over individual goals. It often means neglecting larger social issues and a lack of sympathy toward other groups. Under such survival mentality, upward mobility ultimately means moving out of those areas with poor clientele to areas that are economically better off, less violent, and, perhaps more intensely in Chicago, racially white.

Although a reasonable number of Korean entrepreneurs transition from one area to another, Korean-owned businesses rarely change hands outside of the ethnic group. Such intra-ethnic financial transactions are common in many groups, not only because they are more likely to be informally handed over amid tight networks but also because most of these business owners tend to be first-generation immigrants who are unfamiliar with the mainstream process of real estate transactions. Thus, the most likely scenario for selling a business, outside of word of mouth, is advertising in local Korean newspapers rather than mainstream publications. And, as long as a constant influx of new immigrants continues, the entrepreneurial opportunity is likely to remain within the group.

This limitation is an important point to be made in the context of the Korean–African American relationship, because Koreans are often accused of shutting blacks out of opportunities to own businesses in their own neighborhoods.

Korean local media at one point posed the question of why blacks would display such fierce antagonism toward Koreans, unlike other ethnic groups such as Italians and Jews, who run businesses in their community. Korean newspapers portrayed this phenomenon as the African American community's inability to protest against established whites but instead use Koreans as an easier target or scapegoat. This notion further reinforced the feeling among Koreans that they do not belong in the mainstream, and therefore stressed the importance of ethnic solidarity.

The relationship between these two groups improved over the years, and the tension has subsided. Many Korean business owners made efforts to hire blacks from the community, and there has been less resistance from the African American community to patronize Korean businesses. Structurally, however, the problem remains, because blacks are confined mostly to the South and West Sides, and Korean immigrants commute into these areas from afar. Consequently, the lack of interaction other than business transactions still remains. If history is any indication of the future, the current generation of Korean business owners is likely to move out of black communities and hand them over to another group, just as they have inherited these businesses mostly from Jewish owners.

GENERATIONAL ISSUES

Because most children of immigrants, the 1.5 generation, are more likely to be assimilated and surrounded by mainstream norms, they often feel abashed by their parents' culture and attitude. Some are even aghast at the thought of carrying the tradition down to their own generation. However, their parents' old customs and mentalities influence much of their lives. The Korean immigrants' strong emphasis on education means that their children are likely to attend good schools and receive college degrees. As mentioned earlier, their residential choices are likely to be made based on school performances.

Because so many aspects of their home life are dramatically different from life outside of it, from language to food and ways of interaction, many 1.5- and second-generation Korean Americans struggle to find a compromise medium. Over time, as they grow older, however, especially those with higher education develop the audacity to challenge the mainstream norm and explore their own culture. They also appear to have developed desire for political and social participation outside the Korean community as well.

At the same time, many immigrants have begun to accept the changes in values, especially those from family-oriented to more individual aspirations. For many parents, this means acknowledging their children's differing perspectives on careers, marriages, and even living arrangements.

Although such patterns of interaction are thought to be the norm in the Korean immigrant community, where parents work long hours to provide homes in good school districts and later a good college education, conflicts and problems often go unnoticed. Although mainstream media has described this Korean immigrant experience as being a part of the "model minority," a lack of substantive interaction and understanding between parents and children sometimes leads to a failure to meet expectations, both socially and personally. From the immigrant parents' perspective, working longer hours is often required to provide well for the family, especially for those in the entrepreneurial sector. But that means less time for the supervision of children. From the children's perspective, because academic expectations are seemingly higher than for the mainstream culture, those who struggle to meet them or require guidance tend to internalize their failure. This, in part, could explain the recent increase in gang activities in high schools and the increasing college dropout rates among not only Korean students, but Asian American students in general.

With the growth in proportion of second- and third-generation Koreans, many first-generation immigrants perceive marriage out-side the ethnic group as an inevitable part of the assimilation process. Although many still resist such change, especially marriage with other non-white racial groups, the level of tolerance has been much higher than in years past. For those concerned with the identity issues of the younger generations, the Chicago area does not offer much institutional support, outside of Korean churches offering language schools. Not many schools offer the language, nor are there plans to promote the advantages of learning the language and being bilingual. As is the case in political participation, the only way to make Korean culture and language visible may be by means of coalition with other ethnic groups.

Concerns also are voiced about the elderly Korean population, which is intimately tied to spatial distribution. According to the census data, despite the fact that only 27 percent of Koreans in the six-county area live in the city, 66 percent of Koreans over the age of 65 reside in the city of Chicago, and two-thirds of them earn income below the poverty line. Virtually all those over 65 and living in poverty in the city (97 percent) were immigrants, most of whom (91 percent) have lived in the United States for more than 10 years (Census 2000, SF4 and 5-percent PUMS). The large economic disparity by age and geographic isolation of the elderly population implies a breakdown of traditional family structure among this immigrant community.

CONCLUSION

In her dissertation about Koreans in Chicago, historian Yoon-Jin Kim (1991, 4) described their lives as "isolation but acculturation, strong ethnic identity and solidarity but assimilation." Despite cultural conflicts and tensions across generations and with other ethnic and racial groups, the Korean community in the Chicago area has managed to expand in size and economic strength, and it strives to increase its visibility. In the near future, the younger generations are likely to define the Korean identity in Chicago, rather than the first-generation immigrants and their entrepreneurships. Although most Korean immigrants may be proud of the ways in which they managed to survive in this society, they are likely to admit that their ultimate goal is to achieve a balance between the maintenance of traditional values and assimilation to the mainstream culture.

It is important to point out the distinction between the ways in which mass media has defined successful immigrants and the ways Koreans themselves assess their progress and history in American society. Based on the Confucian elements of their culture, many Koreans tend to consider prestige and status more than material wealth in deciding occupation (Kim 1991, 121). Thus, the much-publicized economic successes of Korean immigrant entrepreneurships through dry cleaning and retail shops do not meet expectations in measuring the level of success. Rather, it would require more representation in more visible and higher-prestige occupations, such as politics, academia, medicine, or law. First-generation immigrants expect such status will be achieved by the subsequent generations, which in many cases it is.

The Korean population in the Chicago area is not likely to experience the massive growth in size that it did during the 1980s through migration. In such a relatively stable and moderate-sized community, three potential issues predominate. First, the composition of the community is likely to change with rapid a increase in numbers from the second and third generations and a disproportionately slower increase in new immigrants. Combined with a higher rate of marriage outside its own group, the faces of the Korean community will have a multiethnic and multiracial association. The level of tolerance and the scope of inclusiveness in Korean identity will determine the cohesiveness and longevity of the community.

Second, the spatial mobility of residential and commercial clusters of Korean Americans will likely depend on their ability to interact with other racial and ethnic groups in Chicago. Unlike in Los Angeles or New York, where Koreans have established commercial areas through decades of building in a concentrated area, Chicago's commercial development has shifted from urban to mostly suburban during a 30-year period, and it is likely to be mobile yet again. As with other ethnic groups, particularly Mexicans and other Asian ethnic populations, Koreans follow similar patterns of migration to similar areas, where competition for space is likely. This has been the case among a number of different racial and ethnic minorities throughout the history of this country, in various metropolitan areas. In this process, Koreans in Chicago are not likely to numerically dominate any given area, but rather to continue to display a scattered pattern. Last, although the relatively small number of Koreans in the Chicago metropolitan area may have remained stable, the number of Koreans in the Midwest region has grown at a much faster rate in recent years, mostly because of the steady number of Korean students who can be found in major universities. It is very common to find concentration of Koreans in campus towns including Madison, Wisconsin; Ann Arbor, Michigan; Columbus, Ohio; Iowa City, Iowa; and Minneapolis, Minnesota. Thus, Chicago will play the role of a hub city to Koreans in the Midwest and will provide goods and services to those who live far from sizable Korean communities.

Yvonne M. Lau

13 Chicago's Chinese Americans: From Chinatown and Beyond

The Chinese Immigrant comes to America as an
economic adventurer.
—Paul Siu

ALTHOUGH THIS DESCRIPTION was written
more than 50 years ago by Paul Siu (1987) in his
doctoral dissertation, *The Chinese Laundryman,*
it aptly describes a significant number of Chinese Americans today. In recent decades, cities
like Chicago have been transformed by changes
in local and global restructuring that include
the transnational migration of labor and capital. Given the higher visibility of Asian American
populations in California and the Northeast,
and the strong presence of Asian American and
ethnic studies on bi-coastal campuses, smaller
centers of Asian American community life in the
Midwest and in cities like Chicago have been
under-represented in academic research and
popular literature. Ethnic enclaves like "Chinatown," both real and imagined, are immediately
linked to cities like San Francisco or New York.

This chapter reviews some of the early history of Chinese migration to Chicago, examining trends in Chinese immigration to Illinois, both in Chicago and compared with the
six-county region. *Within* the city of Chicago,
Chinese Americans represent the largest Asian
community, followed by Filipinos, Asian Indians, and Koreans. They have contributed to
the revitalization and gentrification of Chicago's
neighborhoods, from the far North Side to the
South Loop and southwest side.

To challenge prevailing images that all "Ori-
entals" or "Chinese" are alike, this chapter

highlights the increasing diversity among Chinese immigrants and Chinese Americans. Suggesting that, aside from traditional ethnic enclaves like Chinatown, a number of ways exist
for immigrants to seek and maintain their cultural and ethnic identity, the chapter encourages readers to think beyond Chinatown. For
today's upwardly mobile immigrants, retaining
transnational linkages may not depend on living or working in an ethnic enclave. Using their
larger pools of human, cultural, and social capital, advantaged Chinese Americans may never
be attracted to a Chinatown, and may opt instead to live and possibly work in the suburbs. By
analyzing old and emerging communities, this
chapter delineates geographically bound from
socially constructed communities.

HISTORICAL BACKGROUND: FROM SOJOURNER TO IMMIGRANT

Chinese immigration to the United States occurred over four historical periods: (1) open
immigration from 1849 to 1882; (2) immigration policies of exclusion from 1882 to 1943, except for members of exempted categories such
as merchants, scholars, and the like; (3) immigration quotas permitting limited entry from
1943 to 1965; and (4) revived entry following
the 1965 Immigration Act and continuing until the present. The 1965 Immigration Act ended
the 1924 national-origins quotas and created a
new system of preference categories focusing on
family reunification and occupational skills (Lau

2002, 47); this chapter focuses on this latter contemporary period.

Just as Chicago's Great Fire of 1871 provides the entry point for the century-long trajectory leading to New Chicago, it is also a marker for the first recorded Chinese-owned business in Chicago. In 1872, as the city rebuilt from the Great Chicago Fire, the first Chinese hand laundry opened in Chicago's Loop at 167 West Madison (Siu 1987, 23). Chicago's first Chinatown was established during the 1880s, near Clark and Van Buren—part of what came to be known as the Loop. The small downtown Chinatown fulfilled the basic business and social needs of the early wave of Chinese, who were predominantly single and male. Unlike other urban Chinatowns, Chicago's first ethnic enclave was not a residential center. Chicago's Chinese population was small, overshadowed by those of gateway centers like San Francisco and New York. In 1910, 65 Chinese women and 1,713 men lived in Chicago (Lau 2002, 47).

Furthermore, with hard lessons learned from the American West experience and anti-Chinese movement, most Chinese who made it to the Midwest chose not to live in Chinatown, preferring to "blend in," scattering themselves around town and living invisibly within their storefront businesses. By 1883, a newspaper article reported that 700 Chinese in Chicago had asked Peking to open a consulate in the city because the police had "raided them indiscriminately on the pretense of cracking down on opium dens" (Jew 2003, 167).

By 1910, higher rents, indicative of the growing Loop economy, and internal factionalism in the original Chinatown led the leaders to expand to another Chinatown, south of the Loop, near Wentworth and Cermak, which provided affordable storefronts and apartments. According to documents collected by the largest social service agency in Chinatown, escalating rents and conflicts displaced about half of the Chinese population in the Loop into this Italian and Croatian neighborhood (Chinese American Service League 1996, 2). Some presence in the Loop Chinatown remained (mostly in the form of restaurants) until 1975, when the buildings were razed to prepare for municipal buildings

including the Metropolitan Correctional Center (Tom 1995, 45).

An influx of new immigrants arrived in Chicago during the 1950s, mainly Mandarin-speaking professionals displaced by the 1949 Revolution in China. Because they possessed more human capital (including English proficiency), many of them settled in the suburbs outside of the central city. Newly arrived Cantonese-speaking immigrants and refugees from China and Hong Kong tended to live around Chinatown, joining the second-generation community in renovating and expanding the South Side Chinatown. A smaller group of working and middle-class Chinese immigrants and refugees settled on the North Side, in racially diverse neighborhoods including the Near North Side, Uptown, Edgewater, and Rogers Park, close to public transportation and city jobs. By 1960, the U.S. Census reported about 7,000 Chinese Americans living in Chicago, with a growing number of native-born (Tom 1995, 44).

The passage of the Hart-Cellar Act and the lifting of discriminatory quotas prompted a major surge in the Asian American population. After the 1965 Act allowed for annual quotas of 20,000 per year for each independent country outside of the Western hemisphere, the Chinese diaspora erupted, with waves of immigration coming in from the People's Republic of China (PRC), Taiwan, Hong Kong, and Southeast Asia. The quota was based on the immigrant's country of birth; China and Taiwan would share a quota for 20,000. Persons born in Hong Kong came under Great Britain's quota (McCunn 1998, 161). By 1970, Chicago's Chinese American population had doubled to 14,077, making it the fourth largest population center for Chinese in the country (Tom 1995, 44).

By the late 1970s, another significant spurt of immigration from PRC appeared as the United States and China renewed relations in 1979. China was allocated its own quota of 20,000. Taiwan was given a separate quota of 20,000 in 1982. The Immigration Act of 1986 allowed an increased quota of 5,000 for those born in Hong Kong (McCunn 1998, 161).

The birth of a third Chinese enclave was prompted in the mid-1970s, after two major converging events. With the demolition of remaining buildings situated in the original Chinatown complete, another group of Chinese businessmen representing the Hip Sing Tong decided to venture to the north side of the city. Led by restauranteur and Hip Sing president, Jimmy Wong, tong associates purchased over 60 percent of a three-block section of Argyle, from Broadway to Sheridan Road, on Chicago's North Side. Early Chinese residents of the Uptown neighborhood talked about the poor image of the neighborhood: "No one wanted to go there, to live or shop. There was prostitution, poor Appalachian whites, drunks, and the homeless. Jimmy couldn't get many Chinese to invest. He would've lost everything, but lucky, the war ended," said one interviewee.

After the conclusion of the Vietnam War in 1975, a mass influx of refugees from Southeast Asia buttressed the development of this enclave of refugees and immigrants around this Uptown neighborhood. Represented mainly by ethnic Chinese and natives from Vietnam, Cambodia, Thailand, and Laos, the new Argyle neighborhood provided more affordable business and residential opportunities, especially for newcomers who could not fully access the higher rental or purchase properties common in the more homogeneous and desirable South Side community of Chinatown.

CURRENT DEMOGRAPHIC TRENDS

A thinly veiled frustration in the Chinese community is the public perception that all Chinese are alike. For most Americans, Chinese Americans are usually not distinguishable by nativity, dialect, class, generation, paths of social mobility, or patterns of geographic residence (Zhou 2003, 40). Yet, in Chicago as elsewhere, a tremendous diversity prevails among Chinese Americans, related to their ten-fold growth in the United States between 1960 and 2000. Currently, Chinese Americans are the largest Asian American ethnic group in the United States, totaling 2.88 million. Of these Chinese Americans, about 57 percent are American born, with ancestry from mainland China, Taiwan, or Hong Kong.

Among states with the largest population of Chinese Americans, Illinois is ranked seventh, behind California (1.1 million), New York, Hawaii, Texas, New Jersey, and Massachusetts (Zhou 2003, 40). During the last decade, Chinese Americans, similar to other Asian American groups, experienced a significantly higher growth rate than the Illinois population at large (9 percent). The Chinese American population increased by 72 percent in Illinois, rising to 85,840, and is the third largest Asian population group in the state after Indians and Filipinos (Asian American Institute 2002, 9).

City versus Suburban

Although Chinese Americans are concentrated in three of Chicago's six collar counties—Cook, DuPage, and Lake (Map 13.1, color insert), the largest number of suburbanites by far (48,058) reside in Cook County. Concentrations of Chinese suburbanites, like Chinese city dwellers, are dispersed throughout the three-county region and have risen dramatically in the past decade. Municipalities like Naperville (4,198), Skokie (1,574), Evanston (1,426), Schaumburg (1,388), and Hoffman Estate (896) head the list followed by Palatine (846), Buffalo Grove (758), Arlington Heights (757), Wilmette (705), and Westmont (705). Although some Chinese reside in nearly all of Chicago's 77 neighborhoods, like all other immigrant groups, they too concentrate in some neighborhoods more than others.

Armour Square (7,148) and the adjacent neighborhood of Bridgeport (8,273) account for 48 percent of all Chinese living in the city—nearly 15,500 people. The remaining eight of the ten largest Chinese neighborhoods—as Map 13.2 (see color insert) shows—are scattered in the near west, near north, far north, and northwest neighborhoods of West Ridge (1,489), Hyde Park (1,392), Near West Side (1,316), Edgewater (1,192), McKinley Park (1,132), Uptown (1,069), Brighton Park (977), and Lake View (830).

Foreign-born Chinese represent 76 percent of the Chinese American population, both in Chicago and the suburbs. This is in rather stark contrast to other large immigrant Asian groups—Filipinos, Asian Indians, and

Koreans—who reside primarily in the suburbs. Human capital differences among city and suburban Chinese are the most striking and polarized of any of the large immigrant groups in Chicago. Comparing the median household incomes, Chicago's households average $36,853, whereas suburban Chinese families in DuPage and Lake Counties average $91,393 and $94,506 (Chapter 12, Table 12.2). Educationally, 40 percent of Chinese Americans in Chicago have a college degree or higher, whereas 71 percent in the suburbs are college graduates. Similarly, 43 percent of suburban Chinese have post baccalaureate degrees, and 21 percent of Chinese city residents do. Finally, suburban Chinese are disproportionately more English-proficient than their city counterparts—65 percent versus 40 percent.

Chinese Americans are more likely to live beyond Chinatown and in the suburbs if they have a college or advanced degree, thus reflecting a higher socioeconomic status. Particularly for Chinese American families with children, access to "good" public schools, which are perceived to be mainly located in the suburbs, becomes a key factor in choosing a suburban neighborhood. Residential and socioeconomic mobility are closely linked. Bringing in more human and social capital, middle-class and professional Chinese Americans use their greater access to financing and networks to identify the "best" neighborhoods beyond ethnic enclaves to provide a higher quality of life for their families; they are twice as likely to choose the suburbs if they have a master's, professional, or doctoral degree.

Counter trends are marked by the overall gentrification of Chicago's ethnic neighborhoods and the return of empty nesters and second-generation "yuppies" who can afford new and renovated housing. Attracted to the conveniences of the South Side Chinatown and South Loop areas, these city enclave residents represent those who have remained in the area because of limited human capital and financial resources, and those returning to the old neighborhood.

Two Socioeconomic Worlds

City resident profiles reflect a widening gap in human capital and economic resources, tending towards a bi-modal distribution. For example, although large numbers of college-educated professionals and highly-skilled technicians are contained within the Chinese labor force, there are also significant numbers of low-literacy and low-wage service and manufacturing workers. Contributing factors may be linked with the variations in immigrant occupational backgrounds by period and country of immigration. The bimodal and gendered occupational niches of Chinese Americans are particularly striking among foreign-born Chinese men and women (Chapter 15, Appendix Tables 9 and 10). The largest male concentrations range from cooks (2,101) and chefs (633), to computer software engineers (1,143), computer programmers (1,281), and medical scientists (308). Among foreign-born Chinese women, the largest occupations are represented by accountants (1,498), computer programmers (881), chemists and math scientists (479), and in the less-skilled jobs such as sewing machine operators (803), and cutting workers in the clothing industry (N = 309) (see Chapter 15, Appendix Tables 9 and 10).

A visit to the South Side Chinatown points to the growing inequality among residents in terms of access to goods and services or affordable housing. Chinatown's real estate ranges from old, substandard dwellings to new luxury townhouses on the same blocks. Some residents are linguistically isolated, bound to jobs in the ethnic enclave, often tied to menial, low-wage work. Others are professionals, commuting daily in short trips downtown to their corporate offices and white-collar jobs.

In contrast, suburban Chinese Americans are more homogeneous in socioeconomic status, with sufficient human capital and economic resources to afford the lifestyle linked to suburban communities. Gravitating toward new housing developments, reputable school systems, and high-tech corporate corridors, and lured by the emerging "ethno-suburbs" (e.g., Naperville, Skokie, Palatine, Schaumburg, Arlington Heights) that offer ethnic goods and services, suburban Chinese Americans are more integrated into the dominant suburban culture. They are not dependent on traditional Chinatown for jobs, services, or products, but rather they visit Chinatown on special occasions.

Mainland Chinese, Taiwanese, and
Hong Kong Immigrants

In deconstructing the notion that "all Chinese are alike," it is critical to consider their country of origin and period of migration. Significant differences exist in human, cultural, and social capital when comparing Chinese immigrants from mainland China (PRC), Taiwan, and Hong Kong; these differences lead to different modal patterns of occupational specialization, residential segregation, and overall acculturation. Thus, data on Chinese immigrants must be disaggregated by country of origin and immigrant status.

Such distinctions are needed to uncover the differences in the formation of transnational identities and the extent to which Chinese Americans maintain their ties to their native homeland. With the rich diasporic history of overseas Chinese, dating back to earlier centuries, migration to the United States does not necessarily reflect a contemporary or linear model. Eventual residence in Chicago may be the culmination of a multistage process, interrupted by wars and immigration barriers. Although the country of emigration may be identified, the object of homeland affections and ties can be difficult to measure.

Currently, the cumulative total population of Chinese immigrants in the region is 51,255. Mainland Chinese represent 69 percent of the population, Taiwanese 19 percent, and Hong Kong immigrants make up 12 percent (Figure 13.1). About 60 percent of Taiwanese immigrants and 56 percent of Hong Kong immigrants arrived before 1990. However, 57 percent of immigrants from China had arrived after 1990.

Identifying watershed years for differences in immigration cohorts from the three sending nations leads to a consideration of the effect of U.S. foreign policy and resulting INS laws and preferences. For Taiwan, instead of sharing its quota with China, 1982 marked a turning point as the Reagan administration allotted it a separate quota of 20,000. For the ten years up until 1993, a consistent flow of Taiwanese immigrants arrived in Illinois, from a low of 395 in 1988 to a high of 784 in 1983. For Hong Kong, the Immigration Act of 1986 enhanced the flow of immigrants in later years, reaching a high of 417 in 1992.

Although the normalization of U.S.–Chinese relations dates in 1972, during the Nixon administration, prompted a steady out-migration to states like Illinois, a turning point for mainland

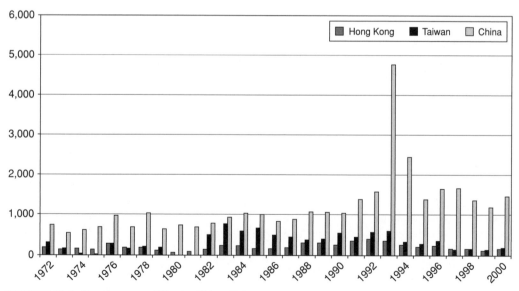

FIGURE 13.1. Immigrants to Illinois: China, Taiwan, Hong Kong, 1972–2000.
Source: U.S. Immigration and Naturalization Service Data, 1972–2000.

immigration occurred in 1993. Given the events following the Tiananmen Student Movement in 1989, many Chinese nationals and students in the United States joined in protest against the Chinese government. By 1992, concern for the safety of the 80,000 Chinese who were studying in the United States led President George H. Bush to sign a Presidential Directive, granting these students and their families permanent resident status. This directive became effective in 1993 (Lu 2001, 218), thus prompting the high rates of adjusted visas for Chinese. Over 65 percent of the total number of valid visas was for Chinese immigrants who applied for a change in status. Only 14 percent of the immigrants in 1993 entered through the Immigration and Naturalization Service (INS) family preferences or reunification programs. The impact of this directive can be seen when comparing the total number of immigrants admitted by the INS. In 1992, 1,592 were admitted from China. In 1993, 4,790 were admitted, and in 1994, 2,466 were admitted.

A review of INS data on Chinese immigrants to Illinois based on occupational and family preferences and year also yields valuable information. General national patterns of visa allocation post 1965 showed more than 75 percent of immigrants enter through family preferences, and about 20 percent enter through occupational preferences (Zhou 1992, 43). Chinese immigrants to Illinois over a decade ago showed a similar trend. In 1991, 83 percent of Chinese immigrants to Illinois entered through family preferences. By 1998, however, the percentage of admittances by family preferences had shifted radically, to 19 percent. The highest number of permanent visas was given to highly skilled and professional immigrants, including their spouses and children, and resulted in the largest adjusted category.

The implications of such a shift point to the declining proportion of visas allocated to new arrivals and the rising proportion of visas adjusted for Chinese already residing in Illinois. Anecdotal evidence suggests that the largest recipients of adjusted visas were Chinese students who, after completing their degree programs and practical training, sought permanent residence in the United States. If they can find a job with an employer or company willing to sponsor them for permanent residency, then their student status may be converted to permanent residency.

A counter trend worth noting from INS occupational data is found for the years 1999–2000. A sharp decline of former Chinese managers and professionals processed through Illinois accompanies the sharp rise of Chinese immigrants with backgrounds in farming, forestry, and fishing. In 1999 and 2000, 46 percent and 36 percent respectively of Chinese recorded their backgrounds in farming, forestry and fishing. This may result from cycles of transitioning immigration status for the large cohort of Chinese students who gained permanent residency in the 1990s. As they become U.S. citizens, they are able to petition for their immediate family (including parents, spouses, and minor children) who may enter as nonquota immigrants. With more Chinese residents achieving permanent resident or citizen status, increasing numbers of Chinese immigrants are eligible for admission through INS family preferences.

As with other ethnic immigrant groups, the second wave of Chinese immigrants tend to have less human capital in the form of lower job skills, and they may be more linguistically dependent if their native language is not English. The relatively recent migration of mainland Chinese to Illinois, compared to those from Taiwan and Hong Kong, partially contributes to the significant proportion of Chinese residents in South Side Chinatown. Compared with other residential Chinatowns across the United States, Chicago Chinatown maintains a large percentage of Chicago's Chinese residents. The Chinese Chinatown population constitutes 26 percent of Chicago's entire Chinese population (31,813). In terms of the other major Chinatowns in the United States, 2 percent of Chinese immigrants live in Los Angeles Chinatown, 8 percent of Chinese immigrants live in San Francisco Chinatown, and 14 percent live in New York Chinatown (Zhou 2003, 41). Whether this residential concentration favoring Chicago's Chinatown reflects the more recent entry of Chinese immigrants or other appealing features of the changing enclave will be an important point of discussion.

SEARCHING FOR *JIA*: CONSTRUCTING CHINESE AMERICAN COMMUNITIES

For first-generation foreign-born Chinese, across class and country of origin, a key issue is how to maintain their "Chineseness." Although adjusting and succeeding in America is necessary and expected, retaining their Chinese identity and roots becomes more problematic. Among Chinese whose ancestors were part of the early Chinese diaspora to Southeast Asia, North and South America, Africa, and the Caribbean, full assimilation, even when legally mandated, was always resisted. How to preserve their Chinese heritage, language, and traditions to pass on to their family perpetually lingers on the Chinese psyche. *Jia*, commonly translated as *family*, may also connote home or homeland. China is referred to as *guojia* or country of family or motherland. When asking Chinese where they are from, you can ask about their jia or *laojia* (old home). Consequently, the immigrant need to recreate jia, especially in the United States, where INS laws may delay the arrival of the whole or extended family, becomes a paramount concern.

South Side Chinatown—Whose Jia?

Celebrating 90 years of history, the South Side Chinatown remains home for more than one of four Chinese Americans. Thirty years ago, the public image of Chinatown was that of a boxed-in enclave. As a resident commented, "Before, we were bound between the elevated train tracks, two interstate highways, a railway yard, and a sanitary canal." Today, it has been proclaimed "a scene of exciting dining finds and hip nightlife" (Wheaton 2004, 78).

For many years, the informal boundaries of Chinatown were Cermak Avenue and the South Branch of the Chicago River on the north, Dan Ryan Expressway on the east, 35th Avenue on the south, and Halsted Ave on the west. This area included two Chicago area communities, Armour Square and Bridgeport. In 1990, Asians represented 42 percent of the population; a decade earlier, Asians represented 24 percent of the population (Tom 1995, 45).

Given the population growth fueled by immigration and the spiraling expansion and development of residential and commercial real estate during the past decade, Chinatown's borders have extended to encompass six census tracts (Map 13.3, color insert). Bounded by 18th Street to the north, the Chicago River on the northwest leading to Wallace to the west, 31st Street to the south, and beyond the Dan Ryan Expressway to Federal and Clark to the east, today's Chinatown area population totals 8,135. Two-thirds (67 percent) of New Chicago's Chinatown residents are Chinese, and nearly three-quarters (72 percent) identify themselves as Asian and Pacific Islanders (APIs), reflecting a growth rate of 31 percent in the past 10 years.

Anchored by a new commercial outdoor mall, Chinatown Square, the area's trendy restaurants and stores attracts tourists and a younger crowd. Adjacent to the mall, Santa Fe Gardens, a modern complex of townhouses, single-family homes, and condominiums has added (to date) about 1,200 new residents. This represents the largest single new housing development in Chinatown's history.

In addition to inflationary housing values, a major shift in housing demographics has also occurred. The 1990 ratio of property owners to renters (2:1) has reversed itself in the last census. Property owners decreased from 66 percent in 1990 to 37 percent in 2000. Renters increased from 37 percent to 63 percent, representing a 106 percent increase. Comparing median housing values by tract, in 1990, the range from highest to lowest was $114,000 to $76,400. By 2000, the range from highest to lowest was $156,100 to $105,600.

Residents of this area are increasingly more educated and more likely to be in executive, administrative, managerial, or professional occupations. Comparing lowest and highest percentages of college graduates or higher, in 1990, the range was 5 percent to 23 percent. In 2000, the range was 6 percent to 39 percent for college-degree or advanced-degree graduates.

In reviewing demographic changes by tract, the fastest population growth of Asians (almost all Chinese) occurred in tracts 3401 and 6003. The latter tract falls into Bridgeport, home historically for generations of Irish Americans including, until recently, the family of Chicago Mayor Richard M. Daley. Once dominated by single-family brick homes, now tear-down or new construction units are interspersed throughout the neighborhood. Chinese families have been moving into the tract for the past decade, (rising to 41 percent), drawn to the better schools and single-family housing.

Tract 3401 is the most northern tract, north of Cermak. Once perceived as the environmentally hazardous Santa Fe Railroad yards, the area has undergone radical transformation into a multiuse complex. Chinese immigrants have been eager to purchase new commercial or residential units and now dominate this neighborhood, representing 70 percent of residents. Ranging from $239,000 for 1050 sq. ft. condos to $460,000 for 2640 sq. ft. single-family homes in its Phase IV and Phase V development (as of August 2003), attractive luxury housing units have sold rapidly in the last several years, with Phase V units almost sold out. Representing the largest single new housing development in Chinatown's history and expanding the boundaries of Chinatown by 32 acres, the Chinatown Square and Santa Fe projects were financed through private and public monies.

Unlike other North American Chinatowns, Chicago has not been on the radar for overseas Chinese investors, who have disproportionately invested in New York, Toronto, Vancouver, and new Chinese suburban enclaves like those in California (e.g., Monterey Park, Arcadia, San Gabriel). The transnational flow of investment capital from overseas Chinese has generally bypassed Chicago. Although foreign direct investment poured in rapidly during the 1990s to bicoastal Chinatowns—particularly prior to the anxiety-producing 1997 return of Hong Kong to the PRC—Chicago, despite its global standing, has not been viewed as a Pacific Rim center. One real estate broker commented that, "People in Hong Kong don't really think of Chicago. They still associate Chicago as a gangster city! There was that first condo development way early in the 80s, Appleville on Canal. Hong Kong investors partnered with a local businessman, but those units sold very slowly. Hong Kong

investors want a fast return. Why invest here when they could go to New York, Vancouver, or Toronto?"

Overseas Chinese investors have historically been eager to safeguard their capital against uncertain political and economic climates by investing in businesses and real estate throughout Southeast Asia and North American Chinatowns and Chinese enclaves. So, to date, Chicago's Chinatown has attracted mainly local investors and businesses. Still, Chinatown is definitely on an upswing, especially in real estate. As housing stock expands and property values escalate, the boom will continue. For Chinese immigrants, owning a home is the first goal and a symbol of making it in America. A local banker comments that "Chinatown is the central point of assimilation . . . immigrants work hard in restaurants . . . they are great savers. They work 24/7 for their children to have a better life . . . They want to buy a house. That's their escape."

He describes the intense housing-goal orientation of typical immigrants and how he supported unconventional criteria for mortgage qualifications: "They would make significant down payments, maybe 40 percent down, planning to pay back in 5 years! No one had financial statements to support these payments. If we used traditional criteria for borrowing, no one would qualify. Can you imagine—a waiter or chef making $1,100 a month gross, putting down 40 percent?"

Given the high rate of savings, in the last decade, Chinatown has attracted numerous banks, including eight Chinese-owned institutions. The rising reputation of Chinatown's banks as repositories of local capital enhances growth prospects for the local economy.

Today's new Chinatown residents are likely to be Chinese Americans or others higher in socioeconomic status. If they are Chinese Americans, they could be empty nesters who enjoy the conveniences of living in Chinatown or younger middle class, second-generation professionals who may be products of suburbia. Living around Chinatown now represents being in a trendy area, convenient to working downtown. The changing demographics have led to new types of businesses, including clubs and Internet cafés.

One interviewee, Todd, grew up in Chinatown, but had little interest in taking over his father's herbal medicine and acupuncture business. After a career as a software engineer, he decided to open up a late-night Asian bubble tea café. "I've gone back to my roots. We've been a hangout for the neighborhood, a comfortable place for teens to play games and relax. I've done something on my own!"

South Side Chinatown: The Other
Side of the Boom

With new waves of immigrants from mainland China and Southeast Asia, acute needs have surfaced for many services, including English-as-second-language (ESL) classes, job training, and bilingual and interpretive services. For those restricted by language barriers to ethnic enclaves, access to affordable housing is paramount. The duality of the ethnic enclave serves to both reward and punish those who are most dependent on it. The communities of Chinatown and (as later discussed), the North Side community of Argyle, provide social capital or ethnic networks of support, in addition to ethnic resources. Although this counteracts the new immigrants' limited pools of human capital (lower skills in English, lower education levels, or restricted transfer of occupational skills),[1] relying on Chinatown brings other consequences.

A dependence on Chinatown or Argyle as the only site for jobs and housing creates a habit of using the enclave to provide for all immigrant needs, creating an economic and cultural "ghetto," according to one agency staffer: "In order to get a better job, you have to go outside of Chinatown. Otherwise, all you can do is work in a restaurant. Even skilled workers are getting laid off post 9/11, so employers have more choices—they want workers to understand English . . . Chinese women want to get any job, as long as they get benefits."

The popular stereotype of Chinatown as a self-sufficient community is a myth. Some adult immigrants languish in ESL classes, drifting in and out for years, without gaining full-time employment. Without basic formal education,

working-class immigrant parents cannot help their kids with schoolwork without being able to read English or Chinese. Some who are juggling two or three jobs often have little time to spend with family, much less time for ESL classes. In the majority of working-class households, if only one parent can work, it tends to be the husband, thus leading to a perception among youth that fathers are usually not available to them. Many working-class families are under enormous stress to meet household expenses and provide for their families. They are struggling to sustain an adequate standard of living while facing limited opportunities for mobility.

The still-limited economy in Chinatown, dominated by service jobs in over 180 shops and restaurants, contributes to the rising unemployment and underemployment in the community. Few factory or manufacturing jobs are available in close proximity to Chinatown; workers must have transportation to get to where the better jobs are.

With a downward economy, two groups of workers prevail: those being laid off and those struggling to keep their jobs. Being largely confined to the secondary labor market or service-sector jobs, enclave residents are most vulnerable to rapidly changing market trends and business climates. With the restructuring of industries and businesses in the Chicago vicinity, better job opportunities may be increasingly available in the suburbs or outside the enclave. Immigrant workers or enclave residents may have less access to the social capital necessary to find and obtain higher-paying jobs in the primary labor market.

Another issue focuses on Chinatown's aging population. The elderly population has risen sharply, to 63 percent since 1990. Chicago's Chinese American elderly complain of being victims of crime, including burglaries. They encounter more transportation, safety, parking, and public access problems. In contrast, suburban elderly express more loneliness and isolation from community life, particularly when they depend on their working children for daily care or for transportation to medical and support services. Also, some elderly believe that they are not getting enough attention and respect from family members. Recent arrivals, who may have waited for long periods before obtaining visas, experience greater adjustment issues in reuniting with family and relating to a new society.

Overall, South Side Chinatown presents some contradictions. Although some residents have chosen to live there, attracted to the services and conveniences, others are more dependent on the immigrant economy. Out of necessity, some newly arrived immigrants must live in Chinatown, sponsored by relatives or friends and sometimes confined to sharing temporary housing. Linguistically isolated, such immigrants are compelled to find work in the ethnic enclave, at least until they gain the needed skills to succeed in the mainstream economy. With median annual household incomes as low as $12,188, Chinatown residents may be confined to substandard housing and dead-end, menial jobs.

The greater diversity of Chinatown residents has also affected the once close and more homogeneous networks of residents. For example, dialect differences have always separated different linguistic groups. One realtor claimed that, in 1975, 90 percent of Chinatown residents spoke Cantonese or Toishan. Today, as numbers of Chinese from the mainland increase, more Mandarin and Fukien speakers reside in Chinatown; by his estimates, about 30 percent of the enclave speaks Mandarin only. The greater diversity of backgrounds, then, has led to greater factionalism and self-segregation. The "old-timers" are known to still control the old Chinatown, south of Cermak and down Wentworth. The newcomers have gravitated north, toward Chinatown Square businesses. Dialect and generational differences also separate some of the organizations and nonprofits, where Cantonese, English, or other dialects may still reign. The largest church, Chinese Christian Union, holds eight different Sunday services in various languages and Chinese dialects in its Chinatown and suburban locations.

With the boom in real estate, many recent arrivals are staying with their relatives or friends for much longer periods. Given the dwindling stock of affordable housing, new immigrants may be locked into renting for many years. As one Chinese American Service League

staffer mentioned, post-9/11, employers are demanding that new workers are proficient in English yet, with the immediate need to provide for one's family, new immigrants are less able to attend ESL or other English classes. Finally, with the growing numbers of middle-class Chinese and non-Chinese moving into the neighborhood, services and businesses are emerging to meet the new consumer demand.

As the character of Chinatown changes, will recent immigrants be able to call Chinatown jia, both in terms of being able to afford living in Chinatown and in the image of what jia represents? Can Chinatown serve as jia for both newly arrived immigrants from rural areas of China and for second-generation Chinese American yuppies? After the old Santa Fe yards have been completely developed, can Chinatown continue to expand while still addressing the needs of old and new residents?

Although there may be conflicting claims for Chinatown as jia to various groups, it will continue to dominate the general public's perception as Chicago's Chinese American enclave. Symbolically, this enclave serves as Chicago's only Chinatown and the focal point for the Midwest's Chinese Americans.

Argyle: The New Chinatown?

The history of the Argyle community dates back to the mid 1970s, when the Hip Sing Tong decided to separate from the southbound On Leong Tong. Two census tracts, 311 and 312, represent the focal point, bounded by Foster Avenue (5200 N) on the north, approximately Clark Street on the west, Lawrence Avenue (4800 N) on the south, and Sheridan Road on the east (Map 13.4, color insert), the area's name and direction have been hotly contested. Reflecting the difficulties in distinguishing "Chinese" from Vietnamese, especially given the disproportionate numbers of ethnic Chinese refugees who fled from Southeast Asia and arrived in Chicago during the 1970s, the battle for which name to use has been going on for over 20 years.

Ranging from New Chinatown, North Side Chinatown, Little Saigon, Asian Village, or just plain Argyle, it seems that Argyle has won the most support. Similar to the factionalism among

South Asians in naming the Devon area on the north side of Chicago, in recent years, area residents have been more accepting of the name Argyle.

Unlike the South Side Chinatown, Chinese and Asian residents are moving out of the community, despite the greater tolerance for different Asian ethnic groups. Since 1990 among APIs, a 15 percent decrease in population has occurred, and other groups have also moved away; Latinos have decreased by 31 percent. Families with children have left the area in high numbers in the past decade, with about 25 percent fewer children living in the neighborhood according to Census 2000. This would support the preferences that Chinese immigrants have for suburban housing and schools. A local social service agency staffer offers: "Chinese immigrants can't afford to live around here now . . . The developers wanted to attract yuppies. It's cheaper for immigrants to move to the suburbs." Housing ownership has increased since 1990, with a rise of 47 percent in owner-occupied housing. The prices of homes within tracts 311 and 312 (Map 13.4) having the highest median housing value, have risen from $110,700 to $194,400. More college graduates also live in the area, along with residents with higher household income. The proportion of residents identified as Chinese or Vietnamese, however, is small. The lower representation of Asians in this neighborhood contributes to the confusion underlying what community Argyle represents and whether Chinese really feel that the area is their jia.

For a significant number of Chinese immigrants and native-born who have accumulated enough human capital or savings, the marker of success is getting a house in the suburbs. In addition to their human capital, which positions them in the housing market, immigrants especially rely on their social and cultural capital to strategize about major decisions like where to relocate. For less advantaged immigrant Chinese, the reliance on an ethnic housing market is even more acute, given the language barrier. Chinese realtors, mortgage companies, banks, and landlords provide a vertically connected housing network to help navigate the first-time immigrant homebuyer through some risky waters.

Research on Chinese immigrants and residential mobility cite this reliance on the ethnic housing market as leading to a high level of residential segregation. In the New York City region, pent-up demand from immigrant Chinese for good housing has increased investment in the surrounding areas in Queens and Brooklyn. Linked through economic ties to Chinatown, the enclave housing market determines the residential patterns of New York's Chinese (Zhou 1992, 213). Similarly, among immigrant Chinese in the Chicago metro vicinity, the residential preferences for first-ring suburbs including Skokie, Evanston, Lincolnwood (known as the first Chicago area municipality to elect a Chinese American mayor), and Oak Park are determined, in part, by this Chinese enclave housing market (Map 13.1).

For those who are tied to this North Side enclave, the executive director of Chinese Mutual Aid Association (CMAA), the largest social service agency around Argyle and serving neighborhood immigrants and refugees since 1981, comments: "Argyle is more convenient, but there are major problems. The five biggest ones would be affordable housing, gaining English proficiency, getting jobs, family or intergenerational issues, and youth problems."

Youth, especially in urban Chicago, face a range of issues including racial harassment in the Chinatown and Argyle vicinities; academic and school-based problems; cultural and personal identity issues; and intergenerational issues. Native-born Chinese Americans are searching for their identity and community base, sometimes feeling invisible as stereotyped model-minority members. Among Chinese-Vietnamese immigrant youth, some feel caught between dual ethnicities and immigrant or native cultures. Some feel the pressure to be "more Chinese" than anything—to speak Chinese and adhere to Chinese traditions. Chinese immigrant and native youths face higher school drop-out rates than is commonly assumed and experience academic problems in elementary and secondary schools. The Chicago Public School (CPS) 2003 cohort drop-out rate for Asian/Pacific students has risen to 20.5 percent (Chicago Public Schools 2004).

A staffer at CMAA, who is also the Family Literacy Coordinator mentions: "We see sixth and seventh graders who can't speak or write English. They come from homes where their parents may have been here for 20 years, and they still can't communicate in English. They don't leave the area, so even if they're struggling to pay the rents here, they don't have a choice."

Many are also latch-key kids who are members of new immigrant and refugee families trying to survive in a new society. They comment on wanting to spend more time with their parents, especially their fathers, and of needing more help at home. Youth are also members of dysfunctional families, in which family conflicts may lead to domestic abuse.

The growing diversity of Asian ethnic languages and Chinese dialects also work to segregate the Argyle community. In the Argyle–Broadway enclave, Cantonese and Vietnamese are commonly spoken. Other popular dialects among the 50 distinct dialects of Chinese include Mandarin (the official PRC dialect), Toishan, Teochiu, Taiwanese, Shanghainese, and Fukien.

Although languages and dialects add to the factionalism within this Uptown community, differences in socioeconomic class are most acute. The gap in median household income between Chinese residents in the western Argyle area (dominated by tract 311, Map 13.4) and the Vietnamese residents in the eastern area (tract 312, Map 13.4) is significant. Chinese families are higher in median household income at $46,719; Vietnamese households show a median income of $25,288. The daily economic struggle faced by Argyle residents dominates the agendas of most community-based organizations.

Another longstanding agency, the South East Asia Center, was founded in 1979 by a group of Vietnamese, Chinese, and Cambodian refugees. The founders were concerned about the interethnic conflicts among the refugees and wanted to build a pan-Asian coalition of common interests. Funded only through individual donations for the first ten years, today, the agency serves about 8,000 families a year, with about 100 volunteers. A leader at this agency, and one of the tireless founders, relates: "When immigrants first come, they don't have education. We help them understand the system here."

Unlike the South Side Chinatown, the Argyle area lacks a strong, unifying identity or a broad infrastructure representing nonprofit and commercial interests. Despite over 20 restaurants, 3 Asian supermarkets, several branch banks, more than 25 retail stores (Chicago Chinese News, 2003), and 4 major social service agencies in the environs, no current community coalitions promote collaboration in community development and planning. One of the few public markers for this Asian enclave, a pagoda on top of the local train station platform, was built in 1992, through the Asian American Small Business Association's work with the City and local businesses to showcase the community.

The future of the Argyle community as a pan-Asian business and residential enclave will depend on changing demographics and economic conditions. Whether the area will continue to experience a decrease in the number of Chinese or Vietnamese residents will likely affect the character, image, and status of the community. As immigrant groups climb the mobility ladder from urban to suburban neighborhoods, they have commonly left tourist enclaves behind in the city. Without a new influx of native-born or overseas Chinese, any association of jia with the Argyle area will diminish. Former residents may return occasionally, to shop and dine, as they do to the South Side Chinatown, but their connections to Argyle will fade. For those who are upwardly mobile, the dream and goal is to move to the suburbs, where you can own your own home and have the security of mind that your children will be safer and have easier access to quality education.

Suburban and Language Communities: Finding Jia beyond Chinatowns

Among suburban Chinese, it becomes more challenging to identify distinct communities beyond their residential borders. Where do different groups of Chinese immigrants congregate to maintain their cultural connections and to find jia? Unlike other recent immigrant groups that may be highly organized by religious affiliations, the majority of immigrant Chinese, especially those from mainland China and Taiwan, are not highly bound to organized religion. Yet, as mentioned earlier, they are very committed to maintaining Chinese language and cultural practices.

The importance of bilingual language retention to Chinese immigrant and Chinese American parents has been recognized by the

Chicago Public Schools system. As the third largest school system in the United States, the CPS has spurred interest among local schools and suburban school districts working with community and parent groups to create Chinese World Language programs since 1998. In addition to almost 800 students enrolled in Chinese transitional bilingual programs in CPS, over 2,300 students were enrolled in Chinese World Language programs in 2003–04. Among English Language Learners (ELL) groups, Cantonese speakers represent the third largest group with 1,325 students; Mandarin ELLs constitute the eighteenth largest group with 130 students.

The high visibility of Chinese World Language programs in CPS reflects strong community advocacy for expanding the foreign-language programs in public schools to include Chinese, as well as encouraging private schools to offer Chinese-language instruction. Coalition-building among CPS officials, parents, teachers, and state officials also led to recent policy changes at the Illinois State Board of Education, providing for the statewide certification of Chinese-language teachers for the first time in 2004. These organizing efforts among parents, community groups, and educators helped transform CPS into the nation's largest public school system provider of Chinese world-language instruction (Chicago Public Schools 2003). The PRC's Ministry of Education has also recognized the CPS commitment to Chinese world-language programs by sponsoring a Confucius Institute in a CPS magnet high school that will serve as a major teacher's training and exchange center for Chinese-language instruction in Chicago.

Chinese Heritage Language Schools: Jia for Mainland Chinese

For suburban Chinese immigrant families, participating in Chinese-language schools becomes an important vehicle for sustaining jia, transnational ties, and cultural capital. Through regular activities in these schools, both parents and children congregate every weekend to refuel their ethnicity. Heritage-language schools have historically played key roles in maintaining ethnic identity and culture for various ethnic groups

in Chicago, including Greeks and European immigrant groups. Given the predominance of mainland Chinese immigrants in the last decade, most of the Chinese-heritage schools have adopted the writing system and curriculum provided through texts from the PRC.

One of the largest networks of Chinese-language schools is coordinated through the Xilin Foundation, which, since 1992, has worked to provide future generations of overseas Chinese with a multifaceted curriculum. The classes range from Chinese oral and written comprehension to Chinese culture, dance, math, art, English, and computer skills. The United Xilin Chinese schools have eight branches enrolling more than 1,500 students. The majority of students are American-born Chinese with mainland-born Chinese parents. Among the reasons parents cite for bringing their children to Xilin include, "To be able to communicate with grandparents and relatives back in China, because we are Chinese, to keep and carry on the Chinese tradition." Participants talk about the school as "not simply a language school, but [one that] has evolved into a community center…" (Lu 2001, 212). For mainland Chinese families, the Xilin schools provide a cultural space and center for community life where parents build friendships and exchange information. The need for Chinatown is only mentioned within the narrow sense of dining out and shopping for Chinese groceries; Xilin has become their social world.

Jia for Taiwanese Americans

Because the majority of highly educated immigrants from Taiwan settled in the Chicago vicinity during the 1980s, they have built networks and institutions across Chicago's suburbs. Many Taiwanese, after completing their graduate or professional training, by-passed enclaves like Chinatown and sought mobility in the suburbs. Feeling a class and language divide with Chinatown residents, Taiwanese immigrants could afford to acculturate into communities outside of Chinatown. Taiwanese Americans geographically concentrated in ethno-suburbs including Naperville, Westmont, Schaumburg, Skokie, and Evanston. In Westmont, and in towns in DuPage County close to the high-tech corridor, they have contributed to a market for Taiwan-affiliated shopping malls, restaurants, and other services. They are disproportionately represented in the high-tech industry as engineers, scientists, computer specialists, and researchers, and in the health professions. Many Taiwanese Americans identify strongly as "Taiwan *ren*" or Taiwan people and feel patriotic toward the Taiwanese government, maintaining strong ties to their Taiwanese families, friends, and national agendas.

An example of their need to maintain cultural ties that enhance being "Taiwanese" may be seen in their own separate network of Chinese-language schools in the suburbs. It is estimated that several Chinese-language schools use curriculum from Taiwanese textbooks in the six-county area; these schools offer weekend classes in Mandarin and Chinese culture. One of the longest established schools, based at Oakton Community College in Skokie, the Chinese Culture School offers all-day Saturday programs in Mandarin and Chinese culture. In addition to the nucleus of Taiwanese American families, they attract other overseas Chinese from Asia and have a core group of about 100 families. There is a strong sense of unity among school families, with regular potluck dinners held on the weekends and socializing outside of the classes. "The school is their social world; outside of their immediate family, these are the people they're closest to" comments one of the former teachers at Oakton.

CONCLUSION

As Chicago has changed in character and structure while retaining its primacy as an immigrant center, so too have Chicago's Chinese American communities evolved and expanded. Recalling the interests of Chicago School sociologists toward the city's new immigrants and migrants over three-quarters of a century, this chapter hopes to spark future research on how immigrants develop and sustain community. Particularly, given the effects of globalization and transnationalism, how do immigrants and new arrivals cope with rapidly changing opportunity structures, immigration and public policies, and other international demographic and political shifts?

Unlike Siu's sojourners, a significant majority of today's Chinese immigrants intend to stay permanently in the United States, raising children and families, and retiring in their adopted country. The Chinese identity is tied to one's group, including extended family, and is not individually based. With close to 80 percent of Chicago and suburban Chinese Americans being foreign-born, maintaining and reconstructing jia will proceed and likely expand into other family or home-building activities and institutions.

Although the Chinese immigrant and native-born populations and its communities will continue to grow and diversify on multifaceted levels, the need for jia and its representative institutions will remain a strong galvanizing force empowering Chinese American communities. Although some may have immigrated as economic adventurers, many who have settled here in the Heartland have engaged in enhancing opportunities for their immediate families and in serving as community contributors to their extended jia.

NOTES

Dedication. This chapter is dedicated to the memory of my father, McKee Lau, who served as my first mentor and guide to our social world of Chinatown. I also dedicate this work to my mother, Grace Lau, who has always inspired me in "growing-up Chinese American," and to my partner, Shu Boung Chan, and daughters Lia and Tiana, for their continuing support of all our family and work activities. Finally, without my interviewees, who generously shared their ideas and time, this chapter could not have been written. While I cannot acknowledge everyone, I would like to thank the following individuals for their gracious commitment to telling their stories: Kwok Gee Chan, Dr. Haiyan Fu, Denise Lam, Jimmy Lee, Raymond Lee, San O, Raymond Spaeth II, Thomas Szymanek, Warren Tai, Bernarda Wong, and Esther Wong.

1. A lack of English proficiency may impede the successful transfer of job skills or career credentials and thus lead to underemployment.

Louise Cainkar

14 Immigrants from the Arab World

COMMUNITIES SHAPED BY EARLY TWENTIETH-CENTURY ENTREPRENEURS AND REFUGEES

Communities created by immigrants from the Middle East and the Arab world are part of the new urban mosaic brought about by changes in U.S. immigration law in 1965.[1] Once country quotas were eliminated, migration from the Arab world and Middle East increased dramatically. These immigrants and their children have changed the physical and social landscape of many American cities, particularly Chicago. Cook County, which encompasses Chicago and its inner ring of suburbs, has the third largest Arab population, the largest Assyrian population, and the largest concentrated Palestinian population in the United States (U.S. Census Bureau 2003b). At the same time, the migration of Arabs, Assyrians, Armenians, and others from this region began long before 1965. Twenty-first-century Chicago communities have been shaped in part by the institutions and relationships built by earlier migrants from the Arab world.

During the Great Migration that occurred between 1880 and 1924, more than 95,000 Arabs migrated to the United States from "Greater Syria" (present-day Syria, Lebanon, Jordan, and Palestine/Israel), as well as smaller numbers of Arabs from Yemen, Iraq, Morocco, and Egypt.[2] Thousands of Assyrians came to the United States from Persia (now Iran) during the late 1800s. They were later joined by Assyrians from Turkey and Iraq. Arabs and Assyrians built churches and established newspapers in nineteenth-century America. The first

Arab-American mosques were built early in the twentieth-century. By 1924, about 200,000 first and second generation Arabs were living in the United States, the vast majority Christians and of peasant origins (Hitti 1924).

A series of laws passed by the U.S. Congress in 1917, 1921, and 1924 caused immigration from all but northern and western Europe to slow to a trickle. Each Arab country was given a maximum quota of 100 new immigrants per year. Only the wives and dependent children of U.S. citizens could migrate to the United States without being blocked by these quotas. Migration from the Middle East and Arab world continued in small numbers in the intervening years, until it began to surge in the late 1960s. The Arab immigrants who came after 1965 differed in a number of significant ways from earlier ones: A majority of them were Muslim rather than Christian, their origins were both urban and rural, their trades and professions were varied, and many were highly educated. They came at a time when the world was increasingly more connected, their departures were not necessarily complete or permanent, and, rather than escaping strife, global strife came to be centered on their lives in the United States.

Chicago's earliest Arab communities were established by Syrian-Lebanese and Palestinian immigrants.[3] Recorded history places their initial settlement in the city during the late nineteenth-century, following their success in trading goods from the Holy Land at the 1893 Chicago Columbian Exposition. Syrian-Lebanese men and women largely engaged in wholesale and retail trade. The Palestinians were predominantly urban peddlers, supplied by local Syrian-Lebanese businesses and New York Palestinian wholesalers. Their primary trade routes early in the twentieth-century were among the newly emerging black communities on Chicago's South Side (Al-Tahir 1952). Assyrians in Chicago worked in skilled trades (laborers, masons, carpenters, painters, tailors), in the service economy (cooks, waiters, and hotel staff), and as factory workers.

By 1920, Chicago's Arab immigrant community had three notable residential clusters, all on the south side of the city. Syrian-Lebanese Christian families lived near 12th and California and 63rd and Kedzie. A mostly male and Muslim community of Palestinians lived in boarding houses near 18th and Michigan. The Arabs were religiously diverse, including Melkite Catholics (Eastern Rite), Maronite Catholics (Roman Rite), Greek Orthodox Christians, and Sunni Muslims, although Christians were in the majority.

RACE AND RELIGION INFORM RESIDENTIAL AND OCCUPATIONAL INTEGRATION

The residential and occupational trajectories of the Syrian-Lebanese and Palestinians were partly shaped by ideas about race that existed during the early twentieth-century and the dominant view that the United States was a Christian country. "Arabians" and "Syrians," as Arabs were often called, were considered Caucasian and therefore "white" in the racial taxonomies developed by American ethnologists. In some places however, they were prohibited from naturalizing because they were seen as not white.

Of course, strictly speaking, race is not an objective category, and the very concept is socially constructed. "Arab" is neither a racial or national category; it is a cultural and linguistic group. Arabs are people who speak Arabic and share a tradition of Arab culture, values, and history. Before western hegemony, Arab-Islamic societies were the genesis of significant scientific, mathematical, philosophical, astronomical, architectural, and literary development. Globally connected and pan-"racial," their knowledge was

eventually passed on to a reawakening Europe. Categorizing people by race and nationality cannot phenotypically capture Arabs because they span the color continuum from white to black. Similarly, the 22 Arab nation-states (including Palestine) extend over the continents of Africa and Asia. Arab countries are also multiethnic and multi-religious, home to diverse groups who share to varying degrees Arabic language and culture. In American society, however, race is an important framing construct, so whether Arabs are a racial group or not is irrelevant; their position on the racial continuum is real in its outcomes.

According to Al-Tahir's (1952) research and interpretation of events as they unfolded in Chicago, the Syrian-Lebanese Christians embraced the whiteness that was offered to them, although not without facing the prejudices and obstacles experienced by other white ethnics at the time. As part of their assimilation, they shunned conducting business in Chicago's black neighborhoods. They followed the path of other "white ethnics": The second generation intermarried extensively with European-origin Christians, abandoned the trading and shopkeeping occupational niche, experienced upward economic mobility, and became residentially dispersed across Chicago and its suburbs.

Palestinian Muslims, on the other hand, saw themselves as sojourners who planned to return to Palestine, with their religious difference from mainstream American society contributing to this intention. Documentation is scarce about how they were viewed and treated by members of dominant, white Christian society in Chicago, but we know that they did not see themselves as part of the dominant culture and did not bring their families from Palestine to Chicago. According to Al-Tahir, as sojourners and Muslims, they were not interested in participating in American racial conflicts. They lived on the edge of or within the expanding Black Belt of Chicago. They peddled goods and opened food and dry goods stores in African American communities. They shared this retail turf with Jews and Italians, who left these areas after the riots of the 1960s. Sociologist Edna Bonacich's (1973) characterization of a "middleman minority" applies well to Palestinian Muslims of the time. They were a group who represented neither the dominant nor the subordinate; they could deal with both but were part of neither. Living in modest conditions in boarding houses or behind or near their stores in African American communities, by the 1940s, they were residentially scattered from 18th to 45th Streets and from Lake Michigan to Cottage Grove.

CHICAGO ESTABLISHED AS A DIASPORIC HOME FOR ASSYRIANS AND PALESTINIANS

Chicago's early Palestinian and Assyrian communities laid the foundations of the largest concentrated Palestinian and Assyrian diaspora communities in the United States. Assyrians are Aramaic-speaking Christians who share a deeply rooted culture and language developed in historic Assyria, an area currently part of northern Iraq, southeastern Turkey, and northwestern Iran, roughly contiguous to the boundaries of historic Kurdistan. Assyrians from Iraq and those who resettled in other Arab countries speak Arabic and share Arab culture, but consider themselves historically distinct from Arabs.

Assyrian dispersion began in earnest when they fled Ottoman Turkey in 1915, following persecution and massacres. The Allies had enlisted them, a minority group, to help defeat the Turks and promised them post-war autonomy in return. In 1918, the Turks attacked them again, in the Persian region of Azerbaijan. When World War I ended and the Allies were victorious, Assyrians were not allowed to re-enter Turkey. They were resettled by the British in Iraq, but denied autonomy. Historic Assyrian areas conquered in war were split by the Allied powers between Turkey and Iraq, with Britain ensuring that the oil-rich Mosul area went to its colony Iraq. Upon Iraqi independence (1932), Assyrian leaders again demanded a homogeneous location and autonomy within Iraq. The Iraqis refused, and thousands of Assyrians left Iraq for French-controlled Syria and Lebanon. When some of them returned for their families, they were attacked and shot by northern Iraqi forces, resulting in a third mass killing of Assyrians (1933).

Since this time, most Assyrian immigrants in the United States have come from Iraq or from Arab countries of secondary exile. The flight of Assyrians from the Middle East continues, and the majority have settled in metropolitan Chicago, largely on Chicago's North Side. Statistically, Assyrians represent a large share of immigrants from Iraq and persons who declare Iraq as their country of origin in the census. Although considerable commercial and professional interaction occurs between the Arab and Assyrian communities on the North Side, their private and institutional community lives are largely distinct. Since, unfortunately, this author does not have the expertise necessary to write about their recent and current status, they will not be discussed in detail in the rest of this chapter.

The outcome of World War I also heralded the future of Palestinians, one that would send them migrating around the world for the next 90 years. While promising independence to the Arabs in return for their military and intelligence support (the topic of the film *Lawrence of Arabia*), the British also promised to support the establishment of a Jewish homeland in Palestine (Balfour Declaration), providing it did not prejudice the already existing Arab population of Palestine. When the State of Israel was created in 1948, some 800,000 Palestinians became refugees (Khalidi 1992). Although most of them fled to neighboring countries, the United States Congress passed two Refugee Relief Acts for Palestine Refugees, in 1953 (the first American immigration law to specifically mention refugees as a type of immigrant) and in 1957. Nearly 3,000 Palestinian refugees, Christian and Muslim, were admitted to the United States under these acts.

When Palestinians who were already in the United States brought their wives and children to live with them during the 1950s, boarding houses and rooms behind stores were not seen as fit for family residence. In Chicago, Palestinian families began moving into homes and apartments just west of the South Side Black Belt in which they worked. In the ensuing years, they would continue to move south and west into transitional neighborhoods being abandoned by whites. By the 1970s, the Palestinian community had reached the Gage Park and Chicago Lawn areas of Chicago's southwest side. These areas continue to be home to an increasing number of new Arab immigrants—largely Palestinians. In 2005, the southwest side and southwest suburbs of Chicago were home to the largest concentration of Arab families in metropolitan Chicago and the largest concentration of Palestinians in the United States.

The 1950s and 1960s also mark the beginning of the Arab brain drain, when Egyptians, Iraqis, Syrians, Lebanese, Palestinians, and smaller numbers of other Arabs came to the United States for their college and post-graduate educations, principally in medicine, engineering, physics, and radiology, with a smaller number in the social sciences. Many accepted professional positions in the United States after completing their educations. They made important contributions to the emergence and growth of Arab American community institutions and national Arab American organizations. In Chicago, these figures included persons such as law professor M. Cherif Bassiouni, political science professors Ghada Talhami and Ibrahim Abu-Lughod, and historian Hassan Haddad. The best-known national figure was literary scholar and author Edward Said.

GROWTH AND DIVERSITY
IN CHICAGO'S ARAB COMMUNITIES

According to the data from Immigration and Naturalization Service, between 1965 and 2000, more than 630,000 Arabs immigrated to the United States. Some 8 percent of them declared Illinois as their place of intended residence, including 15 percent of all Palestinians–Jordanians, and 13 percent of all Iraqis. Changes to U.S. immigration law in 1965—the removal of country quotas, family reunification preferences, and immigrant visas for persons with skills needed in the United States—contributed to changes in the size and character of the new Arab immigrants. Later legislation offered refugee visas to Assyrians, Iraqis, Somalis, and Sudanese. Assyrians, Libyans, and some other Arabs became eligible for political asylum, and Lebanese and Palestinians from Kuwait received temporary protected status. Although they are

TABLE 14.1. Major Arab Immigrant Groups to the United States by Nationality: 1965–2000

Country of birth	Number of immigrants	Percent of group
Lebanon	122,291	24
Egypt	114,812	22
Jordan & Palestine	113,117	22
Iraq	87,499	17
Syria	62,610	12
Yemen	9,959	2
Total	510,288	100

Source: Immigration and Naturalization Service, Country of Birth Data.

the largest refugee population in the world, Palestinian refugees have not been declared eligible for post-1965 refugee visas.

Six Arab countries accounted for 81 percent of all Arab immigrants to the United States during this period—Lebanon, Jordan–Palestine, Egypt, Iraq, Syria, and Yemen (Table 14.1), largely the same places from which the earliest Arab immigrants came, with the exception of Egypt.[4] The remaining Arab immigrants include Sudanese, Moroccans, Libyans, Bahrainis, Omanis, Tunisians, Algerians, Kuwaitis, Saudis, and small numbers of immigrants from other Arab countries. Mirroring the turn of the twentieth-century pattern, Lebanese are the largest Arab immigrant group in the post-1965 period, although Illinois is one of few states in which persons of Lebanese and Syrian descent are outnumbered by Arabs from other countries (Census 2000). If Palestinians could be accurately counted, their numbers would surely surpass those for Egyptians. Because more than 60 percent of the Palestinian people live in diaspora, they are statistically mixed in with other Arab groups, making the true extent of their presence in the United States difficult to measure.[5]

Illinois was the place of intended settlement for 44,633 immigrants from Arab countries between 1972 and 2000. Eighty-five percent of these immigrants were from the seven main countries of Arab migration. Thirty-three percent were either Palestinian or Jordanian, and 25 percent were Iraqi, a large proportion of whom are Assyrians (Table 14.2). In some years, 20 percent of all Palestinian-Jordanian

TABLE 14.2. Arab Immigrants to Illinois, Cumulative Patterns: 1972–2000

Country of birth	Number of immigrants	Percent of United States	Group as percent of main Arab immigrants	Group as percent of all Arab immigrants
Jordan–Palestine	14,701	15	39	33
Iraq	11,247	13	30	25
Syria	4,043	6	11	9
Lebanon	3,763	3	10	8
Egypt	3,626	3	10	8
Yemen	737	7	2	2
Total Selected Countries	38,117	7	100	85
Total All Arab Countries	44,633	8		100

Source: Immigration and Naturalization Service.

immigrants to the United States and 25 percent of all Iraqis chose Illinois as their initial location.

Viewed from another perspective, among Arab immigrants declaring their intention to settle in Illinois, Palestinians and Jordanians are the principle group throughout the entire post-1965 period. During the early 1980s and, to a lesser degree in the mid 1990s, they are followed relatively closely by Iraqis (Assyrians, Arabs, and Kurds). During other periods, Palestinians–Jordanians stand alone in their dominance, composing some 39 to 45 percent of all immigrants from Arab countries intending to settle in Illinois. Their figures are even larger when we add the 3 to 4 percent of "Kuwaitis" (mostly Palestinians born in Kuwait). Table 14.3 also indicates that Arab migration to Illinois has become more diverse since the 1990s; the five main

TABLE 14.3. Arab Immigrants Intending to Resettle in Illinois (National Group as a Percentage of All Arab Immigrants Intending to Resettle in Illinois)

Country of Birth	1972	1980	1986	1995	2000
Jordan–Palestine	45	36	39	31	31
Iraq	16	35	15	26	16
Egypt	15	10	12	9	6
Lebanon	10	8	11	8	5
Syria	6	6	9	5	10
Kuwait	–	2	3	4	4
Total	97	97	89	83	71

Source: Immigration and Naturalization Service.

Arab groups fell to 71 percent of all intended immigrants by 2000. Eighty-five percent of the Arabs and 99 percent of the Assyrians counted by Census 2000 live in the nine-county Chicago metropolitan area (PMSA) (Paral 2004).

The Arab and Assyrian communities of metropolitan Chicago have grown in recent decades in large part because of war, ethnic cleansing, and military occupation in their native countries. In addition to Palestinians, Assyrians, and post-1990 Iraqi refugees, growth in the Lebanese and Yemeni communities is also partly due to these conditions. For all these groups, family migration has been the dominant pattern. Families come seeking safety, stability, better work opportunities, a better life for their children, and for some, the capacity to generate enough capital to support family left back home. Globalization of trade, relatively low local salaries, and slow economic development have made life increasingly expensive in much of the Arab world. These conditions impel people to migrate for economic reasons. Arabs vary in their opinions as to whether life in the United States is qualitatively better than life in their home countries, but most agree that it is economically better (Cainkar, Abunimah, and Raei 2004).

Currently, more than half of the Arab population in Illinois is native-born, although this percentage is lower among Iraqis (25 percent), Jordanians (40 percent), and Assyrians 37 percent (Paral 2004). Youths under the age of 18 comprise about one-third of Arabs and

25 percent of Assyrians in Illinois and the Chicago PMSA. Still, it is surprising how many Arab Americans one finds living in the Arab world. Alienation and dehumanization are continuing problems that drive many Arab families back to their countries of origin, migrating and returning in circular patterns at different points of their life cycle (Cainkar, Abunimah, and Raei 2004).

The post-9/11 period brought about some new trends in Arab migration. Thousands of Arab families left the United States in response to Attorney General Ashcroft's Special Registration program for Arab and Muslim men, many voluntarily and some by force (Cainkar 2003). Other families left because of the hostile climate towards Arabs and Muslims. The proportion of Arabs able to come to the United States for study and work has decreased dramatically since 9/11 (Cainkar 2004b).

COUNTRY MIGRATION PROFILES

The earliest Palestinian immigrants were largely unskilled peasants from villages in the Jerusalem, Ramallah, and Bethlehem areas of Palestine. Because most of these migrants sent remittances to family back home, relatives who followed them to Chicago were a bit more skilled and educated than their predecessors. The majority of the Palestinians migrating in the 1965–80 period, and a significant proportion of those coming later, were relatives of the early Palestinian immigrants. Some of them came from their home of second migration: Jordan. Except for Palestinians in Jordan, most other Palestinians in the Middle East are stateless; without passports, they cannot travel easily. In the 1980s, Palestinian students came to the United States in numbers that exceeded immigrants. Their goals were largely to study engineering and other specializations needed in the Arab Gulf countries so that they could land lucrative jobs. Many ended up staying in the United States when their job options in these countries closed down, thus starting a new family migration. When Saddam Hussein invaded Kuwait in 1990, some 350,000 Palestinians were living there. The overwhelming majority were expelled once Iraq was forced out. Many of those holding visitor visas came to the United States and were able to stay under Temporary Protected Status until the mid 1990s. Then, unable to return to Palestine because of Israeli rules for Arabs, they became part of the small group of "out of status" Palestinians living in the United States. Those who did not adjust their status by the fall of 2001 were expelled by the Department of Homeland Security. Few Palestinians have been granted student visas since the 1990–91 Gulf War. This measure to release economic pressure on Palestinians living under Israeli occupation ended when their employment opportunities in the Gulf were limited.

Jordanian migrants to the United States and Chicago who are not originally Palestinian are predominantly Christians from cities and towns in central and northern Jordan, such as Salt, Irbid, Ajloun, and Fuheis. Many are relatives of the smaller wave of Jordanians that came to the United States during the 1950s. Jordanians are largely participants in the Arab shop-keeping niche, although some have professional and technical jobs.

Iraqis include three major subgroups: Assyrians; brain-drain Iraqi Arabs and their families, who began migrating during the 1950s seeking education or professional employment, or who fled the Saddam Hussein regime in the 1970s and early 1980s; and the post 1990–91 Gulf War refugees, principally Shia Muslims but also Sunnis and Kurds, most of whom had limited educational and socioeconomic means. Illinois received the fourth largest number of these 33,000 refugees; some 2,200 Iraqi refugees and asylees were initially settled in Illinois between 1991 and 1999, the overwhelming majority in Cook County. In 2003, just prior to invading Iraq, the Bush administration launched an initiative to interview 50,000 Iraqis in the United States. Many of the Iraqi refugees were recruited to work in the Pentagon or with American forces in Iraq.

Egyptians did not begin migrating to the United States in significant numbers until the 1950s. Although many Egyptians live in metropolitan Chicago, it is not a major hub of Egyptian resettlement. Egyptian immigrants tend to be families of highly educated professionals. Many are Muslims but, a large number of Coptic Christians and some Protestants are also present. Unlike other Arab immigrants, substantial numbers of Egyptians entered the United States on visas granted because of their skills, not their relationship to an American citizen.

Post-1965 Syrian immigrants are of three groups: relatives of earlier Arab immigrants, mostly Christians; well-educated Syrians, such as doctors, pharmacists, and scientists, seeking better job opportunities in the United States; and students who came to the United States for higher education. The latter two groups are both Christian and Muslim. Lebanese migration to Illinois in the post 1965 era is relatively small and quite varied. Yemenis are the sixth largest group of Arabs to migrate to the Chicago area. Their migration increased after 1990, when about 1 million Yemenis lost their jobs as a result of the 1990–91 Gulf War. Yemenis are a rather unique group among modern Arab immigrants because more than 80 percent of them are unaccompanied men who come to the United States to work, save money, and support their families in Yemen. The main Yemeni occupation in metropolitan Chicago is urban shopkeeper.

AREAS OF RESIDENCE, SHOPPING, AND WORSHIP

Map 14.1 (see color insert) indicates areas of Arabs and Assyrians concentration in Cook and DuPage counties. The southwest side of Chicago and its southwest suburbs are the most densely populated Arab areas, with large concentrations of Palestinians and Jordanians, as well as some Yemenis and a small numbers of other Arabs. The visibility of their businesses, such as grocery stores, bakeries, butchers, restaurants, insurance agencies, realtors, barbers, beauticians, doctors, dentists, and lawyers, attests to their presence.

The North Side is more ethnically diverse than the southwest side and suburbs, being populated by Iraqis, Assyrians, Palestinians, Jordanians, Syrians, and Lebanese. Notable concentrations of Arabs and Assyrians live in Albany Park and West Rogers Park. A number of

Assyrian associations are headquartered in these neighborhoods. A major Arab and Assyrian commercial district runs from Montrose to north of Lawrence Avenue on Kedzie. Middle Eastern cuisine, music, dance, and flavored tobacco smoked in water pipes are increasing in popularity in Chicago urban culture. The concentration of Arabs near O'Hare airport is mainly Iraqis and other Arabs with limousine and taxi businesses. Arabs are also notable in the middle and upper-middle class suburbs of Oakbrook, Bloomingdale, Schaumberg, and Naperville. These areas are home to highly educated, professional Arabs of Egyptian, Syrian, Lebanese, Palestinian, and Jordanian origin.

The Iraqi Shia Muslim community has a small storefront mosque on west Addison Avenue. Two other North Side mosques with Arab congregants are the Muslim Community Center on Elston and a new mosque on Belmont. Mosques in the city of Chicago serve a range of indigenous African American and immigrant Muslim communities (Map 14.2, color insert). Four Assyrians churches stand on Chicago's North Side. Arab Christians are a range of denominations. Their religious institutions include St. George Orthodox Church in Cicero, St. Mary's Orthodox Church in Alsip, St. John the Baptist Syrian Orthodox Church in Villa Park, St. Mary's Catholic Church in Elmhurst, St. Mark's Coptic Church in Burr Ridge, St. Mary's Coptic Church in Palatine, and St. Elias Lutheran Church on the city's North Side. Some 30 mosques in Chicago's suburbs serve multi-ethnic Muslim congregations (Map 14.1).

EDUCATION, OCCUPATIONS, AND ECONOMIC INTEGRATION

Arab immigrants have a wide range of income, education, and skill levels. Like other immigrants, the skills and financial resources they bring with them and the social capital they find where they settle strongly shape their economic fates. The national profile for Arabs and Assyrians shows that they are well integrated into the American economy. Nationally, they have a higher median household income ($47,000) than the overall American population ($42,000). They also have a greater proportion of persons with bachelor's degrees or higher (40 percent versus 24 percent).[6] Seventeen percent of them have post-graduate degrees, compared to 9 percent of the overall American population. Their rate of persons with at least a high school diploma parallels the overall U.S. rate at 85 percent. Some 64 percent of Arabs and Assyrians are in the United States labor force, similar to the national average.

In Illinois, the median Arab household income as measured by Census 2000 is $46,590, close to the statewide median. Egyptian, Lebanese, Syrian, and Assyrian medians are higher, whereas those for other groups are lower (Table 14.4). About 16 percent of Arabs in Illinois live below the poverty level, higher than the statewide norm of 11 percent. Table 14.4 shows that the poor are concentrated among Iraqis, Palestinians, and Jordanians (mostly ethnic Palestinians).

Occupational patterns for Arabs in Illinois (and by extension metropolitan Chicago) mirror national patterns. Arabs are overrepresented in managerial, professional, sales, and office occupations. Seventy-two percent of Arabs are employed in these occupations.

TABLE 14.4. Arabs and Assyrians in Illinois: Median Household Income and Poverty Rates

Group	Median household income	Percent of persons below poverty level
All Arabs	$46,595	15.8
Lebanese	$57,656	7.2
Syrians	$57,422	9.2
Egyptians	$56,944	7.9
Assyrians	$49,027	8.3
All Illinois	$46,590	10.7
Iraqi	$45,991	19.9
Palestinian	$39,804	18.3
"Arab/Arabic"*	$39,349	20.5
Jordanian	$32,703	17.6

*Persons with this response tend to be Palestinians, according to earlier research by the author. Includes many Palestinians.
Source: Census 2000 as tabulated by Rob Paral, 2004.

Another 13 percent work in transportation and production, and 10 percent in service (Paral 2004). Palestinians, Jordanians, Iraqis, Assyrians, and "Arabs" (mainly Palestinians) are less likely to work as professionals than others from the Arab world and are more likely to be a spectrum of managers (largely of their own businesses), sales workers (largely in co-ethnic businesses), and transportation workers (taxi, limousine, and trucks). An analysis of 1990 Census PUMS data organized by industry showed that 79 percent of employed Arabs living on the southwest side of Chicago and 75 percent of those in the southwest suburbs worked in the retail and professional sectors of the economy, the vast majority in retail. The same study (Cainkar 1998) showed that of Arabs employed in sales, 76 percent of southwest suburban Arabs were supervisors and owners, whereas 16 percent were workers. The opposite held for the southwest side of the city, where 65 percent of Arabs in sales occupations were workers whereas only 35 percent were supervisors and proprietors. Compared to Arabs in the United States as a whole, the concentration of Arabs in retail occupations in Chicago and Cook County is striking (Table 14.5).

THE ARAB SHOPKEEPING NICHE

Arab employment and ownership in trading and shopkeeping, a niche established 100 years ago by Lebanese and Palestinian immigrants, remains strong in twenty-first-century Chicago. Most second-generation Lebanese moved out of this niche and into white-collar and professional occupations, but Palestinians have stayed in it over the past century. They were joined in the 1950s by Jordanians and later by Yemenis. By the early 1970s, Arabs owned nearly 20 percent of all small grocery and liquor stores in Chicago, although they were less than 1 percent of Chicago's population (Blackistone 1981). Most were located in African American neighborhoods, where Palestinians had historically worked in trade. Contributing to the Arab retail expansion in these areas was the void left when corporate chains and small merchants pulled

TABLE 14.5. Employed Arabs by Industry, 1990

Industry	Southwest side (%)	Southwest suburbs (%)	North side (%)	United States (%)
Retail	67	55	45	24
Professional and related service	12	20	9	26
Transportation, communication, utilities	12	5	8	6
Business and repair service	7	7	3	5
Personal service	0	0	13	3
Manufacturing durable	2	13	4	7

Source: 1990 United States Census, as tabulated in Cainkar 1998.

their investments out of these neighborhoods in response to the rioting and unrest that followed decades of racial discrimination. Many local properties were damaged and looted, chain stores and small Jewish and Italian merchants left, and Palestinians and a growing community of Jordanians filled the void. Institutional lenders were largely unwilling to provide loans for businesses in these areas, limiting the possibility of African American investment. With years of experience in urban trading and shopkeeping, Arab entrepreneurs with access to loans knew how to survive in small businesses where costs were high, inventory small, and personal safety risky. They had two significant advantages over local African Americans: access to capital through family, friends, and dairy companies; and access to nearly free family labor—siblings and offspring willing work 10 to 12 hour days for little compensation and no benefits. Since the 1990s, Palestinians, Jordanians, and Iraqis have ventured into new commercial arenas, such as gas stations, fast food restaurants, taxi driving, and limousine services.

COUNTING PEOPLE FROM THE ARAB WORLD: THE EFFECT OF RACE, DIASPORA, AND CRIMINALIZATION

Census 2000 counted 52,191 persons of Arab ancestry and 15,664 persons of Assyrian ancestry in Illinois, of which 55 percent of the former and 37 percent of the latter were born in the United States.[7] The overwhelming majority live in Cook and DuPage counties, where Census 2000 counted 40,196 persons of Arab an-

cestry and 14,428 persons of Assyrian ancestry. No one in Chicago's Arab community accepts these numbers as accurate. Polling and research firm Zogby International estimated that at least 177,000 people from Arabic-speaking countries live in Cook and DuPage counties, including Assyrians, Somalis, and Sudanese, who the Census Bureau counts separately. In 1998, the Chicago Commission on Human Relations, Advisory Council on Arab Affairs estimated the metropolitan Chicago Arab population at about 150,000, plus about 65,000 Assyrians.

These discrepancies are not new. In 1980, the U.S. Census counted 25,288 persons of Palestinian ancestry in the United States, while a 1984 Census Bureau study estimated that there were at least 87,700 Palestinians in the United States, a 350 percent difference (Roof and Kinsella 1985). In 1986, demographer Janet Lippman Abu-Lughod (1986) estimated there were some 130,000 Palestinians in the United States.[8] Four years later, the 1990 Census counted only 48,019 Palestinians. This discrepancy emerges again when comparing the number of Palestinian and Jordanian immigrants to Illinois between 1972 and 2000 (14,701) and the number of immigrant *and* U.S.-born Palestinians and Jordanians in Illinois counted by Census 2000 (11,727). For a population that has low levels of permanent return migration, relatively high birth rates, low out-migration to other states, and in which more than half of the population is U.S.-born, one would expect the census figure to be at least three times that of the migration cohort. The sociological issues that surround counting Arabs are discussed below, when we view these discrepancies through the lens of social and political factors. In the case of Arabs, undercounting may reflect the convergence of the global and the local.

COUNTED AS WHITE:
THE RACIALIZATION OF ARABS

Many Arabs in the United States say that they are not effectively counted by the census because, unlike other minority groups, no category exists for them on the census form. This is not exactly true. Arabs are officially considered white and are expected to check the Caucasian box on census forms. This act renders them invisible. Arabs can be counted on the long form's open-ended ancestry question, similar to the way in which other "white" groups (mostly Europeans) are counted. Because the long form is sent only to a 17 percent sample of the U.S. population, small groups tend to be undercounted through this method. More important, since the vast majority of Arabs never see the short form, their belief that the census does not count them is sustained. In the context of other deterrents (discussed later), this belief may lead to low levels of compliance.

Issues of race are germane to counting Arabs because Arabs are forced into a category with which fewer and fewer identify, and in which they cannot be distinguished from Europeans, with whom their American experience has much less in common than it did 100 years ago. Arabs and Assyrians lie on a historically floating, liminal position on the racial construct continuum. Considerable evidence suggests that, since the 1970s, Arabs have been increasingly negatively racialized in the United States (Samhan 1999). While still officially white, Arabs have been progressively cast as persons with values and customs different from and inferior to those held in high regard in American society. Over the passage of time, the negative racialization of Arabs has intensified, so that Arabs have become a symbolic outcast group. A 2004 study of Arab Muslims in metropolitan Chicago by this author reveals that some 65 percent of interviewees do not consider themselves white and another 14.5 percent believe no appropriate racial construct exists for multiracial Arabs.

COUNTING ARAB ANCESTRIES:
GOVERNMENT POLICIES, TRUST, AND
THE CRIMINALIZATION OF ARABS

Studies have shown that Arabs in the United States fear government reporting mechanisms (such as the census) because of government harassment. Since the early 1970s, the FBI has spied on Arab American community leaders and activists. In 1988, the *Los Angeles Times* disclosed a draft Department of Justice plan to round up Arab and Muslim aliens and hold them in a camp in Oakdale, Louisiana (Suleiman 1999). Their fears of being pinpointed for special measures, as were the Japanese during World War II, came to life in 2004, when a Department of Homeland Security staff member requested a Census Bureau report of persons of Arab ancestry data organized by zip code (Clemetson 2004).[9] The Decennial Census Advisory Committee called this action the "modern day equivalent of its pinpointing of Japanese-American communities when internment camps were opened during World War II" (Lipton 2004). Current research shows that a large proportion of Arab Muslims living in metropolitan Chicago fear internment or removal in the event of another terrorist attack on the United States. Despite a subsequent revision of Census Bureau policy, the usefulness of census data for counting Arabs in the United States will likely decrease further as a result of these revelations.

THE MEANING OF PLACES OF BIRTH
IN DIASPORA POPULATIONS

Counting, categorizing, and describing immigrants from the Arab world are tasks that are especially difficult for two large diasporic populations, Palestinians and Assyrians. Neither population can be identified strictly in reference to a place of birth because large segments of both groups live in exile. For example, an analysis of 1990 Census PUMS data for the southwest side neighborhoods of Chicago that are home to Palestinians and Jordanians showed the following places of birth for persons of Arab ancestry: Jordan, 31 percent; Palestine,

27 percent; Israel, 21 percent; Saudi Arabia, 10 percent; Kuwait, 8 percent; Lebanon, 1 percent; and Egypt, 1 percent. The persons born in Saudi Arabia, Kuwait, and Israel are not Saudis, Kuwaitis, and Israeli Jews; they are Palestinians. Similarly, Assyrians may be born in Iran, Iraq, Syria, and Lebanon, among other places. Furthermore, many Arabs report Arab ethnicity and not a nationality group, such as Lebanese, Palestinian, or Egyptian, making profiles of Arabs by nationality problematic. An examination of 1990 census data for Arabs on the southwest side of Chicago, which is mainly inhabited by Palestinians and some Jordanians, showed that 62 percent reported "Arab" as their ancestry (Cainkar 1998).

In an action that corresponds to their current global status, the Census Bureau eradicated the Palestine category altogether for Census 2000; persons listing Palestine as their place of birth were changed to "Asia not specified."[10] Indeed, neither the U.S. Census Bureau nor the Immigration and Naturalization Service (INS) has a nationality, country of birth, or country of last permanent residence category entitled Palestinian or Palestine (except when tabulating the write-in ancestry responses). 1957 was the last year Palestine existed as a country in these official U.S. data sources.

Because Palestinians are the largest Arab population in metropolitan Chicago, estimating their number is important but extremely difficult. Census 2000 reports 11,727 Palestinians and Jordanians in Illinois (excluding the potentially large number of Palestinians and Jordanians who identified their ancestry as Arab). If we assume that 33 percent of all Arabs in Illinois are of Palestinian–Jordanian ancestry (based on migration, Table 14.2), they would total 17,223 using Census 2000 data and 72,600 using Zogby estimates (220,000 in Illinois). The same figures for Cook and DuPage counties would be 13, 265 (Census) and 58,410 (Zogby). Demographers who have studied Palestinians assume that about 350,000 Palestinians live in the United States today. If 15 percent of all Palestinians live in Illinois (Table 14.2), the figure for Palestinians in Illinois would be about 52,000.

THE GLOBAL AND THE LOCAL

These racialization, criminalization, and erasure processes and the ways they are interpreted and acted upon by Arabs, indicate the intersection of politics and social processes. They show how something as seemingly simple as filling out a form becomes politicized. Perhaps the most striking aspect of these processes is the way in which they are set in motion by global, as opposed to domestic, matters. Throughout the 1980s and 1990s, American popular culture produced movies, video games, Halloween costumes, and talk shows that homogenized and dehumanized Arabs (Suleiman 1999; Stockton 1995; Shaheen 1984). Their targets were not the Arabs of America, although these portrayals could not help but color and damage their lives; the representations were of overseas Arabs. Their infusion throughout American popular culture had the effect of discouraging the American public from reflecting on American policies in the Arab world, especially in Iraq and Palestine. School textbooks described Arabs as desert wanderers, terrorists, and a defeated people. The discourse of the culturally inferior Arab had become part of American popular culture. These domestic discourses and representations of Arabs, later expanded to Muslims, show that racialization is not a process set in motion by domestic matters alone; it can be a corollary to a global strategy.

COMMUNITY ORGANIZATION AND COALITION-BUILDING: GLOBAL AFFAIRS PENETRATE LOCAL LIVES

Following the 1967 Israeli occupation of the West Bank, Gaza, and part of Egypt, a battle was waged in the American media for the hearts and minds of the American people. The U.S. government was by this time a global power and had thrown its support to the Israeli side of the conflict. Palestinians and Arabs were portrayed by the mainstream media as uncivilized, violence-prone barbarians (Suleiman 1999).[11] When Arab Americans began exercising their rights to oppose these characterizations, they discovered that their voices were locked out in a one-sided media battle. The Association of Arab American University Graduates (AAUG) was founded in 1970 to provide the American public with an alternative scholarly analysis of the situation, but it too was ignored by mainstream media. Arab academics reported facing pressures to conform to accepted paradigms about Arabs and the Middle East and faced struggles for promotion and tenure in the social sciences and humanities.

In Chicago, members of the Arab community who were shocked and traumatized by the flow of refugees and new Israeli military occupation reached out to local Arab academics for analyses. At the same time, academics sought out the comfort of an Arab community. A bridge was built between the Chicago's Arab intelligentsia and its Arab community, fostered largely by the United Holy Land Fund and later by the Arab American Community Center (now Arab American Action Network). Finding their political and social integration into American society blocked by stereotypes, media censure, government harassment, and denigration of their political aspirations, Arab American communities became fairly insular. Their isolation from mainstream American society nourished their concentration in the Arab shop-keeping niche, where contact with white American institutions and prejudice was limited. The family and community institutions encouraged pride in Arab culture among an American-born generation that heard quite different messages from the outside world and at school. Family and community cohesiveness were evidenced by low rates of criminality, broken families, or substance abuse. Transnational issues permeated American Jewish communities as well, but they were the victors, they were not stateless, and their advocacy did not lead to dehumanization and exclusion, as did Arab advocacy of the Palestinian cause. These political conflicts never spilled over into conflicts between Arabs and Jews in Chicago; some Jewish institutions welcomed Arab speakers and Arab organizations welcomed Jewish supporters.[12]

These issues did, however, affect the social and civic integration of Chicago's Arab American community. Locally and nationally, elected officials and power brokers shunned Arab Americans, refusing their electoral support and returning their campaign donations. Arab American institutions faced closed doors at philanthropic foundations and city government. In Chicago, this political exclusion changed after the 1984 electoral victory of Mayor Harold Washington; Arab Americans had formed part of the multi-racial, multi-ethnic progressive coalition that elected him. Chicago's Arab community was institutionally recognized when Mayor Washington established advisory councils for Chicago's racial, ethnic, and other minority communities within the Chicago Commission on Human Relations, including one for Arabs. This inclusion was built on ties made between Arabs and progressive African American, Latino, and Asian activists, as well as relationships with Operation Push and Jesse and Jackie Jackson, who had played key roles in reducing tensions between African Americans and the Arab grocers who permeated their neighborhoods. The philanthropic block faced by Arab American community organizations ended in the mid 1990s, when the Chicago Community Trust funded a needs assessment for the Arab American community. The Arab American community was mobilized for the first time in national electoral politics as part of Jesse Jackson's Rainbow Coalition and his 1988 democratic presidential bid. Significantly, the Coalition's platform included support for a Palestinian state. When mainstream Democrats embraced the Coalition, this plank was dropped. Although the Arab community had entered the 1990s in a better position locally, some of their strength was eroded when the progressive coalitions of the 1970s and 1980s experienced losses in power locally, nationally, and globally. The lessened power of progressive political coalitions hurt Arab American communities and interrupted their nascent social and political integration as members of people-of-color coalitions. Lack of social and political integration and the loss of a strong progressive movement hurt Arab and Muslim Americans after the September 11, 2001 terrorist attacks, when their communities experienced a surge of violent popular backlash and increased levels of domestic government repression (Cainkar 2004a).

The 1990–91 Gulf War, from which the Palestinians and the PLO emerged politically and financially weakened, led to the demise of many Palestinian community organizations in Chicago. When Palestinian community centers closed or cut back their activities, the community-wide cohesiveness that had provided newcomers and Arab American youth with pride, strength, and resilience in the face of discrimination and political disappointments started shattering. Mirroring changes overseas, the vacuum left in the wake of the destruction of nationalist institutions was filled by spirituality and religion for many, and demobilization for others.

GLOBAL ISLAMIC REVIVAL COMES TO CHICAGO

The Islamic revival movement grew in strength across the Muslim world during the 1980s and surged during the 1990s, when few alternative global movements for justice and equality were to be found, and American hegemony had risen out of the defeat and fall of communism. Islamic revival became apparent in metropolitan Chicago during the 1990s, and was evidenced by increasing levels of religiosity among immigrants and second-generation Arab Muslims, the establishment of Islamic schools and organizations, and the growth in Muslim student organizations on college campuses. Islamic revival is, for the overwhelming majority of Muslims, about faith in God and the quest for peace, justice, and equality. The growing spiritual power of Islam among Arab (and other) Muslims in metropolitan Chicago is a phenomenon with many visible markers, such as increasing mosque attendance, *Halal* meat markets, and Islamic clothing stores. Immigrant and American-born Muslim women who had never before veiled have adopted the *hijab* (head scarf), once uncommon, but now a common sight in the Chicago metropolitan area.

Following the September 11, 2001 attacks on the United States substantial popular and governmental backlash occurred against Arabs and Muslims in the United States. In southwest suburban Bridgeview, the largely Palestinian mosque was surrounded by hundreds of angry, flag-waving young whites, some shouting "death to the Arabs." Bridgeview police called in six suburban police departments to help maintain control. For four days, residents of the neighborhood around the mosque had to pass through checkpoints and show identification to be admitted. Although much of the post-September 11th backlash focused on Muslims and Islamic institutions, Arab Christians, Assyrian Christians, and secular Muslims have also experienced hate crimes and discrimination. In 2002, an Assyrian church on the city's North Side was firebombed and the Arab American Community Center was arsoned.

At the same time, Islamic civic and religious institutions in metropolitan Chicago stepped up their outreach, advocacy, and civic participation. Many mainstream institutions welcomed them, signaling the opening of civic and political space for American Arab and Muslim communities. Despite the fact that numerous investigations, including the Congressional 9/11 Commission, showed that no Arab American or Muslim American collaborated with or assisted the 20 hijackers from overseas, hate attacks and discrimination against Arabs and Muslims have continued. In 2004, when a group of southwest suburban Arab Muslims sought to build a mosque in an unincorporated area near Orland Park, opposition raged. The Orland Park city council (which sought to annex the land) was pressured to hold three public hearings on the matter. The matter was settled when the city council voted unanimously to annex the land slated for the mosque, thereby approving the mosque's construction permit.

Testimony given at the final Orland Park public hearing (April 2004) provides insight into the discourses of opposition to the mosque. The issues raised by most opponents had little to do with Orland Park; they were global. They invoked the war in Iraq, international terrorism, the purported violent essence of Islam, and homeland security. The following quotes provide a sense of the context of opposition:

- "We care about America. We care about what's going on because we don't want you to bring it here. We're not saying that you'll bring it, but you must understand, that because you're tied in with this religion and a possible mosque in Orland Park, it will come to our doorstep."
- "Can you give a guarantee to me that these Muslims and their mosque are not going to be terrorists?"

CONCLUSION

Metropolitan Chicago is home to the largest Assyrian and Palestinian communities in the United States, both of which were established more than a century ago. It is also home to significant numbers of Iraqis, Egyptians, Jordanians, Syrians, Lebanese, and Yemenis. Overall, these communities are faring well economically, although pockets of poverty exist within them. The effect of more recent discrimination on those with fewer assets and less human capital remains to be seen. Their community histories reveal challenges to their social and political integration, largely caused by domestic interests in contested global issues. The post September 11th period witnessed increases in public attacks, government spying, media stereotyping, and levels of personal alienation. At the same time, numerous philanthropic and civic organizations in the Chicago area have come forward to support institutions built by Arabs, Assyrians, and Muslims. While the post September 11th period has been extremely difficult for these communities, their civic and religious institutions are more socially and politically integrated at the local level than at any other time in their history. The full social and political integration of Arabs and Assyrians into American society awaits an end to media stereotyping, an opening up to their voices in domestic debates, and peace and justice in the Middle East. The Arab and Assyrian experience in Chicago is entrenched in the local but at the same time, is intensely global.

NOTES

1. The term "Arab world" is more accurate than Middle East because it is definable. "Middle East" is a Western construct having varying definitions and boundaries. The Arab world is composed of the 22 Arab countries that form the League of Arab States.

2. Between 1916 and 1919, cross-Atlantic travel was limited by war. More than 90 percent of Arab immigrants came to the United States from other countries in the Americas. When Arabs initially boarded ships for "America," their destinations included the Caribbean, South, Central, or North America—all sites of historic Arab communities.

3. Prior to the establishment of Lebanon within former Greater Syria, one must use the term *Syrian-Lebanese* to indicate migrants from Syria and modern-day Lebanon.

4. Jordan and Palestine are combined for a number of reasons, the most important being that some 80 percent of Jordanians migrating to the United States are originally Palestinians. Other reasons have to do with passports and ways that Palestinians are counted.

5. More than 60 percent of the Palestinian population lives in diaspora, the vast majority in Arab countries, some of which have offered Palestinians citizenship. Jordan gave citizenship to the majority of 1948 and 1967 Palestinian refugees and exiles, now numbering in the millions. For a time, it gave West Bank Palestinians citizenship. Israel offered citizenship to the few hundred thousand Palestinians who managed to hold onto their land after Israeli independence. Lebanon offered citizenship to some (relatively few) Palestinian refugees, mostly Christians. The majority of "Kuwaiti" and "Saudi" immigrants are Palestinians who migrated to these countries for work and came to the United States in a third migration. Palestinians are also part of Israeli, Lebanese, and to a lesser extent Syrian and Yemeni migration. Most Palestinian refugees living in Lebanon, Syria, Gaza, and Egypt have no passports, rendering migration difficult.

6. These data are from the Arab American Institute tabulations of Census 2000 and combine all persons from Arab countries, whether Arab or Assyrian, and include Sudanese and Somalis.

7. If we add half of the Armenians to these numbers, assuming they came from Arab countries, the total number of Illinoisans from Arab countries counted by Census 2000 reaches 67,981.

8. A 15 percent rate of Palestinian settlement in Illinois using this estimate would put the approximate number of Palestinians in Illinois at 20,000 in 1986. Both of these researchers used migration

and natural increase data to produce their estimates and excluded Palestinians who migrated to the United States before 1940 and their U.S.-born descendants.

9. The data sharing on Arabs between DHS and the Census Bureau was disclosed by a Freedom of Information Act request submitted by the Electronic Privacy Information Center, a research center focused on civil liberties.

10. This is not the first time "Palestine" has disappeared in official U.S. data. See Cainkar 1998 for a much longer history.

11. This is not to deny the orientalized view of Arabs that predates this period, described so eloquently by Edward Said in *Orientalism* (1978).

12. This information is from my fieldwork in Chicago during the 1980s and 1990s, as well as from national records.

John P. Koval

15   Immigrants at Work

CURRENT CANONICAL LITERATURE about immigration and work contains two articles of faith germane to this chapter.[1] The first canon looks at the demand side of the new economy's job market and asserts that "the leading immigration regions display a prominent tilt toward jobs for which training is required and away from jobs of an easy-entry sort and for which the required skills can be picked up as one goes... places where the new knowledge-based economy is most advanced" (Waldinger 2001, 309).

The second article of faith focuses on the supply side of the job market. It asserts a skill mismatch hypothesis and points out that economic restructuring calls for knowledge-intensive professional and technical occupations while de-emphasizing manufacturing jobs that traditionally provide entry-level work for the less skilled. The result is a serious occupational disconnect for many immigrants and poorly schooled native-born (Kasarda 1993; Wilson, 1987). If these two propositions are true, then Chicago is an exception. Without question, Chicago is a leading immigrant region. It is also without question that Chicago, one of the most diverse economies in the country, has attracted an immigrant labor force of immense educational and skills diversity. Yet, contrary to accepted wisdom, the demand is strong for less skilled immigrant workers. A multiplicity of reasons account for this but the primary one is growth in the service sector, especially in low-skill occupations within it. In fact, a case can be made that a very different skill mismatch looms in Illinois' employment future. In its 2004 Annual Report, the Illinois Department of Labor offers a telling

forecast: "... forty-three percent of all job openings by 2010 will require only a minimal education, at a time when native-born Americans are obtaining college degrees in record numbers and are unlikely to accept positions requiring minimal education" (Illinois Department of Labor 2004, 7). This is one of the ironies of a postindustrial society: The need exists for well-trained and well-educated workers *and* a complementary need exists for large numbers of unskilled and less well-educated workers as well. In the latter case, pay levels further diverge along racial and ethnic lines.

Although Chicago is a quiet charter member of America's new knowledge-based economy club, it also has the largest industrial labor force in the country, with more than a few of its ± 475,000 manufacturing jobs filled by recent immigrants. In addition, the still unfolding story of work in a knowledge-based economy is similar to one aspect of a high-tech military unit. That is, every front-line foot soldier requires several support troops to maintain him. To illustrate this using the burgeoning high-technology medical field, in which Chicago excels, two issues must be underscored: (1) an increase in physicians also means the downstream addition of other workers in health care—some to change beds, mop floors, bus and wash dishes, and others to draw blood, administer EKGs, take and record vital signs and the like; (2) in addition, as those physicians become consumers in the general economy, they produce a demand for dry cleaning, home maintenance, child care, restaurant services, car repairs, and much more. The net result is a double-barreled multiplier effect;

the one for medically related services, the other for personal services.[2] Therefore, a number of service-sector jobs, such as food service, contain a large and growing labor force with a hierarchical structure that, for some, allows for mobility and the acquisition of a middle-class income. Other segments of this emerging economy contain well-paying jobs that require skill and training that can be gotten on-the-job without the necessity of formal education—and some immigrant and minority groups are especially adept at discovering and exploiting such opportunities. It remains to be seen if these opportunities are swept away by an incessant educational inflation that, in many instances, foists unnecessary requirements of post secondary education and formal technical training on emerging as well as existing jobs.

The mathematics of economic restructuring then, not only includes the subtraction of many industrial jobs but also the addition of many service and information technology occupations. Chicago's economic restructuring during the 1970s and 1980s, for example, produced a demand for medical professionals that resulted in the recruitment of doctors from India, nurses from the Philippines, and medical technologists from both countries. During the 1990s, local "new economy" enterprises in the region needed information technology specialists. Not finding them locally, that need was filled by immigrants. Until recently, for example, Chicago's Motorola Corporation employed the largest number of immigrants holding H1-B visas of any single firm in America—including companies from California's Silicon Valley and Seattle's Microsoft Mecca.[3] Their multiplier effect has had major downstream implications for employment growth in both service and nonservice occupations.

CHICAGO'S IMMIGRANT LABOR FORCE

The immigrant labor force in the Chicago metropolitan area more than tripled between 1980 and 2000. The total labor force increased by 17 percent over that same time span. In effect, immigrants account for nearly all the growth in Chicago's labor force during the past two decades. Presently, immigrants constitute 20.8 percent of Chicago's labor force—up from 11.3 percent in 1980 (PUMS, 1980–2000). An examination of the six largest immigrant groups in the labor force, as shown in Table 15.1, shows that the tripling of the immigrant labor force has not been uniform for all groups, however. Poles, Filipinos, and Koreans have roughly doubled; Indians and Chinese have tripled; and Mexicans have nearly quadrupled. And, with the exception of Poles, the five other major immigrant groups vastly outnumber their native-born co-ethnics.

These groups are so distinctive, however, that generalizing to "immigrants" as a social unit is almost meaningless. The range in human and cultural capital among immigrant groups is so great that generalizations would tell us little of substance about immigrant workers and even less about their distinctive engagement with the economy.[4] Many are heavily recruited from

TABLE 15.1. Chicago Metropolitan Area Growth of Ethnic Labor Force: 1980–2000

Ethnicity	1980			2000		
	NB	FB	Total	NB	FB	Total
Mexican	67,840	105,250	173,090	166,151	407,904	574,055
Polish	347,004	44,987	391,991	301,269	100,812	402,081
Indian	940	19,266	20,206	6,536	58,442	64,978
Filipino	1,240	24,282	25,522	8,011	52,295	60,306
Chinese	2,681	11,726	14,407	6,409	38,458	44,867
Korean	160	10,402	10,562	4,305	23,518	27,823

Source: U.S. Census Bureau, 2000 Census, 1 percent PUMS sample.
Note: NB = native-born residents; FB = foreign-born residents.

professional, computer science, and information technology occupations—Asian Indians, Filipinos, and Chinese—because of their valued human capital. Others—such as Mexicans—while not formally recruited, have great appeal to potential employers because of their perceived work ethic and willingness to labor for low wages. Still others, although coming to Chicago as refugees, fill a range of nooks, crannies, and cracks in the employment marketplace. Increasing numbers of immigrants also fill the day-labor hiring halls and acquire the euphemism of a "contingent labor force." Few have resorted to sidewalk or street-side entrepreneurship so common in cities like New York, Paris, or Rome.

Although Chicago is home to immigrants from over 200 regions, many of the ethnic immigrants groups are too small to permit a detailed analysis. In the following pages, we focus on six immigrant groups in Chicago whose numbers are large enough to permit a reliable and detailed occupational analysis. They are, in order of descending group size: Mexicans, Poles, Indians, Filipinos, Chinese, and Koreans.

IMMIGRANT OCCUPATIONAL DENSITY

The metropolitan Chicago labor force consisted of 481 different occupational categories in the 2000 U.S. Census. Yet, as Table 15.2 shows, 75 percent of all Polish and Filipino immigrant workers can be found in only 45 job categories.

TABLE 15.2. Ethnic Immigrant Occupational Concentrations: Number of Occupations Required to Encompass 50–65–75 Percent of Ethnic Labor Force

Ethnicity	Males			Females		
	50%	65%	75%	50%	65%	75%
Mexican	13	23	35	11	19	28
Polish	17	29	45	15	26	37
Indian	15	27	40	15	25	35
Filipino	22	35	46	10	20	29
Chinese	13	22	30	16	26	35
Korean	15	22	29	14	23	30

Source: U.S. Census Bureau, 2000 Census, 1 percent PUMS sample.

Stated differently, three-fourths of this group is concentrated in just 10 percent of all occupational categories. And Poles and Filipinos are the most occupationally diverse of immigrant groups. Mexican workers, for example, are clustered—some say crammed—into an even smaller number of occupational categories. In their case, 75 percent of the male and female labor force is found in only 35 and 28 occupational categories, respectively. The figures are consistent for all six of Chicago's largest immigrant groups. That is:

- Between 10 and 15 occupational categories encompass 50 percent of all immigrant males and females in Chicago's immigrant labor force.
- Between 20 and 30 occupational categories encompass 65 percent of all immigrant males and females in Chicago's labor force.
- Between 30 and 45 occupational categories encompass 75 percent of all immigrant males and females in Chicago's labor force.

It would be mistake, however, to assume that all the workers in these six immigrant groups are routed into the same few occupations. On the contrary, one of the distinctive characteristics of Chicago's different immigrant work communities is how little overlap in occupations or industries occurs among them. So, although a good deal of within-group occupational homogeneity is present, there is also a good deal of between-group occupational heterogeneity. The net result is that, collectively, they are like the so many patches of Joseph's biblical coat. Each is separate and distinctive; yet, when combined, they contribute to the wholeness, breadth, and depth of Chicago's labor force.

That many newcomers are shoehorned into a few occupations is part of Chicago's present immigrant story. The text of that story varies depending on the immigrant group in question, because occupational concentrations are typically the result of several factors and combinations of factors, depending on the group's background and its human and social capital—factors including opportunity, network reinforcement, selective immigration, and the selective occupational recruitment of immigrants.

ETHNIC OCCUPATIONAL AND INDUSTRIAL NICHES: HORIZONTAL AND VERTICAL DIMENSIONS

The magnitude, diversity, and global scope of immigration to this country during the past quarter-century, coupled with the diversity of immigrant skills and occupational backgrounds, has resulted in an ethnic division of labor the likes of which hasn't been seen since the great migrations of the late nineteenth and early twentieth century. This is not entirely a historic coincidence. Curiously enough, this country opened its doors to immigrants as widely as it did at the beginning of the twentieth century, at a time coinciding with the emergence of our postindustrial era. The resultant and ongoing economic restructuring required, among other things, a revamped labor force to fuel economic growth in some sectors and fill unmet needs in others.

The interplay of history and contemporary change has had its effect on Chicago's immigrant mix. On one hand, Chicago's historical ties to Eastern Europe have resulted in the city attracting more Poles, Russian Jews, Serbs, and other Eastern Europeans than most other U.S. regions. And, because of its still large industrial base and its rapidly expanding service sector, it is attracting large numbers of unskilled and semi-skilled Mexicans to manufacturing and service economies. In addition, as Chicago continues to move into its own version of a knowledge-based, advanced corporate-services phase, it both recruits and attracts large numbers of Indian and Chinese computer and information technology specialists. Finally, its traditional role as a major regional medical center, enhanced by growth in medical research, has caused Chicago to reach out and recruit, as well as attract, large numbers of Indian and Filipino doctors, nurses, and medical technology specialists.

This analysis shows that Chicago's claim to economic diversity has a human counterpart—occupational diversity. And, with occupational diversity has come increased racial, ethnic, and cultural diversity, since a global occupational marketplace is one of our new realities. Globalization not only means an increase in the international flow of capital and goods but also of labor—so much so that some countries, among them the Philippines—identify workers as an export commodity. Others, like Mexico, have come to recognize the economic benefits gained through remittances—sending money home to community, family, and relatives—and have established government offices and programs that encourage and reward the flow of such resources. In Mexico's case, for example, remittances recently passed tourism as a national revenue source and have come to be the second largest source of national revenue after oil. In recognition of this fact, the presidents of the Philippines and Mexico have publicly elevated economic emigrants to the status of national heroes.

One of the more thorough analyses of immigrants in urban America was conducted by Roger Waldinger, Mehdi Bozorgmehr, and their colleagues in the book *Ethnic Los Angeles*. There, they conceptualized "a plural city, in which the myriad new ethnic groups have created a segmented system, where each group largely lives and works in its own distinctive social world" (Waldinger and Bozorgmehr 1996, 448). The existence of an ethnic division of labor is an integral component part of this interpretation. In their analysis, the division of labor has horizontal and vertical dimensions. Specifically, " . . . the demographic transformations of the past 20 years have created a new ethnic division of labor in which *ethnicity intersects with class*" (my emphasis; Waldinger and Bozorgmehr 1996, 454–55). That is, not only do immigrant workers come to this country with different skills, which find them loading and overloading in certain occupations and industries, but those different skill and educational levels result in different economic and status payoffs. It is then a short step to propose that "The ethnic ordering of L.A.'s economy can be characterized along the horizontal and vertical dimensions of specialization and rank . . ." (Waldinger and Bozorgmehr 1996, 449). In refining this perspective they make the case that:

> On the horizontal dimension, Mexican immigrants and Korean immigrants, and African Americans define three basic modal types, with Mexicans ensconced in manufacturing, Koreans in self-employment, and African Americans

in the public sector and few points of niche intersection among them. (Waldinger and Bozorgmehr 1996, 449)

Although the scale of involvement differs for each, these three modalities apply equally well for Chicago.

THE HORIZONTAL DIMENSION: INDUSTRIAL AND OCCUPATIONAL NICHES

The section that follows is not intended to be a definitive analysis of occupations and occupational placement of each immigrant community in Chicago. It *is* intended to refine the case for the assertion that Chicago's immigrant labor force is not randomly spread throughout the labor force by showing how each group plays a key role in the restructuring and growth of Chicago's economy—each in its own way. What follows highlights, on a horizontal dimension, the occupational and industrial niches that characterize each immigrant group, and then locates those occupations on a vertical, or hierarchical, dimension that fills out a kind of economic mosaic that constitutes the immigrant presence in Chicago's economy.

The labor forces of Chicago's six major ethnic immigrant communities are reasonably large and, while concentrated, those concentrations are found in sectoral clusters. Their size also tends to produce clusters in more than one industry. One way to statistically get a handle on these clusters is through the Index of Representation (RI). The statistic is configured to give an index of 1.0 if a group's proportional representation in an occupation or industry is the same as its proportion in the labor force. A number higher than 1.0 indicates over-representation and a lower number is indicative of under-representation. An RI of 1.50 or greater, 50 percent over-representation or more, is becoming the conventional criterion for labeling this as loading in an occupational or industrial niche.[5]

The Index not only brings some precision to the concept of occupational concentration but also helps to lay out the pieces of an ethnically based occupational mosaic; that is, not

only are workers in any given ethnic group not randomly distributed among occupations in the labor force, but neither are they randomly distributed among the various industries within the economy. They concentrate both in occupations and industries. And, as these pieces are laid out, the social and ethnic mosaic of the labor force begins to take form.

The tables that follow contain two sets of information. First, they list the four industries for each ethnic group in which the highest proportions of men and women are found, along with their respective industrial RIs. Second, at the end of the chapter are two tables for each immigrant group that list, in descending order, the 10 occupations with the largest number of immigrant workers in that group—distinguished by sex and including the RI for each occupation. For the sake of simplicity, the ethnic groups with their related data are examined serially. As we progress through these data, light is shed on the horizontal intersection and relationship between ethnicity, occupations, and industrial areas across the various economic sectors.

Mexican Immigrants

Nearly 75 percent of male and female Mexican immigrants in the labor force are found in four industries and over half in but two. Men are especially over-represented in manufacturing (RI of 1.74) and even more so in food service (RI of 2.41) which, for them, constitute industrial niches. Construction, with a Mexican RI of 1.38, could well be considered a third niche and if "grounds maintenance" were defined as an industry, it would constitute a fourth Mexican industrial niche—because grounds maintenance workers have an RI of 5.03 and managers of landscaping and lawn service workers have an RI of 2.54. (See Appendix Table 15.1 at the end of this chapter.)

This snapshot is reinforced when the genders are broken out and immigrant men are considered alone. Each of the first four occupations on the list is from one of the four niche industries and is three to five times over-represented in that occupation. In addition, the majority of occupations listed in the table can be slotted into one of the four industries and, in most all cases,

TABLE 15.3. Chicago Metropolitan Area: 2000 Industrial Concentrations of Foreign-Born Mexican Men and Women

Men	%	RI	Women	%	RI
Manufacturing	33.1	1.74	Manufacturing	41.9	3.71
Food service	17.2	2.41	Food service	11.0	1.36
Construction	13.4	1.38	Educ, Health, Soc Serv	10.7	.38
Mgmt, Adm	9.9	.81	Retail trade	9.8	.80

each of those occupations is two to five times over-represented.

More than four of ten Mexican women in the labor force are found in some type manufacturing, and their over-representation is sizeable (RI = 3.71). All but two of the women's Top 10 occupations have RIs of 1.50 or higher—and, in the majority of cases, these occupations have two to five times more workers than their expected proportional representation—statistical evidence of the many crammed into the few occupations.

It is necessary to think outside the box—or table in this case—to fully grasp the information provided in Table 15.3 and the related Appendix Tables 15.1 and 15.2. A conceptual eye is also helpful, because what is *not* there is just as important as what is; that is, no professional, technical, or white-collar jobs are found in the 10 largest Mexican immigrant male occupations. What is also not there are government, transportation, or administrative jobs. Manufacturing, food service, grounds maintenance, and construction jobs permeate the Mexican occupational landscape—all blue-collar jobs.

What these data also do not tell us or alert us to is the large and growing number of Mexican immigrants who fill the day-labor hiring halls and street corners in the neighborhoods of Pilsen, Little Village, and Albany Park at 5:00 a.m. each morning. While waiting for possible work, they can share among themselves the urban equivalent of the California farm workers' joke:

Question: "What's worse than being exploited in Modesto/Chicago?"

Answer: "Not being exploited in Modesto/Chicago."

Polish Immigrants

Poles, like Mexicans, have their heaviest concentration of workers, male and female alike, in manufacturing (Table 15.4). But it would be a mistake to assume that contemporary Polish immigrants mirror those in Thomas and Znaniecki's classic *Polish Peasant in America.* Male Polish industrial workers occupy skilled and technical occupational niches, whereas some of their female counterparts work side-by-side with Mexican women in assembly plants and other forms of light industry.

Although both Poles and Mexicans load high in construction, Polish males occupy a rather distinctive niche within a niche. In construction, they typically team together under an independent contractor and specialize in nonunion home construction, rehabs, and other small construction jobs. Like Mexicans, they too fuel the construction and blue-collar day-labor workers' pool—although from sites adjacent to the Polish communities on the near North Side and southwest side of the city.

TABLE 15.4. Chicago Metropolitan Area: 2000 Industrial Concentrations of Foreign-Born Polish Men and Women

Men	%	RI	Women	%	RI
Manufacturing	32.7	1.71	Educ, Health, Soc Ser	19.5	0.70
Construction	22.5	2.32	Manufacturing	19.4	1.72
Trans, Utilities	9.7	1.15	Prof, Mgmt, Admn	18.7	1.66
Prof, Mgmt, Adm	8.6	0.70	Retail Trade	11.1	0.89

Polish women have a bifurcated occupational profile. A significant portion of well-educated immigrant Polish women work as RNs, LPNs, and health care aides in the medical field and as managers and in other mid level occupations in a variety of businesses. A larger proportion of less-well-educated immigrant Polish women work in light manufacturing and, especially, as maids and cleaning service personnel for businesses, office complexes, and private homes. Many is the office building in Chicago that provides its staff with Polish-language signs that read "Prosze nie wyrzucac," ("Do not throw away") to avoid disasters that could result from English-only signage.

Indian Immigrants

Industrial concentrations are a good starting point for delving into the situation of Indian workers, who are multiple players in multiple industries—at very different levels. At the upper level, Indians have had two different major occupational bubbles over the past 20 years, "professional, management, and administration," and "education, health, and social service" (Table 15.5). Forget the "ands" in each of these two clusters; instead read "professional computer and information technology specialists"—massively recruited in the 1990s—in the former, and "medical doctor"—massively recruited in the 1980s—in the latter. In both instances, these are industrial niches for both Indian men and women, as are several occupations within each industry. The full range of occupations in each industrial niche can be examined in Appendix Tables 15.5 and 15.6. Two, however, are especially illustrative.

In medicine, male Indian doctors are over-represented by a factor of five (RI = 5.15) and females by a factor of nearly seventeen (16.82).

In the field of information technology, male software engineers are found twelve times more frequently than their proportion in the labor force (R = 12.33) and females are nearly sixteen times over-represented (RI = 15.62). The manufacturing industrial niche for Indian women is almost solely accounted for by occupations in the electronic and chemical fields.

The industrial niche of retail trade for Indian men and women is tightly banded in two sectors of franchises in "the food chain"—Dunkin' Donut franchises (more than eight of ten franchises in the metropolitan area) and franchise convenient marts—more than 90 percent for the region. A final area of heavy occupational concentration for Indian men (RI = 6.74) is cab driving: a port-of-entry occupation for many immigrants, but especially for Indians and Pakistanis.

Filipino Immigrants

The Filipino female labor force stands out among all immigrant groups because of the extraordinarily high proportion of women employed in a single industry—health care—primarily as a result of intensive recruitment by Chicago's health care industry over the past 20 to 25 years. Since the census data clusters education, health, and social service into one industrial category, the RI of 1.95, although high, is a very conservative figure because Filipino female occupations are not equally spread among all three occupational classes in the industry, but dominates only one—health care. An examination of Appendix Table 15.8 makes this abundantly clear. There we see that six of the ten largest occupations for Filipino women are in heath care, and all six reflect significant over-representation: registered nurses (7.71), physicians (7.18), home care aides (6.37),

TABLE 15.5. Chicago Metropolitan Area: 2000 Industrial Concentrations of Foreign-Born Indian Men and Women

Men	%	RI	Women	%	RI
Prof, Mgmt, Adm	24.0	1.96	Educ, Health, Soc Ser	38.7	1.39
Manufacturing	21.4	1.12	Manufacturing	17.3	1.53
Retail Trade	15.8	1.59	Retail Trade	10.8	.87
Educ, Health, Soc Ser	12.3	1.45	Prof, Mgmt, Adm	9.9	.88

TABLE 15.6. Chicago Metropolitan Area: 2000 Industrial Concentrations of Foreign-Born Filipino Men and Women

Men	%	RI	Women	%	RI
Educ, Health, Soc Serv	22.5	2.66	Educ, Health, Soc Serv	54.4	1.95
Manufacturing	20.3	1.07	FIRE	11.0	1.12
Prof, Mgmt, Adm	12.4	1.01	Prof, Mgmt, Adm	8.2	0.73
Transp, Utilities	9.3	1.11	Retail Trade	6.8	0.55

FIRE = Finance, Insurance, and Real Estate.

medical technicians (5.61), LPNs (4.12), medical assistants (3.24), and nursing and psychiatric aides (2.56). Their secondary industry, Finance, Insurance, and Real Estate (FIRE), consists almost exclusively of finance and insurance occupations such as accountants, bookkeepers, tellers, and clerks.

Filipino men in health care have also been heavily recruited over the years, although their numbers and proportional share of the male Filipino labor force is markedly smaller than for Filipino women. Still, nearly one in four Filipino males is in a health care occupation, and they are nearly three times over-represented in the field. As with Filipino females, this is a conservative number. At the specific occupation level men's RIs literally soar (see Appendix Table 15.7), whether as physicians (6.77), RNs (20.67), psychiatric nurses (12.79), diagnostic technicians (25.39), or laboratory technicians (12.41). Clearly, Filipino men, like Filipino women, are firmly ensconced in health care as an industrial niche.

Filipino males also have a range of occupational niches in various subfields of computer technology such as software engineers (1.47), computer programmers (1.59), and computer support specialists (6.85). A few business and industrial occupational niches are the exception to the general pattern of professional and technical specialty niches, and those are primarily in health care and information technology.

Chinese Immigrants

Chinese—both males and females—have their occupational feet in contrasting occupational worlds that reflect groups coming to this country with very different human capital, at different time periods, from different regions. Food service, with a set of attendant occupational niches (cooks, chefs, waiters, and waitresses) is an industrial niche for both sexes, as is manufacturing for women (2.04) and nearly so for men (1.21) coming from Taiwan prior to 1990. More recent Chinese immigrants from the mainland—male and female, many with H1-B visas—have niches in health care and information technology occupations. High RIs and large numbers are especially characteristic of Chinese men and women in computer programming and software engineering, and high RIs but smaller numbers are found in health care occupations.

Korean Immigrants

At first glance, the significant over-representation of Korean male and female immigrants in "other services" tells us little except that Koreans have an industrial niche in an ambiguous residual industrial category. In fact, approximately two-thirds of Chicago's approximately 3,000 dry cleaning establishments are owned or operated by Koreans. The vague "other services" industrial category now puts on a very

TABLE 15.7. Chicago Metropolitan Area: 2000 Industrial Concentrations of Foreign-Born Chinese Men and Women

Men	%	RI	Women	%	RI
Manufacturing	23.0	1.21	Manufacturing	23.1	2.04
Food Services	18.8	2.34	Prof, Mgmt, Adm	17.3	1.54
Educ, Health, Soc Serv	14.1	1.67	Food Service	14.8	1.84
Prof, Mgmt, Adm	9.1	.74	Educ, Health, Soc Serv	10.0	.36

TABLE 15.8. Chicago Metropolitan Area: 2000 Industrial Concentrations of Foreign-Born Korean Men and Women

Men	%	RI	Women	%	RI
Retail Trade	16.2	1.64	Educ, Health, Soc Serv	20.6	.74
Manufacturing	14.1	.74	Retail Trade	18.3	1.48
Other Services	13.4	3.00	Other Services	15.2	3.10
Prof, Mgmt, Adm	13.4	1.09	Entert, Food Services	12.4	1.53

specific occupational face, and their major industrial–occupational niche becomes fleshed out. And, with a staggering RI of 31.76 for "laundry and dry cleaning," what a niche it is.

Korean immigrants as *petite bourgeoisie* has come to be as much an ethnic stereotype as has "math and computer whiz" for Chinese. In reality, more-recent Korean immigrants also occupy a range of scientific, professional, and technical occupational niches (see Appendix Table 15.11)—software engineers (RI of 4.22), electrical engineers (RI of 5.76), civil engineers (RI of 7.73), physicians (RI of 3.04), biological scientists (RI of 33.90), and pharmacists (RI of 26.25), among others.

So what does all this mean for Chicago, and what is the immigrant contribution to Chicago's economy? One way to put it is that Chicago's health care system would probably collapse without its present immigrant labor force; manufacturing would grind to a halt; hotels, restaurants, and fast-food services couldn't operate; and dual working households would be under the extreme stress of full-time work while, at the same time, managing their own household maintenance. Elder care would be in chaos—as would some forms of child care. And, of no little consequence, Chicago would be less rich culturally and, at the local level, less capable of adapting to a global economy and a global culture.

For immigrants themselves, the social, cultural, and human capital of each group plays an important part in determining the group's placement in the economy. High proportions of Indians and Filipinos are educated, professionally trained, and possess technical expertise. An English-language facility for both groups is a further asset, as is the reasonably strong co-ethnic social network for Indians and, to a lesser extent, for Filipinos. Not only are they rich in human capital, but that capital is the right stuff—the stuff that the evolving economy is looking for and rewarding.

With Filipinos and Indians, in other words, the skill mismatch hypothesis does not apply. Mexicans, on the other hand, face a serious skill mismatch, as do segments of other immigrant communities—not in the sense that jobs are not available to them but, rather, the available jobs tend to be low paying and dead-end. And, as is addressed later, the ethnic and racial occupational stratification taking shape bodes ill for the entire society, not simply for a few groups within it.

THE VERTICAL DIMENSION

The case has already been made that the demographic transformations in the labor force resulting from the immigration spike of the past twenty years and more has resulted in an ethnic division of labor in which ethnicity intersects with social class. Waldinger and Bozorgmehr found strong evidence for this in Los Angeles and, referring to a vertical dimension of occupational niches, he concluded:

> Chinese and Japanese Americans have moved into advantageous specializations, where they find ample opportunity to work in high-paying white-collar jobs and do better than in industries of lower ethnic density. Other groups—African Americans and Mexican Americans, as well as Koreans, Filipino, and Vietnamese immigrants, for example—occupy the middle ranges of the continuum. . . . Mexican, Salvadoran, and Guatemalan immigrants—the most concentrated of all—do the very worst, crowding into menial employment where the wage ceiling is extremely low. (Waldinger and Bozorgmehr 1996, 450–51)

When we parallel Waldinger's approach to summarizing Los Angeles' ethnic occupational hierarchy, we see that Chicago is a near-mirror image (Table 15.9).

In summary, the match of immigrants to industries and occupations is characterized by a high degree of segmentation. Ethnic segmentation existed in preindustrial and industrial economies as well. Replications of specific earlier patterns also occur, for example, Koreans following Jews into small business and the professions, while African Americans retrace Irish mobility from manual labor and domestic service into municipal employment and teaching.

IMPLICATIONS FOR CONTEMPORARY IMMIGRANTS

Achieving the American dream is likely for some contemporary immigrants and a hopeless struggle for many others. One standard rationale points to the difference in our economy now when compared to the time of the last great wave of immigration, at the turn of the twentieth century. Then, a soaring industrial economy put to work large numbers of unskilled, poorly educated immigrants at the same pace as it consumed coal to fuel its industry. The present information technology service society, so goes the thesis, has a decidedly strong education and

TABLE 15.9. The vertical ordering of ethnic occupations: Los Angeles and Chicago.

Los Angeles	Chicago
The region's **Chinese** and **Japanese** Americans make up a professional middle class integrated into the region's core industries in manufacturing and professional services.	The metro area's **Indians** and **Filipinos** (recently joined by Chinese) make up a professional and middle class integrated into the area's core industries in information technology and professional (medical) services.
Koreans, Iranians, and **Chinese** immigrants make up a diversified business grouping with **Koreans** struggling as an embattled *petit bourgeoisie* and **Iranians** and **Chinese** on the road to high-tech, high-skill entrepreneurship.	**Korean** and **Indian** immigrants are the pre-eminent *petit bourgeoisie* of the immigrant community. **Koreans** stake out privately owned small business; **Indians** purchase franchises from Dunkin' Donuts, Convenient Mart, and the like.
African Americans divide into two middle groupings, an emergent middle-class component linked to government and other large employers and an impoverished lower-skilled segment increasingly excluded from the employment system itself.	Chicago's growing **African American** middle class is anchored in the local, state, and public sector—especially as mid-level administrators in the government sector—as postal and public transportation workers. They also have a strong presence in public and private health care and, for males, in lower-level industrial blue-collar jobs.
	Chicago's male **Polish** immigrants have major niches in skilled blue-collar manufacturing occupations as well as in construction. **Polish** women in the labor force are found both in upper-level medical and business occupations and lower-level service jobs in home health care and building maintenance.
Mexicans are divided into a rank of native-born working- and lower-middle-class skilled laborers and lower-level bureaucrats that overlaps little with foreign-born ranks, and an isolated immigrant proletariat confined to the bottom tiers of the region, where they are joined by **Central Americans,** the latest addition to the region's low-wage labor pool.	**Native-born Mexican** women work in mid- and lower-level business and retail occupations. Their male counterparts are found manufacturing and mid-level positions in retail trade. **Mexican** women mainly work in lower-level manufacturing jobs as assemblers, packagers, and general production. Males work as construction laborers, grounds maintenance workers, and heavy concentrations in a range of jobs in the food service industry.

skill bias with little or no need for large numbers of the untrained or poorly educated. The prevalent prediction is that immigrants with such a profile face bleak economic prospects that will only grow bleaker. Two more layers to the issue exist, however—a segmented economy and the growing reality of an hourglass economy.

A Segmented Economy

With the end of World War II, the machinery of America's wartime output was converted to peacetime productivity to meet the pent-up needs of a product-thirsty civilian population. The economic gold rush that followed produced the phenomenon of structural mobility—a time when a rising tide lifted all boats. That metaphor, and the reality it alluded to, no longer applies. The economy now consists of increasingly more segmented sectors, and a transportation terminal with multiple banks of "Up" and "Down" escalators is perhaps a more apt metaphor. From the perspective of immigrant workers, here is one scenario: Indian and Chinese workers in the e-commerce sector were on e-commerce's "Up" escalator during most of the 1990s, while Mexican and Polish blue-collar workers (as well as down-sized white-collar workers of many ethnic origins) were on industry's parallel "Down" escalators. Then, during the late 1990s someone hit the "Down" switch on the e-commerce escalator; the Indian occupants then descended past other Indian and Filipino workers on health care's "Up" escalator.

Equal opportunity unemployment is also a phenomenon of a new economic world. For the first time in the history of industrial American, save for the Great Depression, skilled and well-educated workers are highly vulnerable to economic downturns—segmental economic downturns. In the past, education and training usually provided thick insulation from the heat of economic downturns. So, in times of recession, for example, whatever the unemployment rate in the labor force at-large, you could count on half that proportion, or less, being the case for the upper strata of the labor force. No longer. Segmental unemployment makes few status distinctions. Still, immigrants are especially vulnerable to this phenomenon and are more strongly affected by it. Because they cluster so densely in occupational and industrial niches, segmental decline has more devastating consequences for them than it does for the labor force at-large.

The Hourglass Economy

The metaphor of an hourglass economy speaks to a bifurcated labor force consisting of extreme economic equality. One group—the well educated, highly skilled, and socially connected—reap great economic rewards. The other occupational group—those with low education, few skills, and meager network connections and little social capital—do poorly. The middle shrinks, a "winner-take-all" society emerges, and the economy increasingly becomes a zero-sum game. Its looming national emergence has been predicted by many, its regional and sectoral here-and-now presence is increasingly cited by others (Massey and Hirst 1998, Milkman and Dwyer 2002, Bean and Lindsay 2003, Sassen 1998, Thurow 2001, Hecker 2001, Reich 1991, and Frank and Cook, 1996).

The arrival of an hourglass economy, if predictions hold, further exacerbates the situation for all, but more critically so for immigrants. An increasingly large body of data identifies the attainment of a college or postsecondary degree as *the* single most important factor in becoming successful in a high-tech, information, and service society. Also, it should be clear that traditional forms of occupational mobility—through increased skill, work experience, a high level of individual competence and ability—now hit a mobility ceiling at a relatively low level. In the new economy, individual merit *must* be accompanied by a higher educational credential to enter the management or technical and professional fields which, in turn, hold the key to entry to the top half of the hourglass. A Bureau of Labor Statistics report unambiguously makes the point:

> The hourglass economy will continue to be fed and shaped: The fastest and largest occupational growth is predicted to occur among professional and related occupations and. . . . occupations requiring a postsecondary vocational award or an academic degree, which account for 29 percent of all jobs in 2000, will account for 42 percent of total job growth from 2000 to 2010. (Hecker 2001, 57)

Immigrants are coming to a society that has a shrinking industrial and manufacturing sector and a growing but bifurcated service sector. Therefore, depending on their human, social, or cultural capital, they receive high or low economic returns for their labor investment. Finally, large clusters of workers within particular immigrant communities are rather homogeneous in the capital they arrive with, thus producing a network of ethnically linked occupational and industrial niches. And, as Alejandro Portes asserts, time is the enemy: "The new immigrants are in a very real race against time to jump from the entry level jobs, pass through the narrow center of the hourglass, and reach the professional mainstream" (*Crosscurrents* 1994–95). Given the present socioeconomic conditions of many new immigrants, it is relatively impossible for them to win the race to which Portes refers.

An hourglass economy, with its two-tiered reward structure, then, bodes an economic crisis for all less-well-educated workers and an economic disaster for minorities. Even more troubling is the impending racial and ethnic composition of each of the two tiers in an hourglass economy—an upper tier dominated by white and Asian workers and a lower tier dominated by Latino, African American, and the white working poor. This time around, the structure of a postindustrial economy is not as mobility fluid as that of yesterday's industrial economy. Some assert that extreme economic inequality is the inevitable result of the new economy. Another response is possible: The inevitable is defined as inevitable only because we chose to do nothing about it.

APPENDIX

TABLE 15.1. Foreign-Born Mexican Men

Occupation	Frequency	RI
Cooks	18,352	3.83
Const	12,881	3.19
Grounds Maint Wrkrs	12,365	5.03
Metal/Plas Wrkr	12,051	4.18
Prod Wrkr	12,018	3.44
Janitors	11,170	1.91
Laborers, Hand	10,864	1.62
Truck Drivers	8,619	0.89
Sprvrs of Prod/Op	7,447	1.89
Assmbly, Fabr	7,385	3.37

TABLE 15.2. Foreign-Born Mexican Women

Occupation	Frequency	RI
Prod Wrkr	12,112	7.37
Assmbly, Fabr	9,115	6.71
Packagers, Hand	8,590	8.87
Mchne Opr/Tndrs	7,862	8.65
Maids	7,464	3.59
Cashiers	6,613	1.22
Metal/Plast Wrkrs	6,536	7.04
Laborers	5,405	4.33
Inspec, Sort, Sample	4,604	4.12
Janitors	3,986	3.10

TABLE 15.3. Foreign-Born Polish Men

Occupation	Frequency	RI
Carpenters	3,292	3.44
Truck Driver/Sales	3,264	1.64
Janitor	2,577	2.15
Machinists	2,070	6.78
Construction	1,924	2.32
Metal/Plast Wrkrs	1,561	2.64
Prod Wrkrs	1,529	2.13
Paint, Constr, Maint	1,346	3.83
1st-Ln Sprvrs, Prod/Op	1,329	1.64
Const Mgrs	1,281	3.87

TABLE 15.4. Foreign-Born Polish Women

Occupation	Frequency	RI
Janitors	4,108	9.93
Maids	3,662	5.48
Cashiers	1,665	0.96
Office clerks	1,593	1.57
Prod Wrkrs	1,512	2.86
Scrtr, Adm Asst	1,390	0.50
Nrsng, Psych, Health	1,376	1.62
Elem, Mid Schl Tchr	1,282	0.77
Sprvrs, Mgrs Janit	1,222	15.09
Retail Sales	1,128	0.72

TABLE 15.5. Foreign-Born Indian Men

Occupation	Frequency	RI
Comp Soft Eng	3,860	12.33
Comp Scntst/Anlyst	2,348	6.44
Phys/Surg	1,204	5.15
Taxi Drvrs, Chffrs	1,204	6.74
Mgrs, All Others	1,173	1.68
Sprvors, Retail Sales	1,173	1.98
Cashiers	972	2.57
Compr Progmrs	958	3.29
Retail Sales	883	1.11
Accntnts, Auditors	774	1.60

TABLE 15.6. Foreign-Born Indian Women

Occupation	Frequency	RI
Phys/Surg	1,758	16.82
Reg Nurses	1,435	2.04
Comp Soft Eng	1,082	15.62
Cashiers	928	1.09
Clinical Lab Tech	792	9.66
Scrtr, Adm Asst	680	0.49
Postsec Tchrs	649	3.37
Data Entry	572	2.49
Prod Wrkrs	572	2.21
Preschl Tchrs	555	3.74

TABLE 15.7. Foreign-Born Filipino Men

Occupation	Frequency	RI
Phys/Surg	956	6.77
Reg Nurses	756	20.67
Nrsng, Psych, Health	712	12.79
Lbrs, Freight Movers	618	1.13
Cooks	572	1.46
Electricians	557	2.59
Accntnts, Auditors	509	1.74
Comp Sup Spclsts	495	6.85
Machinists	493	4.06
Janitors	479	1.00

TABLE 15.8. Foreign-Born Filipino Women

Occupation	Frequency	RI
Reg Nurses	7,292	7.74
Nursing, Health Aides	1,422	2.56
Accountants	1,348	2.73
Bookkeeping	1,006	1.55
Phys/Surg	1,004	7.18
Retail Sales	879	0.85
Home Care Aides	726	6.37
Lab Techs	615	5.61
Med Assts	588	3.24
Scrtr, Adm Asst	585	0.32

TABLE 15.9. Foreign-Born Chinese Men

Occupation	Frequency	RI
Cooks	2,101	6.05
Comp Prog	1,281	8.21
Comp Soft Eng	1,143	6.81
Supvr Retails	680	2.14
Postsec Tchrs	649	4.41
Chefs, Head Cooks	633	9.67
Comp Sci	557	2.85
Prod Wrkrs	557	2.20
Spvr, Nonretail	510	2.36
Nrsing, Home Health	386	7.81

TABLE 15.10. Foreign-Born Chinese Women

Occupation	Frequency	RI
Accountants	1,498	4.82
Comp Program	881	12.29
Cashiers	880	1.22
Sew Mchne Op	803	18.11
Office Clerks	650	1.55
Waitresses	603	1.75
Gen Op Mgrs	539	8.11
Comp Soft Eng	494	8.46
Chem, Math Sci	479	28.46
Paraleg, Leg Asst	474	6.83

TABLE 15.11. Foreign-Born Korean Men

Occupation	Frequency	RI
Sprvr, Retail	1,266	6.54
Sprvr, Prod/Op	680	3.90
Comp Soft Eng	432	4.22
Accountants	371	2.35
Electrical Eng	324	5.76
Retail	311	1.20
Taxi Drvrs, Chauff	309	5.30
Chief Executives	293	1.59
Engineering Techn	279	6.19
Entert, Attendants	278	16.47

TABLE 15.12. Foreign-Born Korean Women

Occupation	Frequency	RI
Retail	711	1.79
Sprvr, Prod/Op	696	12.14
Sprvr, Retail	619	3.23
Elem, Mid Schl Tchr	494	1.17
Pharmacists	464	26.25
Post Serv Clerks	464	19.83
Reg Nurses	448	1.23
Cashiers	398	0.90
Chief Executives	294	7.18
Tailors	294	19.34

NOTES

1. Sections of this chapter appeared in an earlier "Works in Progress" paper, "In Search of Economic Parity: The Mexican Labor Force in Chicago." *Interim Reports*, Vol. 2004.1, March 2004. Institute for Latino Studies, University of Notre Dame, Notre Dame Indiana.

2. The multiplier effect, an indicator that shows how the creation of jobs in one sector of the economy contributes to job creation in other segments, varies from region to region and from occupation to occupation. In Illinois manufacturing jobs have the highest multiplier effect—3.7. Service jobs, in turn, have a multiplier effect of 1.8; that is for every new service job in the state, another .8 jobs are created in other sectors, resulting in a total of 1.8. (See: "The state of Illinois Manufacturing." A Report for the Illinois Manufacturers' Association, Center for Labor and Community Research, Chicago. December, 2003. p.11.)

3. In the decade of the 1980's "physician" was the single largest occupation of male and female Asian Indian immigrants to Chicago; "Computer engineers" and "system analysts" were the two largest occupation of male Asian Indian immigrants in the decade of the 1990's, outnumbering physician and surgeon, the third largest immigrant occupation, by a factor of 4-1. National immigration data for 2002 show that Indians, Filipinos, and Chinese—in that order—outnumber all other immigrant groups for receiving favorable immigration status H1-B visas on the basis of employment specialty.

4. At various times the terms human capital, social capital, and cultural capital will be referred to in this chapter. They simply refer to distinctive and differing resources individuals possess. Specifically: human capital refers the resources that individuals bring with them to the labor market—like interest and aptitudes, formal education, occupational training, and previous work experience; social capital refers to the collective value of all 'social networks' [who people know] and the inclinations that arise from these networks to be of help to one another; cultural capital refers to a set of values, beliefs, norms, attitudes, experiences that equip people for life in society and help them navigate through a culture.

5. The categories used by the census bureau and the Bureau of Labor Statistics to identify occupations and industries change with the times but are still slow to reflect many of the changing realities in the contemporary world of work. The occupation of "chef," for example, was so identified for the first time in the 2000 census. In prior censuses "cook" was a one size fits all occupational designation. Also, the 2000 census does not recognize "Information Technology" as an industry even though the "industry" and its related occupations is core to a postindustrial economy. Similarly, the omission of occupational and industrial categories for the "leisure industry" and other evolving sectors and occupations in the economy could be pointed out. For this reason existing industry categories are not treated here as definitive.

PART IV

Contested Reinvention and Civic Agency: Ten Case Studies

Thus far, in Parts I, II, and III of *The New Chicago*, our contributors have discussed a series of broad forces reshaping contemporary Chicago, and they have profiled the most prominent of the metropolitan area's population groups. In Part IV, we present ten cases of "civic agency," self-conscious efforts to redirect government action, sustain or reinvigorate local neighborhood life, or enhance the overall quality of city and metropolitan development. Our cases are, admittedly, but a slice of local civic action, but we do think they represent a reasonably comprehensive sampling of the characteristic institutional formations, policy aims, and strategies animating civic action in this metropolitan region.

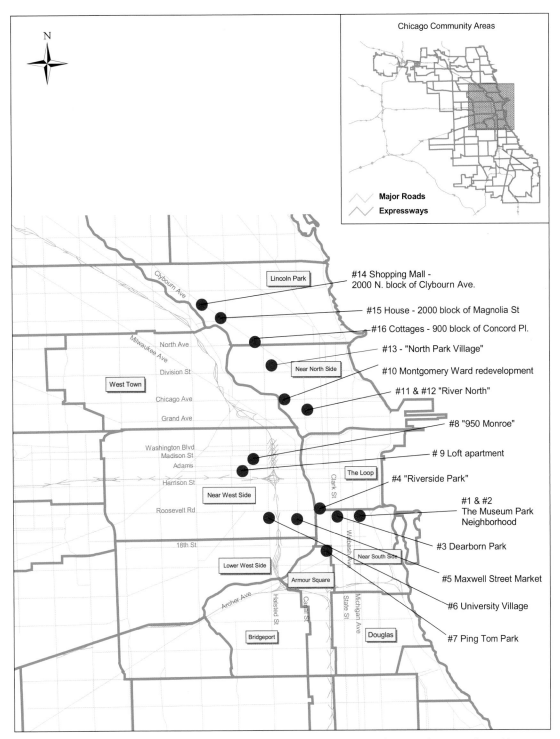

MAP 5.1. Map of Chicago's Central Area. The sites and locations in these photographs generally reside within the "Zone in Transition," made famous by Park and Burgess in *The City* (1925).

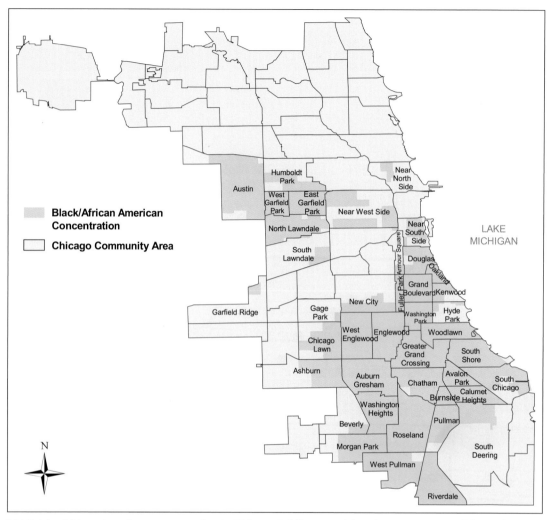

MAP 6.1. African American concentration in Chicago. While comprising about 37 percent of the city's population today, the African American residents of Chicago are concentrated along two axes radiating out from the central Loop area—one to the south and one to the west—that reflect de facto segregation patterns already well in place by the 1960s. *Source:* U.S. Census Bureau, 2000.

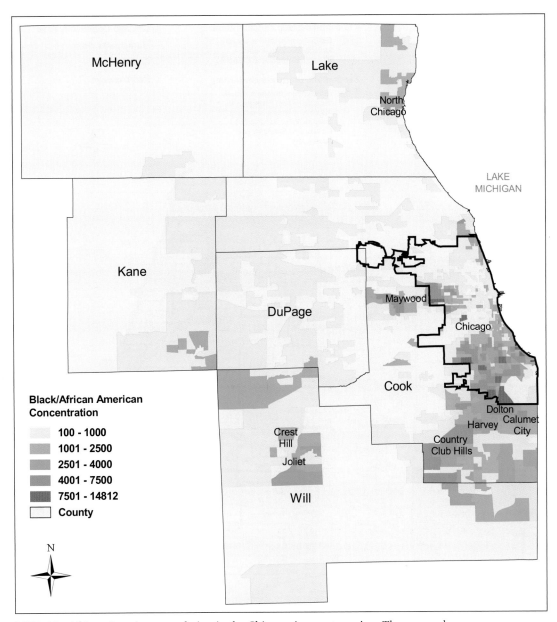

MAP 6.2. African American population in the Chicago six-county region. The nonrandom concentration of African Americans found in the central city is mirrored in the surrounding suburbs and exurbs stretching across six counties. *Source:* U.S. Census Bureau, 2000.

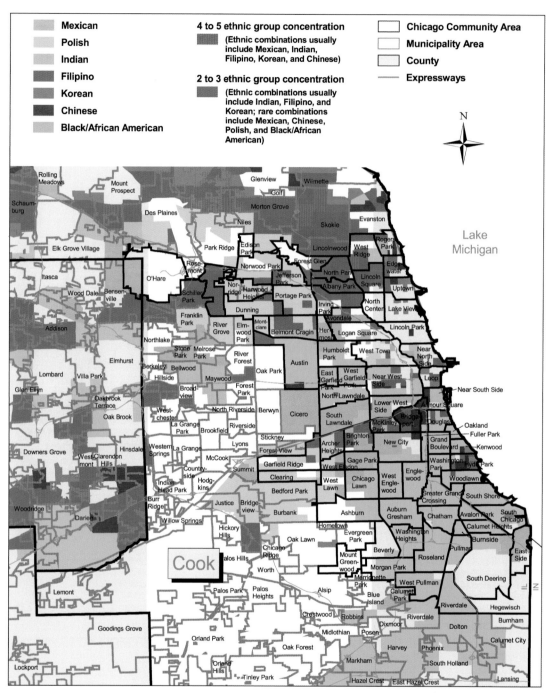

MAP 7.1. City of Chicago: ethnic–racial residential concentrations, 2000. *Source:* Census 2000, Summary File 3.

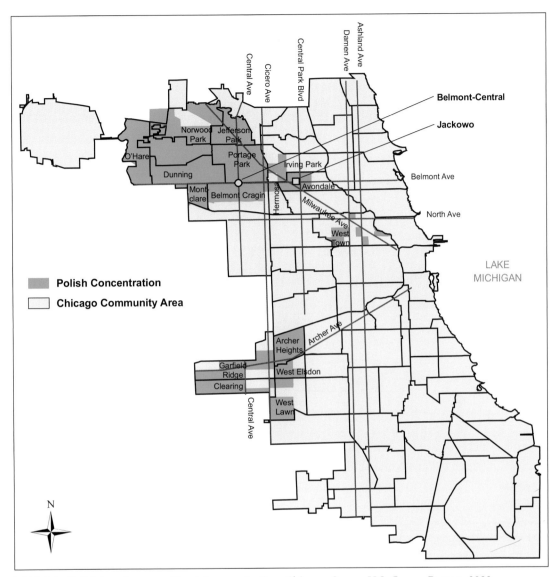

MAP 9.1. Polish immigrant residential concentration: Chicago. *Source:* U.S. Census Bureau, 2000.

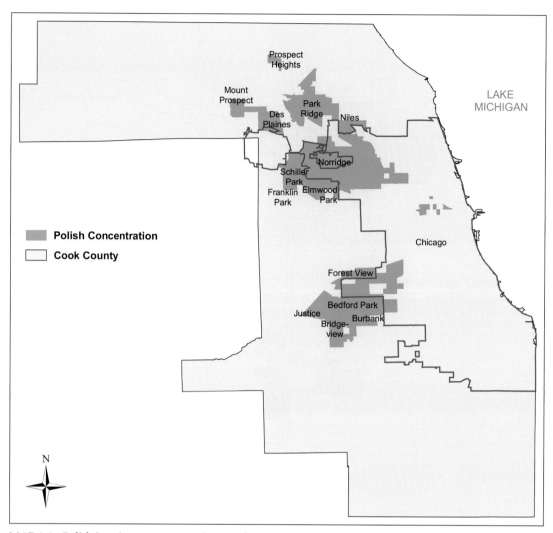

MAP 9.2. Polish immigrant concentration: Cook County. *Source:* U.S. Census Bureau, 2000.

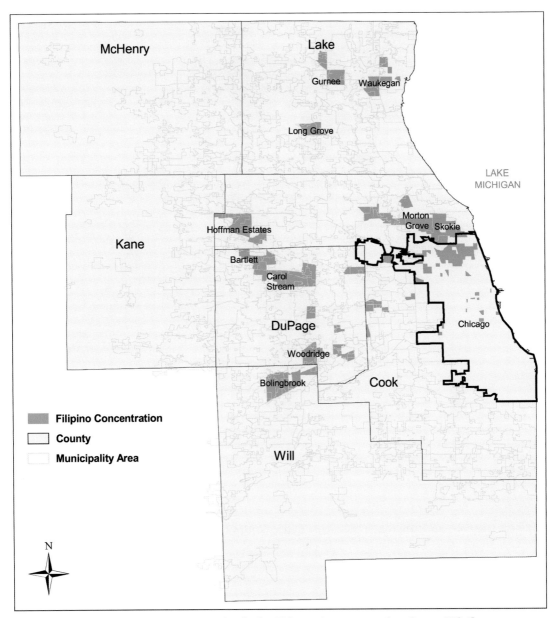

MAP 11.1. Filipino immigrant concentration in the Chicago six-county region. *Source:* U.S. Census Bureau, 2000.

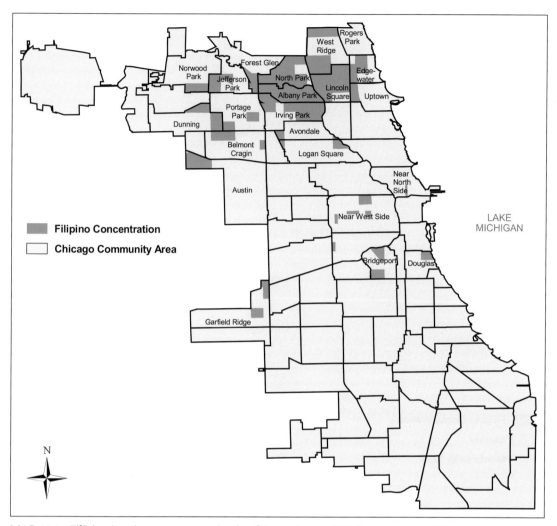

MAP 11.2. Filipino immigrant concentration in Chicago. *Source:* U.S. Census Bureau, 2000.

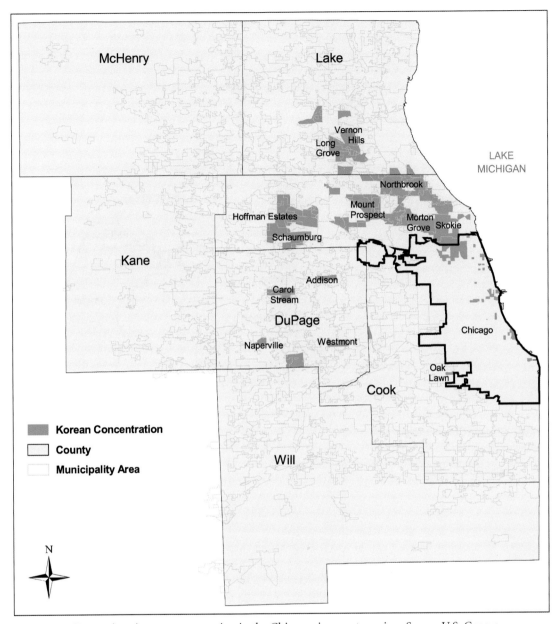

MAP 12.1. Korean immigrant concentration in the Chicago six-county region. *Source:* U.S. Census Bureau, 2000.

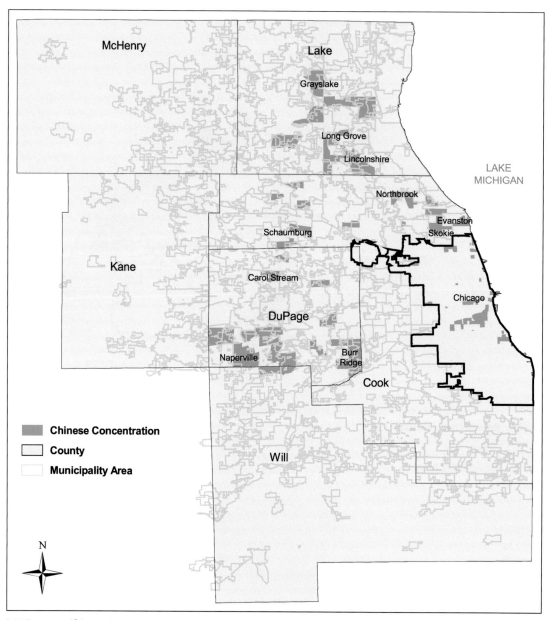

MAP 13.1. Chinese immigrant concentration in the Chicago six-county region. *Source:* U.S. Census Bureau, 2000.

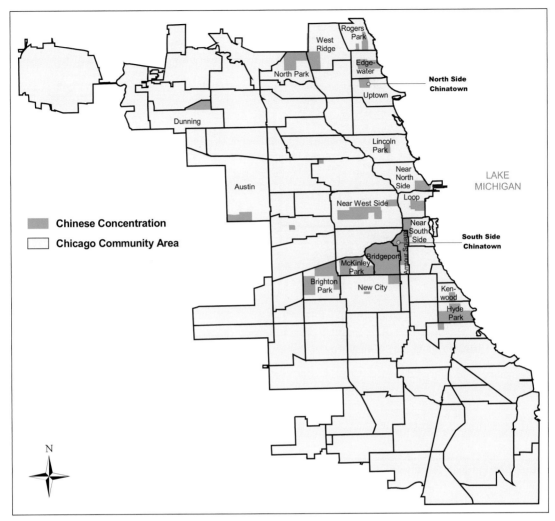

MAP 13.2. Chinese immigrant concentration in Chicago. *Source:* U.S. Census Bureau, 2000.

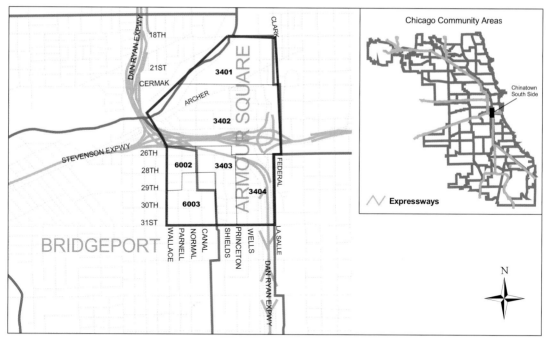

MAP 13.3. Chicago's South Side Chinatown.

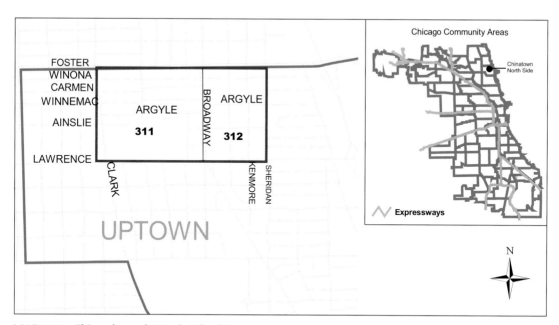

MAP 13.4. Chicago's Argyle North Side Chinatown.

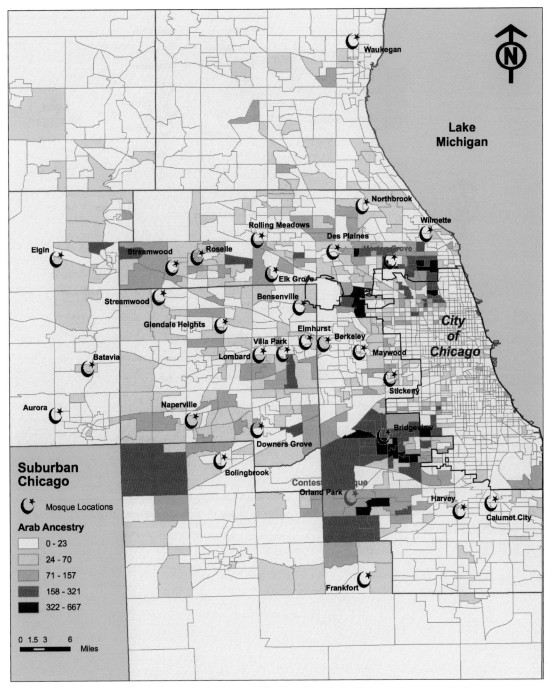

MAP 14.1. Persons of Arab and Assyrian ancestry, Cook and DuPage Counties (crescents indicate mosques). *Source:* U.S. Census Bureau, 2000.

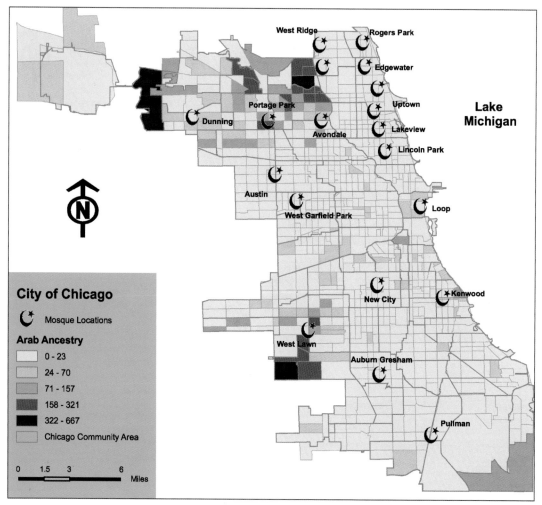

MAP 14.2. Persons of Arab and Assyrian ancestry, City of Chicago (crescents indicate mosques). *Source:* U.S. Census Bureau, 2000.

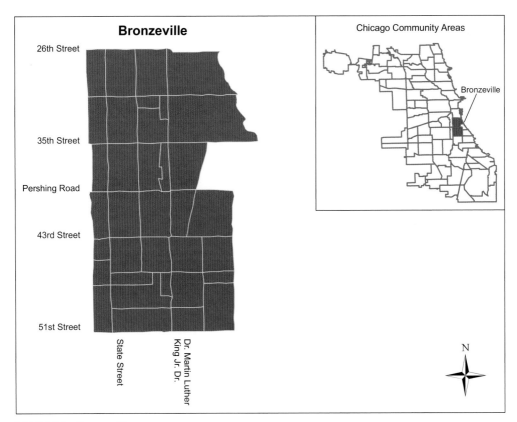

MAP 16.1. Bronzeville.

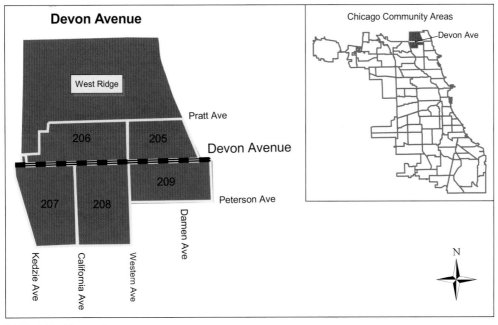

MAP 17.1. Devon Avenue.

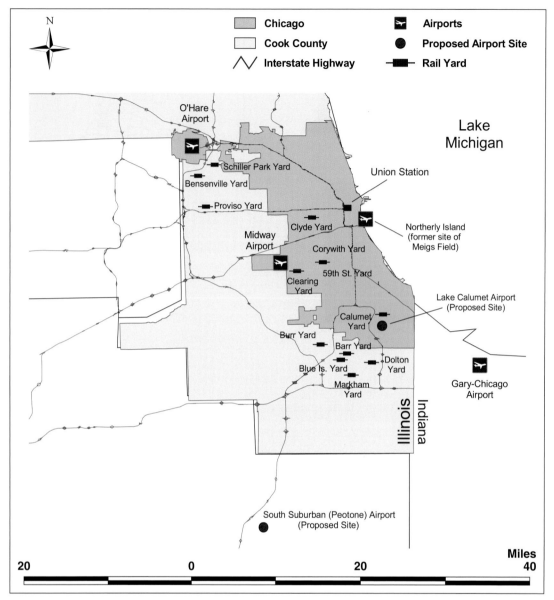

MAP 24.1. Major air and rail facilities of metropolitan Chicago.

Michael I. J. Bennett

16   The Rebirth of Bronzeville: Contested Space and Contrasting Visions

RACE AND CLASS struggles are well known to urbanologists who have studied and written about Chicago for the past century. In the case of Bronzeville, a community created by racial discrimination and then devastated by both urban renewal and urban disinvestment trends, residents and community leaders are now attempting to use racial heritage as an economic engine for community revitalization. In many instances, the cultural heritage theme has been supported and even funded by the city administration and the large white-owned institutions that heavily influence development decisions in this community. Over the past decade, considerable controversy has arisen over questions of land control and visions of the community's race and class mix post revitalization. This chapter presents some of the prospects and dilemmas facing a famous African American community as it grapples with and is being shaped by the political, social and economic realities of the new Chicago.

Grappling and shaping are apt descriptions for the transformation process that the community is experiencing because, since power is not evenly distributed among the political leaders, institutional decision-makers, and resident activists, constant tussles occur among these stakeholders. The rebirth of Bronzeville is truly an illustration of contested reinvention around the redesignation of urban geography, the role of racial identity, and inter-group class conflict.

LIFE IN BRONZEVILLE: THEN AND NOW

Bronzeville's Historical Significance

Author Dempsey Travis (1983) wrote that "East 47th Street was the Magnificent Mile of Chicago's Black Belt in 1928." Its retail shops stimulated the vibrant walking traffic now characteristic of the popular, mile-long stretch of high-fashion shops along North Michigan Avenue known as Chicago's Magnificent Mile. Its dynamics have been about race since the Black Belt emerged from segregation and pronounced de facto residential restrictions. By the early 1920s, the area bounded by 31st Street on the north, and 63rd Street on the south, between State Street and Cottage Grove Avenue, had become home to 300,000 African Americans who migrated from the South in two distinct waves—first from 1840 to 1900, then between 1910 and 1920—to find work and economic liberation in the North. The Black Belt had become the recognized center for black business, politics, and culture by 1925. "Beginning with the establishment of the Binga Bank, the vicinity of State and 35th streets was transformed into the 'Wall Street' of the South Side" (Report of The Commission on Chicago Landmarks 1994, 3). It was the natural spawning ground for black political movements. Oscar DePriest represented the area as the city's first African American Alderman in 1915 and later in the U.S. House of Representatives in 1928 (Report of The Commission on Chicago

Landmarks 1994, 7). Major religious congregations, such as Quinn Chapel African Methodist Episcopal and Olivet Baptist Churches, located at 24th and Wabash Avenue and 31st and South Park (since renamed Dr. Martin Luther King, Jr. Drive) respectively, served to organize social and political responses to community issues (Chicago Fact Book Consortium 1984).

According to Drake and Cayton (1993), "The Black Belt became the Black Metropolis in the 20 years between the close of the First World War and the beginning of the Second" (1993, 77). The years that followed, however, have not been kind to the Douglas and Grand Boulevard communities, the heart of the area known alternately as the Black Metropolis and Bronzeville. Deterioration and decline had already begun before the arrival of black residents, who today make up 97 percent of the area's population (see Map 16.1, color insert).

Myriad forces contributed to the area's ragged, downward spiral. One scenario triggering the demise of black-owned retail enterprises was attributed to white businessmen

> . . . who previously had ignored the area, began to recognize its economic potential. Rather than attempt to break into the prosperous commercial district at 35th and State, white entrepreneurs created an alternate business area along 47th Street, where they already controlled most of the property. The introduction of chain stores and other well-financed enterprises presented insurmountable competition to the independent African American business district and progressively siphoned off its energy and financial base. (Report of The Commission on Chicago Landmarks 1994, 8)

Economic Transformation and Bronzeville

The countervailing impact of deindustrialization and a burgeoning service economy during the 1980s and 1990s shifted the sources of income and wealth for black Chicagoans from the factory to the office to the unemployment line. The changing socioeconomic profile of Bronzeville followed two extremes. The poorest residents clustered in a deteriorating set of public-housing units on the western edge of the community, while upper-income residents purchased magnificent, faded graystones and newly converted condominiums in the central and eastern corridors. One exception is the 3,446 public-housing units of the Clarence Darrow Homes, Madden Park, and Ida B. Wells developments between King Drive and Cottage Grove in the eastern pocket.

The percentage of Douglas–Grand Boulevard residents living below the poverty level declined from nearly 70 percent in 1990 to a deceptive 43 percent just a decade later, primarily because of a population loss of 21 percent during that period. The decline in the percentage of poor residents correlates directly with the number of poor people dislocated as a result of the Chicago Housing Authority's Plan for Transformation.

BRONZEVILLE'S IDENTITY AND DEVELOPMENT AGENDA

Sociologists define community in at least three ways. Landmarks, streets, and rail tracks clearly delineate the boundaries of the *geographic community*. Communities of *common interest* tend to move beyond geographic boundaries to encompass religious, cultural, ethnic, and social interest groups that once may have congregated in a common area but have since expanded throughout the metropolitan area. Members come together to socialize or even strategize around specific social or political actions. The community of *ascribed characteristics* is an aggregate without subscribed membership. Demographers, marketing people, politicians, organizers, and planners ascribe interests to aggregates of people—for example, African Americans, gays, welfare moms, the elderly—that they may or may not have. However, once a functional group mobilizes around a specific issue or set of issues, that aggregate becomes a community of sorts.

Bronzeville is all three communities in one. From a geographic perspective, the community's boundaries are expandable, depending on planning and identity purposes.

For example, the official boundaries of Grand Boulevard (Community Area 38) are 39th Street to the north, 51st Street to the south, the Chicago Rock Island railroad on the west, and Cottage

Grove Avenue on the east. According to the 2000 U.S. Census, the area's population—97.7 percent of which is African American—declined 22 percent from 1990 and 47 percent from 1980, to its current population of 28,043. The geographic identification includes the adjacent Douglas community (Community Area 35), which expands the boundaries north to 26th Street and adds 26,287 people, 85.5 percent of whom are African American. These two communities form the nucleus of Bronzeville.

In the broader planning efforts for the mid South Side area, Bronzeville extends to 55th Street, known to most people as Washington Park. This expanded boundary speaks more to the community of common interests. In its entirety, this area is identified variously as Douglas–Grand Boulevard–Washington Park, the Black Metropolis, and Bronzeville. Each designation carries increasing political and cultural significance. Although the names Douglas–Grand Boulevard–Washington Park appear on Chicago's official community area map, the identity of Black Metropolis is rooted in the forced residential restrictions placed on black migrants from the South, who arrived from the 1930s to the 1950s. Bronzeville, on the other hand, connotes a self-proclaimed, asset-based identity expressive of the area's political, cultural, and economic aspirations. The whole re-birthing effort is banking on the notion that this area holds cultural significance for African Americans citywide and even nationally. The preamble to one grassroots-driven revitalization plan asserts that, "Bronzeville is the most important African American community in the nation outside of Harlem. Its redevelopment has enormous cultural and historic value to the city" (*Bronzeville Vision 2010*, 6).

Yet another perception of the community stems from its history as the site of the largest tract of public housing in the nation, perhaps the world. Prior to recent demolition activities, mostly high-rise public housing stretched more than 30 blocks, from 21st Street south to 54th Street. With the addition of the Wells-Madden-Darrow developments, more than 40 percent of the community's population resided in public housing. The area's resulting association with poor, black, crime-ridden Chicago promotes a set of ascribed characteristics that accompany the tripartite nature of its definition. Middle-income and many low-income residents register strong objections to the negative portrayals of their community, an indication of the ascribed rather than subscribed nature of these characteristics.

PLANS GALORE, BUT DEVELOPMENT FOR WHOM?

The strategic approach of the 1993 *Mid-South Strategic Development Plan: Restore Bronzeville*, a comprehensive land-use plan coordinated by the Mid-South Planning and Development Commission (MSP&DCC), a consortium of community organizations and institutions representing some 3,000 residents, was to leverage the community's historic past to launch new business and cultural development. Its centerpiece was the revival of the Bronzeville Blues and Jazz District and the restoration of eight historic sites. The plan was updated and enhanced by community assemblies and working groups in 1999 and 2002, resulting in *Bronzeville 2010*. The updated version of the plan was expanded to address not only cultural tourism, but housing, education, employment, health, economic development, and safety issues. Harold Lucas, the director of the Black Metropolis Convention and Tourism Council and a member of the MSP&DCC, characterized it as "a plan that improves the neighborhood for the people who are living here now while attracting new residents and businesses" (Lucas 2003).

The historic Chicago Bee Newspaper Building owes its life to the revitalization plan. In spring 1997, the Chicago Public Library established a branch in this building, which was once home to one of Chicago's first African American newspapers. Community leaders later persuaded the Chicago Board of Education to purchase the Eighth Regiment Armory, the former headquarters of a black World War I regiment, which it has turned into a high school academy with an ROTC-oriented curriculum.

The newly expanded McCormick Place Convention Center, anchoring the northern end of King Drive, hosts millions of conventioneers each year. Funds from the Center's McCormick Place Pier and Exposition Authority parent were put into public art along King Drive, including a large bronze street map of Bronzeville and a statue honoring the great Southern migration into the city.

As with most development activities in Bronzeville, cultural development has not come without controversy. Some community activists fear that new investment in business and cultural enterprises may be intended not for their community, but for the targets of the overheated real estate market and upscale development taking shape at Bronzeville's northern doorstep in the South Loop. An article announcing the project in the August 28, 2003 issue of *Crain's Chicago Business* portrays a positive project that will rehab 24,000 square feet of vacant office-building space to house an adjunct to Chicago's nationally known Second City comedy club, five retail businesses, a restaurant, and other offices. "The City Council Committee on Housing and Real Estate on Wednesday advanced a $2.8 million plan to build a Second City comedy club in Bronzeville's Jazz and Blues District." The article quotes Second City alum Dionna Griffin, of Detroit, who will be a producer at the Bronzeville site: "The development will be another venue to support the voice of the African-American performer" (*Crain's* 2003, 7).

A feature story in April 2003, in The Chicago Reporter (Prince 2003, 3), an investigative monthly that focuses on local race issues, poverty, minorities, and politics, "New Theater Opening to Mixed Reviews," quotes critics who view the Second City project as a racial and class-oriented encroachment into black cultural territory.

For some community groups, the crown jewel of the *Restoring Bronzeville Plan* is the Supreme Life Building at the southeast corner of 35th Street and King Drive, the former headquarters of Supreme Life Insurance Company, at one time one of the nation's largest black-owned businesses. Notwithstanding the cooperation and investment of a respectable roster of organizations and institutions, the project had been held up by competition for control and conflict over its eventual usage. The restoration took nearly eight years.

Residential Displacement

The issue dominating public discussion within Bronzeville is the fate of 40 percent of the community's poorest population now living in public housing. For those who have expressed themselves publicly in interviews and community meetings, the prospect of new mixed-income housing to replace public housing is frightening. Grassroots organizations have been trying valiantly to plan a future for Bronzeville that is of, by, and for "the people." However, some community leaders readily admit they have no clout to make those plans a reality.

Harold Lucas observed,

In the historic Bronzeville community, unless a major *Restoring Bronzeville* updated economic development plan is collaboratively implemented by established grassroots community-based organizations like MSP&DCC, Community Weavers, and the Grand Boulevard Federation, within the next six months to a year, 90 percent of the current residents living in Bronzeville who earn less than $40,000 per year will be systematically disenfranchised and displaced by the year 2010! (Lucas 2003)

Although gentrification is a major concern of grassroots activists, its recent history in Bronzeville is complex. In the stereotypical scenario, gentrification occurs in a neighborhood of declining property values, through the efforts of upper-income whites, who displace longtime, low-income residents of color. In Bronzeville, the first wave of gentrifiers was African American professionals. Their number includes a few former residents who have long harbored the wish to return to the neighborhood of their youth. For most homeowners, however, the draw was the bargains in the solidly built, distinguished graystone buildings of The Gap, an enclave between King Drive and Michigan Avenue. The new buyers have returned these subdivided apartment buildings to the single-family residences of their past.

Bronzeville development is not simple. Local institutions such as Michael Reese Hospital, the Illinois Institute of Technology, and the Chicago White Sox baseball organization would undoubtedly welcome its transformation into a "new community." One with a more hospitable image, with close-in living accommodations for employees, students, and faculty, and the perception of "safe passage" for baseball fans, who include many whites from the city and suburbs commuting through the community to reach the ballpark (the newly renamed *U.S. Cellular Field*).

In the opinion of many of the community's black residents, the unsightly public-housing high-rises and their criminal element had to go. Many public-housing residents themselves have raised this opinion, although some observers fear they are misplacing their optimism in the Chicago Housing Authority's (CHA) Plan for Transformation. Released in 2000, that plan reserves 30 percent of its new construction to replace the high-rise developments for former public-housing tenants (Chicago Housing Authority 2000).

The Chicago Housing Authority Plan for Transformation

Few of the various observers following the CHA's attempt to eliminate high-rise public housing and find suitable replacement housing for the residents displaced understand CHA math (Boyd 2000; Synderman and Dailey 2002; Rogal 2002, 2003).

The CHA estimates that 8,500 to 11,000 public-housing residents displaced citywide will need housing. The major question both public-housing tenants and observers are raising is where those being displaced will find decent, affordable housing. The Uniform Relocation Act, passed by Congress in 1974, requires the CHA to make a "good-faith effort" to find housing for these tenants (Snyderman and Dailey 2002). The Central Advisory Council (CAC), a group of elected tenant leaders from each CHA development, recognized the weak commitment the Relocation Act offered and negotiated a much tighter agreement that spells out the rights and responsibilities of both tenants and the CHA. It "ensures that all lease-compliant residents (as of Oct. 1, 1999) are guaranteed a 'Right of Return' to a new or upgraded public-housing unit, if (a) they choose to return to public housing, and (b) they meet the site-specific screening criteria" (Snyderman and Dailey 2002, 5).

However, as the demolition and reconstruction numbers indicate, there is no one-for-one replacement of units at the same locations. Consequently, "most families will have to move at least twice before arriving at their final place of residence" (Snyderman and Dailey 2002, 5). In the interim, they have received Housing Choice Vouchers for private-market housing.

Displaced public-housing residents from Bronzeville will be hard pressed to stay there, considering its substantial loss of housing stock in general and especially rental units, over the past decade. The population also has declined in neighboring Douglas and Grand Boulevard—20.4 percent and 26.3 percent, respectively—with similar losses in the nearby communities that make up "greater Bronzeville." Oakland's population dropped 21 percent, Fuller Park is down 27 percent, and Washington Park lost 30.5 percent of its residents. As these communities succumb to the downward spiral of urban disinvestment—deterioration, abandonment, and demolition—this loss of housing stock and population is intricately related.

At a community meeting on September 10, 2003, MSP&DCC Executive Director Mary Stewart displayed an architectural drawing that showed $750 million in new housing destined for the State Street corridor from 39th to 55th Streets by 2005. In an interview later that month, Sokoni Karanja, the chief executive officer of Centers for New Horizons, said the community is scheduled to receive $1.3 billion in development investments by that time. For whom this community is being developed remains unanswered.

Institutional Plans

The Office of Community Development of the Illinois Institute of Technology (IIT) is a key institutional player with a community-building agenda. That orientation is largely because of Associate Vice President Leroy Kennedy. Kennedy, who directs IIT's Office of Community Development, is a veteran of South Side community involvement, coming out of the Woodlawn community near The University of Chicago (where legendary community organizer Saul Alinsky worked) and North Kenwood–Oakland. IIT is a full partner in Grand Boulevard's development efforts and a valued neighbor for its research and educational resources, and school and community improvement schemes. At times, however, the institution's expansion plans and activities have encountered resistance from community actors with different land-use interests. The distrust this has engendered has led some groups to isolate IIT from their planning processes.

In 1996, IIT launched a development plan calling for 120 units of new residential housing on IIT-owned lots on an eastern block adjacent to the campus, from Michigan to Indiana Avenues between 31st and 32nd Streets—a combination of townhouses and condominiums marketed to IIT faculty and staff, as well as the general public (Illinois Institute of Technology website, Aug. 18, 2003). This new housing is contributing to the residential income mix all parties engaged in Bronzeville's redevelopment favor.

The Politics of Development

Under Chicago's 50-seat city council system, Bronzeville is represented by aldermen from three wards—the 2nd, 3rd, and 4th. Each has an active role, through land-use control, in shaping the community's development agenda; combined, these aldermen have "holds" on 450 parcels of vacant land. City departments, which generally work closely with local aldermen on the land-use plans for their wards, have "holds" on an additional 184 parcels. In essence, 85 percent of the vacant property in the Douglas, Grand Boulevard, and Oakland portions of Bronzeville is under the control or influence of the three aldermen (Quintanilla 1994, 6). The city has acquired this land as a result of tax delinquencies, demolition liens, and abandonment. It then allows a city department, such as Housing or Planning and Development, or a local alderman to place a "hold" on the property to prevent if from further sale without their approval.

Third Ward Alderman Dorothy Tillman, who has 117 parcels "on hold," has a contentious relationship with public-housing residents and their grassroots defenders. She was opposed in the 2002 election for alderman by the former head of the MSPDC. Tillman herself came to prominence through her work as an organizer for Dr. Martin Luther King, Jr., both in the South and during his brief campaign in Chicago. Recently, she has been the city's most outspoken promoter for reparations for African Americans for their "stolen and uncompensated work in building this country" (Muwakkil 2000, 5) In 1984, then-Mayor Harold Washington hand-picked Tillman to fill a vacancy on the City Council created by the previous alderman's conviction for bribery and mail fraud. The Mayor was impressed by her demonstrated vigor fighting for the educational rights of school children and their parents. "When I first came here, I inherited a very corrupt, dirty, nasty ward, and we came in and launched a clean-up campaign," Tillman said (Lawrence 2003).

Many of the battles between Tillman and the grassroots community leaders stem from the development agenda she has launched, featuring the development of residential, cultural, and commercial projects through nonprofit entities she, in turn, has also created. Her critics complain that Tillman takes unfair advantage of her role as alderman to compete for city-controlled development funds. For example, several Bronzeville groups seeking funding from the federal Empowerment Zone program that the city manages have had their request denied. However, Tillman has received direct Empowerment Zone funds and has leveraged other funds for projects she endorsed.

The grassroots responses to local development issues in Bronzeville, as in many changing communities across the country, are fairly well organized. Generally, community groups work in collaboration with the city administration and local institutions in hopes of reaching a consensus around the development agenda. However, clashing concerns and vision for change frequently emerge. In Bronzeville, some community groups complain that local aldermen hold property for their own pet projects or offer prime locations to their favorite developers (who many claim become a favorite as a result of generous campaign contributions) (Quintanilla 1994, 6).

Tillman frequently encounters grassroots opposition from any of three coalitions of organizations that represent Bronzeville residents. MSP&DCC, mentioned previously as shepherd organization of the *Restoring Bronzeville* plan is one. Former MSP&DCC director and deputy commissioner of city planning, Pat Dowell opposed Tillman for 3rd Ward alderman in 2002. Another Tillman opponent is the Grand Boulevard Federation. The two coalitions include community organizations and social-service agencies focused on land use and social-service delivery systems, respectively. The third coalition, the Alliance of Congregations Transforming the Southside (ACTS)—a consortium of churches in and around Grand Boulevard and based at Hartzell United Methodist Church—organizes pastors and congregations throughout the South Side around issues of social justice and community safety.

The alderman's vision for the community's future is the primary point of contention. Some community leaders indicate that Tillman has signaled a lack of support for their "homegrown" agenda through her use of the property she controls for market-rate housing projects, her support of the CHA's demolition plans, and the recruitment of the North Side Second City project.

Although Dowell mounted a formal challenge to Tillman's political leadership, perhaps the most effective informal challenger is Sokoni Karanja, founder and executive director of the 32-year-old Centers for New Horizons. Founded in Bronzeville in 1971, Centers has a staff of 240 and an annual budget of more than $10 million. It is one of the city's largest and oldest community-based organizations. Karanja (a recipient of a prestigious MacArthur Genius Award) and his staff convene most of the community's consensus-building forums, workshops, and strategy sessions. Centers is a founding organizational member of both MSP&DCC and the Grand Boulevard Federation (Karanja chairs Grand Boulevard's board of directors) and plays a significant role in virtually all other community-based collaborations in the mid South Side.

In 1996, under Karanja's guidance, the Centers' Lugenia Burns Hope Center subsidiary launched a structured leadership development program to promote informed resident activism and civic engagement. The participants in the leadership program are members of local organizations who are trained to rally residents to respond to various development plans, which often translate into demonstrations and confrontations with Alderman Tillman.

In addition, Karanja and his staff conducted the Bronzeville Organizing Strategy Session (BOSS), a process that produced the updated *Bronzeville Vision 2010* through the collaboration of some 85 residents and activists. Tillman was not invited into the process, an action which organizers viewed as a direct response to her initiatives.

Significant challenges are attached to the debilitating perception that community residents and their organizations lack the power to influence decisions that are shaping their community's future. One lesson from other community capacity-building initiatives is that people must have a sense that their collective actions can have significant influence over the decisions affecting their communal lives. Evidence suggests that, in Grand Boulevard, people feel relatively impotent over major decisions altering their community. In the words of one agency director, "As a community, we should celebrate the *Restoring Bronzeville* plan and how it was developed. But having the clout to make it happen was another story. It just wasn't there."

BRONZEVILLE AND THE NEW CHICAGO

In the new Chicago, racial separation may not retain historical patterns. This is particularly true on the South Side where, in communities like Bronzeville, new housing sells for upwards of $250,000 and the racial mix is changing slowly. For example, between 1990 and 2000, the white, Asian, and Latino populations increased, albeit by small numbers, while the percentage of migrating African Americans decreased by 24 percent.

Slow demographic changes notwithstanding, the mid South Side of Chicago and especially Bronzeville will be majority black for the next decade. Issues about social ranking within the context of city neighborhoods and political power continue to be steeped in racial terms. The class issue, however, looms large with respect to black-on-black gentrification and the contested reinvention of the cultural fabric—especially for the purposes of tourism (Patillo-McCoy 1999).

Like New York's Harlem, historic Bronzeville could find city-supported cultural tourism to be a real spur to economic development. For this plan to succeed, the perception of Bronzeville as a crime-ridden, poverty-stricken neighborhood with the world's largest collection of public housing must be erased. On this point, consensus exists among city departments, aldermen, local institutions, and community leaders. No consensus exists, however, on how to place its poorest residents in Bronzeville's developmental rebirth.

Padma Rangaswamy

17   Devon Avenue: A World Market

THROUGH THE HEART of Chicago's 50th ward runs Devon Avenue, carrying the commercial lifeblood of a multicultural neighborhood known as the "international marketplace."[1] Devon Avenue is the popular moniker, especially among South Asian immigrants, for what is called West Ridge in the Chicago community area maps and West Rogers Park by many Chicagoans. Devon Avenue's international flavor is evident in its variety of shops and its 22 honorary street names from around the globe, such as Gandhi Marg, Golda Meir Boulevard, King Sargon Boulevard, Mohammed Ali Jinnah Way, Mother Teresa Way, and Sheik Mujib Way. As many as 52 languages are spoken in this area.[2] Under the international umbrella, the many ethnic groups not only cling to their own cultural peculiarities but also cater to them and make a living from them in the local shops, houses of worship, and service centers. As pluralism goes, this may be the finest example of how the Many can co-exist without fusing indistinguishably into the One.

Devon Avenue reflects Chicago in its demographic changes, interethnic relations, globalization, and neighborhood concerns. Demographic shifts throughout the latter half of the twentieth century brought significant social and economic changes. Immediately following World War II, the West Ridge community was occupied by large Jewish and Irish Catholic populations. During the 1970s and 1980s, the post-World War II generation departed as more racially diverse families arrived. The Asian, Latino, and black population of the district rose to 28 percent in 1990 (doubling the 1980 figure), with Asians constituting 17 percent of the population, one of the highest in the city (Chicago Fact Book Consortium1995, 42–43). In 2000, 44 percent of West Ridge residents were foreign-born, twice the proportion in 1970.

The shift to larger, poorer, and more ethnically diverse families affected local educational and business institutions. Schools became overcrowded and were beset by budgetary shortfalls and challenges posed by non-English speaking children. Clashes between old and new business owners, who were quickly establishing themselves as a permanent presence on Devon Avenue, produced conflict. Crime, safety, and congestion became leading issues, while businesses owners struggled to reinvent their products and services to meet the needs of a shifting clientele.

The growth of Devon Avenue east of California Avenue as a major South Asian shopping center specializing in Indian and Pakistani clothing stores, restaurants, groceries, and electronic goods occurred during the 1980s and 1990s, as a result of new immigration from South Asia. Whereas the first wave of immigrants from India had consisted mainly of professionals admitted under preferential quotas of the 1965 Immigration Reform Act, arrivals in the 1980s and 1990s were mostly nonprofessional relatives sponsored under the family reunification clause of the 1965 immigration law. Lacking the professional skills of the earlier immigrants, this second group saw a commercial opportunity to provide ethnic goods and services for an established, still-growing South Asian population. They carved a niche for themselves on Devon Avenue, a site that was convenient, affordable, and available, thanks to the its Jewish population having moved to the suburbs.

This claiming of territory by a new immigrant group is a typically Chicagoan phenomenon but, unlike other neighborhoods where immigrant groups could claim something approaching exclusive possession, Devon Avenue became shared territory, where diverse ethnic groups, old-timers and newcomers, jostled for space. Without a dominant voting bloc, the area continues to be represented by a non-Asian, Alderman Bernard Stone, who promotes Devon Avenue as an international rather than a South Asian marketplace. The fallout from this international identity is that City Hall has little interest in improving or reshaping the built environment since, unlike Chinatown or Bronzeville, it does not fall neatly into an identifiable ethnic category. The residents of West Ridge are well aware of these anomalies, which make them a part of Chicago but also distinguish their neighborhood from others.

Devon Avenue is also part of a globalized world and, regardless of which of the more commonly understood meanings of the term "globalization" we consider, they are all at play here. The same converging forces that have shaped Chicago over the last five decades have shaped Devon Avenue, fostering harmony along with tension. Common economic interests draw people together, but social, political, and religious institutions encourage narrow ethnic identification and pull people in opposing directions. Despite this, or perhaps because of it, Devon Avenue is a vibrant, functioning neighborhood that could become a model for urban development in a world peopled by diverse immigrants.

FROM JEWISH DISTRICT TO WORLD MARKET

During the 1950 and 1960s, Jews of Russian and Polish descent dominated West Rogers Park, frequenting the 20 synagogues that still dot the area. Elegant clothing stores, discount toy shops, and department stores attracted clients from all over the city. Once the Jews were financially stable, many of them moved out to Skokie, Lincolnwood, and other northern suburbs. The 1970s saw the arrival of Southern and Eastern Europeans as well as Middle Easterners, who continued pouring in throughout the next decade, driven from their homes by international forces such as the Iran–Iraq war, conflict in Afghanistan, and the fall of communism.[3] They were attracted to the neighborhood because of its affordable housing and excellent transportation to the Loop. The growth of the South Asian community in Chicago can be traced to the 1965 Immigration Reform Act (see Chapter 10). People from India were among the first to take advantage of these preferential quotas with their pool of well-qualified, English-speaking professionals. They arrived in Chicago, initially settled along Broadway and Lawrence and, as they became successful, moved to suburbs west and northwest of the city. Subsequent immigrants from India and Pakistan settled in Rogers Park and West Ridge, helping to establish and sustain the businesses on Devon Avenue.

The South Asian presence on Devon Avenue did not become firmly established until the 1980s, when the primary immigrants sponsored their relatives, many of whom lacked professional skills and chose to go into retail marketing. By that time, Koreans and Assyrians had opened restaurants, beauty shops, and fruit and vegetable markets. Coincidentally, many of the Jewish stores were closing down because the owners were ready to retire or resettle in the suburbs. The first Indian store on Devon Avenue was India Sari Palace, which opened its doors in 1973, at 2538 West Devon, backed by a parent company, India Emporium of Hong Kong, which had already opened a shop in New York. The manager of the store, Mr. Ratan Sharma, weathered some hard times. Mr. Sharma recalls acts of vandalism and threats of extortion from Jewish merchants but, thanks to the support of the police and the North Town Chamber of Commerce, he persevered (Rangaswamy 2000). Indians bought up leases on Devon Avenue as quickly as the Jews moved out and rented out to other Indians, who found a favorable climate for their businesses. Devon Avenue was humming with renewed activity. The Indians were followed by Pakistanis and Bangladeshis, and soon the mile-long stretch from Western to California had acquired a distinctly South Asian identity without losing its international flavor (see Map 17.1, color insert). Many of the Jewish, Korean, and Assyrian shops continued to do brisk business, benefiting from the increased traffic brought in by South Asians.

TOGETHER YET SEPARATE

Table 17.1 shows a dramatic rise in the Asian population between 1990 and 2000 in census tracts 205 through 209. Indians are the dominant Asian group, comprising between 32 percent and 44 percent of the Asian population in these tracts, followed by the Pakistanis who average 17 percent, and smaller numbers of Filipinos and Chinese. Many African groups, such as the Nigerians and the Sudanese, who are currently moving into the area, are not shown in these tables, which reflect only white and Asian population ratios. The increase in the Asian population is accompanied by a drop in the white population of nearly 20 percent in each one of these tracts. There are still pockets of Irish residents and a large Jewish community that consists mostly of senior citizens. Many of them are concentrated on the north side of Devon or in high-rise apartment buildings closer to the lake.

Indians and Pakistanis are, according to one resident, "compacted" between Devon and Petersen Avenues. Yet the groups are not segregated in the sense of being strictly isolated. According to Police Commander David Boggs, "If you go up and down the Mozarts and the Warsaws, it may be predominantly Jewish, but that doesn't mean you won't find a Southeast Asian or Pakistani living on that block. If they can afford it, they can live there. The word segregation turns me off. It sounds so fiftyish, so civil rights. Segregation means you can't live in a certain block. That's not true here."

State Senator Ira Silverstein, who grew up in the neighborhood and decided to remain and represent its people, agrees. "If you drive up and down Devon Avenue and see the cultures, you will be amazed. If this was the Middle East, there would be war."

Both the Devon marketplace and the adjoining residential blocks share this characteristic of being "spatially integrated" but "socially segregated" (Pacyga 1995). Devon between Ridge and Western is largely Assyrian, Middle Eastern, and South Asian (mainly Pakistani; see Table 17.1 for Pakistani figures for tracts 205 and 209 for the year 2000). More visible than national identity is religious identity, with many grocery stores advertising *halal* (kosher for Muslims) meat. However, the Indian presence is also overtly apparent in some places in this section, as in the storefront Hindu Temple, Gayatri Mandir-Pragya Yug Literature Center. Between Western and California there is a pronounced Indian flavor with its saree shops, boutiques, restaurants, and jewelry stores. This is also where the Gurudwara Sahib of Chicago, a Sikh house of worship, is located. Farther west, between California and Kedzie (parts of tract 206 and most of 207—see Table 17.1), the area is unmistakably Jewish with the kosher delis, Jewish bakeries, and synagogues teeming with Saturday worshippers. This area is also home to the Croatian Cultural Center, founded by a group of Dominican missionaries in the 1970s. Muslims, Jews, Christians, Sikhs, and Hindus live, worship, and conduct business cheek by jowl on Devon Avenue in apparent harmony.

THE ATTRACTION OF DEVON

Who are the Devon Avenue shoppers and why do they come? For a variety of reasons, it would seem, considering their diverse nationalities, religions, and income levels. New immigrants from Russia and Croatia come to snap up bargains in the cheap dollar stores. Chicagoans from all over the city come for the wide selection of fresh fruits and vegetables found nowhere else locally. Wealthy South Asians come from the across the Midwest and beyond to the specialty stores that sell elaborate wedding outfits and jewelry. Suburbanites come to Devon to shop, eat, gossip, and spend the day strolling down the street that reminds them of home. Pakistani cab drivers who live in the area walk to the stores for their daily grocery needs. Yuppies from downtown queue up along the sidewalks for entrance to popular restaurants like Viceroy of India and Indian Garden, which serve authentic Indian food prepared by chefs imported from India's

TABLE 17.1. Distribution of Select Asian Groups in Chicago Census Tracts 205–209, 1990 and 2000

	1990						2000						Change (%)					
	205	206	207	208	209	Total	205	206	207	208	209	Total	205	206	207	208	209	Total
Total	6,040	9,166	7,931	11,524	9,394	44,010	7,084	10,520	8,824	13,163	10,662	50,253	17.3%	14.8%	11.3%	14.2%	14.0%	14.2%
Non-Hispanic White	3,178	7,296	6,026	8,062	4,949	29,511	1,853	6,216	4,936	5,558	3,244	21,807	−41.7%	−14.8%	−18.1%	−31.1%	−34.5%	−26.1%
Non-Hispanic Black	437	78	28	89	855	1,487	683	a	a	501	1,511	2,695	56.3%	–	–	462.9%	76.7%	81.2%
Hispanic	700	558	485	1,196	1,135	4,074	1,442	1,602	979	2,548	2,230	8,801	106.0%	187.1%	101.9%	113.0%	96.5%	116.0%
Mexican	208	230	167	386	420	1,411	778	699	476	1,437	1,482	4,872	274.0%	203.9%	185.0%	272.3%	252.9%	245.3%
Asians	1,672	1,222	1,398	2,137	2,391	8,820	2,624	1,880	2,172	3,697	2,968	13,359	56.9%	53.8%	55.4%	73.0%	24.9%	51.5%
Filipino	130	272	248	451	262	1,363	a	a	a	682	a	682	–	–	–	51.2%	–	−50.0%
Asian Indian	909	304	455	490	1,137	3,295	1,037	567	511	997	1,124	4,236	14.1%	86.5%	12.3%	103.5%	−1.1%	28.6%
Korean	80	377	363	557	328	1,705	a	a	385	a	a	385	–	–	6.1%	–	–	−77.4%
Pakistani	b	b	b	b	b	b	1,014	a	a	504	836	1,340	–	–	–	–	–	–
Other Asian	251	53	51	169	338	862	573	1,313	1,276	1,514	1,026	5,702	128.3%	2377.4%	2402.0%	795.9%	203.6%	561.5%

Source: Census 1990, STF 1, Census 2000, SF3.

a. In Census 2000, the population threshold on Summary File 4 is 100. In addition, there must be at least 50 or more unweighted cases of the population group.

b. The requested table is not available for the following geographic area(s) because the population Pakistani was not a category in Asian groups in 1990.

regional capitals. Beauty salons that offer services such as bridal makeup and *mehndi* (intricate henna designs popularized in the United States as temporary tattoos) are patronized by trendy teenagers and tradition-bound matrons alike. Fans of Bollywood movie stars and singers come to buy DVDs and tickets for concert performances sponsored by the merchants of Devon, or to sign up for Dish Network service that beams Indian television channels into their homes. The customers, it seems, are even more diverse than the shopkeepers.

The American dream has been played out in the lives of many merchants who started small and made fortunes through enterprise and hard work. Many of the restaurants and grocery stores started out as modest, family-operated enterprises but have expanded to hire newer immigrants (such as the Mexicans) and have opened branches in the suburbs. The big chains are conspicuously infrequent on this street. The presence of a Dunkin' Donuts, Domino's Pizza, and Subway are a reminder that Indians and Pakistanis dominate these franchises in other parts of the city. Sav-a-Lot, an out-of-state chain, recently moved into space vacated by the Salvation Army store. There are some worries that Loyola University, on the east end of Devon, may slowly creep westward and forestall the growth of newer small businesses, but for now, the ethnic, family-owned establishment remains the anchor of this shopping district.

ECONOMIC TRANSFORMATION

Devon Avenue has stayed vibrant and increased its reach partly because it has changed with the times. In the days before the liberalization of the Indian economy during the 1990s, when imported goods were coveted in India, stores on Devon Avenue sold Japanese nylon sarees and electronic appliances that Indians in America bought as gifts for their relatives at home. Now that those items are freely available in India, stores are catering to Indian Americans seeking imported silk sarees or Bollywood videos. As a second generation of South Asian Americans comes of age, Devon Avenue has become famous for wedding shopping—from elaborate bridal outfits to shiny 22-karat jewelry in traditional Indian designs—which South Asians favor over the machine-cut, 18- or 14-karat gold jewelry available in American stores. Restaurants that once served mostly the Mughlai cuisine of Northern India now provide far more varied choices that include vegetarian cuisine from the southern states and even hybrid fare called "Indian Chinese." Nowhere other than Devon Avenue can you find such a wide variety of book and music stores—Russian, Arabic, Urdu, Hindi, Punjabi, Gujarati, Tamil, Malayalam. Another sign of the marketplace's response to the special needs of its immigrant population is the proliferation of social agencies offering services from free medical care to English classes, immigration help to childcare. Each ethnic group caters mainly to its own population but keeps its doors open to all.

The viability of the shopping district has helped maintain and even increase local property values. Even when the job market has been weak, property values have risen. According to Rohit Maniar, manager of National Republic Bank, locals who had moved to the suburbs often retained their properties for rental income, and banks were willing to finance purchases of the many two- and three-flat buildings. Although housing is not so segregated as in other parts of Chicago, residents are aware that properties west of California have higher value than east of California, which has more racially integrated, multifamily housing.

LOCAL *IS* GLOBAL

Businesses on Devon Avenue may be family-owned and "small" according to Chamber of Commerce criteria, but they are also global. The grocers, small and large, rely heavily on imports, the boutiques commission their work in the back alleys of Delhi and Karachi, and the jewelry stores order from India, Belgium, and South Africa. When the information technology sector boomed during the 1990s, and the American government raised the quota for H1-B visa immigrants, Indian merchants on Devon reaped the benefits. New, young arrivals from India meant more families to shop on

Devon. And when the boom turned to bust, a visible decline occurred in business as well.

Foreign policy also touches the lives of people on Devon. When war broke out in Serbia, it led to a huge outpouring of fundraising in the Croatian community. Hostilities in the Middle East are a major concern for Jews, Arabs, and Assyrians, most of whom are from Iraq, Syria, Lebanon, and Iran. Events in the homeland strike a chord in Chicago almost instantaneously. An earthquake in Gujarat in 2001 inspired a team of merchants on Devon to fund the rebuilding of an entire village in Gujarat and name it "Chicago Township." On Devon Avenue, globalization is not debated in grand terms of Western economic and cultural imperialism, or devastated Third World economies. It is played out in the everyday lives of its residents through trade, travel, and migration, in the spread of new cultural influences, the dissemination of news and entertainment from the homeland, and the exchange of goods and services from across the world.

THE CHALLENGE OF
CREATING COMMUNITY

Irv Loundy, vice-president of the Devon Bank and past president of the Devon North Town Business and Professional Association (DNTBPA) asserts that his neighborhood has failed to build a strong Chamber of Commerce. The Indian and Pakistani merchants cannot get along among themselves, let alone bond with other members of the community. He deplores the lack of response to his own efforts at greater cohesion. Some successful campaigns have been launched as a result of interethnic cooperation, such as the erecting of banners along Devon Avenue during Diwali, which is an important Hindu religious festival, heralding the start of the New Year and the triumph of good over evil. Known as the Festival of Lights, Diwali is celebrated with great enthusiasm by Indian Americans. For Devon Avenue's South Asian merchants, who ring up their biggest sales of the year during Diwali, it is the equivalent of Christmas for American retailers.

But the merchants do not come to business meetings and do not have a sense of collec-tive purpose. Membership in the DNTBPA has dropped from 200 to less than 150, even though the group estimates there are 500 businesses on Devon and over 1,100 businesses in the adjoining area. Many Devon merchants prefer not to spend time or money cultivating local walk-in business, which they take for granted. They look to their own ethnic communities, catering to the immigrant network of social, cultural, and religious institutions. For example, a large wedding in Oak Brook or an Indian physician's convention in downtown Chicago might be more important for the Indian restaurateur's catering business than an DNTBPA raffle promotion. Loundy's efforts to get older Jewish residents to shop in the Indian and Pakistani stores have not succeeded either: "They prefer to stay in their own comfort zone."

Another point of contention is neighborhood cleanliness. For many years, concerns about litter have prompted local "Clean and Green" campaigns, but such efforts are sporadic. There is much finger pointing as to who is to blame. The older residents assert that the culture of the new immigrants, who had not observed cleanliness in their own countries, has been brought to Chicago. Complaints are heard about bottles being thrown on the streets, sidewalk waste bins overflowing with garbage from establishments that should contract for scavenger service, and parking lots used as dumping grounds. Politicians point to other neighborhoods where shopkeepers themselves sweep adjacent sidewalks. They bemoan the lack of similar civic sense among the South Asians, though they are careful to blame it on individuals rather than the culture. The shopkeepers blame the city government for not supporting a commercial district that brings in so much revenue. Whether it is a matter of educating the storeowners or getting the City to pitch in, no organized effort is in place to make it happen. The suburban scattering of South Asians has produced satellite shopping centers in Westmont, Naperville, Downers Grove, Skokie, and Schaumburg. Although Devon is still attractive because it provides a certain ambience and a "total experience," as one resident put it, competition from outlying areas is a cause for concern.

ETHNICITY AND
NEIGHBORHOOD PROMOTION

A strong local feeling is prevalent that the city government has not promoted Devon Avenue, even as it has invested heavily in heritage tourism in neighborhoods such as Bronzeville (see Chapter 16) and Chinatown. Both Ann Lata Kalayil, past president of the Indo-American Democratic Organization and Rohit Maniar note that, in countless meetings with city officials, residents and merchants have raised the sanitation issue and proposed solutions. "If you look at Chinatown or Argyle Street, the City has made it very attractive for tourism. We need the same thing—a gateway or an arch by Western and Devon," said Kalayil. Irv Loundy, too, asserts, "It's not a secret that this community hasn't received all that much benefit from the City." Alderman Bernard Stone acknowledges that he may be to blame, that he may not have done enough to push the City on this score. A perception exists, borne out by newspaper articles and surveys, that this area is not in danger of decline, that it is affluent and has no need of additional funds.

One of most vexing problems on Devon Avenue is parking. The lack of room for expansion, the weekend congestion produced by out-of-town visitors, and the presence of the large number of South Asian cab drivers who live in the neighborhood but cannot legally park their cabs overnight on the streets, have all compounded to make this an intractable dilemma. Amendments to parking regulations have been made to permit overnight taxicab parking on certain streets, but parking for shoppers on Devon Avenue remains a problem due to lack of consensus. A project to build a privately funded, multiuse facility on Devon and Rockwell that includes some 220 parking spaces may alleviate the situation in the future, but residents and merchants alike feel let down by the City's lack of attention to this matter.

SAFETY CONCERNS

Compared to other parts of the city, Devon Avenue is considered a low crime area. There are local Assyrian, Pakistani, and Punjabi gangs, but like other local inter-ethnic tensions, their activities have been sufficiently subdued not to attract widespread attention. After September 11, 2001, people worried about backlash in a neighborhood with five mosques and a gurudwara for Sikhs. (Sikhs, because of their turbans and long beard, have been confused with Afghans and targeted as terrorists in other parts of the United States.) In fact, a decrease in hate crimes was noted. The most notorious hate crime in the area was committed well before 9/11, in July 1999, by a white supremacist, Benjamin Nathaniel Smith, who went on a murderous shooting spree that left two men dead and six wounded. The attacks started in West Rogers Park, home to Chicago's heaviest concentration of orthodox Jews, continued north to Skokie, and ended in downstate Illinois, where Smith killed himself. This crime reinforced the feeling among residents that, even if they conducted themselves peacefully and showed respect for each other, their neighborhood's all-too-visible ethnic and racial makeup was a source of vulnerability.

Involving the community in preventing crime has been an important strategy for the Rogers Park police district, which was chosen as a pilot site for the City of Chicago Community Policing program (CAPS) in 1993. Commander Boggs takes a proactive approach to community participation, drawing on community representatives to conduct cultural orientation sessions for his staff. He is very sensitive to the mix of cultures under his watch and is helped by Tomi Methipara, a local police officer of Indian descent, the first Indian in the Chicago police force. Among the different South Asian groups, Pakistanis seem to have a disproportionately large number of arrests as illustrated in Table 17.2. The most common crimes are batteries (mostly domestic assaults), shoplifting (often involving women), burglaries, robberies, and other violent crimes. In 2000, about 30 arrests or nearly 15 percent of the total arrests among Indians were for sex-related crimes like sexual abuse, and soliciting and patronizing a prostitute. Younger men were involved in drug-related crimes. Many of those arrested were repeat offenders with long criminal histories.

TABLE 17.2. South Asian Arrest Counts: 1999–2002

Number of arrests	Indians	Pakistanis	Bangladeshis
1999	170	145	—
2000	200	200	2
2001	335	240	12
2002 (Jan. to Oct. 10)	280	178	9

Source: Data provided by Tomi Methipara, Chicago Police Department.
Note: Methipara notes that these statistics do not tell the whole story because accurate statistics for South Asians are difficult to come by for several reasons. They may include only those whose place of birth is South Asia, and exclude the second generation, born in the United States. Ancestry can only be ascertained if the arrested person identifies himself accurately. Many South Asians call themselves "white" or "other" in the intake forms maintained by the police department.

SERVING THE OLD AND THE NEW

Alderman Stone claims that his ward has one of the highest percentages of seniors in the city. The same young parents who pushed their buggies down Devon Avenue during the 1950s have stayed on in the neighborhood, even though their children have left. New immigrants may come and go but, for many seniors, this is the best and last place to be. They stay because this is where they can get the "most bang for the buck" according to Irv Loundy. They enjoy affordable shopping, subsidized housing, social services such as Medicaid, and free meals for seniors.

The area's social-service agencies also offer much needed service for new immigrants. Many of the newcomers, especially women who work in the back kitchens of the restaurants or serve behind the counters in retail establishments, are not even literate in their native tongues. They can attend English classes, get immigration help, and improve their life skills. There is no way of assessing how many of the immigrants in this area are undocumented, but people freely admit that they do indeed exist. It is reported that many of them live in overcrowded conditions in apartment buildings where absentee landlords provide little or no maintenance.

Schools have also come under increasing pressure to adapt to new conditions. Mather High School, who's Class of 1963 was 95 percent Jewish according to alumnus Richard Reeder, now has many Asian children who need English-as-second-language (ESL) classes and whose presence has created a demand for Urdu- and Gujarati-speaking teachers. Overcrowding in the schools is another major concern voiced at PTA meetings. Asian Human Services recently opened a charter school targeting immigrant children.

Immigrants who are eligible for citizenship are targeted by organizations such as the Indo-American Democratic Organization. The 50th ward is heavily Democratic, but the alderman recalled that it was not until 1952, when he became an assistant precinct captain, that it swung to the Democrats as the Irish Catholics gave way to Jews. Recently arrived Russian Jews tend to vote Republican out of loyalty to Ronald Reagan, who they view as their rescuer from the Soviet Union. But the South Asians are solidly Democratic. There are Indian, Pakistani, and African-American precinct captains in the 50th ward, though they do not necessarily work within their own ethnic groups. Still, ethnic voting persists. The closest South Asians come to a concentration anywhere in the city is in this area and, after the 2000 census, serious efforts were made to place them in a single voting district. It is one of the ironies of the American democratic system that, while it idealizes the concept of integration and mutual cooperation, it encourages ethnic division through its political structures.

DIVISIONS ON DEVON

As in other parts of Chicago, and indeed the nation as a whole, local cleavages cut across class, religion, and nationality. The Jews are hardly a monolithic group. Russian-speaking Jews stay aloof from Polish Jews, and the orthodox Jews do not even speak to the reform Jews.

According to Alderman Stone, the Pakistanis are very fractured, with each group wanting its own Independence Day parade, the biggest divide occurring between the established businessmen and the newcomer cab drivers. The leaders of the Pakistani community are from the mosque south of Devon and do not necessarily live in the neighborhood. Mosques unite Muslims of all nationalities on Devon, but Indian Muslims remain socially separated from Indian Hindus. Indians are further divided along regional and linguistic lines. Most of the Indian shops are Gujarati-owned but there are also Punjabi, Sikh, and South Indian storeowners who are more connected to their own language-based groups in other parts of the city than to each other. Running across the entire international marketplace is the language barrier, because so many of the immigrants do not speak English or otherwise share a common language.

While undercurrents among some ethnic groups are acknowledged, especially between Indians and Pakistanis, general agreement is that things don't reach the surface because merchants cannot afford that kind of instability. Common economic interests seem sufficient to prevent tensions from getting out of hand. Harmony is maintained, not through some automatically generated good will, as some residents claim, but through conscious effort on the part of community leaders. According to Alderman Bernard Stone:

> At the time the Muslim shrine was destroyed in India [referring to the Babri Masjid incident in 1992, when Hindus tore down a mosque in the holy Hindu city of Ayodhya], there were fights all over the world and a potential clash here. We had a meeting at the Indo-American Center with Hindus, Muslims, and Sikhs. Everyone was appalled by the violence so they decided to protest the act of violence and do it together and unify, do it publicly to show they were against violence. Young Pakistani kids came in to make trouble at this time but they were told there wouldn't be any disturbances, so they left. Another time, after the Pakistani Independence Day parade, when Pakistan had just gone nuclear, some kids tried to incite Indian merchants by driving up and down the street with cardboard nuclear bombs on the top of their cars. We called the Pakistani elders and appealed to them, and they cut off the trouble where it started.

Similarly, the Croatians who live in the area may not fraternize with Bosnians, most of whom reside outside the area, but they are not averse to frequenting the local Bosnian café or shopping in Bosnian stores, according to John Vopic of the Croatian Cultural Center. Richard Reeder, president of DNTBPA, recalled an earlier time when Bosnians and Serbs experienced common economic and labor struggles in the steel mills and stockyards of Chicago. Currently, no open animosity exists between these groups, but not much togetherness either.

Some local leaders, such as Irv Loundy, would like to see old and new immigrants integrate into one cohesive community and speak with one voice. From this perspective, lack of inter-ethnic cooperation remains a big hurdle. But from the point of view of the new immigrants, who come from tremendously diverse backgrounds, getting along among themselves without erupting into violence is in itself a demanding exercise. They are proud to cling to their culture and happy to allow others to do the same. They have no grander objective than living in peace and working hard for the financial success of their families. As for local political and civic leaders, whose daunting task it is to bring these disparate groups together, they have worked intimately with their constituents in seeking conflict resolution. This has taught them to have realistic expectations, to be satisfied with modest gains, and let their constituents set their own agendas.

AN UNCERTAIN FUTURE

The people of Devon Avenue are acutely aware of the forces that have transformed their neighborhood. Those who resisted change or viewed newcomers as an intrusion have fled. Among the merchants who decided to stay, only those prospered who could do business irrespective of the ethnicity of their customers. Then came the specialty, niche stores for new immigrants, and they built up a varied market that supported the neighborhood ethnics and also drew out-of-towners.

Currently, no vacant stores are found on Devon, but that was not always so. Muhammed Akbar recalled a time when Z Frank, the

Chevrolet dealer, was planning to leave the neighborhood and was persuaded to stay, thanks in part to the efforts of the Indo-Pak community. Observed Mr. Sadruddin Noorani, vice-president of DNTBPA: "Change is positive for newcomers, but not for those who were here before. The English didn't welcome the Jews, the Jews didn't welcome the Indians, and when the Indians move out, it will be because they no longer like it here." Nobody can foresee that day yet, but fears persist that some changes may be beyond the community's control. The possibilities are numerous: new restrictions on Asian immigrants; chain stores pushing out local entrepreneurs; city-mandated redevelopment. But none has happened so far, and Devon Avenue still sits apart from other neighborhoods, shining like a jewel at the crown of Chicago's north end. Irv Loundy was speaking for others, too, when he said: "I hope this street continues to be attractive. The beauty of this street is that you're not necessarily saying it belongs to one ethnic group, but you're inviting groups of all backgrounds under one banner. It's unique. I don't think you'll find another street in the city of Chicago like it."

Overall, Devon Avenue does work. Even if the groups come together only to preempt trouble and live in their own worlds most of the time, there is a supportive enough environment for business and to sustain local peace. Devon Avenue, more than just a commercial street, is symbolic ground on which different groups re-enact their nationalism through events such as Independence Day parades. When the groups who live along Devon Avenue find their countries of origin at war, the potential for a local eruption of violence is enormous. But with so many nationalities whose needs must be balanced and respected, there is no opportunity for any one group to dominate. Things tend to work by consensus rather than majority opinion. The lack of a formal structure to bring together disparate groups may have stymied rapid economic advancement, but the very stumbling blocks to organization may sustain a more informal sort of development that protects the rights of minorities. That, ultimately, is what democracy and pluralism are all about, and Devon Avenue continues to provide a remarkable illustration of these major forces at work in an urban environment.

NOTES

1. The 50th ward is bounded by Ridge in the east, Kedzie in the west, Howard in the north, and Peterson in the south. This chapter focuses on the multicultural corridor of Devon Avenue from Ridge to Kedzie and the residential areas a few blocks north and south of Devon, composed of Census Tracts 205 through 209.

2. From a survey done by the Rogers Park Police Department (24th District), according to police chief, Commander David Boggs. This, and much other information in this chapter, is gleaned from individual interviews and a round-table discussion with community members, including merchants, residents, law enforcement officers, and local and state representatives held on October 10, 2002 at the Indo-American Center, 6328 North California Avenue, half a block south of Devon Avenue. Though these sources are far from comprehensive and do not cover the entire spectrum of the "Devon Avenue population," they do represent an interesting cross-section and reflect, in one way or another, the experiences of other ethnic groups and individuals in the area.

3. Unlike Arabs, Assyrians do not have their own census category. They have a long history in the Devon area, going back to the early 1900s. Like Arabs, they are from the Middle East but, as Christians, they prefer to identify themselves as "white" in the census form. Thus, it is impossible to ascertain the exact number of Assyrians. The Assyrian National Council on Petersen Avenue puts the number of Assyrians living in Chicago at 100,000.

Aurie A. Pennick and Howard Stanback

18 The Affordable Housing Crisis in the Chicago Region

PRIOR TO THE decline of manufacturing in South Side Chicago during the 1970s, relatively open, though unequal access was available to moderate-income employment, despite the intense local segregation of African Americans. As limited as their housing choices were, access to stable and living wages were within reach of most South Siders. However, preceding the decline of the local manufacturing economy and the subsequent contraction of African American household income, white flight from the city of Chicago to the suburbs had begun. A principal source of this massive relocation was white fear of the city's burgeoning African American population, which had been drawn from the South to employment in manufacturing, meat packing, distribution, and transportation, constituting what has been called the "Great Migration" of the early to mid twentieth century. Among its vignettes of post-World War II racial anxiety in the Chicago region, the 2002 Chicago Video Project documentary, "The Shame of Chicago: How Postwar Segregation Took Place" reports on the overt racial motivations of former Chicago residents in north suburban Northbrook, who, in 1955, blocked the construction of market-rate, physically isolated "colored" housing within their community.

The migration of businesses to the suburbs followed the initial wave of residential flight. These firms may have been driven, in part, by savings on real estate costs, but the effect of these presumably bottom line–driven locational decisions was to place thousands of jobs out of the physical reach of incumbent and prospective minority employees. Not only was suburban

affordable housing in short supply, but overtly discriminatory real estate practices and blatant hostility from white residents prevented even higher-income minority employees from relocating to homes near their relocated places of work.

Race relations in the South were built on generations of paternalistic theories of black inferiority that allowed relatively close physical proximity and social interaction between the races. Racial interaction in the North was built on a foundation of black–European immigrant competition for jobs, access to unions, and the quest for decent pay. As migration to northern cities proceeded, specific racial and ethnic populations headed to or were steered to their assigned sections of town, only to emerge with the factory whistle. The closing whistle ended interaction unless residential racial barriers were violated. The anti-black riots in Chicago neighborhoods in 1919, and from 1946 to 1951, were associated with black encroachment on white turf (Spear 1967; Hirsch 1983). The five-day-long riot of 1919 occurred during the first wave of the Great Migration, a period of black movement into formerly all-white workplaces such as the stockyards. The riots of the 1940s coincided with boom periods in the steel, automobile, and transportation industries.

African American population growth on the South and West Sides of Chicago and subsequent white "fight," then "flight," began well before mandated school busing. Efforts at school desegregation, however, may have been the final blow, as middle-income neighborhoods such as South Shore and parts of Beverly and Austin experienced an almost 100 percent racial turnover between 1950 and 1970 (Peterson 1976). Some commentators have argued that mandated school desegregation via busing initiated a major wave of white flight from northern cities, while also producing intense neighborhood-level conflicts that pitted African Americans against poor and working-class whites (Formisano 1991). According to this perspective, whites who could afford to leave indeed did depart urban school districts. In the Chicago area, as African American middle-class families moved to the southern suburbs in the 1970s and 1980s, many white residents simply moved farther south. The continuing isolation of African Americans in the city and south suburbs has increasingly distanced them from areas of economic growth, both in terms of job opportunities and wealth gain from property ownership (Lewis et al. 2002).

Sociologists Douglas Massey and Nancy Denton (1993) have argued that housing segregation is the primary determinant of racial inequality in American life. Massey and Denton's research demonstrates that one of the typically unacknowledged features of America's lingering racial divide is a high degree of residential separation or segregation that, at the collective level, results in many African Americans having to settle for less desirable housing. African American communities rarely are able to make and realize claims on public or private investments sufficient to sustain equal economic opportunity. And, when they do succeed in such claims, the investments are rarely sustained long enough to realize long-term effect. Political and market forces ultimately either shift investments to areas of perceived higher return, or new investments in predominantly African American areas produce a "within-race" gentrification that prices out economically marginal residents and businesses. Without the adoption of policies that restrict residential (and business) flight and promote equal access to jobs and housing, a racially fair distribution of the tools of economic opportunity—education, jobs, and capital—cannot be accomplished. Policies that promote and enforce equal choice must be accompanied by affirmative outreach, education, and recruitment. Generations of discrimina-

tion, hostility, and violence have ingrained fears that tend to restrict the choices exercised by racial minorities, even at the cost of a less than equal standard of economic life and even when the choice is available.

A local newspaper recently featured a cartoon depicting two well-dressed, middle-aged white men apparently engaged in an informal discussion, the caption reading, "Sure, we need affordable housing just so long as it doesn't come at the expense of unaffordable housing." Unfortunately, this not-so-funny sentiment is one that appears to be shared by many. The subject of affordable housing is a highly sensitive and often volatile issue for communities across the Chicago region.

THE STRUCTURE OF THE AFFORDABLE HOUSING CRISIS IN CHICAGO

During the last decade, Chicago has experienced a substantial loss of housing that is affordable to poor and working-class families. Both real estate trends and public policy have led to the destruction of affordable rental units and the conversion of rental units to more expensive for-sale housing. New residential construction is overwhelmingly for ownership. The booming national and regional economies of the 1990s, in combination with very low interest rates, helped generate an exceptional demand for market-rate, for-sale properties. The strong demand for ownership units and the declining supply of rental units in the Chicago region contributed to a cumulative growth in rents that exceeded the overall rate of inflation by an average of 1.2 percentage points annually. In 1999, a local civic organization, the Metropolitan Planning Council, released "For Rent: Housing Options in the Chicago Region: Regional Rental Market Analysis Summary Report" (RRMA). In addition to tracking rent inflation, this report also found that the proportion of renters in the region paying greater than 30 percent of their income on rent increased from 35.2 percent to 37.5 percent between 1991 and 1995, with the entirety of this increase represented by suburban households. Moreover, almost 13 percent of the metropolitan area's renting households paid in excess of

50 percent of their income for housing ("For Rent" 1999, 10).

The RRMA's findings contributed to the larger debate over the future of public housing in the Chicago area. A central purpose of the RRMA—which was produced due to agitation by affordable-housing advocates—was to determine whether the regional housing market could comfortably absorb the relocation of several thousand Chicago Housing Authority (CHA) households into private dwellings, as countenanced by the housing agency's emerging plans to modernize and downsize its operations (Chicago Housing Authority 2000; also see Chapter 22 for a discussion of the CHA Plan for Transformation). In the absence of a region-wide strategy for relocating former public housing residents, all available signs indicate that most of those leaving CHA dwellings will search for housing in traditionally poor, largely African American neighborhoods. A recent report by Lake Forest College economist Paul Fischer (2004) reviews the relocation experience of 3,272 Housing Choice Voucher (HCV, formerly Section 8)-bearing families who moved from CHA developments between 1995 and 2002. More than 98 percent remained in Chicago and, in addition, 85 percent settled in census tracks whose racial composition was more than 80 percent African American. The resettlement pattern revealed in Fischer's report has been construed by some as just another iteration of a longstanding racist proposition: that affordable housing is, by and large, African American housing. Furthermore, Fischer's findings reveal the essential flaw in using housing subsidies as the principal means to access the private real estate market.

However, before turning to an examination of the particulars of the local government action and real estate practices as ingredients in the skewing of this region's affordable-housing market, we will identify some additional, key features of the current situation. The RRMA revealed that 75 percent of Cook County's Section 8 households lived in just 34 neighborhoods and towns ("For Rent" 1999, 45). The report also noted that, in 1999, the only income category for which there was an absolute shortfall of available, affordable units was for households earning less than 30 percent of the area median family income (AMI). The estimated supply of units for families at less than 30 percent of AMI was 125,800 units (which excludes public housing). The estimated demand was 308,200 households, which included CHA households expected to enter the private market ("For Rent" 1999, 30–31).

In reference to the miniscule fraction of CHA relocatees who have moved to predominantly white census tracts, critics of the CHA's Plan for Transformation have argued that this is caused, in large part, by the public housing agency's failure to implement a workable mobility counseling program, which would equip former CHA residents to navigate more successfully in the private real estate market (Independent Monitor's Report 2003). An equally significant determinant of CHA relocatees' choice of new neighborhoods is the longstanding pattern of race- and income-defined boundaries drawn around many of Chicago's suburban communities. HCVs are supposed to "incentivize" private landlords to accept vouchers by permitting them to collect 125 percent of the federal government-defined Fair Market Rent for their properties. Apparently, this economic incentive is not enough to allow HCV holders, especially CHA relocatees, to proceed very far afield. CHA residents have been demonized to the point that a series of distinct terms—"affordability," "low-income household," "African American," and "public housing"—have, in the minds of countless white Chicagoans, become identified with the prospect of crime surges and declining property values. The need to directly confront these widely held associations is critical to defining a successful plan for the provision of affordable housing across the region.

THE TOOLS OF SEGREGATION

Northbrook residents' efforts in 1955 to block the construction of housing marketed to African Americans typifies the exclusionary practices of both real estate interests and suburban communities. Within the city of Chicago, the most important institutional force driving the perceived association of affordable housing with minority housing was the CHA's post-World War II concentration of new developments in the black neighborhoods of Chicago's South and West Sides (Hirsch 1983). Although the original aim of public housing may have been to provide temporary and transitional housing, the stagnation of the South Side manufacturing economy during the 1970s and 1980s shut the door to economic mobility within predominately African American areas.

The combination of increasing unemployment and persistent poverty on the South and West Sides led to the mass exodus of African Americans seeking market-rate housing to Chicago's southern suburbs, the metropolitan area's subregion in which black–white residential proximity has been most prevalent. This pattern was driven by the following: (1) Unlike the western and northern suburbs, there was already a working-class African American population base in south suburban towns such as Dixmoor, Harvey, and Robbins. (2) Market-rate housing in the southern suburbs is older and typically more affordable to households with moderate incomes. Public employees, health care providers, and transportation industry employees could afford to buy into these communities, especially if they were purchasing previously built properties. (3) Exclusionary land-use policies were less prevalent in jurisdictions already developed for a moderate-income market. (4) A substantial share of the early, successful fair housing litigation took place in the south and southwestern suburbs. This pattern was also caused by the greater number of racial minority families seeking housing in these communities. (5) Finally, decades of hostile legal and even violent resistance to desegregation at the neighborhood level makes even the most ambitious African American or Latino reluctant to "be the first." But, where success is gained, there is encouragement to follow. Again, for many African Americans, the southern suburbs were the most promising beachhead for joining the ranks of homeowners.

However, metropolitan-level racial and income segregation are matters of exclusion as well as attraction, and a variety of exclusionary tools were perfected by real estate interests and many suburban communities during the post-

World War II era. The most pervasively deployed of these tools have been local zoning controls, which have the effect of pricing out low- income and working-class residents. Zoning ordinances can prohibit multifamily buildings, limit the number of residential units per acre, and otherwise push up housing prices. Building codes and municipalities' selective enforcement of these codes can also work to prohibit or eliminate local affordable housing (Rubinowitz and Young 1983).

The net effect of these policies is to block affordable housing development in the very areas of Chicago's suburbs in which property appreciation or proximity to employment offer a path to affluence. In the last 20 years, legal advocates for affordable housing have analyzed such practices in order to challenge them through litigation. Here we identify some key features pertinent to these efforts, in reference to three suburban municipalities: Lake Forest and Libertyville in north suburban Lake County, and Downers Grove in west suburban DuPage County. The 2000 U.S. Census reports that racial minorities make up less than 10 percent of the population in each municipality; 80 percent or more of the housing units are single-family dwellings; and median household income exceeded the metropolitan figure by 164 percent in Lake Forest, 72 percent in Libertyville, and 27 percent in Downers Grove. Each municipality has approved zoning and design standards that drive residential construction costs and sale prices well beyond the reach of most moderate-income households by (1) designating more than 80 percent of residentially zoned land for single-family home development, (2) restricting single-family development to lots of at least one acre, and (3) requiring design finishes and infrastructure payments that further increase costs. Each of these municipalities has also failed, within recent memory, to approve any multiunit residential development that would provide shelter for low-income families.

Although the research on these communities has found reasonable cause for legal action based on the provisions of the Fourteenth Amendment of the U.S. Constitution and the Fair Housing Act of 1968 (Title VIII), the problem of "standing" has inhibited litigation. The

U.S. Supreme Court has denied standing to nonresident home-seekers when no specific proposed development exists in which they could find residence. This position essentially limits standing to a party that would propose such a development and be denied approval by the municipality. The potentially injured party would have to be a developer who was willing to endure the financial burden of extended court proceedings to reach victory. Municipal practices such as these are not race specific in segregating populations and, as such, injure whites as well as African Americans. Ironically, many of the municipal employees in these jurisdictions cannot live within them. Retail businesses targeting higher-income households encounter excessive labor costs due to long commute-generated employee turnover and overly frequent training expenditures. Nevertheless, as we prepare this chapter, these individual and family inequities and employer-borne economic costs rest on a firm foundation of home rule-grounded land-use controls.

FUNDING PUBLIC SCHOOLS

The public education funding system in Illinois is one of the primary contributors to the affordable housing woes of the Chicago region. The property tax is the primary source of revenue for local public schools. Under Illinois' tax structure, multiunit rental housing and modest single-family dwellings do not generate revenues sufficient to "pay their way" in respect to local school costs. Even the most socially conscious developer will be unable to overcome the barriers created by suburban municipalities craving upscale "McMansions" whose property tax contributions, in fact, tend to enhance local school district finances. From the standpoint of many suburban communities, their enactment of restrictive zoning laws is a means to protect one of their most prized local amenities: good-quality public schools.

The political salience of the local school finance system was amply demonstrated by the 1994 Illinois gubernatorial election and its aftermath. In that campaign, the Democratic Party's nominee, Dawn Clark Netsch, a long-standing proponent of fair and affordable housing, advanced a proposal to restructure local school funding by increasing the level of state government aid while reducing reliance on the property tax. Netsch and her school funding initiative were hammered by her opponent, the incumbent Republican governor, Jim Edgar. Ironically, the victorious Edgar subsequently submitted a school finance package to the Illinois General Assembly that, in effect, borrowed significant elements of the Netsch proposal. Bowing to fear of an anticipated backlash by their local constituents, state legislators rejected the Edgar version of Netsch's proposal.

VOUCHER DISCRIMINATION: A HOUSING VOUCHER IS NOT A HOME

Crucial to the CHA Plan for Transformation's success is the use of housing vouchers as a permanent, or in some cases, transitional substitute for "hard" public housing units. But vouchers, in fact, do not guarantee access to housing. Source of income, which includes the use of HCVs, is not covered by the federal fair housing statute. However, the City of Chicago Human Rights Ordinance does prohibit landlords from rejecting prospective renters solely on the basis of their carrying a housing voucher. Although the city's ordinance, thus far, has been largely ineffective in derailing such discrimination, it does provide a venue for legal redress (Lawyers Committee 2002). Unfortunately, in the remainder of the metropolitan region, no such venue exists. Moreover, recent attempts to amend the Illinois Housing Rights Act to include source of income, specifically HCV protection, have failed.

The Chicago Area Fair Housing Alliance (CAFHA) recently released new research documenting the problem of HCV use and residential segregation. Mapping the distribution by race of the 59,106 vouchers in the Chicago area (as of June 30, 2003), the report also describes racial and ethnic composition, poverty, and the distribution of affordable housing in the region. Sixty-four percent of all voucher-holders live in areas defined as offering low economic opportunity. Paralleling Paul Fischer's findings, this report also finds that most African American and Latino HCV-bearers live in heavily minority communities (Chicago Area Fair Housing Alliance 2004). It is thus a cruel irony that, just as the Chicago region's real estate sector has geared up to meet the housing demands of the relocating well-to-do, the numbers of low-income and working-class families of color entering the housing market with HCVs has reached an unprecedented volume. Although the well-to-do and down-and-out do not compete for the same units of upscale housing, the pressure to produce upscale housing—especially in formerly undesirable areas such the city's Near South and West Sides, Pilsen, and the Cabrini-Green enclave on the Near North Side—has produced hundreds of apartment-to-condominium conversions and upward property tax pressure. This typically unseen, indirect competition for housing, which pits the rich against the poor, creates a breeding ground for housing discrimination. With so many people competing for a diminishing stock of affordable rental units, the exercise of picking and choosing "the best tenant" routinely translates into widespread discrimination.

TRENDS IN REGIONAL AFFORDABLE HOUSING REFORM

Suburban dependence on exclusionary zoning as a fiscal tool, when considered against the backdrop of seemingly unending regional sprawl, does not simply block racial minority access to areas of economic opportunity. The widespread use of these techniques also produces significant market inefficiencies. For employers, employee absenteeism, workplace distraction, and exhaustion are drags on productivity. For even the most reliable workers, direct transportation costs and the indirect opportunity costs reflected in daily commuting times, which may total three hours each workday, reduce both income and family and leisure time. Moreover, as employers skip outward from community to community, inter-municipal tax base inequality and central-city and inner-ring suburb disinvestment are magnified.

During the region's recent economic boom, Chicago became one of the nation's hottest housing markets ("For Rent" 1999, 9). Coin-

ciding with this economic expansion, several of Chicago's largest private employers relocated their corporate headquarters and other facilities to the suburban counties where, to their surprise, they found little affordable housing. By the mid 1990s, the business sector began to experience the long-predicted negative consequences of the region's jobs–affordable housing mismatch (Leadership Council 1991). In response to this realization, the Civic Committee of the Commercial Club of Chicago, the region's top business and civic entity, embarked on a study identifying major issues affecting the region's economic future. In 1998, the Commercial Club released the thought-provoking product of this exercise, entitled, "Chicago Metropolis 2020: Preparing Metropolitan Chicago for the 21st Century" (Johnson 1998; also see Chapter 23), which provided substantial documentation of the negative economic impact caused by housing segregation and the lack of adequate affordable housing across the region. Following the release of this report, an elite regional planning group that included top business and civic leaders and a number of suburban officials—Chicago Metropolis 2020—was formed. Chicago Metropolis 2020 has joined with affordable housing advocates to advocate opening the entire region to quality affordable housing construction. Nonetheless, few among Chicago's civic leadership have yet to speak out on racial discrimination as a source of the metropolitan affordable housing gap.

Within months of the 2002 Illinois general election, Rod Blagojevich, the first Democrat to be elected state chief executive since the 1970s, appointed a housing task force charged to develop an affordable housing plan for the Chicago region emphasizing the housing needs of families earning less than 50 percent of area median income. In late 2004, the task force completed a draft report calling for a wide range of policies to promote the equitable expansion of and fair access to affordable housing. Among Illinois state legislators, a bipartisan bloc has begun to advocate affordable housing initiatives (*Chicago Tribune* 28 May 2003). Two major proposals became law in 2004. The Affordable Housing Planning and Appeals Act requires all counties and municipalities with insufficient affordable housing, as defined by the statute, to adopt an affordable housing plan. This act also states that developers whose applications for affordable housing projects are denied (or approved, but subject to unfeasible conditions) by those local governments with insufficient numbers of affordable housing units may appeal to a State Housing Appeals Board. The Housing Opportunity Tax Incentive Act provides a tax subsidy to landlords in areas of high job growth who offer apartments to HCV families. Although other desirable bills were not approved during the 2004 session, for the first time in many years, the Illinois General Assembly gave serious attention to affordable housing.

MORE THAN A SUBURBAN ISSUE: NO COMPROMISE ON RACE

Although progress has been slow, and resistance at the metropolitan level both to fair housing principles and the actual development of affordable housing persists, a variety of local initiatives have pointed the way to a more progressive future. Since the early 1970s, Oak Park, Illinois—just west of Chicago—has implemented a series of programs aiming to maintain racial balance. The principal agent of the Oak Park initiatives is the Oak Park Regional Housing Center, a publicly funded organization that promotes the concept of fair housing, publicizes the municipality as a desirable residential community, collaborates with other suburban communities in the effort to promote racial balance, and serves as a "clearinghouse" for landlords and apartment-seekers (Goodwin 1979; McKenzie 2001). A second, landmark program that our organization, the Leadership Council for Metropolitan Open Communities, ran from the mid 1970s until 1998 was the Gautreaux Assisted Housing Program, an outgrowth of the famous *Gautreaux* public-housing segregation case (Rubinowitz and Rosenbaum 2001). During the 22 years of the Gautreaux housing program's implementation, more than 7,000 public housing-eligible families, using Section 8 vouchers, found dwellings in outlying Chicago neighborhoods and suburban communities. It is our

view that the vast majority of families who participated in this "guided" program of housing search assistance and follow-up have found satisfactory shelter. Finally, it is very encouraging to note that Chicago Metropolis 2020 has recruited more than 100 signatories (including BP Amoco, the McDonald's Corporation, and UAL Corporation) for its "Metropolis Principles for Livable Communities." In reference to business location decisions, signatories to the Metropolis Principles endorse the following: "we will give substantial weight to... whether a community has zoning, building, and land-use policies that allow the construction of housing which is affordable to working people..." (*Chicago Metropolis 2020* 2004).

Beyond these important foundational actions, much work lies ahead if we wish to achieve regional equity in racial minority access to good-quality housing and a geographically balanced supply of affordable housing. At present, city of Chicago conditions continue to be the main focus of attention for fair and affordable housing advocates. A growing contingent of Chicago City Council members is pressing the administration of Richard M. Daley to adopt an aggressive affordable housing set-aside mandate (25 percent of new units) for residential developments (Hanney 2003). Although neighborhood-level housing pressure produced by the implementation of the CHA's Plan for Transformation is one source of aldermanic concern over affordable housing, it is in fact the case that the CHA's plans for new, mixed-income residential developments to replace its most deteriorated complexes offers some intriguing opportunities. Many of the mixed-income sites are in increasingly desirable locations, offering access to mass transportation lines and nearby employment opportunities. Given these site attributes, the prospect exists for building multiracial new communities on the foundations of what has been Chicago's housing of last resort. However, without the conscious commitment by governmental leaders and private developers to build and sustain racial and economic diversity in these communities, they will either gentrify out all but the mandated affordable housing, or the market-rate housing demand will evaporate and these communities will revert to ghetto status. Neither of these scenarios is acceptable.

In the coming years—and beyond Chicago's city limits—corporate, civic, and governmental leaders must recognize that a mixture of regional commitments, such as those embodied in the Metropolis Principles, combined with community-by-community advocacy and policy innovation, are the necessary steps in the formation of a metropolitan-spanning, opportunity-based affordable and fair housing campaign. Moreover, we know at present what the content of such initiatives must be: the development of mixed-income, mixed-race residential communities. And we also know such a campaign must overcome, by legal means if necessary, the inclination of many desirable suburban communities to "duck" when the terms "affordable housing" and "fair housing" are uttered. As documented in the CAFHA report, affordable does not mean fair. Despite longstanding fears and a thicket of established, exclusionary policies, currently a unique opportunity exists in the Chicago region to correct the economic inefficiencies and moral deficiencies represented by racial and income segregation. To successfully seize this opportunity, a clear and affirmative call for equity in housing choice must come from all quarters. Failure to do this will only perpetuate segregation in the Chicago region, which in turn will diminish our reputation nationally and abroad while undermining our on-the-ground economic competitiveness.

David Moberg

19   Back to Its Roots: The Industrial Areas Foundation and United Power for Action and Justice

MODERN AMERICAN community organizing traces its roots back to the work during the 1930s of Saul Alinsky, a tough-guy intellectual with an independent leftist outlook, who organized an impoverished eastern European neighborhood near Chicago's famed stockyards. Alinsky saw his Back of the Yards Organization, as well as later groups, such as The Woodlawn Organization (TWO, in an African American, South Side Chicago neighborhood), as the community counterparts of the industrial unions that were organizing at the time (Horwitt 1989). These "peoples' organizations" were intended to mobilize communities to fight for their self-interest outside the normal boundaries of politics and to challenge established political and business powers.

Alinsky's organizing work—but most of all his writing and brilliant knack for public political theater—spawned a wide variety of organizing efforts across the country, but nowhere more so than in Chicago. Although Alinsky's own Industrial Areas Foundation (IAF) continued to organize throughout the country, many other related styles of organizing splintered off and evolved independently, often with different networks of organizers and organizations in competition with each other despite their common goals. Indeed, even the IAF changed significantly after Alinsky's death in 1972, mainly under the influence of its long-time director and Alinsky protégé, Ed Chambers.

Whatever their evolution, most community organizing strategists remain convinced that a need exists to organize citizens based on geographical community as much as on specific policy or ideological interests (as is the base for the Sierra Club) or on electoral action. While some community groups are conservative (and indeed Alinsky's Back of the Yards Organization for many years mainly fought to keep blacks out of the neighborhood), most organizers are politically progressive: They implicitly assume that if low- to moderate-income communities become engaged in civic life and begin to act on behalf of the self-interest of their neighborhoods, the results will be progress towards social and economic justice. Although rarely stated, an assumption also exists that community groups—especially if they work with similar groups across ethnic or racial divides—will forge a common class interest in, for example, safe neighborhoods, affordable housing, better schools, more public and private investment in neighborhood economies, or better access to health care. But most community organizers also advocate participatory democracy, that is, civic life in which average citizens become powerful and in charge of their own lives, not just clients of the more powerful, even if beneficent. It is a sentiment captured in the "iron rule" of the IAF: Never do for others what they can do for themselves.

Each historical stream or contemporary network of community organizing has changed in response, first, to its own internal dynamics and history, and second, in response to changes in political climate, the structure of the economy, and the characteristics of particular urban areas. But there is widespread recognition that the classic Alinskyite model is no longer adequate: Isolated community groups that are not part of a larger-scale organizing effort cannot provide the power that powerless communities need. As John McKnight and John Kretzmann have argued, many urban neighborhoods are increasingly fragmented and deprived of traditional social resources. This is partly a result of the decline of political parties, unions, and, in some cases, organizations of ethnic solidarity, as well as the growth of suburbanization, physical separation of work and home, and economic insecurity. Also, fewer local power centers are useful targets for community organizing (for example, today's neighborhood branch bank, currency exchange, or payday loan office does not wield the power or make the decisions that a local bank once did) (McKnight 1995). Even though many organizers agree on the need for a different scale of operation, community organizations differ widely on the basics of how and whom to organize, how to work with potential allies, and how to engage with electoral politics.

The Industrial Areas Foundation had already begun its transition from the classic local neighborhood model when it established a training school for organizers in Chicago in 1969. Soon afterwards, IAF launched a citywide group called Campaign Against Pollution (later Citizens Action Program, when it expanded to fight a proposed expressway through working-class neighborhoods). But, by 1976, the organization had collapsed, and the IAF training institute moved to New York. The IAF has subsequently greatly expanded, forming more than 45 organizations in 17 states, including the politically powerful Communities Organized for Public Service (COPS) in San Antonio and the ambitious East Brooklyn Congregations, which helped bring about the construction of roughly 4,000 new single-family homes in a deeply troubled neighborhood (Freedman 1994). Increasingly, IAF groups have formed statewide alliances among different cities or expanded to include suburbs as well as the central city, where most community organizations had traditionally been located.

These more recent IAF-organized groups have overwhelmingly been based on religious congregations that joined as members and financial supporters. Religious institutions tend to be anchored in communities and to last longer than many other organizations. They have an independent financial base and an existing or-

ganized group of individuals. Whatever the religion, they are likely to profess a set of values—such as concern for the poor or a critique of commercialism—that challenges the dictates of the market. Originally based mainly in Catholic parishes or black community churches, IAF groups increasingly try to incorporate the Jewish community, Protestant denominations (some of which have been especially supportive of affordable-housing initiatives), and the growing Muslim community in many cities like Chicago.

The aim of IAF is simple, according to Chambers: Help the powerless in society organize to gain power to get what they need. But the strategy has evolved, partly reflecting IAF organizing experience, partly reflecting changes in American cities. In the mid 1990s, the IAF returned to Chicago after an absence of nearly two decades and launched an organizing project designed for a much different Chicago.

The problems of the central city, in Chicago as elsewhere, were linked to metropolitan social, political, and economic patterns. Population, wealth and, to some extent, political power—especially power to influence crucial state government policies—had shifted toward the suburbs. To gain enough power to address central problems of inequality, housing, health care, and education, it was necessary to organize on a broader scale than IAF did in its early years by combining groups from both the city and the suburbs in the same organization. Despite historic city–suburban tensions, many of which were exacerbated during the decades of racial strife and "white flight," new grounds for cooperation had emerged. Many suburbs increasingly shared problems of the central city, and ethnic or religious communities linked city and suburban residents more than they had two decades earlier. More blacks lived in the suburbs, for example, but also ethnic immigrant communities often existed in both city and suburban neighborhoods. Chambers also hoped to bridge the divides of race, religion, class, and geography to create a grassroots strategy that paralleled the motivation of the business elite to undertake the Metropolis 2020 project.

Starting in the mid 1980s, a small group of Catholic priests who were familiar with the IAF began urging then-Cardinal Joseph

Bernardin to underwrite an IAF organizing project in Chicago. They found allies among black Protestants (such as the leaders of TWO) and among white Protestant groups (such as the Methodists, Episcopalians, and Missouri Synod Lutherans, who had helped to bankroll IAF's home-building project in East Brooklyn). On March 6, 1995, these sponsors pledged financial support (eventually $3.5 million, with the aid of additional sponsors) for a six-year organizing effort. After that, the member organizations would take responsibility for the organization and set its direction.

Initially, existing community groups were worried that IAF would monopolize church financial support for organizing and, in so doing, threaten their own work. In addition to many classic, single-neighborhood groups, several distinct networks of organizers and organizer training schools were at work in Chicago. For example, the National Training and Information Center and its national network, National Peoples Action, were based in Chicago and led by Shel Trapp and Gale Cincotta, who had been a pioneer in fighting bank redlining and passing the Community Reinvestment Act. The Midwest Academy training institute was closely associated with the national Citizens Action network and its local Illinois Public Action organization (later more or less reconstituted as U.S. Action nationally and Illinois Citizens Action in the city and state). Illinois Public Action focused on state legislation and politics, even making endorsements and working for candidates, and it included unions, senior-citizen organizations, environmentalists, and some community groups. Like IAF, the Chicago-based Gamaliel Foundation built organizations mainly out of religious congregations, including the South Side Metropolitan Alliance of Congregations. The Association of Community Organizations for Reform Now (ACORN) organized dues-paying members primarily from low-income, minority neighborhoods and worked closely with unions (especially a Service Employees International Union [SEIU] local representing home care workers), engaged in independent politics (working closely for a few years with a chapter of the New Party, which launched an effort to form

a national progressive party in 1992), and campaigned on issues, such as winning a "living-wage" agreement covering the employees of government subcontractors.

An energetic network of community groups focused on local economic development. Another network of community groups focused on neighborhood-based technical assistance and financing for affordable-housing construction and rehabilitation. Several different neighborhood school reform networks existed; they had been instrumental in passing Chicago's school reform and decentralization legislation in the late 1980s. Many groups, including Rev. Jesse Jackson's Chicago-based but nationally active Rainbow PUSH Coalition, claimed to organize and represent mainly black or Latino neighborhoods. A host of policy groups also existed, with a focus on neighborhood interests (such as the Center for Neighborhood Technology and Business and Professional People in the Public Interest). This catalogue does not include all the varieties of community-related organizing in the city during the late 1980s and early 1990s, much of which had been given a boost from 1983 to 1988 by Mayor Harold Washington's "neighborhood agenda" (Clavel and Wiewel 1991). But, shortly before the IAF project was launched, a review of community organizing in Chicago by the Woods Fund, which funded many groups, concluded that the organizations were too small and fragmented to be powerful and effective (Woods Fund of Chicago 1995). Yet a decade after the IAF project was launched, nearly all the major community organizations in the city continue to operate, with the IAF simply adding to the mix.

Eventually, Chambers and his small band of organizers—never more than three—expanded United Power's sponsoring list to include unions (SEIU, American Federation of State, County, and Municipal Employees [AFSCME], the Illinois Education Association and, later, the International Brotherhood of Electrical Workers), the Muslim community, and the Jewish community (although official Jewish community sponsorship lapsed, and only a few congregations have remained active). Community organizations and other institutions, such as community health centers, also became members. However, there was no way for individuals to join, nor has the organization recruited new people. United Power is an organization of organizations, or in the IAF parlance, a broad-based organization.

On October 19, 1997, around 10,000 representatives of roughly 300 congregations and other organizations gathered for the official launch of United Power for Action and Justice. It represented one of the most ambitious efforts anywhere in the country to develop a citizen organization encompassing both city and suburbs and spanning religious and ethnic differences.

BUILDING UNITED POWER FOR ACTION AND JUSTICE

United Power has been organized following the well-honed IAF strategy (Chambers 2003; Gecan 2002). The IAF goal is to organize a set of relationships, starting with leaders who can bring with them other people with whom they have relationships, to achieve social power for those who lack power. The key building block of organizing is the "relational meeting" between two individuals, where the leader or organizer seeks to probe the motivations and values of another to develop a public relationship that permits them to work together. In the organization, as Chambers explains, the community leaders are encouraged to appreciate and make use of the tension between the world as it is and the world as it should be, which includes the tensions between self-interest and self-sacrifice, power and love, change and unity, and imagination and hope. The IAF sees itself organizing civil society as a counterbalance to the power of both the market and the state. Leaders are encouraged through lengthy training and experience to see themselves as actors (indeed, as performers) in public life.

The organization plans actions—public meetings with officials—to win recognition of the group and action on its proposals. Unlike organizing as originally undertaken by Alinsky, who used or threatened flamboyant and confrontational actions with business and political authorities, the actions of IAF organizations are almost entirely limited to meetings (often with hundreds or even several thousand people

attending), which are very tightly scripted and designed to get some figure with political or economic power to agree to a demand, even if it is simply to have another meeting. The organization is extremely disciplined about getting precise counts of how many people a leader pledges to deliver and how many show up (and whether they were on time). A high value is placed on everyone being accountable for their actions to others in the organization.

But IAF formations also value the development and cultivation of both leaders and relationships. United Power is organized around various assemblies, some geographical, some more interest-based. Within these assemblies, leaders either affirm some course of action or make demands on authorities. Although the agenda for the larger organization and the assemblies is typically developed through meetings of the most active leaders (elected by the assemblies) and then approved without much debate in the larger gatherings, a deliberately structured democratic process is followed. Ultimately, however, there are variations in the extent to which representatives to United Power from constituent organizations, such as congregations, are democratically selected by or accountable to their member organizations. Although few professional organizers exist, they can exercise substantial influence on leaders, in part because of their mastery of the model and vocabulary of IAF organizing and through the process of evaluation and criticism after every meeting or action. However, much of the work relies on volunteer leaders.

The leaders of United Power, after undergoing training sessions that last up to ten days, are responsible for deciding on the issues on which the organization will focus: health care for the uninsured (the Gilead campaign), Ezra homes (the construction of a community of affordable single-family homes in Chicago, with the goal of extending the project to the suburbs), and breaking the cycle of homelessness. In addition, regional assemblies or smaller groups get involved with local issues, such as keeping open a battered women's shelter.

In early 2004, four years after it was launched, the Ezra project teetered on the brink of failure. Only eleven homes had been built, but hope existed that a new builder and lower priced—but still union—labor would help the project build 100 more homes within the year and hundreds more in the future. United Power organizers complained about Chicago's bureaucratic obstacles to housing construction, but the project was also one that least mobilized United Power members. It has been a development project detached from the main process of building power for existing organizations. Eventually the obstacles were overcome, and after the first 100 homes in the poor West Side neighborhood of Lawndale were built by the end of 2005, the project hoped to double its size in an additional expansion.

Actions—that is, large meetings—directed toward former U.S. Representative John Porter in the northern suburbs yielded $2 million for supportive counseling services for the homeless, half in Chicago, half in the suburbs. Yet these actions seemed to represent traditional religious charity, realized through a broad-based alliance, rather than the self-interest of suburban member organizations. However, it is possible to see this demand as an expression of the neighborhood and individual self-interest that people, especially from religious backgrounds, have in creating a more just and livable community.

United Power has acted more ambitiously—and more as a true metropolitan organization—on behalf of health care. The group's initial campaign involved meetings of more than 1,000 people with two leading candidates for president of the Cook County Board, asking for more money for community health centers. The campaign failed in its immediate goal, partly because the county government could argue persuasively that, because of a fiscal crunch, the only money available would come from cutting walk-in health centers run by Cook County Hospital, the region's sole public hospital. This conflict also undermined United Power's support base, especially from the unions representing Cook County Hospital employees.

As part of its health care campaign, United Power established the Gilead Center, which organized United Power members to educate and enroll community residents who were eligible for public health care. By the end of fiscal year 2003, the Gilead Center had linked more than 70,000 individuals to public health programs.

In 2003, United Power won $2 million in state funding for education and screening for breast and cervical cancer. But, unlike United Power itself, the Gilead Center relied on unpredictable federal and state funding.

In support of its work, the Gilead Center also commissioned research on the health care crisis. Its 2003 report, for example, showed that 15.9 percent of people under 65 in Illinois and 22.7 percent of that age group in Chicago do not have health insurance. In Chicago, 43.5 percent of residents with less than a high school education have no insurance, but also 23.8 percent of those with high school or some college education and 12.1 percent of individuals with college or higher education are also without insurance. The poor are much less likely to have insurance: 54.5 percent of Chicago families earning $25,000 or less lack insurance for at least one member of the family. Latinos, especially noncitizens, have the highest proportion of uninsured persons among the area's major ethnic or racial groups. Part-time workers (37.2 percent) are twice as likely to be uninsured as full-time workers. Among major industries, construction provided the least adequate coverage (23.1 percent uninsured), compared with education (4.2 percent uninsured); professional, scientific, and technical work (6.1 percent); and nondurable goods manufacturing (9.7 percent) (Rosenberg and Rankin 2004).

Such figures encouraged the campaign, in 2001, to expand the state's KidCare program (the Illinois version of the States Children Health Insurance Program [SCHIP]) to cover their uninsured parents through a new FamilyCare program. At least 17 other states had already received federal waivers and implemented similar plans, and the federal government had already allocated funding to pay two-thirds of the cost (Neal 2001).

The Sargent Shriver National Center on Poverty Law in Chicago had begun investigating the possibility of expanding SCHIP at the time that United Power was developing its initial goals. Some participants in the policy discussions were also involved with United Power, which adopted FamilyCare as a major campaign. Different styles of work were apparent: The Center focused on policy, traditional lobbying, and moving as swiftly as possible for a legislative victory; United Power focused on developing leaders, mobilizing members, and public actions. They both worked with key legislators, especially State Senator Barack Obama. The lobbying combination was central to an ultimately successful campaign that was helped by its broad endorsements—including nearly all major newspapers, the Chicago Association of Commerce and Industry, Blue Cross/Blue Shield, advocacy groups like Voices for Illinois Children, and the Illinois AFL-CIO.

Although the legislation had overwhelming bi-partisan support in the legislature and from Republican Governor George Ryan (who had not, however, initially included it in his budget), it eventually fell victim to a deal between the Democratic leader of the state House of Representatives and the Republican leader of the Senate. Their deal preserved member initiatives (denounced by critics as pork-barrel prerogatives) at the expense of FamilyCare. However, by that time, the campaign for FamilyCare had become so persuasive that Ryan proceeded to apply for a federal waiver and included the first stage of funding in the next budget. In the program's third year, according to Shriver Center director of advocacy John Bouman, funding was available to cover families with incomes up to 133 percent of the poverty level. In the next budgetary cycle, funding was expected to cover families up to 185 percent of poverty and about 300,000 of 340,000 eligible parents.

Although most United Power projects have been planned and executed deliberately, the organization at times has responded to crisis situations. When SEIU janitors in the suburbs struck for decent wages and health care, many congregations offered support, including some whose members included influential building owners. Most dramatically, after the September 11, 2001, attacks on the World Trade Center and the Pentagon by al-Qaeda militants, United Power held a meeting of 4,000 members to discuss Muslims and the Islamic faith in Chicago at the Navy Pier assembly hall. Chambers, who had worked hard to include Chicago's growing but civically uninvolved Muslim community in United Power, encountered reluctance on all sides when he raised the prospect of such

a meeting. (Eventually, very few black churches participated, partly because of old tensions with Chicago's Nation of Islam, which is not part of United Power.) The event, which Chambers called "the finest thing United Power has done," was a significant achievement in moderating tensions after September 11 and keeping the Muslim community even more firmly engaged with the organization.

Chicago, long identified as the United States' most segregated major city, has a history of racial tensions. Blacks resent historic exclusion and discrimination. Some working-class whites felt they were pushed out of the city and into the suburbs as the black population expanded (a history exacerbated by real estate industry "panic peddling" and bank redlining). When United Power lead organizer Stephen Roberson arrived from New York, he was struck by the degree of racial separation in Chicago. He also believed that "groups tend to have had a hunger here to be together because it was so rare in any lasting relationship. Harold Washington and that experience brought forth actualization of working across race. His campaign, his tenure, and his legacy all brought that mixture together, but it seemed rare, and people hungered for more of it." Now both white and black organizations, which are used to define the city in a bipolar way (despite the longstanding Latino presence), face new issues involving immigration, which is likely to become a growing focus for United Power.

In 2003, the IAF and United Power, with seed money from some of its usual denominational funders, launched two new, independent organizations in the northern and western sections of the metropolitan region. Initially, major issues for Lake County United include affordable housing (a response to gentrification, snob zoning, and rising housing prices that affect not just low-income workers but also long-time residents), education for immigrants, health care access, and transportation (including traffic gridlock). People are also motivated to join, according to organizer Tom Lenz, because of their anxiety "about weakening of democracy and civil society, just kind of a sense of, 'Who's in charge?'," especially as their own economic insecurities grow. In the near future, IAF plans to create similar organizations in smaller downstate Illinois cities, such as Springfield and Decatur. In December 2005, 800 young people from varied backgrounds in both the city of Chicago and its suburbs formed a new group for people from late teens to late twenties called Youth United.

VICTORIES, CHALLENGES, AND FUTURE PROSPECTS

Yet, even as it expands or clones itself, United Power faces challenges about its future. It is well established: About 275 member organizations remain active, a slight decline from the beginning, and its funding is relatively secure. However, although IAF groups have prided themselves on independence from government or foundation funding, their reliance on churches poses limitations, too, especially at a time when many historically progressive religious communities are turning inward, or to the right politically. Also, although United Power represents an important expansion of IAF's typical congregational base, the inclusion of some unions and community health care clinics causes problems of organizational integration. To some extent, religious denominations, ethnic groups, unions, or other components of an organization like United Power function as "silos," in the words of former United Power organizer Josh Hoyt, with divergent internal organizations and cultures that often are hard to bridge. IAF organizers, for example, have found it difficult to work with union rank-and-file in the same way that they have worked with church congregations, and they perceive unions as insufficiently committed to joining broader community projects.

For their part, the unions, after initial enthusiasm, gradually have become less involved. Union leaders have been frustrated at the slow pace of United Power, its ponderous internal processes, the lack of political clarity on issues and campaigns, timidity in tackling many issues, and the modest results produced by such an elaborate and expensive undertaking. The unions have appreciated the support from United Power (for example, during the janitors' strike) and the opportunity to form relationships with religious leaders (many of whom influence policies at hospitals and social service agencies that have often resisted unions). But they are also frustrated at United Power's reluctance to provide critical support (for example, on legislation that would have barred nonprofit groups from using tax dollars to fight unions) or engage some major issues that are central to metropolitan politics (such as property and income tax reform or balanced regional development). Activist unions, like AFSCME and SEIU, are typically practitioners of coalition politics and believe in putting organizational power behind social movements; United Power generally disdains coalitions with other organizations or with social movements, which it views as ephemeral. Despite such differences, SEIU Local 1 president and state director Tom Balanoff still offers a positive assessment of United Power, "The idea is really good, and they've had some success and activated some people who've not even thought about activism."

Ed Chambers founded United Power based on his conviction that broad-based organizations must become more inclusive if they are to wield power in contemporary America. But, by 2004, noting that the total metropolis may be "too big a chunk for human scale," Chambers remarked, "There's no way you can get all Chicagoans to change together." United Power did occasionally act effectively as a metropolitan organization, but in its first six years of operation, it has not represented a dramatically new source of metropolitan power. It has also been hard to define the mutual self-interest that could unite city and suburb. Chambers and Roberson note that health care issues cut across divisions of city and suburb, race and ethnicity, and income levels—one reason why United Power's health care initiatives have been its major metropolitan-wide successes. But even the programs promoted by this action mainly addressed the disproportionately greater needs of lower-income families.

Myron Orfield (2002), a Minnesota state legislator and advocate of metropolitan governance, has argued that many suburbs, typically older suburbs or those without a strong tax base in industry, shopping malls, or expensive homes, have much more in common with the central city than they do with tax base-rich affluent suburbs. But United Power rejects what seems a prototypically Alinksyite strategy of uniting the central city and less affluent or older suburbs around common economic self-interest. "That's a class-based strategy," Hoyt said. "That's not how we were organized. We found there were people of faith in wealthy and upper-middle class communities for whom acting with the uninsured or homeless was a very powerful self-interest. They were willing to get into sometimes wrenching confrontations in their communities." Certainly, it is valuable for working-class constituencies to find allies among the wealthy, but there's always the risk that the self-interest of the wealthy will also dilute, neutralize, or redirect the power of a working-class majority in a broad-based organization.

Chicago working-class communities, from poor to upper-middle income, remain politically weakened because they are organizationally fragmented, despite the addition of a large, well-organized, metropolitan group like United Power. If all these communities and their organizations could cooperate, they might have the power to achieve such ambitious goals as progressive tax reform and tax sharing, balanced and sustainable economic development, a single-payer health care system for the state, more affordable housing, and more equitable educational funding. "Not to cooperate is really a decision not to be powerful," argues John McKnight, a veteran organizer and analyst at Northwestern University's Institute for Policy Research. "Lack of cooperation by the IAF leadership is one error they have consistently made, and it weakens the national possibility to bring power to those without power." Cooperation would not be easy in Chicago, let alone nationally, but ruling out efforts to bridge organizational gaps ultimately is as self-defeating as ruling out efforts to reach across religion, race, or geography.

Electoral politics provides one important avenue to power and a basis for cooperation across communities. Since Alinsky's day, community organizations have struggled with the question of how to relate to politicians. In the early days, from the 1930s through the early 1970s, nearly all Chicago community groups directed protests at the all-powerful Democratic Machine politicians in Chicago, to make them accountable or to demand city services or solutions to local problems. By the late 1970s, many community groups were shifting toward creating their own ability to develop local economies, preserve endangered manufacturers, improve local schools, or strengthen other neighborhood institutions.

After Harold Washington was elected mayor, these groups cooperated in implementing city policies favoring balanced development in the city (that is, more attention to neighborhoods and less concentration of public investment in the city center). They indirectly allied with him in his war with the remnants of the old Machine. Under Mayor Richard M. Daley, the working relationship with most community groups—except for a few loyal supporters—has not been as close as it was during the Washington years.

Like smaller organizations, United Power pursues both strategies. It pressures elected leaders to deliver programs (such as health care), and it works with them on local self-help development projects (such as its homebuilding program).

Most Chicago community organizations still do not overtly support candidates for public office. Instead of the old confrontational marches on City Hall, United Power has shifted toward more restrained, civil meetings to pressure politicians. Also, reflecting its broader base, United Power has engaged county and state political figures as much as it has Chicago officials.

Some community groups are edging closer to electoral politics. During the 2004 election year, United Power began registering and mobilizing voters and demanding meetings with candidates. When the Republican candidate for the U.S. Senate dropped out of the race, United Power went ahead with a large candidate meeting, posing questions exclusively to the Democratic candidate, Barack Obama, with whom the organization had collaborated to expand health care. However, without a clear policy agenda, United Power has been unable to make crucial distinctions among candidates to help its members decide how to vote. While remaining nonpartisan, United Power strategists have contemplated how member groups could be more active and even how the organization might cultivate candidates to run for office. If United Power really does want to exercise power, it will have to develop a more muscular way of engaging electoral politics and defining its agenda, even at the risk of provoking attacks by conservative groups, such as its critics from the right wing of the Catholic Church.

United Power represents one important variation of the longstanding effort, which has been pursued in different ways by various organizers and movements, to mobilize the powerless in Chicago. Building on a rich Chicago history, it tries to create new relationships and a new understanding of common interests that can confront divisions of residence, race, ethnicity, immigrant status, and income to create a more socially just metropolitan region. United Power's organizing strategy also seeks to confront some of the new Chicago's crucial policy challenges: lingering and newly seeded racial and ethnic mistrust, unacceptable community variations in the quality of housing and public services, and a frayed social safety net whose holes especially threaten racial and ethnic minorities and families dependent on low-wage, service-sector employment. United Power's experience over the last decade also raises important and still daunting questions of political strategy. It has not yet realized its potential, but it has taken an important step by bringing together people of diverse backgrounds from churches, community institutions, and unions in both the city and the suburbs. Making such metropolitan political organization effective will be crucial in Chicago and its region in the years to come.

NOTE

Research for this chapter included interviews with Ed Chambers from 1995 to 2004, observations of meetings and training sessions, and interviews at various times with staff, leaders, supporters, and critics. When not otherwise identified, quotations from individuals come from those interviews.

Pauline Lipman

20   Chicago School Reform: Advancing the Global City Agenda

IN 1987, SECRETARY of Education William Bennett came to Chicago and pronounced its schools "the worst in the nation." Just 11 years later, in 1998, President Clinton visited the city and declared that Chicago Public Schools (CPS) were "a model for the nation." Indeed, at the millennium, Chicago's school accountability system, based on high-stakes standardized tests, was an exemplar for urban schools districts and a template for the Bush administration's No Child Left Behind federal education legislation. This rapid transition, from disaster to model, in many ways marks the city's transition to global city. But, just as we must look beneath the concrete and steel surface of downtown development and the global production networks to capture the social and economic contradictions that characterize global cities (Sassen 1994), we also must look more deeply into the city's school policies. How are Chicago's school reforms related to the political, economic, and cultural processes that characterize the new Chicago? Are the public schools improving? For which students? And what are the consequences for the city and its race and class inequalities?

Chicago's school reforms are both a product of and response to the converging forces that are reshaping the city. Chicago's drive to become a global city, its deepening economic and racial polarization, restructured economy, and changing dynamics of race, ethnicity, and class (see Chapters 1, 2, and 4) define the social landscape on which the trends and tensions of education policy are played out. Despite its national reputation for school improvement, Chicago's current education policies are contributing to

the exacerbation of economic and spatial inequality along lines of race, ethnicity, and social class. These policies sharpen already differentiated opportunities to learn that correspond with a highly stratified workforce. They support the control of African American and Latino youth, containment and displacement of low-income communities of color, and the development of a new geography of inequality in the city.

CHICAGO'S 1988 AND 1995 SCHOOL REFORMS

In 1995, the Illinois General Assembly gave Chicago's mayor responsibility for the city's public school system. Mayor Richard M. Daley appointed his Chief of Staff, Gery Chico, as President of the Chicago Public Schools Board of Trustees and his Budget Director, Paul Vallas, as CEO of schools. Vallas and Chico immediately installed a corporate-style regime centered on a system of high-stakes accountability based on student performance on standardized tests. They also launched an ambitious array of new schools and programs. Although Vallas and Chico resigned in 2001, the key elements of their policies continue. As a result of these policies, the district has sent thousands of primarily African American and Latino students to mandatory after-school and summer programs focused on test preparation and retained students in grade for up to three years or assigned them to basic skills Academic Preparation Centers (APCs). As many as half the district's schools have been put on probation under central-office oversight, and teachers have been required to use semi-scripted curricula and scripted instruction in failing schools. Under the new policies, bilingual education students are required to take standardized tests in English after three years or less in bilingual education, regardless of their proficiency in English.

The 1995 policies are layered over the 1988 Chicago School Reform Act, which established democratic participation in school governance through local school councils (LSCs) composed mainly of parents and community residents. The 1988 law gave LSCs the power to hire and fire principals, approve annual local school-improvement plans, and allocate discretionary funds. Widely viewed as the most radical democratic restructuring of a school system in the nation, the 1988 reform legislation was the product of a coalition of school reformers, business interests, and grassroots activists (Hess 1991). It was based on the theory that decentralization and grassroots participation would stimulate innovation at the school level (Bryk et al. 1998; Katz 1992). The genesis of the reform and the social forces that produced it are complex, and can only be outlined here (see for example, Hess 1991; Kyle and Kantowicz 1992). The school reform movement should be understood in the context of three intersecting social dynamics: (1) social movements undertaken by African Americans and Latinos for equal and quality education in the decades preceding the 1988 Reform Act, (2) the election of Harold Washington as Chicago's first African American mayor, and (3) business frustration with CPS fiscal crises, a series of teachers' strikes, and the failure of schools to adequately prepare a workforce for the rapidly changing economy.

From the 1960s through the 1980s, African Americans and Latinos organized mass protests against the racial segregation of schools, school overcrowding, inequitable school resources and conditions, school violence, and high dropout rates. They demanded better college preparation, more African American and Latino principals, bilingual education, and the representation of African Americans, Chicanos, and Puerto Ricans in the curriculum. In the 1960s, influenced by the Civil Rights and Black Power movements, African American parents, students, and communities built a mass social movement to force change in Chicago schools (Danns 2002). By the late 1960s, as the Black Power movement took hold, parents, teachers, and students organized conferences, boycotts, and student walk-outs and sit-ins against overcrowding, racist curricula, racist teachers, unresponsive principals, and poorly prepared graduates. Latinos followed suit during the 1980s and early 1990s. In 1984, parents and community members staged a massive march on Clemente High School in the largely Puerto Rican Humboldt Park community, demanding action on the high Latino dropout problem and on gang violence in schools. Four teachers' strikes also occurred between 1980 and 1987, largely because state and local governments failed to fund salary increases and school improvements. During the 1987 strike, the longest in Chicago history, parents' longstanding frustrations coalesced into major demonstrations, and the People's Coalition for Educational Reform, a coalition of African American and Latino parents, set up freedom schools and demanded the mayor resolve the strike.

Despite the gains of these movements, on balance, CPS continued to provide inequitable educational opportunities. In 1990, Gary Orfield, a political scientist at the University of Chicago whose research has followed Chicago school policy, declared, "The great majority of Black and Hispanic youths in metropolitan Chicago today attend schools that prepare them for neither college nor a decent job" (p.131). During the 1970s and 1980s, CPS also faced major financial crises, officially declaring bankruptcy in 1979. The Superintendent resigned; the governor arranged a bailout, and the state legislature established the Chicago School Finance Authority (SFA), chaired by a business leader, to oversee CPS finances. This introduced an element of direct business involvement that would be important in the 1988 reform movement and central to the 1995 reform actions. Programs and staff were cut to pay off bond holders, and teachers had the first payless payday since the Great Depression. Meanwhile, business groups complained that the school system was deterring investors and failing to prepare a workforce with the skills that would enable Chicago to be competitive in the global economy.

The African American and Latino school campaigns of the 1960s through the early 1980s were part of multi-issue civil rights movements in Chicago that helped sow the seeds of the grassroots movement to elect Harold Washington as mayor in 1983. In turn, this grassroots campaign and the potential that Washington would support local economic development and neighborhood initiatives helped energize community organizing, including education organizing. In the autumn of 1986, Mayor Washington convened an education summit, initially to develop a plan to improve the quality of high school graduates and to guarantee that jobs would be available to them when they graduated. The summit included about 40 representatives of business, civic agencies, local universities and junior colleges, the teachers' union, and the Board of Education (Hess 1991). The following year, Washington appointed a Parents Community Council, and parents became key players, along with business, school reform groups, and community activists, in restructuring the school system.

The Chicago School Reform Act that was passed by the Illinois state legislature in 1988 was the product of intense negotiation among these various social forces. The reform was also supported by downstate Republicans, and it was spurred by corruption scandals at the central office and the 1987 teachers' strike. Although some community activists saw decentralization and grassroots participation as a strategy to stimulate innovation and school improvement (Bryk et al. 1998), others involved in shaping the reform and developing the local school councils saw LSCs as vehicles of community empowerment (Katz 1992). It seems that business leaders supported the reform, despite its grassroots character, because they were looking for a dramatic solution for a school system that had gone through years of instability and failure.

Decentralization also made sense to business during a period when corporate restructuring and decentralized management were fashionable (Mirel 1993). In fact, in addition to strengthening local schools and local school councils, the 1988 Reform Act actually gave business more influence over the school system through the close ties major business and financial interests had with the mayor and through business' control of the School Finance Authority (Shipps, Kahne, and Smylie 1999).

As the LSCs developed, there was substantial variability in their effectiveness, the level of community participation, and the degree to which they sparked educational innovation (Shipps 1997). Nevertheless, at least during the first few years of reform, the grassroots character of LSCs and their potential for democratic participation in school governance (Katz, Fine, and Simon 1997; *Catalyst* 1990, 1991) captured national attention. In many communities, LSC elections sparked broad participation and community discussion about education issues, vigorously contested elections, and campaigns to address important local school issues. But there was an inevitable period of development. Untrained LSC members struggled with the technical processes of budgetary and operational issues; principal selections were time-consuming and sometimes fractious; and race and class contradictions, as well as contradictions between school professionals and parents and the community, played out in some LSCs. It was a messy process that reflected the challenges but also the potential of grassroots democratic participation in school governance (Katz, Fine, and Simon 1997).

Business interests and the mayor's office had little patience with this process, and it did not match their larger agenda for the city. The messiness and unevenness of local school reform became the rationale for a shift to recentralization and a corporate leadership style. The break-up of Washington's coalition upon his death and the eventual election of Richard M. Daley as mayor created political impetus to shift school reform to a managerial agenda. By 1995, Daley and business leaders were impatient with the pace of school improvement and ongoing conflicts with teacher and school-employee unions. They again collaborated with Republican legislators, this time to recentralize the system under the mayor's control and to impose a managerial approach to school reform (Shipps, Kahne, and Smylie 1999). The "democratic localism" (Bryk et al. 1998) of LSCs continues to function in tandem with recentralization, albeit in an increasingly weakened form. Although the relationship of democratic local control and centralized accountability varies, in general, the power of the LSCs has been significantly compromised by the overriding impact of recentralization and accountability. The schools under the tightest central office restrictions—low-scoring and probation schools that are located in communities of color—have seen the power of their LSCs sharply reduced. In June 2004, Mayor Daley announced a new school plan, Renaissance 2010, under which 60 "failing schools" would be closed and 100 new schools would be opened—one-third as charter schools, one-third as contract schools, and one-third run by CPS. Under the plan, two-thirds of these schools will not have LSCs. In sum, what began, at least partially, as a grassroots campaign to decentralize power to the local school community, and which held the potential to contribute to a grassroots community empowerment, was marginalized by decisions made by Mayor Daley and allied business elites.

ACCOUNTABILITY AND CENTRALIZED CONTROL OF SCHOOLS

It is not surprising that the 1995 recentralization of the school system resonates with some families and the public in general. The "good sense" (in Gramsci's terms) in these policies is that they mandate decisive action in a system that has profoundly failed to educate all students in Chicago. Finally, schools and teachers are being held accountable for teaching and for students' academic progress (as measured by a single, standardized test score). However, in a system of blatant inequities, CPS has framed standards, tests, and accountability as equality and justice. All students and schools are evaluated by "the same test" and "held to the same standards," and the retention of thousands of students is characterized as "ending the injustice of social promotion" (Vallas 2000, 5). These policies have produced some observable results, including gains in test scores, although scores have fluctuated since 2001. However, the data do not support the efficacy of the retention policy

(Roderick et al. 2000), and there are concerns that high stakes tests and harsh consequences for students exacerbate dropout rates (Haney 2000). Beyond these quantitative indicators, there are broader educational and social implications that are less obvious.

My research suggests that standardized tests are most central and accountability policies most harsh in schools with the lowest scores. Concretely, these schools enroll predominantly low-income African American and Latino student populations. In the low-scoring schools I studied (Lipman 2004), classroom observations, interviews with teachers and administrators, and school documents all pointed to the test-driven nature of curriculum, instruction, and educational decisions. As one teacher summed up, "It's all about the tests." In the weeks before the Iowa Test of Basic Skills (Chicago's high-stakes elementary school test), schools hold Iowa Test pep rallies. "Zap the Iowa" posters festoon school hallways and, in schools across the city, daily announcements exhort students to gear up for the test. In one school I studied, teachers spent about one-third of the year teaching from test preparation booklets purchased from the test maker rather than from classroom texts. Accountability policies promoted or reinforced a narrow focus on specific skills and repeated practice of techniques for taking multiple-choice tests. For example, students spent hours practicing filling in bubbles on answer sheets and reciting test-taking tricks such as "three B's in a row, no, no, no." Improved test scores in these schools may have more to do with test preparation than with learning. This inference is supported by findings of the National Research Council Committee on Appropriate Test Use: "The NRC Committee concluded that Chicago's regular year and summer school curricula were so closely geared to the ITBS that it was impossible to distinguish real subject mastery from mastery of skills and knowledge useful for passing this particular test" (Hauser 1999, 1). In contrast, schools with higher test scores—generally those with larger proportions of middle-class and white students—are less constrained by test preparation. In 2003, CPS put curriculum in low-scoring schools under tighter district controls while the school district increased the flexibility of high-scoring schools (which generally have more affluent students and/or selective enrollments) over curricular decisions.

The data from Chicago and elsewhere (Lipman 2004; McNeil 2000; Newmann, Bryk, and Nagaoka 2001) suggest that, to the extent the new policies prompt low-scoring schools to engage in education as test preparation and basic skills (as opposed to an intensive effort to build capacity for more thoughtful, intellectually challenging pedagogies), they widen educational inequalities by institutionalizing a narrowed curriculum.

The schools' differential responses to district accountability are closely linked to past and present race and class advantages and the political power of their communities. High-scoring schools, magnet schools, special college-prep academic programs in high schools, and elementary schools designated as Gifted Centers are relatively more immune from the pressures of accountability. The consequences of grade retention, assignment to basic skills APCs, and narrow, test-driven curricula have fallen heavily on African American and Latino students. In 2000, Parents United for Responsible Education (a city-wide parent organization) won a civil rights complaint against CPS for adverse discriminatory impact of the retention policy that placed African American and Latino students disproportionately in APCs. In fact, a large percentage of students do not make it through CPS. The Consortium on Chicago School Research calculated that the cohort drop-out rate (following students from ages 13 to 19) was 41.8 percent in 2000, down from 44.3 percent in 1997 (Allensworth and Easton 2001). However, a recent study published by a community organization on Chicago's West Side, using CPS data, calculated that 20 percent of all African American students dropped out in 2002–03, and 25 percent of African American males dropped out within that same period (Olszewski 2003). At Juarez High School, a neighborhood school in the mostly Mexican immigrant Pilsen neighborhood, enrollment of ninth graders at the end of the first semester in 1998 was 547, but only 260 students graduated in 2002, a dropout rate of roughly 52 percent

(Personal communication, Eric Gutstein, August 15, 2002). These figures also probably undercount dropouts because some students never make it beyond eighth grade, or they enroll in an APC only to drop out. Looking at the long-term effects of similar accountability policies in Texas, Walter Haney (2000) found that accountability and high-stakes tests correlated with increased dropout rates, especially among African Americans and Latinos.

Accountability policies are also a form of symbolic politics. They construct definitions of education, organize consciousness around shared understandings of what constitute legitimate classroom knowledge and educational practice, and shape public perceptions of specific social groups. In this sense, Chicago's accountability policies have created a public spectacle of the failure of schools and students in African American and Latino neighborhoods. CPS's get-tough failure, retention, and probation policies signify that these students need discipline and control. Similarly, high-stakes tests in English after three years or less in bilingual education undermine bilingual fluency and symbolically privilege English as the language of importance over students' home languages (teacher interview, June, 1999). These assimilationist policies contribute to the construction of Americanization as the goal for Chicago's immigrant populations.

NEW SCHOOLS, NEW INEQUALITIES

Beginning in 1995, CPS initiated a variety of special programs, schools, and instructional approaches with significant implications in Chicago's new economy. These initiatives have further stratified an already tiered school system by expanding both academically prestigious college prep programs and schools and regimented, vocational, basic skills programs and schools. At the top of this hierarchy are six new selective College Prep Regional Magnet High Schools (particularly three in upper-income areas) and High School International Baccalaureate (IB) programs that lead to a prestigious International Baccalaureate diploma.

The new vocational, basic skills, and highly regimented programs and schools include 12 Education-to-Career Academies (ETCs), which are new vocational high schools that were created out of general high schools and older vocational schools. ETCs have a nonacademic core of courses in addition to core academic subjects (English, mathematics, science, social studies). Nonacademic core course concentrations include cosmetology, secretarial science, and hospitality management. ETCs are all located in low-income African American, Latino, and immigrant communities on the West and South Sides of the city. CPS also established the first two military high schools in the United States, both in low-income African American South Side neighborhoods. A third, small military academy is located on the West Side, in a low-income African American area. The schools, a partnership between CPS and the U.S. Army, are run like military training schools. At the elementary level, schools using scripted Direct Instruction (DI), based on a behaviorist model of basic skills education, were expanded from 7 prior to 1995 to 45 in 2001 (personal communication, CPS Office of Accountability, October 2001). All but four are clustered in low-income African American and Latino areas.

Yet, looking at the school district as a whole, special schools and programs, including ETCs and military schools created after 1995, constitute the *upper* tiers of public schooling in Chicago. They operate alongside pre-1995 magnet schools, college prep programs, advanced classes in general high schools, specialized small high schools, and charter schools across the city. Taken together, these special programs and schools serve a small percentage of students. They are layered over the majority of public schools in the system, the neighborhood elementary and high schools. In most neighborhood schools, advanced courses of study are quite limited. White students are over-represented in advanced college prep classes, whereas African American and Latino students are under-represented (Generation Y 2002). Most important, a large percentage of students do not make it through the system at all. Including these students who drop out is central to grasping the magnitude of inequality in Chicago Public Schools.

SCHOOL POLICY AND GENTRIFICATION

The location of new schools and programs can be mapped onto patterns of gentrification and the geography of race and class polarization in the city. To attract producer and financial services, global cities must offer the lifestyle demanded by highly paid, highly skilled workers (Sassen 1994), and excellent schools are an important element. A series of *Chicago Tribune* articles on Chicago's bid to become a global city noted that key business figures consistently identified the need to "fix" the schools, "both to provide a pool of good workers and to persuade middle-class and upper-class families to settle in the city" (Longworth and Burns 1999, A14).

Good schools are real estate anchors in gentrifying neighborhoods. The intersection of CPS policies and the interests of developers is apparent in the location of four new college prep magnet high schools located in or near upper-income or gentrifying neighborhoods. Three of these new schools are in spacious, state-of-art new or renovated buildings, costing from $33 to $50 million each and in neighborhoods where median home prices are eight to ten times those of the two magnets in far South and West Side neighborhoods (Williams 2000). A fourth college prep magnet is in the middle of the new Mid-South gentrifying area, near the University of Chicago and the Illinois Institute of Technology. A fifth is in the heart of Englewood, one of the lowest-income African American communities in the city. Finally closed for renovation in 2003, it was the last of the college prep magnet buildings to be upgraded.[1] Renovation of the far South Side magnet, which is 80.8 percent African American and 17.2 percent Latino, was accomplished only after political pressure from local elected officials and residents. In addition to unequal facilities between the North and South Side magnets, principals reported dramatic disparities in resources and time to design curriculum and recruit teachers (*Catalyst* 2000, 4). It is also important to note that no regional magnet college prep high school exists in the extensive low-income African American and Latino West Side areas away from the lake.

Magnet schools and International Baccalaureate programs have done little to expand opportunities for the district's overwhelmingly low-income students and students of color. Rather, they have attracted white and middle-class students who otherwise would be attending private schools or would have moved to the suburbs. A CPS official said, the IBs are to "attract more [middle-class] students to CPS. There aren't enough academic offerings for parents—they're all going to private schools. That's why this [IB program initiative] went out" (Personal communication, Feb. 16, 2000). In fact, since the development of the regional college prep magnets and IB programs, the rate at which high-achieving students have been leaving CPS has declined (Allensworth and Rosenkrantz 2000). The student composition of the magnet schools also supports this conclusion. Regions 1 and 2 magnets, the most prestigious, are disproportionately white and have a lower percentage of low-income students than the district as a whole. In 2002, CPS enrolled 90.4 percent students of color and 85.3 percent low-income students. In contrast, Region 1 Northside College Prep enrolled 47.8 percent white and 23.1 percent low-income students. Region 2 Payton College Prep had 31.1 percent white and 37 percent low-income students.

New, highly publicized academic programs and magnet schools serve a dual purpose. They are an incentive for professional and middle-class families to move to or remain in the city, especially in areas of budding gentrification where they provide access to these *separate* high-status educational programs. CPS's open appeal to middle-class families is seen as a legitimate strategy for school reform because it is taken for granted that middle-class children are essential to a good school system. At the same time, small, highly publicized college-prep programs distributed across the city and magnet high schools in each region are used to project an image of equity onto a vastly unequal system.

Altogether, these special academic programs serve a very small percentage of CPS students.

During the 2003–04 school year, 13 high schools (out of a total of 96, including small schools and CPS charter schools) had participating IB programs.[2] In fall 2002, when the initiative was fully underway, the IBs involved just over 1 percent of all high school students; and during the 2002–03 school year (the most recent year for which data are available), they enrolled about 2,100 students, or about 2 percent of all high school students (personal communication, CPS official, August 11, 2004). A total of only 11.5 percent of all high school students were in selective college prep programs or schools in fall 2002—this included the new magnet high schools and those magnets and IBs existing prior to 1995. Yet, the magnet college prep high schools received a disproportionate share of resources. According to *Catalyst*, which has chronicled Chicago school reform since 1988, the new regional magnets got almost half of CPS construction and renovation money between 1996 and 1999 (Schaeffer 2000, 13).

In short, although high-profile, selective academic programs and schools are scattered throughout the city, almost all whole-school college-prep programs initiated since 1995 are clustered in middle-class, white, and gentrified or gentrifying areas. Although IB programs are in high schools throughout the city, including in low-income communities of color and in communities with large numbers of immigrants, they serve only a small percentage of students. On the other hand, new vocational, military, and DI schools, which generally involve all the students in the school, are concentrated in low- and very low-income African American and Latino areas, and their student populations are almost entirely African American and Latino. In the context of a vastly unequal school system and the drive to make Chicago a global city, the aggregate effect of new programs and schools is to support educational inequality *and* heightened economic and social dualities.

SCHOOL POLICY AND THE NEW WORKFORCE

Education reform has been a consistent priority for Chicago's corporate and financial leaders. In a 1990 update to its agenda for city development, the Commercial Club of Chicago (1990, 4) asserted, "The failures of Chicago's public schools in previous years have left us with hundreds of thousands of people untrained and ill equipped to fill the jobs of the new economy.... " In 1988, a survey of 68 top Chicago business leaders also pointed to a poorly educated workforce as a prime reason for business loss (Mirel 1993). *Chicago Metropolis 2020*, a 1998 development plan for the Chicago metropolitan region produced by the Commercial Club and other civic organizations, praised the mayor's school reforms, but again identified educational preparation for a skilled workforce as one of three top priorities to realize its vision of a multi-centered region of "knowledge, expertise, and economic opportunity" (Johnson 1998, 3). The 1995 school reform law can be interpreted as a response to business interests (Shipps, Kahne, and Smylie 1999), and it frames schooling within the language of business—regulation, accountability, and quality assurance.

New programs and schools, coupled with CPS's high-stakes educational accountability system, sharpen already differentiated opportunities to learn with significant ramifications in Chicago's restructured economy. New differentiated high schools parallel a highly stratified labor force. Although new educational opportunities exist for a small number of students, the vast majority, primarily students of color and immigrants, attend schools organized around basic competencies and driven by accountability practices. These students are being prepared with the academic skills and dispositions for the new low-wage service and manufacturing jobs, as well as the large number of part-time and temporary jobs that require the flexibility to adapt to changing job requirements. Basic literacies in reading and math, knowledge of English, and disciplined work habits are essential for this flexible labor force. As Dennis Carlson (1996, 282–83) argues, "The 'basic skills' restructuring of urban schools around standardized testing and a skill-based curriculum has been a response to the changing character of work in postindustrial America, and it has participated in the construction of a new postindustrial working class ... of clerical, data processing, janitorial, and service

industry jobs." Moreover, the regimentation of scripted instruction and test preparation, as well as retention and assignment to APCs, may contribute to weeding out youth superfluous to the labor force. Over 40 percent of CPS students do not graduate. These youth may have little opportunity in the formal economy. These are the youth trapped in what Generation Y (2002) calls "the prison-prep track," more likely to be criminalized and incarcerated than to end up in college or with well-paying jobs.

Although stratified educational experiences and opportunities are not new, educational differentiation takes on new meaning in a context in which knowledge is far more decisive than in the past, when a high school diploma (and sometimes no diploma at all) was sufficient to gain entry to a well-paying, stable job with a relatively predictable future. Equally important, the weight of test-driven, regimented, basic-skills curricula may supplant those educational experiences that give students tools to think critically about the inequalities being produced in their neighborhoods and in the city as a whole. Differentiated schools and programs also equip students with quite different resources from which to construct their identities. The educational practices of specific programs constitute discourses: ways of "talking, listening, reading, writing, interacting, believing, valuing ... so as to display or to recognize a particular social identity" (Gee, Hull, and Lankshear 1996, 10). Thus, the discourses of scripted direct-instruction programs, IBs, ETCs, military academies, college prep magnet high schools, and so on apprentice students to particular identities that have profound implications in a layered society of a "relatively well-paid core of knowledge leaders and workers and a bevy of people servicing them for the least possible price" (Gee, Hull, and Lankshear 1996, 47).

CPS POLICIES AND THE REGULATION OF AFRICAN AMERICANS AND LATINOS

Although racial inequality and segregation have been persistent realities throughout Chicago's history, the city's school policies are unfolding in a context in which the processes of globalization and economic restructuring intersect with historical patterns of structural racism to produce new forms of social isolation and racial exclusion, particularly in very low-income African American communities (see Chapter 2). It is important to reiterate that Chicago's new inequalities are highly racialized. Disparity in wages (Betancur and Gills 2000) and median household income (Mendell and Little 2002) for African Americans and Latinos, when compared with whites, is increasing. Janet Abu-Lughod (1999) reported that the Chicago metropolitan area led all others in the United States in the economic disparity between whites and African Americans. As noted by Fassil Dimissie in Chapter 2, while the low-wage service sector has expanded dramatically, sections of the labor force, particularly African American youth and young adults, are largely excluded from the formal economy altogether. A report by the Center for Labor Market Studies (2003) reported that, in 2000, in the city of Chicago, African American males were nearly six times more likely to be out of school and out of work compared with white males. The study reported that 45 percent of African American males in Chicago between the ages of 20 and 24 were out of school and out of work compared with 8 percent of white male residents of the city (Center for Labor Market Studies 2003, 4). From the standpoint of Chicago's political and business elites, many youth of color are not only superfluous in the labor force but unwanted in a city designed to attract tourism and highly paid managers and technical workers. Regulating and disciplining these youth, concretely and symbolically, is central to producing a disciplined labor force and demonstrating control of those who are excluded from the economy and social life of the city. Chicago school policies cannot be fully understood without examining their relationship to the politics of regulating and controlling African American and Latino youth and their communities.

Military schools are one element of an ensemble of CPS policies that regulate, contain, and sort youth of color, excluding some while selecting others as exemplars of the positive effects of discipline. Since 1995, in addition to the two military high schools and one small military high

school academy, CPS has expanded military programs in neighborhood high schools and created military programs in middle schools. Each of the three military high schools has an enrollment of over 80 percent African Americans, with the remainder being Latinos. The schools are known for strict regimentation and adherence to the military code of discipline, including military-style punishments (push-ups, running laps, scrubbing school walls) for infractions of rules and failure to complete schoolwork. This reputation contributes to the representation of African American and Latino youth as in need of special control. Local media coverage has lauded the schools for bringing under control "dangerous" and "unruly" youth (Johnson 2002).

While youth in military schools are acculturated to a system of rules and authority, thousands of others like them are excluded from school through Zero Tolerance discipline policies, which require automatic suspension or expulsion for specific offenses, and the Safe Schools policy that segregates youth who have been involved in the criminal justice system. CPS data show that, under Zero Tolerance, suspensions increased dramatically and suspensions of African Americans increased disproportionately (Generation Y 2002; Michie 2000). Generation Y reported that, although enrollment in CPS increased by only 665 students between 1999 and 2000, suspensions increased from 21,000 to nearly 37,000, and the biggest increases were for students of color, especially African Americans. The organization's survey of high school students suggested that they are being suspended primarily for minor nonviolent infractions and attendance-related issues. A report produced in 2003, by the nonprofit service agency Hull House, noted that, since the 1995 Safe Schools Law took effect, expulsions have also increased dramatically, especially for African Americans, who have more than three times as many expulsions as Latinos or whites (Hull House 2003). These school-based policies are coupled with aggressive policing of African American and Latino youth in their communities (*Chicago Reporter* website, High Court Is the Final Chapter, 1998). Taken as a whole, this ensemble of policies works, concretely and symbolically, to criminalize youth of color. The policies become a public spectacle of the need for, and the efficacy of, bringing under control African American and Latino youth.

School probation, student retention, and the regimented basic-skills instruction and test-drill curricula that prevail in many low-scoring schools that serve African American and Latino students are another form of concrete and symbolic racialized control. Students in such schools are likely to experience curricula and instruction with fewer opportunities for critical thought and judgment and fewer opportunities to exercise intellectual and personal agency than in more affluent and white high-scoring schools (Lipman 2004; McNeil 2000). This is exemplified by the concentration of DI schools, ETCs, and test-driven probation schools in low-income African American and Latino communities.

School probation and other accountability measures also undermine African American and Latino community participation in school decisions. Although the 1995 School Reform Act diluted the power of LSCs overall, probation schools have lost most power, as outside probation managers contracted by the central office superseded their authority. In some cases, LSCs have been dissolved altogether. The pressure to raise test scores also determines much of the agenda of LSCs in schools in danger of being placed on probation. Renaissance 2010 further erodes LSCs. Thus, recentralization has concretely limited the democratic participation of low-income communities of color where these low-scoring and probation schools are located. Furthermore, the imposition of centralized control and external supervision marks these communities as incompetent to govern their children's schools.

School policies that contain and regulate African American and some Latino students cannot be separated from the history of racial discrimination in the city, but they also serve the interests of real estate developers, banks, and other sources of finance capital, and political elites who are promoting downtown development, gentrification, and Chicago's global-city ambitions. Thus, both concretely and sym-

bolically, school policies function to segregate, control, and displace youth and communities of color. Accountability measures discipline youth who are seen as dangerous in a city that brings together the new gentrifiers and those disenfranchised, displaced, and pushed to the bottom of the new economy. Symbolically, these policies help secure the new urban professionals' claims on urban space much as do the electronic security systems, gated housing, and private security forces that characterize upscale neighborhoods. As public housing is torn down and its residents dispersed to make way for expensive new townhouses and condominiums, the putative need for militarized schooling for African American youth justifies the segregation and removal of their communities, much as the vocabulary of the "urban frontier" justifies gentrification and displacement of working-class residents and people of color in the name of "civilizing" urban neighborhoods (Smith 1996). The historical failure to provide necessary resources and conditions to educate low-income African American students in Chicago (Orfield 1990), when linked with accountability policies that label schools as "failures," also produces the rationale for closing schools, displacing residents, and gentrifying low-income areas.

Saskia Sassen (1998) argues that, "The global city is a strategic site for disempowered actors because it enables them to gain presence, to emerge as subjects, even when they do not gain direct power" (xxi). The urban context is a critical terrain for struggles over power, identity, and the claim to space. This social dynamic is central to understanding educational policies and processes that discipline, demonize, criminalize, and exclude low-income urban youth of color and their communities. These policies also signify that those running the city are taking it back as a space of middle-class social stability and whiteness from dangerous "others" (Haymes 1995; Lipman 2003), especially African American youth. Thus, school policies contribute to the appropriation of working-class neighborhoods as new gentrified spaces and to securing downtown Chicago and its environs as a glamour zone of tourism and upscale cultural venues, leisure spots, and housing.

CONCLUSION

Chicago's school reforms are intertwined with social and economic policies that generate economic and racial inequality, spatial dislocation, and marginalization alongside wealth and opportunity. The dualization of the schools parallels the dualization of the city. Going further, one could argue that recent education reforms are a strategic element in reshaping the city as a global city. School accountability policies are central to the production and certification of a disciplined, highly stratified labor force and key to the attraction of new investment. Fixing Chicago's schools is a key element in attracting both highly paid professionals and guaranteeing a literate and disciplined low-wage workforce comprised of large numbers of immigrants. While there are more selective educational schools and programs for a small number of students, the vast majority, primarily immigrants and students of color, attend schools organized around a basic curriculum that is likely to prepare them primarily for the growing sector of low-wage jobs.

The political economy of the 1995 Chicago School Reform is also intertwined with the cultural politics of race in the city. Selective schools advantage middle- and upper-middle-class, primarily white, students while projecting an image of expanding opportunities systemwide. At the same time, in the name of equity and school improvement, Chicago's reforms concretely and symbolically discipline African American and Latino youth, who are seen as either potential members of the low-wage work force or a surplus population in Chicago's restructured, informational economy. Regimented curricula and instruction, military schools, and the regime of high-stakes testing are part of a process of preparing and certifying a disciplined workforce as well as sorting out those who are no longer needed. These policies are also part of the cultural politics of global city development, directed at controlling or displacing a population seen as threatening to the cultural appropriation of the city as a center of tourism, upscale leisure, and corporate headquarters. Thus, education is another terrain in the struggle over who is fully included in the new Chicago and who will benefit from its renewed economy and reconstruction as a global city.

More concretely, the reform is explicitly designed to attract the middle class to the city. New, academically challenging schools and programs are important to gentrification. And the success of Chicago as a global city is linked to attracting the producer services and corporate and financial headquarters that are at the center of the global economy. Becoming a global city also depends on developing a first-rate cultural, leisure, and arts scene for middle-class consumption and tourism. For the professionals and managers whose work is at the core of these functions, excellent schools for their children—as measured by test scores and quality programs—are essential. Thus, Chicago's school reform is an essential component of remaking the city economically, spatially, and culturally, and it is an important factor in its intensified racial and social inequality and divisions.

NOTES

1. In its last year of operation, 2002–03, not enough applications were generated to run the school as a selective magnet. This was in sharp contrast to the other regional magnets, in which the application process is extremely competitive. The school opened in 2005 with 115 students.

2. A participating program is certified to offer an International Baccalaureate Diploma.

David Plebanski and Roberta Garner

21 Police and the Globalizing City: Innovation and Contested Reinvention

IN 1960, on a cold January morning in a shabby North Side neighborhood, police arrested 23-year-old Richard Morrison, soon to be labeled the "babbling burglar." In his 77-page confession, the small-time crook implicated eight Summerdale police district officers in a burglary and fencing racket. In a vigorous effort at damage control, Mayor Richard J. Daley appointed a new police chief with academic as well as experiential credentials—O. W. Wilson—to launch a major reform of the Chicago Police Department (CPD). Not only were hundreds of police officers suspended, but a general process of structural and technological modernization began (Cohen and Taylor 2000, 252–55; Bopp 1977). In the year of John F. Kennedy's election, O. W. Wilson's appointment signaled impending changes in police work, in Chicago and the nation. Unsophisticated local police forces composed of meagerly educated white men, operating within insulated cultures, were transformed by professionalization, diversification, academic discourse, and managerial efficiency.

Managerialism, as a form of authority, was a major facet of these reforms. It includes depoliticized administrative decision making; discourses of professionalism and expertise; reduced influence for traditional, local power-holders such as aldermen, precinct captains, and ward bosses; and the rejection or marginalization of grassroots initiatives. Managerialism is a strategy with two fronts, opposing both archaic, machine-controlled local centers of power and grassroots citizen movements. Managerial discourses emphasize that decision making should be "above politics," in contrast to these two other forms of authority. Managerial authority thus can be interpreted in different ways—as cleaner, fairer, more modern, more efficient, more knowledge-based, and less racist than old style politics or, alternatively, as anti-democratic and anti-grassroots.

SECTION I: REFORM, INNOVATION, AND MANAGERIALISM

Innovation in policing moved along five tracks: professionalization; racial–ethnic and gender diversification; technological development; improved accountability; and a new proactive and interactive relationship to communities. Changes in the CPD paralleled and were influenced by similar changes in other large-city police departments, reflecting underlying national economic, social, and political forces. The CPD was propelled toward managerialism and community policing, not only by decisions made within the CPD and city government, but also by grassroots activists, the media, and national stakeholders in law enforcement, such as federal agencies and academics. The outcomes in institutional forms and practices are the net result of these contending forces.

Five Elements of Change

Professionalization is a key element of police evolution, subsuming many of the other elements. A major component of professionalization is a higher education requirement, transforming policing from a blue-collar job into a salaried profession, similar to nursing or teaching. In 1965, not even a high school diploma was required for applicants; today, 60 college credits are needed for the application, with an exception made for applicants with armed services experience. A four-year college degree is required for promotion to lieutenant or captain. Another component of professionalization is release of sworn police personnel from support functions, such as lock-up keepers, auto pound personnel, and 911 operators, positions now privatized or staffed by civilians. Professionalization requires the longer training of police officers and new skills and sensibilities, such as attention to cultural diversity, sensitivity training, conflict resolution instruction, and ethical practice.

Professionalization is ambiguous in policing, as it is in most occupations that became professionalized in recent decades. Professionalization has many meanings, including more theoretical training, self-regulation, independence from politics and particularistic ties, merit-based appointment, working conditions akin to those of salaried workers, adherence to standardized and bureaucratically imposed "best practices," new patterns of recruitment, and (in the specific case of policing) less use of "man-to-man" force in favor of sophisticated technology. These meanings can be points of contention; they are not always consistent with each other and represent agendas pursued by competing stakeholders. For example, both self-regulation and standardized "best practices" are elements of professionalization, but reflect different interests within an organization.

Diversification has come to the police department with some difficulty. An especially contentious area of change, diversification took place largely through federal pressure and draconian affirmative action policies, notably a prolonged hiring freeze for white males. Although diversification was the result of contestation, collective action, and federal pressure, local elites also contributed to it as part of the institutional restructuring that brought minorities into the mainstream of city governance during both the Harold Washington and Richard M. Daley administrations. In 1965, Chicago police officers were uniformly white; by the beginning of the century, 26 percent were African American and

13 percent were Latino. Four of the last five recent superintendents (mayoral appointees) were Latino or African American. Women served only as youth officers or prison matrons in 1963; now, 22 percent of the CPD are women police officers. Gays and lesbians are being recruited as officers.

Technological change progressed from Wilson's communication center (a forerunner of the 911 system) to increasing levels of computerization and recent advances in forensics, such as DNA testing and laser prints. An ultra-modern 911 communication center and an automated fingerprint indexing center are in operation. A crime mapping system enables police to portray data clearly and reveals high-profile "hot spots," to focus action quickly and efficiently. The department has installed mobile data computers in patrol cars.

Police accountability, a sensitive point of police–community relations, progressed toward the establishment of multiple offices and procedures to enforce professional standards. The Chicago Police Board began in 1960, after the Summerdale scandal. It is appointed by the mayor, reviews discipline cases, and makes final decisions on suspensions and firings. It proposes candidates for police superintendant to the mayor. The Office of Professional Standards, formed in 1974, hears all excessive-force complaints against police officers, as well as domestic violence cases involving police officers. The Internal Affairs Division handles other types of cases, such as drug abuse. At the level of routine operations, command personnel are now held accountable for explaining criminal activity in their respective areas through department-accountability hearings that are organized by the Office of Strategy and Accountability and patterned on New York City's program.

The relationship to the community was transformed by organizational changes and new philosophies of policing, especially the idea that policing is crime prevention more than crime solving. Community policing and a new model of police–community cooperation accompany this proactive perspective. Wilson's administration addressed police corruption by removing cops from the street and putting them in squad cars to reduce opportunities for illicit contacts. That thinking has come full circle—as communities themselves changed—and police are back in the community, walking beats and talking to residents and merchants as part of the Chicago Alternative Policing Strategy (CAPS), which focuses on crime prevention and the re-solving of local problems and incivilities before they grow into crimes. In this respect Chicago is like other U.S. cities, almost all of which adopted community policing strategies by the 1990s, impelled by a combination of forces—federal support, grassroots pressures, and the challenge of new types of crime (drug gangs and crack). In Chicago, pressures for commu-nity policing came from a variety of sources with distinct ideologies of community policing, and the outcome reflects a shifting balance of forces, tilting away from community activists to more managerial styles of community policing, as we will trace in our case study of community policing.

The cautious term "evolution" suggests that the CPD has become a more complex orga-nization, with better-educated officers, organi-zational and technological sophistication, and greater responsiveness to social issues, academic criminology, and developments in other police departments. It now participates in a national discussion of standards and practices. In an ap-parent paradox, as the CPD becomes more or-ganizationally self-aware, more reflective about the role of police in society, and more sophis-ticated in understanding social problems, it is more strongly shaped by external forces; in fact, it is perhaps precisely because of the external forces that the CPD has become more self-aware.

Change in police departments results from both local and national forces. Each city has its own characteristic power structure, patterns of institutional action, and grassroots activism that result in different details of that change but, ul-timately, all are influenced by uniform national trends that push them in similar directions (Kerr 2001, 78).

In Chicago, change continues to be instituted primarily by the mayor and mayoral staff. Un-derstanding change in the CPD requires trac-ing change in mayors, their policies, ideologies, and management styles (Chapter 4), as well as the role of the superintendant of police. Collec-tive actors, such as the business community and

grassroots organizations, are less powerful forces for change here than they are in other cities.

Among institutional and organizational actors, change results from a complex interplay of public missions and private agendas and ide-ologies; this interplay has both intended and unintended consequences within the structural limits. Reinventors include progressive profes-sionals within the institution, managerially ori-ented administrators, and a range of grassroots activists, mostly outside the institution, but sometimes linked to internal groups. Change can be a profoundly conservative choice when it results from efforts to maintain the overall structure and functioning of an institution by making a series of adjustments to a changing environment.

The Forces: Demographics, Markets, and Crime Patterns

Macro-level, structural forces of change trans-formed neighborhoods, affected crime rates, generated new kinds of crime, and created new public stakeholders in most American cities (Soja 1996). After the 1950s, Chicago changed from an industrial city of segregated racial and ethnic enclaves into a deindustrializing, racially divided city, and then gradually be-came a globalizing and gentrifying city. These phases of economic change were accompanied by distinct patterns of race relations, crime, public sector resources, and police–community relations.

The Civil Rights Era: 1960s to 1980s. Racial polarization and civil rights struggles height-ened pressure to diversify the department and ease tension in police–community relations. Key events during this period show how policing was a focal point and "condensation issue" for the Civil Rights movement. These events included the ambivalent role of police in protecting the 1966 open housing marches led by Dr. Martin Luther King, Jr.; escalating police–community tensions, revealed in the devastating West Madi-son Street riots after Dr. King's assassination in 1968; and responses to unwarranted arrests of middle-class African Americans during the early 1970s. The arrests (one of a dentist who had suffered a stroke at the wheel) contributed to Congressman Ralph Metcalfe's break with the Daley Machine and the formation of the Afro American Patrolmen's League, a group representing a black perspective within the department.

Racial divisions were also expressed in competition for public-sector jobs. African Americans challenged the white monopoly of policing. Patterns of hiring and promotion were changed through federal cases, most notably Judge Prentice Marshall's 1974 decision that the police eligibility examination was discriminatory and that racial diversification had to take place in the CPD. The decision was upheld in 1977, in the federal appellate courts.

Deindustrialization and Neighborhood Deterioration. After stagflation in the 1970s, decline of the Civil Rights movement, and the onset of Reaganomics, the deterioration of deindustrializing neighborhoods precipitated new types of crime—mostly engendered by large, violent drug gangs—that forced police to change practices in many U.S. cities. The nationwide community policing movement was in part a response to the effect of crack and drug gangs. Locally, it involved both grassroots organizations (Chicago Alliance for Neighborhood Safety) and police department innovation (CAPS).

The Postmodern City. Globalization, gentrification, and new class and racial disparities create challenges for policing. With the closing of Chicago Housing Authority public-housing units and gentrification in housing markets, lower-income residents, many of them African Americans, were displaced from the core of the city and replaced by an influx of middle-class residents with high expectations for public safety and security. In the postmodern era, racial disparities remained intertwined with class disadvantage and were dispersed into issues such as excessive and deadly force, the death penalty, removal of the homeless from the central city, and differential enforcement of drug laws. Race has not lost its significance, and the emergent hourglass social structure is extensively racialized; these disparities surface in racially charged but officially colorblind issues that involve policing.

Other Macro-Level Trends Affect Policing. The city's age structure changed, so there are fewer residents in crime-prone age brackets. Raising educational qualifications was not simply a CPD decision, but reflected the rise of credentialism throughout middle-level labor markets.

The Players: Feds, Social Movements, Media, and Criminal Justice Experts

External and internal stakeholders interacted within this larger structural framework to produce contested change. Federal policies stimulated grassroots activism and encouraged local social movements. Activists tried to push media toward more critical coverage of policing issues. Innovators in police departments and their academic allies envisioned new practices and encouraged experimentation.

The Federal Government. The federal government is increasingly a source of resources, regulation, legislation, and broad social policies that affect urban police departments. During the Nixon era, Law Enforcement Assistance Act (LEAA) funding encouraged technological innovation and provided resources for community policing as a grassroots initiative in Chicago (Friedman 2002). Federal affirmative action policies and court decisions radically altered police hiring practices, beginning with the rulings of the mid 1970s. During the late 1970s and 1980s, federal revenue sharing ended; the dismantling of the LEAA and cuts in criminal justice block grants downsized policing resources, while deindustrialization devastated working-class neighborhoods and crack gangs emerged. However, the 1994 Violent Crime Control and Law Enforcement Act distributed funds for the hiring of new officers and encouraged community-oriented policing, thus reinforcing the CPD's decision to move in this direction and providing funds for doing so. Chicago used $70 million in federal funds to pay for 1,100 new officers, in keeping with national trends among police departments in cities over 100,000, half of which developed neighborhood-oriented policies by 1991 and the remainder by 1997 (Skogan et al. 1999, 19–21).

The Social Movement Sector. Non- and partially institutionalized collective actors impact policing. The Civil Rights movement and Black Power groups repeatedly targeted police as a major element in white supremacy. Successor movements to the Civil Rights movement and community-based organizations have made police brutality a focus of collective action. In 1999, Amnesty International drew international attention to coerced confessions, especially in death-penalty cases, and called for stronger civilian oversight of police. External movements also link to activists within the department. During the 1970s, the Afro American Patrolmen's League, under the leadership of Renault Robinson, called for changes in hiring and promotion, coinciding with federal pressures and the activities of civil rights organizations. Police unionization had many characteristics of a social movement within the CPD and led to the recognition of the Fraternal Order of Police as the bargaining agent during Jane Byrne's mayorship. Community activists had a role in launching community policing, as discussed later.

The Media. The media's role in police reform is ambiguous. The media's self-defined role as watchdogs leads them to call for reform, but reporters' reliance on good relationships with police sources constrains criticism. Because the media and many reporters share elite assumptions about city life and favor a gentrified and globalized vision of the city, they are unlikely to question policing as a whole, as long as it is reasonably effective. The media generally support managerialism, and the modernized and apparently depoliticized functioning of the department. Reporters are most likely to expose corrupt behavior by individual police officers, less likely to examine systemic problems, and unlikely to ask broad theoretical questions about the functions of policing in a globalizing and gentrifying city.

Yet, the media accelerated the trend to community policing and more recently began to scrutinize issues such as coerced confessions, specifically in the case of Jon Burge. They helped to shift this story from activists' cause to public issue and contributed to support for Burge's firing and a federal civil suit against him. The *Chicago Tribune* called for opening the records of Chicago Police Board suspension hearings and included the topic of coerced confessions in the series criticizing the death penalty (Anderson 1999; Mills and Armstrong 1999). Critical media coverage of excessive- and deadly force incidents led the CPD to institute new practices, such as videotaping homicide confessions (and homicide interrogations, starting in June, 2005) and the use of tasers (a practice that is itself controversial).

In short, media coverage has ambiguous effects. It can converge with the critical perspectives of activists, but more consistently its net effect is support for professionalization and accountability within a managerial framework.

The Criminal Justice Field: Networking among Police Departments, Academics, and Consultants. Innovations in the criminal justice field contributed to reform in policing. Chicago was influenced by early experiments in community policing in Baltimore County (1981) and Newport News, Virginia (1984), and further innovations in Newark, Boston, and New York. By 1997, every large city had a neighborhood-oriented policy. The sharing of ideas and techniques among police departments is accelerating as police chiefs attend national conferences, network with each other, and share the latest trends and ideas about standards and best practices. Academic and think-tank research on crime and policing also influences urban police departments. Notable examples are the role of Lee Brown, former police chief in both Atlanta and Houston, in advocating police–community partnerships (Friedman 2002), and the intense effect of James Q. Wilson and George Kelling's essay, "The Police and Neighborhood Safety: Broken Windows" in the March 1982 issue of *The Atlantic*. The Rutgers University Safer Cities Initiative brought together police, faith-based groups, criminal justice agencies, social-service providers, and community-based organizations, thus exemplifying the growing national role of universities. Northwestern University and the University of Illinois–Chicago (UIC) evaluated aspects of community policing initiatives, and UIC contributed to a crime-mapping project. In Chicago-area schools of law and journalism, students have engaged in advocacy on behalf of prisoners, especially death-row inmates, bringing about changes in interrogation, such as videotaping of homicide confessions, and the improved use of DNA evidence.

Forces of Conservatism: Police Culture and Chicago Culture

Both police culture and Chicago culture have elements of pragmatic conservatism—resistance against change—that slow down innovation in policing, whether reform is advocated by proponents of managerial reform or by grassroots movements. Pragmatic conservatism not only works against grassroots activism, it also insulates the CPD against extreme innovations, such as the "occupying army" model of the high-technology, low police-to-citizen ratio that characterizes the Los Angeles Police Department (Davis 1988) and the zero-tolerance model of the Giuliani-era New York Police Department (Skogan et al. 1999, 9). Chicago maintains a high police-to-citizen ratio; even at its lower points during the lean 1980s, the ratio was about 4:1,000, compared to New York's 3.4:1,000, and L.A.'s 2.3:1,000 ratios (Rivlin 1992, 280–81). When Harold Washington attempted to cut the force by 500 uniformed officers, opposition in City Council forced him to actually increase it by 500 to 12,500 (Mier and Moe 1991). Chicago's relatively conservative approach to change may also explain why the CPD was "in the middle of the pack" nationally in instituting community policing, neither an early innovator nor a laggard.

SECTION II: COMMUNITY POLICING: A CASE STUDY OF CONTESTED REINVENTION

The institutionalization of community policing illustrates the effect of the many forces discussed so far, the process of contested reinvention in Chicago, and the powerful momentum toward managerial outcomes (Friedman 2002).

Multiple Origins

In the first phase, national actors and grassroots organizations played an important role. The last initiative of the LEAA was the Urban Crime Prevention Program, which offered competitive grants to cities to promote public safety. In Chicago, the Citizens Information Service, a civic organization that had spun off from the League of Women Voters, obtained a grant for a community-based proposal to develop Block Watch Organizing, one of the UCCP options. Block Watch Organizing focused on door-to-door efforts to encourage neighbors to look out for one another. CIS remained fiscal agent for the grant, coordinated the efforts of nine community-based projects, and provided training and technical assistance to community groups. Activists with community-organizing experience in VISTA and other organizations were hired to work with Alinsky-style neighborhood councils and give structure to the block watch organizing by developing phone trees, electing block captains, and holding meetings. About 1,500 block watches were formed. This organizing activity built on and rechanneled existing grassroots concerns about unsatisfactory responses to 911 calls. When federal money ran out, the Ford Foundation provided three years of decreasing funding, and the umbrella structure eventually took the name Chicago Alliance for Neighborhood Safety (CANS).

Meanwhile, ideas about community policing began to circulate nationally in the criminal justice field, influenced by Lee Brown, and by the writing of Wilson and Kelling. These ideas influenced innovators within the CPD as well as community activists. As early as 1984, Mayor Washington had already experimented with a Mayor's Task Force on Youth Crime Prevention after the killing of a high school basketball player. Street intervention workers, victim assistance, youth services, and neighborhood watches were components of this early effort to decentralize crime prevention. The Chicago Intervention Network, with nine neighborhood advisory committees, emerged at the grassroots level of this process (Walker 1991, 161).

In short, during the first phase, national institutional actors had a strong influence on local innovation. These national forces included the federal government, police officers, academic criminologists, and civic organizations in tune with national trends and resources. "An idea whose time has come" as a response to objective structural problems often emerges as multiple, converging initiatives (Freeman 1983).

Converging Action: Implementation

The second phase was more locally driven. Its core dynamic was interaction between community activists and progressive forces within the CPD, but the outcome of this interaction was propelled by the mayor, media, and external institutional forces. This phase took place against the background of a growing homicide rate during the late 1980s and early 1990s. A pilot project proposal was written by a community policing task force, organized by CANS in cooperation with the CPD. When CANS activists felt that Superintendant Leroy Martin was stalling in his response to the pilot-project proposal, they appealed to the media. Their press conference was well attended, and journalists promptly asked Mayor Richard M. Daley whether he supported the proposal's recommendation for community policing. Daley was newly elected, eager to find concerns that would unite white and African American communities, and dismayed by the exceptionally high homicide rate. Because the report came from racially diverse community-based groups, he welcomed it as a project that could bring the city together. He was also aware of growing support for community policing among members of the city council.

The next step was to develop a specific plan formulated by criminal justice consultants. After community and task-force pressure and negotiation, the plan included CPD training for officers, a contract with CANS for training community members, and an evaluation study by Northwestern University.

The implementation phase of the process was characterized by local realization of the community-policing project under pressure from the mayor and local media. Contested, but ultimately convergent, negotiations took place within the CPD, between the CPD and the community activists, and among the CPD, activists, and external criminal justice professionals. The mayor's decision was shaped by media attention, high homicide rates, and his strategy for building coalitions across racial lines—by the larger structures of media, race relations, and crime patterns.

Institutionalization and a Parting of the Ways

The third phase, institutionalization, followed the peak moment of activism and enthusiasm for training, when over 10,000 citizens were involved. Institutionalization was marked by growing divergence of CAPS and CANS, a story told in several versions. CANS activists believe that the CPD preferred a police-centered structure to an equal partnership with community activists. From the activist point of view, both aldermen and the mayor thought that community policing competed with the ward organizations and therefore they tried to limit its participatory potential. On the other hand, CANS activists themselves were divided over the basic meaning and purpose of their activism. Some saw neighborhood safety as the basic issue and were satisfied as long as CAPS reduced crime; others had become community-policing activists because they believed that only fundamental change in police behavior could restore police–community trust. For the latter, activism in community policing meant focusing on excessive force and police disrespect, a position far from the CPD's view of reform. This wing of activists eventually compiled and circulated a report, "The Social Cost of Disrespect," based on a survey of 900 high school students. The mayor was incensed by the report, which concluded there was widespread dissatisfaction among youth because of many unpleasant experiences with police. These tensions precipitated disengagement of CANS from community policing, and CANS eventually lost the training contract. The outcome in Chicago was participatory and effective compared with many other large cities, but it was not the equal community–CPD partnership envisioned in the early stages (Skogan et al. 1999).

A familiar pattern of institutionalization marked the final phase. Grassroots organizations end up believing that they face an inevitable dilemma between co-optation and oppositional marginalization (Garner 1977). They feel forced to choose between accepting the limits of reform defined by institutional actors or expanding pressure for reforms at the risk of losing their institutional ties. The Alinsky model and the civil-rights experiences of Chicago community organizations may have hastened the break with institutional partners (see Chapter 19).

OLD PROBLEMS, NEW CHALLENGES

Various types of issues persist, often associated with links between race and class in postmodern cities: explicit racial tensions, issues of deadly and excessive force and accountability that often have a racial dimension, and ongoing concerns about community policing. These kinds of issues can become "condensation points" for tensions along both racial and class lines, with the racial dimension often being more visible.

Problems Explicitly Associated with Racial Tensions

Despite explicit directives, charges of racial profiling persist, as does litigation concerning racial discrimination in promotion and rank decisions.

Problems of Deadly Force, Excessive Force, Police Brutality, and Accountability. These issues become condensation issues for tensions between police and communities; often there are racial aspects to these tensions, but as the CPD has diversified and improved relations with African American and Latino communities, not every case is clearly polarized along racial lines. The removal of homeless people from downtown locations and a number of cases of excessive and deadly force are interpreted as racial incidents, reflecting the complex intertwining of race and class in postmodern societies.

The Meaning of Community Policing. The success of community policing depends on both community capacity and the quality of planning and implementation by police at the beat level, where sergeants have key responsibilities. Community capacity and beat-level implementation are not related to each other in a simple or direct way (Skogan et al. 1999). When a well-designed and executed beat plan is in effect, it is likely to work best in communities characterized by affluence and homogeneity. These characteristics foster trust in neighbors, density of community organizations, and an ability to focus political pressure on community problems. Poor communities and racially or class divided ones are weaker candidates for good community policing outcomes (Skogan et al. 1999, 224–26). Regardless of the race of residents, communities with more homeowners, higher-income households, and married and two-parent families are likely to have higher levels of participation, more satisfaction with the process, and better outcomes. These findings point to larger ideological issues concerning the meaning of "community." Who speaks for a community? What organizations represent it and where are its boundaries? Is community policing a code word for empowering gentrifiers and middle-class residents, while marginalizing or displacing the poor (Lyons 1999)? These findings and questions do not negate the value of community policing, but suggest subtleties in its evaluation.

The Suburbs: Evolutionary Lag

The suburbs show a marked evolutionary lag compared to Chicago. They are more class and racially segregated, with relatively weaker forces pressing for diversity and improved racial and ethnic relations. Many have large disparities between the proportion of a racial–ethnic category in the population and its representation on the police force: for example, during the late 1990s, Calumet Park, Matteson, and Robbins, Illinois were among suburbs with substantially higher percentages of African Americans in the population than on the police forces. This same situation was true regarding Latinos in Cicero, Summit, Stone Park, and Melrose Park (Gordon 1998a). Suburban communities are more likely than the central city to have racial profiling problems and engage in the restrictive monitoring of minority youth, who are seen as potential gang elements.

Suburban police departments with the highest crime rates have the least resources, reflecting the gradient of suburban affluence (Chapter 5). In south-suburban Robbins, a community with one of the lowest median incomes in the region, starting pay for police was $18,800 in 1998, at a time when it was $33,522 in Chicago and $40,526 in affluent, North Shore Wilmette (Gordon 1998a, 7).

Suburban problems may increase in the next decade as the gentrifying central city pushes poor people into the neediest suburban areas, a process that is accelerating with the closing of CHA buildings.

IMPENDING GLOBAL CHALLENGES

From 1960 to 2000, local policing was increasingly integrated into national structures, but now the CPD is being drawn into transnational issues and practices. In Chapter 2, we noted that the globalization of Chicago has indirectly affected the police department because revalorization of the central business district and its surrounding gentrified areas has shifted police functions toward crime prevention and safeguarding spaces of business and tourism. These shifts have coincided with professionalization and managerialism.

Direct engagement with globalization is still in an early stage and may take several forms, including global conversations about policing in multicultural societies (Chan 1997). Policing in multicultural societies requires diversity as a criterion of police recruitment and a willingness to involve police in reducing inter-ethnic tension, such as that between Korean American business owners and African American community residents in U.S. cities.

A second area in which the global system affects local policing is international crime and transnational criminal organizations. Drugs are already a major transnational commodity, and when a car disappears from Michigan Avenue it may rematerialize in St. Petersburg, Russia. Human beings are also transnational commodities, and city police may be drawn into the interdiction of trafficking in illegal immigrants, who are forced into underground urban enterprises, such as sweatshops and prostitution networks (Conroy 2002).

Social movements and collective action in a global arena are a third transnational policing matter. Police are affected by global movements that scrutinize criminal justice, for example, Amnesty International and the western European movement against the death penalty. Transnational human rights movements and their conscience constituencies amplify the voice of local activists and can force innovations in police accountability and practices. The politicization of policing functions in a global political economy works against movements as well, as signaled by the deployment of Chicago officers to Washington D.C. to help control protestors during a World Bank/IMF meeting in September, 2002, and to provide security for George W. Bush's inauguration in January, 2005.

After the terrorist attacks of September 11, 2001, police are expected to combat violent transnational movements and participate in national security efforts. Yet many departments currently lack the resources and expertise needed to fight terrorism effectively.

CONCLUSION

Policing in the Chicago area changed relatively slowly. It is important not to get carried away by visions of globalization and sci-fi "Robocop" imagery when discussing policing in the new Chicago. The new and old are inextricably linked and layered, creating ambiguity in interpreting change. We can emphasize new features of policing—protecting the work and leisure zones of the global city, managerialism and professionalization, high-tech innovations, and community policing. Or, we can emphasize continuities—the persistence of racial tensions, on-the-ground realities and routines of police work, continued power of the mayor vis-a-vis the department, and the longstanding priorities of securing the central business district and middle-class neighborhoods.

Policing still bears a strong stamp of Chicago's industrial past. Racial issues continue to surface

268 David Plebanski and Roberta Garner

in the public perception of police practices, and the multiplicity of immigrant groups has not yet had a strong effect on policing. New coalitions and a managerial ideology influence the CPD as well as the mayor's choices in police appointments and policies, but the underlying structure remains hierarchical. Managerialism and professionalization have been integrated with older patterns of hierarchical authority and the powerful role of the mayor.

Globalization is a recent force, and its direct effects are not yet clearly discernible. The effect of national trends is more evident. These have reached Chicago through federal law enforcement agencies, academics, and the national networking of police administrators, and their effect definitely moves policing in a managerial and professionalized direction.

Changes in policing are associated with the function of securing the downtown and central-city neighborhoods as areas of consumption and gentrification—a zone of work and leisure for the global city. But safeguarding high-value areas is not a new policing function at all, since the downtown has historically been a high-rent area in need of protection against crime. What is new is that the area around the downtown, the sketchy "zone of transition," has now become revalorized, gentrified, and included in the zone to be safeguarded.

Larry Bennett

22 Transforming Public Housing

DURING THE GLORY days of Richard J. Daley's mayoralty, his admirers characterized Chicago as "the city that works." The expression carried a double meaning. As late as the mid 1960s Chicago's economic might and reputation for sustaining a well-tended social fabric remained unquestioned propositions. And, more pragmatically, Chicago's municipal government was presumed to provide basic services—garbage collection, street cleaning, and the like—of a quality that was unmatched by other American metropolises.

Political scientist Ester Fuchs (1992, 200), in her analysis of fiscal politics in New York City and Chicago, *Mayors and Money*, offers this observation regarding political leadership and governmental structure in Chicago: "Chicago mayors . . . effectively remove special district services from citywide policy debates, politically isolating their constituencies. Political accountability is weak in this type of system, but fiscal control is enhanced because interest groups simply have less influence over the budget." By the 1970s, Richard J. Daley's stewardship of municipal finances was aided immeasurably by the fact of local jurisdictional fragmentation. Chicago's public schools were overseen by an appointed Board of Education and superintendent, who managed a budget separate from the city government's and derived from independent taxing authority. Similar arrangements also structured the operations of the city's mass transit system, the Chicago Transit Authority (CTA), as well as its huge public housing program, administered by the Chicago Housing Authority (CHA).

At the end of the Richard J. Daley era, Chicago—"the city that works"—with the possible exception of the municipal government, was empty rhetoric. The city's public schools were racially segregated and on the brink of financial crisis. The CTA was the proprietor of a badly decayed transportation infrastructure and capable of providing, at best, erratic service. But of these three independent agencies providing crucial city services, the CHA's circumstances were the most harrowing. Extreme racial segregation was the order of the day in developments such as the Cabrini-Green, Henry Horner, and Robert Taylor Homes, and across the CHA's properties, buildings and grounds were starved of basic maintenance expenditures. For Richard J. Daley's successors, the CHA's state of affairs produced a striking political paradox. Conditions at CHA developments were too inhumane to be ignored, but for any public official possessing a grain of career ambition, wading into the CHA mess looked like a shortcut to political retirement.

Since the late 1980s, the CHA has experienced a kaleidoscopic sequence of policy realignments. In part, these have reflected the sheer scale of the policy challenge involved in bringing CHA housing back to reasonable standards of habitability. But in addition, as a new national policy consensus has emerged with regard to New Deal-era initiatives such as welfare and public housing, and as Chicago's municipal and civic leadership has worked to recast the city's position in the global economy, transforming the CHA has become a key element in forging a new Chicago.

FROM PROGRESSIVE SOCIAL ENGINEERING TO HYPER-SEGREGATION

The Chicago Housing Authority was the product of state legislation passed in response to Congressional authorization of the public housing program in 1937 (Hirsch 1983). During its first decade the CHA built residential developments in various sections of Chicago, while also taking over the management of a few complexes that had been previously built by the federal Public Works Administration (Bowly 1978, 17–54). During this period, many CHA apartments were occupied by the families of workers engaged in war-related production.

The CHA was headed by Elizabeth Wood, a social progressive who supported the racial integration of the agency's properties. At the grassroots level, this policy encountered stiff resistance—and occasionally, physical violence—from the white population of residential areas adjoining CHA developments (Hirsch 1983). By the end of the 1940s, public esteem for the CHA had dropped to the point that, when the Illinois General Assembly drafted legislation to enable local implementation of the 1949 federal urban redevelopment legislation, the CHA was bypassed as the local governmental entity in charge of this new program. Elizabeth Wood was removed as CHA executive director in 1954, and the CHA's new leadership reached an accommodation with the Chicago City Council permitting individual aldermen to block the siting of public housing within their wards. From the mid 1950s until the mid 1960s, the CHA embarked on a mammoth building program, with nearly all of its construction in African American neighborhoods on the city's South and West Sides. By the late 1960s, the population of the CHA's "family developments" (multiple-bedroom apartment complexes) was almost entirely African American.

In 1966, a group of African American public-housing residents sued the CHA for using project siting and tenant selection procedures intended to segregate its largely minority residential population. Three years later, U.S. District Court Judge Richard Austin ruled in favor of the *Gautreaux* plaintiffs, directing the CHA to target areas away from the segregated South and West Sides for new public housing (Biles 1995, 171–73). The CHA's response was to stop building public housing. A subsequent ruling in the *Gautreaux* proceedings yielded the Gautreaux Assisted Housing Program, an effort to relocate public housing-eligible families, via Section 8 vouchers, to outlying city and suburban communities. The Gautreaux Assisted Housing Program was managed by a nonprofit organization with no direct ties to the CHA (Rubinowitz and Rosenbaum 2000). For its part, the CHA moved so slowly in building scattered-site public housing, another *Gautreaux* mandate, that during the 1980s a judicially appointed private "receiver" took over the construction of small public housing developments across the city (Henderson 1994).

Apart from the CHA's use as a tool in the campaign to maintain Chicago's residential color line, the agency's internal operating capacity was also compromised. The CHA's inability to adequately maintain its properties derived, in part, from the approach to project development adopted during the 1950s. Facing widespread resistance to public housing, and seeking to acquire land cheaply and build rapidly, the CHA concentrated large numbers of apartments in individual developments (for example, at Robert Taylor Homes, 4,415 residential units), typically in high-rise structures. By the mid 1960s, the CHA estimated that 20,000 children lived at Robert Taylor Homes, a number that simply overwhelmed the development's physical infrastructure:

> Elevators, stairwells, lobbies, hallways, parking lots and alleyways, garbage cans, and laundry rooms became veritable playgrounds. Each possessed a particular set of hazards, which could add to their enjoyment. Parking lots were strewn with broken glass . . . hallways and stairwells were the domain of gamblers and drinkers. (Venkatesh 2002, 24–25)

Once the agency began to experience fiscal pressure during the early 1970s, it never again was able even to begin to address the physical deterioration of its properties. And, as the foregoing description also reveals, substantial resident disorder, in turn, was becoming a fact of public housing life in Chicago.

The CHA became a pariah bureaucracy. Deindustrialization swept Chicago's South and West Sides, eliminating many thousands of jobs and accelerating the impoverishment of public housing residents. For both newly unemployed adults and teenagers without mainstream economic prospects, the allure of the underground economy was substantial. Violent lawlessness caused by the burgeoning drug trade further undermined the quality of life in various developments. At Cabrini-Green on Chicago's North Side, the embattled residents were convinced that police officers simply pulled out, calculating that crime control was most readily achieved by allowing competing gangs to kill one another off (Bogira 1986).

One of the most bizarre incidents in CHA history occurred in March 1981, when Mayor Jane Byrne—accompanied by a battalion of journalists—briefly settled in an apartment at Cabrini-Green. Byrne, whose upset election in 1979 had been fueled by African American voter discontent, claimed that she was trying to bring attention to the plight of public housing residents. Most political observers offered a less generous assessment, perceiving the media-conscious mayor's actions as a desperate effort to win back the support of a constituency discomfited by her pattern of deal making with the entrenched local Democratic Party leadership. In any event, even progressive African American Mayor Harold Washington distanced himself from the CHA during the mid 1980s. In 1986, the U.S. Department of Housing and Urban Development (HUD)—citing its "national reputation for mismanagement and patronage"—added the CHA to its list of "severely troubled" local public housing agencies (Venkatesh 2002, 118).

THE WINDING ROAD TO CHA TRANSFORMATION

Following Mayor Washington's death in late 1987, his successor, Eugene Sawyer, brought in a private real estate manager, Vincent Lane, to oversee the CHA. From 1988 until his departure in 1995, Lane initiated various experiments at CHA developments, but possibly of greater importance, began to articulate a philosophy of public housing redevelopment—emphasizing mixed-income communities—that would become the cornerstone of subsequent CHA restructuring. During the last five years, the CHA has pressed ahead with major redevelopment plans at complexes such as the Cabrini-Green, ABLA, and Henry Horner Homes, while also pledging—via its Plan for Transformation, released in January, 2000—to completely rebuild or rehabilitate its portfolio of properties.

Two Lane-era initiatives illustrate the virtues and limits of his vision for public housing. In the South Side Oakland neighborhood, one of Chicago's poorest communities, Lane authorized the rehabilitation of two CHA high-rises, which were grandly renamed Lake Parc Place (Schill 1997). Recruited as residents were 140 "very poor" public housing-eligible families and an equal number of "working poor" families. Lake Parc Place's new occupants were to test the proposition—dubbed the "Mixed-Income New Communities Strategy"—that the more affluent residents, by keeping alert to and regulating the behavior of other tenants, would serve as the bulwark of a sustainable residential community. Another innovation at Lake Parc Place was the CHA's contracting out of maintenance work to private vendors.

Given the novelty of its tenant selection strategy, coupled with Vincent Lane's insistent advocacy, various social scientists examined Lake Parc Place and produced fascinatingly ambiguous findings. One team of researchers concluded that "Lake Parc Place was successful in persuading nonproject people [that is, the 140 working poor families] to move into public housing in a high-poverty neighborhood and in getting both project and nonproject residents to feel safe and satisfied, to interact with neighbors, to form friendships with neighbors, to support the building's rules and norms, and to volunteer in activities that maintain order and help the community and children" (Rosenbaum, Stroh, and Flynn 1998, 731). But a second study "found that the majority of residents—project and nonproject residents alike—feel a sense of ownership in the success of the complex and feel that their involvement—not management initiatives or role modeling—has been key to Lake Parc Place's success" (Nyden 1998, 743).

Due to the expense involved in rehabilitating just these two high-rises, the variety of mixed-income redevelopment pioneered at Lake Parc Place was not repeated. In 1993, the CHA won a $50 million HUD/HOPE VI grant to demolish three high-rise buildings and rebuild, mainly on Cabrini-Green property, an equivalent number of low-rise residential units. Lane, however, encountered opposition from Cabrini-Green residents, who complained that the CHA was not consulting them, as well as other local government officials, who were unwilling to cooperate with Lane as his dream for Cabrini-Green expanded. By 1994, Vincent Lane spoke in these terms of Cabrini-Green: "We need socioeconomic diversity or we will never solve the problems of the inner city... if we can do this at Cabrini and by McCormick Place and at Henry Horner, I predict you will see people moving from the suburbs back downtown, more commercial space being used and our schools upgraded" (Bennett 1998, 109). Mixed-income development was coming to encompass a much broader slice of the employment and income spectrum than at Lake Parc Place, and Lane was reimagining Cabrini-Green's makeover as a full-scale neighborhood redevelopment campaign.

In 1995, the CHA's Lane era abruptly halted. Due to a variety of internal management problems, HUD took over the operations of the Chicago Housing Authority (Banisky 1995). Until 1999, and the agency's return to local control, the CHA was directed by a former HUD official, Joseph Shuldiner, a tough-talking administrator who energetically reorganized the agency's internal operations. During his tenure, the CHA won several additional HOPE VI grants and pushed ahead with a Cabrini-Green neighborhood redevelopment plan consistent with Vincent Lane's latter, expansive ambitions for that project. The Shuldiner CHA also initiated a viability assessment process, as required by the Congressional Omnibus Consolidated Rescissions and Appropriations Act (OCRA) of 1996. The CHA examined the physical condition of developments holding 20,000 apartments to determine if rehabilitation represented a more cost-effective strategy than demolition coupled with the issuance of Section 8 vouchers to displaced tenants. The result of this exercise was the agency's determination that a majority of the assessed developments could not be economically rehabilitated (Henderson 1998).

In mid 1999, federal officials returned control of the CHA to local administrators and, within a few months, the CHA won HUD approval of its Plan for Transformation, a series of documents defining the agency's course of action for the current decade. The Plan for Transformation envisions a very different CHA. Ongoing demolitions—which ultimately will eliminate all of the agency's "family" high-rise structures (51 as of early 2000)—will reduce the CHA's housing stock to 25,000 units, an 18,000-unit reduction from the agency's maximum portfolio in the 1980s. All these 25,000 CHA apartments will be newly constructed or rehabilitated. Most of the newly constructed units will be located in mixed-income redevelopments at major existing complexes, such as the ABLA, Cabrini-Green, and Robert Taylor Homes. Senior-citizen apartments will number 10,000. The CHA will also contract out social services and building maintenance. As of January 2000, the CHA estimated that 6,000 families (in addition to the several thousand who had left its developments during the 1990s) would be relocated from public housing. The estimated cost of the Plan for Transformation is $1.5 million. The proposed completion date for this massive endeavor is 2010 (Chicago Housing Authority 2000).

The Plan for Transformation proposes to completely reshape Chicago public housing. Nevertheless, its main provisions were perfectly foreseeable. The OCRA-mandated viability assessments found that the cost of rehabilitating most of the CHA's larger developments would exceed the expense of demolition and the issuance of Section 8 vouchers. Since the mid 1990s, at complexes such as ABLA and Cabrini-Green, the CHA had already begun planning processes intended to produce mixed-income redevelopment blueprints.

In mid 1996, resident leaders at several CHA developments formed the Coalition to Protect Public Housing (CPPH). Their impetus was the series of Congressional actions that ultimately eliminated the "one-for-one" rule requiring the demolition of public-housing units be accompanied by the provision of an equivalent number of new public housing or Section 8 units (Wright 2006). Across the country, the elimination of the one-for-one rule has yielded plans to redevelop public housing in which one-third or fewer of new residential units will be reserved for public-housing occupancy (Salama 1999; Goetz 2003, 59–61).

The CPPH, in alliance with advocacy groups such as the Chicago Coalition for the Homeless and the Jewish Council of Urban Affairs, has sought to influence both federal policy-makers and local officials. The coalition, however, has not managed to draw much public attention to the ongoing reshaping of the CHA, nor has it seemed to have much effect on CHA plans for particular developments. Probably the CPPH's greatest success was achieved in 1999, when its public demonstrations and threat to sue induced the CHA to add a relocation contract to CHA leases (Wright 2006). The relocation contract spells out a legal "right to return" for public-housing residents who have fulfilled the terms of their leases but are required to vacate their apartments during project redevelopment.

Even before the approval of the Plan for Transformation, the vacating of CHA buildings produced a stream of relocating former public-housing residents. Many of these individuals and families sought to use Section 8 (in 1999 renamed "Housing Choice") vouchers to find private-sector housing. Others simply moved from their CHA dwellings. For many of these families, the experience of relocation seems not to have been especially successful. Journalists have reported on the unwillingness of neighborhood residents in various parts of the metropolitan area to welcome former public-housing residents (McRoberts and Pallasch 1998). Several researchers have found that most former CHA residents relocate to heavily African American, economically marginal neighborhoods, areas that, in effect, represent but a small step up from public housing (Popkin and Cunningham 2002; Fischer 2004). In January 2003, the independent monitor retained by the CHA to review its relocation services wrote:

> In July, August, and September 2002, the large number of HCV [Housing Choice Voucher]-eligible families still in CHA buildings, coupled with imminent building-empty dates, and the relatively small number of relocation counselors, caused a rush to place families in rental units. This in turn led inevitably to placing families hurriedly, and to relocating families into racially segregated areas already overwhelmingly populated by low income families. We were told ... residents were moved to HCV units without having had any real opportunities to make thorough and thoughtful surveys of available private rental units. (Independent Monitor's Report 2003, 22–23)

The ongoing transformation of public housing in Chicago has, thus far, produced an extremely mixed record. Across the city, thousands of public-housing units have been demolished, whereas new construction and rehabilitation (other than at senior-citizen developments) has proceeded very slowly. Agency–resident relations—long a sore point—have been redefined, but not clearly improved by the CHA's efforts to downsize and contract out supportive services. The deconcentration of Chicago's public-housing population, a policy goal initially advanced by Vincent Lane, has been compromised by the CHA's haphazard relocation services. Even at showpiece developments, such as ABLA and Cabrini-Green, where plans to produce attractive new mixed-income communities have been promoted by the CHA and blessed with the active support of Mayor Richard M. Daley, resident discontent and erratic consultative practices are much in evidence.

TROUBLE IN (MIXED-INCOME) PARADISE

The contrasting paths to redevelopment at the ABLA and Cabrini-Green Homes represent instructive examples of the procedural and political difficulties that have dogged the CHA's transformation. The Cabrini-Green Homes on Chicago's Near North Side—just west of the "old money" Gold Coast neighborhood and sandwiched between a gentrifying gallery district (River North) and the upscale Lincoln Park neighborhood—has long been one of the CHA's most notorious developments. By the 1980s, the Chicago press had begun to trumpet impending change at Cabrini-Green (Ziemba

1986). The focus of real estate attention was the Cabrini Extension and William Green Homes portions of the development, mid- and high-rise structures that were built during 1950s and 1960s. The third portion of Cabrini-Green is the Cabrini Rowhouses, low-rise structures that had been built to house wartime workers during the 1940s.

The initial Vincent Lane-defined Cabrini-Green redevelopment was a modest effort, which in subsequent years grew into a neighborhood-scale proposal. In late 1995, the CHA and City of Chicago issued a request for proposals (RFP) characterizing Cabrini-Green rebuilding as a neighborhood redevelopment initiative. Although none of the proposals responding to this RFP were accepted, city officials—rather fatefully—excluded from ongoing planning meetings Cabrini-Green resident representatives. This CHA–city government nonconsultation with local public-housing residents persisted, even as CHA Executive Director Joseph Shuldiner and Mayor Richard M. Daley, in June of 1996, unveiled the Near North Redevelopment Plan (NNRP). The NNRP proposed the use of tax increment financing to leverage public support for private residential development and also committed the Chicago Public Schools and Chicago Park District to local infrastructure investments. The NNRP's most controversial element was its commitment to expanded demolition at Cabrini-Green (Bennett 1998).

In October 1996, lawyers representing the Cabrini-Green Local Advisory Council (LAC) filed suit in federal district court, claiming that, apart from lack of consultation with development residents, the NNRP would have a "disparate impact" on a resident population of mainly African American, low-income, female-headed families. Over the course of four years, LAC–CHA negotiations yielded an out-of-court settlement. The settlement's main provisions were the following; (1) the CHA and the City of Chicago agreed to build 990 units of housing to be rented to public housing-eligible residents (which would, in effect, yield a Cabrini-Green development with approximately 1,600 units of public housing—a unit reduction of 2,000); and (2) Cabrini-Green residents would participate

in the decision-making team that would review future proposals to build on both Cabrini-Green and adjoining parcels (Ciokajlo 2000).

Since the settlement of the Cabrini-Green litigation, new commercial and residential development has proceeded rapidly. Probably most notable of these projects is North Town Village, a 261-unit development in which 30 percent of the units are reserved for public housing-eligible families. As new residents moved into North Town Village in 2001 and 2002, the property management company encouraged them to participate in a variety of community-building exercises ("Working with Tenants" 1999). In late 2002, when the Cabrini-Green Working Group, which solicits and reviews development proposals, selected the developer for the first phase of new construction directly on Cabrini-Green property, the winning consortium included North Town Village's principal partner, Peter Holsten (Wheelock 2003). However, as of summer 2004 construction had not begun on this phase of Cabrini-Green's rebuilding. Nor have local public-housing resident–CHA relations fallen into an altogether harmonious track. In response to the arrival of notices informing 385 families that they must vacate their apartments within 180 days, in June 2004, attorneys for the Cabrini-Green residents once more filed suit, arguing that the legal settlement of 2000 requires the CHA to construct replacement units in advance of building demolitions (Olivo 2004).

The CHA's ABLA development is the composite name for the Jane Addams and Robert Brooks Homes—both completed before the end of World War II—and the post war Loomis Courts, Grace Abbott Homes, and Brooks Extension buildings. Located near one another on the Chicago's Near West Side, these developments range from low-rise (the Addams and Brooks Homes), to mid-rise (Loomis Courts) and high-rise (the Abbott Homes and the three now-demolished Brooks Extension buildings). Around 1980, the CHA began to manage this group of developments as a single entity. At that time, the ABLA Homes stood to the north and east of a broad swath of deteriorating industrial and residential areas. At present, although residential gentrification is much less advanced on Chicago's West Side than on the city's North

Side, substantial townhouse and condominium development has approached ABLA's northern flank, an area bounded by the University of Illinois at Chicago to the east and a cluster of hospitals to the west.

Preliminary ABLA redevelopment discussions began in the mid 1990s, with the CHA winning substantial HOPE VI grants in 1996 and 1998. Unlike the Cabrini-Green experience, the main sequence of negotiations between CHA officials and the ABLA residents has proceeded smoothly. This may be attributable to the compliant attitude of the LAC leadership, which has not objected to City–CHA plans to demolish most of the ABLA buildings. Press reports suggest that the president of ABLA's LAC, has, in turn, been encouraged to recommend resident allies for employment with contractors and for first call on replacement housing units (McRoberts 1998). A rival tenants' group, the Concerned Residents of ABLA (CRA), formed in the late 1990s and has sought unsuccessfully to displace the incumbent resident leadership (Concerned Residents of ABLA 2004).

Many years of planning, as of mid 2004, have resulted in remarkably little redevelopment at ABLA. The three Brooks Extension buildings have been demolished, as have 45 buildings in the older, low-rise Robert Brooks Homes. The remaining Brooks Homes buildings have been reconfigured as 329 residential units (a reduction of 505 units). Most of the residents have been relocated from the Jane Addams Homes and, although demolition of the Grace Abbott high-rises has begun, several of these buildings continue to provide temporary housing for displaced families. The extremely piecemeal nature of this process, with considerable demolition and numerous building closures accompanied by very little rehabilitation or new construction, has undoubtedly produced much of the resident displeasure directed at the LAC and CHA. On multiple occasions, attorneys representing the CRA have filed suit seeking to stop the ongoing demolitions and tenant relocations at ABLA, but these legal interventions have had no discernible effect on the redevelopment process (*Chicago Tribune* 30 July 1999).

One of the curiosities of these events is that, long before much actual reconstruction had oc-curred, the City of Chicago prepared a document entitled "Holistic Urban Redevelopment: The ABLA Homes Model" that claims to "represent[s] a new public policy standard . . . and sets a new course for creatively redeveloping and revitalizing public housing complexes here and, perhaps, across the U.S." (City of Chicago n.d.). More than 3,000 public housing units will be demolished, with the new mixed-income development to include 966 market-rate units, 845 units of affordable housing (for families with annual earnings between 36 percent and 120 percent of the metropolitan area's median income), and 1,084 public-housing units. Since the release of "Holistic Urban Redevelopment," the pace of project planning has accelerated and included participation by representatives of local institutions such as the University of Illinois, as well as residents of the gentrifying residential area north of ABLA (Mansfield 2001a; 2001b). In the latter months of 2002, a master developer for the entire ABLA area was selected to proceed with a multiphase program of new residential and commercial construction (Grossman 2002). In early 2004, the Chicago City Council finally approved the ABLA redevelopment plan, which renames the development Roosevelt Square (Spielman 2004a).

Although many years of development activity lay ahead of the residents and planners at Cabrini-Green and ABLA, the processes of rebuilding these public housing neighborhoods, thus far, demonstrate one certainty while continuing to sustain an ambiguity of equal significance. Fifteen years ago, few Chicagoans would have anticipated the degree of private developer interest that has accompanied redevelopment efforts at ABLA, Cabrini-Green, and other CHA properties. Moreover, the preliminary results of marketing new, upscale dwellings in the very shadow of these public-housing communities suggests that substantial interest exists, on the part of prosperous Chicagoans, in taking up residence in once dreaded inner-city neighborhoods. That much is certain. What remains to be seen, at Cabrini-Green, ABLA, and elsewhere, is whether or not racially, culturally, and occupationally diverse mixed-income communities can take hold, and as such, yield a type of stable, inclusive neighborhood environment that in Chicago's preceding history has tended to be the exception rather than the rule.

PUBLIC-HOUSING TRANSFORMATION AND THE NEW CHICAGO

The transformation of public housing in Chicago is part of a national trend in domestic policy emphasizing a devolution to the states of formerly federal government-led initiatives in social welfare and housing, as well as the scaling back of public bureaucratic program implementation in favor of market-based solutions (O'Connor 2001, 242–91; Goetz 2003, 1–88). Nevertheless, the current close partnership between the CHA and Mayor Richard M. Daley's city government reflects another set of emerging circumstances. In the last decade or so, a very evident local policy consensus has emerged that seeks to reposition Chicago as an up-to-the-moment postindustrial metropolis. This new consensus reflects how the city's business, civic, and political leadership has come to view the shifting contours of Chicago's economy, and it is very much reflected in the "global city" agenda of the Daley administration.

For the rank-and-file Chicagoan—or the foot-loose conventioneer—this policy consensus has been writ large on the cityscape of central Chicago. Not only has the Daley administration pushed the major infrastructure developments discussed by Costas Spirou in Chapter 25, in many smaller ways, central Chicago-based arts organizations, universities, and other units of cultural capital have received governmental support. The ultimate aim of these initiatives is to enhance Chicago's status as an inviting, varied, and exciting world metropolis.

A secondary effect of this program of core-area physical and cultural enhancement has been the explosion of upscale residential development in neighborhoods adjoining the Loop (see Chapter 5). In the case of both new residential construction and loft conversions, much of this development has occurred in areas once dominated by manufacturing, warehousing, or transportation infrastructure. In effect—and to borrow metaphors from no less than Richard M. Daley (2002)—an emergent Martha Stewart's Chicago is rising directly atop the sands of an ebbing Nelson Algren's Chicago. One of the ironies of the recent boom in residential construction in areas such as the Near South and West Sides, or in the public-housing enclave of Cabrini-Green in the otherwise upscale Near North Side, is that much of the city's public-housing construction during the 1950s and 1960s had been placed in these very neighborhoods. Usually their demographic composition had been African American, or on the verge of becoming so, and just as often in that era, the proximity of these neighborhoods to railroads, factories, and highways was viewed as an environmental liability. In effect, housing for low-income African Americans was wedged into what were perceived to be among the least desirable sections of the city.

What a difference two generations make! As the middle class and wealthy return to central Chicago, neighborhoods formerly dominated by public housing are being domesticated as safe residential havens. Although a low-income, largely racial minority population will remain in areas such as Cabrini-Green, or on the Near West Side margins of the rebuilt ABLA and Henry Horner Homes, these remnant public-housing residents will no longer be the dominant population bloc as subsequent residential development fills in the empty parcels left by public-housing demolition (or before that, by industrial migration and residential abandonment). As Chicago makes the turn into the new millennium, the sharp racial conflicts over neighborhood succession that marked the 1960s, or for that matter, the racialized political conflicts of the Harold Washington mayoralty of the 1980s, seem to have vanished. Nevertheless, in accompaniment to the emergence of a central Chicago that is the workplace, home, and playground of the affluent, great care is being taken to create residential environments and commercial areas that will conform to the up-market expectations of the downtown area's newcomers.

Larry Bennett

23 Regionalism in a Historically Divided Metropolis

ON NOVEMBER 19, 1998, one of Chicago's most venerable civic organizations, the Commercial Club, issued a document ambitiously titled "Chicago Metropolis 2020: Preparing Metropolitan Chicago for the 21st Century" (Johnson 1998). Although each year dozens of Chicago-area civic organizations issue documents aiming to reshape one or another public policy debate, this report was unusual in its scope and was the object of uncharacteristic public attention. Among others, Chicago Mayor Richard M. Daley took notice, observing that "we, the city and suburbs, are all in this together. Only by working together will we be able to tackle the big issues" (Hinz 1999). Mayor Daley's endorsement of Chicago Metropolis 2020's regionalist vision was not shared by all. The *Chicago Tribune* noted this response by a suburban mayor: "The guy who wrote this must be from Moscow. These people are centralized planners, and they are not on our side" (Washburn and Quintanilla 1998).

The regional vision expressed in Chicago Metropolis 2020 is indeed expansive. For its part, the Commercial Club of Chicago can claim to be one of the cornerstones of the city's maturation as a metropolis during the first decades of the twentieth century. In 1909, fabled architect and planner Daniel Burnham issued his "Plan of Chicago" under the auspices of the Commercial Club (Hines 1979, 312–45). In the ensuing decades, the Burnham plan pointed the way for a series of important public infrastructure improvements. More significantly, it and its storied antecedent event, the World's Columbian Exposition of 1893, have become central features of

Chicago's civic mythology. Few Chicagoans have more than a passing familiarity with the details of Daniel Burnham's achievements, but many—often unknowingly taking their cue from the master—will assert that in this city, one "makes no little plans." Indeed, in offering its end-of-the-twentieth-century blueprint for the Chicago region, the Commercial Club took pains to link its contemporary perspectives to Burnham's vision. Published as a book in 2001, the first subsection of Chicago Metropolis 2020's introduction is entitled "The Burnham Legacy" (Johnson 2001). The appendices include an essay on "The Story of the Plan of 1909."

This is not to suggest that Chicago Metropolis 2020 is a document locked in the past. Its genesis is in the considerable efforts by Chicago's civic and business leadership to redefine this city's place in the contemporary world economy, and its metropolitan vision is a clear expression of the emergent "new regionalist" perspective on urban development (Rusk 1999; Orfield 2002). Nevertheless, to evaluate how likely it is that the Chicago Metropolis 2020 vision will leave a substantial imprint on its region, it is necessary to assess the details of this document in light of the Chicago metropolitan area's political, economic, and institutional contexts. Among the subtexts to much of the commentary on Chicago Metropolis 2020 is the question of whether the city's downtown-oriented business and civic leadership has the collective capacity—or indeed, even should aspire—to redefine the economic, governmental, and public policy rules structuring development across the metropolitan region.

Governmentally, the Chicago area is unusually fragmented, with approximately 1,300 local jurisdictions (Hemmens 1998, 122; Johnson 2001, 57). Moreover, the political divide between the Democratic Party-dominated City of Chicago and the many Republican-leaning suburban communities constitutes something akin to a cultural war. For many suburban officials, Chicago is quite simply a place controlled by power-hungry grafters. Indeed, one of the ironies of the Chicago central-city rebirth during the 1990s, coupled with Richard M. Daley's seemingly unchallenged leadership, may have been to redouble the anti-city paranoia that has long possessed some suburban leaders. At the dawn of the new millennium, the city may look less like a decaying bone yard, but efforts by the Commercial Club to think regionally may also seem to signify a drive by a resurgent Chicago to once more dominate its metropolitan provinces.

CHICAGO AND ITS REGION

As historian William Cronon has powerfully demonstrated in *Nature's Metropolis* (1991), Chicago's explosive growth during the period between the Civil War and the Great Depression cannot be explained except in relation to its regional context. Interestingly, and in utter contradiction to one strand of the local foundation myth, Chicago's specific locale—on mud flats at the southwest corner of Lake Michigan—was not an auspicious site for city building. Nevertheless, New York capital and Great Lakes navigation initially made its mud flats hospitable. By the middle decades of the nineteenth century, local commercial interests took advantage of Chicago's larger regional environment and, having lured a disproportionate number of rail lines to their city, pumped a northerly outpost into the commercial and industrial hub for the westwardly expanding continental economy.

Chicago's metropolitan reach was a conspicuous feature of the Plan of Chicago. City planning historian Mel Scott (1971, 103) observes of the Burnham document: "The metropolis portrayed ... extends in a radius of sixty miles from the downtown Loop—as far north as Kenosha on the Wisconsin shore and as far south as

Michigan City, Indiana." In effect, the scale of central-Chicago's economic functions had spawned a series of "satellite cities on Chicago's periphery ... Waukegan, Elgin, Aurora, Joliet, and Chicago Heights developed at the intersections with the Chicago Outer Belt Line (the Elgin, Joliet, and Eastern Railroad)" (Lindstrom 2002, 10). Nevertheless, until the mid twentieth century, the municipality of Chicago clearly dominated its metropolitan region, as late as 1950 holding 70 percent of the area's population. During the subsequent decades, the central city–suburban balance shifted decisively. By 2000, the population of the City of Chicago represented slightly more than one-third of the metropolitan figure. Between 1972 and 1995, the city's share of regional private-sector employment dropped from 56 percent to 34 percent (Persky and Wiewel 2002, xiv).

During the 1960s, Chicago's civic and political leaders interpreted suburbanization as the fundamental threat to the central city's vitality. Chicago's municipal boundaries had been greatly expanded through annexation in the late 1800s but, over the course of the twentieth century, the only significant geographic expansion occurred during the 1950s, with the city's absorption of the O'Hare Airport site. As the metropolitan area's population grew and decentralized, the multiplication of governmental jurisdictions proceeded apace. Many municipalities undoubtedly were birthed in response to local residents' pressing for home rule or, at least, to avoid incorporation within larger, adjoining towns. But in addition to incorporated municipalities, the Chicago region is also awash in single-purpose governments—from local school systems to mosquito abatement districts—that have roots in Illinois municipal-finance regulation. Until the revision of the state constitution in 1970, which relaxed debt limits on municipal governments, towns and cities often found that the easiest way to take on (and finance) new, capital-intensive service delivery responsibilities was through the formation of special-purpose districts (Hemmens 1998, 125).

Chicago's post-World War II suburbanization quickly enough yielded initiatives to increase governmental coordination and impose some order on metropolitan expansion. During the mid 1950s, two new planning-oriented agencies appeared: the Northeastern Illinois Planning Commission and the Chicago Area Transportation Study. Two additional entities with operational responsibilities exist at the metropolitan level: the Metropolitan Water Reclamation District and the Regional Transit Authority (Hemmens 1998). Since the 1950s, nine municipal federations—which typically link city officials within particular metropolitan subregions—have also been founded. It is probably accurate to characterize these councils of government as contributing both to metropolitan cooperation and fragmentation. In the words of sociologist Bonnie Lindstrom (1998, 341), "The councils have . . . become influential actors in articulating subregional economic development strategies. . . . For economic development as the regional level, however, the consensus breaks down. . . . For these issues, each council works in collaboration with other institutional actors in the region to achieve subregional rather than regional goals."

Finally, since 1997, a Metropolitan Mayors' Caucus has brought together the chief elected officials from municipalities across the Chicago region. Although committed to the concept of metropolitan cooperation, in reference to one of the region's persistent public-policy quandaries, the debate over O'Hare Airport expansion versus the development of a new south suburban regional airport, the Mayors' Caucus found that the only acceptable course of action was to exclude discussion of this matter from its proceedings (Hamilton 2002, 412–13).

The ultimate source of political fragmentation in the Chicago area is the longstanding mistrust dividing the City of Chicago and its adjoining jurisdictions. In part, this mistrust is the product of the cultural cleavage between a socially diverse, highly political central city and its more cautious, often more socially homogeneous suburbs. Yet possibly even more fundamental to the Chicago–suburban divide is the legacy of the political arrangement that structured the City of Chicago's dealing with the state government in Springfield during the Richard J. Daley era. When Mayor Daley needed assistance from the state government, he typically cut deals with downstate Illinois-oriented governors. As political scientist Margaret Weir puts it (1996, 31), "Chicago's Democratic mayor and the Governor agreed to measures of benefit to each, generally leaving the suburbs out of the bargain."

In the wake of Richard J. Daley's 21-year mayoralty, City of Chicago–suburban relations have improved only marginally. Since 1989, Mayor Richard M. Daley has often espoused regional cooperation, but some of his most aggressive political maneuvering—notably his advocacy of O'Hare Airport expansion—has drawn him into confrontation with suburban political figures. Nonetheless, political reality may yet produce an alteration in this and subsequent Chicago mayors' approach to their suburban neighbors. The largest geographically defined delegation in Illinois' state legislature is now the suburban Chicago contingent. In the future, Chicago mayors will find it increasingly difficult to solve their problems by "going over the head of the suburbs" to deal directly with Illinois governors. Cooperation—from the ground up—is likely to be forced on Chicago mayors as the necessary principle in governing city–suburban relations.

CHICAGO METROPOLIS 2020

Following its sponsorship of the Burnham Plan, the Commercial Club did not remove itself from civic affairs. For example, during the early 1980s, at the point when Chicago's industrial decline could no longer be denied, the Commercial Club released a report entitled "Make No Little Plans" (1984) urging local leaders to reassess their assumptions regarding the future of the city's economy. Nevertheless, by the 1990s, one of the organization's members described it as a "luncheon club" (Hinz 1999). Some part of the Commercial Club's apparent torpor was, undoubtedly, attributable to the shifting fortunes and reactive strategies of Chicago-based firms during the 1970s and 1980s, an era of withdrawal to the suburbs, takeovers by out-of-town corporations and, in the case of several major manufacturers, outright business failure.

A considerable effort at organizational recommitment accompanied the production of

Chicago Metropolis 2020. The report's author is Elmer Johnson, an attorney and former executive with General Motors. Johnson worked with six policy subcommittees (economic development, education, governance, land-use, taxation, and transportation) whose members were drawn primarily from the city's corporate and civic elites. Moreover, as first the summary report and then the complete document were released in late 1998 and early 1999, the Commercial Club announced the formation of a new organization, Chicago Metropolis 2020 (initially funded with $4 million for three years), to publicize the report's recommendations and promote supportive legislation. The Commercial Club was both advancing a set of regionalist measures and initiating a process of more focused, regional-level policy dialogue.

The published version of Chicago Metropolis 2020 (Johnson 2001) is an elegant volume featuring striking aerial images and graphic representations of the Chicago region. On occasion, its striving for intellectual gravity borders on the comical, as when a verse from T.S. Eliot's "The Rock" accompanies a discussion of rail and truck transport (p. 40). It is, however, a document offering clearly expressed assumptions and articulating a laudable vision:

> We dream of an economically vibrant and environmentally healthy region; one whose concentrated areas of activity enable people of complementary talents to achieve high levels of creativity and productivity; a region where all persons have ready access to jobs, to housing near their jobs, and to good schools and job training; a region in which people are enabled and encouraged to find nourishment in a diversity and complexity of persons, interests, and tastes, and to enjoy an exciting array of cultural, recreational, and intellectual opportunities; and most important, a region that undergirds strong neighborhoods, communities, and families so that they are enabled to nurture the intellectual, moral, and social development of children. (Johnson 2001, 1–2)

Drafted during a period of economic expansion, Chicago Metropolis 2020 largely eschews the rhetoric of urban crisis. Its fundamental contextual premise is global competition, with the report seeking to place Chicago on track to become "one of the ten or fifteen great metropolitan centers of the world economic order that is emerging" (Johnson 2001, 72). Clearly reflecting the thinking of new regionalist advocates such as Myron Orfield and David Rusk, Chicago Metropolis 2020 proposes that metropolitan-level public policy collaboration is essential to sustaining regional economic vitality. For central-city and suburban Chicagoans alike, it is a matter of "self-interest as interdependent residents of one region" (Johnson 2001, 2).

Although avoiding evocations of impending decline, Chicago Metropolis 2020 does specify "three major obstacles that threaten the goals of the plan": "the need to ensure that all the region's children have access to good health care and high-quality education," the metropolitan area's "dispersed and stratified agglomeration of people that is neither village nor city," and the region's "high levels of concentrated poverty and racial and social segregation" (Johnson 2001, 9–10). Following an introductory discussion of these "obstacles," the bulk of Chicago Metropolis 2020 is devoted, first, to discussing "goals, challenges, and guiding principles," which in Chapters 6 through 10 give way to specific policy recommendations.

The number of topics—whether discussed as principles, goals, or recommendations—addressed in Chicago Metropolis 2020 makes summary a daunting task. One analysis of the plan identifies 30 specific policy recommendations, which in fact, represents a distillation of the report's many, very targeted proposals (Hamilton 2002, 416). In fact, given the "three obstacles," many of the plan's recommendations are cross-cutting, tending to affect more than one of the three core problems identified as confronting the region. Nevertheless, a small number of broad policy priorities drive the many specifics of Chicago Metropolis 2020.

At its core, Chicago Metropolis 2020 seeks to produce a metropolitan region in which the rapid suburbanization of the last 60 years would be slowed, and new private investment would flow into sections of the region (several inner-city neighborhoods, a number of inner-ring suburbs to Chicago's south and west) that have been starved of business-related and housing development. The persuasive beauty of this formulation is twofold, and reflective of the document's "everyone's self-interest" premise. If weighed against the cost of the public expenditures necessary to sustain the current, sprawling development of the region, the targeted public works expenditures—such as mass-transit investment and other improvements along transit corridors—would, in reality, save taxpayers hundreds of millions of dollars. Furthermore, transit-oriented development, the densification of currently investment-starved areas, and the slowing of metropolitan expansion would improve the quality of life even in the region's affluent, outlying communities. For the workforce of these areas, traffic congestion and commuting times would be reduced. For residents, disruptive new development and the gobbling up of open space would abate.

Although this grand vision of an alternative metropolitan physical form is Chicago Metropolis 2020's governing aim, the document also expresses a strong commitment to improving inner-city conditions, especially for younger Chicagoans. The lengthy discussions of education measures connect with a variety of pragmatic regional development considerations. New investment in the economically marginal sections of the region is unlikely without a substantial improvement in the educational achievement and work-readiness of these areas' residents. However, Chapter 6, rather than critically examining currently fashionable school-reform measures, chooses to catalog a fairly conventional menu of presumed innovations (higher teacher salaries, more rigorous school performance monitoring, vouchers, and the like). In respect to that thorniest of school issues, funding, Chicago Metropolis 2020 steers clear of controversial specifics. On the page preceding the discussion of education reforms, the document assures readers that subsequent proposals "may well not entail a net increase in state and local taxation for the vast majority of households" (Johnson 2001, 83). Regarding school finance specifically, the report is studiously cautious, calling for a more regular and precise determination of state "foundation" funding for each local school district, in conjunction with some restructuring of the property and income tax systems, and permitting local districts, if they

choose, to raise funds in excess of state foundation support (Johnson 2001, 86–87).

Chicago Metropolis 2020 is less equivocal in discussing transportation improvements. The plan advocates increased investment in mass transit and devotes great attention to the question of intermodal freight centers, transfer points between highway-, rail-, air-, and waterborne means of commercial shipment: "One of the challenges for metropolitan Chicago is to figure out how it can most profitably exploit its position as railway hub of the nation and reposition itself as one of the world's major intermodal centers for the transfer of goods between different rail carriers, between rail and truck, between air transport and both truck and rail, and between water transport and both rail and truck" (Johnson 2001, 39–40). These and related transportation investments are joined to a very specific discussion of funding sources, mainly derived from auto-licensing and related auto-use fees (Johnson 2001, 115).

In reference to the other substantive areas given significant attention by Chicago Metropolis 2020, land use and affordable-housing development, many of the report's recommendations turn on the willingness of the state and federal governments to shift priorities or increase fiscal support. For example, in conjunction with its support for the ongoing demolition of Chicago Housing Authority high-rise apartment buildings, Chicago Metropolis 2020 proposes that the number of locally available Section 8 (since renamed "Housing Choice") vouchers be increased. Similarly, the report supports expanding the Low-Income Housing Tax Credit program to spur more affordable-housing production (Johnson 2001, 120–24). Chicago Metropolis 2020 also recommends the adoption of a state building code to supersede local building codes and enable builders to deliver their product at a lower cost. In reference to land use, Chicago Metropolis 2020 suggests that Illinois might follow the lead of New Jersey and Maryland and increase funding for the preservation of open space in metropolitan areas (Johnson 2001, 136–38).

Chicago Metropolis 2020, even as it calls for increased state and federal governmental action in particular areas, does not wish to make public initiative the guiding force in achieving an ecologically sustainable, socially equitable region: "government policies should be designed to maintain a strong business climate, not to achieve a planned or targeted set of industry-specific goals" (Johnson 2001, 79). Indeed, in the volume's concluding chapter, private businesses are encouraged to accept a "new commercial compact," binding them to locational decision making that considers the strength of local communities' commitments to affordable housing construction and transit-oriented development (Johnson 2001, 139). This commercial compact has subsequently been renamed the "Metropolis Principles," and a prime follow-up initiative has been to sign on firms willing to adjust their corporate decision-making to fall in line with Chicago Metropolis 2020's commitments to smart growth, regionally dispersed affordable housing, and transit-accessible workplaces.

Despite the document's persistent faith in private-sector public-spiritedness—which is paralleled by a wariness of governmental action ("we reject the notion of metropolitan government," p. 57)—Chicago Metropolis 2020 does propose that a new, metropolitan-wide governance unit assume a coordinating function within Chicago's new regional order. The envisioned Regional Coordinating Council (RCC) would encourage metropolitan-conscious physical development strategies, resource sharing, and intergovernmental cooperation, in large measure via the use of incentives. For example, armed with an independent bonding capacity, the RCC could offer fiscal assistance to municipalities engaged in smart-growth initiatives or committed to local affordable-housing development. The RCC's 15-member governing board would be elected indirectly, by the metropolitan area's 270 municipalities whose individual votes would be weighted according to population (Johnson 2001, 111–17). In line with the great attention it devotes to transportation issues, Chicago Metropolis 2020 advocates the following intermediate organizational consolidation: a merger of the Northeastern Illinois Planning Commission and the Chicago Area Transportation Study, with this consolidated agency also absorbing the planning func-

tions of the Regional Transit Authority. This consolidated planning agency "would prepare the way for the . . . new RCC described above" (Johnson 2001, 117).

BRINGING CHICAGO METROPOLIS 2020 TO FRUITION

Reactions to the release of the first version of Chicago Metropolis 2020 in late 1998 assumed a wild variety of tones and amplitudes. Given the Commercial Club's substantial corporate backing, the solemn respectfulness expressed by most city-based figures was to be expected, although *Chicago Tribune* columnist John McCarron's (1998) pessimistic assessment of the report's likely affect—"[c]hances are the Metropolis project is going nowhere"—probably crossed the minds of many otherwise supportive readers. One hostile commentary on the plan, by reporter Harold Henderson (2002) of the weekly *Chicago Reader*, substantially mistargeted its attack. Charging that Chicago Metropolis 2020 was apolitical and technocratic, Henderson failed to mention key instances of careful waffling within the document. These included the plan's call for both expansion of O'Hare Airport and land-banking in preparation for the development of the area's "third airport" in south suburban Peotone (Johnson 2001, 102–03). Although it is not beyond reason that both measures could be pursued, in the short run author Elmer Johnson and associates were clearly seeking to avoid miring their report in the longstanding, seemingly intractable metropolitan airport war. Just as "political" in its caution was the report's mild advocacy of local tax-base sharing without reference to specifics.

To avoid the proverbial fate of ambitious civic exercises that, once completed and written up, find their ultimate place among previous such exercises on the shelves of a few civic leaders, the release of the full Chicago Metropolis 2020 report in the spring of 1999 corresponded with the formation of the like-named organization to shepherd the report's recommendations. Chicago Metropolis 2020 is a lean organization, led by a small number of unpaid volunteer executives working with an equally small full-time professional staff. The 50 members of Chicago Metropolis 2020's executive council (as of August 2004) tend to be drawn from the city's business leadership, but there is also substantial representation of the nonprofit sector (six members) and state and local government (seven members). There is a paucity of corporate "titans," with fewer than ten representatives of international-scale corporations. The driving figures in Chicago Metropolis 2020 are executives associated with second-tier firms and prominent business professionals (mainly attorneys) with a deep commitment to Chicago. The group's work is organized via discrete policy areas: regional learning, transportation and land use, early childhood education, justice and violence, and housing.

Chicago Metropolis 2020's core activities are outreach, consultation, and lobbying. Leading executives associated with Chicago Metropolis 2020, such as King W. Harris and George Ranney Jr.—the latter as the group's president—are tireless editorialists and public-event participants. Since its formation, the group has released reports examining overall regional economic, social, and housing conditions (its Metropolis Indexes of 2001, 2002, and 2004, respectively) and, in the spring of 2003, an updated plan focusing on metropolitan transportation issues. Although Chicago Metropolis 2020 does not wish to be characterized as a think tank, in executive director Frank Beal's (2003) view, his group's transportation modeling work has goaded the Chicago Area Transportation Study into developing more rigorous transportation needs projections.

Ultimately, for Chicago Metropolis 2020's regionalist vision to become reality, there must be a significant buy-in by those constituencies beyond the city limits of Chicago. Toward this end, in the months preceding the release of its 2001 Metropolis Index, Chicago Metropolis 2020 sponsored a goal-setting exercise bringing together 500 civic, governmental, and business leaders from across the metropolitan area. Through a series of meetings combining discussion with priority-identification, Chicago Metropolis 2020 was able to specify a list of 12 overarching metropolitan goals. However, political scientist David Hamilton (2002,

418) suggests that this process of consultation and agenda setting may not have triggered an essential byproduct, an abiding sense of city–suburban mutuality among the elites present: "The forums were short, one-shot affairs and did not create any lasting participant support. In fact, some participants felt that the forums were simply a mechanism for Metropolis to claim public support for its goals." Chicago Metropolis 2020's publications sometimes seem to reinforce this perception. In outlining how public discussion contributed to the articulation of its transportation goals, "The Metropolis Plan: Choices for the Chicago Region" (Chicago Metropolis 2020 2003, 17) observes:

> Over a period of four months, we held a series of workshops around the region in which we solicited input from many of the people who know and care the most about the future of our region: mayors, business leaders, members of the clergy, environmental experts, transportation planners, and other community leaders. We unrolled maps at these workshops and asked the participants the question at the core of how our region will grow and develop: We are expecting 1.6 million new residents by 2020; where should they all go? These leaders made choices that reinforced the principles developed in the original Chicago Metropolis 2020 report....

In one crucial respect, however, John McCarron's anticipation of inconsequentiality has not befallen Chicago Metropolis 2020: Since the group's formation in 1999, it has become a significant player in state-level policy making. In Chicago Metropolis 2020's very first months of existence it offered crucial assistance to then-Governor George Ryan in his successful promotion of a $12 billion public works proposal (Hinz 1999). In 2003, following the election of Democratic Governor Rod Blagojevich, a Chicago Metropolis 2020 staff-member was, first, selected to lead a task force studying the operations of the state Department of Children and Family Services (DCFS), and subsequently, appointed by the governor to head DCFS (Casillas and Chase 2003). In August 2003, Governor Blagojevich appointed a transportation task force mandated to explore another of Chicago Metropolis 2020's central goals, the consolidation of Chicago-area transportation planning and operational functions (Chase 2003). However, the playing out of the transportation task force's proceedings also underlines the current political limits to the organization's regional vision. Following the release of the task force's recommendations to reorganize the governance of the Regional Transit Authority (RTA) and merge the region's commuter rail (Metra) and suburban bus (Pace) agencies, the county board chairs of DuPage, Kane, Lake, McHenry, and Will Counties pledged to fight efforts to dismantle the RTA "by giving the majority of the seats to the city of Chicago and Cook County" (McCoy et al. 2004).

CHICAGO METROPOLIS 2020, CHICAGO, AND THE FUTURE OF THE CHICAGO REGION

The formation and activities of Chicago Metropolis 2020 reflect forces that have been reshaping most North American cities, as well as drawing the anxious attention of municipal elites, for a half-century (Teaford 1990). Like Cleveland, Detroit, Milwaukee, and many other American metropolises, since World War II, central-city Chicago's industrial-based economy has shrunk, and the city's metropolitan cultural dominance has likewise been attenuated. And again, like the civic elites of many other American cities, during the last generation, Chicago's leaders have come to define their principal challenges in terms of global competition. The work of Chicago Metropolis 2020 has already become something of a benchmark for local leaders seeking to redirect the developmental trajectories of other Midwestern metropolitan areas (Kosdrosky 2003; Williams 2003).

More distinctively—and to some degree, surely, an artifact of the timing of the original Chicago Metropolis 2020 plan's release—the regionalist gospel espoused by Elmer Johnson and George Ranney Jr. is couched in strikingly optimistic tones. Inevitably, the economic- and population-growth projections of civic leaders function, in part, to boost the spirits of local residents and win the attention of nonlocal publics. But, in fact, the city of Chicago did experience a turnaround during the 1990s:

registering a decennial population increase for the first time since the 1940–50 period, attracting thousands of new residents and millions of dollars in commercial and residential investment to its near-downtown neighborhoods, and successfully hosting notable events such as World Cup soccer matches in 1994 and the 1996 Democratic Party national convention. Consequently, from the standpoint of Chicago Metropolis 2020's leadership, central-city–suburban mutuality in the Chicago region can be construed as a collaboration in which both parties bring substantial resources to the relationship.

Another distinctive feature of the political and economic context shaping the response to Chicago Metropolis 2020 is the region's unusual degree of governmental fragmentation. Nevertheless, the sheer number of local jurisdictions in the Chicago region is probably not, in itself, that serious an impediment to the development of more comprehensive, region-spanning public policies. Clearly, the evident success of more localized, subregional cooperation via the area's nine councils of government indicates that a limited regionalist perspective has already taken root in Chicago's suburbs. Indeed, one barrier confronting Chicago Metropolis 2020's sponsors may be that, for the bulk of suburban Chicagoans, this is the scope of regionalism that they find most desirable. Grander regionalism, which implies central-city Chicago–suburban cooperation, is a riskier proposition. At present, Chicago Mayor Richard M. Daley is quite fond of espousing cooperative regionalism. Yet practically speaking, Daley's municipal government plays a clearly self-interested variety of inter-municipal cooperation and, as the O'Hare Airport versus third airport conflict reveals, is not averse to backing away from seemingly fixed commitments.

In short, during the first years of the new millennium, Richard M. Daley may be a bit too formidable, and his city a bit too vigorous, for aggressive regionalism to win the hearts and minds of the political leaders and local constituencies north, west, and south of Chicago. In the coming years, with Richard M. Daley's passage from the scene, a more egalitarian regionalism may be possible. Nevertheless, Chicago

Metropolis 2020's leaders, or their successor regional advocates, will still need to come to terms with a seam of public sentiment that no one in the Chicago area can assess with certainty at this time. Do, in fact, most of the two-thirds of the Chicago region's population who live in the suburbs arcing from northwestern Indiana to the southern border of Wisconsin really think that they are "interdependent residents of one region"? The answer to this question is no clearer in the Chicago area than it is in dozens of other metropolitan regions across the United States.

Joseph Schwieterman

24   Coalition Politics at America's Premier Transportation Hub

AT THE HEIGHT of the railroad era, Carl Sandburg described Chicago as a "Player with railroads and the nation's freight handler." Sandburg admired the city for its brawny character, its enterprising spirit, and its seemingly boundless industrial capacity. More than 80 years later, the city immortalized by Sandburg remains the country's busiest freight and passenger interchange.

By most commonly accepted measures, Chicago's dominance in the transportation industry extends from the airline and railroad industries to commercial trucking. Despite a decline of heavy industry in the Great Lakes region, the bankruptcies of some of its largest common carriers, and economic changes favoring more southerly cities, Chicago is still widely considered the railroad capital of the world and the continent's leading aviation hub. The city's location at the southern end of Lake Michigan has made it a natural transportation crossroads (Cronon 1991; Young 1998, 2003).

The future, however, promises to be much different from the past. Patterns of globalization, the restructuring of American transportation, and the region's changing industrial character are shifting the contours of Chicago transportation. In aviation, the expansion and transformation of commercial air travel is necessitating a reassessment of the city's terminals and runways. In rail transportation, the excess capacity once so prevalent on main lines and in terminals has been absorbed by escalating tonnage moving between international points as well as between various parts of the United States. Support for the development of a high-speed system

of passenger trains, meanwhile, is being fueled by rising congestion on expressways and arterial highways.

Broad coalitions of governmental and nongovernmental organizations are leading the push to expand Chicago's intercity transportation system. These strategic alliances weigh heavily in the battles over the direction of public policy that take place between the city and its suburbs as well as between public agencies and residential populations. Years ago, the role of coalitions was less prominent on the transportation scene. As recently as the 1960s, private companies and the city government of Chicago (with assistance from the federal government) were, for all practical purposes, unilateral decision makers in air and rail planning. Although coalitions of governmental, private, and nonprofit organizations exerted influence over decisions, responsibility and leadership rested principally with Chicago officials and private firms.

The landscape of transportation planning dramatically changed after voters approved the creation of the Regional Transportation Authority (RTA) in 1974, a milestone in the evolution of intergovernmental relations in northeastern Illinois. The RTA was given responsibility for public transportation in a six-county area and had a board of directors that included representatives from both the city and suburbs. The agency had a mandate to balance the needs of constituencies that had previously shown little interest in cooperation. By the early 1980s, other intergovernmental initiatives had been formed for the purpose of pursuing shared transportation goals.

Today, coalitions that promote and plan investments in intercity transportation facilities are an accepted part of the political landscape. From dueling coalitions involved in the airport expansion debate, to the largely disconnected coalitions pushing for rail-freight investments, and to the fragile coalition seeking to develop a high-speed regional rail system, the political environment facing transportation decision-makers is both unpredictable and complex.

THE PROBLEM OF AIRPORT EXPANSION

The recent politics of airport expansion in the region underscore the difficulty of launching major transportation projects without the benefit of regional consensus. For more than 15 years, opinions have remained divided about the most effective way to handle the rising number of passengers moving through the city's airports.

Pressure to expand the region's airport system has been almost continuous since the Airline Deregulation Act of 1978, which eliminated federal regulation controlling airline routes and fares. As carriers invested in major hub-and-spoke networks in Atlanta, Chicago, Denver, Pittsburgh, St. Louis, and other cities, prices dropped significantly and passengers received the benefits of greater schedule frequency and a wider choice of destinations (Morrison and Winston 1995). American Airlines and United Airlines made large investments in hub operations at O'Hare and, by the early 1980s, accounted for more than three-quarters of that airport's passenger traffic.

By the middle of the 1980s, significant congestion occurred during certain times of the day at O'Hare—a problem aggravated by the city's severe weather and the less-than-optimal configuration of the airport's existing runways. Between 1981 and 1988, the number of passengers boarding flights at the airport rose from less than thirty-eight million to nearly fifty-nine million—an increase of more than 50 percent. By the end of this period, traffic had grown to absorb virtually all of the airport's maximum theoretical capacity.

New runways appeared to be on the horizon when an alliance of state governments emerged in 1988, with the goal of resolving the inadequacies of the regional airport system. The consortium, consisting of Illinois, Indiana, and Wisconsin, launched the Chicago Airport Capacity Study, which evaluated a variety of locations in the southern part of the metropolitan area, including sites near the Illinois communities of Beecher, Kankakee, and Peotone. In 1992, however, its final recommendation was to build at Lake Calumet (see Map 24.1, color insert), a more centralized location that aviation planners in Chicago were evaluating at the time (Young 2003). This prospective airport, in the middle of an industrial area on the far south side of the city, was to be partially situated on a landfill. In part because of its relative proximity (15 miles) to downtown Chicago, the city publicly endorsed the Lake Calumet site.

A massive airport at Lake Calumet may well have emerged had power-sharing issues not proved to be intractable. Illinois governor Jim Edgar and Secretary of State George Ryan (who later succeeded Edgar as governor), both downstate Republicans, supported this ambitious undertaking. Nevertheless, other officials were opposed, and the city was uneasy with the prospect of delegating critical decision-making responsibility to other governmental units. The fragility of the coalition was evident after the Illinois state government (still under a Republican governor at the time) failed to approve the creation of the airport authority that the study had recommended to oversee the region's airports. Rather than negotiating with the state, Mayor Richard M. Daley abandoned the Lake Calumet airport proposal, derailing the entire initiative. The Mayor also announced that any effort to build a new airport outside city limits would have to proceed without Chicago's cooperation.

The mayor's decision to abandon the Lake Calumet project was driven in part by political and planning issues internal to the city. Building the airport would have been inordinately complex and raised concerns about both the loss of wetlands and environmental justice. By late 1992, it had become evident that these issues could not be easily resolved without requiring the mayor to expend a great deal of political capital. Another problem was the incompatibility of the Lake Calumet Airport proposal with other aviation opportunities presenting themselves in the city, most notably the expansion of flight operations at nearby Midway Airport, which was in the midst of a renaissance. By the early 1990s, Midway had come to exemplify the potential to infuse new vitality into older urban facilities. An airport at Lake Calumet would have created such severe airspace problems that it would have threatened the future of this resurgent southwest-side facility.

DUELING COALITIONS TAKE ROOT

Whatever the inherent difficulties of a Lake Calumet proposal, the manner in which it was abandoned led to a divide among officials supporting airport expansion in the region. The mayor's subsequent refusal to cooperate with planning for a new "green grass" airport (an airport built on a rural site), possibly in south-suburban Peotone or in northwestern Indiana, fostered a deep sense of mistrust among suburban and state decision makers. The governments of neighboring states distanced themselves from the Chicago airport problem, whereas the state of Illinois adopted a largely hands-off policy on matters related to aviation in the city. From this point forward, proposals to resolve the region's airport needs would be advanced by two coalitions from within the region, each with competing agendas.

The first coalition consisted of the City of Chicago and a broad spectrum of local business leaders and urban advocates supporting the expansion of O'Hare. This coalition included groups such as the Business Leaders for Transportation (a group co-sponsored by the Commercial Club and the Metropolitan Planning Council), Chicagoland Chamber of Commerce, and, later, Global Chicago. Also visible in the debate were the editorial writers for the *Chicago Tribune* and various environmental groups who supported "infill" development rather than the construction of an airport on agricultural land. Although the city of Chicago kept most of the critical planning decisions to itself, other coalition members worked to build the case that the economic future of the region hinged on O'Hare's expansion.

Countering this alliance were groups united in their opposition to O'Hare but encumbered by different policy goals, which essentially divided the alliance into two camps. The first camp was led by Jesse Jackson, Jr. whose Congressional district included many African Americans in the south suburbs. This camp opposed expanding O'Hare largely because of a competing interest in building a new airport in south-suburban Peotone (Map 24.1), a location 35 miles south of Chicago that had been evaluated years before by the Airport Capacity Study. Notable among this group was the government of Will County and the South Suburban Mayors and Managers, a council of governments representing suburbs south of Chicago. This coalition was able to solicit the endorsement of essentially every community in the vicinity of the proposed new airport, with the exception of Peotone itself, which remained wary of the airport proposal.

The second camp opposing O'Hare's expansion was led by the Suburban O'Hare Commission (SOC). Among the organization's most active members were the villages of Bensenville and Elk Grove Village, whose mayors brought much visibility to its cause. SOC felt strongly that the airport's expansion would create congestion and major land-use problems as well as undermine the economy of adjacent communities. This group was emphatic in its belief that the noise and traffic generated by the airport would severely affect the quality of life for hundreds of thousands of residents. (Communities west of O'Hare had experienced a sharp rise in noise following the opening of a new runway in 1969.) SOC also heavily publicized engineering studies showing that new runways would necessitate the relocation of many homes and businesses. Not only did SOC pursue legal action to thwart the O'Hare expansion, it enlisted the support of Senator Peter Fitzgerald and Republican voters from affluent northwest suburban communities represented by U.S. Congressman Henry Hyde. This camp appeared to relish its role as an underdog and worked furiously to fracture the coalition supporting the expansion of O'Hare. It made a particular effort to discredit the notion that the city—and especially the mayor—could be trusted to carry out such a complex project in a financially and socially responsible way.

The two camps opposing O'Hare's expansion made strange bedfellows. The SOC camp was primarily white-collar and Republican; the Jackson camp represented more heavily blue-collar and Democratic constituencies. Jackson's camp went to great lengths to build a case that, even if O'Hare was equipped with new runways, the region still urgently needed a new airport. The SOC camp, on the other hand, initially tried to minimize the discussion about new runways as a result of its overriding interest in blocking O'Hare's expansion. In addition, Jackson had an established relationship with Mayor Richard M. Daley (as did his father, the Reverend Jesse L. Jackson) and sought to preserve this relationship; SOC had no such ambition and, indeed, seemed intent on portraying the mayor in a negative light.

The pro-O'Hare faction also suffered from internal weakness and conflict. The city's unwillingness to participate in a regional dialogue about the alternatives was a particularly awkward issue. Moreover, for reasons not entirely clear, during the 1990s, the city did not publicly embark on plans to build new runways, as many pro-O'Hare advocates had hoped. (The city may have been wary of inciting opposition to such a project until it had evaluated all its options.) Many felt the city was not being sufficiently forthcoming about its plans, perhaps even building a war chest to overwhelm opponents of an enlarged O'Hare. Others accused the city of having no plan at all.

As might be expected, financial issues were a driving force behind the behavior of both coalitions. Early in the process, the pro-Peotone camp pushed for an airport authority to put the region's airports, existing and proposed, in the hands of an entity jointly managed by both city and suburban interests. Supporters of a new south-suburban airport sought to tap into existing airport revenues, including passenger facility charges (PFCs) that travelers at Midway and O'Hare are required to pay. Partly to forestall discussion of such an authority (and to safeguard funds generated at its airports), the city created the Chicago–Gary Regional Airport Authority and gave it some oversight power on the operation of O'Hare, Midway, and the newly named Gary-Chicago Airport.

SOC amassed smaller but still significant financial reserves by tapping the general revenues of its members (that is, local governments near O'Hare). It spent its funds judiciously, focusing primarily on legal initiatives and public relations. Although support from some of its members eventually began to waiver, SOC was later instrumental in garnering the interest of private companies in financing the Peotone airport, a development that infused new life into this coalition.

Both coalitions understood the importance of enlisting the support of state government. With Jim Edgar still in the governor's mansion, the idea of building Peotone had a solid political base. The state deepened its commitment to the airport in 1997, when it released its initial engineering study for a Peotone facility. By the end of the decade, it appeared (to some degree because of campaign statements by Governor Edgar's successor, George Ryan, another downstate Republican) that the state had squarely sided with the pro-Peotone coalition. Ryan, who grew up in nearby Kankakee, had a strong interest in promoting economic development in the region.

The airlines opted to keep a safe distance from the verbal sparring between the dueling coalitions. American and United by now had such a commanding market share at O'Hare that some industry observers considered their vast connecting complexes to be "fortress hubs," capable of crushing new entrants. Although these carriers had an incentive to protect the status quo, they felt that some form of airport expansion was inevitable and recognized that an obstructionist stance could have political consequences. The carriers, in turn, aligned themselves with the pro-O'Hare camp, albeit on the condition that the airport's expansion would not result in substantially higher airport landing fees. Nonetheless, American's and United's support remained lukewarm. As many O'Hare expansion advocates rallied in the late 1990s to support the mayor's plans for a major redesign of that airport's terminal facilities (called "World Gateway"), these two airlines quietly voiced skepticism caused by fears of escalating costs.

The mayor made it clear that the city would not allow revenues generated at O'Hare and Midway to subsidize a new suburban airport—a position critical to gaining American's and United's support. Instead of a "green grass" airport, the city sought to promote the development of a third regional airport in Gary. Over the next several years, however, commercial air service to Gary performed relatively poorly, and this left proponents of the Indiana facility struggling to reassert its relevance in the airport debate.

The intensity of the airport debate rose to its zenith during the summer of 2001, when the Daley administration formally announced its plan to reconfigure existing runways and build several new ones at O'Hare. The O'Hare Modernization Plan envisioned a pair of entirely new runways on land acquired by the city, as well as major transit and highway improvements, including a new road for western-access to the airport from DuPage County. The coalition opposed to O'Hare's expansion, and SOC in particular, reaffirmed that it would do everything possible to fight the plan.

A GLOBAL CRISIS INTERVENES

The timing of Daley's announcement proved to be unfortunate because of a severe downturn that pushed the airline industry into a tailspin. Airline boardings dropped dramatically after the terrorist attacks of September 11, 2001, thus precipitating a crisis that bolstered the industry's claims that embarking on both a new airport and an expanded O'Hare was a luxury they could not afford (Schwieterman, 2002).

Adding to the complexity of the situation, certain members of the pro-O'Hare coalition expressed misgivings about entrusting leadership of the airport issue to a city that, they believed, was too inflexible in its approach. These concerns were greatly amplified by the mayor's handling of concession contracts at the city's airports and his stance on Meigs Field, a downtown airfield near McCormick Place. Mayor Daley had been resolute that Meigs Field should be converted into public open space. The increasingly high landing fees charged by the city kept many corporate jets away and greatly angered the general aviation community. In 2003, the mayor downplayed earlier remarks that he would keep Meigs open (if only to bolster state and federal support for his O'Hare plan) and bulldozed part of its only runway. His actions raised protests that he had finally "gone too far" and that he was grossly insensitive to the nuances of the region's aviation debate.

As the politics swirled and airlines struggled to fend off bankruptcy, it became exceedingly difficult to determine the most appropriate scale and configuration of the city's airport system. In the past, the traditional hub-and-spoke systems employed by major airlines had given the city a great deal of stability in forecasting traffic levels. As airlines looked to improve the utilization of labor and aircraft, however, they began de-emphasizing mega-hubs and began using smaller planes. Along with these changes came a shift in market share toward discount airlines, which supported the notion that consumers would be better served by developing a multiple-airport system rather than one limited primarily to Midway and O'Hare.

Although these circumstances necessitated that both coalitions adopt a less ambitious implementation timetable, the pendulum of public and political opinion continued to swing in the pro-O'Hare coalition's favor. Democrat Rod Blagojevich, a Chicagoan and ally of Daley, succeeded Ryan as governor in 2003 and took executive action that allowed the city to continue its effort to expand O'Hare without the risk of interference by the state. Blagojevich also gave the city the authority to expeditiously condemn the land needed for the project, even if this land was in neighboring suburbs. Although the state continued to buy land for the new airport at Peotone, a budget crisis forced it to reduce the scale of this program.

During this phase of the airport battle, the city crafted its plan with the help of consultants, public relations specialists, and an internal strategic-planning process, while putting comparatively less emphasis on galvanizing grassroots support or cultivating public opinion through direct citizen outreach—a manifestation of the "managerialism" discussed in previous chapters that was by this time a pervasive part of municipal policy. The city sought to foster the belief that the O'Hare Modernization Program was all but inevitable and that major decisions were best made internally, without the burden of a protracted public debate.

By early 2005, the pro-O'Hare coalition had apparently persevered in the battle to win the support of the public. Later that year, the city received federal approval to begin work on the first phase of the O'Hare Modernization Program. The city also entered into agreements with American, United, and other airlines to help finance this phase of the airport expansion plan. More than 15 years after the multistate Airport Capacity Study, the logjam blocking runway construction was finally broken.

The coalition opposing the expansion of O'Hare showed little sign of weakening, however, and even developed a working group—the South Suburban Airport Coalition—to spearhead an effort to attract private capital for the Peotone airport. This entity gathered a significant amount of momentum but also brought attention to an underlying weakness in the pro-Peotone coalition: the continuing distrust between the south-suburban faction and the SOC faction. South-suburban communities insisted that the municipalities affiliated with SOC, Bensenville and Elk Grove Village, eventually withdraw from the consortium if the Peotone airport was built. There was also a widening gulf between Representative Jackson and Will County officials, who had differing agendas and visions of the airport's future. Nevertheless, by early 2006, the effort to build a south-suburban airport had once again gathered considerable momentum.

These developments, however, did little to ameliorate concerns about the financial viability of either the O'Hare or south-suburban projects, or the need for costly ground-transportation improvements. At this writing, critical details about the O'Hare financing plan, including necessary highway and rail improvements, have yet to be resolved. A full 17 years after the region launched the Airport Capacity Study, a major increase in the capacity of the region's airports appears, even under the best scenario, several years away.

THE NATION'S RAILROAD HUB

Unlike the airport debate, in which opinions are divided into opposing camps, views are largely unified about the need for investment in the region's rail infrastructure. The rail lines of metropolitan Chicago, radiating from the city like spokes on a wheel, have been engines of regional prosperity for more than a century. These routes are today akin to funnels through which much of the country's rail-freight flows, fostering Chicago's role as a major logistics and distribution center.

Changing patterns of global commerce, growing shipments of time-sensitive freight, and railroad consolidations are attracting new customers to the rails (Reebie Associates 2003). Over the past decade, containerized freight has been growing at a rate far exceeding the growth of the region's economy. Unlike years ago, when manufacturing in the Great Lakes region was the primary driver of local rail-freight movements, the growth of traffic today is heavily dependent on trans-Pacific trade, the North American Free Trade Agreement (NAFTA) regulations, and manufacturing imports from developing countries.

The problems facing the city's rail lines tend to receive little attention in contemporary media reports, partially because of the dearth of railroad companies headquartered in the city. In 1970, Chicago was home to the eight major (Class I) railroads. Rail-industry executives were a prominent part of the region's civic leadership. The Rock Island Lines and Milwaukee Road, however, fell victim to wrenching bankruptcies, and the Chicago & Eastern Illinois, Chicago & North Western, Burlington Route, Illinois Central, and Monon were consolidated into larger carriers with head offices in other cities. During the late 1990s, the Atchison, Topeka & Santa Fe Railway merged with Burlington Northern and moved its headquarters to Fort Worth, thus stripping the Chicago region of its most influential voice in rail-industry affairs. Today, none of the Class 1 carriers has headquarters in Chicago.

Despite the loss of local leadership on this issue, a surge in railroad traffic is placing a burden on local terminals and railyards. Carriers must allow an average of more than 30 hours to move a rail-freight car across the city, a service standard that many shippers consider unacceptable. Railroads haul containers between freight yards by truck to avoid the congestion at yards and terminals, adding to traffic levels on city streets. Some observers liken this practice to using the city's streets as classification yards, which from the standpoint of many neighborhoods is a highly disruptive practice.

In metropolitan areas that support large ocean-going commerce, regional port authority stakeholders have generally served as focal points for public investments in rail-freight improvements. Such intergovernmental consortiums have had particular success in enhancing rail-freight connections in New York and Los Angeles, where the Port Authority of New York and New Jersey and the Port of Los Angeles have taken leadership roles. Chicago does not have an oceanic port, however, and lacks a tradition of strong intergovernmental leadership on rail-freight issues. Neither the Regional Transportation Authority nor the Chicago Port Authority considers major rail-freight investments to be part of their organizational mission.

Efforts to create an alliance of organizations to modernize the rail-freight system have been slowly gathering momentum. Over the past several years, two different coalitions have emerged to improve the rail-freight system. The first coalition centers on the city of Chicago, the state government, and private railroads, which are proposing a $1.5 billion initiative—the Chicago Regional Environmental and Transportation Efficiency Project (CREATE)—to improve the flow of freight through the region. This effort, supported by U.S. Representative William Lipinski (now retired), would take many years to implement and would focus heavily on the elimination of freight bottlenecks on the city's South Side.

A second coalition is an alliance of organizations and officials pushing for relief from a variety of problems related to railroad grade crossings, including the noise from locomotive horns, pedestrian accidents, and trains blocking grade highway crossings for extended periods. A coalition encompassing the Metropolitan Mayors' Caucus, various suburban councils of government, and municipal officials is pushing for state and federal policy changes. Senator Dick Durbin (who began his career as an attorney representing railroads) and Representative Dennis Hastert (whose west-suburban district is deeply affected by grade-crossing issues) have brought visibility to the coalitions goal's on Capitol Hill.

Hastert's role as the Speaker of the House and Durbin's membership on the Senate Appropriations Committee provides a base of political power that could be mobilized to the region's advantage. Lipinski's retirement, however, has been a major blow to proponents of local rail-freight projects.

At present, efforts to improve the rail system are moving from the planning stage to the construction stage. Nevertheless, with critical financial issues unresolved, it remains unclear whether some of the more ambitious plans to reduce rail-freight congestion will become a reality.

THE POLITICS OF PASSENGER TRAINS

The push to expand the capacity in the region's rail system is closely linked to proposals to build a network of modern, high-speed rail passenger routes to and from Chicago. The departments of transportation in nine states (Illinois, Indiana, Iowa, Michigan, Minnesota, Missouri, Nebraska, Ohio, and Wisconsin), have created the Midwest Regional Rail Initiative, an intergovernmental compact that enlists the support of a variety of advocacy groups, most notably the Environmental Law & Policy Center and the Midwest High Speed Rail Association.

These entities are pursuing efforts that could establish Chicago as the epicenter of a 3,000-mile passenger system. Chicago is envisioned as the hub for a network that will link Cincinnati, Cleveland, Detroit, St. Louis, Minneapolis-St. Paul, and several other metropolitan areas. By 2015, several thousand passengers could move across the system daily on trains reaching a maximum speed of 110 m.p.h. Although the coalition pushing for investments in high-speed rail has the advantage of involving governments with extensive budgetary authority and hopes for matching federal dollars (which have been slow to materialize), it also has to contend with a variety of internal problems. First, differing budgetary issues and philosophies toward transportation investments among the states is hampering planning and implementation.

Another issue affecting the performance of the coalition is the inequity of the costs and benefits associated with rail investments. The funds that a given state needs to allocate for high-speed rail corridors are not always closely aligned with the benefits that state receives. Although much of the benefit of the Chicago–St. Louis corridor would be realized by travelers and businesses based in Missouri, for example, this state will likely bear only a small fraction of the costs because only a few miles of this route actually lie within its boundaries. The asymmetries in the benefits and costs of high-speed rail investments have weakened interstate initiatives and led some to conclude that corridor planning must be under the purview of the federal government.

The coalition must also struggle with an ambivalent or even adversarial relationship with the railroad companies owning and maintaining the routes. Freight-oriented railroads making their tracks available for passenger trains have an incentive to demand improvements that will have spill-over benefits for their freight business. Although some carriers, such as Burlington Northern Santa Fe, might be considered appropriately as part of the coalition pushing for rail-passenger service, others are akin to independent contractors.

Amtrak's presence in the coalition also is awkward. A significant share of planners question whether Amtrak can successfully (and affordably) provide the necessary level of quality service for Midwestern high-speed rail to prosper. Amtrak dates back to 1971, when the federal government essentially nationalized a core system of intercity passenger routes. The beleaguered quasi-government agency may not be able to project an image or provide a travel experience that is favorable enough to attract large numbers of passengers away from highway and air systems. The possibility of contracting with private-sector firms to provide such services, however, is constrained by the absence of

agreements giving such firms the authority to operate over the tracks of freight railroads.

The coalition pushing for a high-speed rail system has the advantage of involving the same government agencies that are planning for the expansion of airports. Recognizing an opportunity to provide passengers with convenient air–rail connections, the State of Illinois is considering aligning one of the proposed high-speed passenger routes through Peotone. Nevertheless, an alliance between coalitions promoting airport investment and those pushing for an improved rail system has yet to materialize. Successfully positioning high-speed rail service as a substitute for airport expansion may be necessary if the coalition pushing for this alternative is to achieve a wider base of political support.

CONCLUSION

Perhaps the most basic observation one can make from reviewing the politics of public investment in Chicago's intercity air and rail systems are the differences in the composition and behavior of the coalitions involved. Although the airport-expansion issue was initially envisioned as being decided by a multistate pact, it has evolved into a series of efforts dominated by coalitions with diametrically opposing goals and comprised almost entirely of organizations and leaders in the Chicago metropolitan area.

The effort to expand the region's rail-freight capacity, conversely, has suffered from the disjointed nature of its planning process. The dispersion of effort among various policy forays has apparently denied supporters of rail-freight investment the critical mass needed to overcome the legislative and political hurdles. The leadership positions of Illinois' congressional delegation apparently could be used to greater advantage if these different efforts were consolidated.

The push for a high-speed rail system is being orchestrated by a coalition committed to a common goal but riddled with coordination problems and financial conflicts. Differing assessments of the appropriate allocation of cost have hampered the efforts of government agencies and fostered mistrust among the states and private railroads. Attempts to push decision making into the federal realm, however, have been hindered by the legacy of Amtrak, which has left many stakeholders and leaders in the U.S. Senate wary of a more centralized planning approach.

Chicago—the "Player with Railroads" and the "Nation's Freight Handler"—will for the foreseeable future remain the country's busiest interchange. Its terminals will continue to shoulder a heavy burden, moving freight and passengers through the American Heartland. With the rise of coalition politics, however, the expansion of the region's air and rail systems is less methodical and predictable than before, leaving big plans adrift in the ebb and flow of changing tides.

Costas Spirou

25 Urban Beautification: The Construction of a New Identity in Chicago

DURING THE LAST 20 YEARS, cultural policy has become an integral part of economic and physical redevelopment strategies for many urban centers across the United States. Driven by deindustrialization, population decentralization, and globalization, many cities have turned to cultural strategies as a means to reposition themselves in a rapidly changing economic environment or to reaffirm their standing in an evolving metropolitan hierarchy.

One factor fueling culture-driven strategies in urban development is that citizens now have more leisure-expendable income than ever before. This fact has led city governments to increase expenditures on culture and related specialized bureaucracies. As a result, policy-making bodies have ventured to enhance their provision of cultural services to cater to a growing, more differentiated, and increasingly sophisticated public demand. The outcome of these trends has resulted in the development of an economy of urban tourism. This has encouraged cities and their governments to turn their attention to policies that center on showcasing their cultural heritage, exporting their cultural identity, and translating these policies into revenue streams that can then be used for social and economic transformation. Hence, promoting festivals, arts, sport, music, cinema, conventions, and exhibits has come to be viewed as central activities of this strategy.

This trend is the focus of an April 2000 report published by the National League of Cities entitled *Tourism and Entertainment as a Local Economic Development Strategy: A Survey of City Halls* (Judd et al. 2000), which discusses

how tourist and entertainment infrastructure has recently emerged as a primary form of public investment in American cities. How has this tourism-focused economic restructuring come to fuel emerging urban-planning strategies? Although there is no simple answer to this question, multiple issues can be identified as factors that have caused the ascendance of urban tourism and associated public works activities.

In the past, tourism and related cultural forms did not fit the planning mix and were viewed at best as inconsequential elements of local economic activity (Beauregard 1998). The motivation and rising demand for urban tourism may be found in two fundamental factors. The first can be drawn from a recent and continuing desire by people to explore the unfamiliar and to construct or to solidify their identity through travel and appropriately utilized leisure time (Law 2002). Whether it is the search for self-actualization (Maslow 1970), the acquisition of "cultural capital" (Bourdieu 1984), or identity formation through consumption (Baudrillard 1988) and pilgrimages to famous places (MacCannell 1976), or even the "tourist gaze" as projected onto destinations by the media (Urry 1990), tourism and leisure activities have entered and influenced the realm of human experiences in ways more powerful and profound than ever before.

The second factor relates more directly to the dynamics of city governance and to the contemporary condition of cities. The economic decline following the post war restructuring; the impact of globalization, which substantially reduced the primacy of the U.S. economy in production activities; and diminishing contributions by the federal government to the cities and states, presented a series of challenges for local officials facing the new fiscal reality of shrinking budgets and services. Cities responded by divorcing themselves from their manufacturing dependency; instead, they searched for ways to diversify and strengthen the various remaining sectors of their economy. Within this framework, urban tourism emerges as an appealing alternative, one that slowly has gained favor with local officials and civic boosters alike.

As cities rush to take advantage of this new growth potential, they face numerous challenges, mainly in the areas of urban identity and urban competition. Specifically, how can a city with a formerly strong and nationally or internationally identifiable manufacturing economy convert itself into a tourist destination? Most important, how does it convince potential visitors of its new services and sense of "attractiveness"? Similarly, what are its competitive advantages within this reformulated environment?

The rise of urban tourism increases inter-municipal competition and requires cities to be more entrepreneurial. In *Marketing Places: Attracting Investment, Industry, and Tourism to Cities, States, and Nations,* international marketing guru Philip Kotler along with Donald H. Haider and Irving Rein (1993) definitively make the point that competition is a new reality that cannot be avoided: "Places have to visualize a clearer sense of the functions they perform and the roles they play.... A place that fails to examine its prospects and potential critically is likely to lose out to more attractive competitors" (p. 311). Within this context, the city is no different from the corporation that must engage in image-building activities, market its products, and be prepared to deal with change if it wants to maintain its competitive edge.

The competition to attract tourists has had a tremendous impact on cities as spatial transformation, increased commodification, rapid segmentation of urban form and function, and new economic and planning mechanisms became widely introduced. The "tourist bubble" has emerged as a common restructuring strategy

(Judd 2003; Judd and Fainstein 1999). Convention centers, theme parks, stadiums, and casino and riverboat gambling have reshaped the physical landscape and image of hundreds of dying urban cores. The city of leisure and entertainment, aimed at attracting locals and visitors, has caused a reorganization of planning policies and priorities (Clark 2003; Spirou and Bennett 2003, 37–58).

TOURISM AND URBAN BEAUTIFICATION IN CHICAGO: BUILDING THE CITY OF LEISURE

Tourism and urban beautification initiatives have proved crucial parts of the cultural policy agenda adopted in Chicago during the last decade, and these initiatives are closely connected to the structural changes outlined in the first section of this chapter. As a form of public policy, the promotion of tourism and the showcasing of Chicago have evolved considerably over the years. In the past, tourism and large events—such as the Columbian Exposition of 1893 and the World's Fair of 1933–34—were means to another end, the projection of Chicago's vitality and industrial might. These were also single-purpose, periodic events, without an enduring place in the city's economy. By contrast, today, tourism, leisure, and their related promotions are part of a continuous flow of activities, and one of Chicago's major industries.

Chicago began to promote itself as a site for convention, trade show, and tourism business at the beginning of the twentieth century. In 1907, recognizing the increasing view of the city as a world-class attraction, the Chicago Association of Commerce charged a local business committee to bring conventions to the downtown area. Yet, the city was not a leader in this industry; the Chicago Convention and Visitors Bureau (CCVB) was not founded until 1943. The CCVB was expanded in 1970 to include the Tourism Council of Greater Chicago, thus forming the Chicago Convention and Tourism Bureau. In 1980, the Bureau furthered its responsibilities by becoming the principal sales agent for the McCormick Place, a task held until that time by the Metropolitan Fair and Exposition Authority (MFEA).

It was not until the 1990s, however, under the leadership of Richard M. Daley, that Chicago crafted and promoted a policy that converted tourism, conventions, and leisure and entertainment activities into a central and consistent part of its economic development agenda, one expected to produce significant revenues for city coffers. In 1989, Mayor Daley supported the MFEA's assuming of responsibility for Navy Pier and renamed the agency the Metropolitan Pier and Exposition Authority. This move would focus the group's management activities, thus helping the development and promotion of the Pier. He also supported the expansion of McCormick Place. At his first, full-term inaugural address, Daley (1991) noted: "Chicago's prominence as a convention center is vital to the entire state of Illinois. But other cities across the nation have caught on to the benefits of the convention trade, and they are hard on our heels. We must expand McCormick Place or lose our competitive edge in the battle for convention and tourism dollars."

More recently, the mayor's economic growth strategy has included festivals and large-scale events, even during Chicago's cold winter months. Referring to "Winter Delights," a series of city-sponsored cultural activities running from November to February, Daley noted: "One of the best ways to maintain Chicago's economic momentum is to encourage tourists and Chicagoans alike to enjoy the best of Chicago. January and February are always challenging months. The more we can help the better" (Angelides 2003).

A major part of Chicago's cultural policy agenda is produced by the Mayor's Office of Special Events (MOSE). The Office provides support for year-round family entertainment, neighborhood festivals, parades, and citywide holiday celebrations. MOSE manages 20 major events annually, bringing millions of people to the lakefront. Twelve of these 20 events have been instituted since Mayor Daley took office in 1989. The central aims of the City of Chicago's cultural policy agenda have been to (1) reconstruct Chicago's image as a city of culture and leisure, (2) utilize this identity and translate it into sub-

stantial revenue streams from tourism and related activities, and (3) alleviate the negative social consequences associated with city living, thus making the city a more inviting place for residents and prospective investors. In the end, the rise and role of tourism and urban beautification in Chicago reveal how structural changes inform pertinent local policies that in turn come to reshape municipal identity and affect everyday living.

CHICAGO AND THE NEW ECONOMY OF TOURISM

During the last decade, Chicago's lakefront has been adorned with various new public works. These have included the renovation and redesign of Navy Pier in 1995, at a cost of $250 million; the Lakefront Millennium Project in 2004, at a cost of nearly $500 million; the reconfiguration of Lake Shore Drive and creation of the Museum Campus in 1998, at $110 million; the rebuilding of Soldier Field, newly opened in 2003 at a cost of over $680 million; the proposed conversion of Meigs Field into a $40 million "super park"; and the expansion of the McCormick Place South Building, Chicago's main convention space in 1996, at $675 million (Spirou 2000).

Many of these projects have included massive investments to ensure that green landscapes abound. The plan for Soldier Field, for example, utilizes 17 acres of space and extends from the Museum Campus to McCormick Place East. The area includes a children's garden, a sledding hill with winter gardens, sculptures, and 1,300 trees (Moffett 2001; Wagle 2003). The shifting of Lake Shore Drive to the west added 57 acres to the Museum Campus area. To put into perspective the size of this project, consider that more than 120,000 cubic yards of dirt were displaced, and the ground was lowered by as much as 22 feet to create an imposing tiered lawn (Kamin 1998).

On the convention front, when Las Vegas and Orlando recently upgraded their facilities to match Chicago's 2.2 million square feet of exhibit space and 360,000 square feet of meeting room space, Chicago responded by building McCormick Place West. This expansion, at a cost

TABLE 25.1. City of Chicago Estimated Travel (in millions)

	1997	1998	1999	2000	2001	2002	2003	2004
Domestic	25.60	26.70	28.60	30.46	28.56	28.85	29.04	30.97
International	1.09	1.21	1.27	1.35	1.07	1.01	0.78	0.94
Total	26.69	27.91	29.80	31.81	29.63	29.86	29.82	31.91

Source: D.K. Shifflet & Associates, Ltd., International Trade Administration/Tourism Industries, Chicago Convention and Tourism Bureau.

of $850 million, is scheduled for completion in 2008, and it will be developed in an area bordered by Cermark Road, Martin Luther King Drive, Indiana Avenue, and the Stevenson Expressway. It will include approximately 500,000 additional square feet of exhibition space and 200,000 square feet of meeting space, thus once again surpassing its nearest competitors.

It is clear that Chicago has made a commitment to conventioneers and visitors, and it plans to play a major role in the new economy of tourism. The number of trade and consumer shows hosted by Chicago has increased from 42 in 1989 to 50 in 1997 to 83 in 2003. The net square feet of space utilized has remained around 11 million annually, and the attendance has ranged around three million visitors each year. The convention business struggled in 2004, however, as competition from other cities increased substantially. The total number of visitors to the City of Chicago has also grown in the last few years (Table 25.1). In 2000, it was projected that the total number of visitors to Chicago in 2002 would reach 35.63 million. Chicago's tourism experienced a record year in 2000. However, because of the September 11, 2001, terrorist attacks and the subsequent economic slowdown, tourism volume is expected to hover (at least for the near future) around the late 1990s figures. This is still well above those posted during the early 1990s, when total tourism figures were between 20 and 23 million visitors (Hinz 2003). As 2004 data reveals, Chicago is on its way to rebounding: 2004 posted a considerable increase in domestic travel, bringing the total number of visitors back to the peak numbers of the year 2000.

Apart from Grant Park, the Museum Campus, and McCormick Place, Chicago has recently invested in numerous other destination attractions, notably Navy Pier. The revitalization of the 3,300-foot pier, converted into a center of entertainment and recreation, has produced the city's most popular attraction, drawing over eight million visitors annually. Other recent investments have included a substantial upgrade at the Lincoln Park Zoo, a $40 million modernization of the Adler Planetarium, new construction of exhibits at the John G. Shedd Aquarium, and a $10 million addition at the Field Museum (Mendieta 1999).

A yearly round of nearly continuous festivals and outdoor activities is another means of attracting tourists and day visitors to the city. City sponsorship of such activities has expanded over the years to include many smaller venue events, such as art fairs and exhibits, fireworks displays, outdoor movie presentations at Grant Park, concerts, dances, and festivals (Table 25.2).

The economic impact of these leisure- and entertainment-based activities is especially touted by city officials. During the record-breaking 2000 year, more than 120,000 jobs were attributed to domestic tourism, with over $180 million in local taxes derived from the same source. Given the impact of larger national and international events, these figures declined in 2002, when the local taxes generated from domestic tourism were estimated at about $160 million. Despite this decrease, according to data from the Chicago Convention and Tourism Bureau, in 2002, Chicago remained first as a domestic business-travel destination, eighth for domestic leisure travel, and fourth for total domestic travel.

TREES, PLANTS, AND CHICAGO'S EMERGING MUNICIPAL IDENTITY

The face of Chicago has been significantly altered during the last ten years in support of

TABLE 25.2. Attendance at Festivals in Chicago: 1996–2003

Festival	2003	2002	2001	2000	1999	1998	1997	1996
Taste of Chicago	3,565,000	3,350,000	3,575,000	3,570,000	3,695,000	3,065,000	3,460,000	3,250,000
Air and Water Show	2,200,000	2,100,000	1,950,000	2,200,000	2,200,000	2,200,000	2,400,000	2,100,000
Blues Festival	560,000	750,000	750,000	585,000	700,000	660,000	660,000	600,000
Country Music Festival[1]	525,000	520,000	605,000	600,000	600,000	250,000	600,000	525,000
Venetian Night	600,000	750,000	575,000	550,000	550,000	500,000	500,000	500,000
Jazz Festival	285,000	305,000	315,000	310,000	360,000	310,000	300,000	310,000
Celtic Festival	175,000	195,000	Cancelled	195,000	160,000	150,000	125,000	N/A
Gospel Festival	210,000	225,000	200,000	175,000	150,000	150,000	250,000	200,000
Viva! Chicago	160,000	160,000	160,000	165,000	160,000	160,000	150,000	150,000

[1] Part of Taste of Chicago.
Source: The Chicago Convention and Tourism Bureau, Mayor's Office of Special Events, *Crain's Chicago Business*, Museums in the Park, and individual attractions. June 2, 2003 and May 11, 2004.

the foregoing initiatives, as urban beautification has been placed at the forefront of local urban planning efforts. For example, large stone and concrete planters now define the medians of main thoroughfares, bright flowerbeds and newly planted trees dominate open spaces, and wrought iron fences and old-style street light posts are commonplace. Specialized public exhibits in the central business district and adjacent popular tourist destinations have included cows, couches and, most recently, statues of baseball players. In 2000, Mayor Richard M. Daley even authorized the use of Venetian-style gondolas on the Chicago River (Spielman 2000).

One of the driving forces behind the changes in Chicago has been the introduction of a new Landscape Ordinance. The ordinance was originally put in place in 1991. In July 1999, significant amendments were added to make it even stricter. From the very beginning, Mayor Daley argued for the importance of increased aesthetic appeal in city streets by requiring investment in trees and streetscapes. According to the ordinance, builders of new or substantially renovated commercial or large residential buildings are expected to incorporate landscaping into their plans. In 1999, numerous amendments were added to include landscaping islands and hedges for new parking lots and shade trees for every 25 feet of new building frontage. The effect of this policy was dramatic, because the private sector shared in the expenditures and sharply accelerated the greening of Chicago.

Other city government-sponsored initiatives have shared the goals of the Landscape Ordinance. These include Mayor Daley's Green-Streets Program, which has planted thousands of trees across Chicago and supported community-based planting efforts. As part of the mayor's efforts to further enhance the aesthetic quality of the Loop, River North, and Printers Row districts, 950 hanging baskets were installed along city streets in 2001 (USDA Forest Service 2003). In 2000, the city government (Office of the Mayor 2000) announced a tree-planting program aimed at buffering Chicago's expressways. Many of the Chicago's major streets also have been adorned with stone planters, including downtown LaSalle Street, whose median strip now sports three-foot-tall planters bearing Chicago's municipal motto "Urbs in Horto" (City in the Garden) (Suparno 1999). However, some observers have noted that the planters may be responsible for increased traffic accidents. Atop the planters, tulips as tall as 18 inches can create visibility obstacles, a concern expressed by both the Fire and Police Departments (Hilkevitch 2000). In 1999, Mayor Daley's commitment to environmental enhancement was recognized by the National Arbor Day Foundation, which awarded him with its highest honor, the J. Sterling Morton Award (National Arbor Day Foundation 1999).

The city has also looked abroad to expand its cultural vitality through exhibits such as the Chicago's Cows on Parade Art Exhibit, which took place in the summer of 1999. Sponsored by the Department of Cultural Affairs, the 300 life-size, fiberglass art cows invaded the downtown sidewalks and plazas from June to October.

Originally conceived by Beat Seeberger-Quin and presented in Zurich, Switzerland, during the summer of 1998, the exhibit was reported to have brought more than one million visitors to the city and produced an estimated $200 million in revenues (Chicago Department of Cultural Affairs 1999).

It is said that whenever Richard and Maggie Daley visit European cities, Chicagoans may have to brace for new planning initiatives. Some of those have included the installation of lights at Water Tower Place Park, a $600,000 refurbishment plan designed to mirror the effect generated by public spaces in Paris (Gezari 2000). Other touches to this high-profile park have included Parisian-style landscape designs, ivy and colorful annuals plantings, French park chairs, and puppet performances of the sort performed at the *Jardin du Luxembourg* (Frey 2000). As a long-time, self-proclaimed fan of Paris, the mayor has repeatedly expressed his vision of bringing the atmosphere of "the city of lights" to Chicago. One of those plans has included illuminating and bathing the city's skyscrapers, bridges, and bridge houses in lights while replacing unattractive light posts with ornamental, turn-of-the-century designs (Washburn 1998a).

Historic preservation and the creation of landmark districts has been another strategy employed by the city to maintain the architectural integrity of historic buildings and to promote them as part of Chicago's cultural heritage. Most notable is the recent designation of a mile-long section of Michigan Avenue from Randolph Street to 11th Street. The 12-block stretch includes several distinctive examples of late nineteenth- and early twentieth-century architecture. According to the mayor, "No other street in the city reflects the beauty and evolution of Chicago more than Michigan Avenue.... [these buildings] make a district that is like no other in the world, one that is symbolic of the cultural, commercial and architectural heritage of Chicago." Fourteen of the district's 45 properties are already either on the National Register of Historic Places or official Chicago Landmarks (Department of Planning and Development 2002).

These and other initiatives have helped forge Chicago's new municipal identity. In 2000, for example *Money* magazine identified Chicago as the best place to live in the Midwest, noting the city's major beautification and redevelopment efforts. Similarly, commentaries such as this from Steve Berg (2000) of the *Minneapolis-Star Tribune* hail the transformation of Chicago to outside audiences, while noting the effect of recent beautification initiatives:

> Although a creature of New York, it always seemed to me that Edward Hopper painted Chicago. His brawny buildings, his plain streets, the dreary mood of his urban landscapes captured perfectly a city unable to escape its broad Midwestern shoulders, its functional status as hog butcher to the world.... Now, few boulevards in the world can match the flower-bedecked splendor of Michigan Avenue, and public beauty is spreading like a contagion down every street in the Loop and into the neighborhoods.

A MASTER FORM OF URBAN BEAUTIFICATION: THE TRIALS OF CHICAGO'S MILLENNIUM PARK

Initially unveiled as the Lakefront Millennium Project in 1998, this is the most recent, large-scale, culturally based development effort of the Richard M. Daley administration. The trials of this development reveal the risky side of linking entertainment and leisure investment to economic development. From the beginning, Mayor Daley (1998) characterized the project as "an exciting new cultural destination for families and children, and an economic magnet for visitors and conventioneers," in short, a project with multiple objectives. This exceedingly ambitious public works improvement would be a crucial component of Chicago's orchestrated effort to reposition itself in a rapidly expanding world economy and refine its international image.

The conceptualization of the park was based on formal French landscape designs, such as the gardens of Versailles. Also integral to the planning strategy was Daniel Burnham's decades-old vision of Grant Park as a civic focal point. Millennium Park's design includes both formal elements, such as those found in classic French gardens, and entertainment and leisure opportunities, such as its ice rink. The initially projected cost of $150 million included $120 million to be funded by revenue bonds. Corporate sponsors and private donations were expected to provide the remaining $30 million. The proposed 16.5-acre project would feature an outdoor performance stage, an indoor theater, an ice skating rink, gardens, and concession stands. Summertime Grant Park Symphony performances and the city's other outdoor musical festivals would relocate to Millennium Park. A parking garage would be constructed directly beneath the park, on land formerly home to a rail yard, and proceeds from the parking structure would pay off the bonds. The completion of the project was set for mid-2000 (Shields 1998).

The Chicago Department of Transportation subsequently announced an expansion of the plan, including a "warming house," a restaurant for the skating rink, a larger Music and Dance Theater Chicago (from 500 to 1,500 seats), a commuter bicycle center, a glass greenhouse pavilion, and an improved music pavilion (Department of Transportation 1999). The park's area also grew to 24.6 acres (Strahler 1999). The completion date was postponed until fall 2001, and the cost estimate increased to $200 million. The City issued additional revenue bonds to reach a total of $150 million, with a further $50 million to be raised from private sources. To retire the additional bond debt, parking fees would be increased (Shields 1999).

By late 2001, the transformation of the derelict railroad yard into the glittery park was far from complete. Because of construction delays, the parking garage was not producing the expected revenue. Continuous design changes and errors in the construction process had forced contractors to stop and resume work on numerous occasions. The reworked designs forced crews to revise work that had been already completed. The City pulled the lead contractors, Harston Construction and Schwendener Company, off the project and, in so doing, provoked a lawsuit. The *Chicago Tribune* (Martin and Cohen 2001) reported: "In less than a year, the city issued more than a thousand design revisions piecemeal that caused 'delay, extra work and tremendous loss of efficiency'," forcing

contractors Harston and Schwendener to incur "millions of dollars in additional costs and put the project substantially behind schedule." City Hall responded to these challenges by shifting the oversight of the project from the Department of Transportation to the Public Building Commission and hiring a new construction management firm. The Daley administration also re-estimated the cost of Millennium Park at $320 million, of which $220 million would be publicly funded (Martin and Cohen 2001).

Achieving world-class city status in a rapidly changing economy of culture and leisure requires the investment in renowned architects, sculptors, and design experts. Apart from their presumed skills, bringing such figures on board demonstrates both a city's taste and deep pockets. Heralded architect Frank Gehry had this exact effect on the city of Bilbao, Spain, where, in 1997, he built the highly acclaimed Guggenheim Museum. In turn, Gehry was hired to design the band shell of the Music Pavilion at the Millennium Park. His signature massive steel trellis, unveiled in 1999, would be built over a seating area for 11,000 spectators, the new home of the Grant Park Symphony Orchestra.

The completion challenges experienced by this component of the project encapsulate the trials of Millennium Park as a whole. Initially scheduled for completion in 2000, the band shell did not host its first event until mid-summer 2004. Although the early cost estimate was $17.8 million, the actual cost ballooned to $50 million (Kamin 2003). Moreover, the willful City Beautiful-oriented fan of classical architecture Mayor Daley clashed with the willful, costly, and postmodern-oriented Frank Gehry over the band shell's design. Cost overruns and Mayor Daley's halting acceptance of the design's irregular geometry suggest that the pursuit of civic grandeur can tax even a civic beautifier's enthusiasm.

Throughout the construction process, the Daley administration has proudly promoted its partnership with corporations and the private sector in creating various elements of the park. Although economic recession hampered fundraising efforts, many of the park's features reveal strong public–private partnerships. The names of many of these contributors are prominently displayed at given venues, including the Millennium Monument in Wrigley Square (William Wrigley Jr. Foundation), the Ice Rink at McCormick Tribune Plaza (Robert R. McCormick Tribune Foundation), the Bank One Promenade (Bank One Foundation), and the BP Pedestrian Bridge (BP America Inc.).

Although the 24.6-acre park has been hampered by cost overruns, extensive completion delays, and public feuding, most local commentators have praised the finally completed Millennium Park. According to John McCarron of the *Chicago Tribune* (2004), "Don't even compare Millennium Park to last summer's debut of the new—and improved?—Soldier Field, or to last week's groundbreaking for the umpteenth addition to McCormick Place.... Millennium Park is bigger than those civic debuts, in size and in meaning. Compare it, instead, to the 1893 and 1933 World's Fairs in Chicago ... "

The examination of this initiative provides numerous insights to Chicago and its emerging new urban identity. An assessment of the Millennium Park development process allows for two key observations. The first deals with the dominance of public–private partnerships in the city's public spaces. The second centers on the opportunity costs signified by the huge expenditures for Millennium Park. Both these issues also point to larger sociopolitical considerations, as Chicago endeavors to reconstruct itself as a city of leisure.

When cultural representation comes to be treated as a form of urban capital, the strong association between the corporate and public sectors, as reflected in the Millennium Park case, extends beyond the realm of philanthropic stewardship. This public space, as a highly visible and extensively promoted attraction, becomes a powerful advertising venue. Furthermore, the financial interests of the corporate sector assert substantial influence on the conceptualization and design of public works projects and serve to obscure the demarcation between the public and private. These partnerships, of course, also help cultivate stronger relationships between the Daley administration and corporate entities such as SBC, Bank One (now Chase Bank), and BP America Inc., all of which might choose to offer support to the incumbent in future mayoral elections.

As Millennium Park's price tag increased from $150 million to $500 million, its cost generated considerable local debate regarding scarce public resources and competing public needs. Chicago's public schools continue to struggle and, despite concerted reform efforts over the last ten years, student performance still lags. Criminal activity continues to undermine the quality of life in many Chicago neighborhoods, with the city ranking first among large urban centers in homicides both in 2002 and 2003. Housing issues persist, as more and more residents are forced to cope with the effects of gentrification, displacement, and limited affordable-housing options. Given these social challenges, has Chicago expended its resources equitably? Although Millennium Park will be the jewel of Chicago's lakefront for many years to come, the lack of public debate over the project's conceptualization and execution, as well as questions about the municipal priorities it seems to reveal, will be the unsettling, parallel legacy of this major urban beautification initiative.

PART V

Conclusion

Roberta Garner

26 Learning from Chicago

Who built the seven gates of Thebes? The books list the names of kings. Was it kings who hauled the craggy blocks of stone?
——Bertolt Brecht, *A Worker Reads History*, p. 109

A NEW ACCUMULATION regime is transforming industrial cities. In this volume, we are not developing a one-size-fits-all "New Chicago paradigm," but opening a conversation about change in industrial cities, the causes of similarities and differences in the effect of the new accumulation regime, and the ways in which actors contest and negotiate responses to converging forces.

SECTION I: WHAT HAPPENED? A NEW ACCUMULATION REGIME, 1960–2005

The five converging forces that organize this volume are part of an underlying process of social change, the onset of a new accumulation regime within capitalism, a trend that follows three major phases in capitalism: nineteenth-century industrial capitalism, the period of instability during the early twentieth century, and the "long boom" of the post-World War II years. The new phase is variously characterized by terms such as *postmodern, neo-liberal, postindustrial, flexible capitalism, globalization,* and the *information society,* depending on whether economic, political, cultural, or technological elements of the overall transformation are highlighted. The shift became evident by the 1970s—certainly by the 1980s—with increased transna-

tional flows of capital and people, government withdrawal from welfare and regulatory functions, decreasing unionization and labor organization, a resurgent emphasis on ethnic and religious identity, the appearance of new information technologies, the disintegration of large firms into global webs, and the upward redistribution of wealth in many developed societies following the post-World War II period of leveling. All countries and cities are affected by these processes, but in different ways depending on global region, past history, and the actions of individuals and organizations (Beauregard 1989).

This cluster of changes is almost certainly more than a short-term fluctuation and it may herald a transformation of the magnitude of the Industrial Revolution. The technological basis of the transformation contributes to the irreversibility of the changes, and political forces make it unlikely that there will be a return to the post-World War II welfare states in their original form. The authors of Chapter 1 argue that this transformation is creating a totally new form, a hyper-industrial mode of production and technology, and this may indeed turn out to be the case in historical perspective.

In an accumulation regime shift, major interrelated changes occur in technology, state–economy relationships, forms of enterprise, capital–labor relations, and global structures of power. Each change in turn triggers further changes in technology, the role of the state, capital–labor relations, the global political economy, and forms of enterprise, thus creating a cascade of changes that are unlikely to be reversed. The totality of system change remains within that larger entity called "industrial capitalism," defined by a market economy and private ownership of productive enterprises. In the "postindustrial" era, industrial technology means the penetration of machinery into all areas of life, including intellectual production and information processing (Mandel 1999).

Both structure and agency are present in the transformation. On the agency or instrumentalist side, political decisions are made and implemented by powerful elites. In the instrumental perspective, emphasis is on employer choice to introduce new technologies and move production to low-wage and nonunion locations, as well as pressure from finance capital to deregulate controls on transnational capital flows. The Thatcher and Reagan administrations made key decisions to privatize enterprises, deregulate markets, and reduce social-service spending. Alternatively, from the structural perspective, these choices of employers and governments were conditioned responses to fundamental contradictions that became apparent in the post–World War II accumulation regime. The model of the welfare state and national economic development encountered a decline in profitability when workers increased their share of the economic pie. The choice to initiate the neo-liberal model was determined by this underlying structural problem.

Both elites and ordinary citizens of cities and metropolitan areas experience the new accumulation regime as an external, irreversible, structural force, but hope it can be managed at the local level. The tension between apparently determined macro-level forces associated with the new accumulation regime and a limited but open range of possibilities at the micro level gives the new Chicago an unpredictable, ambiguous character.

The effect of the new accumulation regime, although not a zero-sum game, produces unequal outcomes. Actors are constrained by structures formed in the past. These structures are not identical in all locales affected by current trends and forces; therefore, these multiple micro-diversities, together with the local, ongoing interests of agents, make change different, uneven, and unequal at the local level. Actors respond to what they perceive as trends creating new structures that constrain further action or make it less effective in coping with the flow of events.

SECTION II: THE PAST IS PRESENT: NEW TRENDS AND OLD PATTERNS IN CHANGING CHICAGO

Chicago's current situation is the product of two forces: new trends associated with the new accumulation regime (the focus of this book) and old patterns that persist despite the transformation and intermingle with the new characteristics.

The new trends include an economic shift to corporate services and related dependent economic activities, such as entertainment, education, health care, and retailing; revalorization of the central city, accompanied by the displacement of lower-income African Americans and a crisis of affordable housing; accelerated immigration based on expanding social networks; the hourglass economy, which is not only a class structure but also a structure of racial and ethnic disparities; and a new politics of development and managerialism.

Older trends and characteristics persist, and here we will identify six striking continuities. One persistent feature of life in Chicago is the racial divide. It is now softened by a growth in the African American middle class and the dilution of race in an increasingly diverse society, but it is also hardened by the residential isolation of African Americans (Hancock and Kim 2003; Mendell and Little 2003, Pattillo-McCoy 1999), high dropout rates for African American youth (Olszewski 2005; Chapter 20), high incarceration rates among African Americans, and displacement of lower-income African Americans from the city center. A second persistent pattern is the sectoral spatial organization of the whole metropolitan region, marked by suburban status crystallization. Over recent decades, there has been little change in the relative socioeconomic levels of suburban communities, and in addition to the full range of subtle status differences among communities throughout the suburban arc, a major difference in socioeconomic level and resources persist between affluent, predominantly white northern suburbs and low-income, predominantly African American southern suburbs (Fidel 2003). A third long-standing feature of the Chicago region is that it is a leading manufacturing center of the nation. Far from being postindustrial, the Chicago region retains its manufacturing strength, although the plants have moved from the central city into other parts of the metropolitan region (Chapter 3; Markussen et al. 2001; Phillips-Fein 1998). A fourth pattern is in fact the continuing shift of manufacturing into suburban areas, which began early in the nineteenth century and contributes to the sprawl of both economic activities and residential development (D'Eramo 2002). Fifth, Chicago politics and styles of governing remain stable, as seen in the organization of City Hall, the strength of the mayor, and the centralized patterns of policing and educational decision making. New managerial forms of governance are blended with the older, centralized patterns. Finally, Chicago's new burst of immigration is, in many respects, simply a return to the trend that characterized the region during its industrial take-off—Chicago has long been a port of entry for arrivals from the midwestern heartland, from the South, and from every corner of the globe.

Thus, on closer inspection, the new Chicago is a complex layering of the really new (the five trends most clearly associated with the new accumulation regime) and the not-so-new—trends that began earlier during Chicago's industrial development. These older trends did not come to an end during the new accumulation regime and, in some cases, they actually accelerated and shaped Chicago's response to the new regime.

The way new trends are shaped by the older patterns is exemplified in the displacement of people from the revitalizing central city. Although this revitalization or revalorization appears to be a new trend, it is superimposed on and intermingled with older patterns of inequalities. The people who are displaced and least able to find affordable housing are lower-income African Americans. The closing of Chicago Housing Authority (CHA) housing combines old patterns of racial segregation and exclusion, new trends towards a revalorized central city, and the neo-liberal dismantling of public-sector social services.

SECTION III: A COMPARATIVE PERSPECTIVE: SIMILARITIES AND DIFFERENCES IN ACCUMULATION REGIME EFFECT

"*De te fabula narratur*—this story is about you," said Karl Marx in his Preface to *Capital*, alerting his German readers that German capitalism would follow the English pattern he analyzes. Most cities—certainly all industrial cities in Europe and North America—have been hit by the same massive transformation, the new accumulation regime. They all face similar converging forces: globalization (i.e., survival in a neoliberal global economy, management of new flows of people and capital); economic transformation (postindustrialization and the proportionate decline of the labor force in manufacturing); spatial reorganization (abrupt changes in land values and the built landscape in both the inner city and the larger metropolitan region); demographic and cultural change (absorption of succeeding waves of migrants, shifts from internal to international migration); and new forms of political power and ruling strategies, precipitated by crises of governability, reduced government functions, emergence of new coalitions, and managerialism. But these forces play themselves out differently in each city, depending on history, demographic mix, racial and ethnic stratification, local industrial bases, and the decisions and interests of institutional, collective, and individual actors.

How far can we generalize from Chicago's experiences in an era of globalization and postindustrial development? Does the new accumulation regime determine the form of cities, and is that form discernible in Chicago's transformation? Industrialization in the nineteenth and early twentieth centuries produced a variety of urban forms, similar but certainly not identical in all industrial cities. In some cities, manufacturing took place near the city center. The *raison d'etre* of these cities was industry, and residential areas grew around manufacturing and transportation facilities. But, in other cities, elites intervened to protect older areas from the incursion of industry, to safeguard a historical center or elite residential areas. They succeeded in locating manufacturing in zones away from the center and, in some cases, factories were actually located in the countryside. Metropolitan development in the nineteenth and early twentieth century saw battles over the central city, which often resulted in successful efforts by elites to keep manufacturing out of the city centers and displace the traditional urban poor away from the centers in the name of slum clearance and "hygiene." Although the industrial-centrality model fits Chicago, the safeguarding of the lakefront shows that the elite preservation of central cities operated as well, and the outcome was by no means one-sided.

In short, the structural wave of industrial capitalism did not lead to identical outcomes in all cities. Results were shaped by existing urban forms, traditional economic activities, cultures and subcultures, the balance of class forces, and contending collective actors that included traditional elites, new manufacturing interests, the new industrial working class, and the traditional urban poor. The different patterns and outcomes of industrialization in turn set the stage for differences in "postindustrial" development. Because responses to the new accumulation regime of the late twentieth century grow from the variety of infrastructure and institutional platforms created during the period of industrialization, these responses will not produce identical new cities.

Many former industrial cities, especially in Europe and North America, are likely to share aspects of Chicago's transformation. These cities, like Chicago, were industrial centers, lost jobs and enterprises after the middle of the twentieth century, and are seeking a new identity in an era of globalization. They are distinct from the great world cities such as London, Paris, Tokyo, and New York, which have had financial, cultural, or governing functions for a century or more and were never only or even primarily industrial centers. Second- and third-tier cities that were historically manufacturing cities or transportation hubs, such as Los Angeles, Detroit, Torino, Bilbao, Osaka, Harbin, Lille, and Marseilles offer intriguing comparisons to the clearly dominant financial, political, and cultural world cities like London, Paris, Tokyo. Chicago represents the future of these industrial cities—at least those

in Europe and North America—just as well, if not better, than L.A., which is often hailed as the paradigm of everyone's future, and certainly better than Las Vegas! Chicago, with its history of heavy and diversified industry, transportation centrality, a powerful political machine, a functioning mass transit system, and an architecturally vital downtown, is probably a better candidate for paradigmatic status throughout the industrial regions of the globe than is L.A., with its mid twentieth-century growth, defense-related industrial surge, politically and symbolically weak downtown, centerless sprawl, Hollywood dreams, and total dependence on the automobile. Less quintessentially American than L.A. or Las Vegas, Chicago represents a more typical trajectory into the new era of globalization.

The vignettes of four second-tier globalizing cities bring out differences and similarities in this category. Chicago, Los Angeles, Detroit, and Torino, Italy are all experiencing the effect of the new accumulation regime: the decline in large-scale manufacturing, increased transnational immigration, and the downsizing of the welfare state. Their conditions, however, are shaped by the persistence of past trends as well as different choices by elites and other political actors and different forms of contention among elites and between elites and grassroots movements. Macro-uniformities are present in urban responses to the new accumulation regime, but also powerful micro-diversity—those differences occurring at the local level and produced by local histories and local actors (Kerr 2001).

L.A. is an even newer city than Chicago, with a different industrial past. Its growth was linked to extractive and defense-related industries, and it experienced different demographic patterning and racial and ethnic relations (proportionately fewer African Americans and European ethnics, more Latino and Asian immigrants and working-class WASPs from the rural heartland), and different styles of governance, civic leadership, and grassroots organizing. The outcome of its transformation from the 1960s to the 1990s, so vividly described by Soja (1996) and the L.A. school (Davis 1992), has similarities to the new Chicago. The two areas share rapid flows of immigration, an unequal mosaic of ethnic groups, continued marginalization of many African Americans, a vital new small-scale manufacturing sector, problems in the school system, and spatial "edgelessness" and "fill-in." As in Chicago, lower-income African Americans and Latinos have not fared well during globalization and economic transformation, and the 1992 Los Angeles riot shows that these disparities did not go unnoticed by the disadvantaged. But Los Angeles is different from Chicago in the management of city government and policing, the level of tension between African Americans and immigrants, the types and locations of new industries, its patterns of spatial organization and edgeless development, the persistence of the Hollywood dream factory and its role in image creation, and the cultural feel of the ethnic mix.

Detroit had a far more specialized manufacturing history than Chicago, focused on automobile production. In the mid 1990s, the Detroit metropolitan area remained a leading exporting region (in the same top category as New York and San Jose, with over $25 billion dollars in exports in 1995—see Chapter 2), but this strength was located in the exurban and suburban ring rather than the central city. As industry moved out of the central city, Detroit's narrow and declining base attracted relatively fewer new immigrants than Chicago's diversified economy. Detroit has a very large African American population, subject to all the disadvantages of a racist society. During the years when the automobile industry drew African Americans into the city, a racial divide emerged between the city and the suburbs, polarizing them even more than in the Chicago area. Detroit now has the highest percentage of African Americans (81.2 percent) of any city in the United States (Brookings Institution 2003). A factor in Detroit's decline may have been the relatively low involvement of business elites in city renewal, whether as residents or philanthropists. Despite the large investment of the Ford Motor Company (and other industry giants) in the Renaissance Center, a downtown hotel and shopping complex developed in the 1970s, efforts to revitalize the center turned out to be too little or too late, perhaps because

throughout twentieth-century Detroit development, relatively little elite attention had been paid to the physical landscape and social institutions of the center. Only very recently, for example, has the development of the waterfront as a state park begun.

As a consequence of its particular industrial history, the effect of racial division and disadvantage, and a spotty history of elite engagement, Detroit's global and postindustrial transition has been more difficult than has been Chicago's or L.A.'s. The city population has dropped to half of the 1.8 million that resided there during the 1950s. Large areas were cleared of their inhabitants and are not yet rebuilt for gentrifiers. The city suffers high rates of crime, poverty, and functional illiteracy. Census 2000 data show a net loss of young, single, college-educated residents in the Detroit area (even including Ann Arbor) from 1995 to 2000, whereas the Chicago area gained population in this bracket (U.S. Census Bureau 2003a). Yet, Detroit has its own forms of cultural vitality, a defiant, hip-hop-inflected affirmation of struggle and survival.

Torino, Italy, shares Detroit's story of car manufacturing with associated massive national inmigration, but within a different national and cultural context. It began its modern existence as an elegant capital city, seat of the ruling House of Savoy and starting point of Italian unification. It was transformed into an automobile manufacturing center early in the twentieth century, and its car factories drew migrants first from the countryside of Piedmont and then from Veneto. Under Fascism, the center experienced a "disemboweling" (*sventramento*), similar to that of Rome and Florence, in which an old working-class market area was demolished to create an elegant shopping street, Via Roma. After World War II, a great migration of industrial workers arrived from impoverished areas of southern Italy, exactly paralleling African American migration to Chicago and Detroit. Native Torinesi were initially nearly as hostile to *terroni* from the South as white Chicagoans were to African American migrants. A "hot season" of labor unrest in the car factories characterized the 1970s, featuring collective action similar to the wildcat strikes and spontaneous insurgencies in the automotive industry in the Detroit region during this same period (Barkan 1984; Georgakas and Surkin 1975). The car factories were closed during the 1980s, because of the macro-level forces of neo-liberalism, globalization, search for cheaper labor, and replacement of national industries by global webs of disintegrated production processes.

In the wake of deindustrialization, Torino seeks a new identity by developing financial institutions, sports (the 2006 Winter Olympics), and culture. Cultural tourism is drawn not only to Torino's spectacular baroque palaces, but—postmodern irony!—the transformation of Fiat's Lingotto car factory and test ramp into a stunning exposition center. As in American cities, the historical center of the city is being gentrified and turned from crowded working-class housing into chic, refurbished apartments.

Continuing to struggle with a high unemployment rate and absorbing a new flow of "extra-communitarian" (non-EU) immigrants from Africa and Eastern Europe, Torino (like Chicago) is neither clearly making it nor failing in its transformation into a postindustrial global city.

In short, outcomes are only partially structured by uniform, synchronic, contemporary forces associated with the new accumulation regime and globalization. A closer look shows that these forces are locally splintered or refracted into more complicated patterns— Chicago, L.A., Detroit, and Torino are not all simply "postindustrial" and globalized, but postindustrial and globalized in distinct ways.

What are the similarities and differences among these cities, and how do they provide clues to answering the general question of why cities respond differently to the single tidal wave of the new accumulation regime?

As noted by a large number of observers, similarities (or uniformities) in the responses to the new accumulation regime include:

- Economic transformation through the decline of heavy industry and rise of a diverse tertiary sector
- Revalorization of areas surrounding the city center

- Displacement of residents and activities out of the center through a combination of market processes and government decisions
- Hourglass labor markets and occupational structures
- Increasing immigration and complicated class, ethnic, and occupational patterning, with a new intertwining of class and race–ethnicity, and a trend toward increasing disparities within ethnic groups (Soja 1996)
- Shrinkage, privatization, and marketization of public services (Klinenberg 2002; Genestier 2004)

A final new development that requires a word of explanation is the emergence of new political forms, including "issue contestation" and managerialism. Old forms of contestation have begun to wane, especially the conflict between capital and the working class organized into unions or left-wing parties. New types of contestation appear, organized along racial-ethnic or religious lines rather than class lines. With the shrinkage of state functions in neo-liberal regimes, less conflict exists over public-sector employment, but some of this competition may simply be shifted over into competition for contracts with government agencies. Tax revolts, contention over schooling and policing, zoning disputes, and other quality-of-life issues (such as airport noise) may become the multiple sites or proxy issues where tensions between classes, liberals and conservatives, cities and suburbs, and different ethnic and racial communities are fought out.

Katznelson (1981) believes that the proliferation of such movements after the 1960s was a sign of the death of class conflict in the urban trenches that fortified the state in the United States. Katznelson uses a metaphor introduced by Italian Marxist Antonio Gramsci: In modern democratic capitalist societies, the dominant social order is protected by a system of fortifications where class conflict is constantly shattered and fragmented into other, less explosive types of contention, such as interest group disputes (Gramsci 1971). Because large, class-based divisions were constantly broken up and refracted into myriad local issues at multiple sites, the rise of managerialism was facilitated as an ideology that transforms politics into issue-oriented public policies (Chapter 4). No longer can an organization or movement claim to be a "historical subject" representing the interests of all the subaltern strata. Yet the ideology and practice of managerialism and the customer or consumer model of government and public services are not always able to encompass and tame these disputes. It remains to be seen if grassroots forces will coalesce into a broad progressive movement and form part of an emerging global civil society. Currently, these grassroots movements are neither unified nor consistently progressive.

DIMENSIONS OF DIFFERENCE

Extent of Racial Segregation and Cultural Isolation. Cities differ in the extent to which displaced or vulnerable populations are also racially segregated and culturally isolated.

Patrimony of the Central City. Cities differ in the extent to which they have a patrimony in the central city that can be restored and revitalized to form the basis of a new zone of culture and leisure. Torino and Chicago (the birthplace of modern architecture) have a rich heritage, L.A. is intermediate, and Detroit's downtown attractions are relatively meager. When architectural and institutional patrimony is lacking, the challenge of reinventing the city is much greater and requires new construction and new institutions. A meager patrimony is sometimes characteristic of cities that developed entirely within the orbit of industrial capitalism and had no prior history or *raison d' etre* apart from manufacturing. Detroit is a case in point. Even its waterfront is not nearly as well developed as a recreational and tourist attraction as Chicago's lakefront, which was preserved by visionary planners and philanthropists early in the twentieth century.

Histories of Collective Action. Past contestation sets patterns for the contested reinvention of cities in the new accumulation regime. Some cities have vibrant histories of grassroots movements or a cultural heritage of working-class and labor activism. Yet this heritage may be lost in the transformation as indigenous working classes age, vulnerable immigrant populations are used

as a docile new labor force, and young people define their identities in new ways. The heritage of contestation may survive only in a spectral form, as a feisty spirit.

Elite Attachment to the Central City. In Torino and Chicago, reinvention of the city has been eased (for gentrifiers) by the fierce loyalty of elites, compared with their less consistent engagement in Detroit.

Fit of Immigrant and Host Cultures. The cultural traditions of immigrants influence the responses to the new accumulation regime, and so does the cultural climate into which immigrants must fit themselves. Traditions of entrepreneurship impel immigrants to fill niches in the changing economy of the central city and support revitalization. Strong professional skills (see Chapters 10 and 11, Indians and Filipinos) contribute to a robust response to new economic challenges. At the same time, cities differ in how well immigrants are received, appreciated, and supported by existing communities and institutions and enabled to participate in economic revitalization.

Previous Contention for the Central City. Cities differ in the existence and outcomes of previous battles for the central city. For example, in both Chicago and Torino, much more vital and successful efforts to revitalize the central city are underway than are apparent in Detroit (Los Angeles's efforts fall in-between). In Torino, as in most European cities, the battle for the central city began quite a long time ago, with the Fascist disemboweling of the center city and the consequent construction of the beautiful Via Roma. European elites have a long tradition of contending with the poor for the central city, and they generally won these battles well before the wave of gentrification arrived in United States during the late twentieth century. In Detroit and L.A., both products of the automotive age, the revalorization of the central city requires more invention from scratch.

The Industrial Base. The specific type of industry that existed before deindustrialization makes a difference in economic, environmental, and human outcomes of reinvents. Some types of industry are easy to relocate out of central cities; others leave permanent environmental scars or decaying infrastructure. Industrial or transportation development may have destroyed natural assets, such as lakefront or rivers, which now require new investment to restore and recuperate for their use in central-city revalorization as tourist and recreational areas. Whether this destruction happened in turn depends on previous contests over the central city; for example, in Chicago, the lakefront was largely safeguarded from port and industrial development early in the twentieth century. Finally, some industries leave behind a skilled labor force, others do not.

These examples illustrate reasons for the differences among globalizing industrial cities. The general paradigm of globalization must be understood in a very flexible way, and no single city can claim to represent a universal ideal-type of reinvention.

SECTION IV: SPATIAL FORMS, SOCIAL INEQUALITIES, AND COLLECTIVE ACTION

"It's always D-day under the el," wrote Nelson Algren, in his *Chicago: City on the Make*. Spatial reorganization is closely related to social stratification. Spatial restructuring in the new accumulation regime reflects and to some degree increases class and racial–ethnic inequalities. But, in a global perspective, this intertwining of spatial reorganization and stratification is not at all a new phenomenon. For example, in Europe, the medieval to modern transition was accompanied by a new urban form, the baroque city, characterized by a spacious, open, planned, and gridlike layout; this form also dominated all cities in the Americas, from Calgary to Buenos Aires (Rama 1996). Economic activities, such as tanning and slaughtering, were removed from elite residential areas. In Europe, vestiges of the old warren-like central-city neighborhoods persisted into the modern era, so that their destruction and the removal of their inhabitants to peripheral locations sometimes came as late as the nineteenth century (for example in Edinburgh and Haussmann's Paris). "Hygiene" was often the official reason for much of this destruction,

population displacement, and rebuilding, but social control was also a consideration—wide boulevards gave an advantage to armies and police forces in their encounters with the rioting poor. In Italy, the modernization of many city centers began during the nineteenth century, but was not completed until the Fascist period, when working-class housing was replaced with government buildings, boulevards, and shopping arcades. Furthermore, throughout Europe, an accelerating trend occurred to siting industry and workers' housing at the urban periphery. Elites were attached to the central city and reserved large parts of it for their own residences and for political and cultural activities. Even more complete patterns of segregation, justified by the ideologies of racism, appeared in colonial areas, where the open, clean, spacious city of the settlers contrasted with the cities of the "natives"—ancient, maze-like cities in Asia and North Africa and shantytowns and townships throughout the colonized world, characterized as "teeming" or "warren-like" (Fanon 1986). In apartheid South Africa, the displacement of non-whites from central locations was an assiduously implemented state policy, like the destruction and rebuilding of Jewish neighborhoods during the Nazi period, most notably in Berlin (Jaskot 2000).

In these spatial reorganizations, the process begins with labeling an area as deteriorated, blighted, or unhygienic. The rhetoric of dilapidation and blight is used to legitimate land clearance and population displacement. New, upmarket construction and revitalized commercial activity follow.

After the displacement of people and clearing of structures, open spaces may be allowed to remain vacant for a while, giving the appearance that they are fallow terrain, as if their emptiness were a natural or primordial condition. Eventually, the space is filled with new structures, suited to elite interests and activities. The state supports the process by exercising the right of eminent domain, buying and clearing land (as occurred in urban renewal), and providing police protection for gentrified neighborhoods. In some cases, pioneers (a telling metaphor), artists, and young Bohemians, move into a neighborhood, thus signaling and precipitating its gentrification. In other cases, the neighborhood is seen as too dangerous for pioneers and must lie fallow with an increasing number of abandoned buildings and vacant lots before it is redeveloped (Klinenberg 2002). The local school usually remains the final frontier of gentrification.

Inequality and the "Reconquest" of the Central City

The process of gentrification, revalorization, and displacement unfolding in central Chicago is not unique in comparative and historical perspective. However, the current process has features that distinguish it from its precedents. First, demolition is now focused on recently built public housing—CHA units built as recently as 1960; it reflects the withdrawal of the state from social service and welfare functions, a key feature of the new accumulation regime. The dilapidated and now demolished structures were not old, traditional housing but very recently constructed *public* housing that was allowed to deteriorate through state policies (Fuerst 2003; Venkatesh 2002). Second, the original siting and design of the CHA units reflected a misreading of trends by political leaders, professional planners, and economic elites who believed that the inner city would and should become an area of high-rise low-income housing in which racial segregation would and should continue. These perceptions, and the decisions that transformed them into abiding physical and social structures, turned out to be "off" politically and economically and had to be undone. Third, this process reveals how historical outcomes unfold; while one group of agents make decisions in one direction, another set can be making a divergent set of choices, and several decades may be required before the outcome—the net result—can be discerned. At the very moment that the Robert Taylor CHA complex was being completed, urban renewal was beginning in Hyde Park. Federal money and local power structures supported both projects and only 40 years later do we see that the seed of urban renewal grew into central-city gentrification and revalorization, whereas the seed of high-rise public housing shriveled.

In Chicago, an unmistakable link exists among stratification, racial–ethnic disparities, and spatial reorganization. Low-income African Americans, particularly people living in CHA housing, are being pushed out as part of the middle-class invasion and reconquest of the central city. This displacement is the current moment in a process that has been under way for several decades. The first phase of urban renewal occurred in key neighborhoods (Hyde Park and Lincoln Park) during the 1960s and 1970s. The second phase of economic deterioration was caused by the decline of manufacturing on the South Side, followed by a loss of social services. With little improvement in the school system, education proved an uncertain route out of poverty (Chapter 20) and crime escalated. The tight labor markets of the 1990s offered temporary relief, but the job surge did not produce major wage increases and, in any case, was followed by a recession at the beginning of the twenty-first century. The closing of CHA housing and the shortage of affordable housing, compounded by a shrinking job market and the end of the AFDC-based welfare system, have created a new crisis, resulting in overcrowded housing in the poorer suburbs and enormous stress on individuals and families. The pushing of low-income African Americans into poor suburbs also signals and clears the way for an imminent "filling-in" of fallow areas in neighborhoods like North Lawndale. These are desirable locations, along transportation lines and near the Loop, and the displacement of their populations is a step toward their redevelopment into gentrifying—or at least, gentrifiable—neighborhoods. An important but relatively late stage of gentrification is the transformation of local schools into magnet programs that are attractive to white middle-class families (Chapter 20).

Collective Inaction?

Why does so little contestation arise from people who are most harmed by the outcomes of the new accumulation regime—workers in lower tiers of the hourglass economy and residents displaced in the battle for the central city? The balance of forces in Chicago's contested reinvention is top-heavy, and contenders at the top seem far stronger than the dispersed and disunited activists who claim to represent the strata at the bottom. The contests are muted and almost invisible, and activists seem weak against the forces of development, economic restructuring, and managerialism. The most disadvantaged seem to have become particularly silent, invisible, and demoralized or passive—in contrast to the activist struggles of the Depression Era, Civil Rights movement, and "the Sixties."

An ideological analysis suggests that individual coping mechanisms are now believed to be more effective than collective action, but this analysis remains tautological without a complementary structural analysis. Vulnerability at the bottom increased because the most exploited workers are often undocumented immigrants, without citizenship rights and political resources. Homelessness created enormous demoralization, lack of access to resources, pressures to cope with day-to-day survival problems, and the destruction of the fabric of neighborhood attachments and social support. People at the lowest rungs of the structure are afraid to speak out and organize because they might lose their tenuous hold on jobs and social services or they are silenced by the threat of prison.

Another structural factor is the complicated postmodern intertwining of race and class (Chapter 7, Chapter 22, Chapter 23) that continues to disrupt alliances between lower-income whites and communities of color, especially in the highly segregated spatial configuration of the Chicago region. New structures of class and race also produce barriers to joint action by the middle class, working class, and poor within a racial–ethnic community as these communities become less unified and increasingly divided by class and income (Soja 1996). As noted in chapters on the IAF, school reform, and CAPS policing (Chapter 19, Chapter 20, Chapter 21), cross-class and cross-race coalitions of the subaltern have been historically weak in Chicago.

On a global scale, the new accumulation regime was a decisive overall victory for dominant classes and a defeat of working people and subaltern strata. This victory was based on the weakening of unions and left-wing parties, employment structures that divide workers, managerial and customer-oriented strategies of delivering public and collective goods, and ideological discrediting of government and the public sector. The collapse of the socialist states and the emergence of a mono-polar international system has stripped movements of the leverage they had in the bi-polar global arena during the Cold War, when the two superpowers could be played against each other (Layton 2000). Disarray on the left is not unique to Chicago (Beauregard 1989; Roberts 1999; Davis 2004).

SECTION V: SCENARIOS OF CHANGE

"If you can look into the seeds of time, and say which grain will grow and which will not...," Banquo implores the witches in William Shakespeare's play, *Macbeth*. Social science, like science fiction, tries to identify the trajectories of change, trend lines that will not wilt, cultural dominants that emerge from the profusion of contending possibilities. Social scientists can learn from science fiction writers how to create in a few pages a totalizing vision of change that displays all the converging (and diverging) forces playing themselves out in a particular context. Sometimes they are very wrong, sometimes just subtly off—and their wrongness itself is revealing. Look at Aldous Huxley's biostratified, high-consumption *Brave New World* (1932); Kurt Vonnegut's corporate-computer city (*Player Piano*, 1952); Samuel Delaney's Bellona, the benign wild city of the 1970s (*Dhalgren*, 2001); and William Gibson's Reagan-era globalized cyberpunk megalopolis (*Neuromancer*, 1984). In this spirit, we offer a few scenarios for Chicago and all globalizing postindustrial cities. Despite obvious differences, these scenarios are intricately connected to each other, separated only by the flap of a butterfly wing, and we can convince ourselves that we can discern each one growing in the womb of the present.

The Segregated City

The first scenario is an urban area in which there is a place for everyone and everyone stays in their place. It is segregated racially and ethnically, because the rich mosaic of ethnicity turns out to be a minutely detailed, intricately segmented, and sharply crystallized structure of inequality, with different ethnic groups distinguished by residential location, occupation, education, income, and political power. It is segregated by class, with increasing stratification within each racial–ethnic group. Growing class gaps within racial–ethnic groups make identity politics intense, angry, and ambiguous (Pattillo 2003).

Class and racial–ethnic segregation is accompanied by lifestyle differences and residence patterns. Professional-managerial elites live in the revitalized downtown, commute to work on foot and by bicycle, work hard and play hard, and subsist on coarse bread, bitter herbs, and raw fish. The middle and working classes reside in outer zones of the city and in the suburbs, live in bungalows, work hard for very long hours, and commute long distances in cars. The working poor struggle to make ends meet in contingent labor markets (Peck and Theodore 2001), while hopes for their children's mobility through education fade in the face of failing schools and soaring college tuition. The very poor have been pushed into townships—racially segregated low-income ghettos on the urban periphery. The subaltern strata eat fast foods, exercise little, and weigh more than the urban rich (Neergard 2003).

This structure forms an hourglass in which the lower strata are growing most rapidly and the middle is shrinking. Individual and intergenerational mobility out of the lower tiers is grinding to a halt. The segregated city is indeed globalized, but its inhabitants participate in the global economy on highly unequal terms.

From Ephemeral City to Wild City

The Ephemeral City is a city that can vanish overnight when financial markets pack up and leave, advanced corporate services relocate to far corners of the globe via modern telecommunications networks, and sports teams move away. The Ephemeral City is a product of globalization; new technologies that make constant relocation a reality; and the values, choices, and imperatives that make capital "nestle everywhere, settle everywhere, establish connections everywhere" (Marx and Engels 1848). Advanced corporate services, financial institutions, R and D, software development, retailing, the hospitality industry, gaming, tourism, sports, and their attendant retail and service industries are far more portable than the factories that left the Rust Belt during the 1970s and 1980s (Chapter 2). As Reich suggests in *The Work of Nations* (1991) symbolic analysts and new elites associated with global entrepreneurial webs are not sentimental about place. They are always prepared to shut themselves off from their larger social environment and, if necessary, move on, abandoning their home and neighborhood like a postindustrial version of hunter-gatherers leaving behind a midden heap. When the Ephemeral City vanishes—with its high-rolling traders, risk takers, entrepreneurs, corporate professionals, landscapers, busboys, musicians, cleaners, maids, waiters, sports celebrities, chefs, models, webmasters, and media workers—all that is left is Lake Michigan and a new version of the Wild City.

The Wild City is a scenario vividly imagined by Manuel Castells in the late 1970s, and it could be replayed when the Ephemeral City vanishes:

> ...mass police repression and control and... a largely deteriorated economic setting. The suburbs will remain fragmented and isolated, the single-family homes closed over themselves, the shopping centers a bit more expensive and a lot more surveyed, the highways less maintained and more crowded, the central districts still crowded during office hours and more deserted and curfewed after 5 p.m., city services increasingly crumbling, public facilities less and less public, the surplus population more and more visible, the drug culture and individual violence necessarily expanding, gang society and high society ruling the bottom and the top in order to keep a "top and bottom" social order.... (Castells 1982)

The Wild City is close kin to the Segregated City. It is the flip side of the segregated city, as the latter breaks down from a highly segmented, stratified, and controlled social order into the chaos of high unemployment, high crime, pervasive poverty, intense fears, and racial and spatial avoidance and isolation. The Wild City already exists in parts of Chicago (and in every major urban area in the United States), as an analysis of 1995 heat-wave deaths in North Lawndale illustrates (Klinenberg 2002). It forms vast zones of cities in poor and developing nations (Davis 2004). An economic decline triggered by unmanageable balance-of-trade problems could expand existing wild zones of American cities until they engulf whole cities. The search for lower labor costs combined with increasingly sophisticated telecom technologies could move even the most intellectually sophisticated corporate services into new global locations. Careless federal policies—a shift in interest rates, a plummeting dollar, a new military adventure—could topple literally and figuratively overbuilt structures, driving away financial institutions, sending vacancy rates up, bringing real estate prices down, increasing unemployment, and ultimately pushing the new Chicago into a new version of the Wild City.

The Happy Market

The Happy Market emerges from multicultural commercial development. The Devon world market is its harbinger (Chapter 17), and it has now expanded throughout the region. As in the Segregated City, a mosaic of ethnic cultures exists, but they are less stratified and segregated. The market imposes a certain degree of harmony, order, and civility as everyone tries to make a buck while forgetting old ethnic rivalries. The Happy Market is the global marketplace of the neo-liberal vision writ small and spared the ethnic violence of majorities against market-dominant minorities that springs up in global marketization (Chua 2002). Ethnic communities co-exist, and each embraces, rather than resents, the theming of its culture and historical heritage (Zukin 1991; Sorkin 1992).

In Chicago's Happy Market, the persistent racial divide is finally overcome as racial polarization is diluted and eventually swept away in the flood of cultural diversity. African Americans become one more hyphenated American group to enjoy offering a unique culture in the bustling, vibrant city market. Jazz, blues, soul food, hip-hop, and urban style invite the tourist to partake of the culture, and a rich history of struggle and resilience is displayed in visitor-friendly museums. African American culture finally becomes part of the thrilling mix of city life that includes curries and bagels, sarees and dreadlocks, polkas and salsa, tacos and foo-foo. In the popular imaginary, cultural tourism is located in the exciting space between ghetto fears and candleshop blandness. All cultures can be commodified and in the commercialization of difference lies economic prosperity and ethnic harmony. The Happy Market is as good as it gets in the multicultural cities of the advanced capitalist world.

IN CHARLES DICKENS' vision of London's early industrial capitalism, Scrooge encounters two hideous waifs, Want and Ignorance, while his room is stripped by ragpickers and Tiny Tim dies. The Segregated City, the Ephemeral City, and the Wild City force us to ask with Scrooge: "Are these the shadows of the things that Will be, or are they shadows of the things that May be, only? . . . Assure me that I may yet change these shadows you have shown me. . . ." Is a Social City possible, a city of ethnic diversity, reduced class disparities, functioning public services, excellent public education, and affordable housing?

SECTION VI: NEW CHICAGO—NEW CHICAGO SCHOOL?

We end our discussion of the new Chicago with a brief engagement with the Chicago School of urban sociology. North American social theory during the first part of the twentieth century avoided Marx, understood Weber as a theorist of values and *verstehen*, and construed Simmel as micro-sociologist and proto-symbolic interactionist (before the term existed) as if he had never written on the money economy. Working within these readings and dazzled by the immediate, intense realities of Chicago, the Chicago School remained silent on macro-level issues of structure, conflict, and power.

Our analysis of the new Chicago uses key elements of the Chicago School tradition—a focus on communities and cultures, analysis of spatial organization—but recontextualizes them within a larger, conflict-oriented view of societal and global change.

The Chicago School was characterized by local, micro-level studies of individuals, neighborhoods, deviant subcultures, and ethnic communities. Chicago was conceptualized as a spatially distributed mosaic of cultures and subcultures. The larger context was tacitly accepted and thus naturalized. *The New Chicago* takes a different approach by beginning with larger structural forces and then tracing their effect on neighborhoods and the metropolitan region, their role in producing new communities of immigrants, and their association with new forms of inequality.

The second "silence" of the Chicago School was on the topic of agency, power, and conflict at the macro-level. Chicago School studies were often based on life narratives that show how individuals take action and make choices, but these choices were almost always the limited, locally defined options of people who have little control beyond the boundaries of their neighborhood or subculture. They were rarely decisions of elites, powerholders, and ruling classes that shaped the small worlds the sociologists studied. Consequently little was said about contention, struggle, collective action, and a larger political awareness in the Chicago School perspective. The authors of *The New Chicago* try to fill in these silences, giving attention to collective responses to structural forces at both elite and grassroots levels and emphasizing that responses are always contentious. Elites and powerholders often prevail, yet the process is not smooth and the outcomes are not entirely predictable or predetermined.

In response to the new accumulation regime, Chicago has reinvented itself in ways that are similar but not identical to the reinventions that all industrial cities have to undertake to survive neo-liberal globalization. As Bertolt Brecht's poem reminds us, response and reinvention did not come from "Chicago" as a single, harmonious entity, nor from a "Chicago" unswervingly guided and dominated by monolithic, all-powerful, all-knowing elites. Reinvention of Chicago remains an open-ended, contested process with undecided outcomes.

References

100-Year History of Korean Immigration to America: Story of Korean Diaspora 1903–2003 (in Korean). 2002. Los Angeles: Korean American United Foundation Centennial Committee of Korean Immigration to the United States, Southern California.

Abu-Lughod, Janet. 1986. "The Demographic War for Palestine." In *The Link*. New York: Americans for Middle East Understanding.

Abu-Lughod, Janet. 1995. "Comparing Chicago, New York, and Los Angeles: Testing Some World Cities Hypotheses." In *World Cities in a World System*, P. Knox and P. Taylor, eds. Cambridge: Cambridge University Press.

Abu-Lughod, Janet. 1999. *New York, Chicago and Los Angeles: America's Global Cities*. Minneapolis: University of Minnesota.

Abu-Lughod, Janet. 2000. "Can Chicago Make It as a Global City?" *A Great Cities Institute Working Paper.* Chicago: University of Illinois at Chicago.

Acierto, Maria. 1994. "The Filipino World War II G.I. Brides in Chicago, Illinois—1946 to Today." *Filipino American National Historical Society Journal* 3:69–70.

Acierto, Maria. 1999. *Building Community: The Filipino American Council of Chicago*. Chicago: Nyala Publishing.

Adversario, Patricia. 2003. "Quality of Nursing Education Deteriorating." *The Manila Times* (22 April).

Alba, Richard and Victor Nee. 2003. *Remaking the American Mainstream: Assimilation and Contemporary Immigration*. Cambridge, MA: Harvard University Press.

Allen, John and Chris Hammett. 1995. *A Shrinking World? Global Unevenness and Inequality*. New York: Oxford University Press.

Allensworth, Elaine M. and John Q. Easton. 2001. "Calculating a Cohort Dropout Rate for the Chicago Public Schools: A Technical Report." Chicago: Consortium on Chicago School Research.

Allensworth, Elaine M. and T. Rosenkranz. 2000. "Access to Magnet Schools in Chicago." Chicago: Consortium on Chicago School Research and Mexican American Legal Defense and Education Fund.

Almada, Jeanette. 2003. "Taylor Homes Remake Begins." *Chicago Tribune* (24 August).

al-Tahir, Abdul Jalil. 1952. The Arab Community in the Chicago Area: A Comparative Study of the Christian–Syrians and the Muslim Palestinians. Ph.D. Dissertation, University of Chicago.

Amin, Samir 1977. *Capitalism in the Age of Globalization*. London: Zed Press.

Anderson, Alan B. and George W. Pickering. 1987. *Confronting the Color Line: The Broken Promise of the Chicago Civil Rights Movement*. Athens: University of Georgia Press.

Anderson, Rebecca. 1999. "Civilian Disciplinary Board Lacks Teeth." *Chicago Reporter* (November).

Angelides, Stephanie. 2003. "Chicago Encourages Tourism with 'Winter Delights' Program." *Medill News Service* (13 November).

Año Nuevo Kerr, Louise. 1975 "Chicano Settlements in Chicago: A Brief History." *Journal of Ethnic Studies* (Winter).

Arendt, Hannah. 1982. *Lectures on Kant's Political Philosophy*. Chicago: University of Chicago Press.

Aruri, Naseer, ed. 1983. *Occupation: Israel over Palestine*. Belmont, MA: Association of Arab-American University Graduates.

Asian American Institute. 2002. *A Comprehensive Guide to the Asian Pacific Community in Illinois*. Chicago: Asian American Institute.

Atkinson, Robert, Randolph Court, and Joe Ward. 1999. *The State New Economy Index: Benchmarking Economic Transformation in the States*. Washington DC: Progressive Policy Institute.

Avi Shlaim. 2000. *The Iron Wall: Israel and the Arab World*. New York: W.W. Norton.

Baade, Robert A. and Alan Sanderson. 1997. "Bearing Down in Chicago." In *The Economic Impact of Sports Teams and Stadiums*, R. G. Knoll and A. Zimbalist, eds. Washington, DC: The Brookings Institution Press.

Bagby, I., P. M. Perl, and B. T. Froehle. 2001. "The Mosque in America: A National Portrait." Report from the Mosque Study Project 2000. Washington, DC: Council on American-Islamic Relations.

Bagguley, Paul, Jane Mark-Lawson, and Dan Shapiro. 1990. *Restructuring: Place, Class and Gender.* London: Sage Publications.

Banchero, Stephanie. 1997. "City Offers Toned–Down North Halsted Plan." *Chicago Tribune* (13 November).

Bancroft, Hubert Howe. 1893. *The Book of the Fair.* Chicago: Bancroft Company.

Banisky, Sandy. 1995. "Chicago Housing Authority Watches Its Best Efforts Fail." *Baltimore Sun* (18 June).

Banks, Brian, Maureen Hellwig, and David MacLaren. 2000. "Opportunities in Manufacturing: A Future for Our Region and Its Workers." Chicago: Policy Research Action Group. www.luc.edu/depts/curl/prag/.

Banks, Brian and David MacLaren. 1999. "Mobilizing Citizen Participation in Bronzeville." *PRAGmatics* (Chicago) (Spring).

Barkan, Joanne. 1984. *Visions of Emancipation.* New York: Praeger.

Barreto, Sergio C. 2002. "Chicago Northwest Slips, Slides and Gentrifies." *Neighborhoods* (newsletter of the Chicago Alliance for Neighborhood Safety) (September).

Baudrillard, Jean. 1988. "Simulacra and Simulations." In *Jean Baudrillard: Selected Writing,* Mark Poster, ed. Stanford, CA: Stanford University Press.

Beal, Frank. 2003. Interview by author, 9 May.

Bean, Frank D. and B. Lindsay Lowell, 2003. "Immigrant Employment and Mobility Opportunities in California." In *The State of California Labor, 2003.* Berkeley: University of California Institute for Labor and Employment.

Beauregard, Robert. 1989. "Space, Time, and Economic Restructuring." In *Economic Restructuring and Political Response,* R. Beauregard, ed. Thousand Oaks, CA: Sage.

Beauregard, Robert A. 1998. "Tourism and Economic Development Policy in U.S. Urban Areas." In *The Economic Geography of the Tourist Industry: A Supply-Side Analysis,* D. Ioannides and K. G. Debbage, eds., London: Routledge.

Beauregard, Robert A. 2003. "City of Superlatives." *City & Community* 2 (September): 183–99.

Beaverstock, J. V., P. J. Taylor, and R. J. Smith. 1999. "A Roster of World Cities." *Cities* 16 (6): 445–58.

Becker, Wesley. [1977] 2001. "Teaching Reading and Language to the Disadvantaged." *Journal of Direct Instruction* 1 (1): 31–52.

Bell, Derrick A. 1992. *Faces at the Bottom of the Well: The Permanence of Racism.* New York: Basic Books.

Bennett, Larry. 1987. "The Dilemmas of Building a Progressive Urban Coalition: The Linked Development Debate in Chicago." *Journal of Urban Affairs* 9 (3): 263–76.

Bennett, Larry. 1998. "Do We Really Wish to Live in a Communitarian City?: Communitarian Thinking and the Redevelopment of Chicago's Cabrini-Green Public Housing Complex." *Journal of Urban Affairs* 20 (2): 99–116.

Bennett, Larry. 1989. "Postwar Redevelopment in Chicago: The Decline of the Politics of Party and the Rise of Neighborhood Politics." In *Unequal Partnerships: The Political Economy of Urban Redevelopment in Postwar America,* G. Squires, ed. New Brunswick, NJ: Rutgers University Press.

Bennett, Larry. 1999. "The New Style of U.S Urban Development: From Urban Renewal to the City of Leisure." Paper presented at the Annual Meeting of the Urban Affairs Association, Louisville, KY (April).

Bennett, Larry. 2006 "Downtown Restructuring and Public Housing in Contemporary Chicago: Fashioning a Better World-Class City." In *Where Are Poor People to Live?* L. Bennett, J. Smith, and P. Wight, eds. Armonk, NY: M.E. Sharpe.

Bennett, Larry and Adolph Reed, Jr. 1999. "The New Face of Urban Renewal: The Near North Redevelopment Initiative and the Cabrini-Green Neighborhood." In *Without Justice for All,* A. Reed, Jr., ed. Boulder, CO: Westview Press.

Bennett, Michael I. J. 1980. "Community Development Corporations Bring New Life to Business Sections." *Nation's Cities Weekly* (14 July).

Bennett, Michael, Tom Dewar, and Prudence Brown. 2000. *An Assessment of the Building Community Capacity Program.* A Report to the John D. and Catherine T. MacArthur Foundation.

Berg, Steve. 2000. Chicago Shows What Can Happen When a City Strives for Beauty." *Minneapolis Star–Tribune* (10 September).

Berman, Jay M. 2004. "Industry Output and Employment Projections to 2012." *Monthly Labor Review* (February): 58–79.

Bernstein, David. 2003. "Films Flee the Loop, but Chicago Fights Back." *New York Times* (9 April).

Berry, Brian, Irving Cutler, Edwin Draine, et al. 1976. *Chicago: Transformations of an Urban System.* Cambridge, MA: Ballinger.

Best, Steven and Douglas Kellner. 2004. "Postmodern Politics and the Battle for the Future." www.gseis.ucla.edu/faculty/kellner/kellner.html.

Betancur, John, Deborah Bennett, and Patricia Wright. 1991. "Effective Strategy for Community Development." In *Challenging Uneven Development: An Urban Agenda for the 1990s,* P. Nyden and W. Wiewel, eds. New Brunswick, NJ: Rutgers University Press.

Betancur, John, Isabel Domeyko, and Patricia Wright. 2001. "Gentrification in West Town: Contested Ground." Natalie P. Voorhees Center for Neighborhood and Community Improvement, University of Illinois at Chicago.

Betancur, John J. and Douglas C. Gills. 2000a. "The African American and Latino Coalition Experience in Chicago under Mayor Harold Washington." In *The Collaborative City: Opportunities and Struggles for Blacks and Latinos in U.S. Cities,* J. Betancur and D. Gills, eds. New York: Garland Publishing.

Betancur, John J. and Douglas C. Gills. 2000b. "The Restructuring of Urban Relations: Recent Challenges and Dilemmas for African Americans and Latinos in U.S. Cities." In *The Collaborative City: Opportunities and Struggles for Blacks and Latinos in U.S. Cities,* J. Betancur and D. Gills, eds. New York: Garland Publishing.

Biles, Roger. 1995. *Richard J. Daley: Politics, Race, and the Governing of Chicago.* DeKalb: Northern Illinois University Press.

Black Metropolis Convention and Tourism Council. 2001. "Bridging the Digital Divide in Bronzeville: A Financial Proposal." Chicago: Black Metropolis Convention & Tourism Council.

Blackistone, Kevin. 1981. "Arab Entrepreneurs Take Over Inner City Grocery Stores." *Chicago Reporter* (May).

Black's Guide [Real Estate Industry Market Guide]. 2002–03. "Chicago Market Conditions Report," Black's Guide, Inc., Winter.

Bluestone, Barry and Bennett Harrison. 1982. *The Deindustrialization of America.* New York: Basic Books.

Boarnet, Marlon and Andrew Haughwout. 2000. "Do Highways Matter? Evidence and Policy Implications of Highways' Influence on Metropolitan Development." Washington, DC: The Brookings Institution Center on Urban and Metropolitan Policy.

Bogira, Steve. 1986. "Prisoners of the War Zone." *The Reader* (Chicago) (3 October).

Bonacich, Edna. 1973. "A Theory of Middleman Minorities." *American Sociological Review* 38:583–94.

Bonus, Rick. 2000. *Locating Filipino Americans: Ethnicity and the Cultural Politics of Space.* Philadelphia: Temple University Press.

Bopp, William. 1977. *"O.W": O.W. Wilson and the Search for a Police Profession.* Port Washington, NY: Kennikat Publications.

Bourdieu, Pierre. 1984. *Distinction.* London: Routledge.

Bowly, Devereux, Jr. 1978. *The Poorhouse: Subsidized Housing in Chicago, 1895–1976.* Carbondale: Southern Illinois University Press.

Boyd, Michelle. 2000. "Reconstructing Bronzeville: Racial Nostalgia and Neighborhood Redevelopment." *Journal of Urban Affairs* 22 (2): 107–22.

Brecht, Bertolt. 1947. "A Worker Reads History." *Selected Poems.* New York: Harcourt, Brace, Jovanovich.

Brenner, Neil and Nik Theodore. 2002. "Cities and the Geographies of Actual and Existing Neoliberalism." In *Space of Neo-Liberalism: Urban Restructuring in North America and Western Europe,* N. Brenner and N. Theodore, eds. Malden, MA: Blackwell Publishers.

Bronzeville Vision 2010. A report produced by the Bronzeville Organizing Strategy Sessions, 1999.

Brooking Institution Center on Urban and Metropolitan Policy. 2003. "Chicago in Focus: A Profile from Census 2000." Washington, DC: The Brookings Institution (November).

Brozek, Andrzej. 1985. *Polish Americans: 1854–1939.* Trans. Wojciech Worsztynowicz. Warsaw: Interpress.

Bryk, Anthony S., et al. 1998. *Charting Chicago School Reform: Democratic Localism as a Lever for Change.* Boulder CO: Westview Press.

Bryk, Anthony S., David Kerbow, and Sharon Rollow. 1997. "Chicago School Reform." In *New Schools for a New Century,* D. Ravitch and J. P. Viteritti, eds. New Haven, CT: Yale University Press.

Bubinas, Kathleen. 2003. "The Commodification of Ethnicity in an Asian Indian Economy in Chicago." *City & Society* 15 (2): 195–223.

Burnham, Daniel and Edward Bennett. [1909] 1970. *Plan of Chicago.* New York: Da Capo Press.

Cainkar, Louise. 1991. "Palestinian–American Muslim Women: Living on the Margins of Two Worlds." In *Muslim Families in North America,* E. Waugh, S. Abu-Laban, and R. Qureishi, eds. Edmonton: University of Alberta Press.

Cainkar, Louise. 1996. "Palestinian Women: A Generational Perspective." In *Family and Gender among American Muslims,* B. Aswad and B. Bilge, eds. Philadelphia: Temple University Press.

Cainkar, Louise. 1998. *Meeting Community Needs, Building on Community Strengths: Chicago's Arab American Community.* Chicago: Arab American Action Network.

Cainkar, Louise. 1999. "The Deteriorating Ethnic Safety Net among Arabs in Chicago." In *Arabs in America: Building a New Future,* M. Suleiman, ed. Philadelphia: Temple University Press.

Cainkar, Louise. 2003. "A Fervor for Muslims: Special Registration." *Journal of Islamic Law and Culture* 7 (2): 73–101.

Cainkar, Louise. 2004a. "The Impact of 9/11 on Muslims and Arabs in the United States." In *The Maze of Fear: Security and Migration after September 11th,* J. Tirman, ed. New York: The New Press.

Cainkar, Louise. 2004b. "Introduction: Global Impacts of September 11th." *Journal of Comparative Studies of South Asia, Africa, and the Middle East* 24 (1): 157–60.

Cainkar, Louise, Ali Abunimah, and Lamia Raei. 2004. "Migration as a Method of Coping with Turbulence among Palestinians." *Journal of Comparative Family Studies* (Special Issue on the Middle East) 35 (2): 229–40.

Callimachi, Rukmini. 2003. "The Scars of Nationalism." From the series "Passage from India: Stories of Suburban Immigrants." *Daily Herald* (7 May).

Callinicos A. 1994. *Marxism and the New Imperialism.* London: Bookmarks.

Campaign for Sensible Growth. 2003. "Riverdale: Panel Offers a Vision for the Pacesetter Neighborhood" (16 September). http://www. growingsensibly. org/news/articleDetail.asp?objectID=1466 (accessed 23 January 2006).

Carlson, Dennis. 1996. "Education as a Political Issue: What's Missing in the Public Conversation about Education?" In *Thirteen Questions: Reframing Education's Conversation,* 2nd edition, J. L. Kincheloe, ed. New York: Peter Lang.

Casillas, Ofelia and John Chase. 2003. "DCFS Leader's Been There." *Chicago Tribune* (29 April).

Castells, Manuel. 1982. "The Wild City." In *The Internal Structure of the City,* 2nd edition, L. Bourne, ed. New York: Oxford University Press.

Castells, Manuel. 1996. *The Rise of the Network Society.* Malden, MA: Blackwell Publishers.

Castro, Janice. 1993. "Disposable Workers." *Time Magazine* (29 March).

Catalyst (Chicago) 1990. (February). Chicago: Community Renewal Society.

Catalyst (Chicago) 1991. (June). Chicago: Community Renewal Society.

Catalyst (Chicago). 2000. (December).

Center for Labor Market Studies. 2003. "Youth Labor Market and Education Indicators for the State of Illinois." Chicago Alternative Schools Network (October). www.asnchicago.org.

Chambers, Edward T. 2003. *Roots for Radicals: Organizing for Power, Action, and Justice.* New York: Continuum.

Chan, Janet. 1997. *Changing Police Culture: Policing in a Multicultural Society.* New York: Cambridge University Press.

Chase, John. 2003. "Governor Approves Transport Task Force." *Chicago Tribune* (2 August).

Chase, John and David Mendell. 2004. "Obama Scores a Record Landslide" *Chicago Tribune* (3 November).

Chicago Area Fair Housing Alliance. 2004. "Putting the Choice in Housing Choice Vouchers (Part 3): Mapping the Location of Housing Choice Vouchers in the Chicago Region to Demonstrate the Need for Affirmative Efforts to Provide Greater Access to Areas of Opportunity for Families Using Vouchers." Chicago Area Fair Housing Alliance (July).

Chicago Case Study Working Group of the Great Cities Institute. 2001. *Metropolitan Decentralization in Chicago.* Chicago: Great Cities Institute, University of Illinois at Chicago.

Chicago Chinese News. 2003. *Chinese Yellow Pages.* Chicago: Chicago Chinese News.

Chicago Commission on Race Relations. 1922. *The Negro in Chicago.* Chicago: University of Chicago Press.

Chicago Department of Cultural Affairs. 1999. "Cows on Parade: June 15–October 31." City of Chicago.

Chicago Fact Book Consortium. 1984. *Local Community Fact Book, Chicago Metropolitan Area: Based on the 1970 and 1980 Census.* Chicago: Chicago Review Press.

Chicago Fact Book Consortium. 1995. *Local Community Fact Book, Chicago Metropolitan Area, 1990.* Chicago: Academy Chicago Publishers.

Chicago Federation of Labor and the Center for Labor and Community Research. 2001.*Creating a Manufacturing Career Path System in Cook County.* Chicago: Center for Labor and Community Research, March.

Chicago Housing Authority. 2000. "Plan for Transformation" (6 January).

Chicago Metropolis 2020. 2001. "Regional Realities: Measuring Progress toward Shared Regional Goals." Chicago: Chicago Metropolis 2020.

Chicago Metropolis 2020. 2003. "The Metropolis Plan: Choices for the Chicago Region." Chicago: Chicago Metropolis 2020 (March).

Chicago Metropolis 2020. 2004. "Metropolis Principles FAQ." www.chicagometropolis2020.org/ 10_20faq.htm.

Chicago Politics 1990. 1990. DeKalb: Social Science Research Institute, Northern Illinois University and Chicago Urban League.

Chicago Public Schools, Office of Dropout Prevention. 2004. "Overall Data from CPS-2003 Cohort Dropout Rates." Chicago: CPS.

Chicago Public Schools, Office of Language and Cultural Education. 2003. "At a Glance–February 2003." Chicago: CPS.

Chicago Sun-Times. 1992. "Who Lives Where in the Suburbs?" (7 June).

Chicago Tribune. 1999. "Residents Accuse CHA, HUD of Rights Violations." (30 July).

Chicago Tribune. 2003. "Voice of the People." (letters) (24 January).

Chicago Tribune. 2003. "Special Report: Top 100 Companies." (18 May).

Chicago Tribune. 2003. "Compassion Meets Efficiency." (editorial) (28 May).

Chinese American Service League. 1996."History of Chinatown." www.chicago-chinatown.com.

Chisholm, Michael. 1985. "Deindustrialization and British Regional Policy." *Regional Studies* 19:301–13.

Cho, Wendy K. Tam. 1999. "Naturalization, Socialization, Participation: Immigrants and (Non-) Voting." *Journal of Politics* 61 (4): 1140–55.

Choy, Catherine. 2003. *Empire of Care*. Durham, NC: Duke University Press.

Chua, Amy. 2002. *World on Fire: How Exporting Free Market Democracy Breeds Ethnic Hatred and Global Instability*. New York: Doubleday.

Ciokajlo, Mickey. 2000. "New Cabrini Agreement May End Residents' Suit." *Chicago Tribune* (16 August).

City of Chicago. n.d. "Holistic Urban Redevelopment: The ABLA Homes Model."

City of Chicago, Department of Planning and Development. 2002. "The Chicago Central Area Plan: Preparing the Central City for the 21st Century." (July; updated/revised version May 2003).

Clark, Terry Nichols, Richard Lloyd, Kenneth K. Wong, and Pushpam Jain. 2002. "Amenities Drive Urban Growth." *Journal of Urban Affairs* 24 (5): 493–515.

Clark, Terry Nichols, ed. 2003. *The City as an Entertainment Machine* (Research in Urban Policy, Volume 9). Boston: Elsevier Science.

Clavel, Pierre and Wim Wiewel, eds. 1991. *Harold Washington and the Neighborhoods: Progressive City Government in Chicago, 1983–1987*. New Brunswick, NJ: Rutgers University Press.

Clemetson, Lynette. 2004. "Census Policy on Providing Sensitive Data Is Revised." *New York Times* (31 August).

Cohen, Adam and Elizabeth Taylor. 2000. *American Pharaoh: Mayor Richard J. Daley: His Battle for Chicago and the Nation*. Boston: Little, Brown.

Cohen, Laurie and Andrew Martin. 2001. "Daley Insider Paves Way for Big O'Hare Contracts." *Chicago Tribune* (19 March).

Cohen, Laurie, Jorge Luis Mota, and Andrew Martin. 2002. "Political Army Wields Clout, Jobs." *Chicago Tribune* (31 October).

Cohen, Lizabeth. 1990. *Making a New Deal: Industrial Workers in Chicago, 1919–1939*. Cambridge: Cambridge University Press.

Cohen, Robert. 1981. "The New International Division of Labor, Multinational Corporations and Urban Hierarchy." In *Urbanization and Urban Planning in Capitalist Society*, M. Dear and A. Scott, eds. New York: Methuen.

Coleman, Geraldine Balut. 2004. "Educating Polish Immigrants Chicago Style: 1980–2000." *Polish American Studies* 61 (1): 27–38.

Commercial Club of Chicago. 1984. "Make No Little Plans: Jobs for Metropolitan Chicago." Chicago: Commercial Club of Chicago (December).

Commercial Club of Chicago. 1990. "Jobs for Metropolitan Chicago—An Update." Chicago: Commercial Club of Chicago (August).

Concerned Residents of ABLA v. Chicago Housing Authority et al. 2004. First Amended Intervenors' Complaint (14 May).

Conroy, John. 2002. "A Long Way from Latvia." *The Reader* (Chicago) (13 September).

Corfman, Thomas A. 2003a. "City Subsidy Deal Targets Ward Site." *Chicago Tribune* (23 July).

Corfman, Thomas A. 2003b. "Giant South Side Project Planned." *Chicago Tribune* (31 July).

Corfman, Thomas A. 2003c. "Auction Set at Foreclosed River Bend." *Chicago Tribune* (15 August).

Crain's Chicago Business. 2003. "Bronzeville 'Second City' Plans Move Forward." (28 August).

Cronon, William. 1991. *Nature's Metropolis: Chicago and the Great West*. New York: W.W. Norton.

Crosscurrents. 1994-95. "America 2050: Immigration and the Hourglass. A Conversation with Alejandro Portes" (Winter-Spring).

Cummins, Jim. 2000. *Language, Power and Pedagogy*. Clevedon, UK: Multilingual Matters Ltd.

Czapinski, Janusz. 1995. "Money Isn't Everything: On the Various Social Costs of Transformation." *Polish Sociological Review* 4:289–302.

Daley, Richard, M. 1991. Inaugural Address. *Journal of the Proceedings*, Chicago City Council (6 May).

Daley, Richard, M. 1998. "A Letter to the People of Chicago" (August). http://w4.ci.chi.il.us/trans/html/MayorsMill.htm (accessed 10 April 2000).

Daley, Richard. M. 2001. "Revitalizing Chicago through Parks and Public Spaces." Keynote address to the Urban Parks Institute's "Great Parks/Great Cities" Conference, New York (31 July).

Daley, Richard M. 2002. Speech to Chicago Greening Symposium (8 March). www.ci.chi.il.us (accessed 27 August 2002).

Daley, Richard, M. 2003. Inaugural and State of the City Address (5 May). http://egov.cityofchicago.org/city/webportal/home.do (accessed 20 January 2006).

Danns, Dionne. 2002. "Black Student Empowerment in Chicago: School Reform Efforts in 1968." *Urban Education* 37:631–55.

Davis, Mike. 1986. *Prisoners of the American Dream*. London: Verso.

Davis, Mike. 1988. "Los Angeles: Civil Liberties between the Hammer and the Rock." *New Left Review* (July/August): 37–60.

Davis, Mike. 1992. *City of Quartz*. New York: Vintage Books.

Davis, Mike. 2004. "Planet of Slums." *New Left Review* (March/April): 5–34.

Dawson, Michael. 1994. *Behind the Mule: Race and Class in African American Politics.* Princeton, NJ: Princeton University Press.

Dear, Michael. 2000. *The Postmodern Urban Condition.* Oxford: Blackwell.

Deering, Tara, 2004. "World-Class Look for North Side Shelter." *Chicago Tribune* (14 January).

Dela Cruz, Melany and Pauline Agbayani-Siewert. 2003 "Filipinos: Swimming with and against the Tide." In *The New Face of Asian Pacific America,* E. Lai and D. Arguelles, eds. San Francisco: Asian Week.

Delaney, Samuel. 2001. *Dhalgren.* New York: Vintage Books.

Department of City Planning. 1958. *Development Plan for the Central Area of Chicago.* Chicago: Department of City Planning (August).

Department of Planning and Development. 2002. "South Michigan Avenue Gets Official Landmark Approval." City of Chicago (27 February).

Department of Transportation. 1999. "New Millennium Park Unveiled to Chicago Plan Commission on March 11." City of Chicago (March).

D'Eramo, Marco. 2002. *The Pig and the Skyscraper.* London: Verso.

Dold, R. Bruce and Thomas Hardy. 1989. "Chicago Elects 2d Mayor Daley." *Chicago Tribune* (5 April).

Drake, St. Clair and Horace A. Cayton. [1945] 1993 *Black Metropolis: A Study of Negro Life in a Northern City.* Chicago: University of Chicago Press.

Dreier, Peter, John Mollenkopf, and Todd Swanstrom. 2001. *Place Matters: Metropolitics for the Twenty-first Century.* Lawrence: University Press of Kansas.

Duff, John B. 1971. *The Irish in the United States.* Belmont, CA: Wadsworth.

Dunkin' Donuts Inc. 1998. *Producing, Satellite and Express Bakery Center Locations.* Randolph, MA: Dunkin' Donuts Inc.

Duster, Alfreda M, ed. 1970. *Crusade for Justice: The Autobiography of Ida B. Wells.* Chicago: University of Chicago Press.

Economic Focus. 2002. World Business Chicago (November).

Economic Report of the President. 2004. Washington, DC: U.S. Government Printing Office.

Edsall, Thomas Byrne. 1989. "Black vs. White in Chicago." *New York Review of Books* (13 April).

Eisinger, Peter K. 1984. "Black Mayors and the Politics of Racial Economic Advancement." In *Readings in Urban Politics: Past, Present, and Future,* H. Hahn and C. H. Levine, eds. New York: Longman.

Eisinger, Peter K. 1998. "City Politics in an Era of Federal Devolution." *Urban Affairs Review* 33 (3): 308–25.

Elkhanialy, Hekmat and Ralph W. Nicholas, eds. 1976. *Immigrants from the Indian Subcontinent in the USA: Problems and Prospects.* Chicago: India League of America.

Emmons, David. 1977. "Dearborn Park/South Loop New Town: A Project in the Chicago 21 Plan." Chicago: Citizens Information Service of Illinois.

Eng, Monica. 2002. "Indians Reconnect with Roots." *Chicago Tribune* (17 November).

Engardio, Pete, Aaron Bernstein, and Manjeet Kripalani. 2003. "Is Your Job Next?" *Business Week* (3 February).

"English as a Second Language Goals and Standards." 1998. Chicago: Chicago Board of Education.

Erdmans, Mary Patrice. 1995. "Immigrants and Ethnics: Conflict and Identity in Polish Chicago." *The Sociological Quarterly* 36 (1): 175–95.

Erdmans, Mary. 1996. "Illegal Immigrant Home Care Workers: The Non-market Conditions of Job Satisfaction." In *Przeglad Polonijny,* Vol. 6. Krakow, Poland: Jagiellonian University.

Erdmans, Mary. 1998. *Opposite Poles: Immigrants and Ethnics in Polish Chicago, 1976–1990.* University Park: Pennsylvania State University Press.

Erdmans, Mary. 1999. "Portraits of Emigration: Sour Milk and Honey in the Promised Land." *Sociological Inquiry* 69 (3): 337–63.

Ericson, Richard and Kevin Haggerty. 1997. *Policing the Risk Society.* Toronto: University of Toronto Press.

Erlich, Bruce and Peter Dreier. 1999. "The New Boston Discovers the Old Tourism and the Struggle for a Livable City." In *The Tourist City,* D. R. Judd and S. S. Fainstein, eds. New Haven, CT: Yale University Press.

Espiritu, Yen Le. 1994. "The Intersection of Race, Ethnicity, and Class: The Multiple Identities of Second-Generation Filipinos." *Identities* 1:2.

Espiritu, Yen Le. 1995. *Filipino American Lives.* Philadelphia: Temple University Press.

Espiritu, Yen Le. 2002. "The Intersection of Race, Ethnicity and Class: the Multiple Identities of Second-Generation Filipinos." In *Second Generation: Ethnic Identity among Asian Americans,* P. G. Min, ed. Walnut Creek CA: AltaMira Press.

Fanon, Frantz. 1986. *The Wretched of the Earth.* New York: Grove Press.

Feagin, Joe and Eileen O'Brien. 2003. *White Men on Race: Power, Privilege, and the Shaping of Cultural Consciousness.* Boston: Beacon Press.

Feemster, Ron. 2003. "The Problem with Public Housing: Is Chicago Solving It?" Report prepared for the Ford Foundation.

Ferman, Barbara. 1996. *Challenging the Growth Machine: Neighborhood Politics in Chicago and Pittsburgh.* Lawrence: University Press of Kansas.

Fidel, Kenneth. 2003. "Winners and Losers: Crystallization, Status Persistence, and Urban Ecology over Three Decades." Presented at the annual meeting of Midwest Sociological Society, Chicago.

Filardo, Andrew. 1997. "Cyclical Implications of the Decline of Manufacturing Share." *Economic Review: Federal Reserve Bank of Kansas City* (Second Quarter).

The Filipino–American Community Builder. 2003. "Editor's View" (March).

Fischer, Paul. 2004. "Where Are the Public Housing Families Going? An Update." Report prepared for the Sargent Shriver National Center on Poverty Law, Chicago (January).

Fletcher, Connie. 1994. *What Cops Know: Cops Talk about What They Do, How They Do It, and What It Does to Them.* New York: Pocket Books.

Florida, Richard. 2002. *The Rise of the Creative Class.* New York: Basic Books.

Fogelsen, Robert M. [1967] 1993. *The Fragmented Metropolis: Los Angeles, 1850–1930.* Berkeley: University of California Press.

"For Rent: Housing Options in the Chicago Region." 1999. Regional Rental Market Report prepared for the Metropolitan Planning Council by the University of Illinois at Chicago (November).

Forbes, Kristin J. 2004. "U.S. Manufacturing: Challenges and Recommendations." Comments in NABE's 2004 Washington Economic Policy Conference (25 March).

Ford, Liam. 2002. "Triumphant Mell Out of the Shadows." *Chicago Tribune* (7 November).

Formisano, Ronald P. 1991. *Boston Against Busing.* Chapel Hill: University of North Carolina Press.

Fornek, Scott. 2004. "Obama Takes Senate Seat in a Landslide." *Chicago Sun-Times* (3 November).

Fox, Justin. 2004. "The Great Paving: How the Interstate Highway System Helped Reshape the Modern Economy—and Reshaped the FORTUNE 500." *Fortune* (12 January).

Frank, Robert and Philip J. Cook. 1996. *The Winner-Take-All Society.* New York: The Free Press.

Frazier, E. Franklin. 1957. *Black Bourgeoisie.* Chicago: University of Chicago Press.

Freedman, Samuel G. 1994. *Upon This Rock: The Miracles of a Black Church.* New York: Harper-Perennial.

Freeman, Jo. 1983. "On the Origins of Social Movements." In *Social Movements of the Sixties and Seventies,* J. Freeman, ed. New York: Longman.

Fremon, David K. 1988. *Chicago Politics Ward by Ward.* Bloomington: Indiana University Press.

Frey, Mary Cameron. 2000. "Perking Up City Parks." *Chicago Sun-Times* (27 July).

Frey, William H. and Ross C. DeVol. 2000. "American Demography in the Next Century: Aging Baby Boomers and New Immigrants as Major Players." Milken Institute Policy Policy Brief (8 March).

Friedland, Roger. 1983 *Power and Crisis in the City.* New York: Schocken Books.

Friedman, Warren. 2002. Interview by author, 18 September.

Friedmann, John. 1986. "The World City Hypothesis." *Development and Change* 17 (1): 69–84.

Frisbie, Margery. 2002. *An Alley in Chicago: The Life and Legacy of Monsignor John Egan.* Franklin, WI: Sheed & Ward.

Fuchs, Ester R. 1992. *Mayors and Money: Fiscal Policy in New York and Chicago.* Chicago: University of Chicago Press.

Fuerst, James. 2003. *When Public Housing Was Paradise: Building Community in Chicago.* New York: Praeger Publishers.

Fusco, Chris, Fran Spielman, and Lynn Sweet. 2001. "Daley's $6 Bil. Flight Plan." *Chicago Sun-Times* (30 June).

Gardner, Matthew, Robert G. Lynch, Richard Sims, Ben Schweigert, and Amy Meek. 2002. "Balancing Act: Tax Reform Options for Illinois." Washington: Institute on Taxation and Economic Policy (February).

Garner, Roberta. 1977. *Social Movements in America.* Chicago: Rand-McNally.

Garreau, Joel. 1991. *Edge City: Life on the New Frontier.* New York: Doubleday.

Gecan, Michael. 2002. *Going Public.* Boston: Beacon Press.

Gee, J. P., Glenda G. Hull, and Collin Lankshear. 1996. *The New Work Order: Behind the Language of the New Capitalism.* Boulder CO: Westview Press.

Generation Y. 2002. *Higher Learning: A Report on Educational Inequities and Opportunities Facing Public High School Students in Chicago.* Chicago: Generation Y.

Genestier, Philippe. 2004. "Comment loger les plus pauvres si l'on démolit les HLM?" *Mouvements* 32 (March/April): 126–34.

Georgakas, Dan and Marvin Surkin. 1975. *Detroit: I Do Mind Dying.* New York: St. Martin's Press.

Gezari, Vanessa. 2000. "City Gives Downtown Park a Paris Touch." *Chicago Tribune* (25 June).

Gibson, William. 1984. *Neuromancer.* New York: Ace Books.

Giddens, Anthony. 1990. *The Consequences of Modernity.* Stanford, CA: Stanford University Press.

Gierzynski, Anthony, Paul Kleppner, and James Lewis. 1996. "The Price of Democracy: Financing Chicago's 1995 City Elections." Chicago: Chicago Urban League and the Office for Social Policy Research, Northern Illinois University (September).

Gills, Doug. 1991. "Chicago Politics and Community Development: A Social Movement Perspective." In *Harold Washington and the Neighborhoods: Progressive City Government in Chicago, 1983–1987*, P. Clavel and W. Wiewel, eds. New Brunswick, NJ: Rutgers University Press.

Giloth, Robert. 1991. "Making Policy with Communities: Research and Development in the Department of Economic Development." In *Harold Washington and the Neighborhoods: Progressive City Government in Chicago, 1983–1987*, P. Clavel and W. Wiewel, eds. New Brunswick, NJ: Rutgers University Press.

Giloth, Robert. 1996. "Social Justice and Neighborhood Revitalization in Chicago: The Era of Harold Washington, 1983–1987." In *Revitalizing Urban Neighborhoods*, W. D. Keating, N. Krumholz, and P. Star, eds. Lawrence: University Press of Kansas.

Giloth, Robert. 2002. "Lifting All Boats: Targeted Economic Development in Neighborhoods, Cities, and Metropolitan Areas." Chicago: Center for Urban Research and Policy Studies, University of Chicago.

Ginsburg, Robert, Xiaochang Jin, and Sheila McCann. 1994. *E. J. Brach: A Misadventure in Candyland*. Chicago: Midwest Center for Labor Research.

Goetz, Edward G. 2003. *Clearing the Way: Deconcentrating the Poor in Urban America*. Washington, DC: Urban Institute Press.

Gonas, G. 1998. "The Interaction between Market Incentives and Government Actions." In *Contingent Work: American Employment Relations in Transition*, K. Barker and K. Christensen, eds. Ithaca, NY: Cornell University Press.

Goodman, Peter S. 2003. "White Collar Work a Booming U.S. Export." *Washington Post* (2 April).

Goodwin, Carole. 1979. *The Oak Park Strategy: Community Control of Racial Change*. Chicago: University of Chicago Press.

Gordon, Danielle. 1998a. "Police Forces Trail Suburbs in Pace of Racial Change." *Chicago Reporter* (February).

Gordon, Danielle. 1998b. "High Court Is the Final Chapter in Gang Ordinance Controversy." *Chicago Reporter* (September).

Gordon, David. 1996. *Fat and Mean: The Corporate Squeeze of Working Americans and the Myth of Managerial "Downsizing."* New York: The Free Press.

Gordon, Sally and Colin Grant. 2003. "CMBS: A New Economic Diversity Model for a New Economy." Moody's Investors Service Special Report (9 June).

Gottdiener, Mark, Claudia C. Collins, and David R. Dickens. 1999. *Las Vegas: The Social Production of an All-American City*. Malden, MA: Blackwell.

Grammich, Clifford A. 1992. "The Chicago Area Polish Community: An MCIC Special Survey Report." Chicago: Metro Chicago Information Center.

Gramsci, Antonio. 1971. *Selections from the Prison Notebooks*. New York: International Publishers.

Greenstone, J. David and Paul E. Peterson. 1973. *Race and Authority in Urban Politics: Community Participation and the War on Poverty*. New York: Russell Sage Foundation.

Grimshaw, William. 1992. *Bitter Fruit: Black Politics and the Chicago Machine, 1931–1991*. Chicago: University of Chicago Press.

Grossman, Kate N. 2002. "Development Team Picked for Mixed-Income Housing." *Chicago Sun-Times* (18 December).

Gupta, Sapna. 2004. "The Global Corporation: McDonald's, A Case Study." In *Global Chicago*, C. Madigan, ed. Urbana: University of Illinois Press.

Gyford, John. 1985. *The Politics of Local Socialism*. London: Allen & Unwin.

Hagedorn, John. 2003. Interview on "848." WBEZ Radio (4 December).

Hamilton, David. 2002. "Regimes and Regional Governance: The Case of Chicago." *Journal of Urban Affairs* 24 (4): 403–23.

Hancock, Blackhawk and Kiljoong Kim. 2003. "Racial Geography and Racial Movement in Metropolitan Chicago: Rethinking Models, Methods, and Mobility." DePaul University: Unpublished paper.

Handley, John. 2002a. "New Village on Campus." *Chicago Tribune* (28 April).

Handley, John. 2002b. "Near West Side Boom." *Chicago Tribune* (11 August).

Handley, John. 2004. "Battle of the Builders: National and Local Companies Fight for Area Market." *Chicago Tribune* (27 June).

Handlin, Oscar. [1951] 1973. *The Uprooted: The Epic Story of the Great Migrations That Made the American People*, 2nd ed. Boston: Little, Brown.

Haney, Walter. 2000. "The Myth of the Texas Miracle in Education." *Education Policy Analysis Archives* 8 (41). http://epaa.asu.edu/epaa/v8n41/ (accessed 16 January 2001).

Hanney, Suzanne. 2003. "Affordable Housing Advocates Preparing for 2004." *Streetwise* (Chicago) (December 10–16).

Hannigan, John A. 1995. "The Post-Modern City: A New Urbanization?" *Current Sociology* 43 (Summer): 152–214.

Harrison, Bennett. 1994. *Lean and Mean: The Changing Landscape of Corporate Power in the Age of Flexibility*. New York: Basic Books.

Harvey, David. 1989a. *The Condition of Postmodernity*. London: Blackwell Publishers.

Harvey, David. 1989b. "From Managerialism to Entrepreneurialism: The Transformation of Urban Governance in Late Capitalism." *Geografisca Annaler* 71B (1): 3–17.

Harvey, David. 1993. "From Space to Place and Back Again: Reflections on the Condition of Postmodernity." In *Mapping the Futures: Local Cultures, Global Change*, J. Bird, B. Curtis, T. Putnam, G. Robertson, and L. Ticker, eds. London: Routledge.

Hauser, Robert 1999. "On 'Ending Social Promotion' in Chicago." In *Comment on Ending Social Promotion: The First Two Years*, Attachment B, D. Moore, ed. Chicago: Designs for Change.

Haymes, Stephen N. 1995. *Race, Culture and the City.* Albany: State University of New York Press.

Hecker, Daniel E. 2001. "Occupational Employment Projections to 2010." *Monthly Labor Review* 124 (November): 567–84.

Held, David, Anthony McGrew, David Goldblatt, and Jonathan Perraton. 1999. *Global Transformations: Politics, Economics and Culture.* Stanford, CA: Stanford University Press.

Hemmens, George C. 1998. "Planning and Development Decision Making in the Chicago Region." In *Metropolitan Governance Revisited: American/Canadian Intergovernmental Perspectives*, D. N. Rothblatt and A. Sancton, eds. Berkeley, CA: Institute of Governmental Studies Press.

Henderson, Harold. 1994. "Scattered Successes." *The Reader* (Chicago) (14 October).

Henderson, Harold. 1998. "There Goes Their Neighborhood." *The Reader* (Chicago) (29 May).

Henderson, Harold. 2002. "The Future Is Theirs." *The Reader* (Chicago) (5 January).

Herring, Cedric, ed. 1997. *African Americans and the Public Agenda: The Paradoxes of Public Policy.* Thousand Oaks, CA: Sage Publications.

Herring, Cedric, Michael Bennett, and Douglas Gills. 2000. "Pulling Together or Pulling Apart? Black–Latino Cooperation and Competition in the U.S. Labor Market." In *The Collaborative City: Opportunities and Struggles for Blacks and Latinos in U.S. Cities*, J. Betancur and D.Gills, eds. New York: Garland Publishing.

Hess, G. Alfred. 1991. *School Restructuring Chicago Style.* Newbury Park, CA: Corwin Press.

Hewings, Geoffrey J. D. n.d. "Infrastructure and Economic Development: Perspectives for the Chicago and Midwest Economies." www.chicagofed.org/newsandevents/conferences/midwest_infrastructure/documents/hewings_infrastructure.ppt.

Hilkevitch, Jon. 2000. "Beautification Effort Plants Obstacles for Drivers." *Chicago Tribune* (22 May).

Hilkevitch, Jon and Gary Washburn. 2001. "Expansion of O'Hare Already Hits Hurdles." *Chicago Tribune* (7 December).

Hill, Richard Child. 1986. "Crisis in the Motor City: The Politics of Economic Development in Detroit." In *Restructuring the City*, S. S. Fainstein et al., eds. New York: Longman.

Hill, Richard Child and Cynthia Negrey. 1987. "Deindustrialization in the Great Lakes Region." *Urban Affairs Quarterly* 22 (4): 580–97.

Hill, Richard Child and June Woo Kim. 2000. "Global Cities and Developmental States." *Urban Studies* 37 (12): 2167–98.

Hines, Thomas S. 1979. *Burnham of Chicago.* Chicago: University of Chicago Press.

Hinz, Greg. 1999. "Reinventing the Metropolis: Bold, Regional Vision Lands Commercial Club Executive of the Year Award." *Crain's Chicago Business* (8 June).

Hinz, Greg. 2003. "Pressure Building at McPier." *Crain's Chicago Business* (14 July).

Hirsch, Arnold R. 1983. *Making the Second Ghetto: Race and Housing in Chicago, 1940–1960.* New York: Cambridge University Press.

Hirst, Paul and Grahame Thompson. 1996a. "Globalization: Ten Frequently Asked Questions and Some Surprising Answers." *Sounding* 4: 47–66.

Hirst, Paul and Grahame Thompson. 1996b. *Globalization in Question: The International Economy and the Possibility of Governance.* Cambridge, UK: Policy Press.

Hitti, Philip K. 1924. *The Syrians in America.* New York: George Doran.

Holli, Melvin G. and Peter d'A. Jones. 1995. *Ethnic Chicago: A Multicultural Portrait*, 4th edition. Grand Rapids MI: William B. Erdmans Publishing Company.

Horwitt, Sanford D. 1989. *Let Them Call Me Rebel: Saul Alinsky—His Life and Legacy.* New York: Knopf.

"Households and Employment by County and Municipality." 2002. http://www.chicagometropolis2020.org/2002_index/02_index.htm (accessed 30 September 2002).

Hughes, Everett. 1971. *The Sociological Eye: Selected Papers on Work, Self, and the Study of Society.* New York: Aldine-Atherton.

Hull House. 2003. "Minding the Gap: An Assessment of Racial Disparity in Metropolitan Chicago." Chicago: Hull House.

Hundley, Tom. 1998. "The Draining of Dlugopole." *Chicago Tribune Magazine* (15 November).

Huxley, Aldous. 1932. *Brave New World.* New York and London: Harper Brothers.

Ignatiev, Noel. 1995. *How the Irish Became White.* New York: Routledge.

"Illegal Immigration: INS Overstay Estimation Methods Need Improvement." 1995. Report to the Chairman, Subcommittee on Immigration, Committee on the Judiciary, U.S. Senate (September). Washington DC: Government Accounting Office.

Illinois Department of Labor. 2004. "The Illinois Workforce: Identifying Progress of Women and Minorities." Annual Report. Chicago, IL.

Illinois Institute of Technology Website. 2003. www.iit.edu (accessed 18 August 2003).

Immergluck, Dan and Geoff Smith. 2001. "Who's Buying Where? Part I, Home Buying by Income, 1993–2000." Chicago: Woodstock Institute, November.

Inda, Jonathan and Renato Rosaldo, eds. 2002. *The Anthropology of Globalization: A Reader.* Malden, MA: Blackwell Publishers.

Independent Monitor's Report No. 5 to the Chicago Housing Authority and the Central Advisory Council. 2003. Chicago (8 January).

Indian Reporter and World News. 2003. *Chicago Weekly* (4 April).

Indo-American Center. 2003. *Asian Indians of Chicago. A Pictorial History.* Images of America Series. Mount Pleasant, SC: Arcadia Publishing.

Institute for Latino Studies. 2002. "Bordering the Mainstream: A Needs Assessment of Latinos in Berwyn and Cicero, Illinois." South Bend, IN: Institute for Latino Studies.

Institute for Metropolitan Affairs of Roosevelt University and Office for Social Policy Research of Northern Illinois University. 2002. "Race and Residence in the Chicago Metropolitan Area 1980 to 2000." Chicago: Institute for Metropolitan Affairs of Roosevelt University.

Jackson, Kenneth. 1985. *Crabgrass Frontier: The Suburbanization of the United States.* New York: Oxford University Press.

Jacobs, Jane. 1961. *The Death and Life of Great American Cities.* New York: Vintage Books.

Jargowsky, Paul A. 1997. *Poverty and Place: Ghettos, Barrios, and the American City.* New York: Russell Sage Foundation.

Jargowsky, Paul A. 2003. *Stunning Progress, Hidden Problems: The Dramatic Decline of Concentrated Poverty in the 1990s.* Washington, DC: The Brookings Institution.

Jaskot, Paul. 2000. *The Architecture of Oppression.* New York and London: Routledge.

Jessop, Bob. 1990. "Regulation Theories in Retrospect and Prospect." *Economy and Society* 19:153–216.

Jew, Victor. 2003. "Making Homes in the Heartland." In *The New Face of Asian Pacific America,* E. Lai and D. Arguelles, eds. San Francisco: Asian Week.

Johnson, Dirk. 2002. "High School at Attention." *Newsweek* (21 January).

Johnson, Elmer W. 1998. "Chicago Metropolis 2020: Preparing Metropolitan Chicago for the 21st Century—Executive Summary." Chicago: The Commercial Club of Chicago.

Johnson, Elmer W. 2001. *Chicago Metropolis 2020: The Chicago Plan for the Twenty–First Century.* Chicago: University of Chicago Press.

Johnson, Kenneth M. 2002. "Chicago Census 2000: Recent Demographic Trends in the Chicago Metropolitan Area." *Chicago Fed Letter.* Federal Reserve Bank of Chicago (April).

Judd Dennis, ed. 2003. *The Infrastructure of Play: Building the Tourist City.* Armonk, NY: M.E. Sharpe.

Judd, Dennis and Susan S. Fainstein, eds. 1999. *The Tourist City.* New Haven: Yale University Press.

Judd, Dennis and Dick Simpson. 2003. "Reconstructing the Local State: The Role of External Constituencies in Building Urban Tourism." *American Behavioral Scientist* 46 (8): 1056–69.

Judd, Dennis, R. Winter, William Barnes, William R. and Emily Stern. 2000. "Tourism and Entertainment as a Local Economic Development Strategy: A Survey of City Halls." National League of Cities (April).

Kahn, Mathew. 2001. "Does Sprawl Reduce the Black/White Housing Consumption Gap?" *Housing Policy Debate* 12 (1): 77–86.

Kamin, Blair. 1998. "Reinventing the Lakefront." *Chicago Tribune* (26 October).

Kamin, Blair. 2003. "Steel Appeal." *Chicago Tribune* (6 July).

Kasarda, John. 1989. "Urban Industrial Transition and the Underclass." *Annals of the American Academy of Political and Social Science* 501: 26–47.

Kasarda, John. 1993. "Cities As Places Where People Live and Work: Urban Change and Urban Distress." In *Interwoven Destinies: Cities and the Nation.* H. Cisneros, ed. New York: W.W. Norton.

Kass, John and Rick Pearson. 1996. "State Flying into Gridlock: Schools, Bears Could Now Be More Partisan." *Chicago Tribune* (5 December).

Katz, Michael. B. 1992. "Chicago School Reform as History." *Teachers College Record* 94 (1): 56–72.

Katz, Michael B., Michelle Fine, and Elaine Simon. 1997. "Poking Around: Outsiders View Chicago School Reform." *Teachers College Record* 99 (1): 117–57.

Katz–Fishman, Walda and Jerome Scott. 1994. "Diversity and Equality: Race and Class in America." *Sociological Forum* 9 (4): 569–81.

Katznelson, Ira. [1981] 1994. *City Trenches.* Chicago: University of Chicago Press.

Keiser, Richard A. 1997. *Subordination or Power? African American Leadership and the Struggle for Urban Political Power.* New York: Oxford University Press.

Kelly, Maura. 2003. "Daley Says Casino Would Boost City's Economy." *Associated Press* (22 May).

Kent, Mary M., Kelvin M. Pollard, John Haaga, and Mark Mather. 2001. "First Glimpses from the U.S. Census." *Population Bulletin* 56 (June).

Kerr, Peter. 2001. *Postwar British Politics: From Conflict to Consensus.* London and New York: Routledge.

Khalidi, Walid. 1992. *All that Remains: The Palestinian Villages Occupied and Depopulated by Israel in 1948.* Washington, DC: Institute for Palestine Studies.

Kim, Kwang Chung. 1995. "Asian Americans and the Successful Minority Myth." In *Civil Rights Issues Facing Asian Americans in Metropolitan Chicago,* Illinois Advisory Committee to the United States Commission on Civil Rights. Chicago: U.S. Commission on Civil Rights, Midwestern Regional Office.

Kim, Kwang Chung, Won Moo Hurh, and Marilyn Fernandez. 1989. "Intra–group Differences in Business Participation: Three Asian Immigrant Groups." *International Migration Review* 23 (1): 73–95.

Kim, Yoon-Jin. 1991. *From Immigrants to Ethnics: The Life–Worlds of Korean Immigrants in Chicago.* Ph.D. Dissertation, Department of History, University of Illinois–Urbana-Champaign.

King, Anthony, ed. 1991a. *Culture, Globalization and the World System.* Basingstoke, UK: Macmillan.

King, Anthony. 1991b. "Spaces of Culture, Spaces of Knowledge." In *Culture, Globalization and the World System,* A. King, ed. Basingstoke, UK: Macmillan.

Kleppner, Paul. 1985. *Chicago Divided: The Making of a Black Mayor.* DeKalb: Northern Illinois University Press.

Klier, Thomas and William Testa. 2001. "Headquarters Wanted: Principals Only Need Apply." *Chicago Fed Letter.* The Federal Reserve Bank of Chicago (July).

Klinenberg, Eric. 2002. *Heat Wave: A Social Autopsy of Disaster in Chicago.* Chicago: University of Chicago Press.

Knox, Paul. 1997. "Globalization and Urban Economic Change" *Annals of the American Academy of Political and Social Science* 554:17–27.

Knudsen, Daniel. 1994. "Deindustrialization of the U.S. Midwest, 1965–1988." In *Dimensions of Change: Declining and Restructuring of the American Midwest,* C. Bonser, ed. Bloomington: Indiana University, Institute for Development Studies.

Kolarska-Bobinska, L. 1993. "An Economic System and Group Interests." In *Societal Conflict and Systemic Change: The Case of Poland, 1980–1992,* W. Adamski, ed. Warsaw: IFIS Publishers.

Kosdrosky, Terry. 2003. "Planning in Pittsburgh, Chicago Has Produced Results." *Crain's Detroit Business* (28 April).

Kotkin, Joel. 1996. "Cities of Hope: Thanks for Global Trade Urban America's Potential is Revealed" *World Trade* 9 (4): 24–30.

Kotler, Philip, Donald H. Haider, and Irving Rein. 1993. *Marketing Places: Attracting Investment, Industry, and Tourism to Cities, States, and Nations.* New York: The Free Press.

Koval, John P. 2004. "In Search of Economic Parity: The Mexican Labor Force in Chicago." Institute for Latino Studies at the University of Notre Dame. *Interim Reports* 1 (March).

Kyle, Charles L. and Edward R. Kantowicz. 1992. *Kids First-Primero los Niños: Chicago School Reform in the 1980s.* Springfield, IL: Sangamon State University.

Lang, Robert E. and Jennifer LeFurgy. 2003. "Edgeless Cities: Examining the Noncentered Metropolis." *Housing Policy Debate* 14 (3): 427–60.

Lang, Robert E. and Strobe Talbott. 2003. *Edgeless Cities: Exploring the Elusive Metropolis.* Washington, DC: The Brookings Institution.

Langley, Alison. 2003. "Swiss Maker Of Chocolate Will Acquire Brach's Candy." *New York Times* (2 September).

Lau, Yvonne. 2002. "Chinese Americans." In *A Comprehensive Guide to the Asian Pacific Community in Illinois.* Chicago: Asian American Institute.

Law, Christopher M. 2002. *Urban Tourism: The Visitor Economy and the Growth of Large Cities.* London and New York: Continuum.

Lawrence, Curtis. 2003. "Three Vying to Topple Fillman in 3rd." *Chicago Sun Times* (6 February).

Lawyers Committee for Better Housing. 2002. "Locked Out: Barriers to Choice for Chicago Housing Voucher Holders." Chicago (April).

Layton, Azza Salama. 2000. *International Politics and Civil Rights Policies in the United States, 1941–1960.* New York: Cambridge University Press.

Leadership Council for Metropolitan Open Communities. 1991. "Jobs, Housing and Race in the Chicago Metropolitan Area (A Geographic Imbalance)." Chicago (April).

Lee, Erika. 2003. *At America's Gates.* Chapel Hill: University of North Carolina Press.

Lee, Kwang-Kyu. 1989. *Korean Americans: Comprehensive Analyis.* [Korean]. Seoul, South Korea: Iljogak Publishing.

Legal Assistance Foundation of Metropolitan Chicago and Chicago Urban League. 2003. "Racial Preference and Suburban Employment Opportunities." Chicago: Legal Assistance Foundation.

Lemann, Nicholas. 1991. *The Promised Land: The Great Black Migration and How it Changed America.* New York: Alfred A. Knopf.

Levitt, Peggy. 2001. "Transnational Migrants: When 'Home' Means More Than One Country." Washington, DC: Migration Policy Institute (1 October).

Lewis, James, Michael Maly, Paul Kleppner, and Ruth Anne Tobias. 2002. "Race and Residence in the Chicago Metropolitan Area, 1980 to 2000." Institute for Metropolitan Affairs, Roosevelt University and Office for Social Policy Research, Northern Illinois University.

Lewis, Lisa. 1997. "Law, Policy Changes Dilute LSC Power." *Catalyst* (Chicago) (September).

Lewis Mumford Center for Comparative Urban and Regional Research. 2002. "Ethnic Diversity Grows, Neighborhood Integration Lags Behind." www.albany.edu/mumford/census.

Lichter, Daniel. 1988. "Racial Differences in Underemployment in American Cities." *American Journal of Sociology* 94 (4): 771–92.

Lindstrom, Bonnie. 1998. "Regional Cooperation and Sustainable Growth: Nine Councils of Government in Northeastern Illinois." *Journal of Urban Affairs* 20 (3): 327–42.

Lindstrom, Bonnie. 2002. "Public Works and Land Use: The Importance of Public Infrastructure in Chicago's Development, 1830–1970." In *Suburban Sprawl: Private Decisions and Public Policy*, W. Wiewel and J. J. Persky, eds. Armonk, NY: M.E. Sharpe.

Lipinski-Wnuk, E. 1993. "Economic Deprivations and Social Transformations." In *Societal Conflict and Systemic Change: The Case of Poland, 1980–1992*, W. Adamski, ed. Warsaw: IFIS Publishers.

Lipman, Pauline. 2003. "Cracking Down: Chicago School Policy and the Regulation of Black and Latino/a Youth." In *Education as Enforcement*, K. L. Saltman, ed. New York: Routledge.

Lipman, Pauline. 2004. *High Stakes Education: Inequality, Globalization, and Urban School Reform.* New York: Routledge.

Lipset, Seymour Martin, Martin A. Trow, and James Coleman. 1956. *Union Democracy: The Internal Politics of the International Typographical Union.* Glencoe IL.: The Free Press.

Lipton, Eric. 2004. "Panel Says Census Move on Arab-Americans Recalls World War II Internments." *New York Times* (10 November).

Little, Darnell and David Mendell. 2003. "Income Gap Leaves City Asians Far Behind Suburban Cousins." *Chicago Tribune* (11 September).

Lloyd, Richard. 2002. "Neo–Bohemia: Art and Neighborhood Redevelopment in Chicago." *Journal of Urban Affairs* 24 (5): 517–32.

Logan, John and Harvey Molotch. 1987. *Urban Fortunes: The Political Economy of Place.* Berkeley: University of California Press.

Lomax, Tim and David Schrank. 2003. "2003 Annual Urban Mobility Report." College Station, TX: Texas A&M University.

Longworth, Richard C. and Greg Burns. 1999a. "Chicago: A Work in Progress." *Chicago Tribune* (7 February).

Longworth, Richard. C. and Greg Burns. 1999b. "Global City: Progress, Trouble on Economic Front." *Chicago Tribune* (7 February).

Lowe, Lisa. 1996. *Immigrant Acts.* Durham, NC: Duke University Press.

Lu, Xing. 2001. "Bicultural Identity Development and Chinese Community Formation: An Ethnographic Study of Chinese Schools in Chicago." *The Howard Journal of Communication* 12: 203–20.

Lucas, Harold. 2003. *Bronzeville Online.* www. BronzevilleOnline.com (accessed 11 September 2003).

Ludgin, Mary. 1989. "Downtown Development Chicago 1987–90." Chicago: City of Chicago, Department of Planning.

Ludgin, Mary and Louis Masotti. 1985. "Downtown Development Chicago 1978–1984." Evanston, IL: Center for Urban Affairs and Policy Research, Northwestern University.

Ludgin, Mary and Louis Masotti. 1986. "Downtown Development Chicago 1985–86." Evanston, IL: Center for Urban Affairs and Policy Research, Northwestern University.

Lyons, William. 1999. *The Politics of Community Policing.* Ann Arbor: University of Michigan Press.

MacCannell, Dean. 1976. *The Tourist: A New Theory of the Leisure Class.* New York: Schoken Books.

MacLaren, David. 1999. "If We Work on Problems in Our Neighborhoods: Bronzeville Organizing Strategy Session." Chicago: Policy Research Action Group.

Madigan, Charles, ed. 2004. *Global Chicago.* Chicago: University of Chicago Press.

Main, Frank. 2001. "Cops Facing More Violence, Even as Overall Crime Rate Drops." *Chicago Sun-Times* (27 August).

Maly Rocznik Statystyczny. 1997. Warsaw: Glowny Urzad Statystyczny.

Mandel, Ernst. 1999. *Late Capitalism.* London: Verso.

Mansfield, Gail. 2001a. "Neighbors Come Together to Offer Input on ABLA Redevelopment." *Near West/South Gazette* (Chicago) (6 April).

Mansfield, Gail. 2001b. "Green Space, Restored Street Grid Highlight ABLA Plans." *Near West/South Gazette* (Chicago) (6 July).

Marcuse, Peter. 1993. "What's So New about Divided Cities?" *International Journal of Urban and Regional Research* 17 (3): 355–65.

Markusen, Ann. 1991. *Rise of the Gunbelt: The Military Remapping of Industrial America.* New York: Oxford University Press.

Markusen, Ann. 1996. "Sticky Places in Slippery Space: A Typology of Industrial Districts." *Economic Geography* 72:294–314.

Markusen, Ann and Virginia Carlson. 1989. "Deindustrialization in the American Midwest." In *Deindustrialization and Regional Economic Transformation*, L. Rodwin and H. Suzanami, eds. Boston: Unwin Hyman.

Markusen, Ann, Karen Chapple, Greg Schrock, Daisaku Yamamoto, and Pingkang Yu. 2001. "High-Tech and I-Tech: How Metros Rank and Specialize." Minneapolis, MN: The Hubert H. Humphrey Institute of Public Affairs.

Markusen, Ann, Peter Hall, and Amy Glasmeier. 1986. *High Tech America: The What, How, Where and Why of the Sunrise Industries.* Boston: Allen and Unwin.

Martin, Andrew and Laurie Cohen. 2001. "Millennium Park Flounders as Deadlines, Budget Blown." *Chicago Tribune* (5 August).

Martin, Philip and Jonas Widgren. 2002. "International Migration: Facing the Challenge." *Population Bulletin* 57 (March).

Marx, Karl and Frederick Engels. [1848] 1951. *The Communist Manifesto.* New York: International Publishers.

Maslow, Abraham, H. 1970. *Motivation and Personality.* New York: Harper and Row.

Massey, Douglas and Nancy Denton. 1993. *American Apartheid: Segregation and the Making of the Underclass.* Cambridge, MA: Harvard University Press.

Massey, Douglas H. and Deborah S. Hirst. 1998. "From Escalator to Hourglass: Changes in the U. S. Occupational Wage Structure 1949–1989." *Social Science Research* 27:51–71.

Massey, Douglas et al. 1987. *Return to Aztlan: The Social Process of International Migration from Western Mexico.* Berkeley: University of California Press.

Mattoon, Richard. 2003. "Understanding Isolation and Change in Urban Neighborhoods: A Research Symposium." *Chicago Fed Letter.* The Federal Reserve Bank of Chicago (June).

Mayer, Harold M. and Richard C. Wade. 1969. *Chicago, Growth of a Metropolis.* Chicago: University of Chicago Press.

Mayor's Council of Technology Advisors. n.d. *A New Economy Growth Strategy for Chicagoland.* http://www.chicagotechtoday.com.

Mazur, Alicia. 1991. "Downtown Development, Chicago, 1989–1992." Chicago: Department of Planning.

McCarron, John. 1998. "Mammon and Metropolis: In Illinois, Petty Politics Trumps Idealism Every Time." *Chicago Tribune* (23 November).

McCarron, John. 2004. "Lessons behind the Hype." *Chicago Tribune* (4 June).

McCourt, Jeff and Greg Leroy with Philip Mattera. 2003. "A Better Deal for Illinois: Improving Economic Development Policy." Washington: Good Jobs First.

McCoy, Michael, Joseph Mikan, Robert Schillerstrom, Suzi Schmidt, and Michael Tryon. 2004. "Maintaining a Model for Regional Transportation." *Chicago Tribune* (18 May).

McCunn, Ruthanne Lum. 1998. *Chinese American Portraits.* Seattle: University of Washington Press.

McDonald, John. 1984. *Employment Location and Industrial Land–use in Metropolitan Chicago.* Champaign IL: Stipes.

McKenzie, Evan. 2001. "Fair Housing, Integration, and Diversity: The Changing Dynamics of Racial Policy in a Chicago Suburb." Paper presented at the Annual Meeting of the Western Political Science Association, Las Vegas, Nevada (15–17 March).

McKnight, John. 1995. *The Careless Society: Community and Its Counterfeits.* New York: Basic Books.

McNeil, Linda M. 2000. *Contradictions of School Reform: Educational Costs of Standardized Testing.* New York: Routledge.

McRoberts, Flynn. 1998. "Home Is Where Problem Is." *Chicago Tribune* (25 October).

McRoberts, Flynn and Abdon M. Pallasch. 1998. "Neighbors Wary of New Arrivals." *Chicago Tribune* (28 December).

Mehta, Chirag, Ron Baiman, and Joe Persky. 2004 "The Economic Impact of Wal-Mart: An Assessment of the Wal-Mart Store Proposed for Chicago's West Side." Chicago: University of Illinois at Chicago, Center for Urban Economic Development (March).

Mendell, David. 2001. "Poles Feel Left in the Political Dust." *Chicago Tribune* (21 December).

Mendell, David and Darnell Little. 2002. "Rich '90s Failed To Lift All." *Chicago Tribune* (20 August).

Mendell, David and Darnell Little. 2003. "Poverty, Crime Still Stalk City's Middle-Class Blacks." *Chicago Tribune* (27 July).

Mendell, David and Gary Washburn. 1999. "Daley Says He Didn't Deal Cards in CTA Land Jackpot." *Chicago Tribune* (20 October).

Mendieta, Ana. 1999. "Planetarium Shines New." *Chicago Sun–Times* (30 September).

Mendoza, Jay. 2003. "War, Immigrants, and the Economy: Filipinos in a Post–911 World." Inform! Special Report, January 25, 2003. San Jose: FOCUS.

Messerschmidt, James. 1993. *Masculinities and Crime.* Lanham, MD: Rowman and Littlefield.

Michie, Greg. 2000. "One Strike and You're Out." *The Reader* (Chicago) (8 September).

"Mid–South Strategic Development Plan: Restore Bronzeville." 1993. Prepared by Wendell Campbell Associates, Inc. and Applied Real Estate Analysis for the City of Chicago Department of Planning and Development and the Mid-South Planning Group (September).

Mier, Robert and Kari Moe. 1991. "Decentralized Development: From Theory to Practice." In *Harold Washington and the Neighborhoods: Progressive Government in Chicago, 1983–1987*, P. Clavel and W. Wiewel, eds. New Brunswick, NJ: Rutgers University Press.

Mihalopoulos, Dan and Matt O'Connor. "Feds Go After City Hall." *Chicago Tribune* (19 July).

Milkman, Ruth and Rachel E. Dwyer 2002. "Growing Apart: The 'New Economy' and Job Polarization in California, 1992–2000." In *The State of California Labor, 2002.* Berkeley: University of California Institute for Labor and Employment.

Miller, Donald L. 1997. *City of the Century: The Epic of Chicago and the Making of America.* New York: Simon and Shuster.

Mills, Steve and Ken Armstrong. 1999. "Yet Another Death Row Inmate Cleared." *Chicago Tribune* (18 May).

Min, Pyong Gap. 1998. *Changes and Conflicts: Korean Immigrant Families in New York*. Needham Heights, MA: Allyn & Bacon.

Mirel, Jeffrey. 1993. "School Reform, Chicago Style: Educational Innovation in a Changing Urban Context, 1976–1991." *Urban Education* 28 (July): 116–49.

Mishel, Lawrence, Jared Bernstein, and John Schmitt. 1999. *The State of Working America 1998–99*. Ithaca, NY: Cornell University Press.

Moberg, David. 1993. "Making It." *The Reader* (Chicago) (10 September).

Moberg, David. 1995. "Separate and Unequal." *The Neighborhood Works* (August/September).

Moffett, Nancy. 2001. "$100 Million Front Yard: New Landscape for Soldier Field." *Chicago-Sun Times* (11 June).

Mokhiber, Russell and Robert Weissman. 2000. "GE: Every Plant on a Barge." www. corporatepreda tors.org.

Mollenkopf, John and Manuel Castells, eds. 1991. *Dual City: Restructuring New York*. New York: Russell Sage Foundation.

Molotch, Harvey and Marilyn Lester. 1973. "Accidents, Scandals, and Routines: Resources for Insurgent Methodology." *The Insurgent Sociologist* 3:1–11.

Moody's Investors Service. 2003. "CMBS: A New Economic Diversity Model for a New Economy" (9 June).

Morrison, Steven and Clifford Winston. 1995. *The Evolution of the Airline Industry*. Washington, DC: The Brookings Institution.

Motorola. 2003. Telephone interview with a Human Resources Executive from Motorola Corp., Schaumberg, Illinois (April).

Mumford, Lewis. 1961. *The City in History*. New York: Harcourt, Brace & World.

Mumford, Lewis. 1986. "Home Remedies for Urban Cancer." In *The Lewis Mumford Reader*, D. L. Miller, ed. New York: Pantheon.

Munoz, Romeo. 2002. *Filipino Americans: Journey from Invisibility to Empowerment*. Chicago: Nyala Publishing.

Munson, Nancy. 2004. "Southwest Suburban Manhattan Could Soon Triple in Size." *Chicago Tribune* (22 August).

Muwakkil, Salim. 2000. "Paying Back the Slavery Debt." *Chicago Tribune* (17 April).

Naff, Alixa. 1985. *Becoming American: The Early Arab Immigrant Experience*. Carbondale: Southern Illinois University Press.

National Arbor Day Foundation. 1999. "Mayor Richard M. Daley to Receive Arbor Day Foundation's Highest Award" (1 April).

Neal, Steve. 2001. "Ryan Stands Up for Compassion." *Chicago Sun-Times* (21 May).

Neergard, Lauran. 2003. "Live in Oak Brook? You're Probably Fatter than City Folks." *Chicago Sun-Times* (29 August).

Neighborhood Capital Budget Group. 2002. "Who Pays for the Only Game in Town?" www.ncbg.org.

Newmann, F. M., Anthony S. Bryk, and Jenny K. Nagaoka 2001. "Authentic Intellectual Work and Standardized Tests: Conflict or Coexistence? A Report of the Chicago Annenberg Research Project." Chicago: Consortium on Chicago School Research.

Nijman, Jan. 2000. "The Paradigmatic City." *Annals of the Association of American Geographers* 90 (1): 135–45.

Nishioka, Joyce. 2003. "The Model Minority?" In *The New Face of Asian Pacific America*, E. Lai and D. Arguelles, eds. San Francisco: Asian Week.

Norkewicz, Michael and Rob Paral. 2003. *Metro Chicago Immigration Fact Book*. Chicago: Roosevelt University.

Northeastern Illinois Planning Commission. 2003. "2030 Forecasts of Population, Households, and Employment by County and Municipality" (30 September).

Northeastern Illinois Planning Commission. 2000–2004. "Residential Permits Issued by Municipality, 2000–2004." http://www.nipc.org/forecasting/permits.htm.

Nyden, Philip. 1998. "Comment on James E. Rosenbaum, Linda K. Stroh, and Cathy A. Flynn's 'Lake Parc Place: A Study in Mixed-Income Housing.'" *Housing Policy Debate* 9 (4): 741–48.

Oates, Steven, 1982. *Let The Trumpet Sound: The Life of Martin Luther King, Jr.* New York: Harper and Row.

O'Connor, Alice. 2001. *Poverty Knowledge: Social Science, Social Policy, and the Poor in Twentieth Century U.S. History*. Princeton, NJ: Princeton University Press.

O'Daday, Eileen. 2001. "Durbin, Sikhs, Condemn Hate Crimes" *Chicago Daily Herald* (1 October).

Office of the Mayor. 2000. "Mayor Daley Unveils Tree-Planting Program to Beautify Expressways, Cool City, Reduce Pollutants." City of Chicago (2 December).

Olivo, Antonio. 2004. "Cabrini Residents Sue Over Eviction." *Chicago Tribune* (4 June).

Olszewski, Lori. 2003. "One in Five Blacks Drop Out: African Americans Leave City's Public Schools at Staggering Rate." *Chicago Tribune* (11 November).

Omi, Michael and Howard Winant. 1994. *Racial Formation in the United States*, 2nd edition. New York: Routledge.

Ong, Paul and Loh-Sze Leung. 2003. "Diversified Growth." In *The New Face of Asian Pacific America*,

E. Lai and D. Arguelles, eds. San Francisco: Asian Week.

Ong, Paul and John Liu. 1994. "U.S. Immigration Policies and Asian Migration." In *The New Asian Immigration in Los Angeles and Global Restructuring*, P. Ong, E. Bonacich, and L. Cheng, eds. Philadelphia: Temple University Press.

Orfield, Gary. 1990. "Wasted Talent, Threatened Future: Metropolitan Chicago's Human Capital and Illinois Public Policy." In *Creating Jobs, Creating Workers: Economic Development and Employment in Metropolitan Chicago*, L. B. Joseph, ed. Chicago: University of Chicago Center for Urban Research and Policy Studies.

Orfield, Gary. 2004. *Schools More Separate: Consequences of a Decade of Resegregation*. Cambridge, MA: Civil Rights Project at Harvard.

Orfield, Myron. 2002. *American Metropolitics*. Washington, DC: Brookings Institution Press.

Orlebeke, Charles J. 1983. *Federal Aid to Chicago*. Washington, DC: The Brookings Institution.

Ortiz, Wilma. 1996. "The Mexican-Origin Population: Permanent Working Class or Emerging Middle Class?" In *Ethnic Los Angeles*, R. Waldinger and M. Bozorgmehr, eds. New York: Russell Sage Foundation.

Osborne, David. 1988. *Laboratories of Democracy: A New Breed of Governors Creates Models for National Growth*. Boston: Harvard Business School Press.

Osterman, Rachel. 2004. "Filipinos Carry on Legacy of Nursing." *Chicago Tribune* (25 October).

Oxford English Dictionary, 2nd edition. 1989. "Industrial." J. A. Simpson and E.S.C. Weiner, eds. Oxford: Clarendon Press. www.oed.com.

Pacyga, Dominic A. 1995. "Chicago's Ethnic Neighborhoods: The Myth of Stability and the Reality of Change." In *Ethnic Chicago: A Multicultural Portrait*, M. G. Holli and P. d'A. Jones, eds. Grand Rapids, MI: Wm B. Eerdmans Publishing Co.

Padmanabhan, Anil. 2003. "Brain Drain Reversed." *India Today International Edition* (28 July).

Pager, Devah. 2003. "The Mark of a Criminal Record." *American Journal of Sociology* 108 (5): 937–975.

Papademetriou, Demetrious. 2000. "The Shifting Expectations of Free Trade and Migration." Paper presented at the Urban Affairs Association Annual Meeting, Los Angeles (May).

Paral, Robert. 1994. "Hope and Dreams: A Statistical Profile of the Non-Citizen Population of Metropolitan Chicago." Chicago: The Latino Institute.

Paral, Rob. 2000. "Suburban Immigrant Communities: Assessments of Key Characteristics and Needs." Chicago: The Fund for Immigrants and Refugees.

Paral, Rob. 2002. "Mexican Immigrant Workers and the U.S. Economy: An Increasingly Vital Role."

Washington, DC: American Immigration Law Foundation.

Paral, Rob. 2004. "A Statistical Portrait of Persons with Arab, Middle Eastern and Turkish Ancestry in Illinois." Unpublished paper.

Paral, Robert and V. Alexander Corten. 1998. "New Immigrants and Refugees in Illinois: A Profile of 1990–1995 Arrivals." Chicago: The Latino Institute.

Park, Robert E., Ernest W. Burgess, and Roderick D. McKenzie. 1925. *The City*. Chicago: University of Chicago Press.

Pattillo, Mary. 2003. "Black Gentrification." Illinois Sociological Association keynote address, DePaul University (October).

Pattillo-McCoy, Mary. 1999. *Black Picket Fences: Privilege and Peril among the Black Middle Class*. Chicago: University of Chicago Press.

Peck, Jamie and Nik Theodore. 2001. "Contingent Chicago: Restructuring the Spaces of Temporary Labor." *International Journal of Urban and Regional Research* 25 (3): 471–96.

Perlmann, Joel and Roger Waldinger. 1999. "Immigrants, Past and Present: A Reconsideration." In *The Handbook of International Immigration: the American Experience*, C. Hirschman, P. Kasinitz, and J. DeWind, eds. New York: Russell Sage Foundation.

Persky, Joseph and Wim Wiewel. 2000. *When Corporations Leave Town: The Costs and Benefits of Metropolitan Job Sprawl*. Detroit: Wayne State University Press.

Persky, Joseph J. and Wim Wiewel. 2002. "Introduction." In *Suburban Sprawl*, W. Wiewel and J. J. Persky, eds. Armonk, NY: M.E. Sharpe.

Peterson, Paul. E. 1976. "School Desegregation and Racial Stabilization." In *Urban Politics and Public Policy: The City in Crisis*, S. M. David and P. E. Peterson, eds. New York: Praeger Publishers.

Phillips-Fein, Kim. 1998. "The Still-Industrial City: Why Cities Shouldn't Just Let Manufacturing Go." *The American Prospect* (September).

Pinoy. 2004. "Simbang Gabi Calendar" (December).

Plebanski, David, Kenneth Fidel, and Roberta Garner. 1993. "Perceptions of the Gang Impact on a Chicago Community." Chicago: DePaul University, Unpublished paper.

Plotkin, Wendy. 1999. "Deeds of Mistrust: Race, Housing and Restrictive Covenants in Chicago, 1900–1953." Ph.D. dissertation, University of Illinois at Chicago.

Popkin, Susan J. and Mary K. Cunningham. 2002. "CHA Relocation Counseling Assessment." Washington, DC: The Urban Institute.

Porter, Michael E. n.d. Cluster Mapping Project. Harvard Business School, Institute for Strategy and Competitiveness. http://data.isc.hbs.edu/isc.

Portes, Alejandro and Ruben G. Rumbaut. 1990. "Immigrant America: A Portrait." *Population and Development Review* 16 (4): 783–84.

Portes, Alejandro and Min Zhou. 1993. "The New Second Generation: Segmented Assimilation and Its Variants." *Annals of the American Academy of Political and Social Science* 530:74–96.

Posadas, Barbara. 1999. *The Filipino Americans.* Westport, CT: Greenwood Press.

Posadas, Barbara and Roland Guyotte. 1990. "Unintentional Immigrants: Chicago's Filipino Foreign Students Become Settlers, 1900–1941." *Journal of American Ethnic History* 9 (2): 26–48.

Posadas, Barbara and Roland Guyotte. 1998. "Filipinos and Race in Twentieth Century Chicago: The Impact of Polarization between Blacks and Whites." *Amerasia Journal* 24 (2): 135–54.

Powell, John. 2001. "Envisioning Racially Just and Opportunity-Based Housing for the Chicago Region." A study commissioned by the Leadership Council for Metropolitan Open Communities in Honor of its 35th Anniversary. Chicago: Leadership Council.

PRAGmatics (Chicago). 2002. "Looking into Tax Increment Financing" (Summer).

Prince, Jocelyn. 2003. "New Theater Opening to Mixed Reviews." *The Chicago Reporter* (April).

"Problem Solving in Practice: Implementing Community Policing in Chicago." 2000. U.S. Department of Justice, National Institute of Justice (April).

PURE–Office of Civil Rights Letter. 1999. http//: pureparents@pureparents.org/RletterPURE.htmt (accessed 12 January 2000).

Quintanilla, Ray. 1994. "Aldermen Keep Firm 'Hold' on Bronzeville." *The Chicago Reporter* (January).

Quintanilla, Ray. 1999. "It's Not Just School, It's an Adventure." *Chicago Tribune* (12 August).

Rakove, Milton. 1975. *Don't Make No Waves . . . Don't Back No Losers.* Bloomington: Indiana University Press.

Ralph, James, Jr. 1993. *Northern Protest: Martin Luther King Jr., Chicago, and the Civil Rights Movement.* Cambridge, MA: Harvard University Press.

Rama, Angel. 1996. *The Lettered City.* Durham, NC: Duke University Press.

Rangaswamy, Padma. 1995. "Asian Indians in Chicago: Growth and Change in a Model Minority." In *Ethnic Chicago: A Multicultural Portrait*, M. G. Holli and P. d'A. Jones, eds. Grand Rapids, MI: Wm B. Eerdmans Publishing Co.

Rangaswamy, Padma. 2000. *Namasté America: Indian Immigrants in an American Metropolis.* University Park: Pennsylvania State University Press.

Ranney, David. 2003. *Global Decisions Local Collisions: Urban Life in the New World Order.* Philadelphia: Temple University Press.

Rast, Joel. 1999. *Remaking Chicago: The Political Origins of Urban Industrial Change.* DeKalb: Northern Illinois University Press.

Ravinder, Archana. 2003. "Back to India Jobs Fair in Silicon Valley." *Indian Post News Service* (18 July).

Reardon, Patrick T. 1996. "Lord of His Ward." *Chicago Tribune* (26 August).

Reardon, Patrick T. and Abdon M. Pallasch. 1998. "Poles Leading Immigrant Tide." *Chicago Tribune* (3 September).

Reebie Associates. 2003. "The Economic Impact of Rail to the City of Chicago." Chicago: Reebie Associates.

Reed, Robert. 2003. "Flight Delay." *Chicago Magazine* (November).

Reich, Robert. 1991. *The Work of Nations.* New York: Alfred Knopf.

Report of the Commission on Chicago Landmarks. 1994. "Black Metropolis Historic District." Chicago: Commission on Chicago Landmarks.

Rivera, Blanche. 2004. "RP World's Top Exporter of Nurses to U.S., UK." *Pinoy* (November).

Rivlin, Gary. 1992. *Fire on the Prairie: Chicago's Harold Washington and the Politics of Race.* New York: Henry Holt.

Roberts, Dan and Edward Luce. 2003. "As Service Industries Go Global More White Collar Jobs Follow." *Financial Times* (19 August).

Roberts, Kenneth. 1999. *Deepening Democracy.* Stanford, CA: Stanford University Press.

Rocznik Statystyczny. 1989. Warsaw: Glowny Urzad Statystyczny.

Roderick, Melissa, et al. 2000. "Update: Ending Social Promotion." Chicago: Consortium on Chicago School Research.

Rodgers, Angie and Ed Lazere. 2004. "Income Inequality in the District of Columbia Is Wider than in Any Major U.S. City." Washington, DC: DC Fiscal Policy Institute. www.cbpp.org.

Rogal, Brian, J. 2002. "One year later, CHA program a work in progress." *The Chicago Reporter* (October).

Rogal, Brian, J. 2003. "CHA seals records on relocation—2002 in Review." *The Chicago Reporter* (January).

Rondinelli, Dennis, James Johnson, Jr., and John Kasarda. 1998. "The Changing Forces of Urban Economic Development: Globalization and the City Competitiveness in the 21st Century." *Cityscape* 3 (3): 71–105.

Roof, Michael and Kevin Kinsella. 1985. "Palestinian Population: 1950 to 1984." Washington DC: U.S. Bureau of the Census, Center for International Research.

Rosenbaum, James. E., Linda K. Stroh, and Cathy A. Flynn. 1998. "Lake Parc Place: A Study of Mixed-Income Housing." *Housing Policy Debate* 9 (4): 703–40.

Rosenberg, Deborah and Kristin Rankin. 2004. "Assessing Illinois' Uninsurance Crisis." Chicago: Gilead Outreach and Referral Center.

Rubinowitz, Leonard S. and James E. Rosenbaum. 2000. *Crossing the Class and Color Lines: From Public Housing to White Suburbia*. Chicago: University of Chicago Press.

Rubinowitz, Leonard S. and Scott Young. 1983. *Exclusionary Land Use Controls in Illinois*, Volumes I and II. Chicago: Chicago Lawyers' Committee for Civil Rights under the Law, Inc. and Northwestern University Center for Urban Affairs and Policy Research.

Rusk, David. 1999. *Inside Game/Outside Game: Winning Strategies for Saving Urban America.* Washington, DC: Brookings Institution Press.

Said, Edward. 1978. *Orientalism.* New York: Vintage Books.

Salama, Jerry J. 1999. "The Redevelopment of Distressed Public Housing: Early Results from HOPE VI Projects in Atlanta, Chicago, and San Antonio." *Housing Policy Debate* 10 (1): 95–142.

Samhan, Helen Hatab. 1999. "Not Quite White: Race Classification and the Arab American Experience." In *Arabs in America: Building a New Future*, M. W. Suleiman, ed. Philadelphia: Temple University Press.

Sandburg, Carl. [1916] 1950. *Collected Poems.* New York: Harcourt, Brace and Company.

Sanjek, Roger. 1998. *The Future of Us All: Race and Neighborhood Politics in New York City.* Ithaca, NY: Cornell University Press.

Sassen, Saskia. 1988. *The Mobility of Labor and Capital: A Study of International Investment and Labor Flow.* Cambridge, UK: Cambridge University Press.

Sassen, Saskia. 1991. *The Global City: New York, London, Tokyo.* Princeton, NJ: Princeton University Press.

Sassen, Saskia. 1994. *Cities in a World Economy.* Thousand Oaks, CA: Pine Forge Press.

Sassen, Saskia. 1996. *Losing Control? Sovereignty in an Age of Globalization.* New York: Columbia University Press.

Sassen, Saskia. 1998. *Globalization and Its Discontents.* New York: The New Press.

Sassen, Saskia. 2004. "A Global City." In *Global Chicago*, C. Madigan, ed. Urbana: University of Illinois Press.

Sassen, Saskia and Ralph Lewis. 2003. "Global Cities: Whys, Whats and Hows." Unpublished paper.

Savage, Mike and Alan Warde. 1993. *Urban Sociology, Capitalism and Modernity.* Basingstoke, UK: Macmillan.

Schaeffer, Brett. 2000. "Some See Elite Schools as Drain on System." *Catalyst* (Chicago) (December).

Schill, Michael H. 1997. "Chicago's Mixed-Income New Communities Strategy: The Future Face of Public Housing?" In *Affordable Housing and Urban Redevelopment in the United States*, W. Van Vliet, ed. Thousand Oaks, CA: Sage Publications.

Schneirov, Richard. 1998. *Labor and Urban Politics: Class Conflict and the Origins of Modern Liberalism in Chicago, 1864–97.* Urbana: University of Illinois Press.

Schurenberg, Eric. 2005. "America's Best Places to Live." *Money Magazine* (August).

Schwieterman, Joseph P. 2002. "Stormy Skies: State and Local Politics Complicate Decisions about Much-Needed Airport Expansion in the Chicago Area." *Planning* 68 (1): 16–22.

Scott, Mel. 1971. *American City Planning.* Berkeley: University of California Press.

Scott, Robert E. 2001. "NAFTA's Hidden Costs." *NAFTA at Seven.* Washington, DC: Economic Policy Institute.

Seventy Years' History: 1923–1993, The First Korean United Methodist Church of Chicago [Korean]. 1995. Chicago: First Korean Methodist Church.

Shaheen, Jack. 1984. *The TV Arab.* Bowling Green, OH: Bowling Green State University Popular Press.

Sharoff, Robert. 1999. "To Draw Traffic, Chicago Bets on Theatre." *New York Times* (3 January).

Shields, Yvette. 1998. "Chicago Plans Issue for Park Expansion." *Bond Buyer* (2 April).

Shields, Yvette. 1999. "Chicago Needs More Debt to Pay for Millennium Park." *Bond Buyer* (19 April).

Shinagawa, Larry. 1996. "The Impact of Immigration on the Demography of Asian Pacific Americans." In *Reframing the Immigration Debate*, B. Hing and R. Lee, eds. Los Angeles: LEAP Asian Pacific American Public Policy Institute and UCLA Asian American Studies Center.

Shipps, Dorothy. 1997. "Invisible Hand: Big Business and Chicago School Reform." *Teachers College Record* 99:73–116.

Shipps, Dorothy, Joseph Kahne, and Mark A. Smylie. 1999. "The Politics of Urban School Reform: Legitimacy, City Growth, and School Improvement in Chicago." *Educational Policy* 13 (September): 518–45.

Simmel, Georg. 1908. *Soziologie.* Translated in Park and Burgess (1921) as "The Sociological Significance of the 'Stranger.'" Leipzig: Dunche and Humblot.

Simpson, Dick. 2001. *Rogues, Rebels, and Rubber Stamps: The Politics of the Chicago City Council from 1863 to the Present.* Boulder, CO: Westview Press.

Singer, Audrey, et al. 2003. "Living Cities: The National Community Development Initiative. Chicago in Focus: A Profile from Census 2000." Washington, DC: The Brookings Institution Center on Community and Metropolitan Policy.

Sites, William. 2003. *Remaking New York: Primitive Globalization and the Politics of Urban Community.* Minneapolis: University of Minnesota Press.

Siu, Paul. 1987. *The Chinese Laundryman: A Study of Social Isolation*, J. Tchen, ed. New York: New York University Press.

Skogan, Wesley G. and Susan M. Hartnett. 1997. *Community Policing, Chicago Style*. New York: Oxford University Press.

Skogan, Wesley, Susan Hartnett, Jill Du Bois, Jennifer Comey, Marianne Kaiser, and Justine Lovig. 1999. *On the Beat: Police and Community Problem Solving*. Boulder, CO: Westview Press.

Skolnick, Jerome and David H. Bayley. 1986. *The New Blue Line: Police Innovation in Six American Cities*. New York: The Free Press.

Sly, Liz. 2002. "Dee in Denver or Deepali in Delhi?" *Chicago Tribune* (23 June).

Smith, Michael P. 1988. *City, State and Market: The Political Economy of Urban Society*. Oxford: Blackwell.

Smith, Neil. 1986. "Gentrification, the Frontier, and the Restructuring of Urban Space." In *Gentrification of the City*, N. Smith and P. Williams, eds. Boston: Allen and Unwin.

Smith, Neil. 1996. *The New Urban Frontier: Gentrification and the Revanchist City*. New York: Routledge.

Snyderman, Robin and Steven D. Dailey III. 2002. "Public Housing in the Public Interest: Examining the Chicago Housing Authority's Relocation Efforts." Chicago: Metropolitan Planning Council (February).

SOCDS: State of the Cities Data System. http://socds.huduser.org.

Soja, Edward. 1989. *Postmodern Geographies: The Reassertion of Space in Critical Social Theory*. New York: Verso.

Soja, Edward. 1991. "The Stimulation of a Little Confusion: A Contemporary Comparison of Amsterdam and Los Angeles." In *Understanding Amsterdam: Essays in Economic Vitality, City Life and Urban Form*, L. Deben, W. Heinemeijer, and D. van der Vaart, eds. Amsterdam: Het Spinhuis.

Soja, Edward. 1996. "Los Angeles 1965–1992: The Six Geographies of Urban Restructuring." In *The City: Los Angeles and Urban Theory at the End of the Twentieth Century*, A. J. Scott and E. W. Soja, eds. Berkeley: University of California Press.

Sonenshein, Raphael. 1993. *Politics in Black and White*. Princeton, NJ: Princeton University Press.

Sorkin, Michael, ed. 1992. *Variations on a Theme Park*. New York: Hill and Wang.

Spear, Allan H. 1967. *Black Chicago: The Making of a Negro Ghetto, 1890–1920*. Chicago: University of Chicago Press.

Spielman, Fran. 2000. "Gondolas to Give City a Touch of Venice." *Chicago Sun-Times* (8 June).

Spielman, Fran. 2004a. "D'Angelo Overshadows CHA Deal." *Chicago Sun-Times* (14 January).

Spielman, Fran. 2004b. "I'll Take the Blame Myself." *Chicago Sun-Times* (31 January).

Spirou, Costas. 2000. "Chicago's New Direction: Lakefront and the Economy of Culture." Paper presented at the Urban Affairs Association Annual Meeting, Los Angeles (May).

Spirou, Costas and Larry Bennett. 2003. *It's Hardly Sportin': Stadiums, Neighborhoods, and the New Chicago*. DeKalb: Northern Illinois University Press.

Squires, Gregory, Larry Bennett, Kathleen McCourt, and Philip Nyden. 1987. *Chicago: Race, Class, and the Response to Urban Decline*. Philadelphia: Temple University Press.

SriRekha, N. C. 2003. "200,000 NRI Millionaires in US." *India Post News Service* (23 May).

Stalker, Peter. 2000. *Workers without Frontiers: The Impact of Globalization on International Migration*. Boulder, CO: Lynne Rienner Publishing Company.

Statistical Abstract of the United States. 1997. Washington, DC: U.S. Department of Commerce, Bureau of Census.

Statistical Yearbook of the Immigration and Naturalization Service. 1977–1999. U.S. Department of Justice. Washington DC: Government Printing Office.

Stockton, Ronald. 1994. "Ethnic Archetypes and the Arab Image." In *The Development of Arab–American Identity*, E. McCarus, ed. Ann Arbor: University of Michigan Press.

Stoll, Michael A. 2005. *Job Sprawl and the Spatial Mismatch between Blacks and Jobs*. Washington: The Brookings Institution.

Stone, Clarence. 1989. *Regime Politics: Governing Atlanta, 1946–1988*. Lawrence: University Press of Kansas.

Strahler, Steven, R. 1999. "For This Park Planner, Everyday Is Arbor Day." *Crain's Chicago Business* (26 July).

Strahler, Steven R. 2003. "Escape from Chicago." *Crain's Chicago Business* (10 March).

Suchar, Charles S. 1992. "Icons and Images of Gentrification: The Changed Material Culture of an Urban Community." In *Gentrification and Urban Change: Research in Urban Sociology*, Vol. 2, R. Hutchison, ed. Greenwich, CT: JAI Press, Inc.

Suchar, Charles S. 1997. "Grounding Visual Sociology Research in Shooting Scripts." *Qualitative Sociology* 20 (1): 33–55.

Suchar, Charles S. 2004a. "Amsterdam and Chicago: Seeing the Macro-Characteristics of Gentrification." In *Picturing the Social Landscape: Visual Methods and the Sociological Imagination*, C. Knowles and P. Sweetman, eds. London: Routledge.

Suchar, Charles S. 2004b. "A Tale of Two Cities." *Contexts* 3 (3): 48–55.

Suchar, Charles S. and Robert Rotenberg. 1994. "Judging the Adequacy of Shelter: A Case from Lincoln Park." *Journal of Architectural and Planning Research* 11(2): 149–65.

Sugrue, Thomas. 1996. *The Origins of the Urban Crisis: Race and Inequality in Postwar Detroit.* Princeton, NJ: Princeton University Press.

Suleiman, Michael W., ed. 1999. *Arabs in America: Building a New Future.* Philadelphia: Temple University Press.

Sung, Betty Lee. 1967. *Mountain of Gold: The Story of the Chinese in America.* New York: Collier Books.

Suparno, Riyadi. 1999. "LaSalle Turns into Beast for Beauty." *Chicago Tribune* (11 August).

Suttles, Gerald. 1990. *The Man-Made City: The Land-Use Confidence Game in Chicago.* Chicago: University of Chicago Press.

Swanstrom, Todd. 1988. "Urban Populism, Uneven Development, and the Space for Reform." In *Business Elites and Urban Development,* S. Cummings, ed. Albany: State University of New York Press.

Swinney, Dan. 1998. "Building the Bridge to the High Road." Chicago: Center for Labor and Community Research. www.clcr.org/publications/btb/contents.html.

Takaki, Ronald. 1989. *Strangers from a Distant Shore: A History of Asian Americans.* Boston: Little, Brown.

Taub, Richard, P. 1994. *Community Capitalism: South Shore Bank.* Cambridge, MA: Harvard Business School Press.

Taylor, T. Shawn. 2003. "Chicago Tops Nation in Job Losses in '02." *Chicago Tribune* (6 February).

Teaford, Jon C. 1990. *The Rough Road to Renaissance.* Baltimore: Johns Hopkins University Press.

Terkel, Studs. 1992. *Race: How Blacks and Whites Think and Feel About the American Obsession.* New York: The New Press.

Theodore, Nikolas. 1998. "The Business of Contingent Work: Growth and Restructuring in Chicago's Temporary Employment Industry." *Work, Employment and Society* 12 (4): 655–74.

Thurow, Lester. 2001. *The Zero-Sum Society: Distribution and the Possibilities for Economic Change.* New York: Basic Books.

Tita, Bob. 2003a. "A White Elephant Tramples Harvard." *Crain's Chicago Business* (5 May).

Tita, Bob. 2003b. "Trying to Make a Splash with Harvard Water Park." *Crain's Chicago Business* (21 July).

Tom, Ping. 1995. "The Political Dissection of Chinatown." In *Civil Rights Issues Facing Asian Americans in Metropolitan Chicago,* Illinois Advisory Committee to the United States Commission on Civil Rights. Washington, DC: U.S. Commission on Civil Rights.

Toomey, Shamus. 2004. "Affordable Housing in Oak Brook?" *Chicago Sun-Times* (13 August).

Trachtenberg, Alan. 1982. *The Incorporation of America: Culture and Society in the Gilded Age.* New York: Hill and Wang.

Travis, Dempsey J. 1981. *An Autobiography of Black Chicago.* Chicago: Urban Research Press.

Travis, Dempsey J. 1983. *An Autobiography of Black Jazz.* Chicago: Urban Research Press.

Tritsch, Shane. 2004. "The Mystery of Mayor Daley." *Chicago Magazine* (July).

Turner, Margery Austin, Martin Abravanel, Susan Popkin, and Mary Cunningharn. 2001. "Public Housing Relocatees and the Rental Housing Market in the Chicago Region." Washington, DC: The Urban Institute (March).

Uchitelle, Louis. 2003. "A Statistic That's Missing: Jobs That Moved Overseas." *New York Times* (5 October).

ul Haq, Mahbub, Inge Kaul, and Isabelle Grunberg, eds. 1996. *The Tobin Tax: Coping with Financial Volatility.* New York: Oxford University Press.

Urry, John. 1990. *The Tourist Gaze.* London: Sage Publications.

U.S. Census Bureau. 2003a. *Census 2000: Migration of the Young, Single, and College Educated: 1995–2000,* November.

U.S. Census Bureau. 2003b. *Worker Flows by County.* Washington: U.S. Census Bureau.

U.S. Census of the Population. 1983a. *Ancestry of the Population by States (1980).* Washington, DC: U.S. Department of Commerce, Bureau of Census.

U.S. Census of the Population. 1983b. *Characteristics of the Population. General Social and Economic Characteristics, Illinois (1980).* Washington, DC: U.S. Department of Commerce, Bureau of Census.

U.S. Census of the Population. 1983c. *Detailed Population Characteristics. Part 1. U.S. Summary (1980).* Washington, DC: U.S. Department of Commerce, Bureau of Census.

U.S. Census of the Population. 1993a. *Ancestry of the Population in the United States (1990).* Washington, DC: U.S. Department of Commerce, Bureau of Census.

U.S. Census of the Population. 1993b. *The Foreign-born Population in the United States (1990).* Washington, DC: U.S. Department of Commerce, Bureau of Census.

U.S. Census of the Population. 1993c. *Social and Economic Characteristics, Illinois (1990).* Washington, DC: U.S. Department of Commerce, Bureau of Census.

U.S. Census of the Population and Housing. 1992. Summary Tape File 1A. *The Foreign-Born Population in the United States (1990).* Washington, DC:

U.S. Department of Commerce, Bureau of Census, Data User Services Division.

U.S. Department of Agriculture Forest Service. 2003. "Mayor Daley's GreenStreets Program." Northeastern Area.

U.S. Department of Commerce, Bureau of Economic Analysis. 2001. "Foreign Direct Investment in the United States. Operation of US Affiliates of Foreign Companies–Preliminary Estimates."

U.S. Department of Homeland Security. 2003. *Yearbook of Immigration Statistics, 2002*. Washington DC: U.S. Government Printing Office.

U.S. Department of Justice. 1960–1976. *Annual Report of the Immigration and Naturalization Service*. Washington DC: Government Printing Office.

U.S. Department of Justice, Immigration and Naturalization Service. "Immigrants Admitted to the United States: 1972–1998." Washington, DC: Government Printing Office.

U.S. Department of Labor, Bureau of Labor Statistics. 2002. "State and Area Employment Earnings: 1952–2001, Chicago." www.bls.gov.

U.S. Government, Interagency Task Force of the INS, FBI, CIA and Departments of State and Justice. 1986. "Alien Terrorists and Undesirables: A Contingency Plan" (Unpublished document).

U.S. Immigration and Naturalization Service. 1943. "Eligibility of Arabs to Naturalization." *INS Monthly Review* (October).

U.S. Immigration and Naturalization Service. 2002. *Statistical Yearbook of the Immigration and Naturalization Service 1999*. Washington DC: U.S. Immigration and Naturalization Service.

Vallas, Paul. 2000. "Ending the Injustice of Social Promotion." *The Chicago Educator* 5 (6): 5–6.

Venkatesh, Sudhir Alladi. 2002. *American Project: The Rise and Fall of a Modern Ghetto*. Cambridge, MA: Harvard University Press.

Verespej, Michael A. 1999. "The Atlas of U.S. Manufacturing." *Industry Week* (5 April).

Vonnegut, Kurt. 1952. *Player Piano*. New York: Holt, Rinehart and Winston.

Wacquant, Loïc. 1989. "The Ghetto, the State and the New Capitalist Economy." *Dissent* (Fall).

Wagle, Richard. 2003. "Soldiering Forth." *Chicago Journal* (17 April).

Waldinger, Roger. 1994. "The Making of an Immigrant Niche." *International Migration Review* 28 (1): 3–30.

Waldinger, Roger, ed. 2001. *Strangers at the Gate: New Immigrants in Urban America*. Berkeley: University of California Press.

Waldinger, Roger and Mehdi Bozorgmehr, eds. 1996. *Ethnic Los Angeles*. New York: Russell Sage Foundation.

Walker, Judith. 1991. "Reforming the Role of Human Services in City Government." In *Harold Washington and the Neighborhoods: Progressive City Government in Chicago, 1983–1987*, Pierre Clavel and Wim Wiewel, eds. New Brunswick, NJ: Rutgers University Press.

Wall Street Journal Online. 2003. www.wsj.com (accessed 10 March).

Washburn, Gary. 1998a. "Daley's Plan Hopes to Bring Bit of Paris to Loop." *Chicago Tribune* (9 January).

Washburn, Gary. 1998b. "Building-Permit Delays Spur City Shake-up." *Chicago Tribune* (18 May).

Washburn, Gary. 2000. "City Deal Persuades Quaker Oats to Stay." *Chicago Tribune* (3 March).

Washburn, Gary. 2002. "Daley Gets Suburban Anti-Guns Support." *Chicago Tribune* (31 January).

Washburn, Gary. 2003. "Flush with Victory, Daley Lets Traces of Ire Emerge," *Chicago Tribune* (27 February).

Washburn, Gary and Mickey Ciokajlo. 2001. "Price Was High, But Was It Worth It?" *Chicago Tribune* (11 May).

Washburn, Gary and Laurie Cohen. 2005. "City Hall Discovers Clout." *Chicago Tribune* (24 May).

Washburn, Gary and Jon Hilkevitch. 2001. "Deal Cut on O'Hare." *Chicago Tribune* (6 December).

Washburn, Gary and Andrew Martin. 1997. "Huels Feels the Heat, Resigns as an Alderman." *Chicago Tribune* (22 October).

Washburn, Gary and Dan Mihalopoulos. 2005. "Daley Cleans House Again." *Chicago Tribune* (23 June).

Washburn, Gary and Ray Quintanilla. 1998. "Broad Civic 'Blueprint' Targets Sprawl, Education." *Chicago Tribune* (20 November).

Watson, Tony J. 1980. *Sociology, Work, and Industry*. London: Routledge and Kegan.

Weir, Margaret. 1996. "Central Cities' Loss of Power in State Politics." *Cityscape* 2 (2): 23–40.

Weiss, Mark and John Metzgar. 1988. "Planning for Chicago: The Changing Politics of Metropolitan Growth and Neighborhood Development." In *Atop the Urban Hierarchy*, R. Beauregard, ed. Totowa, NJ: Rowman and Littlefield.

Weissmann, Dan. 1998. "Balancing Power." *Catalyst* (Chicago) (April).

Wheaton, Dennis. 2004. "Rediscovering Chinatown." *Chicago Magazine* (February).

Wheelock, Richard. 2003. Personal communication from attorney representing the Cabrini-Green Local Advisory Council (16 September).

Wille, Lois. 1997. *At Home in the Loop*. Carbondale: Southern Illinois University Press.

Williams, Debra. 2000. "Board Gives North Side Preps Lavish Facilities, Ample Planning Time." *Catalyst* (Chicago) (December).

Williams, Scott. 2003. "Support Sought for Regional Unity." *Milwaukee Journal Sentinel* (15 June).

Wilson, William, H. 1989. *The City Beautiful Movement.* Baltimore: John Hopkins University Press.

Wilson, William Julius 1978. *The Declining Significance of Race: Blacks and Changing American Institutions.* Chicago: University of Chicago Press.

Wilson, William Julius. 1987. *The Truly Disadvantaged: The Inner-City, The Underclass and Public Policy.* Chicago: University of Chicago Press.

Wilson, William Julius. 1996. *When Work Disappears: The World of the New Urban Poor.* New York: Vintage Books.

Winant, Howard. 2003. "The Theoretical Status of the Concept of Race." In *Only Skin Deep: Changing Visions of the American Self,* C. Fusco and B. Willis, eds. New York: International Center of Photography, Harry N. Abrams Publishers.

Woods Fund of Chicago. 1995. "Evaluation of the Fund's Community Organizing Grant Program." Chicago: Woods Fund.

Woodstock Institute. 2002a. "Income and Racial Diversity in Home Buying during the 1990s." Chicago: Woodstock Institute.

Woodstock Institute. 2002b. *2001 Community Lending Fact Book.* Chicago: Woodstock Institute.

"Working With Tenants." 1999. *The Network Builder* (The Chicago Rehab Network Newsletter) (Winter).

World Business Chicago. n.d. [2003] *Investing in the Future: It Works.*

Wright, Patricia A. 2006. "Community Resistance to CHA Transformation: The Coalition to Protect Public Housing's History, Evolution, Struggles and Accomplishments." In *Where Are Poor People to Live?* L. Bennett, J. Smith, and P. A. Wright, eds. Armonk, NY: M.E. Sharpe.

Wyly, Elvin and Daniel Hammel. 2000. "Capital's Metropolis: Chicago and the Transformation of American Housing Policy." *Geografiska Annaler* 82b (4): 181–206.

Young, David. 2003. *Chicago Aviation: An Illustrated History.* DeKalb: Northern Illinois University Press.

Zaghel, Ali. 1977. *Changing Patterns of Identification among Arab Americans: The Palestinian Ramallites.* Ph.D. Dissertation, Northwestern University.

Zarembo, Alan. 2004. "Physician, Remake Thyself." *Los Angeles Times* (10 January).

Zhou, Min. 1992. *Chinatown: The Socioeconomic Potential of an Urban Enclave.* Philadelphia: Temple University Press.

Zhou, Min. 2003. "Chinese: Once Excluded, Now Ascendant." In *The New Face of Asian Pacific America,* E. Lai and D. Arguelles, eds. San Francisco: Asian Week.

Ziemba, Stanley. 1986. "Turf Battle Looms Downtown." *Chicago Tribune* (27 January).

Ziolkowska, Helena. 2002. "Polskie szkolnictwo w Chicago." In *50 lat dzialalnosci Zrzeszenia Nauczycieli Polskich w Ameryce w sluzbie Polonii Chicago 2000.* Chicago: Polish Teachers Association of America.

Zukin, Sharon. 1991. *Landscapes of Power: From Detroit to Disneyland.* Berkeley: University of California Press.

Zukin, Sharon. 1992. "Postmodern Urban Landscape: Mapping Culture and Power." In *Modernity and Identity,* S. Lash, and J. Friedman, eds. Oxford, UK: Blackwell.

Zukin, Sharon. 1998. "Urban Lifestyles: Diversity and Standardization in Spaces of Consumption." *Urban Studies* 35 (5/6): 825–40.

About the Contributors

LARRY BENNETT has taught in the Political Science Department at DePaul University since 1977. He is the author, most recently, of *Neighborhood Politics: Chicago and Sheffield* (Garland, 1997) and (with Costas Spirou) *It's Hardly Sportin': Stadiums, Neighborhoods, and the New Chicago* (Northern Illinois University Press, 2003). He is co-editor (with Janet Smith and Patricia Wright) of a volume on public-housing redevelopment in Chicago, *Where Are Poor People to Live?* published in 2006 by M.E. Sharpe.

MICHAEL I. J. BENNETT is executive director of the Egan Urban Center at DePaul University, where he is an associate professor in the Department of Sociology. His teaching and writing are in the areas of urban policy, and urban and rural community economic development, with an emphasis on low-income and African American communities. He has degrees from Kent State University (B.A. 1968), and The University of Chicago (M.A. 1972 and Ph.D. 1988).

LOUISE CAINKAR is Associate Professor of Social and Cultural Sciences at Marquette University. Professor Cainkar is completing a study of the impact of the September 11, 2001 terrorist attacks in New York and Washington on the Arab–Muslim community in metropolitan Chicago, funded by the Russell Sage Foundation.

FASSIL DEMISSIE is Associate Professor of Public Policy Studies at DePaul University. He is editing a book on *Colonial Architecture and Urbanism: Intertwined and Contested History*, University of South Africa Press (forthcoming 2007). His work has appeared previously in *Housing Studies, Social Identities, The International Journal of African Historical Research, American Anthropologist,* and *African Development.* He is also the Series Editor for *New Directions in the Study of African Cities and Urban Form*, University of South Africa Press.

MAY PATRICE ERDMANS is a sociologist who teaches at Central Connecticut State University. Professor Erdmans is the author of *Opposite Poles: Immigrants and Ethnics in Polish Chicago, 1976–1990* (1998).

KENNETH FIDEL earned his Ph.D. from Washington University and is Associate Professor of Sociology at DePaul University. An urban sociologist, Professor Fidel specializes in community research.

ROBERTA GARNER (Ph.D., University of Chicago) is Professor and Chair of the Sociology Department at DePaul University. Her publications include *Contemporary Movements and Ideologies* (McGraw-Hill, 1996), *Social Theory: Continuity and Confrontation* (Broadview, 2004), and *The Joy of Stats* (Broadview, 2005).

KILJOONG KIM received his B.S. in Sociology from the University of Wisconsin–Madison and M.A. in Sociology from DePaul University. Currently, he is Research Director at the Egan Urban Center and Lecturer in Sociology at DePaul University. He is a doctoral candidate in Sociology at the University of Illinois at Chicago.

JOHN P. KOVAL is Associate Professor of Sociology, DePaul University and a Fellow at DePaul's Egan Urban Center. He is also a Visiting Fellow at the Institute for Latino Studies, University of Notre Dame. His primary interests are in work and society, immigrant labor forces, and economic inequality.

YVONNE LAU Ph.D. in Sociology, Northwestern University, is an administrator in the Office of Academic Affairs and adjunct instructor in the Sociology Department at DePaul University. Ms. Lau was previously Director of Asian and Asian American Studies at Loyola University in Chicago.

PAULINE LIPMAN Associate Professor of Education at DePaul University, earned her Ph.D. from the University of Wisconsin–Madison. Professor Lipman is author of *High Stakes Education: Inequality, Globalization, and Urban School Reform* (2004).

DAVID MOBERG is a Chicago-based journalist who covers labor and urban policy issues. He is a senior editor at *In These Times*.

ROB PARAL is Research Fellow with the American Immigration Law Foundation in Washington, D.C. and the Institute for Metropolitan Affairs at Roosevelt University in Chicago. Mr. Paral has written widely on immigration and public policy issues.

AURIE PINNECK a Chicago-based attorney, is former President and CEO of the Leadership Council for Metropolitan Open Communities, a civil rights and open-housing advocacy group.

DAVID PLEBANSKI a former police officer, teaches at Calumet College of St. Joseph in Whiting, Indiana. Professor Plebanski earned his Ph.D. in sociology from Loyola University of Chicago.

PADMA RANGASWAMY an independent scholar, is author of *Namasté America: Indian Immigrants in an American Metropolis* (2000).

RICHARD SCHAEFER is Professor and former Chair of the Sociology Department at DePaul University. A specialist in race and ethnicity, he is the author of numerous textbooks on general sociology and race–ethnic relations.

JOSEPH P. SCHWIETERMAN of DePaul University's Management of Public Services Program has published extensively on the economics of inner-city transportation and is a longstanding contributor to the Transportation Research Board (TRB), a unit of the National Academy of Sciences. He is Director of DePaul's Chaddick Institute, which promotes effective urban planning in the Chicago region.

COSTAS SPIROU is Professor of Social Science at National-Louis University and Research Associate at the Field Museum's Center for Cultural Understanding and Change. He is co-author of *It's Hardly Sportin'* (2003) and is currently researching cultural policy and the use of public amenities improvements to spur private development in Chicago.

HOWARD STANBACK is an economist and independent lecturer on public affairs issues. He has served as President and CEO of the Leadership Council for Metropolitan Open Communities, and during the mid-1980s was an aide to Chicago Mayor Harold Washington.

CHUCK SUCHAR Professor of Sociology at DePaul University and Dean of the College of Liberal Arts and Sciences, is a leading figure in the field of visual sociology.

Index

Abu-Lughod, Janet, 20, 22, 24, 190, 256
Academic Preparation Centers (APCs), 248, 255
Adamowski, Benjamin, 44
affordable housing, 59, 64, 69, 231–38, 242–43, 313; in Chinatown, 171, 176, 177; housing vouchers and, 233, 235–36, 237; public schools and, 235, 241; race and, 231–32, 237–38; regional reform in, 236–37, 281, 282; segregation and, 231, 232, 233–35, 236, 238. *See also* public housing
Affordable Housing and Planning Appeals Act (2004), 92, 236–37
African Americans (blacks), 13, 54, 193, 309, 316; civil rights activism and, 10, 44; exclusion of, 35, 313; gentrification and, 31, 216, 220, 232; Great Migration of, 97, 231; income growth of, 111; Koreans and, 164–65; middle class, 84–85, 86, 88, 90, 92, 206, 232, 261–62, 306; neighborhoods, 23–24, 101, 123; police reform and, 260, 261–62; population of, 231; Richard J. Daley and, 44, 45, 48; schools and, 248–50, 251, 252–53, 254, 255–58; in suburbs, 78, 232, 234, 266–67, 306–7, 313. *See also under* black; Bronzeville; race and ethnicity
Afro American Patrolmen's League, 262, 263
Algren, Nelson, 56; *Chicago: City on the Make*, 312
Alien Immigration Acts, 97

Alinsky, Saul, 218, 239, 242; community organizing model of, 239, 246, 264, 266
Alliance of Congregations Transforming the Southside, 219
al-Tahir, Abdul Jalil, 183
Americanization, of immigrants, 126, 138, 147, 252. *See also* citizenship
Amnesty International, 263, 267
Amtrak, 293, 294
Andreessen, Marc, 38
Arab immigrants, 182–96; Chicago as diasporic home, 184–85; Christian, 182, 183, 184, 187, 188; communities shaped by, 182–83, 192–94; criminalization of, 191; education of, 188–89; growth and diversity in, 185–87; integration of, 183–84; Islamic revival and, 194–95; language and, 183; migration profiles for, 187–88; occupation niches, 182–83, 189–90, 193; place of birth, 191–92; population, 185–86, 189, 190, 191–92; racialization of, 183, 191, 192; refugee status of, 184, 185, 187, 194. *See also* specific nationality
Argyle Street, as Chinatown, 176, 177–79
Asian Americans, 147–48, 224. *See also specific group*
Asian Indian community, 128–40; building coherence in, 133–36; education of, 98–99, 205; gender and generational issues, 137–38; global service economy

and, 131–32; growth and diversification, 128, 129–31; historical overview, 128–29; occupations of, 130–31, 139n2, 203, 206, 209; political agenda of, 136–37, 139; racial identity and, 138–39; socioeconomic divide in, 132–33, 138, 139. *See also* Devon Avenue
assimilation of immigrants: Chinese, 175; Filipinos, 141, 142, 150, 151, 152; Koreans, 156, 157, 165, 166–67; Polish, 124, 127. *See also* Americanization
Association of Arab American University Graduates, 193
Association of Community Organizations for Reform Now, 241
Assyrian immigrants, 182, 184–86, 188, 189, 230n3

Back of the Yards Neighborhood Organization, 239
Beal, Frank, 283
Beauregard, Robert, 6
Bell, Derrick, 83, 92
Belmont-Central neighborhood, 122, 123
Bennett, Edward, 57
Bennett, Larry, 25–26
Bennett, Michael, 31
Bennett, William, 248
Berg, Steve, 300
Best, Steven, 91
Bilandic, Michael, 45–46
Biles, Roger, 44
bilingual education, 105, 122, 124, 156, 179–80, 249, 252

black and white relations, 14, 35, 46, 82, 91. *See also* race and ethnicity; whites and whiteness

Black Belt, 213–14. *See also* African Americans

Black Metropolis, 83, 86. *See also* Bronzeville

black middle class, 84–85, 88, 90, 92, 232, 261–62, 306; jobs of, 86, 206

Black Power movement, 249, 263

Blagojevich, Rod, 51, 137, 236, 283, 290

Block Watch Organizing, 264

Boeing Corporation, 32, 34, 49

Boggs, David, 223, 227

Bollywood movies, 136, 225

Bonacich, Edna, 183

Bouman, John, 244

Bozorgmehr, Mehdi, 200

Brach's Confections Inc., 32, 34

Braun, Carol Moseley, 90

Brecht, Bertolt, 305, 317

Bridgeport neighborhood, 66

Bronzeville, 31, 213–20; development plans for, 215–19; historical role of, 213–14; identity and development in, 214–15; IIT and, 217–18; new Chicago and, 219–20; politics in, 218–19; public housing in, 214, 215, 216–17

Brown, Lee, 263, 264

Buffalo Grove, 80

Burge, John, 263

Burgess, Ernest W., 59

Burke, Edward, 47, 51

Burnham, Daniel, 7, 35, 57, 277, 278, 300

Bush administration, 173, 187, 248

business, 34, 40, 106, 282, 283; in Polish neighborhoods, 121, 123, 124; schools and, 250, 251, 255

business services, 24, 28, 36–37, 38, 42, 306; corporate headquarters and, 33, 37, 39, 43

Byrne, Jane, 45–46, 263

Cabrini-Green public housing development, 69, 70–71

Campaign Against Pollution, 240

Carlson, Dennis, 255

Carlson, Virginia, 23

Castells, Manuel, 315

Catholicism, 99, 104, 150, 151, 240–41; Latino immigrants

and, 102–3, 105; Polonia and, 120–21, 125–26

Center for Labor Market Studies, 256

Centers for New Horizons, 219

Central Advisory Council (CAC), 217

central area revitalization, 19, 26–29, 56–76, 131, 284; Clybourn Corridor, 73; condominiums, 66, 68, 71, 80, 85, 236; elites and, 26, 308, 312; employment change in, 25; gated communities, 69, 70; gentrification and, 12, 29, 59, 60, 63, 72, 73–74, 311; lack of retail stores in, 40–41; middle class and, 29, 30, 60; Near North Side, 59, 85; Near South Side, 64–65; Near Southwest Side, 61, 63–64; Near West Side, 66–67; photographic documentation, 59–75; residential development in, 29–30, 49–50; revalorization of, 56, 58, 74, 75–76, 85, 267, 307, 312; Riverside Park, 61, 62; West Loop, 57, 66–67. *See also* Loop

Centrum Properties, 69

Cermak, Anton, 44

CHA. *See* Chicago Housing Authority (CHA)

Chambers, Ed, 239, 240, 241–42, 245

Chandrasekhar, Subrahmanyam, 129

"Chicago 21," 27

Chicago, as paradigmatic case study, 6–7, 305

Chicago Alliance for Neighborhood Safety (CANS), 264–66

Chicago Alternative Policing Strategy (CAPS), 227, 261, 265–66

Chicago Area Fair Housing Alliance (CAFHA), 235, 238

Chicago Area Transportation Study, 279, 282, 283

Chicago Association of Commerce, 296

Chicago Bee Newspaper Building, 215

Chicago Building Code amendments, 28

Chicago Central Area Committee (CCAC), 27

Chicago Central Area Plan, 27, 56–57, 58, 59

Chicago Convention and Tourism Bureau, 296

Chicago Department of Transportation, 301

Chicago Freedom Movement, 89

Chicago Housing Authority (CHA), 27, 47, 65, 72, 307; ABLA project, 63–64; affordable housing and, 233, 281, 313; gentrification and, 262; *Plan for Transformation,* 55, 214, 217, 233, 235

Chicago Intervention Network, 265

Chicago Mercantile Exchange, 22

Chicago Metropolis 2020 plan, 14, 57–58, 59, 240; housing in, 236, 237; regionalism and, 58, 277, 279–85; on school reform, 255

Chicago Plan for Affordable Neighborhoods, 66

Chicago Regional Environmental and Transportation Efficiency Project, 292

Chicago River, 60, 63, 66

Chicago School of urban sociology, 6–7, 59, 60, 316–17

Chicago School Reform Act (1988), 249, 250

Chicago Sun Times, 123

Chicago Transit Authority, 45, 54

Chicago Tribune, 11, 52, 61, 66, 82, 288; on Millennium Park, 301, 302; on regionalism, 277, 282; on school reform, 253

Chicago Urban League, 93

Chicago White Sox, 47

Chico, Gery, 248

Chinatown, 66, 67, 101, 169, 171; in Argyle, 176, 177–79; elderly population in, 176–77; population of, 173

Chinese Americans, 168–81; community (*jia*) construction, 174–81; current demographic trends, 170–73; historical background, 168–70; language schools and, 180, 181; in suburbs, 170–71, 177; work of, 171, 204, 209

Chinese Mutual Aid Association (CMAA), 178

"Choices for the Chicago Region," 57–58, 59

Christians: Arab, 182, 183, 184, 187, 188; Protestant groups, 241; South Korean, 164. *See also* Catholicism; Religious groups

Cirera, Alex, 149

citizenship and immigrants, 136, 137, 144, 148, 150, 173

Citizens Information Service, 264

city council, 10, 47, 52, 90

civic beautification program, 49, 50

civil rights movement, 10, 44, 46, 88, 250

Clinton, William, 137, 248

Cluster Mapping Project, 39

coalition politics, 91, 193, 294

Cohen, Robert, 21–22

collar counties, 9, 20

collective action, 311, 314. *See also* labor; union movement

College Prep Regional Magnet High Schools, 252, 253–54

Columbian Exposition (1893), 34–35, 182, 277, 296

Column Financial Inc., 69

Comiskey Park, 47

Commercial Club of Chicago, 57, 255, 277; *Chicago Metropolis 2020* and, 236, 278, 279–80, 282

community development, 76, 213, 239–41; Arab immigrant, 192–94; in Bronzeville, 214, 217–19. *See also* United Power for Action and Justice

Community Development Finance Institutions, 85

community policing, 227, 260–61, 262–66

computer-based technology, 4–5, 132, 204. *See also* high technology firms; information technology

concentric zone theory, 59

condominiums, 66, 68, 71, 80, 85, 236

Confucianism, 167

Congress, U.S., immigration and, 113–14

Consortium on Chicago School Research, 252

contested reinvention, 13–14

contingent labor, 8–9, 37, 199

Contract Buyers League, 84

Cook County, 9, 77; immigrant groups in, 101, 106–7, 108, 123, 130, 170

Coordinating Council of Chicago Community Organizations (CCCO), 88, 89

corporate headquarters, 28, 33, 37, 43; Boeing, 32, 34, 49; in suburbs, 40, 79

Cows on Parade Art Exhibit, 299–300

CPD (Chicago Police Department). *See* police reform

CPS (Chicago Public Schools). *See* school reform

crime, 227, 262, 267. *See also* police reform

Croatian Cultural Center, 223, 229

Cronon, William, 34; *Nature's Metropolis,* 278

culture, 103, 295; Asian Indian, 136, 139; development issues, 215–17; Filipino, 151; urban beautification and, 297, 300

Daley, Richard J. (father), 10, 44–45, 52, 89, 279; central city redevelopment and, 26, 27, 36; police and, 259

Daley, Richard M. (son), 10, 49, 51–53, 237, 246; airport debate and, 279, 287, 289, 290; *Chicago Metropolis 2020* and, 277, 278; downtown transformation and, 27, 49–50; global city and, 22, 29, 49, 50; managerialism of, 10, 48–49, 50; police reform and, 260, 265; regionalism and, 279, 284; school reform and, 248, 250, 251; urban beautification and, 297, 299, 301, 302

D'Angelo, Oscar, 52

Dawson, Michael, 89

day labor, 37, 202. *See also* contingent labor

Dearborn Park, 27, 62

Debs, Eugene, 35

deindustrialization, 7–8, 19, 21, 22–24, 310, 311–12; in Bronzeville, 214; community policing and, 262; inequality in, 20; inner-city working class and, 23–24, 86; in Midwest, 8, 22–23; poverty and, 78

democratic participation, 250. *See also* grassroots groups

Democratic Party, 10, 44, 45, 89, 228, 246; city government and, 47, 278; Daley and, 51–52

demographic shifts, 13, 99, 174–75, 221; in Bronzeville, 214–15, 219. *See also* population

Denton, Nancy, 20, 232

DePriest, Oscar, 89, 213

d'Eramo, Marco, 82

deregulation, 21, 34

Detroit, 309, 311

development, postindustrial, 3, 66, 208, 305–6

Development Plan for the Central Area of Chicago (1958), 26, 27

Devon Avenue, 31, 221–30; attraction of, 223, 225; challenges of community, 226; divisions on, 228–29; economic transformation of, 225; Jewish community in, 222, 223, 228; local is global in, 225–26; population in, 223; safety concerns in, 227; uncertain future of, 229–30; as world market, 222

Dickens, Charles, 316

Direct Instruction (DI), 253, 257

discrimination, 83, 213; in housing, 232, 235, 236. *See also* race and ethnicity; residential segregation

Displaced Persons Act of 1948, 97

Dowell, Pat, 219

DuPage County, 9, 77, 101, 130, 234

Durbin, Dick, 292

Dwyer, Rachel E., 5

economic development, immigrant groups and, 35, 39, 99–100, 104, 297; Arabs, 188–89; in Chinatown, 176; on Devon Avenue, 225; initiatives, 49; Korean, 158; Mexican American, 110, 111; Polish, 116, 126–27

Economic Recovery Act of 1981, 28

economic restructuring, 7–9, 11, 32–43, 57, 92, 198; Asian Indians and, 131–32; black jobs and, 85–88; business services and, 24, 28, 33, 36–37, 39; cohesion and contradictions in, 34–36; contingent labor and, 8–9, 37; deindustrialization, 7–8, 19; globalization and, 33–34, 37–39, 42–43; immigrant labor and, 200, 201;

economic restructuring (*Cont.*);
inequality and, 33, 39–41; new
accumulation regime, 305–6;
new economy and, 4–6, 24–25,
87, 198, 207–8; politics and,
35–36; racial exclusion and,
256; regionalism and, 41–42;
tourism and, 296. *See also*
deindustrialization
Edgar, Jim, 53, 235, 287, 289
edge cities, 24, 37, 77, 79
education, 198, 205, 207, 243, 262,
281; Arab, 185; Asian Indian,
129, 138; Chinese American,
171; Filipino, 98–99, 141, 144,
148; Korean, 155, 156, 158, 161,
165–66; Mexican, 107, 109, 252;
Polish, 117, 118, 123, 124; race
relations and, 88–89. *See also*
schools
Education-to-Career Academies
(ETCs), 253, 257
Egan, Jack, 84
Egyptian immigrants, 187–88
Eisinger, Peter, 46, 48
elderly population, 138, 166,
176–77
Eliot, T. S., 280
elites, 21, 22, 31, 34–35, 60;
business, 52, 251, 283; central
city revitalization and, 26, 308,
311, 312; global competition
and, 284; support for Daley
(son), 10, 50, 51, 54
employment/unemployment, 23,
25, 36, 116; economic
restructuring and, 85–88. *See
also* labor
Empowerment Zone program,
218
"End the Slums" campaign, 83–84
English-as-a-second-language
(ESL), 176, 177, 228
English language, 124, 249, 252;
Chinese and, 171, 173, 176, 177,
178–79; Filipinos and, 147, 148,
149
entrepreneurs, 14, 21, 35, 104;
Arab, 182, 189–90; Korean, 162,
164–65, 167
Espiritu, Yen Le, 149, 150
ethnicity, 104, 174, 228, 316;
division of labor and, 200–201,
205; Filipino, 149–51;
neighborhood promotion and,
227, 229. *See also* race and
ethnicity; *specific ethnic group*

Ethnic Los Angeles (Waldinger et
al.), 200
ethnic solidarity, 165, 240
ethnic succession, 11, 103–4
ethno-suburbs, 171, 180
Evans, Tim, 48
Ezra homes project, 242–43

Fair Housing Act of 1968, 234
family. *See* immigrant families
FamilyCare program, 243–44
Feagin, Joe, 92
federal government, 218, 293, 316;
police reform and, 262–63. *See
also* Congress, U.S.
festivals, 31, 226, 297
Filipino Americans, 141–53, 206;
community and, 151–53;
education of, 98–99, 141, 144,
148, 205; in health care, 145–46,
148, 203–4, 209; history of,
143–44; identity choices for,
149–52; intergenerational
differences and, 149–50;
pensionados, 141, 142, 143,
152; post-1965 immigration,
144–46; residential
concentrations, 146–49; in
suburbs, 101, 147; transnational
ties of, 142–43, 146, 150; unity
among, 141–42
films and film industry, 39, 136,
140n4, 225
financial deregulation, 21, 34
financial institutions, 37, 84, 85,
161, 165
Fischer, Paul, 233, 235
Flaherty, Krystina, 124–25, 126
Ford Motor Company, 41, 309
foreign (direct) investment (FDI),
21, 24, 29
foreign languages, 103. *See also
specific language*
foreign medical graduates
(FMGs), 145
Fortune 500 firms, 21, 22
Fraternal Order of Police, 263
Friedman, Milton, 25
Friedmann, John, 20
Fromstein, Mitchell, 9

Gamaliel Foundation, 241
Garreau, Joel, 79
Gary-Chicago Airport, 289, 290
Gautreaux Assisted Housing
Program, 237
gays and lesbians, 49, 51, 138

Gehry, Frank, 301
gender roles, Koreans and, 162–63
generational progress: of Chinese
immigrants, 177; of Korean
immigrants, 165–66; of
Mexican immigrants, 110–11
gentrification, 11, 14, 29, 158, 171,
310; by Asian Indians, 131;
black, 31, 216, 220, 232; in
central city, 12, 29, 59, 60, 63,
72, 73–74, 311; displacement
and, 85, 312–13; middle class
and, 30, 313; phases of, 74;
police reform and, 262, 267,
268; school policy and, 253–54,
257, 258, 313; transformation
by, 25
geographic restructuring, 9, 23
ghettos, 159, 176, 238
Giddens, Anthony, 20
Gilead Center, 243
global city, Chicago as, 7, 21–22,
33, 205, 284; challenges to,
37–38; command-center
functions of, 20; education
policy and, 257, 258; R. M.
Daley and, 29, 49, 50
globalization, 3, 19–31, 33–34,
280, 295, 307; central city
redesign and, 19, 25, 26–28;
challenges in adapting to,
38–39; civic vision and, 26–27;
contested meaning of, 19–20;
defined, 7; deindustrialization
and, 19, 20, 21, 22–24; Devon
Avenue and, 222, 226;
ephemeral city and, 315; future
of Chicago and, 42–43;
immigration patterns, 98, 186;
inner city working-class and,
23–24; neo-liberal agenda and,
19, 25–26; new economy and,
24–25, 308; outsourcing of
labor, 33, 38, 99, 132; police
reform and, 267, 268; racial
exclusion and, 255–56; top
down and bottom up, 29–31
Gordon, David, 38
Angelo Gordon and Co., 69
government, councils of, 279, 284.
See also state government
governmental reformers, 14
Gramsci, Antonio, 310
grassroots groups, 46, 259, 311;
Asian Indian, 135, 137; in
Bronzeville, 216, 218, 219;
community policing and, 261,

262, 265, 266; school reform and, 249, 250, 251
Great Lakes region, 33, 41
Great Migration, 97, 231
Green Card Gamble, 117
"green" initiatives, 49
Green Streets Program, 299
Griffin, Dionna, 216
Grimshaw, William, 44, 45, 51
Gulf War refugees, 187, 194
Gutierrez, Luis, 51

Haider, Donald H., 296
Hamilton, David, 283
Handlin, Oscar, 97
Haney, Walter, 252
Hansberry, Lorraine: *A Raisin in the Sun*, 83
Happy Market, 316
Harris, King W., 283
Harston and Schwendener (contractor), 301
Hart-Cellar Act, 169
Harvard Institute for Strategy and Competitiveness, 39
Harvey, David, 20
Hastert, Dennis, 292
hate crime, 227
Hawaii, Koreans in, 154
Hayek, Friedrich, 25
H1-B visas, 198, 204
health care, 243–44, 245
health care professionals, 197, 205; Filipino women as, 145–46, 148, 203–4, 209
Health Professions Educational Assistant Act (1976), 145
Held, David, 20
Henderson, Harold, 282
High School International Baccalaureate (IB), 252
high-technology firms, 24, 33, 38–39, 78, 79. *See also* information technology
highway system, 77
Hill, Richard Child, 23, 28
Hindu religious groups, 135, 226, 229
Hip Sing Tong, 170, 177
Hirst, Deborah S., 8
Hispanic Democratic Organization (HDO), 52
Hispanics, 13. *See also* Latinos; Mexican immigrants
historic preservation, 300
Holy Trinity Church, 120

Homeland Security, Department of, 137, 191
home ownership, immigrants and, 123, 124, 149, 232, 234. *See also under* housing
homicide rate, 265, 306
homosexuals, 49, 51, 138
Hong Kong, immigrants from, 169, 172
"hourglass economy," 4, 5, 9, 87, 207–10
housing: Chinese Americans and, 174, 178; discrimination in, 83–84, 106; shortage, 66; suburban, 78, 80. *See also* affordable housing; public housing; residential development
Housing and Urban Development, U.S. Department of, 65, 106
Housing Choice Vouchers (HCV), 233, 235–36, 237
Housing Opportunity Tax Incentive Act, 237
Hoyt, Josh, 245, 246
Huels, Patrick, 52
Hull House, 256
human rights movements, 267
Human Rights Ordinance (City of Chicago), 235

IAF. *See* Industrial Areas Foundation
illegal immigrants, 112–13, 267
Illinois Department of Children and Family Services, 283
Illinois Housing Development Authority, 92
Illinois Institute of Technology, 129, 217–18
Illinois Neighborhood Development Corporation, 85
Illinois state government. *See* state government
immigrant diversity, 99, 197, 221, 222; Asian Indians and, 134, 138; Chinese and, 168, 170; Latino, 106
immigrant families, 113, 221; Arab, 184, 187, 190; Asian Indian, 128, 129, 136; Chinese, 173, 178; Filipino, 147–48, 151
immigrant labor/occupations, 9, 104, 197–210, 208; Arab, 182–83, 189–90, 193; Asian, 203; Asian Indian, 130–31,

139n2, 203, 206, 209; Chinese, 171, 204, 209; diversity in, 197; ethnic division of, 200–201, 205–6; Filipino, 143–44, 145–46, 148, 203–4, 209; in food service, 203, 204, 206; growth and density of, 198–99; "hourglass economy" and, 207–8, 210; Korean, 159, 163, 204–5, 206, 209; Mexican, 201–2, 208; Polish, 117, 118–19, 202–3, 208
immigrants, 3, 14–15, 30–31, 86, 97–104, 311; (1950-2000), 97–99; as agents of change, 102–3; Americanization of, 126, 138, 252; citizenship for, 136, 137, 144, 148, 150, 173; diversity in, 99, 100, 104; economic opportunities for, 99–100; ethnic succession and, 11, 103–4; home ownership and, 123, 124, 149, 178, 232, 234; illegal, 112–13, 267; immigrant effect and, 103–4; integration of, 106, 112; Irish, 82; nationalism and, 230; population and, 37, 98; race, ethnicity and, 13; residential patterns, 100–101; transnationalism and, 101–2. *See also* immigrant labor force; *specific immigrant group*
immigrant women: Asian Indian, 137–38; Filipinas, 145–46, 203–4, 209; Korean, 162–63; Mexican, 202, 208; Polish, 118–19, 202, 203, 208
Immigration Act of 1986, 116, 169, 172
Immigration Act of 1990, 118, 125
Immigration and Naturalization Service (INS), 112, 173
immigration policy, 111–14, 128
Immigration Reform Act of 1965, 97, 118, 129, 144, 155, 221; Arabs and, 182, 185; Chinese and, 168, 169; South Asians and, 222
income and income inequality, 39–41, 87–88; African American, 111; Arab, 189; Asian groups, 161; Asian Indians, 132–33, 134; Chinese American, 171, 179; Filipino, 141, 147, 148; of immigrant sponsors, 113; Mexican, 109–10, 111, 112,

income and income (*Cont.*); 114; middle class, 198. *See also* inequality; poverty (the poor)

India Caucus, 136. *See also* Asian Indians

India League of America (ILA)Foundation, 133

Indian call centers, 132

Indo-American Democratic Organization (IADO), 136–37

Industrial Areas Foundation (IAF), 239–42, 244–45, 246

industrialization, 307–8. *See also* deindustrialization

industrial labor, 3, 22–23, 100. *See also* labor

Industrial Revolution, 3, 4, 305

Industry Week (trade publication), 32

inequality, 5, 20, 33, 39–41, 313; globalization and, 42; in "hourglass economy," 207–8; race and class, 82–83; school reform and, 255. *See also* income and income inequality

information technology (IT), 4–5, 9, 19, 198, 203, 225

infrastructure improvements, 27, 41, 76, 277

inner-city neighborhoods, 23–24, 26, 104, 281

investment, 28–29, 34, 71, 85, 280–81; foreign, 21, 24, 29

Iowa Test of Basic Skills (ITBS), 251

Iraqi immigrants, 184, 186, 188

Irish immigrants, 82

Islamic Circle of North America, 135

Islamic revival, 194–95. *See also* Arab immigrants; Muslims

IT. *See* information technology (IT)

Jackowo (Polish neighborhood), 120–22

Jackson, Jackie, 193

Jackson, Jesse, Jr., 46, 53, 90, 193, 241; airport expansion and, 288, 289, 291

Jacobs, Jane: *The Death and Life of Great American Cities*, 53–54

Jahn, Helmut, 72

Jewish community, 193, 222, 223, 228, 241

Johnson, Elmer, 280, 282, 284

Jones, Emil, 90

Jordanian immigrants, 185–86, 187, 190, 192

Joyce, Jeremiah, 52

Judd, Dennis, 30

Kalayil, Ann Lata, 227

Kamyszew, Christopher, 120

Karanja, Sokoni, 217, 219

Katznelson, Ira, 310

Kelling, George, 264

Kellner, Douglas, 91

Kelly, Ed, 44

Kennar, Jerzy, 120

Kennedy, Leroy, 217

KidCare program, 243

Kim, Yoon-Jin, 148, 156, 164, 166

King, Martin Luther, Jr., 83–84, 88, 89, 92, 261

Kleppner, Paul, 44

Korean immigrants, 154–67; African Americans and, 164–65; in Chicago, 157–61; economic and social issues for, 161–62; education of, 155, 156, 158, 161, 165–66; as entrepreneurs, 162, 164–65, 167; gender roles, 162–63; generational issues for, 165–66; history of, 154–57; language of, 163–64, 166; marriage and, 166; media and social-religious institutions of, 163–64; occupational niches of, 159, 163, 204–5, 206, 209; settlement and assimilation of, 156, 157, 166–67

Kotler, Philip: *Marketing Places*, 296

Koval, John, 87

Kretzmann, John, 240

labor costs, 21. *See also* income; wages

labor market, 313; contingent, 8–9, 37, 199; global, 33, 38, 99, 132; industrial, 3, 22–23, 100; race and, 9, 86, 93, 256. *See also* immigrant labor force

labor unions. *See* union movement

Lakefront Millennium Project, 297, 300–302

Landscape Ordinance (1991), 299

"landscapes of power," 70, 76

land-use disputes, 72, 234, 235, 281

Lang, Robert E., 79

language, of immigrants, 103. *See also under* bilingual education; *specific language*

Latinos and Latino immigrants, 5, 37, 98, 105–14, 266, 309; blacks and, 90–91, 93; Catholic churches and, 102–3, 105; Cubans, 105; hourglass economy and, 5, 87; housing and, 54, 236; neighborhoods of, 23, 66, 103; on police force, 260; in Polish neighborhoods, 120; population of, 105, 114; schools and, 89, 248–50, 251, 252–53, 254, 255–58; in state legislature, 90; in suburbs, 78, 92, 106, 267; vote of, 48, 50, 52, 89, 90. *See also under* Mexican

Law Enforcement Assistance Act (LEAA), 262

Leadership Council for Metropolitan Open Communities, 92, 237

Lebanese immigrants, 185, 187

Lee v. Hansberry, 83

LeFurgy, Jennifer, 79

Legal Assistance Foundation of Metropolitan Chicago, 93

Lenz, Tom, 244

liberalism, 35. *See also* neo-liberalism

Lincoln Park, 12, 59, 72, 85; gentrification of, 73, 74

Lindstrom, Bonnie, 279

Lipinski, William, 292

local school councils (LSCs), 249, 250–51, 257

Logan, John, 14

Loop revitalization, 12, 25, 26–29, 49. *See also* central area revitalization

Los Angeles, 24, 77, 81, 200, 205–6, 308–9

Loundy, Irv, 227, 228, 229, 230

Low-Income Housing Tax Credit program, 281

Lucas, Harold, 215, 216

Ludgin, Mary, 28

Lugenia Burns Hope Center, 219

McCarran-Walter Act of 1952, 144

McCarron, John, 282, 283

McCormick Place, 49, 53, 57, 215–16, 296–98

McDonald's restaurants, 41

McKenzie, Roderick D., 59

McKnight, John, 240, 246

Madigan, Michael, 51
managerialism, 10, 38, 48–49, 50, 290, 310–11; labor restructuring and, 8–9; police reform and, 259, 268; school reform and, 250
Maniar, Rohit, 225, 227
manufacturing, 5, 8–9, 35, 204, 307–8; decline in, 23, 25, 32, 36, 86; Mexicans in, 107, 110, 202, 206; suburban relocation of, 23, 35, 36, 307
Markusen, Ann, 23
Marshall, Prentice, 262
Martin, Leroy, 265
Marx, Karl, 307, 316
Marxism, 91
Masotti, Louis, 28
Massey, Douglas H., 8, 20, 86, 117, 232
Maxwell Street, 64, 65
Mayor's Office of Special Events, 297
Mayor's Task Force on Youth Crime Prevention, 264
Mazur, Alicia, 29
media: Korean language, 163–64; police reform and, 263; portrayal of Arabs in, 192–93
medical professionals, 145, 158–59, 197, 198, 203. See also health care professionals
Meigs Field (airport), 53, 290, 297
Mell, Richard, 51
Metcalfe, Ralph, 262
Methipara, Tomi, 227
"Metropolis Principles," 238, 282
metropolitan area, 12, 79, 91–93. See also suburban areas
Metropolitan Mayors' Caucus, 53, 279, 292
Metropolitan Pier and Exposition Authority, 297
Metropolitan Planning Council, 232
Metropolitan Water Reclamation District, 279
Mexican-Americans, 30, 98, 105, 110, 123; birth rate for, 108; blacks and, 90, 91; neighborhoods of, 101, 103; occupations of, 99, 206; in suburbs, 91
Mexican immigrants, 106–14; demographic history and patterns of, 107–8; education

levels of, 107, 109, 110–11, 252; family and, 113; generational progress of, 110–11; immigration policy and, 111–14; income gap and, 109–10, 111, 112, 114; legal immigration status and, 113–14; in manufacturing, 107, 110, 202, 206; other occupations of, 107, 199, 201–2, 205, 208; population of, 107–9; socioeconomic status of, 109–10
middle class, 5, 9, 35, 74; black, 84–85, 86, 88, 90, 92, 206, 232, 261–62, 306; central area revitalization and, 29, 30, 60; immigrant, 129, 198; police reform and, 261–62; school reform and, 253, 254, 258; suburban, 78, 232; white, 313
Mid-South Planning and Development Commission (MSP&DCC), 215, 217, 219
Midway Airport, 288, 289
Midwest, 3, 8, 22–23, 41, 42–43
Midwest Regional Rail Initiative, 292–93
Milkman, Ruth, 5
Mill, John Stuart, 4
Miller, Donald, 82
Mitchell, Arthur, 89
Moberg, David, 86
Molotch, Harvey, 14
Montgomery Ward complex, 67, 69, 70
Morrison, Richard, 259
Morse, Samuel F. B., 82
Mosques, 103, 135, 182, 188, 194–95, 229
Motorola Corporation, 35, 38, 79, 99–100, 198
multicultural societies, 267
Mumford, Lewis: The City in History, 53–54
Museum Campus, 297
Museum Park, 60, 61, 62
Muslims, 137, 183, 187, 194, 241, 244; Mosques and, 103, 135, 182, 188, 194–95, 229. See also Arab immigrants

Naperville, 78, 80
National Institutes of Health, 145
National League of Cities, 295
National Origins Act of 1924, 154

National Research Council Committee on Appropriate Test Use, 251
Native Americans, 82
Navy Pier, 297, 298
Negrey, Cynthia, 23
neighborhood policing. See community policing
neighborhoods, 14, 54, 226, 239, 241; black, 23–24, 41, 101, 123, 233–34; central residential, 59–75; ethnicity and, 227; gentrification of, 12, 60, 63, 72, 73–74, 313; grassroots activism and, 46; inner-city, 23–24, 26, 104, 281; Korean immigrant, 158, 159; Palestinian, 184–85; Polish, 101, 119–22; revalorization of, 58; Washington and, 241, 246
neo-liberal agenda, 19, 25–26, 27–28, 118, 316
Netsch, Dawn Clark, 235
new accumulation regime, 305–11, 314, 317
New Deal programs, 86, 89
new economy, 4–6, 24–25, 87, 198, 207–8. See also economic restructuring
New Urbanists, 54
New York City, 20; Manhattan, 78
New York Standard Metropolitan Statistical Area (SMSA), 21
Nixon administration, 172, 262
Noorani, Sadruddin, 230
North American Free Trade Agreement (NAFTA), 24, 291
Northeastern Illinois Planning Commission, 77, 279, 282
North Side revitalization, 59, 67–75, 85

Oak Park Regional Housing Center, 237
Oakton Community College, 181
Obama, Barack, 90, 244, 246
O'Brien, Eileen, 92
Office of Professional Standards, 260
office vacancy rate, 71
O'Hare Airport, 52, 78, 278
O'Hare Airport expansion, 49, 287–91; Airport Capacity Study, 287, 291; Daley and, 279, 287, 289, 290; Modernization Plan, 290, 291; south-suburban

O'Hare Airport (*Cont.*); debate and, 53, 54, 282, 284, 288, 289–90, 291
Omi, Michael, 82
open space preservation, 58, 281
Orfield, Gary, 92–93, 249
Orfield, Myron, 245, 280
Orland Park Mosque, 194–95
Ortiz, Wilma, 110
outsourcing, 33, 38, 132

Pager, Devah, 88
Pakistani community, 137, 227, 229
Palestinian immigrants, 182–87, 189–90, 192, 194, 195n5
Paral, Rob, 91
Parents United for Responsible Education, 252
Park, Robert E.: *The City,* 59
parking problems, 73, 227
patronage, 47, 51, 52
People's Coalition for Education Reform, 249
Peotone airport, 79–80, 287, 288, 289, 290. *See also* Third Airport debate
Philippine immigrants. *See* Filipino Americans
Ping Tom Park, 66, 67
place and space, 10–11, 34
Plan for Transformation, 55, 214, 217, 233, 235
Planned Manufacturing District (PMD), 73
"Plan of Chicago" (Burnham & Bennett), 57, 277
police reform, 259–68; accountability in, 260; civil rights era, 261–62; coercion and, 263; community policing and, 227, 260–61, 262–66; criminal justice and, 263–64; diversity in, 260; federal government and, 262–63; media on, 263; professionalization, 259–60
Polish immigrants (Polonia), 97, 99, 101, 115–27; Catholicism and, 120–21, 125–26; community building in, 119–20; educated and undocumented, 115–19; language, 119, 121, 122, 124, 125–26; neighborhoods, 120–22, 122, 123; occupations

of, 117, 118–19, 202–3, 208; suburban, 122–23
Polish Teachers Association in America, 124
political machine, 51. *See also* Democratic Party
political refugees, 184, 185, 187, 194
politics, 35–36, 44–55, 294, 310; of affordable housing, 236–37; Asian Indians and, 136–37, 139; of Bronzeville, 218–19; community development and, 245, 246–47; Filipino, 152; Koreans and, 161–62; race and, 45, 89–91; R.J. Daley and, 44–45, 49; R.M. Daley and, 48–53, 54–55; scandals in, 52–53; Washington mayoralty and, 46–48, 91, 193, 246
population, 37, 284; Arab, 185–86, 189, 190, 191–92; Asian Indian, 128, 129–31; of Bronzeville, 215; Chinese, 170, 172, 174; Filipino, 143, 145, 146–47; immigrant, 98; Korean, 155, 157; Latino, 105; Mexican, 107–8; Polish, 115, 116, 117; suburban, 77, 80, 81
Porter, John, 243
Portes, Alejandro, 208
Posadas, Barbara, 151, 152
postindustrial development, 3, 66, 208, 305–6
postmodern urban landscape, 21, 262
poverty (the poor), 40, 78, 86, 87–88, 92; African American, 214, 234; health care and, 243, 244, 245; housing for, 64–65, 235–36; immigrant, 109, 110, 133, 154, 166
private-public partnership, 26, 65, 280, 301–2
probation schools, 248–49, 257
professionals: Chinese, 173; Korean immigrants, 158–59; of police, 259–60; upwardly mobile, 75, 85. *See also* medical professionals
property revalorization, 56, 74, 85
property taxes, 78, 79, 85, 235, 236
Protestant groups, 241
public health care, 243–44, 245
public housing, 59, 64–65, 69, 70–71; in Bronzeville, 214, 215, 216–17, 220; dismantling of, 90,

215, 313; displaced families, 65, 85; housing choice vouchers and, 233, 235–36, 237. *See also* Chicago Housing Authority
public policy, 50, 280, 281–82
public space transformation, 10–11, 20, 30
public subsidies, 32, 69
public transit, 58, 77, 80, 281
public works initiatives, 7, 45, 49, 50
Puerto Ricans, 105, 249
Pullman Company, 34, 35, 79

quality of life, 43, 54, 77, 85, 186

Raby, Al, 46, 88, 89
race and ethnicity, 14, 20, 45, 47, 82–93, 312, 316; affordable housing and, 231–32, 237–38; Arab immigrants and, 183, 191, 192; Asian Indian, 138–39; black metropolis and, 83; black middle class, 84–85, 86, 88, 90, 92; Chinese, 178; class transformation and, 11–12, 213; confronting resistance in, 83–84; defining whiteness and, 82–83; downtown redevelopment and, 30; Filipinos and, 143, 149–50; health insurance and, 243; immigration and, 13; jobs and economic restructuring, 85–88, 256; Korean immigrants and, 164; in metropolitan area, 91–93; new economy and, 4, 5; occupational niches and, 9; pluralism and, 31; police reform and, 266; politics and, 89–91, 247; schools and, 88–89, 92–93, 257. *See also* African Americans; segregation
Racial Preference and Suburban Employment Opportunities, 93
railways, 281, 286, 291–94
Rainbow Coalition, 193, 241
Ranney, George, Jr., 283, 284
Reagan administration, 172, 306
redevelopment, 56, 72
redlining, 84–85. *See also* residential segregation
Reeder, Richard, 228, 229
Regional Coordinating Council, 282
regionalism, 33–34, 41–42, 54, 58, 277–85; Chicago expansion and, 278–79; *Chicago Metropolis*

2020 and, 277, 279–85; in India, 134; Mexican immigration and, 108–9; public policy and, 280, 281–82; transportation and, 283–84. *See also* Midwest

Regional Rental Market Analysis (RRMA), 232–33

Regional Transit Authority (RTA), 45, 54, 279, 284, 286

rehabilitation projects, 28, 74

Reich, Robert: *The Work of Nations,* 315

Rein, Irving, 296

religious groups: African American, 214; Asian Indian, 135, 137, 223; Buddhist, 164; community development and, 240–41; Hindu, 135, 226, 229; immigrants and, 99, 164. *See also* Catholicism; Muslims

Renaissance 2010, 251

Republican party, 250, 278

Residences at River Bend, 71

residential development: in central city, 27, 29–30, 49–50, 54, 58–75; gated communities, 69, 70; high-density, 80, 81; single-room occupancy hotels and, 29–30. *See also* housing; public housing

residential segregation, 83–85, 88, 91, 178; affordable housing crisis and, 231, 233–35, 236, 238

Restoring Bronzeville plan, 219

retailers, in central city, 40–41

revalorization, 56, 58, 74, 75–76, 85, 267, 307, 312. *See also* central city revitalization

Reyes, Victor, 52

River North area, photographic documentation, 67–75

Dr. Jose Rizal Memorial Center, 142, 152

Roberson, Stephen, 244

Robinson, Renault, 263

Roman Catholicism. *See* Catholicism

Roosevelt, Franklin D., 86, 89

Roosevelt Square Project, 64

Rusk, David, 280

Rust Belt cities, 8, 57

Rutgers University Safer Cities Initiative, 264

Ryan, George, 244, 283, 287, 289

Safe Schools Law (1995), 256

St. Hyacinth Church, 120–21

St. John Brebeuf Church, 125, 126

St. Stanislaus Kotska Church, 120

St. Zachary Church, 126

Sandburg, Carl, 42, 100, 286

Sanjek, Roger, 104

Sante Fe Gardens, 164, 165

Sargent Shriver National Center on Poverty Law, 243–44

Sassen, Saskia, 22, 24, 33, 37; on education policy, 257; on inequality, 40

Sawyer, Eugene, 47–48

School Finance Authority (SFA), 249, 250

schools and school reform, 88–89, 92–93, 180, 228, 241, 248–58; accountability and centralization, 251–52, 255, 257; African Americans and Latinos and, 248, 249–50, 251–53, 254, 255–58; in 1988 and 1995, 248–51; desegregation of, 231–32, 249; drop out rate, 89, 111, 178, 249, 251, 252; funding for, 235; gentrification and, 253–54; Korean immigrants in, 160; Mexicans in, 106, 111, 252; military schools, 256, 257, 258; new workforce and, 254–55; South Loop, 60, 62; testing in, 248, 251–52, 255, 258. *See also* education

Scott, Mel, 278

Second City comedy club, 216

security and commodity brokers, 37–38

Sedler, Eric, 66

Seeberger-Quin, Beat, 300

segregation, 74, 86, 223, 314–15; affordable housing crisis and, 231, 233–35, 236, 238; gentrification and, 12; racial and ethnic, 13, 40, 231; residential, 83–85, 88, 91, 178; in schools, 231–32, 249

September 11 (2001) terrorist attacks, 227, 244, 290, 298; Arab immigrants and, 194–95

service economy, 4, 5, 86, 205; Asian Indian immigration and, 131–32; bifurcated, 208; in Bronzeville, 214; immigrant labor for, 198; inequality in, 9; manufacturing economy and, 8; Mexicans in, 107, 201; Polish

women in, 203. *See also* business services

Service Employees International Union (SEIU), 241, 245

Shakman litigation, 47, 51

Sharma, Ratan, 222

Shelley v. Kramer, 83

shopkeeping, 189–90, 193

shopping malls, 73

Shorebank Corporation, 85

Sikhs, 135, 137

Silverstein, Ira, 223

Simmel, Georg, 316

Simpson, Dick, 30

Singh, Chandra Lachman, 128, 139n1

single-purpose governments, 278–79

single-room occupancy hotels (SROs), 30, 72

Siu, Paul, 168, 181

smart growth, 282

Smith, Benjamin Nathaniel, 227

social class/status, 75, 76, 87, 123, 310; community development and, 239; immigrant, 119, 142, 148; race and, 63, 74, 90, 91, 92, 314, 315

social science, 6–7

"The Social Cost of Disrespect," 265

socioeconomic divide, 56, 214; Asian Indians and, 132–33, 138, 139; Chinese American, 171, 175; Mexican immigrant, 109–10. *See also* hourglass economy; inequality

Soldier Field, 53, 297

Solidarity (Poland), 115

South Asians, 228. *See also* Asian Indians; Devon Avenue

South East Asia Center, 179

Southeast Asian immigrants, 170

Southern Christian Leadership Conference (SCLC), 89

South Korea, 156–57, 162. *See also* Korean immigrants

South Loop, 60–61, 62

South Suburban Airport Coalition, 291. See also Third Airport debate

Southwest Side corridor, 66

Spanish language, 121

Spathies, B. J., 71

special-purpose districts, 278

Stalker, Peter: *Workers without Frontiers,* 118

state government, 53, 88–89, 92, 240, 279; airport expansion and, 287, 289; high-speed rail in, 293; KidCare program, 243; public schools and, 235, 250; transportation and, 283. *See also under* Illinois
Stewart, Mary, 217
Stone, Bernard, 222, 227, 228, 229
Stone, Clarence, 26
strikes, by teachers (1987), 249, 250
Stroger, John, 51, 90
suburban areas, 12, 35, 77–81, 147, 243, 244–45, 280; affordable housing in, 234; African Americans in, 78, 232, 234, 266–67, 306–7; Asian Indians in, 129, 130; Chinese Americans in, 170–71, 178; city-suburban balance and, 278; collar counties, 9, 20; corporate headquarters in, 40, 79; downtown revitalization in, 80, 284; ethno-suburbs, 171, 180; immigrants in, 100–101; Koreans in, 160, 161; Latinos in, 106, 108; manufacturing relocated to, 23, 35, 36, 307; minorities in, 92–93; Palestinians in, 185; police reform and, 266–67; Polish Americans in, 122–26, 127; residential development in, 30; social costs in, 40; Taiwanese in, 180–81; white flight to, 13, 84, 231–32, 240
Suburban O'Hare Commission (SOC), 288–89, 291
Sunbelt industries, 22, 35, 39
Supreme Court, US, 235
Supreme Life Building, 216
Syrian-Lebanese immigrants, 182–83, 188

Taiwanese immigrants, 169, 172, 180–81
taxation, 28, 40, 42, 237, 246; property, 78, 79, 85, 235, 236; Tobin tax, 33, 43n3
tax increment financing (TIF), 50, 69
teachers' strike (1987), 249, 250
temporary jobs, 8–9, 37, 112
Terkel, Studs, 86
terrorism, 267, 290, 298; Arab immigrants and, 194–95; Asian

Indian community and, 135–36, 137; September 11th (2001), 227, 244, 290, 298
Third Airport (south-suburban) debate, 53, 54, 79–80, 287–91; O'Hare expansion and, 279, 282, 284, 287, 288–89, 290, 291
Tillman, Dorothy, 218–19
time-space compression, 20
Tobin tax, 33, 43n3
Torino, Italy, 309–10
tourism, 30, 295–96, 310, 316; on Devon Avenue, 227; institutionalized, 11; Polonia and, 121
Toynbee, Arnold, 4
transnational corporations, 20, 21
transnationalism, 101–2, 172. *See also* globalization
transportation, 26, 77, 279, 281, 282–84, 286–94; railways, 281, 286, 291–94. *See also* O'Hare airport expansion
Travis, Dempsey, 83, 213
Trojska Polska (Polish Triangle), 119–20
Twain, Mark: *Life on the Mississippi*, 56
Tydings-McDuffy Act (1934), 144

Uniform Relocation Act (1974), 217
union movement, 35, 86, 88, 239, 241, 245; decline in, 33, 44; police and, 263; Polish Solidarity, 115
United Power for Action and Justice, 239, 241–47
United States, self-image of, 3
universities, Korean students in, 155, 167
University of Chicago, 6, 90, 253; Indians in, 129; Urban Poverty Project, 23
University of Illinois at Chicago (UIC), 11, 26, 63, 264
University Village, 61, 63, 65
upper class, 74, 78, 253. *See also* elites
urban beautification, 295–302; Lakefront Millennium Project, 297, 300–302
Urban Crime Prevention Program, 264
urban pioneers, 75, 85
urban policy agenda, 19, 25–26, 27–28

urban populism, 47
urban renewal, 12, 21
urban theorists, 6–7, 20

Vallas, Paul, 248
venture capital, 38, 42. *See also* investment
Vietnamese immigrants, 179
Vivekananda, Swami, 129
voters, 46, 228, 246; white, 45, 48, 50, 90
Vrdolyak, Edward, 47

wages, 5, 36, 41, 100. *See also* income
Waldinger, Roger, 200, 205–6
Wal-Mart stores, 41
War Brides Act of 1946, 154–55, 159
Washington, Harold, 41, 46–48, 54, 218, 244; coalition politics of, 91, 193; death of, 250; decision making of, 50, 51; election of, 10, 27, 89; neighborhoods and, 241, 246; police reform and, 260, 264; school reform and, 249, 250
Water Tower Place Park, 300
Weber, Max, 316
Weir, Margaret, 279
whites and whiteness, 20, 88, 123; blacks and, 14, 35, 46, 82, 91; defined, 82–83; rioting by, 83, 84, 231; voters, 45, 48, 50, 90; white exodus/flight, 13, 84, 231–32, 240
Whyte, William H., 80
Wild City, 315–16
Wilson, James Q., 264
Wilson, O. W., 259, 260
Wilson, William Julius, 82–83, 86, 88, 90, 91, 92
Winant, Howard, 82
Wirth, Louis, 159
women. *See* immigrant women
Wong, Ernest, 67
Woods Fund, 241
Woodstock Institute, 84
The Woodlawn Organization (TWO), 239
working class, 35, 36, 66, 176, 246; affordable housing and, 232, 236; blue-collar, 8, 201–2; gentrification and, 12, 257; globalization and, 23, 42; suburban, 78

World Business Chicago, 37
world economy, 20, 132. *See also*
    globalization
world market. *See* Devon Avenue

Yemeni immigrants, 188

youth groups, 85, 245, 255;
    immigrant, 178, 186–87

Zakrzewska, Maria, 122
Zero Tolerance discipline policies,
    256, 264

Ziolkowska, Helen, 122
Zogby, 192
zone of transition, 59–60, 268
zoning ordinances, 234, 235, 236
Zukin, Sharon, 29; on "landscapes
    of power," 70, 76